THE ROYAL BALLET
The first 50 years

THE
ROYAL BALLET

The first 50 years

ALEXANDER BLAND

WITH A FOREWORD BY
DAME NINETTE DE VALOIS

THRESHOLD BOOKS
Sotheby Parke Bernet

Produced and published by Threshold Books Limited,
200 Buckingham Palace Road, London SW1,
on behalf of the Royal Opera House.
Distributed by Sotheby Parke Bernet Publications,
Russell Chambers, London WC2.

ISBN 0 901 366 11 0

Editor: Jane Moore

Designer: Ronald Clark

Picture research: Sarah C. Woodcock

Editorial Assistants: Damian Grint, Kate Robertson,
Suzannah Hawkings-Byass, Marabel Hadfield

Statistics compiled by Sarah C. Woodcock, with the help of
Kathrine Sorley Walker; the Ballet Press Office, Royal Opera House;
the Stage Management of The Royal Ballet and Sadler's Wells Royal Ballet;
the Archives, Royal Opera House; Gwen Cherrell;
the Vic-Wells Association; the Archives, London Coliseum.

Cover photograph: the Corps de Ballet in Rudolf Nureyev's
production of La Bayadère.

Printed in England by Balding + Mansell
of Wisbech, Cambridgeshire
and bound by Webb, Son & Co.

The book has been published with financial support from Midland Bank.

Contents

Illustrations

Illustrations

Illustrations

Illustrations

Photographs by J. W. Debenham, Gordon Anthony, Edward Mandinian, Houston Rogers and de Marney are from the Theatre Museum London, Crown copyright.

Cover photograph: corps de ballet in *La Bayadère*. (Zoë Dominic).

PHOTO BY ANTHONY

NINETTE DE VALOIS
VIC WELLS BALLET

Foreword

Fifty years. What does that make England's Royal Ballet but a great-great grandchild of the European School of classical ballet? Let us take this as an opportunity to pay homage to France, Italy, Denmark and Russia – listed in the order of their emergence into the history of three hundred years of professional dance. The world had danced for many centuries before the executants of the courtly capers of the seventeenth century changed their outlook. The world had danced in every corner of the earth; each country dancing with the exuberance of its own particular temperament; dancing to express its special physical highlights; dancing to its own musical heritage. So what did the more sophisticated dance lovers embark on? They set about harnessing the steps of the soil of many countries, seeing to their further development and eventually giving to the world the historically based classical ballet of today.

I think we can regard our national theatres as the universities of our theatre world in general. Here is the chess board where 'moves' and a long-term strategy are pursued with concentration and foresight reinforced by an ancient and sturdy hindsight. What soul-searching creativity, what academic enquiries into the pedagogy of classical ballet have not sprung from three hundred years of research and development – inspired by the ancient dance of man as an expression of himself? The periodical shortcomings of such ventures are usually the result of an unchanged system that has sustained its artists through the years; but the system can and must periodically be modified – an operation to be carried out with a detachment producing a calm contemplation of any temporary moments of stagnation as it passes on to the next move.

Let us recall the early and late middle of the last century, the era of ballet stars with the 'rent-a-corps' atmosphere which prevailed, and the unstinted homage paid – rightly – by all to the great figures of the dance. (It may be noticed that history repeated itself in the middle of the present century.) But when it was over the chess board had to come out again. What were some of the moves? A musical revival, returning to the standards of the eighteenth century with the advent of Delibes in France and Tchaikovsky in Russia: a choreographic revival through the works of Bournonville (via France) and Petipa in Russia (also via France). Pedagogy sprang up refreshed and expanded to restate itself through the school of Bournonville and his disciples, and Italy's school of Blasis put out its final flowering through the influence of Enrico Cecchetti. Then followed an era of great classical ballets, created for their own sake, and an era of dancers who added their demands for a change . . . The result? Diaghilev with Fokine and Stravinsky. Equality was born in dance, music, choreography and décor. The famous ballerina pas de quatre of the middle nineteenth century was replaced by a pas de quatre of wider implications by the early twentieth century.

This may be just history, but it is the epoch directly behind us, influencing The Royal Ballet of England, the newly formed Dutch and German schools and the classical ballet scene in America. An epoch that will remain a lasting challenge to us all – because of its balancing of the part to the whole.

How do I personally regard the fiftieth birthday of The Royal Ballet? I regard it as a national effort on the part of a few in the past for the many in the future. The few have my love, my thanks and my gratitude, and the many the hope that they guide our national ballet into the future as a group of adventurous traditionalists.

Ninette de Valois

Author's Note

Writing this book has proved enjoyable as well as instructive, both in reviving memories and offering excursions into unfamiliar and sometimes legendary territories.

Though many people have helped in its preparation, it remains very much a one-man report. The necessarily summary judgements meted out and the opinions expressed are purely personal and they make no claim to finality. The administration of The Royal Opera House offered me a free hand; if any bias is to be detected in the result, it arises from my own taste. I am all too aware of omissions and imperfections, and I hope that they will be repaired when in the future more detailed studies of particular aspects of the story come to be written.

One major delusion impressed itself on me as I traced the ups and down of the increasingly complicated venture. This is the fallacy that a dance company consists only, or mainly, of the artists whose names are mentioned in reviews or histories. These, inevitably, come and go. But behind them stands a steady nucleus of dancers – not only members of the corps de ballet, but a host of soloists – who constitute the final, vital shape and image of the company. It is to all the dancers whose names do not appear in this chronicle that I would like to dedicate it.

Among the many sources I have consulted, pride of place must go to Mary Clarke's invaluable study of the first twenty-four years of the Company, *The Sadler's Wells Ballet*, to which all future historians must be indebted. I have also profited freely from Dame Ninette de Valois' amazingly prescient writings and from Dame Margot Fonteyn's vivid *Autobiography*. Consistent springs of information and current thinking have been two dance magazines, *Dance and Dancers* and *The Dancing Times*.

I owe special gratitude to Dame Ninette de Valois for continuous self-effacing encouragement; to Sir John Tooley, General Administrator of the Royal Opera House, for his patient and constructive suggestions and to his colleague, Ken Davison, a tower of discrimination and support; to Sarah Woodcock of the Theatre Museum who, besides providing what may prove to be the most valuable part of the book, contributed a steady stream of facts and additions; to Boris Skildelsky and Francesca Franchi, ever-ready researchers in the Covent Garden Archives; to Kathrine Sorley Walker whose sharp eye and retentive memory were consistently helpful; and to Barbara Cooper, the vigilant publisher, who steered the project to its conclusion.

Last but not least I would like to thank Stuart Graham of Midland Bank for his imaginative gesture in making the production of this book possible.

I *Overture*

The Royal Ballet is the offspring of two artistic ancestors. On one side it is descended from the entertainments of Louis XIV via the Court company of St Petersburg and Diaghilev's Ballets Russes; on the other from the London commercial theatre. Out of this mixed blood a new and separate creation has evolved, democratic but not vulgar, royal but not – except when occasion demands – regal. It is a hybrid which is typically British.

Throughout history the English and their monarchs have been fond of dancing, but in 1649, just four years before Louis XIV, resplendent in silk and gold, was to appear in the Louvre dancing the role which was to give him his title 'Le Roi Soleil', the head of Charles I rolled across the scaffold in Whitehall. The English branch of the spreading tree of Court entertainment had been lopped and it was to be three hundred years before a British ballet company received the royal accolade.

However, more than an execution was needed to stem altogether the English love of dance. Diverted from Court patronage it sprang up in more humble surroundings. The commercial theatre took over where royal bounty had vanished. At first, drama predominated, together with opera, but during the eighteenth century London became a favourite centre for top dancers of the day, from Vestris, père et fils, to la Guimard, Vigano and Didelot. Ballet was, however, strictly an import business, and there was never the slightest move to extend royal patronage to the theatre. The art of dance remained firmly in commercial hands.

Towards the end of the nineteenth century, Western taste in dance entertainment moved towards popular musical spectacles; in London ballet became an ingredient of the music-hall. At the Alhambra and Empire Theatres, which specialised in such shows, the standard of performance was high even if the taste of ballets themselves was low. The visiting artists were by now mostly from Milan, then the strongest technical school in Europe, although the resident star at the Empire Theatre, Adeline Genée, had been born and trained in Denmark.

The departure of Genée from London in 1908 left a gap which was soon filled by Russian ballerinas, though dancers like Phyllis Bedells, who became the ballerina at the Empire Theatre in 1919, and Ruth French upheld a high standard among English-born artists. In the years before the début of the Diaghilev Company at Covent Garden, London saw many leading dancers from Moscow and St Petersburg. The sensation created by Diaghilev's Ballets Russes in 1911 was not primarily due to his artists. What bowled the audience over was the style of his productions. The snob public which had despised the entertainments provided by the popular theatres rallied round this offshoot of the Russian Imperial Ballet. Diaghilev had created an entirely new public for ballet in London. The boisterous, conservative and easily-pleased crowds at the Empire and the Alhambra, the descendants of the mobs who had cheered Vestris and booed the manager at the King's Theatre in the eighteenth century, had been joined by the English version of the discriminating aristocratic abonnés of the Imperial Theatre in St Petersburg. When Diaghilev died suddenly in 1929, London had two ballet audiences – the neglected traditional and popular one, and a new aristocratic one now abruptly deprived. Their different demands were soon to be satisfied by a single new organisation launched by a single figure. Her name was Edris Stannus and she danced under the pseudonym of Ninette de Valois.

The Royal Ballet's origins are so deeply bound up with the character of de Valois that her own origins have become part of its history. She was born in Ireland in the shadow of the Wicklow Mountains in 1898, the second child of a retired army officer, and brought up in the comfortable surroundings of the landed gentry. There was no grandeur, but the kind of sheltered security which was an ideal background for the development of an imaginative little girl. The Protestant upper-class virtues of fair play, frugality, patriotism, common sense, industriousness and orderliness must have been imbued in her from the earliest age, providing a rock-firm base from which her individual fantasies could rise. Thence, too, came the cheerful assumption of responsibility, the autocratic eccentricity, the confidence in her own opinions – however often she changed them – which were to lend such strength and individuality to her leadership.

There seems to have been a good deal of day-dreaming solitude. She has recalled two significant adventures. One was a visit to the Gaiety Theatre in Dublin; prophetically the pantomime was *The Sleeping Beauty*. The other was when, at a children's party, a sudden compulsion seized her to leave the skirts of her nanny, to which she had been clinging, and to advance on to the dancing floor and perform an Irish jig. The dance over, she fled to privacy as before, 'hiding behind my nurse'.

A move to the English seaside at the age of seven introduced her to the local dancing class, and a further move to London when she was eleven brought her to a well-known academy run by Mrs Wordsworth, where she embarked on 'fancy dancing' and was taken to matinées to see Pavlova and Diaghilev's Ballets Russes. At twelve her mother entered her for a school for professional theatrical performers. She was launched on her career. It was a quick and rather brutal launching. While only fourteen she found herself touring the country with a troupe called 'The Wonder Children', performing eight times a week for a salary of £4, of which £1 went on lodging and board.

The outbreak of war in August 1914 found her performing on Southsea pier. The company was disbanded, but a few months later came her first professional engagement, dancing in a pantomime at the London Lyceum. She appeared there regularly throughout the war and began to take serious lessons, first with Edouard Espinosa, ballet-master at the Empire Theatre, and then, when the war ended, with the famous Enrico Cecchetti, teacher to the Ballets Russes.

During the next few years de Valois danced at most of the London music-halls. They were exhausting engagements, sometimes involving three shows a day, and artistically unrewarding. She was learning the facts of theatrical life the hard way, in the commercial theatre. But she kept working steadily at her dancing, attending lessons, now that Cecchetti had returned to Italy, with the Russian teacher Nicholas Legat in Hampstead: and in 1919 came the chance to make her break with the music-hall. She was invited to take an audition for the first summer opera season in London since the war, and at the age of twenty she passed for the first time through the stage door of the Royal Opera House.

Soon after, in 1921 at the age of twenty-three, she launched her first venture in the field of choreography and management. She took a troupe of ten English dancers on a music-hall circuit, performing a twenty-minute divertissement that she had choreographed herself. The tour lasted for only six weeks, but it gave her first taste of both group choreography and management. A few weeks later she joined a troupe of Ballets Russes dancers led by Lopokova, Sokolova and Massine, all of whom were out of work following Diaghilev's financial losses from his London production of *The Sleeping Princess*. With this little band she danced in Massine divertissements at Covent Garden and the Coliseum; one programme was a double bill with a film, another was 'Jazzaganza' featuring the comedian George Robey. Both failed, but de Valois had enjoyed a taste of the Diaghilev style – in one of his pieces Massine had employed Milhaud for the music and Duncan Grant for the designs – and she had made some useful contacts. In 1923 she received an invitation to leave her West End variety shows and to join the Ballets Russes in Paris.

The company was very different from the troupe which Diaghilev had introduced to Europe fourteen years earlier. The first wave of dancers had left, and the early choreographers, Fokine and Massine, had been replaced by Nijinska, Nijinsky's sister. The St Petersburg inheritance was weakened. These were the days of experimental ballets inspired by the School of Paris. De Valois danced in the corps de ballet in old favourites such as *Schéhérazade* and *Les Sylphides* but was also given some small solo roles, appearing in ballets by several choreographers. Her most rewarding experiences, it seems, were when Nijinska mounted on her the role of the Hostess in *Les Biches* (which Nijinska herself created on stage) and when she danced in *Les Noces*. It was hard work, with incessant touring and a relentless round of performances (she took mental note of the injuries arising from overwork). But the atmosphere of dedication and experiment was an eye-opener after her commercial dates in the London music-halls. Her engagement ended after two years, in 1925, but she went on making occasional appearances with the company, and the whole experience was to leave a lasting impression.

De Valois has confessed to remaining obstinately 'English' in the somewhat exotic atmosphere of Diaghilev's late period. Her Protestant spirit seems to have remained undimmed. She had absorbed many lessons from her two years with the Ballets Russes, but when she returned to Britain her impulse was to carry her in the opposite direction to that of Diaghilev. She came back to London determined to found not a roving avant-garde troupe like the Ballets Russes but a British version of the very organisation against which Diaghilev had rebelled – a state company with a school and a theatre of its own.

She had sensed at first-hand the feeling of a 'world theatre' and its close relationship with developments in the other arts, but she knew that she did not really fit in with the motley group of emigrés, their gypsy life and their sophisticated friends. What she valued most from her time with the Ballets Russes was not its thirst for experiment but the deep tradition from which it sprang. She admired above all Diaghilev's cultural background: 'His strength lay in the fact that his familiarity with the value of the known and the tried was so great that he could advise with conviction and discard with impunity; he could light the path of the unknown and untried with the torch of knowledge.' She realised that for dancers rootless liberty can become as restricting as established convention and that the material hardships of unrelenting tours can cause as much damage as the stagnation of a static organisation.

The idea of a home-grown company in London was in the air already. In 1924 an article in the *Old Vic Magazine* had called for a British ballet. The following year Anton Dolin opened a school which he hoped might grow into a performing group; it was hailed in one newspaper as 'The Nucleus of British Ballet'. Then a critic, Cyril Beaumont, joined with the dance teacher at the Old Vic Theatre, Flora Fairbairn of the Mayfair School of Dancing, to form a group of British dancers. Both of these schemes proved abortive – de Valois was more successful because she was more methodical. In 1926 she opened a dancing school in Kensington, announcing forcefully the belief at which, paradoxically, she had arrived while skipping through the complex rhythms of *Les Noces* or posing in a Chanel swimsuit in Cocteau's modish romp *Le Train Bleu*: 'The true aim of modern ballet is a serious practical effort to extend the authentic methods of the classical ballet . . . There is no question that the teachings of the Classic School are the sure and only foundation.' Her school was a trifle sententiously entitled 'The Academy of Choreographic Art'. It offered courses in stage design, and a music and drama reference library. De Valois herself conducted the classes, armed, as was then the custom, with a stick to beat time, assisted by Ursula Moreton and Molly Lake. Among the occasional pupils was a slim boy from Ecuador called Frederick Ashton.

De Valois seems to have been positive about her aims and how to achieve them. She realised that to establish an independent ballet organisation was not practical at that time. She would form a nucleus of classically trained dancers and attach them to an existing repertory drama company. She proceeded with her plan with characteristic energy.

She had left the Ballets Russes in July 1925. The next March she opened her school and at about the same time she wrote to Sir Barry Jackson, Director of the Repertory Theatre in Birmingham, enclosing her scheme for a resident ballet company. He turned down her

The Academy of Choregraphic Art

Advertisement in *The Dancing Times*, September 1928.

proposal, and in April she tried a change of tactics. She wrote to Lilian Baylis, Manager of the Old Vic Theatre. Then, wearing her best hat, she made her way to the Old Vic during a matinée to present herself and her project.

It was a momentous occasion. Lilian Baylis was an extraordinary person and by good luck her eccentricities meshed in exactly with de Valois' equally individual, but in many ways similar, temperament. Had they been of the same age the meeting between two agressively ambitious ladies might well have produced an explosion. But Baylis was fifty-two and de Valois was twenty-eight. Affinity of temperament generated not rivalry but compatibility. There was an instantaneous and incalculably fruitful click.

Both by the act of faith which was to set in motion the whole long process which ended finally in The Royal Ballet, and through her personal influence on de Valois, the spirit of Baylis was to haunt the whole formative first period of the Company, and her character is a vital ingredient in its story. She had been born in London into a half-German family with a musical background and she had seemed destined for a career as an instrumentalist. While she was still in her teens her family moved to South Africa and began to tour as a concert group calling themselves 'The Gypsy Revellers'. Lilian was billed as 'soprano, vocalist, violinist and acknowledged premier lady Mandolinist and Banjoist of South Africa'. She also found time to give ballroom dancing lessons (one of her pupils in 'The Lancers' session was the American writer Mark Twain). An illness left her with a permanently twisted lip which doubtless handicapped her as a performer, so she was invited by her aunt, Emma Cons, to return to London to help run the Royal Victoria Hall (traditionally known as the 'Old Vic'), a theatre devoted to productions of Shakespeare and opera at prices within the range of working men and women. When Emma Cons died in 1912, Lilian Baylis took over as Manager of the theatre, where she quickly became a legend: her combination of homely simplicity, frugality and piety aroused mixed emotions of loyalty, amusement and affection.

For the dance episodes in her productions Baylis had been relying on pupils from various dance schools and a local church school – all unpaid. She realised the need for a dance company to correspond to her opera and drama groups, particularly as she was planning to open a second theatre at Sadler's Wells. 'When are we going to have a British ballet?' she would demand from the Editor of *The Dancing Times*, Philip Richardson (who had organised a succession of 'Sunshine Matinées' featuring leading British dancers). Baylis was therefore sympathetic to the proposals laid out in the doubtless soundly-argued letter that she had received from de Valois, though she was dubious about the proposer. 'With writing like that and a name like that she shouldn't waste too much of our time', her assistant, Evelyn Williams remarked. But half an hour with de Valois convinced Baylis. 'I like your face, dear. I think you're practical. And you seem to have had a great deal of experience.' Baylis agreed to visit the Academy of Choreographic Art to check the applicant's credentials. Hardly had de Valois gone out of the room when she turned to Evelyn Williams. 'Ninette de Valois is going to form a ballet company for us. When we open at the Wells it will be on a whole-time basis.' Little did she know how richly this prophecy was to be fulfilled.

Baylis's visit to the school having proved successful, de Valois found herself officially attached to the Old Vic. The financial rewards were on a starvation scale, but her first ambition was achieved: she had embedded herself in a permanent repertory company. The work was stimulating and instructive; the company had some fine actors and the

Lilian Baylis, General Manager of the Old Vic and Sadler's Wells, at the Old Vic Theatre *c*1929.

repertory was remarkable – it included all Shakespeare's thirty-seven plays, besides opera performances. As well as her dancing engagements she taught at her own and other schools. She also accepted with enthusiasm the post of resident choreographer, and occasional dancer, at the Festival Theatre in Cambridge, a new experimental theatre opened by a wealthy but eccentric cousin, Terence Gray. In his own way, Gray was a miniature Diaghilev – autocratic and culturally avant-garde. De Valois must have learned much about stagecraft from this experience.

In the same year, 1926, a final ingredient was to be added to the recipe from which de Valois was to compound her future company. One day in the darkness of the auditorium at the Festival Theatre she was approached by a figure who asked her, in a strong Irish accent, whether she would come and work in Dublin. It was the poet W. B. Yeats. He proposed that she should send over a teacher to the famous Abbey Theatre and visit it personally every three months to produce and perform in his series of 'Plays for Dancers'. She accepted without hesitation, and over the next six years mounted several plays and short Irish ballets suitable for young dancers. The easy-going, talkative informality of the company must have made a pleasant contrast for de Valois to the disciplines so necessary in her Academy. The 'romantic spark' in her character was rekindled, and the acceptance of other people's idiosyncrasies, which was so fruitfully to counter the streak of dogmatism in her personality, was reinforced.

Back in London the threads which were to go into the fabric of her company were drawing together. De Valois herself ventured to put on three evenings of ballet, danced by herself and her students, at the Royal Court Theatre in Sloane Square. They included *Rout*, a vaguely Futuristic ballet to music by Arthur Bliss which she had already given privately in her studio, and a number of other short items. She lost £200 on the venture, but *The Morning Post* remarked that the performances showed that 'given the opportunity we could produce a very good Ballet in England'. Philip Page of *The Times* went even further in long-range prophecy, alluding to de Valois' school. 'Not yet can it tack the word "Royal" in front of its name, but after its activities at the Royal Court Theatre yesterday it is obvious that this must come in time.'

The moment of birth was not far away. On 13 December 1928 de Valois presented the first ballet performance at the Old Vic, a curtain-raiser to the Christmas production of the opera 'Hansel and Gretel'. It was a pastoral romp arranged to Mozart's *Les Petits Riens* with Watteau-style costumes. De Valois herself and her assistant at her school, Ursula Moreton, were the principals; Stanley Judson and Hedley Briggs led the men. It was successful enough to be followed five months later by another curtain-raiser, *The Picnic*, with music by Vaughan Williams. For the principal part of a satyr Marie Rambert lent her leading male dancer, Harold Turner, later to become a star at Sadler's Wells. At the end of the season the Old Vic's annual report remarked 'Perhaps its most far-reaching and important events were concerned with the Old Vic's tentative efforts at founding a school of English ballet. Such a development of the operatic side of the work has always been an ideal the Manager has set in front of her, and in the indomitable hands of Ninette de Valois this ideal has been translated into an achievement.' It bravely mentioned further developments, 'preparations for which ... are now in train'. Baylis intended to found a twin theatre to her South London one, which would house the operatic side; this, clearly, should be the home of her new, fast-growing, dance venture. She had settled on a derelict old theatre in North London – Sadler's Wells at Islington.

Sadler's Wells Theatre. ABOVE The auditorium in 1926. BELOW The exterior after restoration.

It had a history going back two hundred and fifty years to 1684 when it started life as a riverside inn run by a certain Dick Sadler, who by a stroke of luck had found in his garden two springs or wells which he shrewdly described as medicinal. The resort flourished and Sadler offered his customers musical turns as an added attraction. The entertainments proved more convincing than the healing powers of the waters, and by the beginning of the nineteenth century the establishment had grown into a theatre. Kean recited there as a child prodigy and the clown Grimaldi became the reigning star. Later, as fashions changed and the pattern of London altered, the theatre fell on hard times. When war broke out in 1914 it was briefly turned into a cinema, and in 1915 it was closed altogether. However, the shell remained and could be bought cheaply. In 1925 the Duke of Devonshire launched a public appeal for £60,000 to buy and re-equip Sadler's Wells as a theatre. The Carnegie Trust offered to pay the entire purchase price and on 1 July a letter to *The Times* announced that the property had been 'definitely acquired'. Support grew on all sides. The *Daily Telegraph* opened a subscription list which attracted donations ranging from £500 from the Duke of Devonshire to 10s. 6d. from 'some employees of W. H. Smith and Son'. The new theatre rose fast and one day Baylis took de Valois to look at her future home, to be greeted by a large rat scuttling across the road. But the old story of ever-mounting estimates presented itself. By April 1930, £65,000 had been raised; £80,000 was needed – and the appeal was being awkwardly rivalled by a scheme for a British National Opera. An opening date in the autumn was proposed and then postponed. On 5 December *The Times* announced the new plans, and for the first time the proposed inclusion of a ballet ingredient was mentioned. 'Opera will be played six times a week at one theatre or the other, for six, eight or nine months . . . Ninette de Valois will also run a *school of ballet* in connection with Sadler's Wells which will supply dancers for the opera, Miss de Valois herself being *prima ballerina* and choreographist.'

The fateful hour was clearly imminent. Diaghilev had died in August 1929. Almost immediately the several small springs which were to merge and form the mainstream of British dance had begun to bubble. In 1920 Marie Rambert, an ex-member of Diaghilev's company, had opened a dance school at Notting Hill in London and in 1926 had presented the first of Ashton's ballets, *A Tragedy of Fashion*, in a revue at the Lyric Theatre Hammersmith. Now, in 1930, she put on a whole fortnight of ballet by her own little company at the same theatre and in the same year founded her seminal Ballet Club. In October 1930 the Camargo Society, an association founded by the ballet critic Arnold Haskell and Philip Richardson, Editor of *The Dancing Times*, organised an impressive Sunday evening performance by an assembly of some of the best British dancers led by de Valois and Dolin and conducted by a young musician called Constant Lambert, who had recently worked for Diaghilev. Finally, in the last weeks of 1930 the new Vic-Wells Opera Ballet troupe gave its very first performance – at the seaside resort of Bournemouth. All the buds of British ballet had begun to open and if plans had gone straight, the new Sadler's Wells Theatre would have opened that year too, and 1930 would have become the key date in the history of the Company. But at the last minute the work was delayed and the historic event was put off until the New Year.

2 Early Stages

On Twelfth Night, 6 January 1931, the Sadler's Wells Theatre was officially opened to the public with a performance of a Shakespeare play – 'Twelfth Night', of course. Under the terms of the Old Vic Foundation, the theatre was: 'obliged to provide seats at prices within the means of labourers and artisans, and financial gain is strictly debarred. The same will apply to Sadler's Wells.' Drama and opera were to be presented for alternate fortnights. The first opera, 'Carmen', was performed on 20 January and in it the ballet company made its first appearance, providing dances devised by de Valois. One great achievement from the ballet point of view was that a practice-and-rehearsal room had been included in the building (the wooden floor was paid for by an anonymous well-wisher) and the dancers were engaged on a permanent basis. There were six of them, all pupils from de Valois' Kensington school, which by then she had sold. The names of these pioneers, led of course by de Valois herself, were Ursula Moreton, Freda Bamford, Sheila McCarthy, Joy Newton, Beatrice Appleyard and Nadina Newhouse. Most of them were to remain for some years

Ninette de Valois with her dancers in the studio at Sadler's Wells Theatre, 1931.

with the Company. The idea of a full-time male colleague was still unrealistic, and so it was this tiny bevy of girls who constituted the original 'Vic-Wells Opera Ballet' which was to grow and change so dramatically over the next decades.

The girls appeared regularly in the opera ballets, travelling across London to the Old Vic on the South Bank when drama was being played at the Wells. Finally, Lilian Baylis arranged to entrust them with a whole programme to themselves. This took place not at Sadler's Wells but at the Old Vic, on 5 May 1931 – the event thus becoming the official candidate for the honour of being the first-ever performance of the Company. The programme – all by de Valois – consisted of a collection of short pieces: a new work, *The Jackdaw and the Pigeons*, and *Les Petits Riens, Danse Sacrée et Danse Profane* (played in masks), *Hommage aux Belles Viennoises, Suite of Dances* and *The Faun* (a revised version of *The Picnic*). To these Anton Dolin added the lustre of his reputation as a Diaghilev star by dancing a *Spanish Dance* – as well as appearing in *Suite of Dances*. Besides Dolin, the actor Leslie French (who mimed the title role in *The Faun* with Ursula Moreton as a Nymph) and two boys (Stanley Judson and Ivor Beddoes) were roped in, and eight girls were added, making a troupe, including de Valois, of nineteen.

The evening was long but resoundingly successful. 'It is always the wonderful and beautiful thing that happens at the Old Vic', reported the *Morning Post* next day. 'It happened again last night in the victorious arrival of a reborn British Ballet. With the

The Jackdaw and the Pigeons, early 1932. (Left to right) Joy Newton, Marie Nielson, Beatrice Appleyard (crouching), Joan Day, Ailne Phillips, Ninette de Valois, Sheila McCarthy (sitting on stairs), Nadina Newhouse and Gwyneth Mathews.

establishment of a permanent weekly programme of ballet, the old Surrey-side theatre has now set just the same splendid example to the rest of London as it has done in Shakespearean productions. This "magnificent venture", as Mr Anton Dolin called it in a delightfully modest and graceful little speech, at the end of which he threw a rose to Miss Lilian Baylis, is another proof of what loyalty and courage can do.'

The courage was largely that of de Valois and it was rewarded by the entire programme being repeated at Sadler's Wells ten days later. On 15 May the little troupe presented the first full ballet programme in what was to become its home theatre.

A further impetus to set the wheel of a British national ballet in motion was provided a few months later from another source when, in July, the Camargo Society mounted its fourth programme. As well as including two ballets by the promising young Frederick Ashton it presented a major new production by de Valois, *Job*, 'a masque for dancing'. This highly original work was patently British, with its score by Vaughan Williams, its designs by Gwen Raverat and poses derived from drawings by William Blake. It also provided a star role for the only famous British male dancer, Anton Dolin: with his performance in this work, British ballet staked a claim to be considered in the same league as that of foreign companies. The conductor at all the Camargo evenings was Constant Lambert.

The cast which was to perform the miracle of building a permanent British ballet company was now almost assembled. There were several distinguished dancers in London whose help might be acquired. The Camargo Society had Lydia Lopokova as its Choreographic Director, and it was presided over by Adeline Genée, now fifty-three years old and on the point of retiring to devote herself to what later became the Royal Academy of Dancing. Among the ex-members of Diaghilev's company working in London at this time was George Balanchine, who applied unsuccessfully for a permanent working permit. (Had he obtained it, the history of ballet in Britain might have been different.) Another distinguished figure from the Ballets Russes was Tamara Karsavina, who had married an Englishman and opened a ballet school in London. She was on the advisory committee of the Camargo Society and danced in 1930–1 with the Ballet Rambert, but for some reason was not associated with the Vic-Wells Ballet except for occasional advice on special roles.

Dolin's offers of collaboration were always accepted with pleasure by de Valois and Lilian Baylis, who kept a shrewd eye on the box office, but he was too busy with appearances elsewhere to accept a permanent engagement. Another star of Diaghilev's company, Alicia Markova (Alicia Marks), who had appeared in several Camargo performances and with Marie Rambert's Ballet Club, was invited to appear a few months later. At first this was only for individual guest performances.

De Valois was evidently anxious to 'build British' from the foundations and to dissociate herself from the foreign glamour of the Ballets Russes in order to start again from Lilian Baylis's concept of a 'People's Theatre'. What she seemed to be aiming at was a demotic version of the Imperial Ballet of St Petersburg – a paradoxical ambition which, against all the odds, she was, at least partly, to achieve.

Of the team which was now coming together to give substance to her dreams the most important was Frederick Ashton. He already had a rich ballet experience behind him. Born in Ecuador, he had been educated in England and had studied briefly with Massine then with Marie Rambert. It was Rambert, with her sympathy and knowledge of Diaghilev's outlook, who had provided Ashton's first contacts with the world of dance and

LEFT Frederick Ashton with June Brae, 1938.
RIGHT Constant Lambert studying a score, during the early part of the War.

who had encouraged him in 1926 to choreograph his first ballet. He later joined Ida Rubinstein's company in Paris and there he had the chance to work with Massine and, most fruitfully, with Nijinska. On his return to England Ashton created dances for, and appeared in, shows of many kinds, ranging from cabaret to *Le Lac des Cygnes* (the Act II pas de deux with Markova, on the miniscule Ballet Club stage), making appearances with de Valois at the Old Vic and developing as a choreographer with the Camargo Society and Rambert's company, where he partnered Diaghilev's great ballerina Karsavina and arranged a ballet for her. By 1931 he had already produced half a dozen short ballets and had a wide knowledge – wider perhaps than that of de Valois – of the dance and art world. Unlike her, he was temperamentally attracted by the atmosphere of Diaghilev's late period. De Valois' choreographic influence seems to have stemmed from Massine, with his angular idiom based on his own physique, and the serious-minded expressionism of Central European dance. Ashton's leanings were decidedly towards Paris with its aura of neo-classical elegance. This inclination may have been developed in the fashionable atmosphere of the Ballet Club whose select audiences permitted greater sophistication than would have been suitable in Lilian Baylis's worker-orientated theatres.

The third member of what was to become the Sadler's Wells triumvirate seems to have attached himself to the enterprise almost as though through a natural process. Constant Lambert was not only the right man to look after the musical side of the activity – he was the only one. Wherever ballet was being presented in London in these first post-Diaghilev years, Lambert was sure to be there, either in the orchestra pit or at the piano. Born in Russia, the son of an Australian painter, he had been something of a child prodigy at the Royal College of Music, with a quick mind and a face of deceptively cherubic beauty. Diaghilev had invited the attractive youngster to compose a score for him, and his *Romeo et Juliette* was given in Paris and London while he was still only twenty-one. It turned out to be a disappointment and he was violently unhappy. Not unnaturally both Diaghilev and his company had ridden roughshod over his youthful ideas. This experience doubtless coloured Lambert's later views. Part of his sympathy with the aims of de Valois must have arisen from a distaste for the rarefied and fashionable atmosphere of the Ballets Russes in which, like her, he did not feel at home. Back in London he earned a precarious living by playing the piano for dancing classes and writing occasional reviews of films and concerts. Though he could easily hold his own at intellectual parties such as those given by the Sitwells, he moved more naturally in the raffish but stimulating groups of writers, artists, and musicians who frequented the pubs and bars of Soho and Chelsea, a circle which led him into the habit of drinking but which opened up a wide and international range of artistic interests. In 1926 he composed a ballet, *Pomona*, which during the next year was mounted in Buenos Aires by Nijinska, whom he had met with Diaghilev. The same year, inspired by a Negro troupe's appearance in London, he had arranged a setting to a poem by Sacheverell Sitwell, *Rio Grande*, later to become a favourite ballet at Sadler's Wells.

During the next two years Lambert's name slowly became established through small compositions and conducting, notably in Ashley Dukes' dramatisation of Feuchtwanger's 'Jew Süss', which included a short ballet by Ashton. The first concert performance of *Rio Grande* in 1929 rocketed Lambert into fame. 'A new work of great genius', commented the *Daily Express*. 'A conductor born to conduct', said the *Daily Telegraph*.

Diaghilev had died a few months previously and Lambert's association with him made him an obvious choice for English ballet enthusiasts. Marie Rambert hired him to play for her troupe in Hammersmith, where de Valois visited him. 'A very vague young man,' was her first reaction to him. But soon she was convinced of his potential and chose him to orchestrate Mozart's music for *Les Petits Riens* for the tiny Old Vic orchestra. He conducted the first programme of the Camargo Society which included a new version, by Ashton, of his own *Pomona*, and he became the musical helmsman of the Society (Edwin Evans, the noted critic and friend of Diaghilev, was Music Director). Lambert was caught up irrevocably in the world of dance, conducting regularly for de Valois' ventures. When the question of a conductor, and then of a Music Director, arose at Sadler's Wells there was no conceivable alternative candidate.

By now, in 1931, the three architects of the new ballet company were assembled. They made a wonderfully apt and complementary team, very different in character yet united in their ultimate aims. De Valois, aged thirty-three, provided inexhaustible drive, a clear and far-seeing brain and great administrative gifts. Lambert, aged twenty-six, contributed not only a sharp musical sense (curiously, he was deaf in one ear) and a determination to maintain high standards in the orchestra pit as well as on the stage, but also a feeling for and knowledge of the arts in general. Ashton, aged twenty-seven, had been blessed with an abundant talent for choreography, directed by a nature at once sensitive and worldly. Although he had never worked with Diaghilev it was he, oddly, who was nearest to him in temperament, divining instantly the slightest new movement in the arts and turning it to advantage with impeccable flair and taste.

Now that de Valois was entrenched in a large theatre, with the opportunity – indeed the obligation – to present regular ballet programmes, something more substantial than her little group of ex-pupils, strengthened by occasional visitors, was clearly necessary. To establish British ballet as a serious competitor with the companies to which London was accustomed, a high standard of performance was essential. After the death of Diaghilev and before the birth of Colonel de Basil's big touring company, de Valois had been granted a breathing-space to make her plans. She knew that something was needed to lure the sceptical followers of Russian ballet into her theatre.

The obvious answer was Dolin; he was not only British, but a well-known star and an established box-office draw. He had lent his support to the first ventures at the Old Vic and had put British ballet firmly on the map through his virile performances in *Job.* He was invited to appear in the first ballet evenings at Sadler's Wells, obtaining leave from a West End musical to do so. For the second programme, presented at Sadler's Wells on 21 May 1931, he was joined by another ex-Diaghilev dancer, Lydia Lopokova, wife of the wealthy balletophile economist John Maynard Keynes.

The success of the new venture surprised even its instigators. The Vic-Wells Annual Report that year remarked on 'a large and enthusiastic public eagerly waiting for the presentation of this difficult and eclectic form of art, which has not hitherto been treated seriously in London unless it hailed from a foreign country'. It was decided to present ballet programmes once a fortnight from the beginning of the 1931/32 season, starting on 22 September, and Lambert was given a regular engagement as Music Director. The autumn season opened at the Old Vic with Dolin in *Job,* which the Camargo Society had lent for the

Fête Polonaise, the 1934 revival with (centre) Ruth French and Robert Helpmann.

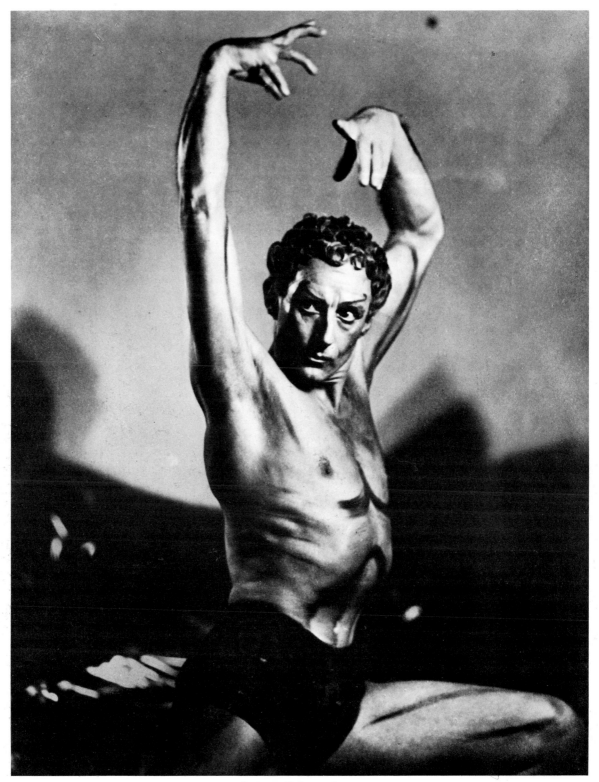

Job. Anton Dolin as Satan.

occasion. 'God, white-bearded and wearing a red night-shirt, sat on a throne surrounded by a heavenly host and took part in the ballet *Job* last night at the Old Vic', reported the *Daily Herald*. 'Although the young dancers lack training yet, of course, the conception was almost one of genius . . .' This first evening of the season ended with *Regatta*, a comic nautical ballet by Ashton. These 'true-blue romps', as *The Times* described them, were his first modest contribution to the Company with which he was to be associated for the next fifty years.

The new creations for the season were less noteworthy, unless we are intrigued by Ashton's interpretation of the eponymous role in a short piece by de Valois with the eccentric title of *The Jew in the Bush*, which was included in a Christmas programme oddly paired with *Hansel and Gretel*. But the new year at Sadler's Wells brought a major development. It was becoming impracticable for de Valois to sustain for long the triple post of Director, chief choreographer and principal ballerina of the Company (now increased to twelve and including Ailne Phillips, who was later to be Ballet Principal of the Sadler's Wells Ballet School, among the newcomers). A new ballerina was badly needed, and Alicia Markova was invited to join the Company as regular Guest Artist.

Job. Satan banished from Heaven by the Sons of the Morning.

Diaghilev had included two English ballerinas in his company. One was Lydia Sokolova, born Hilda Munnings in Wanstead, who had joined the Ballets Russes as early as 1913 as a character dancer and was now, in 1932, thirty-six years old. She was not suitable as a classical ballerina and somewhat beyond her best, though she was still appearing in musicals. The other was Alicia Markova, who had been Diaghilev's last and youngest ballerina, joining his company in 1925 at the age of only fourteen. She had scored a big success in her first roles, but Diaghilev had died before she had had a chance to develop as a classical ballerina or to establish herself as a name with the public.

Markova had undergone some difficult times after Diaghilev's death, but in 1931 Ashton had created a new ballet, *La Péri*, for her at Rambert's Ballet Club and she had become a regular performer with this little company (at a salary of 10s. 6d. per performance), appearing in many Ashton roles and also in excerpts from the classics.

At the beginning of 1932 Markova accepted an invitation from de Valois and made two appearances on the same day, 30 January, with the Vic-Wells Company. Her success was immediate. Even the demanding critic of *The Observer* was impressed. 'There is much to learn and the principal thing is to dance. Only one of the company does that at present, Miss Markova, as Procris; the rest are busy with gymnastics.' But he was not fully satisfied. 'Five ballets on end are too much . . . What about a few songs, or even a one-act play in between?'.

De Valois was never one to be put off by a grumpy critic, and the evening was to prove a portentous one. Markova was immediately engaged to appear again a few months later with Dolin in a special season, at a fee of five guineas each. So began what was to be a vital period of collaboration with the de Valois Company and a long partnership with Dolin. The ability to present two Diaghilev stars was an important coup for de Valois, who hitherto had been working at some disadvantage vis-à-vis the Rambert troupe which had Ashton and Antony Tudor as choreographers, and Guest Artists including not only Markova but occasionally Karsavina and Léon Woizikovsky. Now de Valois was in a position to exploit her larger resources and fulfil her ambition – to mount full-scale nineteenth-century classics and so establish a real continuation of the St Petersburg tradition. In June, Markova – who had been dancing in the final, extended season of the Camargo Society at the Savoy Theatre (in which both the Rambert and the de Valois dancers took part) led by Spessivtseva and Lopokova, appearing alongside British artists such as Phyllis Bedells, de Valois, Ruth French and Dolin – received a letter from Lilian Baylis proposing that she should join the Company again for the next season, this time for weekly performances.

In the meantime the still sporadic evenings of ballet at the Old Vic and Sadler's Wells were filled with a repertoire devised almost entirely by de Valois. For an eleven-week spring season these had been supplemented by two ballets from Diaghilev's early period. Fokine's *Le Spectre de la Rose* was revived for de Valois and Dolin – not very successfully, as it had to compete with Karsavina's production danced two years earlier by herself and Harold Turner with the Ballet Rambert. Then, only two months after her début with the Company Markova with the help of de Valois revived *Les Sylphides*, drawing on her memories of the Diaghilev production – a formidable achievement for such a young and relatively inexperienced artist. She herself danced the mazurka and the pas de deux with Dolin. Ursula Moreton (later to become Principal of the Royal Ballet School) took the Prelude and Marie Nielson the Waltz, and *The Times* voted it the best revival of the ballet

ABOVE *Les Sylphides*, photographed *c*1933 with (centre) Beatrice Appleyard, Stanley Judson, Ailne Phillips and (lying at their feet) Ursula Moreton. BELOW *Le Lac des Cygnes*, 1934. Alicia Markova as Odette, Robert Helpmann as Prince Siegfried, William Chappell (far left) as Benno.

since Diaghilev. For this season de Valois engaged six male dancers led by Stanley Judson, formerly a member of Pavlova's company.

A prestige-building interlude came in the autumn when de Valois was invited to take a group of dancers to Denmark on a visit organised by what is now the Royal Academy of Dancing, and its Danish-born president, Adeline Genée. For this, the first foreign tour ever undertaken by a British troupe, the leading dancers were Markova and Dolin. Also in 'The British Ballet Company' were Phyllis Bedells, Ruth French, and the gifted Harold Turner on loan from the Ballet Club. At the final performance, Genée herself, now aged fifty-four, appeared in a little set of dances, partnered by Dolin. The occasion was a big success. The Danish Royal Family lent its support and everybody admitted, with surprise, that there were good dancers in England. The ballets themselves were regarded with a mixture of delight and puzzled respect – only *Les Sylphides* seemed to represent tradition. After *Job*, one Danish newspaper suggested 'To understand the text fully one must preferably have a Bible at hand.'

The size of the troupe was expanding and on its return de Valois continued her long-term plan to establish the old classical tradition. Finally, in October 1932, the romantic 'White' Act II of *Le Lac des Cygnes* was presented with Markova and Dolin. In retrospect this first production of at least a part of one of the greatest traditional nineteenth-century classics can be seen as a milestone in the history of the Company, but at the time it attracted little attention. It was presented as the last item in a mixed programme, and most newspapers gave it merely a two-line mention at the end of a review. *The Times'* critic wrote of the opening performance: 'It gave ample scope to Miss Alicia Markova's capabilities and to her superb technique. Mr Anton Dolin was her partner, but the male honours in the ballet went to Mr Stanley Judson, who generally does the right thing and looks right in it'. Dolin's performance must have been unusually self-effacing: Judson was cast as Benno, the Prince's friend, whose only duty, in the old version, was to catch the Swan Princess in one backward bend in the pas de deux.

Dolin was to recover his ebullient form a few weeks later when he introduced for the first time a solo to Ravel's *Bolero* which was to become a favourite with audiences for years to come, though it was always looked at askance by artistic directors. Two more men had been added – Keith Lester, who had partnered both Karsavina and Spessivtseva on tour, and Antony Tudor, from the Ballet Rambert. Tudor was to claim that he joined only with the prospect of choreographing for the Company.

That winter a note of confidence for the future began to creep into the accounts of the Company – astonishing in some ways, since these cruel months marked the worst period in the Great Depression, with unemployment running at three million and descriptions of misery, violence and starvation filling the newspapers. But from Sadler's Wells the view looked very different. 'London has definitely gone "ballet-minded",' reported the *Yorkshire Evening Post*. 'All sorts of people are wending their way to Sadler's Wells or the Old Vic, and inside a week I have sat next to a Bishop . . . and discussed the future possibilities of ballet with a railway porter, whose two little girls had been awarded a prize by Anton Dolin.'

De Valois herself was refining and defining the ideas that had formed in her mind five

---

The Rake's Progress. Costume sketches by Rex Whistler for the 1942 revival, annotated by Whistler and de Valois. The original costumes were lost in Holland at the beginning of the War.

VIGNETTE 9"

years before. In a series of articles in *The Dancing Times* that winter she set out opinions to which she was to remain faithful throughout her career. She took a firm line with her Company ('dancers must be prepared to put up with a certain lack of space'), and laid out her basic beliefs about her art. 'Ballet, i.e. dancing, is inseparable from music. Dancing, i.e. movement, is inseparable from the theatre.' She held that every choreographer should have some knowledge of drama production. She surprisingly forecast a greater future for abstract ('architectural') ballets than for narrative ('pictorial') ballets, and set down some far-sighted declarations about the Company that she was still in the process of forming.

Meanwhile its month-to-month existence depended on a steady supply of new works. The successes of Diaghilev's Ballets Russes had set the fashion for a flow of novelties, and for the moment it fell mainly on de Valois to provide them, with Ashton as her still somewhat inexperienced alternative. The results of their combined efforts proved acceptable though not enduring. According to *The Music Lover* magazine, de Valois' *The Jew in the Bush* had 'some lustrous spots'. The score by Geoffrey Toye, and his conducting of it, was praised, as was that of a comedy ballet by de Valois, *Douanes*. (Most of the reviews at this time were written by music critics and the orchestra received much attention, usually favourable.) Ashton's Tennysonian *The Lord of Burleigh*, originally created for the Camargo Society, was paired with de Valois' *The Origin of Design* with modified success. 'Both ballets suffer somewhat from uneventful happenings', reported *The Times'* critic in a striking phrase. *The Scorpions of Ysit*, an exotic Egyptian fable dreamed up by Terence Gray and originally choreographed by de Valois for her Academy of Choreographic Art, left the audience uncertain as to whether it was intended as a tragedy or a comedy. 'When the leading scorpion (Miss Bamford) sat down on the dead babe, laughter was provoked in the wrong place', reported the *Daily Mail*.

Ashton's version of *Pomona*, another legacy of the Camargo Society, was considered 'a synthetic ballet rather than a dance-creation' by *The Times*, though Beatrice Appleyard in the title role earned flattering notices. *The Birthday of Oberon*, an attempt by de Valois and Lambert to extract a ballet from Purcell's 'The Fairy Queen' by combining the operatic and dancing talent of the theatre, seems to have proved unsuccessful. *The Music Lover*, mysteriously labelling it 'A nightshirt ballet', thought that 'Miss de Valois, who otherwise did most admirable things with the choreography, would have been better advised to do one of two things: keep the singers out of sight or make them sit down'.

Choreographically speaking, this was evidently a makeshift period. But in March 1933 the Vic-Wells Ballet presented *Coppélia*, starring one of Diaghilev's most popular ballerinas, Lydia Lopokova. The sparkling charm and warmth of this diminutive dancer had enchanted London audiences. What is more, she had married an Englishman. To add to the general excitement there were even rumours that the two performances she promised were to be her farewell to the stage. A less widely noted but, in retrospect, more vital contribution to the new production was the import of a Russian to supervise it. Nicholas Sergeyev was a living link with the great St Petersburg company from which the Diaghilev troupe was descended. He had been the régisseur of the Maryinsky Ballet from 1904 until the Revolution and in 1921 Diaghilev had called him in to help reconstruct *The*

A Wedding Bouquet. ABOVE backcloth and BELOW drop curtain designed by Gerald Berners, 1937.

Douanes, 1932. (Left to right) Anton Dolin as the Man from Cook's,
Antony Tudor as the Passport Officer, Ninette de Valois as the Tight Rope Dancer.

Sleeping Princess at the Alhambra. After this he settled in Paris and in 1932 he had been summoned to London to mount *Giselle* for the Camargo Society. Now de Valois invited him to help reconstruct *Coppélia*.

Sergeyev seems to have been an eccentric, old-fashioned little man. Interested in the craft rather than in the art of ballet, he was more concerned with the props and mechanics than with the expressive concept, a kind of Dr Coppélius of choreography. De Valois refers to him as 'completely devoid of any real stage sense' and also as 'unmusical to a degree bordering on eccentricity'. His chief asset was a collection of notebooks in which he had recorded a large number of the Maryinsky productions in a system of movement-notation devised by the dancer and teacher Vladimir Stepanov. With the aid of these he reconstructed the choreography that he had supervised in St Petersburg, doubtless with modifications to suit the small company and the modest technical powers of the dancers.

'I had the good fortune to be the pupil of some of the greatest dancing teachers who have lived, such as Marius Petipa, Johansson, Ivanov, Gerdt', he declared in an interview in *The Observer*, 'I call these teachers the walking chronologies, because they all lived to be a hundred. In Italy and France the ballet has greatly deteriorated . . . I therefore hope and believe that there will be a large enough public in London to keep up the most beautiful and most difficult of the arts.' The skeleton, if not the flesh and blood, of the Maryinsky style had been transferred from Imperial Russia to a modest theatre in Islington.

Coppélia, 1933. Lydia Lopokova (centre) as Swanilda, with Nadina Newhouse, Sheila McCarthy, Gwyneth Mathews, Hermione Darnborough, Freda Bamford, Ailne Phillips.

Coppélia – with the last act omitted as had been normal almost since the première in 1870 – was a huge success. Its tuneful comedy was evidently more to the taste of the still unsophisticated audiences than the mournful *Le Lac des Cygnes*, and Lopokova partnered by Stanley Judson was as bewitching as ever, personally coached by Madame Zanfretta who had danced the role of Franz (*en travestie*) in Paris. Predictably, perhaps, Lopokova announced after the curtain had fallen that she might not retire after all. De Valois herself took over the part of Swanilda for later performances and scored a big success. The introduction of a two-act ballet was an important step. Not only did it influence an audience which had been accustomed over many years to mixed programmes of short works, but it also opened the minds of young choreographers and dancers to the potentialities of what was then considered an old-fashioned form.

This *Coppélia* held another, more immediate, source of future triumphs. Now and then the lighting would flash back from an unusually shiny black pate in the back row of the corps de ballet, drawing the eye to the small big-eyed face beneath it. Robert Helpmann, newly arrived from Australia, was making sure, with the aid of a good supply of brilliantine, that his presence did not go unnoticed. His unerring sense of theatre was to serve both him and the Company well for the next seventeen years. In 1933 he was already twenty-four, with a good deal of experience behind him. The son of a frustrated actress, he was a performer from the cradle. He took his first dancing lessons at the age of five and by twelve had begun to appear in revues and plays. At fourteen he was taking lessons from Laurent Novikov, a member of Pavlova's company which was touring in Australia, and he spent six months travelling with the great ballerina. In 1932 he arrived in London with a letter of introduction to de Valois from the well-known actress Margaret Rawlings. 'She tells me she is sure that he has something very special in him,' wrote de Valois later. 'I look up and see a figure in the doorway . . . He is wearing a huge camel-hair coat. Portrait of a young man, very pale, with large eyes. I am struck by a resemblance in some strange way to Massine . . . Everything about him proclaims the artist born.' What she actually said to him at the time was 'I think I can do something with that face'.

'She would have welcomed anything male on two legs', insisted Helpmann later; but in fact de Valois had already sized up his gifts. 'On the credit side: talented, enthusiastic, extremely intelligent, great facility and vitality, witty, cute as a monkey, quick as a squirrel, a sense of the theatre and his own possible achievements therein. On the debit side: academically weak; lacking in concentration; too fond of a good time and too busy having it.' To Helpmann's mortification, she put him in the corps de ballet. But he was not to stay there long. Within six months he was starring in the biggest male role in the repertory – as Satan in *Job*. That he had the nerve to tackle it is a tribute to his self-confidence, for the male contingent at Sadler's Wells had been temporarily strengthened by the addition of one of the top technicians in Diaghilev's company, Stanislas Idzikowski. Helpmann's eyes must have opened even wider when he watched the diminutive Russian in Fokine's *Carnaval* and partnering Markova in *Le Spectre de la Rose* and in the Bluebird pas de deux from *The Sleeping Princess*.

The presence of two such exceptionally light, quick dancers as Markova and Idzikowski inspired Ashton to devise for them in his very first creation for the Company a ballet which was to bring out in full his personal kind of lyricism. *Les Rendezvous*, 'simply a vehicle for the exquisite dancing of Idzikowski and Markova', as he has described it, was a set of classical variations to a collage of tuneful pieces by Auber cunningly put together by Lambert, with designs by William Chappell, a dancer from the Rambert company. Its inventive felicity made it an instant success and it has remained a favourite showcase for many different casts. At the time it was hailed as an example of a still unfamiliar genre, the abstract ballet. 'The possibilities of the square, and of its lively cousin the rhombus, have never, I am sure, been so adequately worked out', reported *London Week*.

Idzikowski was only a fleeting visitor, but Markova was now a full member of the Company. For her, in January 1934, Sergeyev mounted again the *Giselle* that he had produced for the Camargo Society. Dolin, who on that occasion had partnered Spessivtseva, was her Albrecht, with Helpmann as a presumably rather less than rustic Hilarion. Markova inspired glowing compliments for her performance. She was the embodiment of everyone's ideal ballerina, a creature so delicate that it seemed as if the smallest touch of tragedy would shatter her poise, and Dolin made a vividly romantic lover. But the ballet itself was enjoyed rather condescendingly. 'Whether ballet of this type will ever capture again the favour that is now bestowed on the more modern type may be doubted', wrote *The Times* critic cautiously.

By the beginning of 1934 de Valois had two full nineteenth-century classics and part of another one in her repertoire, with a ballerina to star in them, Markova. Encouraged by their success, she prepared, only four weeks after her new *Giselle*, yet another classic, *The Nutcracker* or, as it was then called, *Casse-Noisette*. In many ways this was a more

ABOVE *Giselle*, 1934. (Left) Alicia Markova as Giselle, (right) Anton Dolin as Albrecht.
BELOW (left) *Carnaval* Harold Turner as Harlequin, a role which he first danced in 1935.
(Right) *Les Rendezvous*, 1933. Alicia Markova and Stanislas Idzikowski.

Casse-Noisette, 1937 revival. Act III, with Margot Fonteyn as the Sugar Plum Fairy
and Robert Helpmann as the Nutcracker Prince.

ambitious enterprise than *Giselle*. It was the first-ever production of the ballet outside
Russia, with complicated changes of scene designed by the dancer Hedley Briggs, and with
a very large cast of nearly forty dancers as well as a troupe of children. Once again
Markova scored a personal success, as the Sugar Plum Fairy. Her partner this time was
Stanley Judson, Dolin being unavailable. The charm of Tchaikovsky's score and the
variegated numbers combined to make the ballet as popular as ever. Sergeyev again
supervised the production. According to *The Times* critic (who did not reveal the basis for
his opinion) the Russian had incorporated 'a few alterations'. Some of these were
undoubtedly in the *Danse Arabe* in the last Act, which was entrusted to a publicity-
attracting young actress, Elsa Lanchester. Foreseeably, she received particular attention
in the press reviews but *Casse-Noisette* was also noteworthy for another reason. One
evening, sharp eyes might have noticed among the Snowflakes a small dark girl with a
slightly oriental face which would change instantly from gaiety to sadness, and a specially
soft, easy way of moving. The date was 20 April and she appeared in the programme as
Peggy Hookham, but a few months later this was changed into the stage name of Margot

Fontes, soon to be modulated into Fonteyn. She had only recently joined de Valois' school at Sadler's Wells and was still a student, called in as an extra to fill out the regular company of thirty-six dancers. Born fourteen years before, in Surrey, to an English father and a half-Brazilian mother, she had begun her training with White Russian teachers in Shanghai, where her father was working, and she had continued in London with another Russian, Serafina Astafieva. Her family history and her dark, foreign features misled de Valois when she first arrived in the classroom. '"Who's the little Chinese girl in the corner?" she asked'. 'I noticed', Fonteyn was to write later, 'that the new arrivals fell into two categories as far as Miss de Valois was concerned: "She's a nice child" or "She's an absolute devil, but very talented". It was the latter group that always seemed to get on.'

Fonteyn was considered obstinate and wrongly taught. 'I came in for a good deal of shouting,' she recalls. But de Valois had spotted her potentialities at once. 'It was obvious that something wonderful and beautiful had come into our midst . . . elegance . . . was discernible, even beneath the careless breadth of adolescent movement. Children are generally either gauche or graceful. Miss Hookham was both.'

Gently influenced by her mother, dance had crept into the young girl's life almost unconsciously; she was too retiring and sensitive by nature to have theatrical ambitions of the kind that Helpmann had nurtured. The first performance of *Casse-Noisette* clinched her career. 'It was something of a nightmare until we reached a point near the end where we all knelt as a group, waving our snowflake wands while paper snow rained about our heads. At this moment the opera chorus was singing, Tchaikovsky's inspired music had reached its most beguiling climax, the lights were dimmed to a soft blue and the curtains swung gently together, muffling the applause on the other side. I felt an incredible elation; this was theatre, this was the real thing. All discouraging self-criticism was forgotten. From this moment on there could be no turning back.'

Greatness is often attended by good luck, and the arrival of Fonteyn at this particular moment is a striking proof of de Valois' claim to that attribute. So far, imported stars had carried her budding venture along. Without Dolin in the earliest stage and Markova during the first formative years the whole enterprise might have foundered, and would certainly have faltered. Here now was talent, still immature but expanding, which could and would unfold in step with the Company's demands. It was part of the slow-burning fuse which de Valois had lit so deliberately and courageously.

Fonteyn's first solo role came very soon. In April 1934 de Valois staged a Gothic fantasy called *The Haunted Ballroom*, based on a story by Edgar Allan Poe. The ballet was cunningly conceived to exploit the histrionic gifts of Helpmann as a doomed country laird, a role which demanded as much acting as dancing, and Fonteyn, after the first performance, took the small but important mime part of his son. With a theatrical score by Geoffrey Toye and a romantic setting by Motley it proved an excellent vehicle to launch Helpmann on his long career as a dramatic dancer. So successful was he in the part that in the autumn de Valois entrusted him with the role of Albrecht in *Giselle*, partnering Markova.

For this season de Valois and Constant Lambert were working on her most ambitious project to date – the full version of *Le Lac des Cygnes* (it was not to be renamed *Swan Lake* until 1963, nearly thirty years later). Markova was Odette/Odile and Helpmann was again her partner in another role confined mainly to mime. Elizabeth Miller and Pamela (then billed as Doris) May danced the Pas de Trois with Walter Gore from the Ballet

Rambert, who also partnered Ursula Moreton in the czardas. The ballet was designed by Hugh Stevenson, one of Rambert's discoveries.

This was a vital moment in the Company's history, particularly as the production had to compete with that of a new Russian company, Colonel de Basil's Ballet Russe, which was presenting some of Diaghilev's former stars in revivals of their original roles. The Russians had descended on London the previous summer with a glamorous repertoire ranging from old Fokine favourites to works by Balanchine and Massine, and a dazzling array of dancers including the St Petersburg-trained Danilova and the three 'baby ballerinas' Tamara Toumanova, Irina Baronova and Tatiana Riabouchinska. They inherited most of the old Diaghilev audience and dominated the headlines. During that summer, Massine had introduced to English audiences his 'symphonic' ballets which aroused deep controversy, and all the attendant publicity. With his large company, fine repertoire and opera-house standards of production, de Basil dominated the London ballet scene. In June they were presenting *Le Lac des Cygnes, Act II* with Danilova and Paul Petrov. A few months later on the small stage of Sadler's Wells de Valois offered her full-length production, in which only Markova had an international reputation. It was a gesture of impressive confidence. Her courage was amply rewarded. For the first time in the Company's history, the première was treated as a London social event, a charity gala in the old style, even if not quite in full opera-house splendour. 'Lady Hinchinbrooke was one of the many hostesses who wore a diamond fillet in place of the more ornate tiara', noted the *Daily Telegraph*. After consultations with Sergeyev in Paris, de Valois herself had taken over the production. Lambert, of course, was in charge of his beloved Tchaikovsky score: the *Daily Telegraph*

LEFT Julia Farron as Alicia in the 1942 revival of *The Haunted Ballroom*. RIGHT Margot Fonteyn as the Creole Girl and William Chappell as the Creole Boy in *Rio Grande*, 1935.

remarked that he 'did not insist on the excessively fast tempo demanded by other conductors'. The décor was by Hugh Stevenson.

A spectacle of such magnitude stretched the Company's budget to its limits. The unromantic critic of the *New Statesman*, who considered that 'the ballet depends largely for its effectiveness on the magnificence of the Third Act', found the effect insufficiently splendid and imaginative, while *The Times* found the First Act 'dull'. Markova, given a chance to deploy her classical style to the full, scored a triumph. The distinguished critic Adrian Stokes wrote that she could rightly be compared with Pavlova, and he had fairly kind words for Helpmann as her Prince. 'His build is not altogether a happy one for a dancer. Nevertheless he performs exceedingly well. His movements are concise and he bounces with great verve.' The *Daily Telegraph* critic was more generous, writing that Helpmann's 'springs and leaps were like nothing seen since Nijinsky'. The Company might not yet have achieved the overall standard needed to fulfil the full potential of *Le Lac des Cygnes*, but largely through the star quality of Markova the great classic was established as part of the English repertoire.

The success of the production encouraged Lilian Baylis to launch a public appeal for funds. An article in *The Times* reminded its readers that her two theatres were legally bound to provide performances of 'high class drama, especially the plays of Shakespeare, of high-class opera and other entertainments and exhibitions suited for the recreation and instruction of the poorer classes', and reported that 'the average price last season of the 3150 seats at the two theatres was two shillings and a halfpenny. In these circumstances it has been impossible in recent years to maintain the steadily improving standard without loss'. A sum of £25,000 was the target of the appeal.

In the spring of 1935 (during which a promising boy from the Ballet Club, Frank Staff, joined the Company) de Valois offered one of Ashton's cheerful trifles, a revival of a ballet devised three years earlier for the Camargo Society, to Lambert's popular score *Rio Grande*. It had then been called *A Day in a Southern Port* but had now reverted to its true name and had been given an amusing décor by Edward Burra. The role of the Creole Girl, originally danced by Markova, was given to Fonteyn. The ballet did not make a great impression, but Fonteyn did. *The Dancing Times* presciently recorded her first appearance in a leading role as 'the most notable event of the past few weeks'.

However, it was becoming clear that the Company could not continue for ever on a shoestring basis. Markova had announced her intention to leave so that she could lead an independent career. Now an occasion arose to put her decision into effect. Laura Henderson and Vivian van Damm, the owner and manager of the Windmill, a variety theatre where Markova's sister was appearing, saw one of her performances and immediately offered to back the Company for a season, with Markova dancing at every performance. Since her usual partner, Helpmann, was under contract for a revue, Dolin was signed up in his place.

The Henderson/van Damm season was to start with two weeks at Sadler's Wells followed by a week at the Shaftesbury Theatre in the West End and then a provincial tour, the first to be undertaken by the Company. It was scheduled to open in May 1935 with a new ballet, stipulated in the contract. It turned out to be a worthy milestone to mark this important stage in the Company's history. De Valois' *The Rake's Progress* was the first authentically English ballet to be created for the Company, and it epitomised all its best qualities – the imaginative subject, drawn from Hogarth's famous series of engravings;

Rex Whistler's designs, which brilliantly recreated them in stage terms; the bold tuneful score by Gavin Gordon; and above all, de Valois' choreography – theatrical, vigorous, concise. Yet paradoxically it had by no means an easy birth. The idea had originally been proposed to Ashton, who had turned it down and passed it over to de Valois. Because she fell ill the ballet could not be included in the spring programme as intended. It was postponed and finally chosen to open the Henderson/van Damm season, which thereby got off to a flying start. Apparently it was not the Rake of Walter Gore, a brilliant character dancer in his first major role, who initially made the biggest impression, but Harold Turner, a vital young virtuoso who had started with Rambert and had recently joined the Company; he took the smaller roles of the Dancing Master and the Gentleman with a Rope. Markova, as The Betrayed Girl, was admired in a role which did not extend her classical talent, and most people were impressed by Rex Whistler's imaginative and carefully drawn frontcloth. But *The Dancing Times* complained that the sets were too dark, with too much 'smoky sepia'. 'Life in such an interior would have driven any impressionable young man to end his days in the mad-house.' In the second week at Sadler's Wells, Markova crowned her career with the Company in *Giselle*, now newly designed at Mrs Henderson's expense by William Chappell. Her appearances on the tour which followed (the repertoire included *The Jar*, another recent small de Valois ballet with a Massine flavour), were to be the last that she would make with the Company for many years.

Markova's departure in the summer of 1935 marked the end of the beginning of the Company's history, some three and a half years after its first tentative performance. This first tour undoubtedly reinforced its confidence and sense of identity, as touring usually does. From now on the Company was to develop from within, absorbing some elements, rejecting others, but always retaining the consistent character which comes from firm control and basic conformity. One of the first rejects was the young dancer, Antony Tudor, who, disappointed at not being offered an opportunity as choreographer, returned to the Ballet Rambert (later he was to form his own company, the London Ballet, and then to move to America). Walter Gore left soon afterwards. But, as well as Harold Turner and Mary Honer, both brilliant technicians who had much experience in commercial companies, de Valois acquired from the Ballet Rambert Pearl Argyle, a long-legged dancer noted for her beauty. Finally she made what was to be her shrewdest investment. She signed up Frederick Ashton on a permanent basis as performer and resident choreographer. He was contracted to produce at least three new ballets in the year, at a salary of £10 a week with no royalties.

From now on all ballet performances were at Sadler's Wells, since alternating with the Old Vic had proved cumbersome and expensive. In the new autumn season Ashton dominated the scene. He revived his *Façade*, already a popular success with the Camargo Society and Ballet Rambert audiences, with Fonteyn dancing the Polka and a new Country Dance number (later dropped). His *Les Rendezvous* was already a favourite with audiences and it, too, was included in this season's programme. He also scored a success as a dancer when he took over the role of Pierrot in *Carnaval*, though the revival proved in general unpoetic. At the same time Ashton was working on a serious ballet to be presented a few weeks later, Stravinsky's *Le Baiser de la Fée*, an ambitious project as no choreographer had yet managed to overcome the work's awkward structure. Ashton's solution, with the help of atmospheric designs by Sophie Fedorovitch, his favourite collaborator since their first year together with the Ballet Club, was as good as any. It

Pearl Argyle as the Fairy in *Le Baiser de la Fée*, 1935.

cleverly exploited Turner's virtuosity as the Bridegroom and Argyle's cool lustre as the relentless Fairy and it gave Fonteyn her first big romantic part as the Fiancée. This was the first collaboration between Ashton and Fonteyn, whose combined talents were to mould the whole future dance-style of the Company. It began more as a confrontation than a collaboration. Ashton found Fonteyn lacking in precision. 'I got very cross with her at times and went on and on at her relentlessly.' Finally she burst into tears, flung her arms around his neck, and the conflict was resolved. *The Manchester Guardian*, which found the first act 'vapid' and the second act only 'adequate' praised Fonteyn's pas de deux with Turner as 'a really excellent effort in the classical style'. *The Sphere* described the ballet as 'both ingenious and beautiful and not too ingenious to be beautiful'.

Ashton's arrival in 1935 was the beginning of the long upward swing of classical ballet in Britain, a movement carried forward in a rush by his next works, which were even more successful. They exploited brilliantly the lyrical vein which he had uncovered in Fonteyn and, importantly, in the rest of the Company. While his natural wit and sense of chic inventiveness continued to run riot in the many dances that he went on mounting for commercial shows, he poured into his Sadler's Wells ballets the flood of romanticism that he had hinted at in earlier pieces for Rambert. First came a brief, dreamy pas de deux for Argyle and Helpmann called *Siesta*, the forerunner of many such tenuous duets that he was to devise for gala occasions; and it was followed in February 1936 by a major work for the whole company, *Apparitions*. This was an essay in the High Romantic style, originally conceived by Constant Lambert, with a libretto adapted from the theme of Berlioz's 'Symphonie Fantastique', about a drug-addicted poet who dreams of his ideal love as the potion takes effect. It was clearly to be an elaborate production and Ashton persuaded Maynard (later Lord) Keynes and his colleagues in the Camargo Society to contribute £300. Boosted by an extra £100 from Lord Rothermere, this sum just covered the costs. As a piece of imaginative but inexpensive stagecraft it can seldom have been surpassed. Helpmann, as the Poet, was given the chance to display his theatrical panache in a role which called more for mime than for dance, while Fonteyn again emerged as the epitome of romantic glamour – gentle, sad and seductive. Her musicality was remarked on, and the piquant contrast between her style and Helpmann's dramatics were praised. The *New Statesman*'s critic morbidly savoured 'his last meeting with her in an orgy of scarlet-robed monks and nuns who force upon him the caresses of her lips, already green with putrefaction'. This was a new kind of pleasure for visitors to Islington.

Fonteyn was now firmly established as the Company's ballerina. Two months earlier she had proved herself by taking over as Odette in *Le Lac des Cygnes*. The virtuoso part of Odile in Act III was danced by Ruth French, a skilful technician who had danced in Pavlova's company. The experienced critic Arnold Haskell, whilst criticising the corps de ballet, was carried away by Fonteyn. 'Margot Fonteyn in the famous role gave a truly great performance', he wrote in an extended article. 'She has fully earned that rare title "ballerina".'

The Ashton-Fonteyn-Helpmann collaboration was now successfully launched and they were an impressive team. Beatrice Appleyard left at this time, but the dancers still included the limpidly classical Pearl Argyle, Pamela May and June Brae; Mary Honer, Elizabeth Miller, both lively technicians; the young Julia Farron, a strong dancer with a gift for character; and among the men Harold Turner, Leslie Edwards and in the corps de ballet Michael Somes aged nineteen. Ashton's ballets had begun to dominate the repertoire, but

ABOVE LEFT *The Rake's Progress*. Robert Helpmann as the Rake, Ray Powell as the Gentleman with a Rope. ABOVE RIGHT *Apparitions*, with Margot Fonteyn. BELOW Sophie Fedorovitch at a costume fitting.

Barabau. Molly Brown in the 1937 revival, with Frederick Ashton as the Sergeant.

de Valois did not immediately abandon her commitment as choreographer. She balanced *Apparitions* with a complete contrast in her own more muscular style, a new arrangement of Rieti's comedy *Barabau*, originally composed for Diaghilev. This was followed in October 1936 by an assault on a peak which has continued to baffle choreographers, Beethoven's only ballet, *Prometheus*. Once again the heavy comedy of the story and over-insistent rhythms of the score swamped de Valois' choreography and gallant attempts by Mary Honer, June Brae, and Helpmann and Turner (alternating as the 'hero') to breathe life into it. The mood of the piece seemed to be wrong for the moment.

The right mood was evoked, though, in *Nocturne*, another ultra-romantic short work by Ashton which followed a few weeks later. This was a small-scale updated echo of *Giselle* – a young man emerging from an elegant ball flirts with a flower seller but then abandons her for a rich girl. The nostalgic music by Delius (his 'Paris' nocturne), Fedorovitch's evocative setting, and eloquent performances by Helpmann and Fonteyn, with a moving vignette of a detached onlooker by Ashton himself, made a heady mixture. The autumn of 1936 brought one of the first of many appearances of the Company on television – at that time still a luxury for a small élite; it was to be featured over a dozen times in the next two

Giselle, 1937, with Margot Fonteyn as Giselle and Robert Helpmann as Albrecht.

years. A few weeks later Fonteyn made her début in *Giselle*, partnered by Helpmann, with Pamela May as Queen of the Wilis.

Ashton's next work, *Les Patineurs*, an apparently lightweight piece consisting only of a suite of classical dances held together by a single theme and arranged to the frothiest of scores, was, paradoxically, to be one of the Company's most solid stayers. Lambert had the idea of using music composed by Meyerbeer for his opera 'L'Etoile du Nord', and he made the orchestral arrangement. *Les Patineurs* was announced in *The Dancing Times* in January 1937, with de Valois named as choreographer. But, as Ashton has related, he overheard Lambert playing the score and it struck him as more suitable for his own style. Luckily for him, de Valois was too busy to tackle it and he took over. The result was a ballet with a hoar-frost charm and a sparkling invention which proved irresistible. Fonteyn and Helpmann were as cool and elegant as icicles in the pas de deux, and the technical feats of the first captivating Blue Boy, Turner, and of the first spinning Girls in Blue, Mary Honer and Elizabeth Miller, were to set a challenge for their many later replacements.

The Company was now reaching towards international recognition, and Ashton's next ballet, launched only seven weeks later, had a positively Parisian flavour. *A Wedding*

Bouquet was the fruit of the mutual admiration and friendship between four highly sophisticated people: Lord Berners, who conceived and composed it, Gertrude Stein, whose words were written into the accompaniment, Constant Lambert, who during the war was to replace the original Chorus and to speak the text himself from the side of the stage, and Ashton. The characters included witty caricatures of de Valois as a disciplinarian housekeeper, of Stein's pet dog, and of ballet convention such as the traditional pas de deux. The fun, which revealed for the first time Helpmann's comic genius in the role of the Bridegroom, was charged with a wistful sadness – wonderfully conveyed by Fonteyn's faintly mad Julia – which was pure Ashton. The whole confection had the piquant flavour and the light, crisp texture of a French pastry.

The contrasting and complementary gifts of Ashton and de Valois were never better illustrated than by this ballet and its sequel two months later. If in *A Wedding Bouquet* Ashton had touched a Gallic note, de Valois' approach to *Checkmate* had a British forthrightness and solidity. Paradoxically, Ashton's ballet was launched in Islington while de Valois' production was given its first showing at the Théâtre des Champs-Elysées in Paris, the Company by now being held in such esteem that it had been exported to represent British culture during the 1937 International Exhibition.

The season made little impact on the Parisians, but when *Checkmate* was presented in London in November, it aroused keen interest, even if opinions were varied. *The Observer* described the theme as 'not mere chess but passionate metaphysics', and *The Sunday Times* described the score as 'the best ballet music that has been written for many years'. The *New Statesman*, on the other hand, complained that 'at moments the din was so distressing that one could hardly watch the movements on stage,' the *Sunday Pictorial* criticised the ballet as 'strange and tedious', and *The Sunday Referee* described Helpmann's performance as the feeble Red King as 'palsying about'. From English audiences the almost Central-European angularity of the chessboard choreography, Arthur Bliss's emphatic score, and the post-Cubist designs of McKnight Kauffer, the American poster artist, drew a sympathetic response. June Brae's darkly dramatic Black Queen, Helpmann's faltering Red King and Turner's athletic Red Knight set the tone of a production which still packs a powerful punch.

Sadly, on 25 November 1937 Lilian Baylis suffered a stroke and died. In a sense, her mission was accomplished; Shakespeare and modern drama were firmly entrenched at the Old Vic, opera was flourishing at Sadler's Wells, and her ballet venture was not only standing, but dancing, on its own feet, an acknowledged rival to any ballet company in the West. Baylis had been committed to both of her theatres with equal passion. One day, so it was related, she crashed her old car and lay half-conscious under the wreckage. 'It's Miss Baylis! Miss Baylis of the Old Vic', exclaimed a passer-by. She opened her eyes for a moment, '. . . and Sadler's Wells', she murmured. Her death left personal grief in Rosebery Avenue. It had been her habit to go the rounds of the dressing-rooms at the start of each season distributing white heather to the artists. That autumn she had, instead, inexplicably given to each of them a sprig of rosemary. For remembrance? It was not necessary. Her inspired faith in the future had already materialised in an enterprise too

Les Patineurs. Set and costumes designed by
William Chappell, 1937.

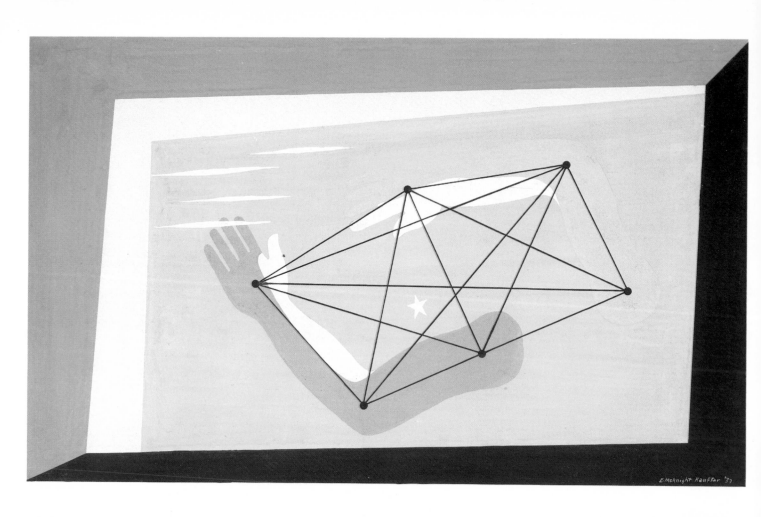

substantial to be threatened by the disappearance of any individual.

Appropriately, the immediate tribute to Lilian Baylis's memory took the form of an appeal for funds. A sum of around £40,000 was needed to complete the building plans for the two theatres, and the Duke of Kent gave his patronage in asking the public for help for 'the nearest thing to national drama, national opera and national ballet that we yet possess'. Meanwhile, activities at Sadler's Wells went on uninterrupted, with a new ballet from Ashton promised for the spring – a spring already darkened by the shadow of Hitler's threats. The new work, *Horoscope*, introduced in January 1938, reflected the atmosphere of the time. Once again the original idea came primarily from Constant Lambert, but, characteristically, Ashton concentrated on private rather than on public tensions, following the theme of two lovers kept apart by their predestined differences of temperament. The score, by Lambert himself, was dedicated to Fonteyn, of whom he had become a passionate admirer, and she danced the part of the gentle heroine – partnered for the first time by a promising dancer with a fine presence and a handsome jump, Michael Somes. Pamela May made a special success of the serene part of the Moon, and the handling of the corps de ballet marked a new maturity in Ashton's style. Once again Sophie Fedorovitch added her delicate personal touch to the designs.

One of the last conversations between de Valois and Lilian Baylis had been about a project which was to become a landmark in the history of the Company, a full-length production of *The Sleeping Princess* (later to be called *The Sleeping Beauty*). The intention had been to include it in the programme for the spring of 1938 but neither the backstage accommodation at Sadler's Wells nor the size of the stage itself – fourteen feet shallower than it is today – was able to do justice to a work which had been designed to exploit the full splendours of the vast Maryinsky Theatre in St Petersburg. The plan was postponed until the theatre could be improved and unfortunately it did not come to fruition in time for Lilian Baylis to see it crown her achievements.

In the meantime two small ballets were mounted during June 1938, a short-lived fable by de Valois, *Le Roi Nu*, and an equally ephemeral trifle by Ashton, *The Judgement of Paris*, to a score by a young British composer, Lennox Berkeley. This was arranged for a Royal Gala in aid of the Baylis Memorial Fund, which closed the Sadler's Wells season. The theatre was then given over to the builders. Moving out of London, the Company went on a provincial tour – to Oxford, Bournemouth, Dublin and Cardiff – before disbanding for the summer holiday.

The international situation was steadily deteriorating and in August came the Munich crisis and the meeting between Hitler and Chamberlain. After many delays, during which the Company performed in two outlying theatres, at Streatham Hill and Golders Green, Sadler's Wells Theatre reopened in October 1938 during the lull provided by the abortive truce between the Nazis and the Western Powers. The atmosphere was tense but performances went on and the Company worked hard on rehearsals for *The Sleeping Princess*. To tide over the weeks while it was still in preparation, and perhaps to raise public spirits, Ashton staged a light-hearted piece, *Harlequin in the Street*. Set to a charming score by Couperin, it had originally been devised for the Arts Theatre in Cambridge. Its most

ABOVE *Checkmate*. Drop curtain by E. McKnight Kauffer, 1937.
BELOW *Le Lac des Cygnes*. Set by Leslie Hurry, 1943 (the first of several versions).

striking features were the nimble dancing of Alan Carter in the title role and some memorable backdrops and costumes by André Derain – fated to be discarded and painted over during the war.

Mustering all the now considerable resources of her company, de Valois announced the première of *The Sleeping Princess* for 2 February 1939. The production was carefully prepared. Sergeyev came over from Paris to supervise rehearsals and he aimed to restore the ballet as near to its old Maryinsky form as the still modest forces at his disposal permitted. Several alterations made by Diaghilev for his 1921 production, which Sergeyev himself had helped to mount, were eradicated – for instance, the Chinese dance in Act III which he had borrowed from *Casse-Noisette*. Similarly, other passages were restored, such

LEFT Margot Fonteyn as the Young Woman, Michael Somes as the Young Man, in *Horoscope*.
RIGHT June Brae as the Black Queen in *Checkmate*.

as the Cinderella pas de deux in the same Act. The coda to the final grand pas de deux was rescued from the Three Ivans to whom it had rather incongruously been allotted.

The idea of reproducing this mammoth spectacle, the very symbol of the splendours of the Imperial Ballet in St Petersburg, in the sober Islington theatre with a company not yet ten years old and entirely made up of home-grown British dancers, marked the peak of de Valois' early ambitions. Her aim had been to plant the classical tradition on English soil; and here was its most prestigious blossom, not seen in the West since the glorious Diaghilev production, on the point of opening. The venture received appropriate publicity. In January a send-off dinner was organised at the Café Royal attended by de Valois and Sergeyev. The *Evening Standard* carried a paragraph about the designer, Nadia Benois, niece of Diaghilev's famous collaborator, daughter of the architect of Warsaw Cathedral and herself 'a painter of landscapes alternated occasionally with portraits of her cook'. The première was celebrated as a charity gala, attended by Queen Mary; and in a dense fog an elegant audience made their way to Sadler's Wells. The Queen was presented with a bouquet by the youngest pupil from the School. She was aged eleven and her name was Beryl Groom – to be changed, when she joined the Company, to Beryl Grey.

The performance of *The Sleeping Princess* was a resounding success. As Aurora, the nineteen-year-old Fonteyn (who, as if to 'play herself in', had danced her first full *Le Lac des Cygnes* three months earlier) was acclaimed for 'probably the best performance of her career'; Helpmann's Prince was described as elegant and noble. June Brae's Lilac Fairy, the Bluebird duet of Mary Honer and Harold Turner, and Ursula Moreton in the Cinderella dance, Pamela May as the Diamond Fairy and Elizabeth Miller, Julia Farron, William

Harlequin in the Street. LEFT Alan Carter as Harlequin.
RIGHT John Hart as the Bread Boy.

Chappell, Claude Newman and Frederick Ashton in 'subsidiary roles' were all highly praised. John Greenwood, borrowed from the opera company to mime Carabosse, was saluted as 'suitably scarifying'. The orchestra was universally admired for its rendering of the score over which its conductor, Constant Lambert, had spent so much loving care. Only one feature of the production came in for some criticism – unfortunately an important feature – the designs. De Valois had a theory that the 'failure' of the Diaghilev production had been partly due to Bakst's too heavy and elaborate costumes; simplicity and lightness (less expensive in any case) were to dominate this production. Inventiveness and imagination would have been needed to wed these qualities to Petipa's massive vision, and they were lacking. The sets were painfully trite and the austere costumes – not one jewel was permitted – looked poverty stricken. Some of the dancers tried to add surreptitious sequins when 'Madam's eyes were elsewhere', and Fonteyn has described

The Sleeping Princess, 1939, Act I. Margot Fonteyn as Princess Aurora.

how she nearly cried when she saw her costume. The overall muted tints of grey and brown and mauve hinted prophetically at the drabness which was to overtake the whole world during the next few years.

The occasion involving seventy dancers (thirty of whom were students), two hundred costumes and four sets, had been by far the biggest enterprise undertaken so far. It proved an instant success with the public and a few weeks later Acts I and III were presented at Covent Garden at a gala in honour of the French President. Following up such a triumph was not easy and a little piece presented by Ashton in May, *Cupid and Psyche*, fell flat. But the general prospect looked rosy. Plans were made to increase the number of ballet performances in the autumn to three a week, and the Company left London in good spirits for a provincial tour followed by the annual holiday.

The dancers reassembled in Manchester in an atmosphere of foreboding; the news coming out of Germany became more and more threatening. After a week in Manchester they moved on to Liverpool, where they appeared for another week at the Royal Court Theatre, and on Saturday 2 September they closed with a performance of *The Rake's Progress*, *Horoscope* and Act III of *The Sleeping Princess*. On Sunday morning they boarded a train for their next destination, Leeds. When they arrived at the station a few hours later they learned that during their journey the Prime Minister had made a broadcast announcing that as from eleven o'clock that morning Britain was at war with Germany. After an anxious night at a hotel in the hastily improvised 'black-out', they were told to go home. All theatres had been closed and the Company was temporarily disbanded.

3 The War Years

The outbreak of war descended on the Company like an overnight frost. Immediate plans – such as a new three-act *Coppélia* due to be presented at Sadler's Wells in a few weeks time – were shrivelled and the whole future was in doubt. What followed, in fact, proved to be like the scene in *The Sleeping Beauty* during which the hero battles his way through the dark woods towards his goal. The vision of future triumphs had already been vouchsafed; when the darkness finally vanished and the curtain rose on the next Act in the Company's history the scene would have changed and it would awake to a new splendour. But meanwhile the situation demanded urgent planning and stocktaking.

This was the kind of crisis which showed de Valois at her best. Only two years before, in a book entitled *Invitation to the Ballet*, she had announced details of her aims for the Company, as precise and orderly as any Petipa dance formation. Now was the time to compare actuality and ideals. She had forecast sagely that though different in origin the new democratically based repertory company might prove to be the new version of the old monarchic state ballet. But she envisaged a more homely atmosphere. While insisting that ballet was just a special form of theatre, she rebelled against such stage conventions as star worship and floral tributes. Her rules for the audience were as spartan as those for the performers: applause for individual artists was disapproved ('when this starts, the magic of the theatre is lost'). In fact she clearly would have liked to control the whole operation: 'It is for artists to remember that they are servants of the theatre, and for the audience to be reminded that they are honoured guests'. The tone, authoritative but courteous, seems an echo of Lilian Baylis and a reminder that de Valois came from a military family.

De Valois was equally firm about the number of dancers that the Company should include and of what kind they should be (twenty women and ten men, divided into classical and demi-caractère), how many Company choreographers (two), how many performances they should give (three a week) and how many ballets they should perform (a repertoire of twenty-four works for each nine-month season). These should consist of four different categories: 1. Traditional-classical and romantic works, 2. Modern works of future classic importance, 3. Current works of more topical interest, 4. Works encouraging a strictly national tendency in their creation generally.

To draw up such an orderly programme was a wildly romantic gesture, but looking back at the end of this first lap de Valois could have felt well satisfied with the way her prospectus had worked out. In 1939 the Company numbered between thirty and forty dancers (plus members of the Opera Company for mime roles), with at least the mandatory four principals – Fonteyn, Helpmann, Honer and Turner – and a good variety of age and talent among the soloists. There were two choreographers as recommended (herself and Ashton). Performances averaged three a week. The repertoire had grown to fifty-two ballets, though not all, of course, were kept in rehearsal. In most ways the venture had developed as pre-ordained. The only unpredictable element was the nature and type of the new ballets. Of these de Valois herself had provided twenty-eight, with sixteen by Ashton (mostly in the last five years) and the rest by other choreographers: three were revivals of ballets by Fokine. All her prescribed categories were included.

Of the output of forty-five new works (some of which had been inherited from the Camargo Society), eleven were to survive the war – *Job, Les Rendezvous, The Haunted Ballroom, The Rake's Progress, Façade, Apparitions, Les Patineurs, A Wedding Bouquet, Nocturne, Checkmate* and *Dante Sonata*. Of these, six are still in the regular repertoire today – *The Rake's Progress, Façade, Les Patineurs, Les Rendezvous, A Wedding Bouquet* and *Checkmate*. A survival rate of nearly one in ten, though not approaching Diaghilev's extraordinary record, is good by modern standards, especially when it is recalled that during the first two years the novelties were hastily improvised on a minimal budget.

In some ways putting on a new production was more difficult then than it is now, in other ways it was much easier. Performances were relatively spread out but rehearsal time and space were severely restricted. 'We have one good rehearsal room and the stage for two hours a week provided that opera rehearsals permit. The most the full ballet company can rehearse is two and a half hours a day.' A yearly routine had been established; a London season from September to May (while de Basil's company was absent) followed by a provincial tour and then holidays. The Company was small, and a cheerful family atmosphere reigned. Many of the dancers lived near the theatre and made a little community, in which success and failure was shared by all and help was freely given, unrestricted by union rules. Often a dancer would find herself helping to teach a newcomer, or stitching her own costume, or lending a hand with moving the sets. The presence of de Valois, alert and sympathetic, could be felt everywhere. Discipline was strict, but at the same time elastic. De Valois' well defined principles were modified by a cheerful inconsistency. She had, for instance, a clear personal conception of the true classical style but welcomed teachers with different methods as being preferable to falling into a rut. Though something of a martinet, she would willingly accept an excuse based on private difficulties. She agreed without bitterness to Markova's shattering decision to pursue her career in more financially rewarding fields, and her low opinion of the commercial theatre, based on personal experience, did not stop her from allowing her dancers to supplement their small salaries in it when they could. Ashton especially, whose languid manner concealed a fierce fire of energy and invention, was frequently arranging numbers in revues and cabarets even during the Sadler's Wells seasons. De Valois' distaste for any form of indulgence did not cloud her friendship for and admiration of Lambert, whose life-style was decidedly Bohemian. Her missionary zeal justified all contradictions and infected the whole Company. The jealousies and disappointments, the fatigue and isolation endemic to all dancers with their unremitting fourteen-hour work schedules were transmuted into the pleasures of working for a single shared aim. Life at the Wells in those early years was illuminated by all the fun and vitality and uncaring prodigality of effort that is the blessing of an adolescent enterprise. This was the springtime of the Company, never quite to be recaptured.

Now the enforced standstill was used as a breathing-space for rethinking and reorganising. If London theatres were closed, there were plenty of audiences elsewhere, and in wartime it was the duty of everyone to contribute what they could. Two weeks after their temporary dismissal the dancers were summoned to Cardiff in Wales to prepare for an unlimited provincial tour around Britain. There was to be a small repertoire. Two pianos, played by Lambert and his assistant Hilda Gaunt, would replace the orchestra. The Company, which included all the principals, would be expected to dance an average of nine performances a week. Salaries would be cut drastically, with any profits shared out between the artists. A few dancers left the Company, including Elizabeth Miller. Among the replacements for the tour, which lasted for two months, was John Field, a youngster newly arrived from the north of England.

No signs of air-raids or other disruptions being yet visible in London, the Company returned, on Boxing Day 1940, to Sadler's Wells, and resumed its normal course. It even mounted a new work by Ashton which illustrated vividly his quick reaction to circumstances. During the summer holidays he had been occupied in composing a large-scale ballet, *Le Diable s'Amuse*, for the Ballet Russe de Monte Carlo, whose Artistic Director was Léonide Massine. The ballet, which had a fanciful plot and an elaborate décor by Eugene Berman, was cancelled because of the outbreak of war. His new work for Sadler's Wells, *Dante Sonata*, was different in every way. The international crisis seems to have opened up an emotional level in Ashton's artistic personality which had not previously been tapped and the theme of Dante's 'Inferno' was completely alien to everything he had tackled before. Lambert found the music, Liszt's 'Fantaisie d'après une lecture de Dante'.

The Wise Virgins, 1940. Michael Somes as the Bridegroom, Margot Fonteyn as the Bride.

Dante Sonata, 1940. LEFT Pamela May and
RIGHT Margot Fonteyn and Michael Somes, as Children of Light.

Fedorovitch, who had been entrusted with the designs, took Flaxman's engravings for the 'Inferno' as her inspiration. Rehearsals began during the provincial tour and *Dante Sonata* had its première at Sadler's Wells in January 1940. The ballet's almost hysterical mood, which explored the conflict between Light and Darkness and twice suggested a double crucifixion, was danced with theatrical intensity by Fonteyn – her dark hair flying – and Somes, as the Children of Light, opposite June Brae and Helpmann representing Darkness. Pamela May contributed a memorably anguished solo. The highly-charged sincerity of the choreographer struck an answering chord in the anxiety-ridden audience. Nothing could have illustrated better de Valois' conception of a 'topical' ballet; this one spoke for its time. Its success was immediate, though some critics found its violence alarming. One of them compared the symbolic struggle with that between two teams at a rugger match 'with a magnificent scrum at the end.' However, another thought that in this ballet 'Sadler's Wells capped their season's, perhaps their life's, work'.

After another short 'austerity' tour the Company returned with the postponed production of *Coppélia*, newly designed by William Chappell and with the recalcitrant Third Act – always a stumbling block to producers – added. This time Sergeyev openly took credit for some of the choreography (the final pas de deux, the male solo and the finale). The production revealed a fine line-up of principals. Helpmann was the hero, Franz, and Mary Honer was a delightfully vital Swanilda, with Pamela May as Dawn, June Brae as Prayer and Claude Newman as the doddery Dr Coppélius. *Coppélia* was followed almost immediately by another Ashton ballet, *The Wise Virgins*. This was like a soft answer

Dante Sonata. June Brae (kneeling, at left) and Robert Helpmann, as Children of Darkness; Margot Fonteyn
(between the two groups), Pamela May (kneeling, at right) and Michael Somes as Children of Light.

to *Dante Sonata*, a wistful farewell to the *douceur de vivre* which was to disappear so soon.
With a honeyed score of choral preludes by Bach, arranged and orchestrated by William
Walton, and a sumptuous décor by Rex Whistler (which today provokes anguished
regrets that he did not design the first *The Sleeping Princess*) it was a vehicle for Fonteyn at
her most gently satisfying, a kind of angelic requiem for peace.

War now began to bite seriously into the arts, including ballet, even though there was
still virtually no fighting. The carrying of gas masks was compulsory, rationing had been
introduced; anti-aircraft balloons floated over the cities and by night the streets were
plunged into almost total darkness. Public transport was restricted and petrol was in short
supply. Audiences inevitably dwindled. But there were other problems for the
management. Turner had already left to join a newly formed troupe, the Arts Theatre
Ballet; Frank Staff had returned to Rambert, and some of the male dancers had become
liable for service in the armed forces. De Valois was not sympathetic to the idea of asking
for exemption for her dancers, and she had to face the prospect of a steady depletion of the
male contingent in her Company. Dancers would be called up as they became eligible.
Fortunately Helpmann, being Australian, was immune from war service, and he and later
the South African Alexis Rassine would bear the main burden of male dancing. De Valois
could not be expected to create all the ballets as well as handling the complicated wartime
administration of the Company. One of the first major tasks which confronted her was to
prove more taxing than she had anticipated. The Government had made the decision –
which constituted a recognition of de Valois' achievements – that the Vic-Wells Ballet

would make a valuable cultural export to help consolidate the still untried Western alliance. A short tour of the Netherlands was planned, and the call-up for male dancers was deferred until after it was over. Early in May 1940 – in retrospect an unlucky piece of timing – the Company boarded a small Dutch boat for Rotterdam. The crossing was made in wartime austerity, which gave way on arrival at The Hague to full peacetime splendour, with plentiful food, blazing lights and formal dress for the Opera House performance.

There was, however, an almost desperate bravado about the determined high spirits and good living. News of troop movements inside Germany was spreading, and the frontier was rarely more than half an hour away from the towns where the Company appeared. The performance of 9 May was at Arnhem, only a few miles from the German border, and the Company returned by bus to The Hague during the night, arriving around three o'clock in the morning. At four o'clock de Valois was woken by the sound of aircraft and guns. Annoyed, she left her room to ask who was disturbing her sleep. 'Excuse me, Miss de Valois, but I really think it must be the Germans', replied one of the corps de ballet. By ten, de Valois was at the British Embassy discussing plans for evacuation. Leaflets dropped from German aircraft were lying in the streets: they announced: 'Strong German

Leaving for Holland in 1940. (Left to right) June Brae, Mary Honer, Robert Helpmann, Margot Fonteyn, Frederick Ashton, and Ninette de Valois.

troop units have surrounded the city. Resistance is of no use.'

After an uneasy day and night spent in the hotel, the Company set out in a bus for the coast. The short cross-country journey took two days, ending in a midnight walk through woods with their few precious belongings. One small bag was the only luggage that they were allowed, besides a packet of food. After nights spent in country houses crammed with refugees, the dancers, divided into seven groups, each under a leader – de Valois, Lambert, Ashton, Helpmann, Joy Newton, Claude Newman and John Sullivan, the Stage Director – reached the coast and were taken on board a cargo boat. Fifteen hours later the bedraggled party disembarked at Harwich and on 14 May the Sadler's Wells Ballet Company (as it was now called for the first time) arrived in London. There had been no casualties, but some serious loss of property, though Ashton's dinner-jacket had been saved by being worn by de Valois over her summer clothes. The scenery, costumes and music for six ballets – *The Rake's Progress, Checkmate, Dante Sonata, Horoscope, Façade* and *Les Patineurs* – had been left behind, and most serious, the one and only manuscript score for *Horoscope* had been lost for ever.

But the spirit and the performing drive of the Company was undamaged. Only three weeks later it opened a new season at Sadler's Wells, including in the programme *Dante Sonata* danced to a gramophone record. More serious tests were to come. The war had now begun in earnest and developed rapidly into a disaster for the Allies. Audiences continued to dwindle and spirits fell as the news from Europe worsened each day. On 22 June France capitulated and everybody knew that the crisis had come. Alone, painfully vulnerable, but determined and in some way relieved that the issue had become simple and the outcome dependent only on themselves, Londoners carried on like patients before a vital operation. Theatres stayed open and the Sadler's Wells Company presented its programme as usual.

More than that, during June 1940 a new ballet was in preparation. De Valois was gallantly rehearsing *The Prospect Before Us*, a characteristically lively and sharply observed work which was intended as a relaxation from wartime stresses. Based on an original but rather awkward libretto concerning the rivalry between two eighteenth-century theatre managers, with a score arranged by Lambert from the work of William Boyce, and designs by Roger Furse after Rowlandson, its chief merit was that it offered Pamela May a memorable role as the heroine and showed Ashton impersonating his great predecessor, the choreographer Noverre. Also it allowed Helpmann, as the drunken Mr O'Reilly of the Pantheon Theatre, to let himself go in a brilliant piece of clowning with a comic solo which brought the house down. Humour rather than romance matched the prevailing mood and Ashton's *Façade*, one of the ballets which had lost its décor in the Netherlands, was brought back with a new, slightly altered set and costumes, two new numbers (the Foxtrot and a Peruvian solo for Ashton himself) and a rather broader approach to the comedy which has persisted ever since. The satirical *Barabau* was also revived, though less successfully.

These brave attempts at keeping a cheerful face in days of national anxiety proved to be a defiant farewell to the Company's years in its home at Sadler's Wells. Air-raids on London had begun to interrupt performances and on the last night of the season, 6 September 1940, there was an 'alert' half-way through the programme. Next day the Company disbanded for its annual holiday. The dancers bade each other good-bye; the prospect before them was ostensibly three weeks of rest and then the start of a new season in their familiar home. But it was not to be. The next day the full-scale Blitz on London began and casualties mounted dramatically. A week later Sadler's Wells Theatre was closed as a place of entertainment and taken over as a rest centre for air-raid victims. The Company was homeless.

The sudden end to the established Sadler's Wells schedules meant some drastic rethinking about the future structure of the Company. De Valois threw herself whole-heartedly into the task, assisted by Tyrone Guthrie, the producer who on the death of Lilian Baylis in 1937 had been appointed to take her place as overall Administrator of the Old Vic and Sadler's Wells. In this capacity he was responsible for both the Sadler's Wells Opera and the Ballet Companies, as well as the Old Vic Drama Company. His first problem

The Prospect Before Us. Robert Helpmann as Mr O'Reilly.

was to find a new administrative centre for them which would not be liable to the constant disruptions of air-raids, now a regular part of London life. The answer was the Victoria Theatre in Burnley, a small town in Lancashire. From here in November 1940 the new wartime career of the Ballet Company was launched. This started of necessity as a touring routine. The Company was sent out with two pianos and a small repertoire on a busy round of dates which included provincial centres and military garrison theatres, a tough professional life which introduced the dancers to makeshift conditions and a variety of audiences, many of whom had hardly heard of ballet. Led by Fonteyn and Helpmann, the Company adapted imperturbably – though not always uncomplainingly – to the hard conditions of a touring troupe, made all the harder by wartime restrictions. De Valois was an inflexible inspiration. Hardship and enforced austerity were just the kind of stimulus to which she responded best. 'I thought of the theatre only as a part of the war,' she wrote later, 'and the ballet only as part of the wartime theatre.' 'We would all unhesitatingly defend her and obey her commands,' wrote Fonteyn. 'Part of her secret, like that of all great generals, was that she cared deeply about our lives and our personal problems as well as our careers.' It was at this time that the Company, at the suggestion of one of its members, Gordon Hamilton, began to call her 'Madam' instead of 'Miss de Valois'.

The banishment of the Company from London was not to last as long as had been anticipated. It soon became apparent to the authorities that a total cessation of normal recreation was more damaging to Londoners than a few bombs. It was decided to reopen theatres and cinemas. The very morning after a raid which had completely ringed St

Nicholas Sergeyev teaching, 1943. Ailne Phillips is second from right.

Paul's Cathedral with fire, de Valois was back in London. First she paid a call at the Ballet School at Sadler's Wells, which, in spite of its big glass windows, had been permitted to continue its activities in the rehearsal room under the control of de Valois herself and Sergeyev. Then she made her way to a theatre in the West End, whose manager Bronson Albery had offered to provide a temporary London base for the opera, ballet and drama companies which had been banished from Sadler's Wells and the Old Vic. Soon she had fixed up for the Ballet Company to open a season there. On 14 January 1941 the Vic-Wells Ballet made its first appearance in the marvellously well-situated New Theatre in St Martin's Lane. The programme was *Les Sylphides, Façade* and *Dante Sonata*.

The smaller size of the New Theatre and of its stage held many advantages. It lessened the financial risks and helped to conceal the depleted size of the Company. The two pianos filled the small auditorium well enough, and a suitable repertoire was selected. To begin with, matinées only were given, allowing the audience time to return home before darkness, when air-raids usually began. When the days became longer, early evening performances were added. Business was good: ballet, like concerts and plays, offered a welcome escape from the preoccupations of war, and prices at the New Theatre, though somewhat higher than those at Sadler's Wells, were still cheap, ranging from one to eleven shillings. A new routine was established, the Company performing alternately in London and for short spells in the provinces, with two weeks holiday a year. It was hard work for the Company. In the provinces, now filled with evacuated Londoners, audiences increased every season, and it danced to full houses.

Its success caused some strain in the Old Vic-Sadler's Wells administration. Carried on a flood tide of public demand, the Ballet Company not only survived but made money. Guthrie hit on the idea of making it help to pay for the less easily marketable opera performances. 'De Valois was resentful', he wrote later, 'that I wished to make the comparatively easy success of the Ballet favour and further the aims of its sister company, the Opera. De Valois considered her work was being frustrated and possibly even ruined.' By the end of the year the rivalry between the two Companies had reached a point where action was called for. De Valois took the initiative. 'She suggested and I agreed', wrote Guthrie 'that the Ballet should be managed by Bronson Albery. From 1941 onwards the Company, for all practical purposes, ceased to be part of the organisation which Miss Baylis had set up.'

The four years that the Company spent based at the New Theatre were to be something of a gestation period, during which the creative process played a subordinate part compared with the extraordinary development of public interest in the art of ballet in general. Of the new works presented during the war years, only one, *Hamlet*, was to survive for more than a few seasons. The first production for the New Theatre was in fact ambitious. Once again Ashton ventured on a ballet of deep emotional complexity, with suggestions of spiritual anguish. Originally the subject was to have been Shakespeare's 'The Tempest', set to Tchaikovsky's incidental music, but in the end the score selected was one which could be acceptably performed on the Company's two pianos, Schubert's 'Fantasia in C', known as 'The Wanderer'. A programme note explained that the journey was a psychological one, a theme underlined by backcloths by the painter Graham Sutherland which in effect were enlargements of his normal painting style. The somewhat expressionist mood of *The Wanderer* was conveyed in movements which seemed to show the influence of Massine's recent 'symphonic ballets', with their heroic symbolism and acrobatic movements. Helpmann was the central figure – flanked for part of the time by militaristic companions in khaki shorts – with Fonteyn displaying a new virtuosity as his vision of success. A striking feature was a sensuous pas de deux for Pamela May and Michael Somes which came in for some criticism. The choice of a classical score also worried some reviewers, mostly music critics who had similarly cavilled at the use of Bach's church music for *The Wise Virgins*, but the sheer dance-invention was much praised. The next production was de Valois' ingenious solution to the problem of the shrinking supply of dancers. Her *Orpheus and Eurydice*, deriving from a production which had been planned earlier, combined the Ballet Company with two singers. Though beautifully designed by Sophie Fedorovitch with looping draperies, its serene mood and slow tempo proved unsuitable for the prevailing wartime atmosphere, and it did not survive for long.

The Wanderer, designed by Graham Sutherland, 1940. The finale, with Robert Helpmann (held aloft),
Michael Somes and Pamela May (kneeling) and Margot Fonteyn (far right).

Boldly, de Valois chose this moment to fight for and win, against many cautious arguments by the management, a revival of the Company's most ambitious work, *The Sleeping Princess*. There were no boy pages for the Queen and indeed no male courtiers at all. The already austere production must have looked positively penurious on the New Theatre's tiny stage, but it proved popular with the public. It gave Fonteyn a fine chance to establish her position as prima ballerina and, above all, it won from the management the restoration of the orchestra in place of two pianos – a vital victory. It was followed by a serious setback. In May, Ashton was called up. At the same time Michael Somes and Alan Carter bade an enforced, if temporary, farewell; Leslie Edwards, Richard Ellis, and Stanley Hall had already gone. During the early months of 1940 there had been some discussion in the Press about the possibility of exempting male dancers from military service. Bernard Shaw, rather surprisingly, had sprung to the defence of 'these irreplaceably rare and highly skilled artists providing a most delectable entertainment' and other celebrities had supported him. Arnold Haskell recalled that Richelieu had used ballet as propaganda and Osbert Sitwell, more down to earth, suggested that calling them up would 'mean considerable financial loss to the nation'. But a correspondent pointed out that Benvenuto Cellini and Michelangelo had both served in the army without any apparent damage to their careers. De Valois remained staunchly patriotic, and the idea of exemption was dropped. As substitutes, sixteen-year-old students joined the Company straight from the

School: they could stay for two years before being called up for the forces.

The loss of so many of the Company's male dancers was taking its toll. Even rarer than dancers were choreographers, and Ashton's departure to join the Royal Air Force was a crippling blow. But Helpmann, a young man who seemed to be able to turn his hand to anything theatrical, readily provided the solution to the problem. He would not only dance but would choreograph as well. With characteristic cleverness he avoided in his first ballet any pure dance creation which might compete with those of his colleagues. He turned to his advantage his sense of theatre and devised a masque which incorporated speech as well as dancing. He adapted Milton's 'Comus', leaving in two of the speeches, which were recited by the choreographer; the score was selected from Purcell, and Oliver Messel was the designer. Presented in January 1942, it was a decorative occasion rather than a dramatic one, but it received both popular and critical acclaim.

A more substantial contribution by Helpmann was to mark the Company's 1942 summer season at the New Theatre. Once again he exploited his interest in straight theatre, choosing *Hamlet*, set to Tchaikovsky's overture of that name. Faced with the problem of conveying a full length play in eighteen minutes, Helpmann, encouraged by his friend the theatre director Michael Benthall, hit on the device of presenting the whole drama as a flashback in the mind of the dying Prince, in which all the threads become entangled and mix with Freudian interpretations of the play, much discussed at that time. To design the nightmare setting Helpmann chose Leslie Hurry, an unknown young artist whose work he had chanced upon in a West End gallery.

In addition to choreographing, Helpmann was showing himself to be the most versatile of dancers. His dramatic skill and theatrical flair enabled him to give acceptable renderings even of a virtuoso part such as the Blue Boy in *Les Patineurs*. He could be poetic or noble, romantic or comical, and during this season he took over the grotesquely sinister role of Carabosse in *The Sleeping Princess* doubling the role with that of Prince Florimund and the crabby old toymaker in *Coppélia*, turning him into a comedy character.

The part of Hamlet, which he was later to perform in the theatre, was an obvious vehicle for him. Fonteyn was perfect for Ophelia, indeed the parallel with the mad-scene in *Giselle* was awkwardly close; for the flower-picking scene common to both roles Helpmann substituted a curious tic of the hands which he had once observed in a Bournemouth café. Celia Franca, a new arrival from the International Ballet, was a dramatic Queen. The dream formula proved ideal; the confusions between the characters, the hectically melodramatic idiom, the compressed intensity and the speed of the action were artistically justified, and Helpmann's highly emphatic style fitted perfectly into the expressionistic mood. *Hamlet* was a powerful example of mime-drama (there was not much dancing), and though it was too highly flavoured for some critical palates, it proved immensely popular.

It acted also as a good introduction to the world of ballet for the rapidly growing audience. In the sordid, and often boring, austerities that the war brought to London's civilian population the arts had taken on a new vital function. Ballet, with its music and spectacle, offered an escape from reality and was embraced with enthusiasm by a public reaching far outside the previously limited and recherché circle of balletomanes. During

Hamlet. Costume design by Leslie Hurry, 1942.

Hamlet

the long daylight hours of summer, evening performances had been resumed and business flourished. Fonteyn and Helpmann were transformed from a minority cult into popular star attractions. Soldiers on leave replaced the aesthetes from Bloomsbury and Chelsea in the gallery. By 1943 seats at the New Theatre had to be rationed when the Company was appearing – not more than four for each patron for any one performance – and at one time three performances were given on Saturdays. Unexpectedly, and indeed inexplicably, the conditions of war were to provide the hotbed in which the young seedling of British ballet swelled and grew to popularity and maturity. It was fortunate that this metamorphosis had not taken place earlier, for by now the Company had a strong repertoire to rely upon.

Helpmann's next contribution, *The Birds*, with charmingly piquant ingredients – a score by Respighi and designs by Chiang Yee – was specifically intended to give a chance to some of the younger dancers such as Moyra Fraser. The light comedy style proved unconvincing, but it did reveal the talents of two dancers who were to leave a distinctive mark on the Company, Alexis Rassine and Beryl Grey, a tall, strong young dancer who only five months earlier, on her fifteenth birthday, had set a new Company record by triumphantly dancing the full-length *Le Lac des Cygnes*. The next ballet also proved unsuccessful. Ashton was given special leave from the Royal Air Force to create something new for the Company. The result, perhaps naturally, was heavily tinged with patriotic sentiment. *The Quest* was drawn from Spenser's poem 'The Faerie Queene' and featured Helpmann as St George, battling against not only a band of Saracens but against all seven of the Deadly Sins. In spite of a commissioned score from William Walton and some romantic designs by John Piper (his début in the theatre), the ballet was complicated and inconclusive. It did, however, show off two gifted young dancers who would soon become principals, Beryl Grey again, and a red-headed girl from Scotland who had studied in Rhodesia and then with Nicholas Legat, Moira Shearer.

Before the next production a rather sad celebration took place. Sergeyev, the unassuming little ballet-master who had handed on to the Company his knowledge of the St Petersburg productions of the classics, resigned from the Sadler's Wells School where he had been teaching, to be replaced by another Russian, Vera Volkova. The occasion was marked by a special performance of *Le Lac des Cygnes*, in the Maryinsky première of which Sergeyev had participated. The new production was designed by Leslie Hurry, who contrived to conjure up an illusion of splendour from exiguous wartime materials, and who was to redesign it two or three times in later years, setting his personal stamp firmly on the Company's versions of the ballet.

De Valois contributed the next production, in October 1943, a short suite of light-hearted dances called *Promenade*, arranged to music by Haydn. Two interesting revivals followed. *Job* came back into the repertoire, with Helpmann as riveting as ever in the part of Satan and David Paltenghi, a Swiss dancer from the Ballet Rambert, as Elihu. This was followed by *Le Spectre de la Rose* in which Fonteyn was coached by Karsavina, who had created the role in 1911, with Alexis Rassine in the Nijinsky role. The next new ballet was *Le Festin de l'Araignée* (*The Spider's Banquet*) by a young choreographer from the Ballet Rambert, Andrée Howard, to a score by Albert Roussel which had already been used by

---

The Birds. Costume and set designs by Chiang Yee, 1942.

ABOVE *Comus*, first produced in 1942, with Robert Helpmann as Comus. BELOW *Le Festin de l'Araignée*, 1944: Celia Franca as the Spider, with Gordon Hamilton and Ray Powell as the Praying Mantises.

ABOVE *Hamlet*. The Prince with the Gravedigger. BELOW *Le Lac des Cygnes*, 1943.
Act II, with Margot Fonteyn as Odette, Robert Helpmann as Prince Siegfried.

several other choreographers. In spite of ambitious designs by the artist Michael Ayrton it proved short-lived. The Butterfly (Moira Shearer) fluttered, the Spider (Celia Franca) crouched and clawed and crawled up and down her web, but there was an air of contrivance about the whole work. It was not strong enough to hold its own with the public's state of excitement, for a change was in the air. Only three weeks before the première the Allies had landed in Normandy. The tide of war had turned. It was time for a well-earned holiday for the Company; and while it was away, on the morning of 24 August 1944, the radio announced that Paris had been liberated.

Le Festin de l'Araignée was to be the Company's last ballet at the New Theatre. A new age was dawning, and when the dancers reassembled they found themselves in a larger theatre with a larger stage, the Prince's Theatre in Shaftesbury Avenue. There was no difficulty in filling it for a long season, but clearly a new production was needed. It was Helpmann's turn to contribute and he chose another highly dramatic subject, which called for more mime than dance. *Miracle in the Gorbals*, presented in October, was a slice of social realism, a morality story set in the slums of Glasgow to a commissioned score by Arthur Bliss, with designs by Edward Burra. A Christ-figure (labelled The Stranger and played by Helpmann himself) appears and works miracles among the poor, only to be denounced by the Establishment and killed by the people whom he had come to help. This melodramatic tale with its blend of religiosity and violence (a programme note advised

Miracle in the Gorbals, 1958 revival. Robert Helpmann as the Stranger
and Leslie Edwards as the Beggar.

patrons 'not to bring young children to performances of this ballet') was shrewdly attuned to the mood of the time and proved to be a big success with the public, though it was not to everyone's taste. Arnold Haskell called it 'masterly' but Cyril Beaumont, doyen of the critics, expressed a doubt as to whether 'this is not one of those occasions when the desire to achieve a sensational work has not overruled a proper sense of the fitness of things'.

The fresh horizons opening up for the Company were soon extended. After a tour in the provinces it was invited to embark on another trip to the Continent. This was carried out under the auspices of ENSA, the organisation which provided entertainment for the troops, and the dancers were fitted out in khaki uniforms (de Valois wore a khaki scarf wound round her head while Fonteyn and May sported turbans designed for them by the Queen's milliner). On a bitter day in January 1945 the troupe of eighty dancers and thirty musicians set out for Brussels, where they were booked to dance for the British troops and also to appear before the public at the Théâtre Royale de la Monnaie. Conditions in the Belgian capital were no more comfortable than in London. There was no heating or hot water and the snow lay thick, but the three-week season was enthusiastically received. From Brussels they proceeded to Paris, a train journey which took them fifteen hours. There they found living conditions hardly better than in Brussels, but they spent a happy month in the French capital, enjoying the sense of release which came from their first outing from England, and dancing every night to packed houses – first to ENSA audiences

On an ENSA tour for the forces, Brussels 1945. (Left to right) Moira Shearer, Alexis Rassine, Margot Fonteyn, Douglas Steuart, Pamela May, Elizabeth Kennedy, Eric Hyrst.

at the Théâtre Marigny and then for a week at the Théâtre des Champs-Elysées.

So far as creativity was concerned this was a period of marking time: no new ballet had been presented since *Miracle in the Gorbals* nine months before, and there was to be nothing else for the next fourteen months, by which time the Company would be launched on a new course. Meanwhile its status and popularity were being strongly consolidated. It returned to the New Theatre for an unprecedented run of ten weeks, fortified by the reappearance of Turner and Somes, both recently discharged from the Army for medical reasons. Ashton was also released from the Air Force and rejoined the Company. He had somehow contrived to rehearse and to appear in a revival of *Nocturne* during a season at the Prince's Theatre in his old role (which demanded almost only one dramatic last gesture): 'I want to tell you how pleased I am to discover that, after three and a half years' absence, I can still raise my arms', he told the enthusiastic audience.

As if making a farewell visit to its old home, at the end of the New Theatre season the Company moved back to Sadler's Wells. It appeared there for eight successful weeks, though it had now outgrown the theatre. Almost at once there followed another ENSA tour, this time entertaining the troops in Germany, a fitting conclusion to a period during which the Company had amply illustrated de Valois' axiom about ballet being part of the war effort. Profiting brilliantly from the absence of imported rivals it had proved itself not only well able to maintain the standards to which peacetime audiences had been accustomed but also to be a tough and resilient organisation able to survive gruelling working conditions, loss of personnel, changes of venue, and the hazards arising from the wartime strains of fatigue, anxiety, cold, undernourishment and overwork. The entr'acte had been turned into a triumphantly surmounted trial of strength, and the Sadler's Wells Ballet Company emerged from the war respected, loved and, above all, enjoyed. When it returned from its continental tour it was faced with a new and exciting challenge, demanding positive proof of its capacities. It was to make its entry on to the larger, grander stage of the Royal Opera House, Covent Garden.

4 *The Move to*
Covent Garden

The translation – or promotion – of the Sadler's Wells Company to Covent Garden was not as sudden as it appeared to be. The move had long been secretly discussed and prepared. At the beginning of the war a committee to foster the arts in Britain, the Council for the Encouragement of Music and the Arts (the ancestor of today's Arts Council), had been set up and had provided financial help for several theatrical enterprises including Sadler's Wells Ballet. Lord Keynes had become Chairman of CEMA in 1942 and soon began to take an interest in the future of the Royal Opera House which had been leased to Mecca Enterprises as a dance-hall. In 1944 the lease expired and, with the encouragement of the prospective new tenants, Boosey and Hawkes, a Trust was set up under Keynes's chairmanship to negotiate for the return of the theatre to its normal use.

In retrospect, the discussions concerning the future use of the Royal Opera House have a touch of unreality about them. The year 1944 was a very critical period in the war. To sit debating the conditions in which opera and ballet should or should not be presented at Covent Garden after the end of hostilities while the Nazi army was still virtually intact now seems a sign of manic self-confidence. There can be few more vivid illustrations of the resilience of the British than the relaxed but businesslike discussions concerning the transfer of the Sadler's Wells Ballet and its sets, scores, ballet copyrights, and other assets, to the Opera Trust which went on during those weeks when the Allied Forces were still desperately grappling with the German army in Europe.

The transaction was not straightforward. To begin with there was the legal difficulty of persuading Mecca Enterprises to abandon its waltzing and fox-trotting in the Opera House, a matter which was to drag on for many months. Then there were plans to celebrate and cement our alliance with France and Russia by visits from their opera and ballet companies as soon as travelling became possible. In July 1944, a few weeks after D-Day, Keynes had reported to CEMA discussions on the subject with some Russian representatives. 'It might be well to explain that unless something goes astray, or their Delegation crashes on their return journey to Siberia, there would also be a direct approach in Moscow.' There were other possibilities. In September 1944 the Russian dancer Léonide Massine was writing privately to Keynes. 'I have heard', he wrote, 'that you have been named President of the Covent Garden Board of Directors. This is wonderful news, as I am sure you would want to see at Covent Garden the best in every field and would help to purify the ballet from musical comedy element and bring back the great Diaghilev tradition . . .' He was very ready to effect this reform personally.

Keynes replied cautiously. 'We shall, I expect, have to feel our way and see the war, if not over, at any rate nearer to its conclusion, before we can embark on the creation of a new ballet attached to Covent Garden. There is also the position of Ninette de Valois' Sadler's Wells company to consider.' In fact, the proposal to move the Ballet Company to Covent Garden was already decided in Keynes' mind, though some of his colleagues evidently had doubts about the Opera Company. Two months later Keynes wrote to David Webster, a Liverpool businessman with an interest in music (he had been Chairman of the

Liverpool Philharmonic Society) who had been brought in as administrator of the Covent Garden Preliminary Committee: 'So far as the opera is concerned, I expect it is wise to keep Sadler's Wells away from Covent Garden until they are much stronger. About the ballet, on the other hand, I feel differently. I should expect that Ninette would like to come to Covent Garden and, rightly handled, I should hope that they [the Sadler's Wells Directors] would change their minds'. De Valois was not, as it happened, immediately convinced of the advantages of being absorbed by the Covent Garden management; she had experienced the difficulties arising from sharing a theatre with an opera company and there would clearly be advantages in establishing the Company independently in a theatre such as His Majesty's, but she quickly became convinced that the Royal Opera House was the proper home for what was virtually a national company.

Negotiations between Covent Garden and Sadler's Wells, represented by Sir Alan Barlow, became narrowed down to finance. Meanwhile a struggle began between Boosey and Hawkes and the reluctant Mecca Enterprises to regain possession of the theatre. By May 1945 the negotiations and the war situation had so improved that a definite date in 1946 for re-opening the Opera House could be envisaged. 'We look forward to opening at Covent Garden in February 1946', wrote Keynes to Lord Lytton, Chairman of Sadler's Wells. 'Our hope is that the Sadler's Wells Ballet will share the programme at the opening with an opera company from Paris and we should like to see the Ballet in continuous residence through the spring and early summer . . . Subject to the advice of Miss de Valois our intention would be to take over all the dancers and choreographic staff. We should also expect Mr Lambert to remain as chief conductor . . . We should also take over responsibility for the Ballet School.'

'The Finsbury people', as Keynes called them, were to go on haggling over the terms for some time; they insisted on the earning capacity of the Company, quoting some impressive profit figures – £4055 for the 1939/40 season, £2855 for 1940/41, £12,146 for 1941/42 and £15,661 for 1943/44. But the hand-over was virtually settled. Only the question of a name for the Company remained. Should it be changed or not? In April Keynes seems to have made up his mind and he wrote to Webster: 'There is maybe a very good case for our keeping the name of Sadler's Wells Ballet, which I believe, has a distinct value.' Finally, in December 1945 the transaction was concluded. The visit of the Paris Opéra faded away in a cloud of practical and financial obstacles and while the Company was touring for ENSA in Germany, de Valois was finalising her plans. On 1 January 1946 Webster was able to write to Keynes: 'The suggested opening night is Wednesday 20 February and the opening show *The Sleeping Princess*. The production is heavy and involves much work but I hope we shall be in a position by 15 January to say definitely that *The Sleeping Princess* can go on the first night.'

The move by the Sadler's Wells Company involved changes of a magnitude which

---

The Prospect Before Us. Costume design for Vestris by Roger Furse, 1940.

OVERLEAF *The Sleeping Beauty*, 1946 production, designed by Oliver Messel.
LEFT Act II, (above) the Vision, with Margot Fonteyn as Aurora, Robert Helpmann as Florimund,
(below) Beryl Grey as the Lilac Fairy, with Helpmann.
RIGHT Act III, (above) Jean Bedells and David Davenport as the King and Queen,
with Leslie Edwards as Catalabutte, (below) the Wedding, with Fonteyn as Aurora.

"The Prospect
Before us!"

Vestris
Monsieur ~~Didelot~~
in the Pantheon
Ballet.
x a waistcoat

turned into a qualitative alteration. The Royal Opera House has a glamorous history going back almost two hundred and fifty years. The first theatre on the site, which was once the garden of a convent attached to Westminster Abbey, was built by John Rich in 1732. In 1808 it was burned down. Twelve months later a new theatre was opened to replace it, and here in 1832 Taglioni appeared in *La Sylphide*, the ballet which her father had just devised for her. Only a year later her rival, Fanny Elssler, was dancing on the same stage.

In 1846 the theatre was handsomely redecorated and soon became one of the chief homes of opera and ballet in London. After ten years this theatre, too, was burned down, but a replacement designed by Edward Barry, son of the architect of the Houses of Parliament, was built in only seven months. On 15 May 1858 the present theatre, which seats about two thousand people, was opened. Many famous dancers appeared in it at this time, and in 1911 Diaghilev's Ballets Russes made their London début there. They returned several times, giving their last performance in 1920. In 1931 Ida Rubinstein brought her company to it for a season, and later the theatre became the regular home of de Basil's Ballet Russe de Monte Carlo – a company with an enthusiastic and faithful audience, a good part of which Ninette de Valois now inherited.

'We were setting out', wrote de Valois later, 'on the adventure of making this building extend its hospitality to us throughout the year, challenging it, at the beginning, with nothing more than a bedraggled war-weary Company. It could be likened to a crazy nightmare, wherein I might be given Buckingham Palace, a few dusters, and told to get on with the spring cleaning.'

The Company which the Covent Garden Trust had acquired from Sadler's Wells might be war-weary but its assets were impressive. It consisted of an irreplaceable Founder-Director in Ninette de Valois, aided by a first-class choreographer, Frederick Ashton, and an inspired Music Director, Constant Lambert. The Company was led by two stars of growing magnitude, Margot Fonteyn and Robert Helpmann, and had a repertoire of sixty-seven ballets (of which sixteen were to be deemed suitable for Royal Opera House presentation). It is not surprising that there were serious misgivings among some members of the Sadler's Wells Board about letting it go. It is perhaps symbolic of the friendly, informal way in which the negotiations were carried on between the two old friends, Lord Keynes and Lord Lytton, that there appears to have been no formal contract. In view of 'certain guarantees' from the Arts Council, no payment was made except for the assets taken over. To judge by a few figures which survived (productions were purchased at two thirds of their cost price, so that *Le Lac des Cygnes* fetched £1690 and *The Rake's Progress* went for £416) Covent Garden got a bargain.

Her mind once made up, de Valois had no doubts. 'I knew that we had outgrown the Sadler's Wells theatre in size; that we were ripe, at this very moment, for further expansion.' She seized the opportunity with courage and energy, and with her particular kind of passionate commonsense she embraced without alarm the complications which the change would incur. The easiest of these was the establishment of an expanded branch of her school in Baron's Court, paid for largely out of the Company's wartime profits. A more difficult and risky new venture was the founding of a touring company (now Sadler's

---

ABOVE John Piper's backcloth for the 1948 revival of *Job*.
BELOW Costume designs by Isabel Lambert for *Tiresias*, 1951.

Wells Royal Ballet) to carry on at Sadler's Wells Theatre and in the provinces – a major undertaking, the history of which is related in Chapter 9.

To tackle this three-pronged exercise at a moment when Britain itself was exhausted and poverty-ridden after more than five years of war would have been challenge enough for most people; but de Valois now turned her mind to mounting a production fit to celebrate the first appearance of her Company in its new and noble home. It was to be *The Sleeping Princess*, now restored to its original title, *The Sleeping Beauty*, and this time it was to re-awaken to a fanfare of splendour. Oliver Messel was commissioned to design the production while Lambert worked on Tchaikovsky's full score for seventy musicians and de Valois and Ashton invented some new dances. Clothing coupons (rationing was still strict) were stretched to provide silks and satins, gloves and shoes. The scene-painters struggled with cheap pigments and wartime canvas. In the theatre, workmen hammered away to remove the two bandstands and the ballroom floor which had stretched across the whole auditorium. The re-opening of the Royal Opera House became a symbol of the beginning of peacetime, as opposed to the mere ending of the war.

At last the great day arrived, 20 February 1946. An elaborate gala had been organised, attended by the Royal Family, the Prime Minister, a cluster of ambassadors and countless British dignitaries of society and the arts. Pomp was garnished with good sense: 'Evening dress, uniform or day clothes' were prescribed, and a social commentator could only count

The night of the reopening of the Royal Opera House with
The Sleeping Beauty, on 20 February 1946.

four tiaras, including the Queen's. The curtain went up early, at 7pm, for transport was still a problem. A setback occurred when Lord Keynes was suddenly taken ill, and his wife, Lydia Lopokova, had to receive the guests until he had had time to recover. The fact that ballet rather than opera was filling the stage on this almost solemn occasion was in itself a tribute to Ninette de Valois who darted, bright-eyed and quick-tongued, from the wings to the circle throughout the performance. That evening rests like a crown on her career. 'It was more than auspicious; it was festive,' pronounced *The Times*. 'Princess Elizabeth enjoyed herself so much that she returned incognito for a second visit and, evidently inspired by the dancing, she went on to a nightclub where she was reported as joining in a rumba, a bahia, a samba and a slow bolero.' Six years of austerity had vanished as if by a wave of the Good Fairy's wand.

By later standards the dancing may not have been overwhelming. Traces of the constrictions necessitated by the small stage of Sadler's Wells were to haunt the Company's style for many years. This was highlighted by the introduction of a recent arrival from the Bolshoi, Violetta Prokhorova (later Elvin) in the Bluebird pas de deux on the second night; but the production as a whole struck a bull's-eye. It was far from the heavy, stiff tradition of the Maryinsky. It was equally different from the Diaghilev-Bakst production. Its tone was emphatically English, giving the ballet a fresh, light lyricism which suited exactly the British temperament, the British physique and British taste.

Margot Fonteyn standing on the half-painted backcloth for
Act III of *The Sleeping Beauty*.

Symphonic Variations, 1946.
ABOVE Moira Shearer, Henry Danton, Margot Fonteyn, Michael Somes, Pamela May.
BELOW Frederick Ashton rehearsing Georgina Parkinson and Antoinette Sibley, with Michael Somes.

Its overwhelming success, ironically, was to become something of a millstone around the Company's neck in future years when efforts to revive or replace the production were to become necessary.

In the part of Aurora, Fonteyn was already experienced, having first danced it seven years before and many times subsequently. She had felt her way with characteristic thoroughness and intelligence into a role in which, she declared later, she at first felt lost. ('There was nothing to act except a young girl celebrating her birthday'.) Helpmann, with a more varied stage history, found little difficulty in projecting into the big auditorium, doubling as the Prince and the wicked Carabosse and thereby mingling 'a stately grace' with 'forceful mime'.

The performance inevitably took on the character of a social occasion as well as a theatrical event, but in both respects it was a resounding success. Messel's designs, 'refulgent, plumed and gauzy' were praised for their taste and imagination: Fonteyn's Aurora was saluted as outstanding, though the *Manchester Guardian* noted that she still lacked 'the ballerina's grandeur which is needed to match the fine, loud blatancies of Tchaikovsky's superb ballet music': Beryl Grey's Lilac Fairy, and the Bluebird pas de deux of Pamela May and Alexis Rassine earned warm approval. *The Sleeping Beauty* played for seventy-eight consecutive performances – no rival to Diaghilev's three-month record in 1921, but still a worthy send-off for the Company's first Covent Garden season.

Meanwhile, Ashton had been preparing a ballet to a César Franck score, one which would have made the perfect new offering by the Company in its new home. Unfortunately an injury to Michael Somes delayed its first performance, so British choreography at Covent Garden got off to a rather shaky start with an ambitious but confused piece of symbolism by Helpmann called *Adam Zero*. To present a new ballet only six weeks after the mammoth première of *The Sleeping Beauty* was a feat in itself; but *Adam Zero* was not popular in spite of a theatrical score by Bliss, elaborate stage effects, and powerful performances by Helpmann and June Brae. Two weeks later, in mid-April, the postponed Ashton ballet was launched, and this time there were no doubts about success. The ballet was *Symphonic Variations*, one of Ashton's greatest achievements, destined to occupy a unique place in his choreographic repertoire and also in the history of British ballet. It has remained a distillation of the English style of this period.

It was both appropriate and lucky that *Symphonic Variations* was born at the very beginning of the Company's new career. Coming almost immediately after *The Sleeping Beauty*, that rich reminder of the traditions in which the repertoire was rooted, it pointed the way to future developments, totally different in scale and style and yet none the less rewarding. The ballet's small demands – only six dancers against a simple backcloth – and its limited virtuoso requirements were completely in contrast to the massive Maryinsky spectacle. It also appeared as a sudden dive into pure, interpretation-of-music abstraction, a field still foreign to British choreographers. In fact, Ashton originally had conceived it with a strong theme, revolving round a mystical marriage symbolised by the changing seasons, and with a large cast including a corps de ballet. Gradually he pared away the performers and refined the choreography until all that was left was a suite of classical dances in which emotion emerged all the more strongly for being controlled within a discipline as immutable as a ritual. The extra time granted by the ballet's postponement had been used for final adjustments and the result was an exceptionally well-finished work. The dancing seemed to float on the lyrical music, following every inflection with perfect simplicity and naturalness, and the original cast – Fonteyn, May, Shearer, Somes, Henry Danton and Brian Shaw – has never been surpassed. Once again Sophie Fedorovitch made a vital contribution to her friend's choreography, placing the scene in a kind of geometrical setting which faintly suggested the arches of a forest in spring and seemed to marry Ashton's dances with the fresh, gentle score. The ballet won instant recognition. 'He has done more than fit appropriate movements to Franck's music', reported *The Times*, 'He has created a sense of lyrical poetry that matches its moods.' Another critic, moved by what he described as the ballet's 'lawnlike background', wrote that 'one might be watching a kind of heavenly tennis while the band plays'. The ballet still has the power to elevate the spectator to a plane of existence where time seems to stand still, and Ashton still guards it carefully, permitting only rare performances.

The success of *Symphonic Variations* helped to give the Company a triumphant beginning in its new home, with a season which was eventually extended to one hundred and thirty performances. Pamela May, Beryl Grey and Moira Shearer all tackled the formidable role of Aurora with success, and *Giselle* reappeared in an elaborate new production, with lavish designs by James Bailey, which slightly overwhelmed Fonteyn's delicate interpretation.

When the season ended, the dancers dispersed for their holidays and Covent Garden was taken over by American Ballet Theatre, which shook British audiences out of their patriotic complacency by its vitality, the virility of its male dancers, and its stimulating repertoire. It introduced ballets by Balanchine, Jerome Robbins, Agnes de Mille, and the British choreographer, Antony Tudor. The pre-war Russian companies were still missing, but an exciting breath of new invention was introduced by a small troupe from Paris, Les Ballets des Champs-Elysées, which brought works by Roland Petit, décors by Bérard and Clavé and new, exciting dancers such as Renée Jeanmaire and Jean Babilée. Once again London was a competitive open market for ballet. The Sadler's Wells Company had to look to its laurels.

The administrators and artists on whom the Company relied at Covent Garden were virtually the same as those who had attended its salad days at Sadler's Wells, and the golden trio, de Valois, Ashton and Lambert, still guided its artistic policies. Markova and Dolin had moved on, though they were to reappear as Guest Artists, and the Sadler's Wells Company was now led by Fonteyn, the undisputed *prima ballerina*, supported by a team which included Pamela May, Moira Shearer, Beryl Grey, Julia Farron and Pauline Clayden. Helpmann and Turner were still the male leads, with Somes, John Field, John Hart, Alexis Rassine and (briefly) David Paltenghi. Ashton and Leslie Edwards from the old company were still going strong in character parts, while young dancers filled the war-depleted ranks. This was to be the core of the Company over the next ten years.

The overall policy, which was now more and more concentrated on the single figure of de Valois, with the unfailing support of David Webster, the Opera House's General Administrator, took a new turn. De Valois quickly became aware of the different demands made by the large stage and the more international audience of Covent Garden. Not all of the Sadler's Wells ballets survived the transfer successfully: for instance a new version of *Coppélia*, with designs by William Chappell, was thought by some to have lost the subtle appeal of the old, more modest production. An ambitious attempt to revive Purcell's multi-media masque *The Fairy Queen*, a long-cherished project of Lambert, pleased neither the opera nor the ballet audience; and *Les Sirènes*, a comedy trifle invented by Ashton for the

ABOVE *The Three-Cornered Hat*, with Léonide Massine as the Miller, Margot Fonteyn as his Wife.
BELOW *La Boutique Fantasque*, with Pamela May and Harold Turner as the Can-Can Dancers.

autumn season, was not a success. Seeking variety, de Valois looked around for a choreographer who was both widely known and experienced in handling large-scale ballets. Her choice fell on a man whom she had admired ever since she first joined the Ballets Russes: Léonide Massine. She invited the Russian star to mount revivals of two of his best-known ballets, *The Three-Cornered Hat* and *La Boutique Fantasque* in the spring of 1947, and a more recent work, *Mam'zelle Angot*, in the autumn. To add piquancy to this project, Massine agreed to appear in his original roles. It was a shrewd move, for it brought back those members of the Russian ballet audience who had been reluctant to transfer their allegiance to the home-grown Company. In *The Three-Cornered Hat* the Picasso décor and the sun-drenched de Falla score came up fresh and vibrant as ever and the fifty-one-year-old star, still taut and slim, worked his usual magic as the Miller around whom the comedy of the ballet revolves, while Fonteyn took the chance to show a new, mischievous personality as the Miller's Wife.

Three weeks later *La Boutique Fantasque* was revived. On its first appearance the ballet achieved less than its full effect. Later, however, it was to prove popular when revived by the Touring Company. In principle, the two Massine productions with their imaginative Ecole de Paris designs and their nostalgic echoes of pre-war triumphs amply fulfilled their function – to set the mantle of the Ballets Russes firmly on the shoulders of the Sadler's Wells troupe.

The other Massine ballet, *Mam'zelle Angot*, was not a legacy from Diaghilev but had been written for Ballet Theatre in America during the war. It was a work in light opera style, a genre in which Massine excelled, and it abounded in character roles of the type which de Valois, following in Massine's footsteps, liked to create and which deployed the dramatic abilities that she encouraged in her artists. Fonteyn was not quite the soubrette needed in the title role (later Julia Farron and Nadia Nerina were to take more happily to the part). Alexander Grant scored a brilliant hit as the Barber, but the fizzing dynamism demanded by this kind of piece does not come easily to British dancers, and in spite of a distinguished new décor by Derain the ballet as a whole never took off.

This third Massine work was not presented until the following autumn, and by then there had been some significant developments in the Company's activities. In the New Year's Honours List for 1947 de Valois had been made a Commander of the British Empire, an honour which symbolised acceptance of her Company's national status. It had taken part in the first Edinburgh Festival and it had undertaken an extensive European tour which took it to Brussels, Prague, Warsaw, Poznan, Oslo and Malmo. But a momentous sign of change came with the resignation of Constant Lambert from his position as Music Director. He was going through a difficult period in his private life; he was over-working, undertaking numerous conducting engagements; and his increasing drinking made him unreliable and difficult. After a protracted dispute with Covent Garden over the fee allotted to him for his work on *The Fairy Queen*, the failure of which must have been painful to him, he abruptly resigned in July 1947. He received a formal letter from Sir John Anderson, the Chairman of the Covent Garden Trust, icily thanking him for his past services as composer and musical archivist. No mention was made of his conducting. The breach seemed

---

Daphnis and Chloë. Costume design by John Craxton for
Michael Somes as Daphnis, 1951.

[90]

ΔΑΦΝΙΣ

Shepherds

serious and irreparable; but before a year had passed Lambert had accepted an invitation to rejoin the team as one of the three Artistic Directors of the Company alongside de Valois and Ashton, and he was soon back in the orchestra pit as Guest Conductor.

Another change in the Company's character was Helpmann's connection with it. Always attracted by straight drama, he temporarily abandoned his dancing to appear at the Duchess Theatre in a repertory season. He was to make no further choreographic contributions for some years, though he continued to dance with the Company. His place as partner for Fonteyn was gradually to be taken over by Rassine and by Somes, whose handsome, manly presence and noble style were ideal for the classics.

The Company was now firmly settled into the Opera House, from which in 1948 it made a one-week visit to Holland. Among the productions it presented there was *Scènes de Ballet*, a short piece by Ashton recently launched at Covent Garden which represented a follow-up to his successful *Symphonic Variations*. It was a more severely geometrical abstraction, with an astringent impersonal quality replacing the gentle lyricism of *Symphonic Variations* – the result of the very different character of Stravinsky's acerbic score, which had originally been composed for a revue. With its acceptance of totally non-narrative, non-emotional pattern-making, it marked a decisive point in Ashton's development but, perhaps foreseeably, it did not at first prove popular though its brilliance was recognised. There were no qualifications, however, in the disapproval of the next ballet, on which high hopes had been placed – a new work by Massine with décor and costumes by the famous Parisian designer, Christian Bérard. Danced to the Haydn score, *Clock Symphony* turned out to be trivial and uninteresting. One interesting production during that summer was a revival of *Job*, with striking new designs by John Piper. Helpmann was Satan. Later, Dolin resumed the role and he and Markova also gave some memorable guest performances this season, in *Giselle, Les Sylphides, Le Lac des Cygnes* and, for the first time, the full-length *The Sleeping Beauty*. Autumn brought one of Ashton's few real failures, *Don Juan*, a piece to Richard Strauss's tone poem in which Helpmann played his last romantic Ashton role. But now Ashton was to embark on something new – a series of full-length ballets in the old tradition, which were to re-shape the whole style of the Company, with important consequences.

The first of these was *Cinderella*, launched, appropriately, on 23 December. Prokofiev had composed the score for the Bolshoi Company only three years earlier, and Ashton followed the carefully worked-out scenario very closely. Undaunted by the task of filling out a whole evening with a single ballet in the nineteenth-century manner, a feat which had not been attempted in the West in this century, Ashton revealed at once his professional craftsmanship with an uninterrupted flow of invention. Within six weeks he completed the choreography for the ensembles, solos, pas de deux, comedy mime scenes and varied numbers which Prokofiev's score demanded. On the first night of *Don Juan*, Fonteyn had torn a ligament, so the part of Cinderella was arranged for Shearer, whose light, fast lyricism was reflected in the role – Somes was the Prince. Elvin, partnered by John Hart, followed her, and a few months later Fonteyn took over the role and immediately invested it with her own special wistful pathos.

Don Quixote, designed by Edward Burra, 1950:
ABOVE Backcloth, BELOW Costume designs for village girls.

Though Ashton has maintained that he was not influenced by British pantomime, the playing of the two Ugly Sisters by male dancers lent to the work an ineradicable flavour of that ever-popular Christmas theatrical treat. This happened as an afterthought because Moyra Fraser, who originally had been cast as one of the Ugly Sisters (Margaret Dale was to have been the other) temporarily left the Company. Ashton himself stepped into Dale's role, and he and Helpmann made such a success of the double-act clowning, with Ashton's hesitant gaucherie underlining Helpmann's bossy over-confidence, that they tended to change the balance of the work. Handsomely designed by Jean-Denis Malclès, richly orchestrated and offering a wide variety of classical roles, the ballet was to prove a reliable favourite and resistant to any changeover to female Sisters. It was an instant guide to one of the ways in which the Company might develop, a pointer to the modern three-act ballets which were to become a feature of its repertoire.

The spring brought some nostalgic memories for devotees of de Basil's Ballet Russe. In March Alexandra Danilova and Massine once again appeared in their old roles of the Can-Can dancers in *La Boutique Fantasque*. Danilova followed these up by dancing *Coppélia* with Frederic Franklin as her fellow Guest Artist. She then gave two performances of *Giselle* with Franklin, as well as dancing Act II of *Le Lac des Cygnes* with him – a strenuous schedule, especially as she was suffering from a strained tendon which forced her to cancel

Moira Shearer as Cinderella, 1948.

one or two appearances. During the season all efforts were concentrated on what was to prove decisive in the fortunes of the Company – its first visit to North America.

The prospect of a visit to the United States and Canada had been under discussion for some time. Sol Hurok, the famous New York impresario, had been impressed by *The Sleeping Beauty* at Covent Garden in 1946 and had proposed presenting the Company in 1948 at the City Center Theater as part of a Dance Festival. However, after inspecting the theatre David Webster decided that it would be too small to accommodate the production. The visit was postponed until October 1949, when the Metropolitan Opera House (at that time located on Broadway between 39th and 40th Streets) would be free. The decision to open with *The Sleeping Beauty* was a bold one. New York ballet audiences were quite unused to full-length works; indeed they were geared to the spare, lean idiom of Balanchine, who was inclined to concentrate on pure dance at the expense of all the other ingredients of ballet. Not content with *The Sleeping Beauty*, Hurok and the Sadler's Wells administration proposed to include among the twelve productions in the Company's repertoire *Le Lac des Cygnes* and the three-act *Cinderella*. It was a gamble which paid off so resoundingly that it was to shape the image of the Company for many years in the American mind and to influence its whole future development at home. The Hurok administration went into top gear in announcing the imminent arrival of the mammoth

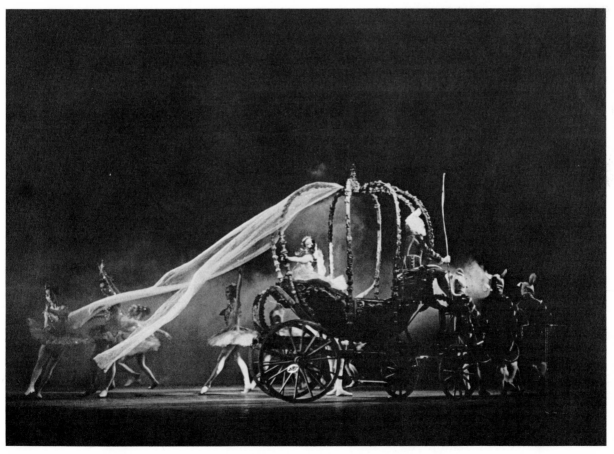

Cinderella, 1965 production. Cinderella leaves for the ball.

organisation which would involve the transportation of sixty-five dancers, a large technical and administrative staff and seven thousand pieces of scenery and costumes, adding up to fifty tons of freight – a $750,000 venture according to David Webster. The publicity stressing the magnitude of the operation, added to the glowing reports of the unknown dancers, suggested that the mantle of Tsarist splendour had fallen upon the British company. It worked wonders: there was a record advance booking before the Sadler's Wells Ballet had even arrived in the USA, and long queues formed around the theatre.

Such resonant fanfares were new to a Company whose roots lay not in imperial magnificence but in the workaday frugalities of Islington, and they engendered among the dancers a mood of intense excitement mingled with nervousness. De Valois was still doubtful whether American audiences would accept full-length ballets. It was a do-or-die enterprise; and the triumph of the première on a stiflingly hot October night was all the more rewarding. It was an important social occasion as well as a theatrical one. The centre boxes at the back of the 'Golden Horseshoe', decorated with the Union Jack and the Stars and Stripes, were occupied by the British Ambassador, the Mayor of New York, distinguished members of the government and diplomatic corps and, of course, the Sadler's Wells management. 'The atmosphere inside the Opera House was like a jungle minutes before a tropical storm,' Fonteyn wrote later. 'In the audience, applause greeted the Oliver Messel décor before anyone danced a step. When I ran out on to the stage there was a burst of sound. It drowned out the music and also some part of my mind, for I have never been able to remember anything between those first minutes of deafening applause on my entrance and the incredible reception after the third-act pas de deux.'

The reception was vividly described by *The Christian Science Monitor*: 'After the . . . ballet had triumphantly concluded, Ninette de Valois, the Director, thanked the overflow 'Met' audience and confessed that "we were terribly frightened of you." They needn't have been. Applause was recurrent, even impatient, throughout the evening. It rippled distractingly against some of the solos. It burst out in great tides when the scenes were finished. It rose to a roar of cheers for the curtain calls which finally ended around half-past eleven. The immense garlands of flowers brought on to the stage after the finale were pretty well matched by garlands of praise in the New York press.'

'So far as the quality of the demonstrations and the manifestations of enthusiasm are concerned, the première of the Sadler's Wells Ballet at the Metropolitan Opera House on 9 October 1949 was the most outstanding of my entire experience,' wrote Hurok six years later. 'In those days dance-hysteria was still unknown in New York, and the unanimity of the acclaim was striking.' The reviews were ecstatic – for the production, the designs, the orchestral playing and the dancing. 'This was ballet in all the grandeur of pageantry and finish of technique,' wrote another commentator two weeks later. 'For those who expected virtuosity there was little, for those who appreciated ballet as theatrical design expressed in fluid movement, the Sadler's Wells company gave the finest exhibition to be given here in many years.'

Many salient points emerged from this opening performance. First was the special style of the Company as it appeared to American eyes, creating an impression which became a fixed ideal not easily replaced. New York critics remarked on the 'fine and dignified leisureliness' of the dancing, on its 'graciousness and unity of style', on its 'mannerliness, unhurriedness, correctness of detail'. They noted that 'an ensemble performance as was

Ninette de Valois with her Company on the last night of their
first New York season, 6 November 1949.

shown last night could not conceivably be achieved except by a company which works all the year round, with financial and artistic security and a set of high ideals'. They also relished the return of spectacle and the 'grand manner', but noticed at the same time that this contrasted with the American emphasis on 'grandness in size of movement', and they noticed a British stress on phrasing rather than on rhythm.

The third point was that New York confirmed Margot Fonteyn as 'a star of the first magnitude'. In one performance she was precipitated from national adoration to international adulation, 'a ballerina among ballerinas' with a special place among the world's superstars. 'Star is a singularly unsuitable term for Miss Fonteyn,' recorded *The New York Times*, 'for there is nothing at all stellar, nothing at all "grand" about her; it is by a quiet sweetness, an effortless beauty entirely innocent of bravura that she takes her place among the elect.' Popular as were the appearances of Moira Shearer – known to wider audiences than Fonteyn through her success in the recent film *The Red Shoes* – she was no longer a threat, as at one moment she had appeared to be, to Fonteyn's supremacy.

The triumph of *The Sleeping Beauty* was, if anything, surpassed by the full-length *Le Lac*

[97]

Ballet Imperial, which Balanchine revived for Sadler's Wells Ballet in 1950.

des Cygnes, which came as a revelation to audiences accustomed only to the Second Act extract. *Newsweek* found it 'a little shorter than *The Sleeping Beauty* . . . and danced to a better score . . . It would make an excellent addition to any company's repertoire'. *Cinderella*, perhaps unsurprisingly, could hardly compete with such heady successes; both the music and the choreography were found less interesting, though the Ugly Sisters made the same comic impact as in London. Of the shorter ballets *Façade* seems to have been the favourite. The atmosphere of excitement at each performance in New York was to be recreated by enthusiastic audiences at the Company's subsequent appearances in Washington, Chicago, Richmond, Philadelphia, East Lansing, Detroit and three cities in Canada: Toronto, Ottawa and Montreal. It was intoxicating to the dancers and initiated a tradition that they would always respond to New York audiences by performing with extra vitality. They returned to a reception party at the Royal Opera House (of which the lease had just passed to the State). Significantly, the Chancellor of the Exchequer, Sir Stafford Cripps, paid a special tribute to their achievement: 'You have no idea what pride that has aroused in the fastnesses of the Treasury Chamber,' he remarked. The tour had netted $75,000.

When the Company re-opened at Covent Garden on Boxing Day in *Cinderella* they received an ovation, and Fonteyn made a speech thanking the audience for its warmth. But a sobering mood of anti-climax set in when the first new ballet of 1950 was presented, de Valois' *Don Quixote*. Though in theory ideally cast, with Helpmann as the Don, Fonteyn as Dulcinea and Alexander Grant as Sancho Panza, with striking designs by the British artist Edward Burra and a danceable score by Roberto Gerhard, the ballet never got going. However, something of the glories of the American tour was reflected in a brilliant gala presented by the Company for the French President Vincent Auriol. The theatre was decorated by Oliver Messel to harmonise with his designs for the last Act of *The Sleeping Beauty* which ended the programme. During the intermission de Valois was decorated by the President with the Légion d'Honneur.

Soon the Anglo-American connection was to be cemented. Ashton had returned to the USA in February to mount a new ballet, *Illuminations*, for the New York City Ballet. In return, its Director, George Balanchine, arrived in London to direct his *Ballet Imperial*, an abstract work first launched in 1941, set to Tchaikovsky's Second Piano Concerto in characteristic classical style. Its references to the great Maryinsky tradition – reinforced in this production by lavish designs by Eugene Berman – came easily to the British company, but the dancers found the sharply articulated, clear and vigorous idiom hard to assume after the softer, more insinuating approach of Ashton. Beryl Grey quickly found her way into the role of the Second Ballerina, but Fonteyn at this time, musical and moving as she was, seemed too gentle for the fast, brilliant dances allotted to the leading part. The exhilarating choreography proved difficult at the first performance and was criticised as mere virtuosity, but it was a very evident tonic to the Company, the first of many experiments in which the American approach – athletic, open and somewhat impersonal – would be adapted to the British temperament and physique.

While the Sadler's Wells Company had been at the Metropolitan Opera House in New York, Roland Petit's Ballets des Champs-Elysées had been performing at a neighbouring theatre. Discussions between the two companies took place about a new ballet by Petit for the Sadler's Wells Ballet. The result, presented at a gala in May 1950, was *Ballabile*. It was in every way opposite to the Balanchine ballet: allusive instead of abstract, mysterious and irrational where the other was lucid and geometrical, strong in characterisation but short on virtuoso dancing, with a lively score by Chabrier and dashingly modern designs by Antoni Clavé. But the French flavour proved even less acceptable to British taste than the American and it was received without much enthusiasm.

By now the Company was accustomed to such disappointments – the normal theatrical pattern of alternating successes and failures. In fact it was taking on the character of an established national organisation. Its status was confirmed when it 'came of age' and celebrated its twenty-first birthday with a party and gala at Sadler's Wells Theatre, its old home, in the presence of Princess Margaret. The programme was both nostalgic and lively and was hailed by the audience with obvious satisfaction. Late in the day it was discovered that there had been a mistake in the date and that it was, in fact, only the twentieth birthday. This in no way diminished the party spirit. After an especially realistic rendering of the orgy scene in her ballet *The Rake's Progress* by some of the original cast, now no longer young, de Valois is reported to have remarked: 'I shall always have that danced by married women in future'.

Hurok was keen to follow up quickly the success of the Company in America, and when the dancers split up in July for their summer holiday they learned that on their return to Covent Garden they would give only one week of performances and then would leave for a long tour of the USA and Canada. This time the visit was to last nineteen weeks and cover thirty-two cities, and once more it would start at the 'Met' in New York.

The opening ballet was *Le Lac des Cygnes*, with Fonteyn and Somes leading the Company, and again the production was greeted with unqualified praise. *The Sleeping Beauty* was also welcomed back without reservations. But inevitably the excitement of discovery was missing, and a few criticisms began to appear. Fonteyn was found less appealing in *Giselle* than in her other roles; and the production was thought to be only moderately successful, though Shearer was admired in it. As on the first visit, the new short ballets, apart from *Façade*, had a lukewarm reception.

The New York engagement was followed by a strenuous tour which took the Company south as far as New Orleans, across to the West Coast, then up to Chicago for Christmas and on to Canada. 'The longest tour in its history and the most successful tour in the history of ballet,' as Hurok described it, was a remarkable financial success. During the five months the flag of British culture had been carried over twenty-one thousand miles to the far corners of the North American continent, with the Company travelling in a special train made up of six sleeping-cars, four scenery wagons and a restaurant-car. When they returned to London in the February of 1951, they were able to celebrate their welcome home with the knowledge that in the New Year Honours List, the Director of the Company had been created a Dame Commander of the British Empire and Margot Fonteyn had been honoured with the CBE.

This peak in the Company's career, marked by its triumphs in America and its coming-of-age celebration (even though premature), was paradoxically to be followed by a downward turn in its fortunes. In America, Helpmann had announced his resignation. After the return to Britain, Moira Shearer, Pamela May and Beryl Grey fell ill. The dancers were tired after their exertions abroad, and at home the first fire of public enthusiasm for the Company seemed to have dimmed. Of the sixteen ballets to be presented at Covent Garden between 1950 and 1955 only two, *The Firebird* and *Sylvia*, were to survive in the repertoire for more than a few months, and the management began to come in for some

Ballabile by Roland Petit, with décor by Antoni Clavé.

critical sniping. The first signs of this was the public reception in April 1951 of Ashton's new ballet for the Company, *Daphnis and Chloë*. This seemed to have every prospect of popular success. Ravel's score was well-known, admired and loved. Ashton had for many years been thinking about a new approach to it (Fokine's version for Diaghilev had been short-lived). The designer, John Craxton, a respected modern artist living in Greece, seemed the ideal choice. The ballet also offered a part in which Fonteyn could perfectly exploit her quality of innocent charm opposite the sturdy manliness of Somes as her young shepherd lover. Elvin and John Field fitted naturally into the contrasted character roles of the rival lovers, Grant was a dashing pirate chief and there was plenty of scope for ensemble dancing. The ballet had, in fact, many appealing moments; but the difficulties which have always dogged it, the symphonic element in the music and the lack of drama in the story, outweighed Ashton's characteristic felicities, and the work was coolly received. It was to prove more popular later, especially in America.

Even more disappointing was the reception a few months afterwards of Ashton's next creation, *Tiresias*. This was a project thought up by Lambert, who composed the score while his wife Isabel designed the décor. The highly complicated story strained credibility

Daphnis and Chloë, 1964 revival, with Margot Fonteyn as Chloë and Christopher Gable as Daphnis.

to breaking point – it necessitated Somes changing into a woman (danced by Fonteyn) as a result of breaking a sex taboo – and the hour-long entertainment had only a single pas de deux which was of interest. The press reviews were almost universally unfavourable. Lambert, already very sick, died six weeks afterwards while the Company was away at the Edinburgh Festival. This understandably caused some public protests that his condition had been worsened by the ungrateful response to the ballet. The whole management came under attack for what looked like an ill-prepared venture. Ashton must have been even more disappointed than Lambert, and he was not to compose a ballet for a year.

Meanwhile three works by other choreographers were mounted – none very successful. In December 1951 Massine returned to put on *Donald of the Burthens*, a venture into the Scottish idiom which could have proved a perfect vehicle for the Russian choreographer's feeling for national dance and character roles. The ballet was strikingly designed by a pair of Scottish artists, Robert MacBryde and Robert Colquhoun, and the score had been specially commissioned from a Scottish composer, Ian Whyte. There were, in fact, some moving passages, but in spite of strong, sinuous dancing by Beryl Grey as Death threatening Alexander Grant as Donald, the old-fashioned story and some uncertain translations of folk-dance into ballet bogged the piece down. It had to be notched up as one more misfire in a disappointing season: significantly, Fonteyn was absent during most of it owing to illness. Her place in *The Sleeping Beauty* had been filled very pleasingly by Grey, Elvin and two youngsters, Rosemary Lindsay and Nadia Nerina, a brilliant and lively

Beryl Grey as Death in *Donald of the Burthens*, 1951.

technician from South Africa who had joined the Sadler's Wells Theatre Ballet in 1946 and moved to the main Company the following year.

By the spring of 1952 Fonteyn was back again, but the next new production, Andrée Howard's *A Mirror for Witches* – with another commissioned score, this time by Denis ApIvor – was arranged for Anne Heaton, a dramatic performer who had started her career in the Theatre Ballet and was now well cast as a fey, haunted heroine persecuted by her Puritan neighbours. This ballet too, failed to excite either the audiences or the critics. The list of disappointments ended with a comedy-ballet by another South African dancer, John Cranko, previously choreographer of Sadler's Wells Theatre Ballet for which he had recently created an outstanding success, *Pineapple Poll*. His new *Bonne-Bouche*, also to a commissioned score (by Arthur Oldham) was a broad joke packed with witty gags, and designed by Osbert Lancaster in his most tongue-in-cheek mood. It was a brave attempt at creating that most difficult of theatrical forms, farce. The public was not amused.

When the Company disbanded for the summer holiday, spirits must have been low, especially as Shearer had announced that she was leaving; in future she would appear as a Guest Artist; but hopes were doubtless raised by the news of the imminent launching of another venture in the genre which had brought the Company's biggest triumphs, the full-length narrative ballet. A success was badly needed to restore morale and public confidence. Ashton's new version of *Sylvia* went a long way to providing it. The tuneful 1876 Delibes score, the pretty Second Empire pastiche designs by Robin and Christopher

Sylvia. Frederick Ashton's 1952 production, Act I.

Ironside, the enchanting classical dances for Fonteyn, and the wealth of supporting roles craftily spread out across the evening, gave Ashton the chance to display his inventiveness and charm to the full.

Not content with mounting *Sylvia*, the Company was hard at work preparing a new production of *Le Lac des Cygnes*, one of its most reliable successes but now, nine years after it had last been revised, showing signs of fatigue. Leslie Hurry reworked his designs and costumes and Ashton contributed some effective new numbers – a pas de six in the First

LEFT Nadia Nerina in *Ballet Imperial*. RIGHT Svetlana Beriosova as Odile in *Swan Lake*, 1954.

Act and a tarantella in the Ballroom Scene which, danced with electrifying dash by Julia Farron and Alexander Grant, brought the house down on the opening night. Fonteyn had contracted diphtheria a few weeks before the première, and the first performance – a royal gala – was danced with huge success by Beryl Grey and her regular partner, John Field. Other young dancers who made their début in the ballet this season were Nerina, the New Zealand-born Rowena Jackson and (in Act II only) Svetlana Beriosova, a Lithuanian-born dancer who, after starring with the Metropolitan Ballet, had recently joined the main Company from the smaller Sadler's Wells Theatre Ballet and scored an instant success with her lucid, elegiac style.

But the road back to acclaim was not to be smooth. Neither of the first two productions of 1953 found much favour. Fonteyn was still ill, and these new ballets were both devised for other ballerinas. In March, John Cranko composed for Beriosova *The Shadow*, an old-fashioned romantic ballet to a Dohnanyi score with figures symbolising Love and Death. It was effective in its style and Beriosova was much praised for her performance, but the genre already looked dated. The next production, *Veneziana* by Andrée Howard, was written for Violetta Elvin. An extended divertissement set in Venice to music by Donizetti, it had a melancholy interest in that its attractive designs were by Sophie Fedorovitch, who had died in an accident only two months before. Following so closely after the death of Constant Lambert, this was another sad blow to the British ballet world.

LEFT Margot Fonteyn as the Queen of the Air in *Homage to the Queen*, produced in Coronation Year, 1953.
RIGHT Violetta Elvin.

A few weeks later the Company was rehearsing a celebration ballet. This was *Homage to the Queen*, devised by Ashton, that master of the *pièce d'occasion*, to be included in a gala marking the Coronation of Queen Elizabeth II. The programme, on 2 June 1953, began with Act II of *Le Lac des Cygnes* danced by Fonteyn and Helpmann, and ended with the new ballet. The short but exhilarating piece, constructed around the theme of the Four Elements, designed (not very happily) by Oliver Messel, and danced to a cheerful score by Malcolm Arnold, served as an excuse for the Company to display four of its principal ballerinas. The stars were Fonteyn, Nerina, Elvin and Grey; unhappily Shearer was missing from the list, having had to retire altogether because of an injury.

After the summer holiday and a two-week season in London, *Homage to the Queen* provided a bracing send-off for the Company's third visit to North America. The American tours, which were to take place every two or three years over the next two decades, had superseded visits to British provincial cities. These were now regularly served by the smaller Sadler's Wells Theatre Ballet, the main Company appearing for only a few weeks each year in three or four of the larger towns. Once again the American tour was presented by Sol Hurok, a firm and friendly supporter of the Company. It opened in September at the 'Met'. The Company had not been seen in New York for three years but its reputation was secure and tickets were sold out in advance for the entire season. The première coincided with a stifling heat-wave and the new production of *Le Lac des Cygnes* which opened the season was not universally liked, though Fonteyn and Somes were praised for their dancing. However, *The Sleeping Beauty*, offered a few days later, restored confidence in a Company which New York not only admired but loved. This time, Ashton's short ballets also began to win warm admiration. As before, it then set out on a long tour, this time through twenty cities in the United States and four in Canada, making a total of one hundred and thirty-six performances spread over nineteen weeks.

After their return to London, the dancers were allowed a three-week breathing space and in February 1954 opened a season which within the first fortnight was to include a new version of *Coppélia*, with fresh, crisp designs by Osbert Lancaster. The principal part was danced by Nadia Nerina, who had recently shown that she could shine in lyrical as well as in soubrette roles, partnered by a promising young dancer recently transferrred from the Sadler's Wells Theatre Ballet, David Blair. Ashton – always a formidable character-dancer – gave a personal twist to the character of old Dr Coppélius, making him lovable as well as comic. Two new *Giselles* were greeted in London this season, Anne Heaton (with John Field) and Pauline Clayden (with Alexis Rassine). In June, Beriosova made a sensational début in *The Sleeping Beauty*.

This autumn the twenty-fifth anniversary of the death of Diaghilev was being featured at the Edinburgh Festival, and to honour the great Russian director as well as taking advantage of the presence in London of Diaghilev's former régisseur, Serge Grigoriev, the Company mounted a production of Michel Fokine's *The Firebird* with the Stravinsky score and Goncharova's colourful décor. In the orchestra pit was Ernst Ansermet, the famous Ballets Russes conductor. The première was handicapped by the cramped conditions of Edinburgh's little Empire Theatre, but shortly afterwards when the ballet was presented at Covent Garden it scored an immediate success. The title role proved a superb vehicle for Fonteyn. Compensating for her lack of a striking jump with her glamour, musicality and dramatic powers, she found in the part of the magic bird a new vein of glittering vitality. The London showing was the occasion of a controversy full of interest and, indeed, instruction. While most critics praised Fonteyn's performance, one of them attacked it vigorously; this was none other than Cyril Beaumont, a veteran observer who had seen the original interpreter, Karsavina, in the role in 1910. He declared that she had presented 'a beneficent, fairy-like being' whereas Fonteyn gave the part a fiercer tone, almost that of 'a bird of prey'. It was quickly pointed out that Karsavina herself had coached Fonteyn in the role; but Beaumont stuck to his guns, provoking an unusually outspoken letter from Karsavina in the *Sunday Times* in which she remarked that 'If Mr Beaumont doubts the accuracy of my memory after twenty years of frequent appearances in this part, he must

---

Veneziana. Costume designs by Sophie Fedorovitch, 1953.

perhaps concede me some knowledge of Russian folklore and enough integrity not to distort the ideas of Fokine.' It seems likely that even Beaumont's sharp memory may have been clouded by nostalgia. In any case, in later performances, Fonteyn tended to add, if anything, to the sharpness of her attack, supported by Somes as an ideal rustic Prince, rugged and handsome. The work proved to be the Fokine ballet best suited to a Company which has normally looked better in works created for the Maryinsky company on which it had been modelled.

In the autumn of 1954 a long delayed exchange with the Paris Opéra Ballet at last took place. The visits, however, were not very successful on either side: French and British taste in ballet proved to be wide apart and neither company could claim to have scored a success. The Sadler's Wells subsequent tour, in Italy, was more warmly received. This year, however, marked a pause in the Company's development. Apart from the revival of *The Firebird* there were no new productions, and 1955 proved equally unfruitful. It began with three new Ashton works, indifferently received. *Rinaldo and Armida*, to a score by Malcolm Arnold, was another old-fashioned symbolic-romantic vehicle for Beriosova: pretty, but superficial in spite of her beautiful dancing. *Variations on a Theme of Purcell*, to Britten's 'Young Person's Guide to the Orchestra', was even less convincing. Three months later, in April 1955, Ashton presented yet another short work, *Madame Chrysanthème*. This was a delicate little piece based on a novel by Pierre Loti and re-calling Puccini's opera 'Madame Butterfly'. The hazardous task of setting the story to new music was entrusted to Alan Rawsthorne and the designs were by Isabel Lambert. With Elaine Fifield, imported from the Sadler's Wells Theatre Ballet, as the heroine, it was a work of considerable charm, but its appeal was to prove ephemeral. Perhaps the most striking portent for the future came this same year with the first performance of the full-length *Le Lac des Cygnes* in which Beriosova again revealed herself to be a pure classical dancer of exceptional quality. It had been a thin period during which – maybe coincidentally – Fonteyn had been largely absent.

One more work was given its first performance by the Company before it set out on its fourth North American tour, *The Lady and the Fool*. This was a romantic ballet to music by Verdi revolving round a clown's love for a society beauty, which Cranko had created for the Sadler's Wells Theatre Ballet the previous year. In preparation for New York, *Les Sylphides* was also revived under the careful eyes of Grigoriev and Tchernicheva, and Ashton's *Tiresias* was given a second chance to establish itself. With one American critic, John Martin of *The New York Times*, it definitely did so; he described it as 'rich, noble and underestimated . . . as great a work as he has ever accomplished'. But his isolated voice was not to prove powerful enough to preserve the ballet in the Company's repertoire.

The five-week season in New York had again been sold out in advance and was acclaimed once more by the critics. *The Firebird* was hailed as a convincing reconstruction of Fokine's important work, though Balanchine's 1949 version was still preferred by some. Beriosova and Nerina were praised for their performances as Aurora, Grey for her La Capricciosa in *The Lady and the Fool*; Somes and Brian Shaw were picked out from the

The Firebird. Margot Fonteyn, 1959.

LEFT John Field as Prince Siegfried in *Le Lac des Cygnes*, *c*1952. RIGHT Alexis Rassine as Albrecht in *Giselle*.

rather less admired male contingent. But once again it was the classics which made the most impact, and Fonteyn was held to be outstanding in them. 'Dame Ninette's charming people are truly at home and unsurpassed in the dazzling Never-Never-Land of romantic ballet', declared one newspaper. The usual round-America tour – somewhat less financially profitable this year – followed New York, and on New Year's Eve the eighty-six-strong Company was back at home, this time to enjoy a big welcome at Covent Garden. Once again they opened with *The Sleeping Beauty* and of course Aurora was danced by Fonteyn. Next morning in the New Year Honours List for 1956 it was announced that she had been created Dame of the British Empire.

5 Royal Company

The honour, combined with the fact that during the previous year Fonteyn had been married, provoked the first of many rumours of her 'imminent' retirement. It was true that in the future her ties with the Company would be slightly loosened, but in fact her own qualities and achievements had become a permanent ingredient of its personality. Blessed with an ideal figure and a small, oval, large-eyed face which registered gentle sadness in repose and dazzling joyousness when she smiled, she had a soft, easy and musical way of moving which was the perfect expression of delicate sensitivity. She was never a virtuoso and she concentrated on her other qualities – purity, precision, harmony and a sustained control which made even difficult passages look effortless. This quality of quietness developed by de Valois and Ashton, but above all by her own exceptionally clear-headed and resolute efforts, turned her into the epitome of the Royal Ballet ballerina – restrained, unshowy, dependable and touchingly feminine. The honour bestowed on her was thus justifiably taken as a tribute to the whole Company. It came at a significant moment. This year, 1956, which had dawned so auspiciously, was to inaugurate an outstanding decade. In the next twelve months the Company would celebrate a series of anniversaries; it would be involved in a drama which was of concern to the whole nation; and it would finally enjoy a change of status which would set it on a unique footing in the world of British dance.

The organisation was in excellent shape. At its centre were sixty-seven dancers, who were led by an exceptional team. There were two experienced choreographers to draw on, de Valois and Ashton, as well as two highly promising young aspirants in this field, John Cranko and Kenneth MacMillan. The repertoire now embraced almost all the surviving nineteenth-century classics from Russia as well as a rich supply of works from the Diaghilev repertoire and many modern creations, two of them full-length productions. Few companies in the world could now match the resources or outshine the performance standards of the Sadler's Wells Ballet.

During the spring de Valois and David Webster had flown to Moscow to complete arrangements for a visit to Russia in the autumn, with a reciprocal season of the Bolshoi Ballet at Covent Garden. Meanwhile there were new productions to be mounted. The first of these was *La Péri*, a new version by Ashton of a pas de deux to a Dukas score first devised with the Ballet Rambert as far back as 1931 for Markova and himself. On this latest occasion he was severely restricted by a last-minute decision by the music publishers to insist on strict obedience to Dukas's original instructions – that the male role should be limited to mime and partnering. The little ballet thus became virtually a supported solo for Fonteyn, with a be-turbanned Somes in walking attendance. The décor unsuccessfully tried to marry the Parisian chic of André Levasseur's costumes with a neo-romantic pastoral setting by a British painter, Ivon Hitchens. In the circumstances there could be little left but some Oriental swayings and posturings, and the ballet was unenthusiastically received. 'The waving of coloured scarves by invisible hands is fit for the parish hall and not for the Opera House', wrote the critic Arnold Haskell severely.

The next new production, *Noctambules*, was of great import for the future. Presented in

March 1956, it was the first ballet written for the Covent Garden Company by the young Scottish choreographer Kenneth MacMillan. A product of the Sadler's Wells School, he had reached some eminence as a dancer and had already composed two successful ballets for the Sadler's Wells Theatre Ballet. His new work was strikingly original in both subject and approach. It concerned an embittered hypnotist who ended up by subjecting his whole audience to his powers. The treatment was high-pitched and weird, a mood matched by Humphrey Searle's commissioned score, considerably more modern than anything heard so far in ballet at Covent Garden, and by the iridescent décor of a Greek designer, Nicholas Georgiadis, who was to become a frequent collaborator with MacMillan. The production, which had Maryon Lane, a South African dancer recently transferred from the Theatre Ballet, as heroine, was found 'confused' by some critics while others complained of the 'violent, complicated music' and the 'screaming rainbow-change' of the designs. But the signs of a new, original talent were unmistakable.

The Company's Silver Jubilee was celebrated two months later, on 5 May. Curiously, this important occasion was not honoured by any royal patronage as the mistimed twenty-first anniversary had been, nor did it even count as a gala. This may have been due to the avalanche of anniversaries and special occasions which had called for celebration in 1956. On 6 January the twenty-fifth anniversary of the re-opening of Sadler's Wells was

The Queen and Prince Philip with Margot Fonteyn and
David Webster after a gala performance at
the Royal Opera House.

marked by the resident Theatre Ballet with a gala. On 23 January another gala, this time at the Stoll Theatre, commemorated the twenty-fifth anniversary of the death of Pavlova. On 20 February the tenth anniversary of the re-opening of the Royal Opera House was celebrated with a whole week of *The Sleeping Beauty*, in which Aurora was danced by six successive ballerinas, Fonteyn, Elvin, Grey, Nerina, Beriosova and (making her début) Elaine Fifield. On 22 March the Royal Family attended the annual Benevolent Fund Gala, and on 5 April a gala was organised in honour of a visit by the Soviet President Bulganin and Premier Khruschev. In contrast to these glittering occasions, the Silver Jubilee performance was more like a private family reunion. The programme opened with Helpmann and Farron in *The Rake's Progress* and ended with *Façade*. The nineteen-year-old Merle Park was the Milkmaid and Fonteyn and Helpmann danced the Tango so stunningly that they were encored. (Twenty-three years later at Fonteyn's sixtieth birthday performance their interpretation was to prove equally popular.) Also included was a short suite of dances constructed very rapidly by Ashton, to a Glazunov score arranged by Robert Irving to display the prowess of the Company. Called *Birthday Offering*, it consisted of an *entrée*, seven solos for the seven ballerinas, a mazurka for their partners, and a finale. It was intended as an ephemeral *pièce d'occasion* for a single performance. However, it turned out to be so deftly made that it was to be revived on several suitable

Birthday Offering. (Left to right) Elaine Fifield with Brian Shaw; Violetta Elvin with David Blair; Svetlana Beriosova with Bryan Ashbridge; Margot Fonteyn with Michael Somes; Beryl Grey with Philip Chatfield; Rowena Jackson with Desmond Doyle; Nadia Nerina with Alexander Grant.

occasions, a vivid demonstration of Ashton's personal adaptation of the classical idiom. 'The best suite of dances composed since English ballet began', declared one critic, while another claimed that it proved Ashton to be the equal of Petipa. The grand parade on this first occasion consisted of Fonteyn, Grey, Elvin, Nerina, Beriosova, Jackson, Fifield, Somes, Chatfield, Blair, Grant, Bryan Ashbridge, Desmond Doyle and Brian Shaw. At the end of the show de Valois made a speech in which were mingled pride, hope, gratitude and good sense. 'Twenty-five years old. That means we can take two paths. We can sit back and remember what we have achieved, or we can sit up and remember what we have still got to do.' There was no doubt which posture the Director would adopt.

If 1956 is taken as the beginning of a new stage in the Company's history some concomitant endings can be seen as inevitable. During the last few years Shearer, Turner, Helpmann and Rassine had all left the Company. That summer, Violetta Elvin gave up dancing altogether. The changes might have been serious, but fortunately a strong entry of young dancers was ready to take over – such as Annette Page, Anya Linden, Merle Park, Doreen Wells, Antoinette Sibley, Lynn Seymour, Gary Burne, Graham Usher and Ronald Hynd. There was no American tour this year, and after the summer holiday the Company went north to Edinburgh to take part in the Festival. Here it launched a new ballet, *The Miraculous Mandarin*, by the South African-born Alfred Rodrigues, who had already choreographed three ballets for Sadler's Wells Theatre Ballet. Like most attempts to dramatise Bartók's dramatic score, it proved unsatisfactory. Somes was miscast as the sinister but pathetic central figure, and Wakhevitch's realistic setting contrasted awkwardly with the heavily symbolic story, but Fifield was a striking seductress and Grant a dynamic hoodlum.

While the Company was away in Scotland, Covent Garden was host to Ballet Theatre from America, which was less successful than on its previous visit ten years earlier. This season all eyes were turned towards the forthcoming arrival of the legendary Bolshoi company, which was to be followed by the British Company's four-week visit to Moscow. The impact of the Bolshoi would certainly have been immense in any case, but it was made all the more powerful by the publicity which preceded its arrival; and this was increased a hundred times by an accident which hovered breathtakingly between farce and tragedy. Two weeks before the arrival of the Russian company a discus-throwing lady from a Soviet athletics team was accused of stealing hats from a store in Oxford Street. She received a summons to appear in court, but failed to show up. Headlines flared, and on 22 September a long letter appeared in the Moscow paper *Izvestia* signed by the Director of the Bolshoi, its principal ballerina Ulanova and several others, declaring that they would not feel safe from similar 'provocation' in London and that the forthcoming visit would therefore have to be cancelled. Over the next ten days this dramatic move made front-page news. Messages flashed between Moscow and London. Ambassadors and Members of Parliament were involved. It was reported that the Cabinet was discussing the next move. Eighty tons of Russian scenery, already unloaded, lay in the London docks. But at the last moment the Soviet authorities relented and the Bolshoi company arrived, with only a few hours in which to rehearse its first appearance. The opening ballet was *Romeo and Juliet* and it made an impact which was to reverberate for many years. Shrewd critics had foretold that the sight of Western productions would revolutionise ballet in Russia; in the event, the influence was to be almost as strong in the opposite direction, at least as far as the Sadler's Wells Ballet was concerned. While the Russians were basking in popular, as well as a great deal of critical, acclaim at Covent Garden, the home Company was engaged to appear in the suburb of Croydon before leaving on a tour to Coventry and Oxford – a workaday preparation for the Moscow visit.

It was on 31 October 1956, while the Company was in Oxford, that the Governors were handed a solemn document. It read:

'Elizabeth the Second, by the Grace of God of the United Kingdom of Great Britain and Northern Ireland of our other realms and Territories Queen, Head of the Commonwealth, Defender of the Faith. To all whom these presents shall come, greeting! . . . Now therefore know ye that We by virtue of Our Royal Prerogative and of all other powers enabling Us in that behalf have of Our special grace, certain knowledge and mere motion granted, willed, directed, ordained and declared and by these Presents Do for Us, Our Heirs, and Successors grant, will, direct, ordain and declare as follows: The President, the Vice-President and Governors for the time being of the corporation hereby constituted shall be and are hereby created one body corporate with the name of 'The Royal Ballet' with perpetual succession and a common seal.

The first aim of The Royal Ballet was defined as: 'To promote and advance the art of the ballet, and in association therewith the literary, musical and graphical arts and to foster public knowledge and appreciation of the same'.

This honour – not to be announced publicly until 15 January 1957 – was not, as it appeared, an instant gesture to give the Company a good send-off in Russia. Two years earlier, de Valois, disturbed to find that both of the financial grants from which her two Companies benefited were tied to the theatres on which they were based, had drawn up a memorandum for the Board of Directors suggesting a new title. It should cover both the Covent Garden and the Sadler's Wells Companies, as well as the School which had been set up by the Sadler's Wells Foundation, and would thus 'enable our ballet to face its existence as an entity, and so ensure its continuity whatever conditions may prevail'. The emphasis on continuity was characteristic, and she was impelled by a second motive – to separate the interests of the ballet from those of the opera. She compiled a list of possible titles; there were six, headed by 'The Royal English Ballet'. All of them were prefixed by 'Royal'. The Chairman of the Board of the Royal Opera House, Lord Waverley, had in fact applied for the grant of a Royal Charter some months previously, and confidence was evidently felt that it would be granted. The special committee which was set up to examine de Valois' proposals was called, in fact, the 'Royal Ballet Board of Directors'.

The timing of this accolade, which would have been of obvious benefit to the Company during its Russian tour due to start two weeks later, was upset by a sudden international crisis. The opening in Leningrad had been planned for 14 November, with a programme including *The Lady and the Fool*, *Birthday Offering* and *Daphnis and Chloë*. All seemed in order, and the scenery, costumes, props and scores had been sent off and reported as having arrived safely in Russia. Then, in late October, the newspapers carried reports of an uprising in Hungary. On 4 November listeners to the radio heard a voice from Budapest appealing for help against the Soviet army, which was moving in 'to restore order'. On 7 November David Webster, General Administrator of Covent Garden, cabled to his

The Prince of the Pagodas, 1957. Svetlana Beriosova as Princess Belle Rose,
David Blair as the Prince of the Pagodas.

opposite number in Moscow (presumably after consultation with the Foreign Office): 'In view of public opinion in this country which strongly condemns the renewed suppression by Soviet forces of Hungarian liberty and independence . . . it has been unanimously agreed that in present circumstances the projected visit of the Sadler's Wells Ballet to Moscow cannot take place'.

An alternative tour for the Company was hastily arranged. On 21 November it was back again at Covent Garden with a performance of *Cinderella* to open a short improvised season while it awaited the return of its scenery. On 10 December it was taking part in a gala at Sadler's Wells in aid of Hungarian Relief. Incongruously one of the hits of the evening was *Valse Eccentrique*, a lunatic pas de trois by MacMillan danced in Edwardian bathing costumes. A year which had been eventful in many ways closed with a performance of *The Sleeping Beauty* with Nerina and Rassine, who had recently left the Company and was appearing as a Guest Artist.

The next year, 1957, opened with an éclat which seemed to counteract recent misfortunes. For many months the Company had been planning the most ambitious project that it had yet mounted – a full-length ballet by a Commonwealth choreographer to a commissioned score by a British composer with British designs and mainly British dancers. The ballet was *The Prince of the Pagodas* and the choreographer was John Cranko. Now thirty, Cranko was, with MacMillan, one of the young choreographers whose talents had been developed in the Sadler's Wells Theatre Ballet, for which he had already arranged four productions (including the immensely popular *Pineapple Poll* and *The Lady and the Fool*) as well as two for the main Company. Born in South Africa in 1927, he had shown precocious talent, creating at the age of fifteen for the Cape Town University Ballet a new version of Stravinsky's *The Soldier's Tale*. In 1946 he arrived in London and after a brief period at the Sadler's Wells School joined the Theatre Ballet. Quick-minded, mercurial, and charming with a ready smile and wide, childlike eyes which seemed alert to every new idea, he had a strong sense of theatre which had revealed itself in an original commercial revue, 'Cranks', devised and directed by him in 1955. His choice for this new ballet venture, which was to combine tradition and experiment, seemed a happy one.

The première had been planned for the previous September, so that the work could be included in the Moscow tour, but Benjamin Britten, the chosen composer, fell ill and the ballet finally opened on New Year's Day 1957, with Britten conducting. 'Please clap as at an ordinary performance,' Cranko requested the over-respectful audience at the dress rehearsal, 'because Mr Britten hasn't conducted for ballet before and he doesn't know how to judge the applause.' Cranko, always full of inventive ideas, had decided to stick to the traditional structure of a nineteenth-century classic. He constructed a fairy-tale plot of his own, a blend of 'Beauty and the Beast', 'Cinderella', and 'The Sleeping Beauty', with a touch of 'King Lear' thrown in, devised as an excuse for traditional mime, solos, pas de deux and ensembles. The result, however, was too clever to be effective. The décor by John Piper, which included unsuccessful trick effects, did not blend with Desmond Heeley's costumes and the choreography was ostentatiously modern. Beriosova made an appealing heroine, with Julia Farron as her delightfully spiteful sister. Blair suffered from an awkward role, half prince and half lizard; but a young Rhodesian, Gary Burne, had an unexpected success with a solo as the black-faced King of the South. Britten's score was colourful but undramatic and it became apparent that in such a long work narrative ingenuity was no substitute for emotion. The ballet, the first full-length work to a modern commissioned score to be presented in the West, was undoubtedly a milestone, but not a very impressive one.

The resignation of Beryl Grey a few weeks later, to pursue her career elsewhere, was an unexpected blow, but fortunately she had not been cast in *Petrushka*, the Company's next production. This Diaghilev classic had so far been avoided by de Valois because she felt that its style was so firmly based on Russian folk-dance that it would not suit a British company with its very different roots. The continued presence in London of Grigoriev, who had supervised the original production, overcame her doubts, but her initial misgivings proved well founded. Over-respect for correct reconstruction, together with a lack of the national verve which the crowd scenes demand, robbed this revival of vitality. Grant, handicapped by his strong build and broad shoulders, was touching but not very puppet-like, and Fonteyn was too lyrical for the Doll. The result was a faithful copy rather than a fresh revival. As though exhausted after these two major productions, the Company relied for the rest of the year on old favourites. It was joined in the summer by Markova, who gave some performances of the classics partnered by Blair, now an experienced star, and by Philip Chatfield.

The summer of 1957 was marked by a development which did not at first work out quite as intended. In June it was announced that a decision had been made to co-ordinate the work of the Royal Opera House Company and the Sadler's Wells Company, with a regular exchange of productions and dancers. The title The Royal Ballet would cover both organisations. The Royal Opera House Company would be known simply as 'The Royal Ballet' while the smaller unit (it was strictly taboo to refer to it as 'the second company') would be called 'The Royal Ballet, formerly the Sadler's Wells Theatre Ballet'. The new arrangement would, it was hoped, put an end to confusion. This was, in fact, the logical consequence of the recent grant of the Royal Charter, a proposal fortified by the example of the visiting Bolshoi company, which had numbered a hundred dancers and yet still left an even bigger troupe in Moscow to carry on in their absence. The aim may have been admirable but the confusing and impractical result was greeted with dismay. The problem of unifying three separate units – the two Companies and the School – into a trinity in which each would continue to preserve its own identity defeated the Board of The Royal Ballet, and has continued to plague it, in spite of changes of title for the smaller Company. 'Royal Ballet Muddles Fans' read a headline in an American paper preparing its readers for the next tour by the Covent Garden Company.

This fifth American tour, which started in September, was to be the longest so far. A four-week season at the 'Met' in New York began with *The Sleeping Beauty*. Subsequent programmes included the new *Prince of the Pagodas* – not much liked – as well as *Petrushka* and two MacMillan ballets, *Noctambules* and *Solitaire*, taken over from the Sadler's Wells Theatre Ballet. The Company then set out across the length and breadth of the USA and up into Canada on a tour which covered seventeen cities and lasted seventeen weeks – an exhausting schedule. Every five or six days the dancers would arrive in a new city with a different stage to dance on – sometimes in the open air, sometimes in an opera house – and after half a dozen performances the special train, with its one hundred and forty passengers and its freight-cars packed with scenery and costumes and musical instruments, would be off again. The climate changed from New York in September to Montreal in January. It was not until 19 February 1958, five months after it set out, that the Company was back home in London, with a spirited performance of *Sylvia* in which the comic Turkish duet by Brian Shaw and Peter Clegg won special applause. Meanwhile, the former Sadler's Wells Theatre Ballet had been carrying the flag of The Royal Ballet at the Opera House, the first example of the new administrative system.

Back from its prolonged tour, the Covent Garden Company saw the return to its ranks of one of its first stars. In March Helpmann rejoined it to give a series of performances which included his original parts in *The Rake's Progress*, *Coppélia*, *Miracle in the Gorbals*, and *Hamlet*, as well as an attempt – less successful than had been anticipated – on the title role in *Petrushka*. Interesting débuts included Merle Park with Gary Burne in *Coppélia* and Anya Linden in *The Sleeping Beauty*. The 1944 *Miracle in the Gorbals* was revived but looked melodramatic now that the dark mood of wartime had lifted, in spite of strong performances by Helpmann, John Hart as the Official and Leslie Edwards in his old role as a beggar. In May The Royal Ballet paid a flying visit to Brussels and on 10 June it was back at Covent Garden to take part in a gala to celebrate the hundredth birthday of the Royal Opera House with a performance, very suitably, of *Birthday Offering*.

The ensuing summer season was outwardly uneventful but in fact rehearsals were going on for two adventurous productions. The first of these, *Agon*, marked a major step forward by the Company in the direction of modern dance. Stravinsky had composed this ballet for Balanchine, and the work had been produced by New York City Ballet seven months previously. With remarkable alacrity MacMillan – who three years earlier had used a Stravinsky score with success for his *Danses Concertantes* – studied the score and digested it sufficiently well to consider composing his own choreography. It was presented at Covent Garden in August 1958. The music, with its sharp short rhythms and epigrammatic structure carried much further the idiom with which Covent Garden audiences had only slowly come to terms in Ashton's *Scènes de Ballet*. The wry, enigmatic mood suggested by MacMillan and his designer Georgiadis introduced a new and very personal note, as was to be seen when Balanchine brought his own production to London seven years later.

The other new production of 1958, presented when the Company returned from its summer holiday, was on a larger scale.

For many years Ashton had been searching around for a subject for a full-length ballet suitable for Fonteyn, and for a score by a contemporary composer. After considering 'The Tempest', 'Macbeth' and 'The Dybbuk', he finally chose *Ondine*, the story of a water-sprite who falls in love with a mortal, a fable already used by several nineteenth-century choreographers. In 1956 he had asked William Walton to compose the music for it, but Walton was busy and suggested instead Hans Werner Henze. Early in 1957 the German composer came to London, and slowly the work took shape. The ballet was finally presented in October 1958, after a postponement due, among other difficulties, to an injury to Ashton in a car accident.

Like *The Prince of the Pagodas, Ondine* was devised according to nineteenth-century

Ondine, 1958. LEFT Margot Fonteyn as Ondine. RIGHT Fonteyn as Ondine, Michael Somes as Palemon.

tradition, with a romantic exposition, a dramatic development in the middle Act, and a finale mainly composed of divertissements. Its success was largely due to the skill with which Ashton exploited Fonteyn's personality and style. The chief supporting roles, Tirrenio (danced by Grant) and Berta (Julia Farron) were not much developed, and the hero, Palemon (Somes), was a cipher without even a solo. Everything depended on the ballerina, and Fonteyn, with her fluid, lyrical, wistful style, proved ideal. *The Times* described it as 'a concerto for Fonteyn' and she carried it off triumphantly. The pastiche elements – such as the famous *pas de l'ombre* when the sprite plays delightedly with her new-won shadow, the make-believe shipwreck, a 'swimming' passage and a vision appearing magically within a picture-frame – were skilfully absorbed by the designer, Lila di Nobili, into a fantastic Gothic design. The score was appropriately iridescent and danceable, though not particularly adventurous. A few voices were raised complaining that the idiom of the ballet was old-fashioned, but it proved, as *The Prince of the Pagodas* had not, the validity of a full-length work entirely created by living artists, thus giving impetus to the development of the three-act ballets which were to become so closely associated with The Royal Ballet.

Ondine was to be the last major role created for Fonteyn with the Company for five years; the next would be *Marguerite and Armand*. New choreographers and new dancers were coming forward, and the repertoire was to reveal a glorious overlap of the generations with a seemingly endless supply of talent. One of the most gifted among the younger ballerinas was Svetlana Beriosova, now aged twenty-six. Although trained in her youth in the United States and Canada she was Lithuanian by birth and her essentially classic style was characteristically broad and liquid. Andrée Howard's *La Fête Etrange*, a success when in 1947 it was revived for the Sadler's Wells Theatre Ballet, was brought into the repertoire for her. It provided a chance to display her aristocratic poise and line. As in 1947 the young boy was danced by Pirmin Trecu, a Basque who had arrived in England as a refugee during the Spanish Civil War (his real name was Aldabaldetrecu), and who had joined the Sadler's Wells Theatre Ballet before transferring to the main Company.

The new year, 1959, brought an award – Michael Somes received a CBE in the New Year Honours – and a film. In January, Paul Czinner, a director who had made a successful record of a stage production of the Bolshoi's *Giselle* while that company was in London, shot a full-length feature film called 'The Royal Ballet', filmed in the Opera House over two days and a night. It consisted of Fonteyn, partnered by Somes, in *Ondine*, *The Firebird* and Act II of *Le Lac des Cygnes*.

The spring programme offered many full-length works, especially featuring Nerina and Beryl Grey who returned as a Guest Artist, partnered by a Swedish dancer, Caj Selling, as no sufficiently tall British dancer was available. The Company was busy preparing a revival of two ballets originally created for the smaller Company. On 5 March, Cranko's *Harlequin in April*, originally presented by the Sadler's Wells Theatre Ballet in 1951, was given. As on its first showing, it was found interesting rather than convincing; the symbolism was decidedly confused, but Blair slipped back effortlessly into his old role as Harlequin opposite the delicate young Antoinette Sibley, newly promoted as a principal. A week later another work from Sadler's Wells was introduced, MacMillan's *Danses Concertantes*, which on the big stage made an even stronger impression, with Maryon Lane and Pirmin Trecu dancing with great attack, supported by Merle Park and a recent acquisition from the Theatre Ballet, Doreen Wells.

Only a few days later another revival formed the centrepiece of a programme, this time a gala in aid of the Royal Ballet Benevolent Fund. Ashton had created his version of Ravel's *La Valse* the previous year for the company of La Scala, Milan, as part of a programme devoted to the French composer. The music had originally been commissioned by Diaghilev but when it arrived he had rejected it as unsuitable for ballet because it lacked 'scenic action'. This had not discouraged countless choreographers from using it, and Ashton himself had danced in a version devised by Bronislava Nijinska. His arrangement was very different – an ultra-chic swirl of waltzing couples in elegant costumes designed by André Levasseur. It was a decorative *pièce d'occasion*, too short and sweet for most normal programmes but ideal for a gala. Several of the Company's stars were away, on a long tour of New Zealand and Australia, and on her way home Fonteyn was briefly arrested in Panama on a charge of revolutionary activities connected with her husband, Roberto Arias, a former Panamanian ambassador.

After a revival of her *Job* with David Blair as Satan, de Valois paid a visit to Russia – the first since the cancellation of The Royal Ballet's visit there. Inevitably rumours began to circulate suggesting a revival of the abandoned project. These were denied, but the atmosphere was friendly and de Valois returned to London full of new enthusiasms, especially for the talent of the boy students and for the Russian teachers whom she had watched. During the summer season Merle Park danced a memorable *Coppélia* and on 6 May Lynn Seymour made a highly acclaimed London début in *Le Lac des Cygnes*, with a promising young partner from Scotland, Donald MacLeary. Fonteyn shared *The Sleeping Beauty* with several younger dancers including Nerina, Beriosova, Jackson, Annette Page, and Anya Linden; in July a decision was taken to make her a Guest Artist and to charge higher prices when she appeared – a significant change in Covent Garden's policy.

After the summer holiday an experiment was made. The two Companies, mustering one hundred and eighteen dancers, combined to present a season from both their repertoires. Though the experiment did not make a particularly strong impact, the season was extended by four weeks. At the end of September the Covent Garden Company went off to appear in the suburbs of London, first at Golder's Green, where Antoinette Sibley danced her first full-length *Le Lac des Cygnes*, and then at Streatham, before returning in October to begin an eight-month season at the Royal Opera House: it lasted until June and amounted to one hundred and fifty-four performances. To open it Cranko presented *Antigone*, a short ballet which was in complete contrast to anything he had done before. Derived from Sophocles, it was a tragedy of ancient Greece: the story of a young girl who faces death rather than dishonour her brother by leaving his body unburied. It seemed to be a subject more in the genre of Martha Graham than of a classical choreographer, and Cranko abandoned the point shoe for this work. Beriosova made a touching heroine, with Gary Burne and David Blair as her warring brothers. The score by the Greek composer, Mikis Theodorakis, and the brooding set by a Mexican artist, Rufino Tamayo, helped to produce a dark, fateful mood which was still a rarity in the Company's programmes. Though the strong drama had its admirers and certainly added a new dimension to Cranko's British repertoire, the simplification of the tragedy produced only stereotyped characters and situations, and in general the work was not enthusiastically received. For most ballet-goers it was probably a relief to get back to *Cinderella*, already established as a Christmas favourite.

The New Year, 1960, opened auspiciously with the news that David Webster who as

La Fille Mal Gardée, 1960. ABOVE Act I: (centre) Alexander Grant as Alain, (left) Stanley Holden as Widow Simone, Leslie Edwards as Thomas. BELOW Nadia Nerina as Lise, David Blair as Colas.

General Administrator of the Royal Opera House had played such a vital part in the steady development of the Company, had received a knighthood. It was not long before the British ballet world was to enjoy a more memorable event – the birth of Frederick Ashton's best loved and most characteristic and successful work, *La Fille Mal Gardée*. Ashton was by now one of the world's most experienced choreographers, with over fifty ballets to his credit. His specialities were wit and charm and delicate romanticism. Now, suddenly, he moved into new territory, abandoning modern sophistication and nineteenth-century sentiment for an apple-cheeked country comedy redolent of the eighteenth-century. This 'tribute to nature', as he called it, seemed to tap new sources of inspiration and to offer fresh openings for his felicitous invention and theatrical ingenuity.

The original ballet had been devised by the French choreographer Jean Dauberval and was first presented in 1789 in Bordeaux. It was a key work at that time, a bold step away from the gods and goddesses of conventional ballet, introducing into dance a new set of characters taken from life and from a humble stratum of society. The scene is not Parnassus nor a palace but a farm; the hero and heroine are country youngsters and their love affair involves no fine sentiments but money, property and – significantly – sex. When they are accidentally locked together in a bedroom the audience has no doubt about how they spend their time. The ballet had provided the great dancer Tamara Karsavina with one of her favourite roles and it was she who encouraged Ashton to revive it and showed him passages from the Russian version. In the main, though, Ashton completely rewrote the choreography, while retaining such traditional motifs as the butter-making scene and the use of ribbons. In place of the customary foreign national dances he introduced English folk-dances, such as a clog number for the Widow Simone and a men's ensemble with clashing sticks. Alexander Goehr and Malcolm Arnold having turned down the proposal to compose a new score, John Lanchbery, who had started conducting ballet at Sadler's Wells in 1951, made a delightful confection from the original music combined with later alternatives and additions; and Osbert Lancaster contributed pretty, affectionately mocking designs. A perfect cast was to hand – Nerina as the mischievous Lise, Blair as her spunky young admirer, Grant as the pathetically droll simpleton whom Lise is supposed to marry and Stanley Holden *en travesti* as her mother, the Widow Simone. From the start the mixture of pastoral innocence, theatrical variety, humour and choreographic charm was a winner at Covent Garden. It was eventually to captivate audiences everywhere, though its gentle appeal and rural theme took time to catch on with provincial British, and New York, ballet-goers accustomed to high romance and spectacle.

In April a new ballet by MacMillan was launched for which there were great expectations. Stravinsky's *Le Baiser de la Fée*, the composer's tribute to Tchaikovsky, had enjoyed only a partial success when Ashton had mounted it for the Vic-Wells Ballet in 1935. Neither Nijinska, the original choreographer, nor Balanchine who tackled it soon after Ashton, had managed to make it work satisfactorily. But the story, derived from Hans Andersen's *The Ice Maiden*, and the score, were so attractive that high hopes were pinned to this new version. The casting seemed ideal – Beriosova as the cool, implacable ice fairy, Lynn Seymour as the warm-hearted bride, and MacLeary as her ill-fated bridegroom; while Kenneth Rowell, the Australian designer, contributed some striking décor. But the ballet, hampered by the awkward scenario devised by Stravinsky, failed, in spite of some beautiful passages.

No new ballets were planned for the summer, but *The Sleeping Beauty* was presented in June with costumes refurbished by Oliver Messel. The production was now fourteen years old and had played for over five hundred performances; the need to renew it offered a chance for a change. As it turned out, the use of more expensive materials than had been available in the post-war London and the addition of extra buttons and bows detracted rather than added to the spectacle, and the colours seemed not so much fresh as harsh. But there were some improvements: the 'panorama scene' and the role of Carabosse were expanded to great effect. These first changes provided an augury of many subsequent attempts to bring up to date a production which in its time had been almost perfect.

When the Company dispersed for the summer holidays the dancers knew that it would be their last rest before a year of exceptional activity. In spite of the doubts occasioned by the previous American tour, a sixth had been arranged. It opened on 11 September 1960 at the 'Met' and was almost as long and just as strenuous as before, lasting nearly five months and covering twenty-six cities in the United States and Canada, mostly on visits of only two or three nights. By the time that the tour ended, in New York on 29 January, the Company had given over one hundred and forty performances, resulting in a considerable profit. The keystones of the programmes had been *The Sleeping Beauty* (there were a few complaints about the new costumes); *Le Lac des Cygnes* (particular praise for Beriosova, partnered by MacLeary); Nerina and Blair in the new *La Fille Mal Gardée*, which was received rather cautiously, as an ineffective version had been in the repertoire of the American Ballet Theatre; and *Ondine*, which brought Fonteyn another shower of compliments.

The New Year, 1961, opened with an important announcement. On 10 January it was revealed that the Company's long awaited visit to Russia was to take place in the summer. Negotiations had been slow. Only three months after the first cancellation, the Soviet Minister of Culture had put out feelers towards a revival of the project, and it was soon afterwards that de Valois had visited Moscow and Leningrad. Though not planned as such, it was to be a reciprocal arrangement. A Russian company would dance at Covent Garden while The Royal Ballet was in Russia – not the Bolshoi this time, but the Kirov from Leningrad. Rumours about the visit had been current for some months. Now, nearly five years after the first attempt, the great exchange of companies was to be effected.

Meanwhile the long Covent Garden season continued. The first new production for this spring, a revised version of *Giselle*, had already been presented in New York the previous September and was to be included in the programmes in Russia. It had been undertaken by Ashton with help, as in his recent *La Fille Mal Gardée*, from Karsavina, who had danced it with Nijinsky. Missing passages from the score were restored and the action expanded accordingly – for instance the crowning of Giselle as Queen of the Vintage. Karsavina also contributed her memories to the revival of some mime scenes, such as the moment when Giselle's mother foretells the fate which may await her daughter. Many of the changes were welcomed, but some voices of dissent were raised against the production (which had again been charmingly designed by James Bailey). The new ending – actually a restoration of the original, with its last-minute reconciliation between the hero and his aristocratic

---

Les Biches, first produced by The Royal Ballet in 1964,
with Georgina Parkinson and David Blair.

fiancée – was particularly criticised, and later was to be discarded.

The rest of the spring season of 1961 was uneventful. All thoughts seemed to be turning towards Russia. The programmes to be taken this time were different from those planned for the 1956 trip. It was to include, besides triple bills, *Ondine*, *La Fille Mal Gardée* and *The Sleeping Beauty* which was at the same time the 'signature ballet' of The Royal Ballet and the very symbol of the Maryinsky style and theatre to which the Company was now to pay tribute. To take *The Sleeping Beauty* back to the stage on which it had been born seventy-one years before was an act not only of piety but of boldness. How would the efforts of the thirty-year-old British company stand up to comparison with the Russian dancers with their two hundred years of glorious tradition? Even de Valois was nervous.

On 15 June The Royal Ballet presented its first performance in Leningrad, and four days later the Kirov opened in London. Curiously, neither company presented *The Sleeping Beauty* on the opening night. Whereas the Kirov began with *The Stone Flower* the Royal Ballet, which had arrived in the USSR four days earlier with fifty-five tons of scenery, launched its tour with *Ondine*. Though historically less apt than the Petipa classic, it was a good choice. As a romantic three-act ballet, its format was familiar in Leningrad, while at the same time details of the choreography represented Western modernity. Above all it offered a fine example of Ashton's stagecraft, and Fonteyn at her very best. The ballet, a dancing rapprochement between fantasy and realism, and its interpreters, had a warm reception. Fonteyn's grace and enchanting femininity were especially singled out, and Somes's dignity and Grant's attack were praised in the measured style of Soviet critics. Henze's score presented difficulties for many in the audience, and the last Act aroused less enthusiasm than the first two; but at the end of the evening there were armfuls of bouquets, twenty-one curtain calls and shouts of 'Fonteyn!'. The next night *La Fille Mal Gardée* was evidently easier to love, and proved the big success of the tour. Nerina, the Lise of the première, was already known in Russia as she had danced in Moscow with the Bolshoi the previous year, and her strong, lively style was much admired. Blair's warm personality and confident technique also made a good impression and the comical Alain of Alexander Grant was much appreciated. Ashton's handling of the whole ballet, which was still in the Russian repertoire – in a different version, of course, with different music – won universal praise; 'full of bright colours and the joy of living, happiness and humour in which elements from national folk-lore combine with elegant and beautiful classical dances'.

The first *The Sleeping Beauty* seems to have made less of an impact. 'I think I gave my worst performance ever' wrote Fonteyn afterwards. Like the rest of the Company she was evidently too nervous to do herself justice. The changes introduced by Diaghilev such as the Three Ivans' pas de trois and the Florestan pas de trois (quite apart from more recent alterations and additions) were predictably criticised, but at the same time the 'festive and fairy-like' spectacle was considered to be pleasingly near to the current Soviet version. The dancing, though acknowledged to be creditable for a relatively young company, could hardly be expected to rival native Russian standards. It was remarked that the British dancers were less strong in the back than their Russian counterparts, and that they used

---

La Fille Mal Gardée, drop curtain, 1960, and *Pineapple Poll* backcloth, 1951,
both designed by Osbert Lancaster.

less épaulement. Of the short ballets, Cranko's *The Lady and the Fool*, de Valois' *The Rake's Progress* and Ashton's *Les Patineurs* were especially admired: unexpectedly Fokine's *The Firebird* made little impression. The footwork of the British ballerinas was praised; the Bluebirds of Brian Shaw and Graham Usher pleased by their speed and dexterity; and the 'clowning' of Grant and Ray Powell (a dancer not usually much noticed in London) was singled out. The musicality and absence of exaggeration was approved and, with the exception of the abstract *Danses Concertantes* ('it suggests that the choreographer composed it for a bet'), the whole season was held to be 'a great creative achievement, near

The Company at the Kirov Theatre, Leningrad, in June 1961 after a performance of *Ondine*.

to our conception of art'. For Fonteyn and Ashton the tour was undoubtedly a triumph; for the rest of the Company it won admiration and respect.

After its two-week tour, the Company returned for the summer holidays exhausted but justifiably satisfied and eager to hear about the exploits of the Kirov Ballet in London. It had received an ecstatic reception in spite of the fact that its brightest young star had not arrived, having defected in Paris; his name was Nureyev. De Valois quickly arranged for reports on his travel plans and performances to be relayed to her. (He had joined the Grand Ballet du Marquis de Cuevas in Monte Carlo.) The reassembled Company launched almost immediately into two new creations, presented simultaneously. One of them, *Jabez and the Devil*, was not a success. It was choreographed by Alfred Rodrigues, his seventh ballet for the two Companies. The main features of the ballet – a sardonic reworking of the Faust legend – were the provision of a strong part for Grant as the Devil and the first role to be created for Sibley, as Mary. The other new work, *Diversions*, was by MacMillan. Taking Bliss's 'Music for Strings' he made it the basis of a long, flowing set of abstract manoeuvres for a group of twelve dancers. The music and the original and becoming designs of Philip Prowse set up a brooding mood in which two contrasting pairs, Beriosova with MacLeary and Maryon Lane with Usher, linked and parted in fluid movements which suggested emotion without demonstrating it.

Perséphone, 1961. Svetlana Beriosova as Perséphone, Keith Rosson as Pluto.

With no American tour that winter, the Company settled into a long season at Covent Garden. After the marathon foreign travels of the past season it was not to venture abroad again for nearly two years, when it would resume biennial visits to America. It had now virtually abandoned all touring in Britain, as the Touring Company now included in its repertoire several full-length nineteenth-century classics as well as ballets transferred from Covent Garden, in addition to its own commissioned ballets, so that it was well able to fulfil the demands of audiences outside London.

One new production was launched at the Royal Opera House in the winter of 1961, *Perséphone*. This was a completely new working by Ashton of a ballet originally choreographed in 1934 by Kurt Jooss (the creator of *The Green Table*) for Ida Rubinstein and her company. The music was by Stravinsky; the story, based on a Greek myth, was by the French writer André Gide, as were the short speeches to be spoken by the heroine, and the text, to be sung by tenor and chorus. It was an elaborate and lavish piece in three separate scenes, with a multitude of small incidents, a large corps de ballet and heavily loaded multi-colour designs by Nico Ghika, the Greek artist. Cumbersome in construction, the tale of Perséphone's abduction into the Underworld advanced slowly, as if unfolding on a tapestry. Beriosova struggled gamely with the title-role which demanded dancing with a microphone (built into her costume) into which she declaimed Gide's French text. Keith Rosson was her statuesque abductor, ruling over a Hades which proved more lively than the world above. The stools between which the ballet fell were all distinguished but the end result was none the more convincing.

Nothing new was promised to enliven the spring of 1962, but interest rose when it was announced that Rudolf Nureyev the young defector from the Kirov, was to appear at Covent Garden in March. He had made a sensational London début at a gala the previous November, following which two thousand people signed a petition calling for him to be invited to dance with The Royal Ballet. Fonteyn, who had hesitated to dance with him at the gala, was anxious to have him as a partner now that she had seen him perform. De Valois, willing as always to allow exceptions to her preference for British artists when special talent appeared, seems to have made a swift decision. After his pas de deux at the gala she watched him take a curtain call. She knew exactly what she wanted. 'I could see him suddenly in one role,' she wrote later, 'Albrecht in *Giselle*. Then and there I decided that when he first danced with us it must be with Fonteyn in that ballet.' And so it was. On 21 February. after weeks of frenzied publicity, with tickets selling at huge prices on the black market, the curtain rose on a performance which was to launch a partnership that would affect the fortunes and character of The Royal Ballet for over a decade.

The question naturally arose of Nureyev's becoming a full member of the Company. This could not be a straightforward decision. De Valois had insisted from the first on the importance of establishing and maintaining a clear individual character for the Company, rather than allowing it to be a back-up team for visiting stars. Occasional foreign Guest Artists had been admitted, such as Danilova, Chauviré, Massine and Selling. Now the question arose of inviting a dancer with a totally different background and style, and a reputedly difficult and demanding temperament, as a guest on a long-term basis – perhaps even a permanent one. Would not the impact of such an explosive and magnetic star shatter the structure which had been built up so carefully over the years? It was decided that he should be invited to become what Lord Drogheda, Chairman of the Opera House, was to call 'a sort of permanent Guest Artist'. As such he was soon appearing frequently with the Company. He caused widespread flurries by his demanding and dedicated individuality, but the general stimulation of his performances, especially the raising of the standards of male dancing, was undeniable. De Valois, in what was to be almost her last contribution to the Company that she had created, insisted on the importance of injecting this heady new strain into its now sturdy constitution, and she never deviated in her support of Nureyev's continued presence.

A further sign of de Valois' confidence in her Company was the arrival as Guest Artist only a few weeks later of another male star, Erik Bruhn, the great Danish dancer regarded as the epitome of the classical style. This had been arranged some time before Nureyev's appearance on the scene, but had been delayed. Thus in one month British ballet-goers

they provided the introduction to a major new work by MacMillan, a revised version of *The Rite of Spring*, starring one of the new young soloists, Monica Mason.

This ballet, originally commissioned by Diaghilev and choreographed by Nijinsky, had created a furore of protest when it was first performed in 1913. To match the elemental scale and massive force of Stravinsky's score demands superhuman powers from the dancers and the designer. MacMillan asked the Australian artist Sidney Nolan to design it and Nolan based the tribal sacrificial ceremony on Aboriginal dances, with costumes suggesting patches of colour applied direct to the skin to create a grotesque disguise. A huge cast was assembled to perform a series of intricate, jerky, violent manoeuvres in which primitive rhythms mingled with revue-style ensembles, the whole work building up to the climactic solo by the Chosen Maiden. This demanding dance was performed by Monica Mason with an intensity, commitment and physical prowess which scored a triumphant success. Born in South Africa, she had already made her mark in the classics with her strong, sure dancing; now a new facet of her talent, as well as of MacMillan's, had been revealed.

Guest Artists were much in evidence that summer. Chauviré danced once in *The Sleeping Beauty* and four times in *Les Sylphides*, while Bruhn made several appearances

The Rite of Spring, 1962. Monica Mason as the Chosen Maiden.

[135]

The Good-Humoured Ladies, 1962. (Left to right) Ronald Hynd as Leonardo, Antoinette Sibley as Mariuccia, Stanley Holden as Luca, Brian Shaw as Battista.

with Nerina. By June, Chauviré and Bruhn had gone, but a new partner for Nureyev arrived, the roving Bulgarian-born ballerina Sonia Arova. On two successive evenings *Le Lac des Cygnes* was danced by this new partnership, followed by Fonteyn and Blair in the same ballet, and soon afterwards Fonteyn and Nureyev joined each other again to dance *Giselle*. With Beriosova, Park, Page, Grant, Gable, MacLeary and Usher all taking principal roles on other evenings, this was a rich period in the Company's history.

The season ended with an encouragement for the future – Ashton's elevation to a knighthood – and a tribute to the past – a production of Massine's *The Good-Humoured Ladies*. This one-act comedy had been created for Diaghilev in 1917 and de Valois had danced in it during her years with the Ballets Russes. As a final gesture of admiration to a choreographer whom she both loved and respected, she invited Massine to revive the work for the Company and it was presented in July. In spite of its past record, its distinguished score by Scarlatti, and its décor by Bakst, and the participation of the 66-year-old ex-Diaghilev star Lydia Sokolova, the revival fell rather flat. Opinions differed over the cause: was it dated choreographically or was it unconvincingly performed? The simple answer probably was that the revival was mistimed. It was dogged by misfortune before it even

[136]

opened. Sadly, only nine days before the première, Harold Turner, one of the earliest members of the Company, who was to have returned to take a leading role in the revival, collapsed and died leaving a rehearsal on stage.

A new work by MacMillan announced for a few days later was postponed, but sharp eyes picked out an exceptional young dancer in the Bournonville divertissement which had remained in the programmes since Bruhn's visit. This was Anthony Dowell, slim and trim as a reed, in one of the *Napoli* solos, his first featured role. With raised seat prices dampening enthusiasm for a rather moderate performance of a revival of Ashton's *Les Rendezvous*, the none-too-popular *The Good-Humoured Ladies*, and the formidable *The Rite of Spring*, the first few weeks of the season passed quietly. The major new asset was a work acquired from the Touring Company's repertoire, Ashton's *The Two Pigeons*. Both Lynn Seymour and Christopher Gable, the dancers who had created the ballet's leading roles, were now full members of the main Company, and there was no problem in transferring the gentle pathos of the work to the larger group. The return of the Fonteyn-Nureyev partnership in November suddenly raised excitement to full pitch. For their first appearance they introduced *Le Corsaire*, a short pas de deux which had been one of Nureyev's show-pieces in Russia. Extracted from an early Petipa ballet, the romantic-virtuoso choreography, in which Nureyev managed to combine both qualities, opened up new excitements from him as well as a new sparkling facet of Fonteyn's talent. Their sensitive performances together in *Les Sylphides* were equally successful, and expectations ran high for a ballet which Ashton was said to be preparing for them. Unfortunately Nureyev injured his ankle and Fonteyn left for a holiday, so the project was postponed.

In the New Year, 1963, the Opera House found itself making headline news when on 31 January a section of a cornice crashed down into the street causing the upper sections of the auditorium to be closed, much to the indignation of those who had bought seats in that part of the house. The main attention of the Press, however, was fixed on the imminent Ashton ballet, now announced for March. Meanwhile the new work by MacMillan, *Symphony*, was launched at last. This was the second recent MacMillan addition to the repertoire – his dramatic, highly successful *The Invitation* having been taken over from the Touring Company before Christmas. *Symphony* was in marked contrast to it in style – a rather complicated abstract accompaniment to, or interpretation of, Shostakovitch's First Symphony in which the dancers were somewhat overwhelmed by the vivid sets and costumes designed by Yolanda Sonnabend.

At last, in March 1963, after protracted and at times almost hysterical publicity (there was even a Press dispute over the right to photograph rehearsals), Ashton's *Marguerite and Armand* was finally revealed. It was a compressed and distilled version – what Ashton himself called 'capsule form' – of the famous story by Dumas fils, 'La Dame aux Camélias'. The treatment took the form of a sick-bed dream, ending in the heroine's death in her lover's arms, in which the whole drama was contained within a single sonata by Liszt. Pitched in a high emotional key and elegantly designed by Cecil Beaton, it proved an ideal vehicle for the two stars, deploying Nureyev's gift for passionate romanticism and releasing in Fonteyn new depths of dramatic pathos. The ballet was an instant success and became a signature-work for the celebrated pair. No other artists have ever danced it.

Only three days later, on 15 March, the mood of elation over this new success changed to consternation when an official announcement broke almost unimaginable news – that de Valois was to retire at the end of the season. Eleven years earlier she had secured the succession by appointing Frederick Ashton as her Associate Director and during the past two years she had confided in her close collaborators her determination to withdraw in 1963, when she would reach the 'retiring age' of sixty-five. Now that her decision became public the full effect of the change became clear and many tributes to her achievements were made in the Press.

Meanwhile the season had to go on and, a few weeks later a sensational, not to say lurid, new ballet by Helpmann was launched, *Elektra*. It had originally been intended as a component for a gala; but wisely it was postponed and grew into a short highly-charged sex-and-violence exercise with an effectively Expressionist design by a fellow-Australian, the artist Arthur Boyd. The choreography was vigorous, with Nerina, neurotically obsessed by her axe, being tossed acrobatically from group to group until all except she were dead, but it often lapsed into a crudity bordering on vulgarity.

Soon after this unusual experiment, the Company left London for the USA, where it opened its seventh American season in New York. Covent Garden was occupied in its absence by the Bolshoi Ballet, making a second visit. After four weeks at the 'Met' the Company moved out on a tour which lasted nearly two more months and ended with a week in two vast auditoria in Los Angeles, first The Shrine, then the Hollywood Bowl. Predictably *Marguerite and Armand* and *Le Corsaire* were popular hits of the season; the other new ballets in the repertoire were less well liked, though Lynn Seymour in *The Invitation* received much praise. Neither Ashton's *The Two Pigeons* nor MacMillan's *The Rite of Spring* was much to the American taste.

The last appearance of the Company in New York, on 19 May 1963, proved to be an emotional occasion. The performance of *The Sleeping Beauty* which, in keeping with tradition, had also opened the season, ended with a huge ovation for Fonteyn. The evening concluded with a short speech by de Valois. After thanking the public for its generous response to the performances, she went on to bid a double farewell, first for the Company and then on her own behalf. This was to be her last appearance as Director, in New York or anywhere else.

The knowledge that her successor was Ashton, who had been her close collaborator from the earliest days and who was universally recognised as one of the architects of the Company, made the hand-over seem like the deft passing of a baton in a relay race. Nothing reflects the aim and achievement of de Valois more clearly than this skilful and painless handling of the succession. From the very beginning she had been intent on constructing a lasting organisation, not a personal monument. It was thirty-five years since she had mounted her first little ballet for Lilian Baylis at the Old Vic; thirty-two years since the première of the first performance by the Vic-Wells Opera Ballet Company which was to grow into The Royal Ballet. During that time she had guided her dancers through the war years, watched over their promotion to Royal status, and led them triumphantly to America and Russia. She had branched out into the formation of a second Company as well as a School. She had fostered choreographers, encouraged designers and musicians, and coached generations of performers into artistry. She had also become a Dame of the British Empire.

But although presiding over one of the most glamorous institutions in the country, de Valois had never been remotely touched by ambitions of glamour for herself. She was a shrewd and practical organiser, seeing her own path towards her vision and sticking to it with fierce but far from single-minded determination. To a virile forcefulness she added the

Dame Ninette de Valois with the Company after the gala performance
in her honour on 7 May 1964.

fickleness of a woman and a delightful contrariness. English tenacity was mixed with Irish flexibility. She could be ruthless yet thoughtful, solemn and frivolous, purposeful but suddenly and effectively indecisive all in one afternoon. She had learned much from Diaghilev but taken from him only what she admired. She had based her early successes on established stars but had developed a steady opposition to the 'star system'. She had mostly limited the ranks of her dancers (though not her designers or composers) to native talent – and then, in her last two years she had abruptly reversed direction by opening up her Company to foreign Guest Artists. She cherished the ideal of British fairness but she had strong likes and dislikes. She understood and tolerated the uses of criticism but she sometimes hit back when attacked. Above all, through every twist and turn of circumstance and personal vacillation, she kept her eye steadily on her target – the establishment of a dance organisation as tough and lasting as the British monarchy. 'It is the belief of the present Director', de Valois had written in an article in 1932, only three years after the birth of her Company, 'and this is the point to be driven home, that if the Ballet does not survive many a Director it will have failed utterly in the eyes of the first dancer to hold that post'. So far it had not failed. Like a rocket still rising from its launching-pad, the Company shed its first vital stage without a tremor and proceeded serenely on course.

[139]

6 The Ashton Years

The first years of any new institution are usually the most exciting, and nothing in the Company's story is likely to surpass the formative period under its founder which had just come to an end. Ashton was well aware of the ensuing change. 'I feel rather like James the First succeeding Queen Elizabeth', he remarked when he took up his duties as Director in September 1963, after the holidays. The comparison was perceptive – stepping into the shoes of an inspired matriarch is never easy – but it was over-modest, for King James had not helped to create his predecessor's realm nor had he contributed to its achievements, as Ashton had contributed to the success of de Valois' Company. Now fifty-six years old, he had been an essential part of the organisation since its cradle days and was universally recognised as one of its architects.

In most ways the new régime was a continuation of the old, particularly as de Valois remained a very active force both as Supervisor of the Ballet School (the post which she now took up) and as an ever-present guide and adviser to the Company. Ashton instituted no great changes either in policy or in personnel, but his temperament was very different from that of de Valois, as were his gifts. Essentially he was a creative artist with a sensitive reaction to individuals. He needed time and privacy in order to concentrate on his choreography, and he had no natural inclination towards planning and administration. From the first he delegated to his Assistant Directors, Michael Somes, John Field and John Hart, much of the routine work which de Valois had enjoyed looking after herself, devoting himself particularly to rehearsing and coaching the dancers and planning the programmes. What he immediately contributed were his own ideas for the repertory. His tastes were based on an affinity with French culture; on an admiration for the achievements of Diaghilev's company, especially those of Nijinska; and on an inherent and passionate loyalty to the classical tradition.

This last ingredient in Ashton's artistic personality was to be rewardingly illustrated in the first new production under his leadership. When the Kirov company from Leningrad had visited London two years earlier one of its most popular items had been an extract from an early full-length ballet by Petipa, *La Bayadère*: the Kingdom of the Shades scene, in which the spirit of the dead heroine appears to the hero together with her companions, rank after rank of remote but radiant figures weaving and bending like a field of corn in the moonlight. The leading male dancer in the Kirov production was to have been Nureyev, who now offered to mount the work for The Royal Ballet Company. It seemed risky to entrust such an enterprise to a young and notoriously temperamental artist, but Nureyev proved to have a phenomenal memory and great gifts as a coach. The première, in November, with Fonteyn and himself as the leading pair, was an unqualified success. Their combination of glamour and style was irresistible, and the three soloists, Park, Seymour and Mason, brought off their fiendishly difficult variations with perfect aplomb. The whole Company absorbed the Russian style with extraordinary skill, and the work was to be a favourite showcase for displaying the distinction and classical purity of The Royal Ballet. In particular it showed off the corps de ballet, which never failed to win a round of applause for its first ensemble.

La Bayadère, 1963. Margot Fonteyn as Nikiya, Rudolf Nureyev as Solor.

A shadow had been cast over the final rehearsals of the ballet by an event which broke through the time-hallowed conventions of the Royal Opera House. It happened just five days before the première of *La Bayadère*, on 22 November 1963, and the programme that night consisted of *Ballet Imperial, Marguerite and Armand*, and *The Invitation* with Seymour and Gable. When the final curtain fell, Ashton stepped out to make an announcement. During the performance, he told the audience, the radio had reported the assassination of President Kennedy, and he asked that everyone should stand for one minute as a tribute to the President's memory. There was a gasp and then a frozen silence as the minute dragged by. Then, with no curtain calls, the theatre emptied swiftly and solemnly.

The next revival undertaken by Ashton, *Swan Lake*, revealed in its full mature complexity the Russian romanticism explored by Petipa, with inspired simplicity, in *La Bayadère*. The direction was entrusted to Helpmann, but three choreographers were asked to add new dances to the Petipa-Ivanov original. There was a new Prologue by Ashton in which the Princess was seen being turned into a swan. Act I included a polonaise by Nureyev, and the melancholy solo for the Prince which he had introduced in 1962, while Ashton devised a pas de douze and a pas de quatre. In Act III there was a new mazurka by Nureyev, a czardas by Maria Fay, a Hungarian-born dancer who was teaching in London, and a Spanish dance by Ashton. In addition, Ashton rewrote the whole of the last Act. The result was deemed interesting rather than completely successful, and conservative voices sighed for the plainer virtues of the old production. The elimination of Ivanov's Act IV, one of the very rare examples of his choreography, proved particularly controversial. But the new production became an admirable vehicle for Fonteyn, Nerina, Sibley, Beriosova, and Page, partnered respectively by Blair (who at the première replaced an injured Nureyev), Gable, MacLeary and Desmond Doyle.

In March 1964 a new candidate for the succession to Fonteyn arrived on the scene when, in the Company's four hundredth performance of *The Sleeping Beauty* at Covent Garden, Antoinette Sibley appeared as Aurora, partnered by the South African-born Desmond Doyle. The production had been slightly revised, with the Awakening coming before, instead of after, the last interval. Sibley's delicate swallow-swift interpretation contrasted vividly with a strong, warm performance in the same role a few nights later by the French-born ballerina from New York City Ballet, Violette Verdy, partnered by Blair. Verdy joined a long list of distinguished foreign artists who had moved in and out of Covent Garden during the last year.

Swan Lake, 1963, pas de quatre.
(Left to right) Antoinette Sibley, Brian Shaw, Merle Park, Graham Usher.

Meanwhile an important date was approaching which offered both an opportunity and a challenge – the national celebration, on 23 April 1964, of the four hundredth anniversary of the birth of Shakespeare. Already the Company had produced one ballet derived from a Shakespeare play, Helpmann's *Hamlet*. It was agreed that Ashton and MacMillan should each add a new work. The three ballets were given together on 2 April at a surprisingly low-key occasion; there was no gala and the Quatercentenary was not mentioned in the programme. However, the ballets themselves turned into a celebration. Nureyev, predictably, proved to be an alluringly moody Hamlet, with Seymour as a touching Ophelia. MacMillan's new work, *Images of Love*, was a series of nine dances based not on a play but, more originally, on individual lines from plays and sonnets. Barry Kay devised a seminal golden structural setting but the work was handicapped by Peter Tranchell's score, and the variations were uneven. The most effective was judged to be the ambivalent love-triangle between Nureyev, Seymour and Gable, derived from Sonnet 144: 'Two loves I have of comfort and despair'.

What turned out to be the most popular of the three ballets was Ashton's *The Dream*. This was a straightforward translation of Shakespeare's *A Midsummer Night's Dream*, with

Swan Lake, 1963, Act II. Svetlana Beriosova as Odette,
Donald MacLeary as Prince Siegfried.

its lovers and fairies and 'mechanicals', arranged to the incidental music by Mendelssohn. Taking the score as the main clue to the style, Ashton offered a Victorian vision with picturesque settings and costumes by Henry Bardon and David Walker. The emphasis was on the lyrical poetry of the play, with cleverly interlaced comic scenes for the lovers and a rich part for Alexander Grant as Bottom, which included a little caper on tiptoe to imitate the hooves of a donkey. Nowhere had Ashton better used his skill in conveying narrative through action and dance: within fifty minutes the whole complicated story was unfolded, with a minimum amount of mime. The ballet was important, too, in that by exploiting their special qualities it launched what was to become a famous partnership, that of Antoinette Sibley and the twenty-one-year-old Anthony Dowell. Sibley's Titania was light and fragile as a dew-spangled cobweb; Dowell as Oberon darted and spun with electrifying speed and nimbleness in a part that skilfully showed off his long, elegant line.

Since taking over the Directorship, Ashton had already offered the public ballets by two of his colleagues, Helpmann and MacMillan; to these, in May, he added another choreographer whom he greatly admired, Balanchine. *Serenade* was a very early work, dating from 1934. Though hardly representative of Balanchine's current preoccupations, it was an ideal choice for the Company. The flowing style deftly married to Tchaikovsky's romantic score proved a natural vehicle for Nerina, Beriosova, Page, Blair and MacLeary, who led the opening cast. It was an instant favourite.

The première of *Serenade* on 7 May, which was preceded by *La Création du Monde*, a short, rather unfocused work recently created by MacMillan for the Touring Company, crowned a momentous commemoration. The occasion was a gala organised to honour Dame Ninette de Valois as Founder and, for thirty-three years, Director of the Company. The programme was a felicitous blend of pomp and friendly affection. At the end the curtain rose on a gigantic flight of steps, rank after rank of dancers appeared from the back of the stage and descended to their places, starting with diminutive pupils from the School and their teachers. Dancers from the three Companies – the Covent Garden Company, the Touring Company from Sadler's Wells and the Covent Garden Opera Ballet – were finally joined by Sir Frederick Ashton, his co-choreographer Kenneth MacMillan, and his three Assistant Directors, Hart, Somes and Field. Finally de Valois herself, resplendent in a sky-blue dress and long white gloves, slowly walked down the steps to be presented with a bouquet, accompanied by a roar of cheering from the audience. The massed dancers turned and bowed as she paused to make her speech, in which she expressed her pleasure at seeing the fulfilment of her dream that the Company should continue to flourish after she had retired. The programme included not only the two new ballets but also short pieces chosen to allow many of the principal dancers to shine. By ill luck, Fonteyn and Nureyev – her first discovery and her last acquisition – were abroad.

Soon after this occasion the Company had to move from the Royal Opera House because of structural alterations. During June and July they appeared at the nearby Theatre Royal, Drury Lane, where they presented a season of triple bills and of full-length ballets. It was a

---

Romeo and Juliet, 1965.
ABOVE Act I, Scene 4, the Ballroom; Margot Fonteyn as Juliet, David Blair (with mandolin) as Mercutio.
BELOW Act III, Scene 4, the Balcony Scene; Fonteyn as Juliet, Rudolf Nureyev as Romeo.

triumphant ending to Ashton's first season as Director, one which raised in the Press the question as to whether the Company might not benefit from moving out of Covent Garden and adopting Drury Lane as its home – an idea which was to crop up repeatedly over the next ten years.

While the Company was away enjoying temporary lodging, its general reputation was suddenly greatly increased by the launching at a gala on 1 June of another, and very successful, film introducing its work to the cinema public, *An Evening with the Royal Ballet*, directed by Anthony Havelock-Allan. It was a record of stage performances of Ashton's *La Valse; Le Corsaire* and *Les Sylphides* with Fonteyn and Nureyev; and Act III of *The Sleeping Beauty* with Fonteyn partnered by Blair.

With the autumn opening of the new season came a revival of Massine's *Mam'zelle Angot*, which paid tribute both to him and to his admirer de Valois. The November programmes were noteworthy for an unusual feature, an unprecedented succession of performances of *Swan Lake* – nine in a row, with six ballerinas, who now included Sibley and Seymour. Rehearsals were also in progress for one of Ashton's favourite and most successful ventures, the rescue from oblivion of *Les Biches*, a ballet originally created in 1924 by Nijinska. She was now aged seventy-three and living in Los Angeles and her ballets had become neglected. Curiously she and Ashton had never met in America, but when he wrote and invited her to come over to London and produce *Les Biches*, she accepted immediately. Even after fifty years in the West she spoke no English but her memory and her discipline were as sharp as ever. She rehearsed the ballet scrupulously, taking great pains to see that the style of the Twenties and Marie Laurencin's beautiful designs were reproduced faithfully. The new production was first performed in December 1964, and scored an immediate success, with Beriosova in the taxing role of the sophisticated cigarette-smoking, necklace-twirling Hostess, and Georgina Parkinson as the mysteriously androgynous Garçonne. The marriage between classical enchaînements and the style of the period – arguably the first of all neo-classical ballets, predating Balanchine's *Apollo* by four years – was meticulously observed, and the wit and concealed emotions were subtly conveyed by a company to whom, under the eye of de Valois and Ashton, acting and dancing had become almost synonymous.

Les Biches was the essence of Parisian light-hearted chic. The New Year, 1965, brought a complete contrast. With another American tour planned, a major new creation was urgently needed. After the visit to London in 1958 of the Bolshoi company it had been announced that, in an exchange by which Ashton would produce one of his ballets in Moscow, Leonid Lavrovsky would shortly be mounting his *Romeo and Juliet*, a spectacle-drama much admired at Covent Garden, but this had proved impracticable. Ashton had produced his own version of *Romeo and Juliet* for the Royal Danish Ballet in 1955 (it was later shown in the Edinburgh Festival) and Cranko had choreographed a new version for the Stuttgart Ballet in 1963. Ashton had doubts whether his production, which had been mounted on a smaller company, might look lightweight after the massive Bolshoi affair. He accordingly invited MacMillan to take on the project.

Romeo and Juliet, 1965, décor by Nicholas Georgiadis.
ABOVE Projected design for Juliet's ante-room, Act I, Scene 2.
BELOW Design for two angels in the Ballroom Scene, Act I, Scene 4 (see previous page).

The Dream, 1964. ABOVE Keith Martin as Puck.
BELOW LEFT Alexander Grant as Bottom, RIGHT Antoinette Sibley as Titania, Anthony Dowell as Oberon.

MacMillan had seen the Cranko version in which Lynn Seymour, for whom he was to arrange the role of Juliet, had danced. In any version the main line of the action is laid down by the construction of Prokofiev's score, but MacMillan gave it a slant of his own by concentrating on the personal, family aspect of the drama, using the public scenes only as a background. As designer he chose Nicholas Georgiadis, with whom he had collaborated several times already. The final result was first presented in February and scored a huge success, receiving forty-three curtain calls, described in the Press as setting some kind of record. The sumptuous costumes and sets rivalled the pomp and spectacle of the Russian production and, enhanced by the special qualities of the Company, the drama and dancing took on a new shape. Though the ballet was rehearsed with Lynn Seymour and Christopher Gable, the gala was allotted to Fonteyn and Nureyev who, predictably, made an ideal pair of lovers; the tender singlemindedness of the one set off the romantic ardour of the other to give the drama a heartbreaking intensity, and their individual approach set the style for two essentially different ways of playing the drama. The alternative reading of Seymour and Gable won equal, and from some people even more, praise. The main difference between the two pairs was that Fonteyn's Juliet was a helpless victim of her own passion whereas Seymour's was headstrong, scheming and positive; Nureyev's Romeo was a wayward and sophisticated playboy who found his true direction only after his meeting with Juliet, while Gable presented a cheerful, single-minded youth who, from the first, tackled obstacles with full-blooded vigour. These interpretations, equally valid, were

Romeo and Juliet, 1965. Lynn Seymour as Juliet,
Christopher Gable as Romeo.

Monotones 2, 1965. (Left to right) Anthony Dowell, Vyvyan Lorrayne and Robert Mead.

to influence many later performances. Merle Park – a Rhodesian-born dancer with a dazzling technique – partnered by MacLeary, and Sibley and Dowell, quickly followed the other two pairs in the leading roles. David Blair scored a popular success in a part which might have been thought unsuitable, as the volatile and sardonic Mercutio. Gerd Larsen lent her warmth and wry humour to the Nurse, Desmond Doyle was the brutal Tybalt, Dowell was the first inimitable Benvolio and Michael Somes and Julia Farron made convincingly human characters of Capulet and Lady Capulet.

The next production was doubtless inspired by the continued presence in London of Diaghilev's former régisseur, Serge Grigoriev, and his wife, Lubov Tchernicheva, and of yet another Russian, Nureyev. Fokine's arrangement of the *Polovtsian Dances* from Borodin's opera *Prince Igor* had been revived frequently by many companies and there now seemed a good opportunity to introduce it into The Royal Ballet repertoire. It was the main item in the annual Benevolent Fund Gala in March, with a short new pas de trois by Ashton and a Russian pas de six revived by Nureyev also in the programme. As it turned out, it was the Ashton piece, *Monotones*, which stole the show. The animal energy needed

Lubov Tchernicheva and Serge Grigoriev rehearsing the *Polovtsian Dances from Prince Igor,* 1965, with Deanne Bergsma and Rudolf Nureyev.

to convey the spirit of the Borodin dances did not come naturally to the British, and Nureyev, though suitably Tartar in temperament and appearance, proved too classical for the barbaric warrior. *Monotones* fitted the Company's style and attainments like a glove. A cool, elegant and austerely simple arrangement to Erik Satie's haunting 'Trois Gymnopédies', the gentle weaving and interlocking of three white-clad young dancers (Vyvyan Lorrayne, Anthony Dowell and Robert Mead) serenely reflected the plainsong undertones in the music. The only drawback to the piece was that it was awkwardly short for a normal programme, but this was soon to be overcome by the addition of a second section.

The 1965 American tour (the eighth so far) began early, in April. The opening at the 'Met' was another triumphant send-off to what was perhaps the Company's most highly acclaimed New York season. Nureyev was at the peak of his popularity, the centre of worldwide publicity. He and Fonteyn scored a smash-hit in the new *Romeo and Juliet*, which was as successful in New York as in London; and the other three pairs were all greatly praised. The new producton of *Swan Lake* was more appreciated than it had been

Les Noces, 1966. ABOVE The Company with (in the background) Svetlana Beriosova and Derek Rencher as the Bride and Groom. BELOW Bronislav Nijinska and Frederick Ashton during rehearsals

in London. After nearly a month at the 'Met' the Company embarked on one of its most arduous tours, which took them to seventeen cities across the United States and up into Canada, where they finished in Vancouver. Almost immediately on their return to London they set out again, this time for Italy where they appeared in Milan, Rome, Naples and Bologna, with the Fonteyn-Nureyev combination dominating attention. They arrived back in Britain at the end of October after four months of travelling, with only a two-week break.

After such a long period on tour the Company's autumn programmes were understandably drawn from stock, with Ashton's *Cinderella*, newly designed with a Second-Empire setting by Henry Bardon and David Walker, as the perennial Christmas favourite; Annette Page, a small, elegant dancer who had joined the Sadler's Wells Theatre Ballet in 1950, making her début (very much in the Fonteyn style) in *Romeo and Juliet* with Gable; and a superlative performance of *Giselle* by Beriosova, with MacLeary as Albrecht. The first new production of the season was not presented until February 1966. This was *Brandenburg Numbers 2 and 4*, an abstract arrangement set to Bach's music by Cranko, who came over from Stuttgart to carry out his first Royal Ballet assignment for five years. A Balanchinean exercise for eight girls and eight men in practice tights, it earned respect rather than enjoyment and proved to be something of a curtain-raiser to Cranko's *Card Game*, which was introduced the following week. He had created this for his own Stuttgart company the previous year. The dry astringency of Stravinsky's score, written for Balanchine in 1937, was given a more slapstick flavour by Cranko, and the choreographer's childlike sense of fun seemed at odds with the composer's sophisticated wit. In spite of some energetic clowning from Seymour, Page and Gable the ballet proved less popular in London than in Germany.

Ashton, however, had a winning card up his sleeve. In March 1966 came a second ballet by his beloved Nijinska which proved to be an even more important acquisition than the first. *Les Noces* had been arranged for Diaghilev's company in 1923 and had been one of his favourite ballets. Stravinsky's strange score, with its four pianos (originally intended to stand on stage), its rattling percussion and its chanting and declaiming singers, conveyed a haunting and overpowering sense of Russia, aided by Goncharova's austerely ethnic designs. Nijinska had set to it tightly-plaited dances mostly arranged – as in her brother's *L'Après-midi d'un Faune* – in uncomfortable profile poses and to rhythms as complicated as those of *Le Sacre du Printemps*. *Les Noces* was rehearsed by Nijinska herself over a long period and, with Beriosova as the Bride and Georgina Parkinson and Dowell leading the impeccable ranks of twisting, jumping wedding guests, the ballet emerged to an enthusiastic reception. It was paired with the same choreographer's *Les Biches*, and the two ballets – the evocative Russian ritual and the sharply-observed comedy of Parisian manners – were to remain the most distinctive contributions of Ashton's Directorship.

1966 was to be a bumper year, crowning a bumper decade. A month after *Les Noces* came Ashton's promised addition to his *Monotones*. The second pas de trois (paradoxically performed before the first) danced to Satie's music for 'Trois Gnossiennes', was a subtle variation on the same style and perfectly complemented it. The whole work was now labelled, not very adroitly, *Monotones Numbers 1 and 2*. During the three weeks which followed, *The Sleeping Beauty* was revived after an absence of two years and then came yet another winner, MacMillan's *Song of the Earth*, which he had arranged for Cranko's Stuttgart company the previous year. He subtly translated the death-haunted melancholy of Mahler's songs with their elusive Chinese allusions into movements blending modern and classical style, hinting at dark and strong emotion without ever clearly revealing it. The Stuttgart ballerina Marcia Haydée came over specially to repeat her dynamic and moving performance as the Woman, and she was matched by MacLeary as the Man, and Dowell in an uncharacteristic role as the gently but implacably persistent Messenger of Death. Danced in an austere setting designed by Georgiadis, the ballet set a mood which never relaxed during its sixty-five minutes. The unanimous acclaim for it was offset by reports that MacMillan had proposed it for Covent Garden two years earlier, only to be told that objections had been raised, on the grounds that dance could add nothing to the self-sufficient score. Curiously there was to be an echo of this a decade later when MacMillan proposed a ballet set to Fauré's 'Requiem' but found that the atmosphere for creating the work would be more congenial in Stuttgart, where it was eventually produced with great success.

Misgivings in some quarters about artistic judgment at the Royal Opera House, which paradoxically had been aroused by the very success of *Song of the Earth*, were magnified by the fact that just two weeks before the première the management had announced that MacMillan had been released from his contract with the Company to take over the Directorship of the German Opera Ballet in Berlin. With Cranko in Stuttgart, this was the second gain by Germany from Britain of that rarest of creatures, a gifted choreographer.

There was no American tour this year, but three weeks after the *Song of the Earth* première the Company broke new ground during a trip to Europe which started in Monte Carlo and proceeded to Athens, Florence, Luxembourg, Prague, Brno, Bratislava, Munich, Belgrade, Sofia, Bucharest and Warsaw. They were led by Fonteyn, but not by Nureyev; obviously in some of the countries visited his presence might have raised political complications. It was not until the end of October 1966 that the dancers arrived back in England. After two weeks' well-earned holiday they opened their autumn season in London – but without Nadia Nerina, who had resigned as a full-time member of the Company at the end of the summer. On the first night in November an important new acquisition was launched, Balanchine's *Apollo*. Created for Diaghilev's Ballets Russes in 1928, it continued the representation by the Company of the 'late' Diaghilev period, already illustrated by *Les Biches* and *Les Noces*. It was a witty re-thinking of the hallowed Greek myth, in the crisp Art Déco manner of the period, which contrived at the same time to preserve a serious attitude towards the subject. Stravinsky's score was alternately playful and solemn, and the story of the birth of the god and his assumption of the leadership of the Muses was related by Balanchine in an individual style based on pure academic choreography which made the ballet a rival to *Les Biches* as the foundation stone of modern neo-classicism. Donald MacLeary danced Apollo, with Beriosova, Monica Mason and Georgina Parkinson as the Muses. Although some critics claimed that only Balanchine-trained dancers could interpret the choreography correctly it was generally agreed that the ballet was a worthy addition to the repertory.

Cinderella, 1965. The Ballroom, with Frederick Ashton and Robert Helpmann as the Ugly Sisters and Wayne Sleep and Derek Rencher as their Suitors.

OVERLEAF *Swan Lake*, 1971, Act IV.

Later in the month Fonteyn returned in *Ondine* with Attilio Labis from the Paris Opéra, for whom Ashton inserted an extra solo. Christmas brought *The Sleeping Beauty*, *Cinderella*, and a series of performances of *Giselle* by the magical Fonteyn-Nureyev partnership. A succession of injuries and departures at this time produced alterations in casting and a sense that change was in the air, as indeed it was. Nerina had gone; now Gable, though only twenty-six, gave his last performance before taking up a career as an actor. Page, too, was planning to leave during the following year. But the Company's image received a boost when in November another Paul Czinner film opened in London. This time it was *Romeo and Juliet* with Fonteyn and Nureyev, made in 1966 a few months after the première of the ballet.

The next year, 1967, introduced to The Royal Ballet a choreographer who had hitherto been a notable absentee from its programmes, Antony Tudor. A resident of New York since 1939, Tudor had first made his name at Marie Rambert's Ballet Club with a series of psychologically-slanted ballets which were the complement to Ashton's delicate inventions. Notoriously demanding and independent, Tudor could be relied upon to make an individual contribution. He devised *Shadowplay*, a short ballet built around a score by a little-known composer, Charles Koechlin, with an unusual theme, a reflection of Tudor's own interest in Buddhism. It depicted a young man searching for his own identity, beset by earthly and spiritual distractions. The ballet's somewhat mystical subject debarred it from popular success, but it was hailed by the critics as an original addition to the repertory and it had the extra merit of discovering new dimensions in the personality of Dowell, whose elegance was tending to limit his roles. His interpretation of the 'Boy with Matted Hair' had an innocent but enigmatic quality which was to prove a key to his future development.

The public demand to see Fonteyn and Nureyev persisted. The scheme for charging special prices for Fonteyn performances, introduced in 1959, had also been applied to Nureyev in 1965 (it was later abandoned). A new ballet for the pair, *Paradise Lost*, by Roland Petit, was launched in February 1967. It would be hard to find a greater contrast with Tudor's meditative experiment. Taking a poem by Jean Cau as his theme, Petit gave it a shock-element by adopting for the two exponents of classical-romantic style an angular modern idiom and, in place of the grave Miltonian sonorities suggested by the title, he offered a Pop Art version in which the creation of Man took place to a countdown recorded in neon lights. The first scene, which ended with Nureyev diving through the scarlet lips of a vast pin-up lady, went with a fine swing; but the second scene tailed off, and the ballet, though both popularly and critically acclaimed at first, did not survive for long. It did, however, form part of the Company's repertory on its next American tour, which opened in New York in April with a performance of *Cinderella*. Extra drama was added when, in a fit of over-enthusiasm from her attendants, Beriosova was accidentally toppled out of her coach almost into the orchestra-pit, fortunately without injury. Fonteyn and Nureyev joined the Company for the last part of the six-week season at the 'Met'. Then the whole troupe went off on the usual coast-to-coast tour up into Canada and down again, to finish in St Louis at the beginning of August – a four-month excursion, under the customary

ABOVE Backcloth for *Paradise Lost* designed by Martial Raysse, 1967. BELOW *Jazz Calendar*: 'Monday's Child', danced by Vergie Derman, with backcloth designed by Derek Jarman, 1968.

management of Sol Hurok. The tour included a much-publicised incident in San Francisco when Fonteyn and Nureyev spent a night in jail after attending a party where there was a suspicion that marijuana was being smoked. The Assistant General Administrator of Covent Garden made a hurried appearance on London television screens to announce that both dancers were non-smokers.

When the next London season opened in October routine programmes of *Swan Lake, Romeo and Juliet, La Fille Mal Gardée* prevailed, interspersed with mixed evenings which included revivals of Ashton's *Sylvia* (reduced, not very successfully, to one Act, an abbreviated version for the Touring Company having proved unpopular) and *La Valse*. Ashton ballets still dominated the programmes, but it was eighteen months since he had introduced anything new, and people began to think that his duties as Director had extinguished his gifts as choreographer. But 1968 had hardly begun when he sprang one of his surprises with *Jazz Calendar*. Although composed by a serious musician, Richard Rodney Bennett, the score was in the popular jazz style, and for it Ashton devised a set of brisk variations danced by small groups, each based on the theme suggested by the nursery doggerel beginning 'Monday's child is fair of face'. With its clean and lively designs by a young painter, Derek Jarman, the result was not far from revue material, but

Song of the Earth, 1966. (Left to right) Donald MacLeary, Anthony Dowell, Monica Mason.

its cheerful zest made it a useful as well as a popular ingredient of many programmes.

The Company's next production was a major undertaking, Tchaikovsky's *The Nutcracker*. Since its creation in 1892 with choreography, now mostly lost, by Ivanov, it had always been a Christmas favourite and the mainstay of many a company's repertory for audiences at holiday times. It was one of the old Sadler's Wells Ballet's best-loved productions, mounted in 1934 with Markova as a sparkling Sugar Plum Fairy, but its nursery charms would not fit into the setting of the Royal Opera House. A solution was found when Nureyev proposed a new treatment befitting the grand style of much of Tchaikovsky's music. The story would be seen through the eyes of a child, the monsters and visions reflecting the anxieties of the heroine, who would dominate the whole ballet, thus acquiring a full ballerina role. Nureyev had just mounted his new version in Stockholm and it was intended to introduce it at Covent Garden for Christmas. This proved impracticable, and the première was postponed until the Benevolent Fund Gala in February 1968. With entirely new choreography, and designs in the grand manner by Georgiadis, the childlike fable was turned into a work in the same genre as *The Sleeping Beauty*. Some people lamented the loss of the simple virtues of conventional productions, but the musical gains were manifest, and in addition big dancing roles were offered to the

Shadowplay, 1967. Antony Tudor rehearsing Anthony Dowell.

heroine and her prince, danced at the opening performance by Merle Park and Nureyev himself. The result proved to be one of the most popular ballets in the repertoire, and was something of a breakthrough for the technically scintillating Park.

Though the première went off smoothly and though outwardly the Company was in good shape, strains were developing. For some time Ashton had let it be known privately that he was thinking of retiring in 1970, and as early as 1966 Webster had actually proposed to MacMillan (who accepted) that he should take over the Directorship simultaneously. However, Webster seems to have kept other alternatives in mind, for in 1967 it was rumoured that among the changes planned for 1970 he was contemplating the appointment of John Field, currently in charge of the Touring Company, as Ashton's successor. In February 1968 the need for a decision suddenly became crucial. In that month Sir Donald Albery, Director of the London Festival Ballet, announced his resignation and Field received a private invitation to succeed him. Field naturally informed Covent Garden. Webster seems to have reacted over-hastily (de Valois was absent in Turkey at the time). Fearing to lose Field to the rival company he persuaded him to decline the offer: Field gained the impression that he would succeed Ashton, a proposition which was then modified to take the form of co-Directorship with MacMillan. To clinch the arrangement, Ashton was formally told – apparently to his surprise – that his intention of retiring in 1970 was to be implemented. These ill-co-ordinated negotiations resulted in suspicion and misunderstanding (both Field and MacMillan seem at first to have thought that they were to be in sole control) and rumours spread to the dancers.

The main Company was due to leave in April for another American visit – a four-week season in New York undertaken at short notice when the Bolshoi Ballet cancelled its engagements at the 'Met'. The mainstays of the programmes were the classics, with other ballets such as *La Fille Mal Gardée* (which was becoming popular in the States) and *Marguerite and Armand. Symphonic Variations* was presented, for the first time in the USA since 1949, and now began to attract enthusiastic comment.

But the season was an uneasy one. A few nights after the première on 23 April, Webster, who had accompanied the Company to New York, called the dancers together and broke the startling news of Ashton's retirement to them. The announcement was greeted with some vigorous protest. Meanwhile the Assistant General Administrator John Tooley, was officially informing the Touring Company which was appearing at Covent Garden. On 26 April 1968 the news was made public; the Royal Opera House announced that in 1970 Ashton would retire and would be replaced by MacMillan and Field as joint Directors. The matter was settled, but cracks had opened up both within the administration and between the management and dancers.

By the end of May the main Company was back from New York, with Sibley and Dowell leading a series of different partnerships in *Romeo and Juliet.* Neither Fonteyn nor Nureyev took part in this season as they were in Europe with the Touring Company, and the young English pair had the chance to consolidate the ever-growing reputation of their partnership. But at the end of the season the Company broke up for the summer holiday in an atmosphere of some anxiety. On their return their first notable engagement was a gala, on 24 October. A mixed ballet-and-opera programme was presented, as Sir David Webster explained, to celebrate the fact that 'we have been going ever since the war, for twenty-one, twenty-two or twenty-two-and-a-bit years'. Because of the different opening dates of

The Nutcracker, 1968. Merle Park as Clara, Rudolf Nureyev as the Prince.

the opera and ballet companies, this anniversary was marked by a somewhat nondescript programme which included excerpts from *Fidelio, Aïda* and *The Nutcracker*.

A more suitable contribution from the Ballet Company would have been *Enigma Variations*, the new Ashton production, which was introduced the next night, 25 October 1968. The idea of basing a ballet on Elgar's well-known suite had originally been conceived by a young designer, Julia Trevelyan Oman, as far back as 1950. Ashton had seen her drawings; sixteen years later he recalled them and began to work on the idea, following the hints which Elgar had given concerning the characters of the friends whom each variation depicts. The setting was an English country house at the end of the nineteenth century, with suggestions of croquet and cucumber sandwiches; the costumes were uncompromisingly contemporary, watch-chains and all, and Ashton introduced naturalistic details to an extent that he had not tried before – two of the series of solos and pas de deux began with the dancers making their entries as cyclists.

Though ostensibly it was about the happy start to a career and included some comic sketches, the overpowering atmosphere of the ballet was one of autumnal sadness, lending it a poetic nostalgia. With Derek Rencher as an amazingly convincing re-incarnation of Elgar, Beriosova as his gentle wife, Sibley expressing the springtime charm of Dorabella in a captivating little solo, and a fast and furious dance for Dowell as Troyte, it proved an ideal vehicle for the Company's skill in dramatic dancing. In retrospect, the affectionately backward-looking mood seems very appropriate. This was to be the last ballet (apart from gala pas de deux) which Ashton was to create for the main Company for eight years.

The success during the previous year of Tudor's *Shadowplay* encouraged this elusive choreographer to pay another visit to London in November 1968 to mount one of his earliest ballets, *Lilac Garden*. First presented on the tiny Mercury Theatre stage in 1936, it had subsequently entered the repertoire of American Ballet Theatre, surviving surprisingly well the transfer to a vastly bigger stage. Great care was taken over the London revival of this historically important ballet, which had introduced into dance for the first time contemporary characters with believable emotions and realistic backgrounds. Though danced by Beriosova as the heroine and MacLeary as her secret lover, sadly it failed to achieve the intensity necessary for its theme. Tudor's highly individual style eluded the dancers, and the Proustian atmosphere of tight-laced passion was dissipated in somewhat generalised romanticism. However, Tudor's visit was not unfruitful, for he found time to mount a short ballet for the Touring Company, *Knight Errant*.

Meanwhile a major project was under way – no less an undertaking than a new production of the Company's most treasured jewel, *The Sleeping Beauty*. The famous 1946 Sergeyev – de Valois – Messel version, now twenty years old, was beginning to lose its freshness. To attempt to replace this enormously successful production with a new version which would recapture the original vividness and excitement was a bold venture – a challenge which was to haunt the Company for years to come. Ashton did not undertake the new version himself but entrusted it to Peter Wright, a former Royal Ballet dancer who, after working with the Sadler's Wells Theatre Ballet, had become Cranko's assistant in Stuttgart where he had produced a successful *Giselle*, recently adopted by the Touring Company. He had mounted *The Sleeping Beauty* for the Cologne Ballet; Ashton flew to Germany, saw the production and liked it, and asked him to take charge of the new version in London.

For his new production Wright adopted a relatively simple approach, stressing the fairy-tale element in the ballet rather than the symbolic or spectacular (this was very much in line with de Valois' view of the work). It was given an appropriate new look: the Renaissance period imagined by Petipa and Tchaikovsky being replaced by Henry Bardon's mediaeval setting, with costumes by Lila di Nobili and masks by Rostislav Doboujinsky. There were several cuts and alterations, as well as some new dances by Ashton, notably a pas de deux after the Awakening – effectively romantic and lyrical but not very much in the Petipa style. Sibley and Dowell fitted ideally into the lyrical interpretation and danced impeccably, with Deanne Bergsma, a tall strong dancer from South Africa, as a graceful Lilac Fairy and Julia Farron conveying genuine venom as Carabosse, a part given to a woman for the first time in a Royal Ballet production. The Prologue, which was enacted in the royal bedroom, was imaginative and splendid to look

Enigma Variations, 1968. The 'Nimrod' variation, with Desmond Doyle as Jaeger,
Svetlana Beriosova as Elgar's Wife, Derek Rencher as Elgar.

at but it was not matched by the later scenes, and some of the changes in the production were not popular. The first of what were to be many efforts to kiss *The Sleeping Beauty* back to full youth and life had been only partly successful.

There was no special Christmas production this year, but Sibley and Dowell – by now a partnership second only to that of Fonteyn and Nureyev, and representing the very essence of the lyrical Royal Ballet style – appeared in a succession of performances of *Swan Lake* and *Romeo and Juliet*. The first new offering of 1969 was a slight one and, as it turned out, exceedingly ephemeral. Plans had been laid for MacMillan to introduce at Covent Garden one of the ballets that he had composed for his company in Berlin. Difficulties over the casting of the work which he proposed, *Cain and Abel*, led to its replacement by a short piece entitled *Olympiad*, inspired by the Olympic Games which had been held the previous year in Mexico. But the action fitted very awkwardly Stravinsky's 'Symphony in Three Movements', the score that he had chosen; on top of this, The Royal Ballet's male dancers were not at that time athletic enough to be convincing.

The next venture was hardly more successful. In view of yet another American tour in the summer of 1969, it was essential to find a new vehicle for the Fonteyn-Nureyev partnership, which was so important to the box office. At a late date, after some false starts, it was decided to call on Roland Petit, a quick worker who was familiar with the two dancers. To Schoenberg's symphonic poem *Pelléas et Mélisande*, Petit devised for the pair an extended pas de trois with Keith Rosson as the hero's half-brother, Golaud, and occasional invasions by a corps de ballet. Turgid and overlong, it fell rather flat. The following night brought another première, the first performance of the last Act of *Raymonda*. The full ballet had been mounted on the Touring Company by Nureyev in 1966 and Act III was now adapted as a separate item for the main Company, stylishly led by Beriosova and MacLeary in a glittering gold-and-white setting by Barry Kay.

Both ballets formed part of the programmes for the eleventh North American tour on which the Covent Garden Company embarked three weeks later. These operations were becoming more and more expensive to organise and correspondingly less profitable financially. The 1969 venture, a three-month coast-to-coast tour from which Canada was omitted, was to be the last extended visit for some years. It started with a long season at the 'Met' in New York, a six-week engagement which celebrated the twentieth anniversary of The Royal Ballet's New York début and which was as successful as ever. By now the Company was a regular and much-loved part of the summer dance scene, and it always responded to the demonstrative American audiences by performing with extra zest. This year the programme opened unconventionally with a mixed bill – *La Bayadère*, *Enigma Variations* (appreciated by connoisseurs) and *Jazz Calendar* (not liked). As in London, *Pelléas et Mélisande* was unpopular, but the Fonteyn-Nureyev partnership redeemed itself in *Swan Lake* and in the revised *The Sleeping Beauty* (controversial), while Sibley and Dowell were hailed as their successors. *Coppélia* and the *Raymonda* extracts were unexpected triumphs. The tour continued across the States and ended with appearances at the Hollywood Bowl and at St Louis.

During the Company's absence the Bolshoi Ballet had been presenting a season at

The Sleeping Beauty, 1968. Costume design for
Bluebeard and Cinderella, by Lila di Nobili.

273

<u>BLUEBEARD</u>

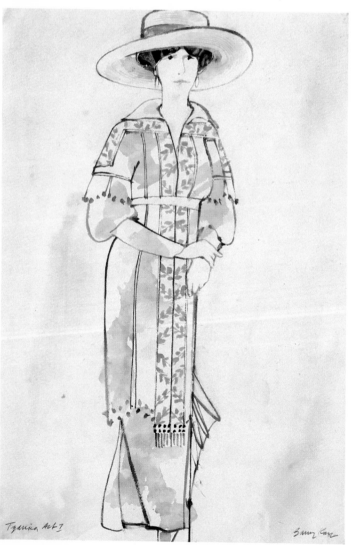

Covent Garden which included its powerful *Spartacus*. This virile spectacle, combined with some derogatory remarks about British male dancing which MacMillan had let drop during a radio interview, brought some criticism of The Royal Ballet when it reassembled after the summer holiday. The season – which was interrupted in October by three performances in Vienna – turned out to be rather unadventurous. For the moment the springs of invention seemed to have run dry. After *Pelléas et Mélisande* there was to be no new creation, apart from a gala pas de deux, for nearly a year.

Creativity may have been temporarily at a low level, but much activity was going on behind the scenes administratively. On 7 January 1970 a press conference was called, presided over by the Chairman of the Royal Opera House Board, Lord Drogheda, and attended by the General Administrator-elect John Tooley, with Kenneth MacMillan and John Field. It was officially confirmed that Sir Frederick Ashton – who had been made a Companion of Honour in the New Year Honours List – would be resigning at the end of the season and would be replaced by MacMillan and Field. At the same time a drastic re-organisation of the Company was outlined. It had been decided, partly for artistic, partly for financial reasons, that the Sadler's Wells Company would be merged into the main Company and replaced by a small group of soloists. (The change is described in the section of this book devoted to the Touring Company, Chapter 9). Thenceforward the main Company, now constituting about one hundred and ten dancers, would as usual appear at Covent Garden throughout the autumn and winter and would also present a continuous season of two or three weeks at the Royal Opera House in August. (The Opera would be compensated by a continuous season in the spring.) The result of the new arrangement would be some reduction in the total size of the Company, the concentration of big productions on Covent Garden and an important financial saving. The idea of merging the two Companies had been considered ever since the 1956 visit of the Bolshoi with its monolithic structure. In theory the advantages were impressive, but practical difficulties emerged almost at once and the scheme was to be short-lived; it was quickly modified and then virtually abandoned.

The previous winter season had been uneasy, disturbed by the prospect of change, but it had introduced some promising new talent – the Canadian-born Jennifer Penney in *The Nutcracker*, Ann Jenner in *Coppélia*, and a production of *Cinderella* in which Laura Connor and Lesley Collier, a young dancer who had attracted attention in a Royal Ballet School performance of *Les Deux Pigeons*, appeared for the first time as soloists. Now a new Ashton work was announced for the Benevolent Fund Gala in February 1970. This was *Lament of the Waves*, a pas de deux for two very junior dancers, Marilyn Trounson and Carl Myers. Set to a score by Gerard Masson, with costumes by Derek Rencher, the theme was of a young couple drowning and reliving their love in their last moments together. With light-projections in place of scenery it was a slight, ephemeral but moving piece, not intended as a lasting addition to the repertory.

The Company's first major production this year, *The Ropes of Time*, written for Nureyev, Monica Mason and Diana Vere, came a few weeks later. The choreographer was Rudi van Dantzig, Director of the Dutch National Ballet, and he provided the Opera House audience

Anastasia, 1971, designed by Barry Kay, Act I. ABOVE Model for set.
BELOW Costume designs: (left) the Tsarina, (right) the Grand Duchess Olga.

The Sleeping Beauty, 1968, Act I. (Centre) Leslie Edwards as the King,
Antoinette Sibley as Princess Aurora, Gerd Larsen as the Queen.

with a surprise. In place of the classical-romantic roles with which Nureyev was mainly
associated, van Dantzig created for him a part demanding plastic modern movements with
severe abstract designs by Toer van Schayk, and danced to the sound of an electronic tape.
The symbolic theme, a Traveller's path through Life attended by Death, was somewhat
obscurely conveyed and the attempt to adapt modern dance movements to the Company's
classically-trained dancers resulted in an indecisive compromise. It did, however, furnish
some ingenious effects and the chance for Nureyev to show his versatility.

A few weeks later, in April 1970, the Company embarked once again on a visit to New
York. During the past twenty years these trips had become regular events, but it was now
suggested that they were coming to an end. There was no coast-to-coast journey this time;
instead the Company appeared for five weeks at the 'Met' opening with *Romeo and Juliet*
followed by a single performance of *The Sleeping Beauty*. *The Ropes of Time* did not please,
but the Ashton ballets were warmly received, and the highlight of the visit was the last
night, 31 May, which took the form of a gala in honour of Ashton before his retirement. He
insisted that the programme should start with *La Bayadère* so that the corps de ballet
would share in the occasion.

With Ashton's retirement imminent, the season when the Company returned to London in June turned into a small-scale Ashton festival. As well as a triumphant London début by Sibley in *Giselle*, on 21 June, it offered a succession of Ashton's ballets ranging from *La Fille Mal Gardée* and *Marguerite and Armand* to *Scènes de Ballets*, and the recent *Lament of the Waves*. The climax came on the last night of the season, 24 July 1970. A special performance was planned in secret and presented as a surprise tribute to the man who had so fundamentally contributed to the birth, growth and flowering of the Company. The programme was devised and produced by three of Ashton's closest colleagues, Leslie Edwards, John Hart, and Michael Somes, one of whose special responsibilities was to look after the Ashton ballets. A linking narrative written by William Chappell, yet another of the early members of the Company, was spoken by Helpmann, and extracts from no less than thirty-six of Ashton's ballets were presented to an audience foremost among whom was Queen Elizabeth The Queen Mother. Some performances – such as Fonteyn in *Apparitions* and *The Wise Virgins* and Somes in *Daphnis and Chloë* – revived familiar roles of long ago; other dances were lovingly reconstituted for new interpreters, such as Alexander Grant in a solo from *Rio Grande* and Vyvyan Lorrayne as the Moon in *Horoscope*. More recent ballets such as *Enigma Variations* featured contemporary casts. Sibley and Dowell danced the Awakening pas de deux from *The Sleeping Beauty* and Fonteyn and Nureyev the Garden Scene from *Marguerite and Armand*. Finally, the whole Company joined in the waltz from *A Wedding Bouquet*. A huge cheer rang out as the hero of the evening (having been surreptitiously led backstage during the final scene) appeared on stage to acknowledge the applause. The occasion also saw the last appearance as General Administrator of the Royal Opera House of Sir David Webster, in whose honour an opera gala had been organised a few weeks earlier.

Frederick Ashton's departure marked the end of the first-generation phase in the history of The Royal Ballet – a period dominated by the aims and methods devised in its first formative years. He had written forty-eight ballets for the Company, and he embodied a continuity which had survived war, changes of theatre and a new title and status. His own preferences and ideals – primarily a sophisticated romanticism demanding delicacy and elegance, though he was equally at home in the bouncing comedy of *Façade* or *La Fille Mal Gardée* – had moulded the style of the dancers. Experienced as he was in the commercial theatre, where he had learned theatrical ingenuity and professional craftsmanship, he nonetheless retained a sense of restraint and an innate good taste which permeated all his work, qualities which had rubbed off on the Company so strongly that in the end the 'English style' became almost synonymous with the 'Ashton style'.

Ashton's fastidious sensitivity, coupled with a shy and rather melancholy personality and a low boredom-threshold, had made the administrative duties of Director irksome to him. He had never set out to reshape the Company, only to continue on the course which he himself had helped to set. During the seven years of his Directorship there had been a series of important additions to the repertoire, while the standard of performances during that period was never higher. Ashton handed on his inheritance intact and enriched.

7 The Seventies

The simultaneous retirement during 1970 of David Webster and Frederick Ashton – one of the Assistant Directors, John Hart, also left during this year – clearly marked the end of an era. The challenge for Kenneth MacMillan and John Field was to make it the beginning of a new one. MacMillan, now forty-one, arrived with several years' experience of running a German company. A Scotsman by birth, he had spent the whole of his career with the British Company until he left for Berlin, and he knew most of the dancers well; but his exceptionally sensitive and withdrawn temperament made administrative work unpalatable. In this, John Field was much more at home; he, too, had grown up as a dancer with the Company and for fifteen years had run the large and almost independent Touring Company.

On the face of it, MacMillan and Field made an ideally complementary pair, but they faced formidable difficulties. The first of these and the most obstinately enduring was the legacy of the awkward change-over. The second was the implementation of the still untried re-organisation of the Company's two components. Fortunately anxiety was allayed almost at once by a smash-hit première – Jerome Robbins's *Dances at a Gathering*. It

Choreographer Jerome Robbins in rehearsal.

had been created for New York City Ballet in May 1969 and had received instant and universal acclaim. Though superficially it was modest in scale and conventional in style, it was in fact revolutionary. It was abstract and yet warmly human, with the dancers responding to each other as individuals; it was technically difficult and strictly rehearsed but always casual – Robbins allowed different interpretations from different dancers; and the form of the ballet itself, an hour of uninterrupted variations accompanied only by a single piano, was startlingly new. The music consisted of assorted Chopin pieces, mainly waltzes, études and mazurkas, and the dancing suggested cheerful open-air encounters; the men wore boots and there were hints of a rolling Polish landscape. The Royal Ballet cast, chosen by Robbins, proved a shade more dramatic than the American one: the dancers, trained in the choreography of de Valois, Ashton and MacMillan, could not fail to give a touch of character to the roles. Sibley, sunny and lyrical, Seymour, seductive and witty, and Monica Mason, athletic and speedy, were matched by the lithe power of Nureyev, cheerfully contending with Dowell's stylish vitality, Wall's easy swing and Michael Coleman's darting vigour. The invention never flagged and the audience sat rapt, as one dance succeeded another. The ballet, just as successful in London as it had been in New York, gave the new régime a flying start.

The next offering, two weeks later, was not so successful. During the previous June the Touring Company had fulfilled one of its last dates in its old form by taking part in a Beethoven Festival at Bonn, which celebrated the composer's birth in the city two

Dances at a Gathering, 1970, with Rudolf Nureyev, Laura Connor and Ann Jenner.

hundred years previously. For the occasion Ashton had created a new work to the only ballet-music that Beethoven ever wrote, *The Creatures of Prometheus*. The original plot involving classical gods and goddesses now appeared unconvincing, and Ashton approached it with his tongue in his cheek. His version, with its original interpreters Doreen Wells and David Wall, was introduced into the main Company's programme at the end of October, but with its heavy setting and its uncharacteristically laboured humour, it fell flat.

Another production from the repertoire of the now defunct Touring Company proved to

Giselle, Act II. The Wilis with Myrtha, their Queen.

be more popular. This was *Concerto* which MacMillan had originally devised for his Berlin company in 1966. Set to Shostakovitch's Second Piano Concerto, its fluent abstract style sat happily on The Royal Ballet dancers, some from the old cast and some new, including David Blair, who had happily returned after three years' absence, and Alfreda Thorogood. The corps de ballet combined dancers from both the Touring and Covent Garden Companies. Another transfer was Peter Wright's production of *Giselle*. He had mounted this cleverly thought-out version for the Stuttgart Ballet in 1966 and later he revived it for the Touring Company. Now it was transferred intact to the main Company and launched by Sibley, as a rather modern-minded heroine with Dowell an elegantly deceitful Albrecht, and Deanne Bergsma as a cool and commanding Myrtha.

There were few highlights during the winter of 1970 and the new administrative arrangement was already showing signs of strain – reflected in a note of criticism which crept into Press comments, expressing anxieties that much-loved stars and favourite ballets might be eclipsed. It had been observed that on the programmes John Field appeared not as co-Director but as Administrative Director. On Christmas Eve it was suddenly announced that he had resigned. He was not replaced, but Peter Wright, who had been put in charge of the 'New Group', as the small touring section was to be known, was appointed Associate Director with MacMillan. The première of *Anastasia* was postponed and the air was full, as one writer expressed it, of 'alarms and sicknesses, resignations and rumours, changes of cast and changes of programmes'.

Meanwhile the spring season at the Royal Opera House went on, with varied results. In February 1971, after six months without a nineteenth-century classic in the repertoire, (the corps-de-ballet of the two Companies were in the process of being integrated) a revised version of *Swan Lake* was introduced, with no special producer credited. It was danced by a succession of pairs in the leading roles, beginning with Sibley and Dowell. Though the performances of the principals were praised – particularly those of Fonteyn with Wall as a heroic Prince Siegfried – the overall standard of dancing was criticised. Some of the changes, notably the introduction of short tutus for the swans, came under fire, and the new recipe, a mixture of the Company's two versions, found little critical favour. After an exceptionally long period at the Royal Opera House, the Company left London in April for a series of appearances in the provinces – the first tour by the Covent Garden Company for fifteen years.

It was towards the end of the 1971 summer season that the long-awaited *Anastasia* was launched. It proved to be a surprising and significant invention. MacMillan had long shown an interest in abnormal psychology, and he was also intent on bringing ballet into contemporary focus by dealing with modern themes. In 1967 he had boldly merged these two trends for his Berlin company in a short Expressionist ballet based on the case of a patient in a German hospital who purported to be the Grand-Duchess Anastasia, youngest daughter of the Tsar Nicholas. The ballet showed her in hospital, mentally insecure as the result of her youthful sufferings. In his new version of *Anastasia* MacMillan enlarged the narrative to include the events leading up to her illness – the outbreak of the 1914 War, the Revolution and the murder of the Imperial family. For the music he used two Tchaikovsky symphonies – the First for a 1914 forest scene, the Third for a St Petersburg ballroom – retaining the Martinu score for the original ballet, which became the last Act.

It was an imaginative idea, offering Seymour, as Anastasia, a huge part in which she could display her dramatic and lyrical talents to the full. She was enchanting throughout, and in the finale heart-rending. The ballet was beautifully designed by Barry Kay, and there were many attractive details, such as a melancholy Russian dance by Beriosova as the Tsarina and a lively number for three officers, brilliantly executed by Dowell, Wall and Michael Coleman. But the long symphonic scores dragged out the first two Acts, and the naturalistic style of these scenes contrasted awkwardly with the last Act's tense hysteria.

In the very last week of the season there was an addition to the repertoire, *Field Figures*, which was not only interesting in itself but seemed to presage a fresh artistic policy. It was an uncompromisingly modern ballet by Glen Tetley, an American choreographer who had until recently been working with the Nederlands Dans Theater. He had created it for the experimental New Group at Nottingham the previous autumn and it was now introduced into the Covent Garden repertoire. Consisting of fifty uninterrupted minutes of taped sound-mix effects by Stockhausen with a geometrical setting by Nadine Baylis, the ballet demanded a totally different, unclassical style of dancing. That such a novelty, arranged to a difficult score, should be absorbed into the Opera House repertory, particularly at a performance which happened to be attended by the Queen Mother, was disconcerting to some. The dancers, however, led by Bergsma and Desmond Kelly from the original cast, attacked the new movements with enthusiasm and the experiment showed just the spark of enterprise needed to convince the public that a new approach was on the way. It made a promising ending to the Company's first year under the new directorship – one of the most difficult years in its history.

Attendances at the Royal Opera House had temporarily fallen off to some extent and public response to the Company in the provinces in the spring had been less enthusiastic than expected. But with *Anastasia*, a solid achievement in a traditional idiom, and *Field Figures*, a bold thrust into a modern one, a positive policy for the future became evident. In August 1971 the foundation on which that future would be built was eloquently defined in a three-month exhibition entitled 'Covent Garden: Twenty-five Years of Opera and Ballet', at the Victoria and Albert Museum.

The first excitement of the autumn season was provided by a Benevolent Fund Gala shortly before Christmas which introduced some new short works. The principal contribution, *Afternoon of a Faun* by Jerome Robbins, was a welcome addition to a repertoire which was short of American ballets. The work had been created in 1953 for New York City Ballet and had appeared in the repertoire of several companies. With impressive self-confidence Robbins had taken the old 1912 Nijinsky-Debussy version, moved it into a modern dance studio (coyly named 'a room with a mirror') and turned the erotic fantasy into an actual, if fleeting and delicate, encounter. It was a sweeter conception than that of the original, but in Rouben Ter-Arutunian's pretty set it was very effective, and it was sensitively interpreted by Sibley and Dowell. The gala audience also saw the same pair in *Meditation from Thaïs*, a seductive little pas de deux by Ashton set to Massenet's music, with costumes designed by Anthony Dowell.

MacMillan had deliberately created in *Anastasia* a ballet which only a large opera house company could tackle. His new piece, *Triad*, presented in January 1972, was so small in scale that it might have been mounted equally well on the New Group. The story of jealousy between two closely attached brothers, it had a post-adolescent feeling reflected in the score, Prokofiev's youthful First Violin Concerto, and this character was sustained by the choice of especially slim, slightly-built dancers to interpret it: Sibley as the girl, with Dowell and Wayne Eagling, an agile newcomer from Canada in his first principal role, as the rivals. The choreography was original and brilliantly danced, but the effect in dramatic terms was rather lightweight, with the mood dominated by an airy, lyrical setting. *Triad* made a striking contrast with an imported work introduced a few weeks later, *Poème de l'Extase*, danced to the Scriabin score of the same name. The ballet had been created nearly two years earlier by Cranko for Fonteyn and his Stuttgart company, on the theme of an ageing beauty dreaming of her former lovers. Its acrobatic style was influenced by Russian choreography, with Fonteyn tossed from torso to naked torso, an odd creation for Britain's foremost classical ballerina which failed to impress either public or critics. Its most inspired features were the striking Jugendstil draperies of Jürgen Rose inspired by Klimt. The spring season continued with an exceptional variety in the programmes – eighteen productions were listed in the first three months.

Anastasia, 1971, Act III. Lynn Seymour as Anna Anderson.

On 24 April the Company began a six-week season in New York. From 1967 to 1970 they had visited America every year. Now two years had passed since the last visit and this thirteenth appearance under a new Director was particularly important. It opened with a very mixed programme (including no fewer than three pas de deux), which met with a very mixed reception. *Triad* made little impression and a comic pas de deux, *Side Show*, devised earlier by MacMillan for Seymour and Nureyev, did not amuse; but *Thaïs* was very popular and so was *The Mirror Walkers*, a duet from a ballet originally composed by Peter Wright for the Stuttgart company. As the season progressed it was the classics that were most successful. Though Fonteyn and Nureyev still dominated the scene, Sibley and Dowell were attracting much favourable attention, but both were forced to withdraw through injury and illness. Park, Mason and Wall (dancing his first *La Bayadère* in New York) all scored big successes. *Anastasia*, the main new offering, was not much to the taste of New York critics, nor was *Poème de l'Extase*, which had been danced there before by the Stuttgart Ballet; *Field Figures* was also coolly received. On the whole the dancers seem to have been appreciated more than the works in which they appeared and there was still public dissatisfaction at the seemingly enforced retirement of Ashton which had been announced during the Company's last visit: especially as MacMillan did not appear until the last week (he was busy in London choreographing his *Ballade* for the New Group).

Two weeks after its return the Company was back at Covent Garden for the summer season, which had a notable beginning. On 20 June 1972 Natalia Makarova made her début as a Guest Artist in her most famous role, *Giselle*, partnered by Dowell, followed by two performances of *Swan Lake* with MacLeary. Her interpretations aroused enormous interest, ranging from wild fervour to disapproval. She made few, if any, concessions to the Royal Ballet style: her performances were memorable for her very individual manner – unmistakably Russian but with an accent all her own.

Meanwhile another drastic novelty was in the pipeline. In July, Tetley's *Field Figures* was succeeded by an even more ambitiously contemporary work, *Laborintus*. As in *Field Figures* a small cast was deployed – three couples led by Seymour and Nureyev, with two 'attendants' – whose intense and sometimes tortured movements combined hints of classical technique with modern plasticism. With a score by Luciano Berio, a severe but mysterious set by Ter-Arutunian and important lighting effects by John B. Read, the distinguished cast gave a vivid impression of some infernal struggle, the choreographer having been inspired by a Pollaiuolo drawing. Though it was predictably incomprehensible to some, it was strikingly different from most of the works in the Company's repertoire: it seemed to reinforce the evidence that The Royal Ballet was being led towards the world of modern dance. As it transpired, *Laborintus* was to represent the limit of this development, at least for many years.

The autumn season was preceded by an experiment which was so successful that the Covent Garden Company was to repeat it in the future – performances priced at only 50p, with all the seats in the orchestra stalls removed so that a large audience, predominantly young, could sit on the floor. Prices in the rest of the theatre were also reduced. In the first try-out most of the performances had been of opera, with only two of ballet, but later the ballet had an equal share. These performances sponsored by Midland Bank were called 'The Covent Garden Proms', after the celebrated Promenade Concerts.

The autumn season of 1972 opened with an all-Stravinsky programme and continued with mixed bills fortified by a revival of de Valois' forty-one-year-old *Job. Swan Lake* was revived in a form which recognised the criticism of the recent version. The production, supervised by MacMillan, reverted almost completely to the Sadler's Wells version, replacing Ashton's Act IV with the original but keeping his pas de quatre, now moved more appropriately to the Ballroom scene; Nureyev's Act I solo was also retained. This version was much preferred to the earlier revised production.

The first real excitement of the season came in November, with the Benevolent Fund Gala, which brought another new ballet by Jerome Robbins, *Requiem Canticles* – his third work for the Company in the last two years. It had formed part of New York City Ballet's Stravinsky Festival in June and consisted of a succession of nine episodes in different styles for a large but sparingly used cast, set to a complicated score for singers and orchestra. This gnomic 'celebration of death' proved ill-suited to a gala occasion, but the programme also offered Makarova dancing in *Les Sylphides*, and in the *Don Quixote* pas de deux partnered by MacLeary. In addition there was a new duet by Ashton, *A Walk to the Paradise Garden*, set to Delius's music of the same name – a typically felicitous little piece arranged for Park and Wall, with some unusually acrobatic Russian-type lifts and a theatrical ending when Death enfolds the lovers in his cloak.

The year 1973 marked the entry of Britain into the Common Market and was celebrated at Covent Garden in January with 'Fanfare for Europe,' a glittering gala to which many European companies contributed. The Royal Ballet offered excerpts designed to show off principal dancers; the contributions included a piece specially composed by MacMillan for the occasion, a gentle duet to Fauré's *Pavane*, danced by Sibley and Dowell. February brought no new ballet but some significant new performances: Merle Park making a long-delayed début in *Swan Lake*, partnered by Desmond Kelly; Lesley Collier and Wayne Eagling in their first *Romeo and Juliet*; and Dowell making a striking appearance as Colas in *La Fille Mal Gardée*, a role which seemed to open up a new extrovert side to his normally reserved stage personality.

Only two weeks later, on 25 January, major acquisitions by the Company were unveiled when a single programme presented a triple bill consisting of three more Balanchine works, which brought The Royal Ballet's total by this choreographer to six. The newly acquired ballets represented three stages in his career. *Prodigal Son* was an early creation, having been devised for the Ballets Russes in 1929, a popular but curiously uneven work, which Diaghilev did not like. It revolved around a single star role which was as much mime as dancing. Nureyev, well cast, was the powerfully dramatic young rebel, with glamorous Deanne Bergsma as his seductress. *The Four Temperaments* dated from Balanchine's middle period, having been composed in 1946; subtitled 'A Dance Ballet Without Plot', it was one of his early abstract works, interpreting the Hindemith score in a series of brilliantly demanding dances.

The most original of the three ballets was *Agon*, dating back to 1957, characteristically rigorous and inventive – and completely without content, whether of mood, narrative or character. Arranged to a score by Stravinsky, it was specially composed for New York City Ballet in 1957 and MacMillan had created another version of it for The Royal Ballet the following year. Of the three works, *Agon* taxed The Royal Ballet dancers most, but considering that all three had had to be rehearsed simultaneously the result was astonishingly successful. The precise and stylish dancing of Vergie Derman and Laura Connor, Dowell, Wall and Eagling was marginally smoother and less rhythmic than that of Balanchine's own company, but it was completely convincing. This trio of Balanchine ballets constituted one of the most important additions to the Covent Garden repertoire for a long time.

The triumphant mood was clouded later in the spring of 1973, when yet another version of *The Sleeping Beauty* was introduced. MacMillan had added a few new dances and had made some amendments to the choreography and to the production, but they were not considered to be significant improvements and the new designs by Peter Farmer were generally disliked. Sibley and Dowell were very highly praised as the Princess and Prince, Alfreda Thorogood and Michael Coleman made a stylish pair in the Bluebird pas de deux, and Bergsma was a regal Lilac Fairy. Once again, however, the curse of Carabosse seemed to have robbed the ballet of a true re-awakening. Disappointment was all the sharper because the production had been mainly financed by the American Friends of Covent Garden and it had been intended to take it to New York the following spring. This ambitious production ended the season at Covent Garden and in April the Company flew to Brazil, on its first visit to South America.

The tour was a strenuous one; there were three days in Porto Allegre, two in Belo Horizonte, five in São Paolo, twelve in Rio de Janeiro, and one in the vast 19,000-seat open-air stadium at Brasilia. Here enthusiasm was so intense that half way through the disciplined opening ballet, *La Bayadère*, the dancers thought that a revolution had started. The tumult was caused by riot police dealing with crowds trying to break into the overbooked auditorium. The high altitudes and constant travelling inevitably imposed a strain on the dancers and on their return they were given a few days' rest. Then, on 8 May, they opened again in London – but in another theatre, the London Coliseum (the Opera Company was occupying Covent Garden). The four-week season included a dazzling succession of triple bills, alternating with a few performances of *Giselle*, *Anastasia* and *Romeo and Juliet*, which deployed the entire range of the Company's ballerinas and male dancers.

Two days later the Company returned to the Royal Opera House with a notable performance of *The Sleeping Beauty* in which the celebrated ex-Kirov dancers Makarova and Nureyev danced here together for the first time. Their début as a pair was not entirely harmonious, and the magic which is generated by two stars in true conjunction emerged only a fortnight later when Makarova appeared in MacMillan's *Romeo and Juliet*, again partnered by Nureyev and giving the role a feverish desperation matching his mercurial passion. In this performance Michael Coleman was Mercutio, dancing with his usual swift lightness and giving the character his own touch of raffish humour. Between Makarova's two Juliet performances there was a sad evening when David Blair gave his last performance, as Colas in *La Fille Mal Gardée*, before retiring. Next day brought more sadness when the news came that John Cranko had died suddenly while returning with his Stuttgart company from New York.

A performance in July furnished dramatic proof of the advantages arising from a distinctive and uniform company style. On 12 July Desmond Kelly was making his début as Prince Florimund in *The Sleeping Beauty*, with Ann Jenner as Aurora. At the end of Act I, Jenner became seriously ill (with what turned out to be appendicitis), and had to retire. During the interval, Brenda Last, a ballerina of the Touring Company who had twice danced the role eight years earlier – and who herself was recovering from an operation – went backstage to visit Kelly. Within a few minutes she found herself dressed in Aurora's tutu and making her entrance on stage in the Vision Scene. She completed the rest of the ballet with triumphant aplomb, and received an enthusiastic ovation as the curtain fell. (Eight months later Collier almost rivalled this feat when she went on to dance the principal role in *La Bayadère* without a single rehearsal.)

During the season, MacMillan, who seemed to have become no less productive since his appointment as Director, was rehearsing the revival of a slightly unusual ballet *The Seven Deadly Sins*. This curious hybrid was a typical example of the Bertolt Brecht-Kurt Weill collaboration. Half sung, half danced, it had been commissioned for Balanchine's 'Les Ballets 1933' and he had choreographed it himself. MacMillan had produced his own version for the Edinburgh Festival in 1961, with the small Western Theatre Ballet. He now revived it, considerably enlarged and with a warm-voiced singer, Georgia Brown, replacing the caustic-sounding creator, Lotte Lenya. The attempt to restore the bitter-sweet flavour of the original, produced a nostalgic impression of the decadent Twenties and a few effective scenes, but the overall result was uneven. The most successful elements were the giddy designs of Ian Spurling and an irresistible interpretation by Jennifer Penney of the innocent, waif-like dancing half of the heroine, Anna – a performance watched from the stalls by the original Anna, Tilly Losch. The ballet was followed by a revival of Balanchine's *Ballet Imperial* which, following the choreographer's wishes, was now

Kenneth MacMillan with dance notator Monica Parker in rehearsal for *The Seven Deadly Sins*, 1973. Reflected in the mirror are Jennifer Penney and the singer, Georgia Brown.

[181]

Manon, 1974, Act I. Anthony Dowell as Des Grieux.

completely denuded of the last of its Tsarist-style costumes and décor (replaced by a discreet grey-brown background designed by Terence Emery) and renamed *Piano Concerto No. 2*, after Tchaikovsky's concerto in G Major.

The autumn season began in October with a small but telling new offering, Robbins's *In the Night*. This spin-off from his *Dances at a Gathering* had been given its première in 1970 by New York City Ballet. It used the same formula as *Dances at a Gathering*, a suite of Chopin pieces played on the piano while the dancers, six this time, danced first as pairs and finally all together. The score, as the title suggests, was drawn entirely from the Nocturnes, which gave a more sweetly romantic flavour. Danced with lyrical sensitivity by Sibley and Dowell, Mason and MacLeary, Park and Wall, it was immediately popular, but it inevitably appeared as something of a postscript to the earlier ballet. A week later the Company took *The Sleeping Beauty* and a triple-bill programme to Brussels for six performances as part of the biennial Europalia celebrations – devoted this year to the entry of Great Britain into the Common Market. The critics, accustomed to the local modern company of Maurice Béjart, were somewhat baffled by the traditional classical repertoire.

There were no new creations in the autumn: programmes concentrated on revivals. Christmas was ushered in with a slightly revised *The Nutcracker* and some mixed bills which even included, contrary to tradition at Covent Garden, a popular divertissement in which Makarova and Wall danced the famous virtuoso *Don Quixote* pas de deux. With the return of Fonteyn, Makarova and Nureyev and of favourite ballets such as *Marguerite and Armand, Romeo and Juliet, The Sleeping Beauty* (with Monica Mason) and *La Fille Mal Gardée*, audiences were as large and as enthusiastic as ever.

Apart from the brilliant Balanchine trio, the acquisitions of the previous year had been slight as well as short, but the balance was restored at the Benevolent Fund Gala in March 1974 by an addition to MacMillan's impressive list of three-act ballets. It was another example of a genre which he was to make very much his own – the psychological dance-drama expanded into a three-act spectacle. The new ballet, *Manon*, was taken from the Abbé Prevost's eighteenth-century story of Manon Lescaut. The tale of young love corrupted by Parisian society and then redeemed, had been turned into an opera by Jules Massenet in 1884. In using music by Massenet, drawn not from the opera of the same name but from other operas mingled with oratorios, orchestral pieces and songs, MacMillan risked giving a nineteenth-century flavour to the story, a risk which he did not entirely overcome. The action was stretched in a rather leisurely fashion until it suddenly burst into frantic desperation in the final ten minutes. However, the eighteenth-century scene, evoked by Georgiadis in a sumptuous style cunningly hinting at the rags and squalor which lay beneath the surface, made a fine vehicle for the acting capabilities which have always been a hallmark of Royal Ballet dancers. In particular it created a wonderful role for the heroine. In the first cast Sibley conveyed to perfection Manon's childlike egotism, even if the hard selfishness of the character eluded her; Dowell was touching as her naïf and besotted lover; but it was Wall who stopped the show with his comical and sympathetic portrait of the heroine's drunken brother. Later casts gave their own personal twists to the characters: Seymour marvellously expressed the heroine's tinsel rapacity, Nureyev stressed the hero's rustic innocence, while Dowell when he took over Wall's role as the brother gave it a more sinister emphasis. The ballet as a whole proved a substantial addition to the repertoire, a mixture of that spectacle and drama (perhaps blending Petipa and Fokine) which has been MacMillan's chief contribution to The Royal Ballet.

Soon afterwards, in April, the Company paid one of its now rare visits to a provincial city, giving sixteen performances in Bristol, which started with a bomb-scare on the first night. Attendances were rather disappointing but the reviews in the Press were encouraging for future visits. During the season a new scheme, introducing children to the art of ballet through talks and glimpses of class and rehearsal, was introduced by the Associate Director, Peter Wright: the programmes were later named 'Journey Through Ballet'. In May the Company set off on another visit to America, opening on 7 May 1974 at the Met in New York. It was the fourteenth tour and the Company's first since the death in March of the impresario, Sol Hurok, who had introduced them to American audiences. A three-week season in New York was followed by nearly two weeks in Washington. *Manon* was popular with the public though not so much approved by the critics: but they, unlike their London colleagues, hailed the new production of *Swan Lake*. As always, the Company's dancing was highly praised. For the first time Fonteyn was missing, and Nureyev received most of the publicity, but the Sibley-Dowell partnership was noted with admiration.

With only a week for the dancers to recover and rehearse, the Covent Garden season continued through June and July with Makarova and Nureyev as Guest Artists (though following a well-publicised tiff they were tactfully not cast together). The programmes included revivals of *The Two Pigeons*, in which Lesley Collier made a lively début opposite David Ashmole, with Ann Jenner as the seductive Gypsy Girl; and of *Shadowplay* with Dowell and Park. The season ended with a gala in honour of Lord Drogheda, who retired after seventeen years as Chairman of the Royal Opera House Board, a position which had given him the chance to take a keen and often active interest both in the running of The Royal Ballet and in its achievements. The summer ended with a dashing new experiment. Spurred by demands from the provinces to see the Covent Garden Company and its productions of the classics, and yet unwilling to cut them down to fit into small stages, the management arranged a two-week trial season at Plymouth – sponsored by Midland Bank – in a capacious tent known as the 'Big Top'. The venture had its disadvantages, however. During one performance a violent rainstorm rattling on the roof nearly drowned the orchestra; scenery and lighting were somewhat limited; and the stage at first proved noisy. Nevertheless it drew in large and enthusiastic audiences. No full-length works were tackled, but the programmes included single Acts from *Swan Lake* and *The Sleeping Beauty* as well as a number of short ballets. This attempt to break out of the restrictions imposed by the large scale and regal image of the Company was counted a resounding success.

The return to the Opera House in October 1974, after the holidays, was celebrated on the first night by a new MacMillan ballet, *Elite Syncopations*. This was not one of his 'blockbusters' but a short and cheerful frolic to a suite of ragtime piano tunes by Scott Joplin and some of his early twentieth-century contemporaries, played on-stage. The harlequin-bright costumes by Ian Spurling set the Company's top dancers jerking their shoulders and elbows and joggling their hips in a series of dizzy, difficult, syncopated dances – a challenge which they met with an infectious glee. The idiom looked rather odd in the grandiose Opera House setting; but it was an immensely popular work from the start and has proved to be an enduring favourite. The rest of the autumn season, though mostly uneventful, was notable for some London débuts, such as those of Sibley in two performances of *Swan Lake* with Nureyev, and of Makarova in *Song of the Earth* and *Manon*, a role in which, with Dowell as des Grieux, she seemed instantly and marvellously at home, giving it a heartless feminine allure. Soon after the New Year, 1975, Lesley Collier danced her first Aurora, with David Ashmole.

A specially commissioned work was introduced on 31 January 1975, *Four Schumann Pieces* by Hans van Manen of the Dutch National Ballet, a choreographer new to Covent Garden though he had mounted four short works for the Sadler's Wells Company. This abstract ballet, more classical in shape than much of his work, was specially built around Dowell's smooth and fluid style. To the music of Schumann's A Major Quartet, the choreographer set a series of swift entrances and exits for ten dancers linked by the continual presence of Dowell. It was not the kind of work to arouse sharp opinions, and the pastel-coloured costumes by Jean-Paul Vroom stressed its gentle understatement; but everybody agreed that it offered a striking role for Dowell. The programme had opened with *La Bayadère* and at its conclusion de Valois presented to the corps de ballet an award

Manon, 1974. Anthony Dowell as Des Grieux, Antoinette Sibley as Manon.

[184]

from the London *Evening Standard* for the best achievement of the year in dance – a well-deserved tribute to the dancers and to their teacher, Jill Gregory, who was celebrating forty-three years of almost unbroken service with the Company. Lynn Seymour was to win the award in 1976 and David Wall in 1977.

The Benevolent Fund Gala in March included two short pieces for Fonteyn and Nureyev, but the main offering of the gala evening – and, as it turned out, a lasting asset for the Company – was another Jerome Robbins ballet, *The Concert*. Like his *Dances at a Gathering* and *In the Night*, this was another piece performed to a solo piano. In fact *The Concert* pre-dated the other two by thirteen years, having originally been composed for New York City Ballet as far back as 1956. Once more it was arranged to music by Chopin – but this time the whole ballet was a joke, a disrespectful impression of an earnest audience attending a recital. Good comic ballets are the rarest of all dance material, and this one contrived to alternate wit and fun, ranging from the music-hall joke of a lady trying on hats to a mysteriously poetic number consisting simply of people walking about under umbrellas. Its comedy offered ideal chances for The Royal Ballet dancers to exploit their subtle sense of timing and acting. Lynn Seymour was already known as a comedienne; but Georgina Parkinson, Michael Coleman flourishing an outsize cigar, and a young dancer called Graham Fletcher all emerged in a new, hilarious light. The short, unusual ballet was a triumph at the gala, and was to pass into the repertoire.

The next night *The Concert* was included in a programme introducing yet another new ballet by MacMillan, *The Four Seasons*. It was an unassuming but overlong set of pure classical variations to music composed by Verdi for the ballet episodes in three of his operas – light, pretty tunes leading to some charming dance numbers. Their effect was undermined by the setting of the action outside an inn bearing the name of the ballet, a fussy structure designed by Peter Rice, and later to be discarded.

Soon after this double occasion, a welcome sign of vigorous creative activity, the Covent Garden Company embarked on its first visit to the Far East. (Thirteen years before, in 1961, the Sadler's Wells Company had undertaken a four-week tour which had included Japan, Hong Kong and the Philippines.) During the four-week tour of Japan, which took it to Tokyo, Yokohama, Osaka, Kobe, Fukuoka, Hiroshima and Chiba, the accent was on full-length works. On its way out the Company made a stop in Korea for three days to present three performances to an audience which, having been accustomed to the Russian style, seemed at first rather nonplussed by some of the dancing. In Japan, however, balletgoers took more readily to the British style, though The Royal Ballet production of *The Sleeping Beauty*, a work already familiar to them, was less admired than the dancing, which won high praise, especially that of Park partnered by Dowell. *La Fille Mal Gardée* was popular as always and Wayne Sleep's nimble Puck in *The Dream* delighted the normally undemonstrative audiences. For the Company the tour was a refreshing and stimulating experience.

On the dancers' return to London in June they were due to start a six-week season at the Coliseum while the Opera Company took over Covent Garden, but because of a sudden dispute with the Coliseum stage staff about pay the season had to be cancelled at short

Elite Syncopations, 1974.
Costume designs by Ian Spurling.

Elite Syncopations, 1974. LEFT Merle Park in 'Stop Time Rag'. RIGHT Wayne Eagling in 'Hot-House Rag'.

notice. However, Midland Bank came to the rescue, providing the necessary financial backing for an alternative venue. The Big Top, which had been used in Plymouth the previous summer, was hurriedly erected by the Thames in Battersea Park, and the two Royal Ballet companies joined for a hastily improvised season. As the marquee held only about half the audience of the Coliseum it was an expensive operation. However, though the stage conditions were not much better than the rejected facilities of many provincial theatres, the reduced prices drew a largely new audience, and the change of atmosphere worked like a tonic on performers and management alike. The four-week season opened in pouring rain with Makarova and Dowell in *Swan Lake*. In these unusual conditions there were several débuts, including Makarova in *Elite Syncopations*, Collier in her first Giselle in London, and Eagling as Prince Siegfried in *Swan Lake*. Once back at the Royal Opera House a revival of MacMillan's abstract Shostakovitch *Symphony* was mounted, with new designs by Yolanda Sonnabend. July was also notable for seven evenings during which the Russian conductor Yuri Ahronovitch coaxed magical sounds from the orchestra in *Romeo and Juliet* (though synchronisation with the dancers was somewhat spasmodic).

The 1975 autumn season opened with two weeks in Newcastle, the second provincial city to welcome the Big Top, where only two ballets were presented, *Swan Lake* and *Romeo and Juliet*. On the Company's return the repertoire was dominated by these two and *Manon*, with Makarova much in evidence. She was joined by another ex-Kirov star, Mikhail Baryshnikov – though they did not dance together. Baryshnikov, who had defected in Canada during the previous summer, appeared in two performances of *Romeo*

LEFT *The Concert*. Michael Coleman in the first production by The Royal Ballet, 1975.
RIGHT *A Month in the Country*, 1976. Wayne Sleep as Kolia.

and Juliet and three of *Swan Lake*, in each case partnering Merle Park. He had never danced Romeo in Russia and in this eagerly awaited début with the Company he brought to the role a special extrovert freshness contrasted with unalloyed despair. The part of Prince Siegfried was familiar to him and he performed it in true Russian romantic fashion, blending the pure Kirov style with his own individual virtuosity. The third ex-member of the Kirov, Nureyev, rejoined the Company a few weeks later to dance Petrushka.

Just before Christmas 1975 yet another new ballet by MacMillan, *Rituals*, was given its première. It had evidently been inspired by the Company's recent visit to Japan. To Bartók's 'Sonata for Two Pianos' the choreographer arranged three mysterious and seemingly unconnected episodes, starting with some Kung-Fu acrobatics (Wayne Eagling versus Stephen Beagley, refereed by David Drew), continuing with an impression of Bunraku puppets (Vergie Derman and David Wall, manipulated like dolls) and ending with a scene suggesting Japanese reactions to the birth of a child (Lynn Seymour attended by Monica Mason). The movements were strictly non-classical and impassive, the mask-like make-up entertainingly impenetrable and the setting and costumes by Sonnabend airy and beautiful; but the idiom was too remote for general enjoyment. *Cinderella* returned once again for Christmas, with Ashton and Helpmann still dominating it to the extent that it was facetiously christened 'The Ugly Sisters Show'. It provided Makarova with another telling role as Cinderella, which she interpreted with a characteristic blend of humour, vitality and elegance.

The New Year, 1976, began sadly with the last performances together at the Royal

Opera House (apart from a pas de deux) of Fonteyn and Nureyev, in *Romeo and Juliet*. The important event of the spring was a première in February of a ballet which had been keenly awaited for a long time, Ashton's *A Month in the Country*. He was now seventy-one and this was the first work, apart from a gala duet, that he had created since *Enigma Variations* eight years earlier. It was a testing time for him and for the Company. As a subject he had chosen the well-known play by Turgenev concerning a married woman's last romance, in the setting of a Russian country house. For music he chose Chopin (definitely the composer of the decade as far as The Royal Ballet was concerned), and Julia Trevelyan Oman set the scene in an elegant salon. This was, literally, a 'chamber work' – the dancing took place around tables and chairs – in Ashton's favourite distilled form. He devised a set of ingeniously embroidered dances which simultaneously revealed the personalities of the characters and at the same time skilfully and rapidly recounted Turgenev's story – the devastating impact on the family of an attractive young tutor who leaves only after innocently causing emotional havoc.

A Month in the Country, 1976. Lynn Seymour as Natalia Petrovna,
Anthony Dowell as Beliaev.

successful in the USA as it had been at home, *Rituals* and *Elite Syncopations*. Among the New York débuts were Makarova in *Romeo and Juliet*, *Manon* and *Song of the Earth*; Collier and Nureyev in *La Fille Mal Gardée*; Collier and Eagling in *Swan Lake*; and Nureyev in *The Dream*. Some critics found the repertoire rather conservative, but the general standard of dancing was recognised to be as high as ever and the reception by the public was as enthusiastic, with MacMillan this time constantly on hand to supervise. After New York the Company went on for two weeks in Washington and one week in Philadelphia. It was rumoured, correctly, that this would be its last visit for some time. Transatlantic tours were becoming complicated as well as costly, and the pressures which they exerted on rehearsal and production schedules loomed increasingly large. It was to be five years before The Royal Ballet returned to New York. At the end of the tour Alexander Grant – one of the finest character dancers that the Company has ever produced – left to take up his appointment as Director of the National Ballet of Canada, and on the Company's return to Britain the sudden death of David Blair caused general sadness.

After three weeks back in Covent Garden the Company went off on another tour, to dance in the Big Top at Plymouth. This season was very successful and ran for the entire three weeks before the summer holiday. The autumn season did not open until mid-October, and in November a new work was introduced, *Voluntaries* by Glen Tetley. This was the first ballet by the American choreographer to be acquired since his two modern-style works *Field Figures* and *Laborintus* in 1971 and 1972. It had been created for the Stuttgart Ballet in 1973 as a memorial to John Cranko, and they had already danced it in London. The Royal Ballet's interpretation of the vigorous, emotionally exalted and sometimes acrobatic choreography, arranged to Poulenc's dramatic 'Concerto for Organ, Strings and Percussion', was gentler and more flowing than that of the Stuttgart dancers, with Seymour and Wall in roles created for Marcia Haydée and Richard Cragun. The basically classical idiom which Tetley employed in this work fitted the Company well, and the ballet was warmly received.

Only a few days later, on 22 November 1976, the Benevolent Fund Gala brought another new piece, van Manen's *Adagio Hammerklavier*. This slow-moving, abstract series of pas de deux for three couples set to the adagio movement from Beethoven's Hammerklavier Sonata had been created in 1973 for the Dutch National Ballet. It was not very appropriate gala material, but it was eloquently danced by contrasting pairs, Makarova and Wall, Mason and Eagling, Penney and Mark Silver, and it proved again that a solo piano is a valid accompaniment to dance, even in an Opera House. During this season Sibley and Dowell had both been suffering from injuries; and MacLeary, who had retired earlier in the year to become the Company's Ballet Master, returned to partner Makarova in *Swan Lake*. The leading British pair were also absent from the list of dancers who featured in performances of *The Nutcracker* which marked the Christmas holiday season, and from performances of *Swan Lake*, *Romeo and Juliet* and *La Fille Mal Gardée*, which dominated the programmes in the first month of 1977.

February was to have seen the introduction of *Onegin*, a ballet that Cranko had planned to choreograph for the Company but which had been rejected, partly on musical grounds: the idea of translating an opera into a ballet was considered undesirable. Originally intended for The Royal Ballet as a vehicle for Fonteyn and Nureyev, it had been mounted in Stuttgart in 1965 for Haydée and Cragun. In London, difficulties arose about the fireproofing of the scenery and the project had to be dropped. A later work by Cranko, *The*

Taming of the Shrew, was substituted, not too happily. An ingenious full-length piece following Shakespeare's play very closely, it was choreographed to a modern arrangement by Kurt-Heinz Stolze of a selection of Scarlatti pieces which were hardly in keeping with the knockabout comedy. The roles of Kate and Petruchio, created for Haydée and Cragun, were danced by Park and Wall, followed by Seymour and Eagling and Collier and Stephen Jefferies. The robust style did not suit the Royal Ballet dancers, who did not convey the full vigour and comedy-timing of the Stuttgart cast, but in some guest performances Haydée and Cragun brought back to the ballet the punch and conviction which it had lacked. While in London to mount it, Haydée and Cragun had also given a memorable performance of *The Song of the Earth*, together with a third member of the original Stuttgart cast, Egon Madsen, as the Messenger of Death. During February Sibley and Dowell both succumbed once again to injury or illness, but Baryshnikov returned in March to dance in *Romeo and Juliet*, this time with Seymour, and to learn the part of Colas in *La Fille Mal Gardée*. In April he danced the role with inimitable zest and precision, partnering two of the young principals, first Ann Jenner and then Lesley Collier. His visit coincided with the première of *The Fourth Symphony*, the first ballet for the Company by the Hamburg-based American John Neumeier. It was an evocation of childhood which interpreted hints dropped about the work by its composer, Mahler. Wayne Sleep was the central figure, a boy involved in scenes with his parents, some of his companions and a pair of lovers. Although this was an interesting work which helped to give the repertoire a more contemporary look, it was not liked and it survived only a few performances.

The Company paid another visit to Bristol in May for a two-week season, returning to the Royal Opera House to take part in a gala celebrating the Silver Jubilee of the Queen's accession to the throne. For the occasion Ashton composed *Hamlet Prelude*, a pas de deux for Fonteyn and Nureyev, and MacMillan produced an arrangement of the dances from Benjamin Britten's opera *Gloriana*, marked by a startling passage in which the royal personage was turned upside-down. The Company then moved over the Thames to Battersea Park for a second season in the Big Top. The programmes were light and varied, with some of the junior principals such as Laura Connor, Stephen Jefferies (a leader of the Touring Company newly returned after a year with the National Ballet of Canada) and the young Derek Deane given the opportunity to dance principal roles. This policy of trying out new casts was continued when the Company returned to Covent Garden – with Marguerite Porter, Wendy Ellis and Ann Jenner all taking turns as Juliet.

The last few weeks of the season had been overshadowed by an announcement made on 13 June which came as a total surprise to the ballet public – the resignation of Kenneth MacMillan as Artistic Director. The circumstances in which he had taken over from Ashton, coupled with the almost immediate resignation of his Administrative Director, John Field, had given him a difficult start and had proved to be a persistent handicap. He also had the awkward task of inaugurating the re-formed structure of the Company's two component parts. His positive contributions had been impressive, especially the introduction of American choreographers. He had continued to keep up a stream of new works of his own, ranging from short ballets for the New Group to full-scale productions for the Covent Garden Company, which explored new developments of the three-act ballet. He had encouraged the younger dancers, while phasing out Fonteyn and Nureyev; on the other hand Makarova had been a constant Guest Artist, performing in many ballets, with Baryshnikov also making a few appearances. One of MacMillan's chief

Sol Hurok, the American impresario, at a luncheon given in his honour at the Royal Opera House.
From left to right: Lord Drogheda, Anthony Dowell, Antoinette Sibley, Sol Hurok,
Merle Park, Rudolf Nureyev, Donald MacLeary and John (now Sir John) Tooley.

contributions as Director was his attempt – short-lived though it turned out to be – to introduce contemporary-style works into the repertoire. Shy, complicated and introverted, he concealed his intelligence and charm beneath a veil of privacy and remoteness and found many of his directorial functions uncongenial. He retired proud of his achievements: but he summed up the laying down of his administrative duties as 'a great relief'.

He left the Company in good dancing shape, and its repertoire was the richer by at least half-a-dozen new ballets of lasting value, several of them his own. (An attempt to revive *The Prince of the Pagodas* with new choreography by himself and designs by Georgiadis regrettably lapsed after discussions with Britten over changes in the score.) Although of a different generation from de Valois and Ashton, MacMillan was, nonetheless, in direct line of succession (having been with the Company since 1946, apart from his few years in Berlin). A total break with the past came with the announcement that his successor was not to be an heir moving up from the ranks of The Royal Ballet, but someone from outside, ex-Director of Ballet Rambert, Norman Morrice.

8 Yesterday and Tomorrow

Before his appointment as Director, Norman Morrice's connections with The Royal Ballet Company had been only slender. Born in 1931 in Mexico he was, at forty-six, two years younger than Kenneth MacMillan. He had joined the Ballet Rambert at the age of twenty-two, becoming first a principal dancer and then choreographer, with nine ballets for it to his credit. He was also producing works for other companies, including *The Tribute* for the Royal Ballet Touring Company in 1965. In 1966 he had been appointed Assistant Director of the Ballet Rambert and carried through a complete transformation of the company, turning it from a classical group into a team specialising in modern dance, which he had studied during a stay in New York in 1961. In 1974 he had resigned from his administrative post in order to work full time on choreography, as MacMillan had done. His name was still familiar only to a specialist public, and his tastes and opinions were hardly known outside the small Rambert company. The appointment of a figure so manifestly outside The Royal Ballet circle looked like the signal for drastic change.

For Morrice the change in scale was dramatic. The Royal Ballet was a large and complex organisation, closely meshed with the overall policies of the Royal Opera House which were concerned with opera as well as with ballet. It included two separate companies – the Opera House Company, the Touring Company based at Sadler's Wells and a small educational group 'Ballet for All' – totalling one hundred and twenty-five dancers, the schedules for whom were always fixed many months and, in some respects, such as touring, years ahead. Those who now looked for dramatic and immediate new developments were inevitably to be disappointed. Morrice, a quiet, diffident and accessible character, spent some time patiently studying the Company and its problems, making few noticeable alterations in its running. He emerged with only one major change in mind, an increase in the number of performances by the Company's dancers, even if this meant the temporary banishing of all Guest Artists. The decision was understandable. His own background in the Ballet Rambert had accustomed him to the concept of a tight, self-contained team which outsiders would have disturbed. Any dissatisfaction among the Company's dancers would be cured by more appearances, a greater variety of roles and quicker promotion. Morrice's aim was to strengthen morale and build for the future by giving more prominence to junior talent within the Company. This was a bold and controversial measure which over the next two years was to provoke a good deal of comment, both favourable and unfavourable. It involved a lowering of the temperature of public excitement and, according to some critics, of performing standards, while a new generation of British dancers was developing. There was to be some restiveness from a public which complained that it was paying for present not future enjoyment, but there was also support from those who were anxious to encourage talent. The idea of a top-ranking company deliberately pulling back in the hope of future benefits was courageous: inevitably it involved some loss of glamour and a sense of dismay among a section of the audience; but it brought compensating benefits. As it happened, the decision was taken in the face of fierce outside competition. A galaxy of stars, including Fonteyn, Makarova,

Nureyev, Baryshnikov, and the American Ballet Theatre Company had been performing in London during Morrice's first season as Director. The endeavour to match this kind of competition solely from within the Company's own resources was a brave gesture.

Morrice's new measure was to be tested almost immediately. The first production, planned earlier, but mounted only after he took over the Company's direction in the autumn of 1977, was the supreme symbol of tradition and continuity, a revival of *The Sleeping Beauty*, which had its première in October. This latest attempt to re-awaken the obstinately dormant masterpiece – an admission that the last one had failed – was produced by Ninette de Valois. She rejected all attempts at modernisation in favour of a near-restoration of the famous 1946 version, the production which had conquered Covent Garden at first sight. The effort was in many ways successful, with Collier and Dowell a distinguished pair of principals and Seymour a balefully elegant Carabosse in the modern style. But this gentle and undramatic version had a built-in handicap: it inevitably invited comparison with its predecessor conceived and performed in the first flush of the Company's youth. The new designs by David Walker were pretty but conventional, with the transformation effects reduced to a minimum. Ashton's romantic-style Awakening pas de deux was restored and also a showy little Hop o' my Thumb solo which MacMillan

Norman Morrice with Sir Frederick Ashton and Monica Mason after
a television performance of *The Sleeping Beauty*.

had added for Wayne Sleep in 1973. The style and the dancing of some of the smaller roles were criticised in the light of nostalgic memories of the glamorous post-war version, and the inevitable charge of 'carbon-copying' was levelled at an otherwise acceptable production.

The rest of the autumn saw few innovations, though there were several personal successes. On 25 October 1977 it was announced that Ashton had been awarded the Order of Merit; that night his *Enigma Variations*, conducted by Sir Adrian Boult, and *Symphonic Variations*, together with his beloved *Les Noces* (which owing to a dispute with the musicians was played without percussion), were in the programme, and he received a suitable ovation.

During January 1978 Ashton ballets dominated the repertoire. In *A Month in the Country* Marguerite Porter, who originally danced the role of Katya, the maid, made a wistful heroine while Michael Coleman, not a dancer often cast in romantic roles, brought an effective virility to the character of the tutor. The next month was to see the launching of *Mayerling*, a new and important full-length dance-drama by MacMillan, marking a further step in his search for a modern replacement for the traditional nineteenth-century format for a full-length ballet. As in *Anastasia*, he turned away from fiction to historical fact and, as in several of his earlier works, he chose psychological abnormality as his subject. The setting was Imperial Vienna at the end of the nineteenth century, offering an opportunity for Georgiadis to provide another of his rich and detailed spectacles. The ballet's originality lay in its sordid subject: the slow descent through drugs and syphilis to the eventual suicide of the neurotic Prince Rudolf, heir to the Austro-Hungarian Empire, dragging his adoring young mistress with him. This story of sex, violence and neurosis carried ballet into a world far from Petipa's fairyland. Told in a series of short film-like sequences, the drama was slow-moving but in the end compelling, with a succession of brilliantly inventive and characteristically acrobatic pas de deux and a host of rather vaguely suggested minor characters. The parts of Prince Rudolf and that of his death-infatuated young mistress offered rich dramatic possibilities. Powerfully created by Wall and Seymour, the roles were also taken over by Eagling and Collier, Jefferies and Thorogood; their interpretations varied greatly and showed the range that this kind of ballet can display. Park was outstanding as Countess Larisch, one of Rudolf's ex-mistresses, as was Parkinson as his mother, the Empress. The music was full-bloodedly romantic, though not particularly neurotic: an assortment of forty Liszt pieces artfully stitched together and orchestrated by John Lanchbery, an experienced ballet-musician who had been the Company's principal conductor from 1960 to 1972 and who was now Music Director of Australian Ballet. Some people found the treatment too literary and operatic – there was actually a sung episode – but, considering its sombre subject, the ballet was well received. It remained in the repertoire throughout March and was featured successfully in a 'Prom' performance on 1 April (it was also to be the subject of a Thames Television programme which won the Prix d'Italia in September).

This month introduced some two-ballet programmes, consisting of *Song of the Earth* and *The Firebird*, which proved surprisingly popular. Shortly afterwards the dancers left London for a visit to the Empire Theatre, Liverpool, where the stage had been recently enlarged, thus making it, with the Bristol Hippodrome, one of the only provincial theatres suitable for the Company. From there they left for an extended tour of South Korea and America. When they had visited South Korea on their way to Japan in 1975 it had been

Mayerling, 1978. David Wall as Prince Rudolf, Lynn Seymour as Baroness Mary Vetsera his mistress.

only for three days; on this tour they stayed in Seoul for ten performances in two weeks. From there they crossed the Pacific to Los Angeles, where they opened with the new production of *The Sleeping Beauty*, which was far more warmly received than in London. This time Fonteyn was present, and for her *Les Sylphides* and the Ashton *Hamlet Prelude* pas de deux were included in the second night's programme, with *Mayerling* making its début in the second week. It proved to be a big popular success, though some critics found it too heavy. The same programme pattern was repeated throughout the tour, which included a week in Houston and another in Chicago. This was the Company's first American tour since Sol Hurok's death and under new management – not a triumphant progress nor greatly profitable, but reaping high praise for the dancers. Back in London for a final week before the holiday the Company revived *Anastasia* and celebrated de Valois' eightieth birthday with, naturally, a performance of *The Sleeping Beauty*. Immediately afterwards they left again, this time for Athens, where they presented *The Sleeping Beauty* and *Romeo and Juliet* in the Roman open-air theatre of Herodes Atticus, on the slopes of the Acropolis.

The 1978 autumn season opened with the disturbing awareness that two of the Company's principal dancers were about to leave. Lynn Seymour had accepted the post of Director of the Munich Ballet, which meant the loss of an outstandingly dramatic dancer.

The Company on tour at the Herodes Atticus Theatre in Athens, 1978.

In July, before the summer holiday, it had been announced that Anthony Dowell, the Company's leading male dancer now rising to the peak of his career, had decided that the time had come to widen his experience by joining American Ballet Theatre in New York. The departure of these two outstanding artists was a serious blow to a Company already beset by illnesses and injuries, and opposed to foreign Guest Artists. New talent was becoming difficult to recruit. Australia and Canada now had large national companies offering good openings for their own young dancers and, to make matters worse, a recent decision by the Government limited the employment of dancers from the Commonwealth. This robbed the Company of a rich source of supply; sometimes over one-third of The Royal Ballet artists, including many of the principals, have come from countries such as Australia, New Zealand, South Africa, Rhodesia and Canada. For several reasons (one of them being the higher salaries paid on the Continent) dancers from Europe, though permitted, could not be counted on to fill the gap. British dancers of top quality had now become all the more indispensable.

Under this shadow the season opened with *Mayerling*, the gloom of which was relieved as usual by the antics of Graham Fletcher as the eccentric coachman. A more cheerful note was soon struck with triple bills consisting of *Serenade*, *A Month in the Country* (with the young dancer Mark Silver making a convincingly innocent Tutor) and *Façade*, one of the oldest survivors from the early years of Sadler's Wells but now losing its edge through the exaggeration of the comedy. *Les Sylphides* was revived in a careful production by Ashton.

The early weeks of 1979 brought more revivals, among them Ashton's *Scènes de Ballet*, a work which now seemed perfectly accessible, the years having softened the shock-effect of its angular acerbity. Coupled with it was another Ashton piece, *Birthday Offering*, which had also undergone a transformation. Dazzling when first seen in 1956, it now seemed rather old-fashioned. Another ballet which passing time seemed to have modified was MacMillan's *Rite of Spring*; many of the dances which had at first looked arrestingly modern now appeared jazzy. The season saw several interesting débuts including, in February, a 22-year-old soloist Rosalyn Whitten as Aurora. In March Margaret Barbieri, from the Sadler's Wells Royal Ballet, and Stephen Jefferies danced Juliet and Romeo together, and Mark Silver gave his first performance as the Prince in *The Sleeping Beauty*.

The first new ballet of the year, indeed the first for over a year, came in March, once again from MacMillan. The sombre atmosphere which had marked much of his recent work gave way to a cheerful mood. *La Fin du Jour* was a salute to the Thirties, the period when the score, Ravel's Piano Concerto in G, was composed, just as the ballet's sister-piece, *Elite Syncopations*, had reflected the early years of the twentieth century, when its music had been written. A kind of fantasy arising from wax models wearing the fashions of the period, *La Fin du Jour* conjured up a world similar to that of *Les Biches*. The light and airy Art-Déco setting by Ian Spurling, married to Ravel's danceable score, made a light-hearted and elegant divertissement through which the Company moved with ease. Park and Penney slipped gleefully into the period, with Eagling and Hosking almost unrecognisable under doll-like make-up. In the same programme *Diversions* was restored, but sandwiched between the new ballet and the equally sprightly *Elite Syncopations*, it now seemed rather bland.

Great hopes had been pinned on Balanchine's *Liebeslieder Walzer*, composed in 1960, an acquisition which was presented in April, having been postponed since the previous

November. It was a favourite with critics in America and had been popular in London during the last visit of New York City Ballet. Its construction is simple – an hour-long succession of thirty-three songs by Brahms (accompanied by a piano duet) to which four couples perform a closely linked chain of waltzes; in the first half they are dressed for the ballroom; then, after a pause, the lights go dim, stars come out, and they reappear in ballet costume, with the girls in long tutus and point-shoes executing more acrobatic steps. The craftsmanship looked as impressive as ever, but the smooth and elegant style of the Company glossed over the differing variety of the dances, and a gimcrack setting and cabaret-style costumes gave a curiously provincial, old-fashioned flavour to the whole entertainment. Contrary to expectation the London audience – perhaps sated by two recent productions by other ballet companies based on Viennese waltzes, Australian Ballet's *The Merry Widow* and the London Festival Ballet's *Rosalinda* – did not rise to the occasion, and what had looked set to be a winner misfired. Fortunately it had not been made the keystone of the May programmes, which were enlivened by an evening celebrating Margot Fonteyn's sixtieth birthday. Since it was rumoured that it might also be her last appearance with the Company, the pleasure was mingled with nostalgia: this was a farewell party, not a gala but a 'private' occasion, in which affection, respect and simple star-worship blended in a kind of wistful euphoria. The highlight of the programme which started appropriately with *Birthday Offering* was the appearance of the guest of honour herself. Glamorously dressed by her long-time friend and colleague William Chappell, she dreamed her way through a solo cunningly devised by Ashton to include tiny steps from many of the ballets he had created for her – a summary of the fifty-seven roles she had danced with the Company. It was set to a piece by Elgar suitably entitled *Salut d'Amour* and ended with the choreographer himself entering to make a révérence before his ballerina, then leading her off stage. Predictably it brought the house down, and had to be repeated. A fine performance of *Symphonic Variations* followed; then Fonteyn appeared in a characteristically cheerful Tango from *Façade* with her first partner, Robert Helpmann, now seventy years old. Having witnessed the tributes to de Valois in 1971 and to Ashton in 1970, many members of the audience must have felt that as the flowers rained down from the gallery they were saying goodbye to the Company's first years. But plans for the future were full and varied. Only a week later the dancers flew off for another tour of America, visiting Washington, Montreal, Vancouver, San Francisco, Los Angeles and Mexico City. They returned to the Royal Opera House in October to present a fine performance of *Romeo and Juliet*, with Merle Park as Juliet. The audience welcomed back not only the Company after five months absence, but also Anthony Dowell, as Romeo. Henceforward he was to rejoin the Royal Ballet for intermittent appearances.

The only new undertaking in this autumn of 1979 was a slightly modified and renovated version of *Swan Lake*. Like the recent revival of *The Sleeping Beauty* this kept fairly close to the original Sadler's Wells production. The designs were by Leslie Hurry (who died before the première) and incorporated costumes from earlier versions. More controversially, Ashton's choreography for the last Act, replacing Ivanov's, was restored.

ABOVE (left) *Giselle*, 1968, Bathilde; (right) *The Sleeping Beauty*, 1973, a courtier:
costume designs by Peter Farmer.
BELOW *Mayerling*, 1978. Costume designs by Nicholas Georgiadis:
(left) Countess Larisch, Act III, Scene 1; (right) Baroness Helene Vetsera, Act II, Scene 3.

Isadora - The Marseillaise - Act II sc 16

Barry Kay

Lesley Collier danced with her usual impeccable vitality as Odette/Odile; still a relative newcomer to the role, she had an experienced partner in Wall who, during Dowell's prolonged absences, now took his place as the Company's leading male dancer.

The spring of 1980 brought a revival of *Mayerling*, *Four Schumann Pieces* (with Eagling taking over Dowell's part), and Merle Park making her début opposite Mark Silver in an impetuous rendering of Natalia in *A Month in the Country*. A special item introduced during March was a revival of *Mam'zelle Angot*, dedicated to the memory of Léonide Massine, who had died in 1979. Though on the opening night the critics were not generally impressed, the ballet played to enthusiastic audiences, forming part of a successful triple bill with *Voluntaries* and *La Fin du Jour*. The most notable event of the season was a new ballet by MacMillan, *Gloria*. Like his *La Fin du Jour* this had a nostalgic quality but it was a total contrast in style. The title was taken from Poulenc's setting of the words from the Roman Mass, a mainly exultant work for orchestra and a large choir. Unexpectedly MacMillan used this to accompany a sombre evocation of the 1914 War, inspired by a poem written in 1931 by Vera Brittain. The shades of post-war girls mingled with the shadows of their lost lovers, still wearing the ravaged battledress and tin hats in which they had been killed. There was no explicit story or action. The dancing centred around two girls, Penney and Ellis, and two men, Eagling and Hosking. As they emerged from the trenches at the back of Andy Klunder's stark setting, their changing moods were conveyed in a succession of dances, often against a background of resting, sleeping and dying soldiers. The style was classical, with arabesques and pirouettes, but mixed with inventive new movements. Eagling's speed and agility were particularly exploited and the action veered from melancholy stillness to acrobatics. The movement-idiom and the use of voice-and-dance recalled MacMillan's *Song of the Earth*, but this time the music and the dancing were used against, not with, each other. The sincerity and skill of this sophisticated work, coupled with the elegance of Penney's interpretation, established for it a successful place in the Company's repertoire.

A refreshingly adventurous programme in May introduced no less than three additions to the repertoire. The evening opened with *Troy Games* – a pioneering work in that it was the first ballet acquired by the Company from a contemporary-style dance group. The choreographer was Robert North, an ex-pupil of the Royal Ballet School who had joined London Contemporary Dance Theatre and was now its resident choreographer. It was that rarity a ballet for men only, in this case a light-hearted frolic based on oriental Kung-Fu and western athletic contests, originally created for North's own company. Some Royal Ballet dancers had performed it and had enjoyed the chance to display their acrobatic prowess – so much that it was now taken, to popular acclaim, into the repertoire.

The second novelty was a MacMillan work created by the Stuttgart Ballet in 1978: *My Brother, My Sisters*. Set, adventurously but successfully, to Schoenberg's 'Five Pieces for Orchestra, Opus 16' followed by Webern's 'Five Pieces for Orchestra, Opus 10', and 'Six Pieces for Orchestra, Opus 6', this was one of MacMillan's explorations of family sex-problems – a descendant of his *The Invitation*. Inventive and intense, the emotional entanglements of five sisters and a spoilt brother develop into a violent climax beneath a

---

Isadora, 1981. Costume design by Barry Kay:
Isadora dancing the Marseillaise.

LEFT *Gloria*, 1980. Jennifer Penney and Julian Hosking. RIGHT *Rhapsody*, created by Frederick Ashton
in honour of Queen Elizabeth The Queen Mother's eightieth birthday,
with Lesley Collier and Mikhail Baryshnikov.

brooding sky designed by Yolanda Sonnabend. Finely danced at the première by Penney,
Wall and Collier, the leading roles were played with extra assurance a few nights later by
the original Stuttgart pair, Birgit Keil and Richard Cragun.

The last work was also a notable event, being the first work for the main Company by a
young choreographer developed by the Sadler's Wells Royal Ballet, David Bintley. For the
occasion he played rather safe: his *Adieu* was a conventional abstract-experiment piece
arranged to Andrzej Panufnik's Violin Concerto. Competent and pleasing, it was a hopeful,
if not very personal, introduction.

After a brief excursion to Liverpool, the Company returned to the Royal Opera House
with a revised production of *Giselle*. Supervised by Norman Morrice it seemed to be an
attempt to recreate the style of the 1960 production, using the same designer, James
Bailey. Such resuscitations are notoriously difficult and this one had a somewhat cool
reception from the critics.

The visit by two Guest Artists from Stuttgart was followed later by an invasion from
America. The first star to appear was Natalia Makarova, dancing in the new *Giselle* with
Anthony Dowell who was also now mainly based on American Ballet Theatre. Next came
Mikhail Baryshnikov as Romeo – a role he had danced on his first visit five years before –
with Lesley Collier as Juliet.

A few nights later there was an even more striking performance when Gelsey Kirkland –
yet another American Ballet Theatre dancer – made her début with the Company as Juliet.
Partnered by Dowell, with Stephen Jefferies as Mercutio, she brought to the part a passion

and technical fluency which had never been surpassed, changing from immaturity to tragic womanhood in a single sweep. All four artists appeared at a Benevolent Fund Gala on 17 July. Makarova danced in two evocations of the Twenties, Ashton's *Façade* tango and Lorca Massine's *Fantaisie Sérieuse*; Baryshnikov performed some Robbins dances with David Wall; and Dowell, as well as twice partnering Makarova, danced the final pas de deux from *The Dream* with Kirkland as Titania, an intense and individual interpretation which suggested that she could shine in many Ashton works.

The summer season came to a climax at another gala on 4 August, organised to celebrate the eightieth birthday of Queen Elizabeth The Queen Mother, for which Ashton created *Rhapsody*, his first new ballet for four years. It was very much a party piece, contrasting strongly with the delicate lyricism of his *A Month in the Country* which preceded it. Full of fast, glittering passages, it centred round Baryshnikov, whose virtuosity was displayed in short bursts of bravura dancing. There was no perceptible theme, though one violin-playing gesture recalled that the music was Rachmaninov's 'Rhapsody on a Theme of Paganini'. Baryshnikov, an Apollo figure with gold-dusted hair, and Lesley Collier, who also performed some brilliant solos, were the central figures in a series of difficult evolutions with six other pairs. The whole ballet had a showy flavour – a daring and unusual quality for Ashton – accentuated by William Chappell's costumes. The effect, away from the context of the glamorous gala, was over-ornate. *Rhapsody* was followed the next evening by Makarova in a new and eloquent interpretation of the heroine in *A Month in the Country*, with Dowell in his old role as the Tutor, and a promising youngster, Karen Paisey, as Vera.

It is, appropriately, with Ashton's celebratory fireworks, which demonstrated a remarkable vitality (slightly reminiscent of his *Scènes de Ballet*), that this record must end – though several months are still to elapse before The Royal Ballet officially reaches its half-century. The Company's Director, Norman Morrice, has no revolutionary plans for the intervening period, but there are many projects in hand, culminating in a visit to the United States and Canada. It is planned to celebrate the anniversary with a major production – Kenneth MacMillan's *Isadora*, another milestone in the progress of The Royal Ballet which will surely be long and varied. Its first steps were planned and executed with a determination that sets its general direction firmly, but its eventual destinations remain excitingly unpredictable. The next fifty years will reveal some of them.

9 The Touring Company

The story of the main Company of The Royal Ballet is one of steady and continuous development. That of its sister Company, which opened as 'The Sadler's Wells Opera Ballet' has been more erratic, with fluctuations in its title which reveal shifts of purpose and changes in policy. It has often had a struggle to create and to maintain an individual image, and the experience has made it sturdy and independent, with the capacity not only to survive but to thrive in many conditions and environments. The actual rhythm of its activities was to be modified extensively as time passed, and it went through three different, though overlapping, transitions before arriving in its present situation. As it happens, the changes coincided fairly precisely with the appointments of new Directors.

Sadler's Wells Theatre, put at her disposal by Baylis, gave de Valois the permanent base that she needed, and up to the outbreak of war in 1939 the Company was firmly rooted there. It was home, and it rightly lent its name to the Company that it had nurtured. But the changes brought about by war, the long absences, either in the provinces or at the New or Prince's Theatres, and the unexpected expansion of general interest in ballet, set a question-mark over the Company's peacetime return to Sadler's Wells. The invitation to move to Covent Garden was irresistible and the Sadler's Wells Ballet acquired a new home at the Royal Opera House. This, too, raised difficulties. Who would now undertake the Company's obligation (which had lapsed, of course, during the war) to perform in the opera productions at Sadler's Wells? More important, should the patiently built-up connections with that theatre be thrown away? And what about the obligations and potentialities of touring? There could really be only one answer to these problems: the setting up of a second Company which should stay behind at Sadler's Wells. This could fulfil the ballet obligations to the opera and it could also act as a stepping-stone for young dancers who were not ready for the Royal Opera House. Being smaller in size the second Company could take over some of the touring dates from the main Company and open up new venues. It would also be better suited for experiments, as well as for the first efforts of budding choreographers, designers and musicians.

The project went forward simultaneously with the plans for moving the main company to Covent Garden, and on 17 October 1945 the opening of de Valois' 'second front' was announced. The new troupe was to be under the general directorship of de Valois. Ursula Moreton, one of de Valois' first stalwarts and now her Personal Assistant, was to be in immediate charge. Peggy van Praagh, an ex-member of the Ballet Rambert who had joined the Company in 1941, was to be Ballet Mistress. There would be thirty dancers, who would be fortified by Guest Artists from Covent Garden. The new Company would be called 'The Sadler's Wells Opera Ballet' and would be the responsibility of the Sadler's Wells Trust, both financially and administratively. Its birth was warmly welcomed, but immediate doubts were expressed about its name, which seemed cumbersome and to some degree misleading. The point might appear trivial, but it touched on a major and enduring difficulty – the relationship between the two Companies. This was fraught with complications. The new Company was to be both a part of the old Sadler's Wells Ballet and yet almost totally independent of it. It was to serve as a training ground for young talent, yet not to be considered in any way inferior in status to the Covent Garden Company. It was to be formally attached to the Sadler's Wells Theatre but in practice was linked to the Royal Opera House through the person of de Valois, who was Director of both Companies.

Some of these snags were to be surmounted in due course, but others were to arise in their place. The built-in contradictions were to result in a whole series of changes, adjustments and even subterfuges. The Company's title has been altered several times; its size has swollen and shrunk; it has swung from being a vehicle for the classics to serving as

Peggy van Praagh, first Ballet Mistress of Sadler's Wells
Theatre Ballet, in rehearsal.

a commando group to open up new territory. It has been hailed at one moment as the livelier member of the linked pair of companies and attacked at the next as an inferior substitute. But somehow it has gone on resolutely performing up and down the country, in London and abroad, introducing new talent, creating and developing, and sometimes just holding the fort. Without losing its individuality and confidence it has survived punishing schedules and loss of dancers to the Covent Garden Company as well as changes in policy and even in name. In 1947 it was known as The Sadler's Wells Theatre Ballet, which in 1956 was changed to The Royal Ballet (Touring Section) – usually referred to as the Touring Company. In 1970 it became the New Group and since 1976 it has been established as Sadler's Wells Royal Ballet.

The Company's first title, 'The Sadler's Wells Opera Ballet', was unpretentious but temporarily appropriate, for its first appearance at Sadler's Wells was in Smetana's opera *The Bartered Bride*, on Boxing Day 1945, nearly two months before the main Company made its début at Covent Garden. The real opening, on 8 April 1946, could hardly have been happier. Margaret Dale, and Norman Thomson from Canada, were borrowed from Covent Garden to dance *Casse-Noisette, Act III*. De Valois' *Promenade*, a cheerful divertissement to a Haydn score created three years earlier, gave Anne Heaton one of her first successes. *Assembly Ball*, a new work by Andrée Howard, from the Ballet Rambert, now Resident Choreographer, was also light and pretty. A characteristically fluent and musical ballet, arranged to Bizet's Symphony in C, it was charmingly danced by June Brae, returning after a five-year absence. Also in the cast were Leo Kersley, who had started with Rambert but had joined the Sadler's Wells Ballet in 1941, and Claude Newman, who had returned from war service. The ballet proved to be one of the most popular in the new troupe's repertoire, a winner at first strike. The evening was received with enthusiasm and it was noted that this time de Valois' dancers had succeeded without any outside help in the form of guest celebrities, such as Markova or Dolin.

Alternating with the Opera, the Company gave four performances in April and five each in May and June, adding small-scale classics such as *Les Sylphides* and *Le Spectre de la Rose* (with Kersley and Brae) to the repertoire. In May came a new ballet, *Khadra*. Choreographed by Celia Franca, another of Rambert's pupils who had been a Sadler's Wells Ballet principal since 1941, it was a Persian study arranged to music from Sibelius's

Khadra, created for the Theatre Ballet in 1946 by Celia Franca, with décor by Honor Frost.

'Belshazzar's Feast', with striking designs by Honor Frost. Soon afterwards the Company embarked on a month's provincial tour which ended close to where it had started: in the open-air theatre in Finsbury Park, London. The autumn season at Sadler's Wells saw rather more performances, including three new works: two of them choreographic débuts, *The Catch*, a pas de trois by Alan Carter, and *The Vagabonds*, a drama adapted by Anthony Burke from a poem by Thomas Hardy. The third, Andrée Howard's *Mardi Gras*, was a nightmare fantasy which brought to light two dancers who were to become principals, Nadia Nerina and Donald Britton. The Company was already beginning to develop a character of its own, with strong performances of a variety of works which included plenty of new material; already it was acting as a pool of future talent for the main Company: John Cranko, Kenneth MacMillan and Peter Darrell, all future choreographers, were among its original dancers.

The fluctuating fortunes of the Company while it was finding its feet and its proper function were evident in the nature of its activities. In its first year it had actually spent less time in the provinces than the Covent Garden Company, but during 1947 as well as offering forty-nine performances at Sadler's Wells it presented fourteen weeks of provincial touring. During this time two works were added to the repertoire. One of them, *Adieu*, though only a trifle, was the first production for the Company by a choreographer who was soon to become famous, John Cranko; the other was to prove successful enough to be taken later into the Covent Garden repertoire. This was Andrée Howard's *La Fête Etrange*, originally created for the small London Ballet during the war. Conceived by Ronald Crichton, it was a mysteriously haunting evocation of the betrothal party described in Alain-Fournier's novel, 'Le Grand Meaulnes', with a snowy setting by Sophie Fedorovitch and wistful music by Fauré. June Brae was the tragic chatelaine and Donald Britton her rustic admirer. At the time not everybody was convinced of its value. 'If this work is to survive it needs drastic cutting,' wrote Arnold Haskell: but its fragile lyricism was to prove inexplicably enduring. Another ballet added to the Sadler's Wells repertoire was Ashton's romantic *Valses Nobles et Sentimentales*, arranged to the Ravel music which he had used for Rambert's company fourteen years earlier in his *Valentine's Eve*. As then, Fedorovitch was the designer, providing a simple but evocative décor of screens which intermittently hid the dancers led by Anne Heaton, Donald Britton and Michael Boulton.

All through 1948 the Company was presenting one or two performances a week at Sadler's Wells, mostly at Saturday matinées, with ten weeks of touring. New ballets were few that year, but there were several revivals, the most important being Ashton's *Les Rendezvous*, first presented on Boxing Day 1947, which gave an opportunity for the Australian-born Elaine Fifield to display her technical prowess. *Capriol Suite* was another of Ashton's small pieces originally composed for the Rambert company and now happily revived – simple but clear, strong, and apt. None of the new works had much to add: the most substantial was *Selina*, a send-up by Andrée Howard of conventional nineteenth-century romanticism, with a deliberately preposterous story and some subtle satire. The costumes were designed by Peter Williams, later Editor of *Dance and Dancers*. The leading male role was danced by Hans Zullig, a gifted Swiss who had been a principal dancer of the Ballet Jooss in Essen, but contrived to change from this 'modern dance' background to the classical idiom with surprising ease.

In the summer of the following year, 1949, a major development was the introduction of Act II of *Le Lac des Cygnes* in the original Vic-Wells production. This was a test piece which would reveal the Company's technical standards. The première, in the little Arts Theatre in Cambridge, passed off well. Fifield danced Odette with striking success, smoothly partnered by David Poole, a South African who had entered the Company in 1947. With only four huntsmen in pursuit of eight swans and four cygnets it was a miniature production, but it worked. Beriosova, who joined the Company after the collapse of the short-lived Metropolitan Ballet (founded in London in 1947), was to make her Sadler's Wells début in it as Odette. In 1949 touring included a week at Stratford-upon-Avon, previously a frequent date for the main Company; and the Theatre Ballet made its first appearance on a foreign stage at the Gaiety Theatre in Dublin, where it premièred *Sea Change*, a sombre study of fisher-folk by Cranko with designs by John Piper. It included the first leading role created for David Blair and a strong part for a young Spanish dancer, Pirmin Trecu. Cranko also contributed an extended pas de deux on the old theme of *Beauty and the Beast*, arranged to Ravel's 'Mother Goose' suite. The year ended with a new departure, a mammoth season at Sadler's Wells which was to continue well into 1950 – eight months of regular appearances totalling sixty performances.

In the spring the one new ballet was *Summer Interlude*, a slight but charming little romance by Michael Somes, his only piece of choreography. On 15 May the Company took part in the gala which celebrated the twenty-first birthday of the Sadler's Wells Ballet, the programme opening with many of the original cast in *The Haunted Ballroom* and including *A Wedding Bouquet* in which de Valois performed her old part of Webster – with the pointwork removed. After a short 'summer interlude' of provincial touring, the Company reassembled for another lengthy season at Sadler's Wells, over nine consecutive months at their home theatre. During the first part of this season a major addition to the repertoire was planned. That summer New York City Ballet had been in London, and the opportunity had been taken to ask Balanchine to write a new work specially for Sadler's Wells Theatre Ballet. This was part of an exchange: Cranko had created for New York City Ballet a new work, *The Witch*, to Ravel's Piano Concerto in G. It had been performed only twice and then withdrawn owing to difficulties over the musical copyright. Balanchine fulfilled his part of the bargain with *Trumpet Concerto*, to music by Haydn, first presented in Manchester in September. Alas, the result was far from a triumph. Balanchine had seized on the military suggestions in the music to devise geometrical manoeuvres as stiff and dry as those depicted in some old German print. It was a disappointment, and the ballet soon had to be dropped. But the next year, 1951, was to offer a succession of successes. First came an over-hasty revival of de Valois' *The Prospect Before Us*. Without the hilarious presence of Helpmann, who appeared as Guest Artist in only three performances, and in spite of some inspired clowning by Stanley Holden, a gifted young character dancer, it proved too complex for the Company. But it was soon followed by Cranko's *Pineapple Poll*, one of the most successful of all the Theatre Ballet's productions. It is a translation into dance of W. S. Gilbert's 'The Bumboat Woman's Story' to music drawn from several of Arthur Sullivan's operettas (which had just been released from copyright) and arranged by Charles Mackerras. The news that the music, which had previously been the monopoly of the D'Oyly Carte Opera Company, was going to be used for a ballet had caused such alarm that Miss D'Oyly Carte herself invited de Valois to lunch in order to discuss it. She looked doubtful when she was assured that if the ballet were a success it would pre-empt all further attempts. De Valois' forecast was to prove right: there has never been another. *Pineapple Poll* has been performed so often that its novelty may have worn off but its durability is based on solid virtues. Light entertainment is as difficult and risky a genre in ballet as it is in other media, but Cranko managed to seize on the Gilbert and Sullivan formula of one part sentiment to six parts joke and infuse it with a bubbling vitality all his own. Osbert Lancaster, famous for his witty cartoons, struck just the right note in his designs, and the comic-strip characters have provided several generations of dancers with demi-caractère parts which fit the style of the Company perfectly. In its breezy way, this is one of the most perfect British answers to Diaghilev's demand for a true marriage of the three components of a ballet – dance, music and design. The opening dancers were Fifield as the saucy little Poll, Blair as her gallant pin-up ideal and David Poole as her sentimental Pot Boy admirer. They may have been equalled since, but they have never been bettered.

Only seven weeks later another major contribution from the same choreographer had its première, *Harlequin in April*. Commissioned for the Festival of Britain, this was very different from *Pineapple Poll*. Taking as inspiration the opening lines of T. S. Eliot's poem *The Waste Land* ('April is the cruellest month, breeding/Lilacs out of the dead land . . .',) Cranko devised an obscure but moving allegory, with romantically ragged designs by Piper and a commissioned score by Richard Arnell, in which 'Harlequin completes full circle and embraces the winter of death without having achieved his ideal'. This oblique approach, full of hints and symbols which were never made explicit, represented a new phase in Cranko's development and opened up an alternative to the rather rigid abstract or narrative formulae into which ballets were tending to fall. Blair gave a moving account of the aspiring young Harlequin-hero, with Patricia Miller as his ideal Columbine and Stanley Holden as the obstinately earthy Pierrot.

LEFT John Cranko with Margaret Knoesen, in costume for a performance of *Sweeney Todd*.
RIGHT *Pineapple Poll*, 1951, with Elaine Fifield as Poll.

Two revivals filled out what was to be a bumper year, preparing the Company for its most important tour so far – to Canada and the United States in the autumn. One was *Coppélia*, in the original Sergeyev production but with new designs by Loudon Sainthill. It was the first full-length work to be tackled by the Theatre Ballet, and was a considerable trial of strength. There were three accomplished Swanildas in Fifield, Beriosova and Maryon Lane; three lively Franzes, with Blair, Trecu and Britton; and a brilliantly individual pair of toymakers, Holden and Poole. The other revival was more unusual – a version of *Casse-Noisette* by Ashton which missed out the Christmas party in Act I altogether, turning the work into a set of divertissements, with a chaste white décor and costumes by Cecil Beaton. The result was over-refined, in spite of good dancing by Beriosova in the Snowflake scene and Fifield as the Sugar Plum Fairy.

Both of these ambitious new productions were launched at Sadler's Wells within a week of each other just before the Company sailed for North America. After dancing in three cities in Canada – Quebec, Montreal and Toronto – they embarked on a six-month tour of the United States which took in no less than sixty-three cities, often for one night stands, with only one week's break, at Christmas, in Los Angeles. It was a gruelling operation but of the kind which knits a company together as a team. One hundred-and-eighty performances in a row, many more than the total given during the whole previous year, not only shook down the organisation but gave the dancers irreplaceable experience in their roles, appearing night after night in front of new and widely differing audiences.

Harlequin in April, with Patricia Miller as Columbine.

After an unnervingly cool reception on the opening night in Quebec, audiences were enthusiastic and reviewers praised what they took to be a team of teenagers. 'We had come to accept as normal ballet dancers of a middle-aged twenty-six or even a totally senile thirty-two. The new Sadler's Wells brings back the litheness, simplicity and artistic innocence that prevail when no one in a ballet company is a split second older than twenty.' The Company as a whole was thought to compare well with its Opera House counterpart, 'different in personnel and in repertoire rather than in quality'. Fifield's sparkle was universally acclaimed; Beriosova was especially praised in *Le Lac des Cygnes*; and one critic wrote that Blair was 'touched by Destiny'. *Pineapple Poll* was a favourite everywhere, almost equalled by *Coppélia*, 'as crisp, gay and charming as a lace-edged old-fashioned nosegay'. The more serious critics were impressed by *Harlequin in April*. The only unenthusiastic responses were in San Francisco and Chicago and to a lesser extent New York, where the Company arrived exhausted at the end of its six-months' tour to appear on a tiny stage in the huge and unattractive Warner Theatre.

On their return to Britain at the beginning of April 1952 the dancers, not unreasonably, were allowed two weeks off. They spent the summer at Sadler's Wells, performing now about five times a week. A big asset during this season was the restoration of de Valois' *The Rake's Progress* to the Company and to the Sadler's Wells Theatre for which it had been created. With Alexander Grant as a powerfully moving Rake (Blair was to take over the part on tour) and Sheilah O'Reilly as the Betrayed Girl, the ballet recovered the impact

Members of the Theatre Ballet 'relaxing' on the beach at Miami, Florida, during their 1952 tour of the United States and Canada.

which had been partly lost during its time in the Covent Garden repertoire. The summer of 1952 ended with a week at the Edinburgh Festival during which the indefatigable troupe mounted a new work, a short and, alas, short-lived, piece by Cranko called *Reflection.*

The Company was now mainly directed by Peggy van Praagh, who from the outset had been an active influence as Ballet Mistress, since Ursula Moreton had taken over an additional responsibility as Director of the Sadler's Wells School and consequently found her interests beginning to move towards teaching. Van Praagh had an unlucky start. If 1951 and 1952 had been rich years for the Company from the creative point of view, the next twelve months were something of a trough. Two new choreographers were introduced, Margaret Dale (*The Great Detective*, her first ballet, featuring MacMillan as Sherlock Holmes) and the more experienced Walter Gore (*Carte Blanche*), but neither had much success. The most striking new production was Alfred Rodrigues' *Blood Wedding.* This was a genuinely powerful piece in which the brooding story, based on a play by Garcia Lorca, was matched by Denis ApIvor's score, with sets and costumes by Isabel Lambert. Fifield was the Bride, fought over by Poole and Trecu, while MacMillan and O'Reilly as the Moon and Death looked on.

Extensive touring was clearly making the creation of new ballets difficult. During April 1953 the Company went overseas again to Belgium, Germany and Holland. In July a new continent was invaded when ten days were spent at Bulawayo in Rhodesia, a country which has contributed several notable dancers to The Royal Ballet. September saw a visit, now almost an annual event, to the Edinburgh Festival. All these excursions were in addition to forays into the Midlands and Wales. It was on a visit to Oxford in the following February, 1954, that another resounding success was launched. *The Lady and the Fool* was a romantic follow-on by Cranko to his comedy-hit *Pineapple Poll*, and it proved equally popular. The tale of a famous beauty's love for a forlorn clown, it was set to music from several of Verdi's operas, again arranged by Mackerras, and offered openings for comedy and spectacular ensembles as well as tender pas de deux. The key roles of the pathetic pair of clowns were movingly danced by MacMillan and Johaar Mosaval, who had joined the School from South Africa, with Patricia Miller as the glamorous Capricciosa, the first of many. The choreography was not particularly notable, but Cranko's sense of theatre was always evident. Even today it still rarely fails to grip and amuse audiences.

There were very few performances at Sadler's Wells this year – only thirty in all. The whole of June and part of July were spent in South Africa, and this excursion was followed by four months in the provinces, the conditions of which were tough. In those days dancers received no touring allowance and could rarely afford to stay in a hotel; though theatrical 'digs' were plentiful they were certainly not luxurious. It was unheard of to own a car, and difficult to take a break either at home or in London. The long hours spent together in draughty rehearsal halls and on sluggish Sunday trains fostered a group-identity, magnified by the main advantage of this nomadic life – frequent performances before a wide variety of audiences who were less specialised than the dance-addicts of the capital, and who accepted ballet as just another form of theatrical entertainment. In these gruelling but exhilarating conditions the dancers grew up fast both artistically and theatrically.

The New Year of 1955 found the Company in London and almost at once recording another success with *Danses Concertantes*. This was MacMillan's first professional ballet, a startlingly confident work and an important landmark in his development. It was an abstract suite to astringent Stravinsky music with angular designs by Georgiadis. The debt to Balanchine was clear but the way in which MacMillan paid it was different from that of Ashton in his *Scènes de Ballet*: more eccentric, with a quick, wry invention which was to reappear often in later ballets. Again the Company spent most of its time in the provinces, penetrating as far afield as Glasgow in Scotland and Llandudno in Wales and twice crossing over to Dublin, but it gave only thirty-four performances in London. These included a striking new ballet by MacMillan, *House of Birds*, an adaptation of a characteristically alarming fairy-tale by the Grimm brothers with sadistic overtones.

The Lady and the Fool, 1954. Johaar Mosaval as Bootface,
Kenneth MacMillan (right) as Moondog.

Georgiadis's designs, especially the costumes with a sharp-beaked witch and captive girls with cages around their heads, contributed to the menacing mood.

That summer of 1955 was a watershed in the history of the Sadler's Wells Theatre Ballet, bringing a sharp change in its policies. At the end of the season Peggy van Praagh resigned as Director. An active, practical character with some of de Valois' brisk and unassuming authority and an instinctive sympathy with the humblest dancer, she had successfully led the Company through its vitally important early days, and had strongly influenced its independent character. She was later to become Director of The Australian Ballet. Until now the size of the Theatre Ballet had remained relatively small with about thirty dancers, just enough to put on a small-scale classic such as *Coppélia*. However, since it was becoming more and more difficult for the Covent Garden Company to tour the

On tour in the North of England, 1966.

provinces owing to its size and its other commitments, it was decided that the smaller troupe should be enlarged sufficiently to take major works such as *Le Lac des Cygnes* and *The Sleeping Beauty* to the provinces. One result of the new arrangement was the fact that the Company's dancers would now rarely be available to perform with the Sadler's Wells Opera. A special group was therefore set up to appear with the singers under the direction of Peter Wright, who had enjoyed wide experience with the Ballet Jooss, the Metropolitan Ballet and other companies before joining Sadler's Wells in 1949. The successor to van Praagh was John Field, one of the senior principals of the Covent Garden Company who at thirty-five was ready to move away from dancing. He took over at very short notice and without a break in his activities; on 4 January he was dancing Prince Siegfried in *Le Lac des Cygnes* at Covent Garden and on 5 January he joined his new colleagues at Stratford-upon-Avon, where he found himself, somewhat to his alarm, immediately involved in a strange nineteenth-century production of *Coppélia* which made him wonder what he had taken on. But it was an auspicious place in which to begin; Stratford was always a favourite venue, for not only was the theatre convenient and modern but there was always good accommodation in the town.

Field's brief from de Valois had been characteristically vague. 'Do something about the classics', he had been told. This did not involve much new training, for classical ballets such as *Coppélia*, *Les Sylphides* and *Le Lac des Cygnes, Act II* were already in the repertoire. The number of dancers, however, had gradually to be almost doubled, rising from about thirty to nearly sixty. After a long tour in the provinces, the Company returned to Sadler's Wells at the end of May 1956 for a season, a short one of only twenty performances. One of them included the première of what was to be another immensely popular ballet by Kenneth MacMillan, *Solitaire*. MacMillan was in the process of taking over as principal choreographer from John Cranko, who was widening his sphere of activity in the theatre, including the creation of a revue entitled 'Cranks'. *Solitaire*, described in the programme as 'a kind of game for one', explored the feelings of a young 'outsider' (danced by Margaret Hill), a theme which was to permeate MacMillan's later ballets. The melodious score by Malcolm Arnold and airy designs by Desmond Heeley gave the work hints of whimsical sentimentality, but the sophisticated wit of the movement was individual and appealing.

MacMillan's first-ever ballet, *Somnambulism*, set to a jazz score, was also shown during these weeks. It had been tried out three years before with the Sadler's Wells Choreographers' Group – a short-lived venture organised by David Poole which was to be succeeded in 1967 by the Royal Ballet Choreographic Group, a more regular and influential organisation run by Leslie Edwards, in whose programmes several choreographers have made their début. *Saudades*, a pseudo-Oriental piece which Rodrigues had created the previous October while the Company was on tour, did not prove to be successful. In contrast was the new *Coppélia* with its updated designs by Robert Medley, which some people found drab. When it came to presenting the classics the Company was still small. Field himself was the most experienced classical partner and during the first year he continued to dance until his responsibilities as organiser, teacher and producer made it impossible. His team in those early days included Anne Heaton, Margaret Hill, Sara Neil, Elaine Fifield, Donald Britton, Michael Boulton, Walter Trevor, Alexander Bennett, Doreen Tempest and Miro Zolan, and several names among the corps de ballet were later to become well-known, among them Lynn Seymour, Donald MacLeary, Bryan Lawrence and Susan Alexander.

The Company's first tour under Field's direction was very successful and in August it was received with acclaim when it appeared at the Santander Festival in Spain, where it mounted *Giselle* with Nadia Nerina as Guest Artist. But complications – indeed disaster – threatened. When Field had taken over, David Webster had warned him that he might be 'joining a sinking ship'. Funds, as usual, were alarmingly low. Sure enough, early in 1956 Sadler's Wells, which was going through a financial crisis, decided that it could no longer afford to maintain the Ballet Company, which was losing £6000 a year. Covent Garden acted immediately. 'Come back to us and bring all your dancers with you', Webster telephoned to Field. 'I don't know how we'll raise the money; but let's try.' In this moment of duress a new, closer relationship between the two companies was conceived. By November 1956 it was an accomplished fact.

When, during that month, the Royal Charter was signed, by which the Sadler's Wells Theatre Ballet was formally linked to the newly designated Royal Ballet, the Company was performing in Glasgow. It was now referred to as the 'Touring Section of The Royal Ballet' and during that autumn and winter and in the spring of 1957 it certainly earned the title, accomplishing a nine-month non-stop stint around Britain, then overseas for a long season in Spain, Germany, and Switzerland, ending up in Holland. This hard but rewarding tour was completed on the Company's return in July by what proved to be its last visit for many years to its old home theatre – before it moved, for the last week of 1957, to Covent Garden.

The short season at the Royal Opera House opened on Boxing Day with two new works, *The Angels* by Cranko, which proved short-lived, and Peter Wright's *A Blue Rose* which enjoyed a modest success. A third, MacMillan's *The Burrow* – introduced soon after – was not only interesting in itself but full of portents for the future. It showed the choreographer in a new mood – sombre, dramatic, factual – which was to colour many of his later works. Inspired by, though not actually based on, the war-time diary of Anne Frank, a young Dutch victim of the Nazis, *The Burrow* was set in a besieged attic, the claustrophic atmosphere of which was vividly created by Nicholas Georgiadis, with Anne Heaton giving a powerful performance as a trapped woman. The ballet also introduced, as the adolescent girl, a young Canadian-born dancer, Lynn Seymour, who was later to be the heroine of many of MacMillan's productions. Donald MacLeary was her sensitive lover, and Donald Britton appeared as a harshly irritating character called 'The Joker'.

Ironically, the year in which, under the new Charter, the Sadler's Wells Theatre Ballet was grafted more closely onto the Royal Opera House organisation, had clearly proved the Company's artistic individuality. It was naturally given identical billing with the main Company, a well-meant gesture emphasising the equal (or nearly equal) status of the two troupes, but one which led to widespread confusion and sometimes to complaints. Provincial theatre managements, understandably wishing to promote the well-known title of 'Sadler's Wells Ballet', tended to ignore or play down the new title of 'Royal Ballet' on their playbills – a situation which was to be reversed in later years. For some time, hoping to get the best of both worlds, the Company was actually advertised as 'The Royal

---

Coppélia. ABOVE Model for Act I, 1954, by Osbert Lancaster.
BELOW The 1979 production, designed by Peter Snow, with Marion Tait as Swanilda,
David Ashmole as Franz.

Ballet (formerly Sadler's Wells Theatre Ballet)'. Inevitably the touring dancers came to be called 'The Second Company', a title sternly discouraged officially, but popularly used for many years.

The year 1958 saw the Touring Company embarking on yet another round of regional tours with only a very short season in London during June and July, when there were four performances at Covent Garden, including the Company's first presentation of a full-length *Le Lac des Cygnes*. In the ballerina role was the New Zealand-born Rowena Jackson, seconded from the Covent Garden Company, whose brilliant technique gave a special sparkle to the Black Swan (her thirty-two fouettés were dazzling) while Philip Chatfield, also from Covent Garden, proved a strong partner. The ultimate test of presenting a full-length classic in the Opera House had been surmounted with honour. But the high point of the year was another major overseas tour – thirty-four weeks in Australia and New Zealand, presenting one hundred and thirty-eight performances. It opened with a prodigious eight-week engagement in Sydney, the repertoire including *Le Lac des Cygnes*, *Giselle* and *Coppélia* and favourites such as *The Rake's Progress* and *Pineapple Poll*, as well as a variety of short works ranging from *Les Sylphides* to *The Burrow*. Helpmann, as Guest Artist, helped to draw in the crowds, especially in a revival of his *Hamlet*, and dancers such as Beriosova, Linden, and Blair strengthened the team. The season in Sydney was followed by another eight weeks in Melbourne during which Seymour and MacLeary formed a much-acclaimed partnership in *Le Lac des Cygnes*. After visits to Adelaide and Brisbane the Company flew on to New Zealand. Helpmann had left, but they were joined by Fonteyn and Somes and enjoyed tumultuous receptions. On the final night in Wellington enthusiasm was so great that during the last Act of *Giselle* a hired limousine had to be driven into the theatre through the scenery gates at the back of the stage. When the performance was over, Fonteyn and Field got into the car, the streets to the airport were cordoned off, the gates were opened and the car, ringed by police, edged out through cheering crowds who banged on the windows and ran behind it until it slowly disappeared from their sight.

On the Company's return to London in May 1959 at the end of the tour, it embarked on a two-month provincial tour, followed by its June holiday. In August it was back at Covent Garden to take part in a new experiment, a season shared with the main Company. The venture was not a great success. There were some changes of repertoire and a few exchanges of dancers – for example six corps de ballet dancers were swopped at regular intervals – but as a rule each Company offered its own works. The dancing of Doreen Wells and Christopher Gable, Beriosova and MacLeary in the classics were acclaimed. *Pineapple Poll*, long absent in the provinces, had all the success of a favourite's return, and the young Lynn Seymour was highly praised. It was, however, felt that the combination of the talents of the two Companies had proved less impressive than expected and the idea of an exchange of soloists was soon found to be impractical.

The rest of 1959 was spent in the provinces. In September at the Grand Theatre, Leeds, the Company presented the largest and most prestigious of the nineteenth-century classics, *The Sleeping Beauty*, in a faithful reproduction of the 1946 Royal Opera House

The Invitation, 1960. Costume design for
the Two Older Sisters, by Nicholas Georgiadis

production. Aurora and her Prince were danced by Anya Linden and Desmond Doyle from the Covent Garden Company. Over the next few years most Covent Garden principals appeared with the Touring Company in the full-length classics and the younger dancers were often sent out to gain experience in the major classical roles. This did not mean that the Touring Company did not develop its own ballerinas – its first 'home-grown' Aurora was Susan Alexander, who was partnered by Desmond Doyle. Later exponents of the role included Doreen Wells, Shirley Grahame, Judith Maden, Jane Landon, Margaret Barbieri and Alfreda Thorogood, with Christopher Gable, David Wall, Paul Clarke and Stephen Jefferies among their partners.

The acquisition of this work to the repertoire gave the troupe the status of a full-scale company, an alternative to the Opera House Company and not merely a secondary substitute, with three of the great classics in its repertoire (strangely it never presented a full-length *The Nutcracker*). Thus fortified, the Company continued through the winter on a long tour round the provinces, during which it presented another new work, Cranko's *Sweeney Todd*. How the dancers found time to rehearse is a mystery. There were classes every day, and Sundays were usually spent travelling in slow local trains, while the stage scenery followed in special trucks which served as storage space, parked overnight in local car-parks. Conditions in many of the theatres were primitive. Discipline was strict – girls, for instance, were not permitted to leave the theatre in trousers without permission. In February 1960 came a break in the gruelling and often monotonous routine with a tour of South Africa, which lasted three months and took in Johannesburg, Durban and Cape Town, with a stop-off at Pietermaritzburg. Sibley joined the Company for this trip and danced, among other roles, her first *Giselle* and her first Aurora in *The Sleeping Beauty*.

On its return to Europe the Company set off almost immediately for a three-week visit to Ireland followed by a fortnight in the provinces before opening in London for another joint season at Covent Garden. *Sweeney Todd* and *Le Lac des Cygnes*, with Doreen Wells, now the Company's ballerina, partnered by Gable and MacLeary, were the ballets most enjoyed. Three months later, at Oxford, MacMillan came up with another winner, *The Invitation*. Set in the Edwardian period to a danceable score by Matyas Seiber (who had been killed in a road accident a few months earlier) with imaginative designs by Nicholas Georgiadis, the ballet gave full rein to MacMillan's skill in exploring psychological problems. It showed with unnerving truthfulness frigidity implanted in the mind of a young girl by a violent experience. The unusual subject and the details of the narrative – girls giggling at the anatomy of statues, a squabbling married couple, and an orgasmic rape – opened up new paths for choreography and provided new opportunities for its interpreters. Passionately danced by Seymour as the girl, Gable as her innocent admirer, with Desmond Doyle as her sinister but pathetic ravisher and Anne Heaton as his neurotic wife, the ballet was an instant success. Its subject, understandably, caused some raised eyebrows; while it was being rehearsed in Sheffield a local paper reported a rumour that rape was being practised in the church hall. But in Newcastle the news that it had been withdrawn from a matinée programme, in which it had been included by mistake, produced a packed house for the evening performance. *The Invitation* was introduced to London audiences in the last days of 1960 when the Touring Company came together with some dancers from the Royal Opera House for a long season there while the rest of the main Company was away in America. After a few weeks, in February 1961, it scored another success, with Ashton's *Les Deux Pigeons* (soon to be re-named *The Two Pigeons*). Reshaping La Fontaine's fable, he

ABOVE *Danses Concertantes*, 1955. Donald Britton (at centre) with, in the back row,
Sara Neil, Maryon Lane and Annette Page. BELOW (left) *The Invitation*, 1960. Lynn Seymour as the Girl.
(Right) Margaret Hill in *Solitaire*, 1956.

transferred the action to the nineteenth century and gave it his own individual flavour, mingling comedy and sentiment. With a gentle score by Messager and pretty designs by Jacques Dupont, enhanced by the introduction of a pair of well-trained white doves, it seemed at first a lightweight, conventionally sentimental affair; but the sensitive and

The Two Pigeons (Five?) with Lynn Seymour as the Young Girl and Christopher Gable.

always musical choreography and Ashton's sure feeling for character gave it unexpected stamina. From the first it was an ideal vehicle for Seymour, using her seductive femininity and her delicate footwork rather than the dramatic power which MacMillan had exploited in *The Invitation*. The role of the fickle young artist showed off the fresh vigour of Christopher Gable. This part had been originally conceived for the older and technically stronger Donald Britton, but an injury forced Britton to be replaced, necessitating an adjustment of the character which it is hard to regret.

The Covent Garden season of 1961, which continued until the end of March, was followed by another major foreign tour. In mid-April the Company, again led by Fonteyn as Guest Artist, opened in Tokyo for a season involving appearances in three theatres in two weeks – a routine common in Japan. In one theatre the stage was nearly two and a half times wider than that of Covent Garden. Fortunately all the scenery had been specially rebuilt in Japan in extra-large sizes, to match photographs sent by air from London. Tokyo was followed by a few days in Osaka and then back to Tokyo for another week in a fourth theatre. The Company was relieved to find the taste of Japanese audiences similar to that of the British public – their applause might be less vociferous but it went on much longer. Wherever the Company danced, Field was in big demand as teacher in the local ballet schools and the dancers enjoyed a round of receptions and sight-seeing tours. The critics were impressed, especially by Fonteyn, whom they remembered from a previous visit with Somes. One writer compared her performances with those of a Noh play, while another remarked that it was not strange that 'in London they charge 5% more for her performances'. Her interpretation of *Giselle* – in which they found that the scenery 'looked like a Christmas card from the Royal Family, rich beyond expectation' – was found particularly attractive, 'symbolising with extreme purity and beauty the memory of a maiden who disappears from everybody's mind leaving only a sweet scar'.

Foreign travels at this time were frequent. After Japan, the Company made a short excursion to Hong Kong and thence to the Philippines, sponsored for the first time by a commercial organisation, the San Miguel Brewery. At the end of a month, back to Britain, in outer London and the provinces, then off again, this time to the Middle East – first to Lebanon to take part in the Baalbek Festival, where they performed *Swan Lake* (as *Le Lac des Cygnes* was now billed) with Fonteyn and Blair in the ruins of the Temple of Bacchus. This short appearance was followed by another one in Damascus to boost a British Trade Fair, with a more glamorous date on the way home, when they gave three performances in Athens in the old Roman theatre on the slopes of the Acropolis. Their schedule when they returned to Britain was more humdrum: three months of travelling around the provinces, though a treat awaited them at Christmas when they flew to Monte Carlo for a week's season in the famous Salle Garnier.

Few companies in the world could now compete with their touring record, and their hectic routine continued in 1962. Spring was spent in the provinces but at the end of May they crossed over to Dublin and then proceeded to the Continent, on a tour which took them through six countries and was to last until mid-October, with one intriguing interruption. In June they flew back from Munich to England to appear for a week at the Bath Festival in *Swan Lake Act II*, led by Fonteyn and Blair, with Yehudi Menuhin playing the violin solo. After a few days they were away again, appearing in the first Festival at Nervi, outside Genoa, this time led by Fonteyn and Nureyev, who danced their first *Swan Lake* together, this being Nureyev's first appearance with the Touring Company. A round of provincial visits completed the year, during one of which Ashton's full length *La Fille Mal Gardée* was added to the repertoire.

The tour continued without a pause into May 1963, when the Company opened at Covent Garden. This was its first appearance in Central London for almost two years and it had many new dancers to display. Among them were Doreen Wells, now its principal ballerina, Shirley Grahame, Elizabeth Anderton and a newcomer, Brenda Last, who was to become one of the most popular members of the Company. The men included Ian

LEFT *La Fille Mal Gardée*, with Brenda Last as Lise, Gary Sherwood as Colas.
RIGHT *Concerto*, 1967. Doreen Wells and Richard Farley in the Second Movement.

Hamilton, Gary Sherwood and Michael Coleman. During touring schedules, programmes were arranged as far as possible to give the young artists, most of whom arrived straight from the Royal Ballet School, a chance to acquire experience in old ballets and to try out their talents in new ones. The principals became celebrities as they returned year after year to the same theatres. There was no shortage of talent, but with the ever increasing popularity of the Company, and with the growing pressures which this involved, there were few opportunities to create new works. Since the fruitful winter of 1960/61 which had seen the birth of *The Invitation* and *The Two Pigeons* not one new ballet had been launched. In this current Covent Garden season of May 1963 the Touring Company now presented two new pieces, *Toccata* by Alan Carter, which had been created on tour the previous December, and the ephemeral *Le Bal des Voleurs* by Massine. During this season the Company was strengthened by Guest Artists – Carla Fracci from Milan with John Gilpin, formerly London Festival Ballet's leading male dancer, and Melissa Hayden of New York City Ballet with Flemming Flindt from the Royal Danish Ballet.

It was during this year that de Valois announced her retirement and was succeeded by Ashton. Field remained in charge of the Touring Company, which found its independence even more firmly established. 1964 saw the now usual round of visits to provincial theatres followed by just two appearances at Covent Garden during the special evening performances arranged to honour de Valois. On the first of these, the Company presented for the first time in London a ballet created during the spring tour by MacMillan, *La Création du Monde*. This was an interpretation of the Genesis story in the style of the currently fashionable Pop Art. But the joke did not amuse, and another disappointment had to be recorded.

However, the Company had no time to be down-hearted. An extensive tour of Northern Europe had to be completed, two months of travel which took it to Germany, Switzerland, Belgium and Holland. Finishing in Amsterdam, it proceeded to the Spoleto Festival in Italy, where it was due to mount another elaborate three-act ballet, *Raymonda*. Originally choreographed by Petipa to a score by Glazunov, it was revived and re-staged by Nureyev. Unhappily, just before the dress rehearsal Fonteyn received news that her husband, in hospital in Britain after being severely injured in an assassination attempt in Panama the previous month, had had a relapse, and she flew off to be at his side. Her place in the long and taxing role of the heroine in *Raymonda* was taken at the shortest notice by Doreen Wells who, partnered by Nureyev, had a big success. Happily Fonteyn was able to return for the last performance and to proceed to the Baalbek Festival. *Raymonda* had proved that the Company could cope very capably with this kind of super-classical Maryinsky-style choreography, but the unexpectedly sparse designs of Beni Montresor did not satisfy the choreographer, or anyone else, and the production was not retained in the Company's repertoire.

Spring 1965 found the dancers continuing their round of the provinces. During this time one new work was offered, not a very considerable one, but interesting in retrospect. *The Tribute*, set to a modern score by Roger Sessions with designs by Ralph Koltai, was a bold attempt to marry classical technique and modern-dance style, courageously tackled by its young interpreters, Patricia Ruanne, David Wall and Richard Farley. It did not prove successful, but it introduced Norman Morrice, a choreographer from the Ballet Rambert, who twelve years later was to become Director of The Royal Ballet. The Company returned to London in May for the now annual season at Covent Garden, which was longer than usual, lasting right through the summer until the holidays. An important addition to the repertoire was a new production by de Valois of *Swan Lake*. The new, freshly decorated, version was launched by a ballerina from Covent Garden, Nadia Nerina, partnered by Attilio Labis.

The winter was spent as usual in the provinces, and the customary foreign tour which covered some new ground – Finland as well as Norway, Belgium, Holland and Germany – took place in May. To open the 1966 London season in June a repertoire of reliable favourites was chosen: the new *Swan Lake*, finely led by Doreen Wells and David Wall; a new presentation of Act III of Nureyev's *Raymonda*, handsomely re-designed by Barry Kay and launched earlier in Finland; and some very successful performances of *La Fille Mal Gardée*. The programmes were becoming very similar to those of the main Company and another overlap appeared in the autumn when Ashton's *The Dream* was presented in Oxford with new designs by Peter Farmer, and Doreen Wells and David Wall as Titania and Oberon. These two dancers, the one slim and fair the other athletic and red-haired, had turned into the Company's best-loved partnership. In the provinces their names on the bill-board filled the theatre more effectively than any visiting celebrity from the Covent Garden Company. On one tour an outraged citizen was to complain to the local Customs and Excise Department and to claim damages under the Trades Descriptions Act because David Wall, whose appearance had been announced, did not dance on the relevant night.

In February 1967 Ashton found time to mount a short ballet for the Touring Company, *Sinfonietta*, an abstract work danced against projections of moving lights, a device much in vogue at this time in the art world, designed by students of an art college. It was memorable mainly for a long adagio section in which the heroine, Doreen Wells, was almost continuously held aloft and passed around by a group of male dancers.

Ballet formed part of a very long summer season at Covent Garden, the longest that the Touring Company had enjoyed there, with forty-four performances in a row. MacMillan at this time also chose to present an abstract work, his attractive *Concerto* with its eloquent adagio pas de deux. In 1967 there were no more new works and no foreign tour. Instead, a new rhythm of performances was instituted in the provinces throughout the winter, with a consecutive four-week season in Glasgow, Manchester and Stratford-upon-Avon, a sign of the steady growth of the Touring Company's popularity, boosted by regular visits from Fonteyn, partnered by Wall. Even smaller cities such as Bournemouth, always a 'good date', and Sunderland, now offered a fortnight's stay.

In 1968 the Opera House season was once again mostly devoted to favourite classics, with a new production of *Giselle* by Peter Wright (the changes included turning the peasant pas de deux into a pas de six) which was to prove internationally successful. Doreen Wells and David Wall danced the first performance, and the indisposition of Lucette Aldous, a tiny New Zealander who had been a ballerina with the Ballet Rambert, brought some unscheduled débuts; of Elizabeth Anderton, partnered by Wall, and then of the Touring Company's youngest partnership, twenty-one-year-old Nicholas Johnson and the twenty-year-old South African Margaret Barbieri in a highly successful performance. Aldous was later partnered by Paul Clarke, an athletic young dancer with an attractive personality who had joined the Company in 1964. He had proved himself to be a useful soloist and was taking over most of the leading roles. There were also revivals of two Massine ballets, *La Boutique Fantasque*, with Doreen Wells a rather over-refined Can-Can dancer, and *Mam'zelle Angot*, led by Lucette Aldous; both ballets had been launched in Stratford-upon-Avon earlier in the year and the zestful Massine choreography suited the Company to perfection. As soon as the season finished, the Company set out on a two-month foreign tour, which took it on a zig-zag course across Europe. The name of The Royal Ballet was now well-known abroad, but it was the Touring Company, not the one at Covent Garden, that had built up its reputation on the Continent.

On its return to Britain in the autumn the Company had the experience of working with Antony Tudor, who now lived in New York but was in London to work on a revival of his *Lilac Garden* at the Royal Opera House. In November 1968 Manchester was the setting for the première of *Knight Errant*, a characteristically dry, ironic comedy based on the book by Laclos, 'Les Liaisons Dangereuses'. Unfortunately at the last minute David Wall, the lynch-pin of the whole ballet, sustained an injury, and the work, in any case somewhat over-sophisticated, did not survive long. But Field was keen to discover new choreographers in the Company instead of relying on visitors, and in January 1969 two Royal Ballet dancers, Geoffrey Cauley and David Drew – who had been 'discovered' by Leslie Edwards' Royal Ballet Choreographic Group, one of the ventures supported by the Friends of Covent Garden – were given the chance to try their hand. At Stratford-upon-Avon they produced *In the Beginning* and *Intrusion*, both interesting but immature works. These two ballets were also presented during the Touring Company's three-month summer season at Covent Garden.

ABOVE *Giselle*, 1968. David Wall as Albrecht, Doreen Wells as Giselle. BELOW *Mam'zelle Angot*, 1968. Lucette Aldous as Mam'zelle Angot, Paul Clarke as the Caricaturist, Ronald Emblen as the Barber.

After a flying five-day excursion to Cairo, where they danced in the open air at Giza by the Pyramids, the dancers set off on their usual round of the provinces. At Leeds in December 1969 they mounted Geoffrey Cauley's *Lazarus* – a rather over-delicate ballet originally devised for the Choreographic Group – with a score by Bloch. A third ballet by the same choreographer, launched when the Company was at Covent Garden in May 1970, proved disappointing. *La Symphonie Pastorale* was an old-fashioned narrative ballet, a version of André Gide's fable about a blind girl whose sight is restored with fatal results. Its chief pleasure was a touching performance by Alfreda Thorogood as the unhappy heroine. The Company was plagued by illness and accident (Elizabeth Anderton, Margaret Barbieri, Patricia Ruanne, David Wall and Kerrison Cooke all missed performances) but it managed a brave revival, de Valois' *Job*, not seen for eleven years. Cooke was a fine muscular Satan in the Dolin tradition, Nicholas Johnson stood out as Elihu, and the performance, conducted by Sir Adrian Boult, received a warm welcome. A few days later a young dancer still in his first season, the eighteen-year-old Stephen Jefferies, made a striking début in the role. The Company's last performance of the season at Covent Garden was of an all-Ashton programme – *The Dream* and *The Two Pigeons*. That summer they set out on a European tour, ending in June at Bonn in Germany where they took part in the Beethoven Bicentenary Festival, with *The Creatures of Prometheus*. Ashton, the choreographer, had boldly treated the 1801 libretto as a joke, an experiment received by the Germans with a delight which was not to be repeated when it was presented at Covent Garden four months later. Their return to England was attended by alarums, rumours and sadness, for word had leaked out that their whole future was in danger. The feeling that the two Royal Ballet Companies were overlapping had been causing concern. In any case changes were imminent: Ashton's period as Director was coming to an end and the management had decided not to extend it. Field, the Director of the Touring Company, had found himself invited to join MacMillan as Joint Director of the Covent Garden Company, an arrangement which got off to a shaky start. On top of these considerations came the scare of a financial crisis which would make the support of two large companies difficult. Eventually it was decided that the touring section in its current form should be scrapped and be replaced by a much smaller group.

With some reluctance Field fell in with the new proposals. The idea was that the 'New Group', as it was unofficially called, should consist of twenty-two soloists (there would be no corps de ballet) who would regularly be replaced from the Opera House Company and strengthened from time to time by the loan of its leading artists. The new team would not attempt the classics but would concentrate on short experimental works, and would thus offer opportunities to young choreographers without the financial risk of trying them out in London. The new team was to be under the artistic direction of Peter Wright, who had been invited to replace Field at the head of the Touring Company before the reform was announced, and who willingly agreed to give the new experiment a try. The change was to take effect at the end of the summer season. On its return home the Company gave two more weeks' performances before disbanding. In Wimbledon on 25 July 1970 it presented *Swan Lake* led by Doreen Wells. Desmond Kelly, former principal dancer with London Festival Ballet and National Ballet of Washington, deputised for the injured David Wall. It was a farewell occasion. With that performance the old Touring Company died.

Four months later the New Group was born in Nottingham. Here, in November at the Theatre Royal, the first programmes were tried out, and decidedly promising they looked.

To begin with, one of Balanchine's most outstanding ballets, *Apollo*, was transferred from the Covent Garden Company, and was finely interpreted by Keith Rosson; with it was Ashton's masterpiece, *Symphonic Variations*, performed by one of the regular London casts. The evening was completed by a new work of a far more avant-garde nature than anything hitherto attempted by The Royal Ballet, *Field Figures*, a piece specially composed by the American choreographer Glen Tetley. Until now Tetley had been known in Britain mainly for his modern-dance works for the Nederlands Dans Theater and Ballet Rambert, and *Field Figures* was revolutionary by Royal Ballet standards. Bergsma and Derman showed a ready sympathy for the new choreography, and were well matched by Kelly and Johnson. The Stockhausen score, Nadine Baylis's metallic setting and the athletic movements were defiantly modern. A few nights later the Group presented another famous work imported from the Royal Opera House repertory, Tudor's *Lilac Garden*. These were ballets that any small company would have envied. Yet another brave new work, *Checkpoint*, was launched a few weeks later in Manchester. It was a claustrophobic piece by MacMillan in which Beriosova and MacLeary crawled across walls covered with stretch-material. The result was unconvincing, but the idea was interesting and novel. The New Year, 1971, dawned on what seemed a promising experiment.

However, change and trouble were in the air. Just before Christmas John Field had

Field Figures, 1970. Desmond Kelly and Deanne Bergsma.

[233]

resigned from the Joint-Directorship, and Peter Wright found himself reluctantly taking over the administration of both companies. John Auld, born and trained in Australia, former Assistant-Director of the London Festival Ballet and Director of the Gulbenkian dance company in Lisbon, was invited to join as Assistant to MacMillan, to relieve Wright of some of his burden. Peter Clegg, who had joined the Sadler's Wells Ballet in 1946, was appointed Ballet Master to the New Group. Meanwhile this troupe was encountering difficulties. As might have been foreseen, the avant-garde ballets were not very popular with provincial audiences who were little accustomed to modern dance. From The Royal Ballet people expected the classics, and attendances fell off. Shrewdly, the next production for the Company, launched in Norwich in February, was something very near to a revue number. *The Grand Tour* was by Joe Layton, an American choreographer and director who had worked in many musicals. Arranged to music by Noël Coward (who attended one of the performances), the ballet was an evocation of the 1930s, with the dancers impersonating celebrities of the period – a witty entertainment carried out with manifest enjoyment against a clever shipboard Art Déco design. Gary Sherwood and Deirdre O'Conaire entangled their cigarette-holders as Noël Coward and Gertrude Lawrence; David Drew was Bernard Shaw, Doreen Wells and Paul Clarke impersonated Mary Pickford and Douglas Fairbanks Senior, Nicholas Johnson appeared as a dumpy Gertrude Stein and Vyvyan Lorrayne was disguised as an elderly American passenger. Two more useful small-scale ballets from the Covent Garden repertoire were also added, MacMillan's *Diversions* and Ashton's *Monotones 2*. But the programmes were mainly composed of survivals from the old repertoire such as *The Rake's Progress*, *Les Patineurs* and *Pineapple Poll*, now made possible by increasing the size of the company to thirty-four dancers. The New Group was still half-wedded to the old. When it came to London for its summer season it was to Sadler's Wells Theatre, the birthplace which it had not visited for fourteen years. Here the Tetley ballet received respectful notices while Layton's *Grand Tour* was regarded with compensatory amusement; and *Las Hermanas*, a melodramatic work based on a Lorca play, by MacMillan (composed for Stuttgart eight years previously), enabled the Company to show its acting powers, an opportunity seized with relish, especially by Seymour. Cauley and Drew were both given the chance to produce new works, but neither hit the target.

After a lengthy rehearsal period the Group went on tour in the autumn, opening at Wimbledon with two short ballets by another American, the choreographer who was later to turn film director, Herbert Ross. His *Caprichos* was already over twenty years old and looked it. However, *The Maids*, a weirdly imaginative translation into dance of Jean Genet's play – with Nicholas Johnson and Kerrison Cooke portraying the two servant girls without benefit of female costume, as Genet had prescribed – remained as disturbingly theatrical as it had been when it was first produced fourteen years earlier. The tour finished in mid-December, followed by a long pause for rehearsals, and the Group did not perform again until two months later, February 1972 in London. The new schedule reflected its new character. Under the revised system there was more rehearsal time, less foreign touring, and a couple of seasons a year at Sadler's Wells. Emphasis now was on new productions and in fact this year saw the introduction of a large number of novelties, few of which, unfortunately survived. The first was *O.W.*, a strange and abortive new ballet by Joe Layton, in which the voice of Sir John Gielgud was heard intoning Oscar Wilde's 'De Profundis' while Michael Somes appeared, surprisingly but very effectively, as

Grosse Fuge, 1972. Lois Strike and Paul Clarke.

the maturely florid writer. On 25 February a midnight matinee, organised by the dancers themselves at a moment's notice in a spontaneous gesture to help the financially-threatened Sadler's Wells Theatre, raised over £7000. The most substantial new ballet this year was *Grosse Fuge*, introduced at Golder's Green in North London in April. A bold abstract arrangement to a Beethoven score – one of the few successful ballets with music by this composer – created the previous year by Hans van Manen for the Nederlands Dans Theater, it was notable for the fact that the men (all eight dancers had equal billing in the programme) wore oriental-type skirts. The strong rhythms of *Grosse Fuge* seemed to fit the Group ideally. After a two-month trip overseas the season ended with an appearance with the English Opera Group at the Aldeburgh Festival in Suffolk. After the holidays, followed by four performances to fill a gap at Covent Garden, the Group was back at Sadler's Wells where it presented two more ballets, making a total of six new works in one year. Unfortunately no one seemed to like MacMillan's *The Poltroon*, and Ronald Hynd's *In a*

Card Game, 1973. Stephen Jefferies as the Joker.

Summer Garden, pleasant though it was, did not last long. The most striking addition to the New Group's repertoire in this highly productive year was *Triad*, taken over from the main Company. Its modest scale made it an excellent addition to the Group's programmes.

In the spring of 1973 yet more novelties were added to the repertoire, and this time they were mostly successful. At Stratford-upon-Avon in February Balanchine's sparkling 1956 *Allegro Brillante*, an abstract arrangement to Tchaikovsky's Third Piano Concerto, was introduced, a major test of classical dancing for ten performers led by Vyvyan Lorrayne and Barry McGrath. It demanded a somewhat sharper virtuosity than the Group could at present muster, but it stood as a clear sign that the modern trend was beginning to be modified in favour of classical revivals. However, a few days later a dashingly experimental and decidedly successful short work was launched, another piece by van Manen. This was *Twilight*, an odd flirtation-cum-confrontation set to a score by John Cage for 'prepared' piano, in which, halfway through the ballet, the girl shed her high-heeled shoes. Van Manen had composed it, like his *Grosse Fuge*, for Nederlands Dans Theater and it was now performed with electric vitality by Patricia Ruanne and Paul Clarke. It came to London in the spring season at Sadler's Wells, together with *Tilt*, a third piece by van Manen. This was an intriguing series of dances set to Stravinsky's String Concerto in D

Rudolf Nureyev, Lois Strike, Lynn Seymour
and Anya Evans in *Apollo*.

(played twice) in which three pairs constantly kept exchanging partners and choreography.

In August the New Group, now a greatly enlarged team of forty dancers led by Seymour and MacLeary with Nureyev as Guest Artist, travelled to Israel. The tour opened in intense heat in Jerusalem; a few days later in Tel Aviv a revival of Balanchine's *Prodigal Son* with Nureyev as the Biblical hero was launched. This ballet, with its strong central male role, had been revived for the Govent Garden Company in January and was to prove a rewarding addition to the New Group's repertoire, though its venerable provenance was yet another sign that the Group was departing from its original character as a progressive pioneer. The restive atmosphere was emphasised by the sudden departure to the Festival Ballet of three of the Group's principal dancers – Patricia Ruanne, Kerrison Cooke and Paul Clarke. Coincidentally, Alain Dubreuil, a Monte Carlo-born dancer, moved from London Festival Ballet to The Royal Ballet.

Another import from Covent Garden, Cranko's *Card Game*, also stressed the male dancer, in this case Stephen Jefferies, performing as an almost alarmingly dominating Joker. Other ballets featured were old favourites like *Les Patineurs*, *Pineapple Poll*, *Façade*, and *The Rake's Progress*. In spite of strong efforts to widen the repertoire which had been made during 1973, with ten new ballets, the avant-garde image of the Company was obviously fading. This trend was underlined by a revival the following January of Andrée Howard's thirty-four-year-old fantasy *La Fête Etrange*, with Vyvyan Lorrayne as the Bride and Stephen Jefferies as the Country Boy. In the following spring, however, the Group staged another decidedly contemporary work, *Septet Extra* by van Manen, which originally had been composed for the Dutch National Ballet the previous year. Van Manen's personal style, which mixed modernity and tradition in equal parts, seemed to fit the Group comfortably. However, the ballet's rather nebulous character, set to a Saint-Saëns score, made less impression than had his previous works for Sadler's Wells. Neither of the next two productions added to the repertoire in the summer was successful. These were Ronald Hynd's *Charlotte Brontë*, a sombre piece which appropriately had its first performance in Yorkshire, and *The Entertainers*, a set of divertissements by Ashley Killar, one of the Company's young dancers. The Sadler's Wells season ended with a rousing programme to commemorate the centenary of the birth of Lilian Baylis, with Stephen Jefferies and Margaret Barbieri in *The Rake's Progress* and Brenda Last affectionately imitating de Valois in her old role as the comical parlourmaid in *A Wedding Bouquet*.

In 1974 the Group found itself with fewer touring dates than usual. There were three seasons in London and a week's excursion to Holland where de Valois was presented with the Erasmus Prize, a cash award which she promptly donated to the Royal Ballet Choreographic Group. The autumn season brought another distinctly modern ballet, *Unfamiliar Playground* by Christopher Bruce, performed to an electronic score. Bruce, a dancer-choreographer with Ballet Rambert for whom he had composed many works, seemed less at home with The Royal Ballet than with his own company, and though June Highwood attracted attention in her short solo, the work had to be counted as another disappointment. The dance-power of the Group was not in doubt – it still had the benefit of experienced artists such as Brenda Last, Margaret Barbieri, Lois Strike, Marion Tait, David Morse, Alain Dubreuil and Stephen Jefferies. But it seemed in danger of losing its strong individuality.

In the spring of 1975 a change came. First there was a tour of the provinces during which two decidedly more successful works were mounted, *Arpège*, a pleasant abstract piece by Peter Wright in a completely classical style devised originally for the Royal Ballet School; and *Shukumei*, a picturesque Japanese-cum-classical melodrama by Jack Carter, a British dancer who was now widely employed as a choreographer. The Group then found itself back for the first time in two years at the Royal Opera House, while the Covent Garden dancers were in the Far East. It successfully presented a restaging by Wright of the main Company's *Coppélia*, using the same sets and costumes, with Brenda Last and Alain Dubreuil in the leading roles. A few evenings later this was followed by *Giselle*, eloquently interpreted by Barbieri, a dramatically romantic dancer, also partnered by Dubreuil. The wheel had come full circle. Though the New Group naturally differed from its predecessor at Sadler's Wells, under the new management it had very much reverted to the old repertoire and style. For better or for worse The Royal Ballet again had two branches performing largely similar programmes. This fact was illustrated at the end of the Royal Opera House season when, after a brief excursion to Paignton in Devon, the two Companies

---

ABOVE *The Rake's Progress*. The 1970 Touring Company production, with Kerrison Cooke as the Rake.
BELOW *The Prodigal Son*, 1973. Scene 1, designed by Georges Rouault.

[238]

actually came together in the Big Top performances at Battersea. These were followed by another visit to Athens to appear in the Roman amphitheatre, with Fonteyn leading the Group. For the next date, at the Edinburgh Festival in September, they were joined by Seymour and Nureyev, Nureyev dancing – among other ballets – *The Dream*, with the young Marion Tait. In Edinburgh a new work was introduced, Peter Wright's *El Amor Brujo*, to the score by de Falla. It was dramatic if not particularly original, with Vyvyan Lorrayne and June Highwood as a sinuous pair of gypsies and Stephen Jefferies and Peter O'Brien as the somewhat histrionic lovers, one dead and the other alive. At the end of the Edinburgh visit the departure of Nicholas Johnson to the London Festival Ballet deprived the Group of one of its most dependable and versatile artists.

El Amor Brujo was also featured in the Group's autumn season at Sadler's Wells, an otherwise very traditional affair featuring old favourites such as *Les Sylphides, Les Patineurs* and *Checkmate*. Through the ensuing winter and spring months the Group was on tour, and at Stratford-upon-Avon in January 1976 one of the dancers, David Morse, composed the choreography for a short-lived ballet called *Pandora*, to a score by Roberto Gerhard, which appeared briefly in the early summer at Sadler's Wells. There was also another of Jack Carter's theatrical pieces, a version of Wedekind's *Lulu*, one of the few ballets written for Merle Park, who made a seductive siren, with Jefferies doubling as the Ringmaster and Jack the Ripper. The Milhaud score set a somewhat incongruously cheerful mood and the work fell between Grand Guignol and revue. Once again it was *Coppélia* and *Giselle* which provided the solid successes. Another trip abroad occupied the month of July, taking in the Nervi Festival, a visit to the ravishing La Fenice theatre in Venice and a performance in the open air on the Ile Sainte Marguerite at Cannes.

The concept of the New Group as an experimental outpost of the main Company was over. This was formally recognised when the Sadler's Wells dancers appeared under a new name at a gala at the theatre on 29 September 1976 to commemorate the twenty-fifth anniversary of Constant Lambert's death. The New Group became 'Sadler's Wells Royal Ballet', with an arrangement whereby it would once more be closely connected with the Islington theatre. It would not only continue to have regular seasons at 'The Wells', but there would be an additional rehearsal room specially designed for the Company, as well as wardrobe accommodation and administrative offices. Peter Wright, the Director, found himself at the head of a company of forty-five dancers, led by Barbieri, Lorrayne, Tait, Dubreuil, Kelly and two newcomers, Carl Myers and David Ashmole, a young dancer who had recently been seconded from the main Company to replace Jefferies who had left to join the National Ballet of Canada.

The new season opened with a recent acquisition, Ashton's well-loved *La Fille Mal Gardée*, with Brenda Last as Lise and Desmond Kelly as her rustic lover, Colas. A few nights later the Company presented another classical ballet which it had taken over from Covent Garden while on tour in the spring, Balanchine's *The Four Temperaments*, with Maina Gielgud, an experienced dancer who had appeared both with the Béjart Ballet and London Festival Ballet, as Guest Artist. In a season that was designed to establish the 'new' Sadler's Wells Royal Ballet Company firmly in the public mind, Seymour appeared in *Las Hermanas*

The Sleeping Beauty, 1977. Dame Ninette de Valois
with Merle Park and David Wall.

and *Concerto*, and Egon Madsen, a guest from the Stuttgart Ballet, danced the part of the Joker in Cranko's *Card Game* which had originally been created for him. Two other works also celebrated the occasion, *Summertide* by Peter Wright, a pleasantly classical-style abstract ballet, set to music by Mendelssohn, and *Rashomon*, a reworking by Lynn Seymour of the famous Japanese sex-and-violence folk-tale. Seymour's promising choreographic début was enhanced by the brilliant décor of Pamela Marre. June Highwood danced the part of the all-too-seductive wife, Desmond Kelly was her hapless husband and Robert North, borrowed from the London Contemporary Dance Theatre, a ferocious bandit.

The regional tour, which occupied the autumn of 1976 and the spring of 1977, included four two-week seasons, bookings which proved the popularity of the new organisation. This was followed by the Company's first foreign trip under its new name – three performances in Frankfurt and Luxembourg. It returned for a single week to Bournemouth where another short ballet by Seymour, *The Court of Love*, was introduced to celebrate the Queen's Silver Jubilee. This slight piece was included the following week in the opening programme of the reconstituted Company's second season at Sadler's Wells. The main new offering was *Gemini*, by Glen Tetley. Originally created for The Australian Ballet, this was a work for two couples set to Henze's Third Symphony, with designs by Nadine Baylis. Its athletic style, less exclusively 'modern' than Tetley's pieces performed earlier at Sadler's Wells, suited the four dancers, Maina Gielgud, June Highwood, Desmond Kelly and Dale Baker, an Australian dancer specially flown in from Stuttgart where he was working, to replace the injured David Ashmole. The traditional character of the Company was confirmed with performances of *Coppélia*, in which Helpmann returned triumphantly in his old role of Dr Coppélius; *Checkmate* (with Helpmann once again as the Red King), and *La Fille Mal Gardée* with Galina Samsova, the Russian-born ex-Festival Ballet ballerina, as Lise. Tradition was further emphasised in the summer, at Cambridge, when in the somewhat difficult conditions of the Big Top, Balanchine's *Concerto Barocco* was introduced. One of his most severely classical ballets dating back to 1940, it was danced to an abstract arrangement of Bach's Double Violin Concerto.

This year, 1977, in which Norman Morrice succeeded Kenneth MacMillan as Director of The Royal Ballet, saw the Sadler's Wells Royal Ballet presenting its two three-week seasons at its home theatre and making two short overseas tours. The first trip abroad, for a week in September, was at the Flanders Festival in Belgium; the second, in October, went much further afield, to Teheran and to Salonika in Northern Greece. The winter was spent in the provinces on short one-week visits. During the spring while in Stratford-upon-Avon the Company mounted MacMillan's *Elite Syncopations*. The technically demanding choreography was brilliantly performed and the atmosphere of this balletic evocation of an American ragtime dance-hall proved more convincing on the smaller stage and in the more relaxed surroundings of the Stratford theatre than it had in the majestic setting of the Royal Opera House. It was also to have a big success when the Company eventually brought it to Sadler's Wells.

Meanwhile at Birmingham in March 1978 a new young choreographer, David Bintley, who had been with the Company only two years but had already contributed to Choreographic Group programmes, was given the opportunity to devise a ballet. *The Outsider*, an Expressionist exercise evoking the days of silent films, showed welcome promise of an individual talent and it was introduced to London audiences in the Sadler's

The Outsider, 1978. Stephen Wicks as Meursault, David Morse as Dariol, Lois Strike as Renée.

Wells spring season. It contrasted strikingly with a far more sophisticated work with which it was paired, *Brouillards*, a restrained, intimate, slightly uneasy ballet of inconclusive episodes and ambiguous moods set to Debussy piano preludes by Cranko for his Stuttgart company in 1970. *Game Piano*, an eccentric experimental piece by a young choreographer, Jonathan Thorpe, who had written ballets for the Northern Ballet Theatre, was also tried out this season, while old favourites such as *Les Sylphides*, *Giselle*, *La Fille Mal Gardée* and *The Dream* were revived, and the eighty-two-year-old Massine specially rehearsed the Company for a revival of *La Boutique Fantasque*. This was certainly an echo of The Royal Ballet of earlier years.

After a two-month provincial tour, which ended with three weeks in the Big Top at Plymouth, the autumn season at Sadler's Wells saw the launching of more new works. *Take Five*, a trifle specially created by David Bintley for a gala at Sadler's Wells in September 1978 in honour of de Valois' eightieth birthday, was paired with a short piece, *6.6.78* (the date of the anniversary) by MacMillan. A few days later came *Rhyme Nor Reason*, a cheerful little ballet by another young dancer, Michael Corder. What proved to be an adventurous three weeks was completed by *Intimate Letters*, a complicated psychological ballet by Lynn Seymour, devised in a style slightly reminiscent of Antony Tudor. It was eloquently danced by Samsova in a 1905 period salon designed by Georgiadis, accompanied by a Janáček quartet played on-stage, but the dancing sank under the complicated theme and setting. The creative activity was sustained when, after three

Playground, 1979. Marion Tait as the Girl with Make-Up, Desmond Kelly (lying down) as the Youth.

months in the provinces, the Company allowed itself a full six-weeks rehearsal period, followed in February 1979 by a new production of *Coppélia*, its most reliable stand-by, which, following tradition, had its première at Stratford-upon-Avon. Thoroughly rethought by Peter Wright, it had a refreshing open-fields setting by Peter Snow contrasting with some ingenious dolls in the middle Act. Marion Tait was a crisp, almost over-sharply mischievous Swanilda, with Alain Dubreuil as Franz, and John Auld, the Company's Assistant Director, as the old Toymaker.

A few weeks later David Bintley introduced another ballet, *Meadow of Proverbs*. Like Carter's *Lulu*, it set a sombre subject – impressions of Goya's 'black' paintings – to a frivolous score by Darius Milhaud. The result was an awkward but original and inventive blend of sincere emotion and unsophisticated antics – Goya's profound pessimism was far away – which left Bintley's promise still only half fulfilled. His next work for the Company, *Punch and the Street Party*, set to the score of 'Triumph of Neptune' which Lord Berners wrote for Diaghilev in 1926, was also rather puzzling: its naïve style seemed to hark back to the Company's Old Vic beginnings. It was introduced at the 1979 Edinburgh Festival, in the Big Top, together with a striking new work by MacMillan, *Playground*, a daringly experimental piece worthy of the pioneering days of the New Group. Pursuing his interest in psychological abnormality and the situation of the alienated 'outsider', MacMillan set the action in a mental institution. Desmond Kelly, a patient, becomes involved with the plight of one of the girls, danced by Marion Tait. Performed to a dramatic score by Gordon Crosse in a cage-like setting by Yolanda Sonnabend, it was realistically mimed rather than danced, the one or two arabesques seeming inappropriate. But it was a forceful work, carrying to an extremity MacMillan's attempt to open up serious areas for the dance-theatre to explore.

In the spring season of 1980 a fresh note was introduced with *Papillon*, an affectionate send-up by Ronald Hynd of the whole nineteenth-century classical ballet tradition. In celebration of the centenary of Offenbach's death, it took the form of a new version of the composer's only ballet, *Le Papillon*, which had originally been devised by Marie Taglioni for her favourite pupil, Emma Livry, in 1860. Two years later at the age of twenty-one, Livry died after being badly burned in a stage fire, and the ballet was subsequently lost.

Parody is a dangerous weapon but this production did partly succeed, by treating the whole thing as a friendly joke and turning into caricature all the roles except those of the hero and heroine. In Britain, pantomime has already generously exploited the comic potential of Victorian drama, and though the ballet barely rose above this level of Christmas entertainment it provided a pleasant evening, with pretty tunes and attractive designs and costumes by Peter Docherty. It had been first created for the Houston Ballet in the USA, and none of the Sadler's Wells Royal Ballet's ballerinas was cast quite in the ethereal Taglioni-Livry mould, but at the opening performance Margaret Barbieri adopted the period manner very adroitly, with Jefferies extracting every ounce of comedy from the part of an amorous Shah, and Dubreuil as a balefully vain witch. The most successful sections were the passages of pure dance in scenes which recalled *La Sylphide*. The ballet was preceded in the opening programme by MacMillan's *Danses Concertantes*, with striking new designs by Georgiadis which suggested a slightly sinister Twenties night-club.

Only a week later, at Stratford-upon-Avon, Bintley introduced another new ballet, *Homage to Chopin*, a romantic piece arranged to a score by Andrzej Panufnik and distantly

LEFT *Papillon*, 1980. Margaret Barbieri as Papillon. RIGHT Peter Wright rehearsing
Alain Dubreuil and Marion Tait.

recalling *Les Sylphides*. After a Sadler's Wells season which centred on *Papillon* but
also introduced to London the new production of MacMillan's *Danses Concertantes*, the
Company continued its policy of creating new productions with Michael Corder's *Day into
Night*, first presented at the end of March in Norwich. Like his *Rhyme nor Reason*, it was a
near abstract piece, set to Martinu's cheerful 'Sinfonietta La Jolla' the core of its three
celestial sections being a double duet in the central Moon movement. In April, Galina
Samsova mounted in Bournemouth the *grand pas* from Petipa's *Paquita* in a rich setting by
Peter Farmer. Led by Samsova and Ashmole this was a successful test of the Company's
classical powers. In June at Exeter, the very young Jonathan Burrows introduced a lively
and unpretentious set of dances for eight performers, entitled *Catch*; this was the last
production of the summer season.

In retrospect, the story of the Touring Company can be seen as describing the gentle
swing of a pendulum which has left it today as an improved and enlarged version of the
organisation of 1946. The changes – first the transformation into a larger company
virtually exiled from London, then an over-violent reversion to a small experimental
group, then a slow return to its former size with much of its former repertoire – were
largely dictated by forces outside its control, centred on the main Royal Ballet organisation
at Covent Garden. The oscillation emphasises the interdependence of the two Companies
and their constant interaction. With dancers, repertoire, directors, designers, conductors
and members of the administrative staff moving constantly from one troupe to the other,
the story, particularly between 1970 and 1973, has been inextricably tangled. The fact
remains, however, that for a substantial period the Touring Company – second in time

sequence, if not in quality – operated outside London for most of the year, and it thus has acquired an independent character and reputation. Moving continually from place to place, practising and rehearsing in a variety of conditions – usually very far from ideal – performing night after night instead of at long intervals, and before widely differing audiences instead of before faithful followers, results in a close-knit group in which life outside the theatre must take a secondary place and in which loyalty is strong and natural. The simple demands of performing outweigh all other complications, and the lack of a fixed background concentrates interest on life within the Company.

Conditions have changed and are still changing, but the Company's popularity, at home and abroad, is as great as ever. In the autumn of 1980 it went to the Far East on a triumphant tour which included South Korea, the Philippines, Singapore, Malaysia, Thailand and Hong Kong, followed on its return home by an extended tour of the provinces. Back at Sadler's Wells once more, Cranko's *The Taming of the Shrew*, adapted from the Covent Garden production, was presented in a Christmas season as well as a new ballet by Bintley, *Polonia*, again to music by Panufnik.

The Company's creative impulse has never slackened, nor has its steady supply of home-grown stars. The 'Touring Company' – to use the unofficial name by which it is still often affectionately known – has its own part to play, and plays it with skill, zest and pride in the history summed up in its title, Sadler's Wells Royal Ballet.

Ballet for All

A modest little group, which was soon to launch out on its own, flourished for some years in close association with the Touring Company. It was known as 'Ballet for All'. Born in 1964, it was an educative organisation aimed at adults and teenagers, and it was the brain-child of an Oxford graduate, Peter Brinson (later to become Director of the British branch of the Calouste Gulbenkian Foundation). It grew from a series of extra-mural lectures on ballet which he gave at Oxford, Cambridge and London Universities in the late 1950s and early 1960s. These engendered a keen popular demand for information about dance, and he approached Barbara Fewster, senior teacher at the Royal Ballet School, with the idea of expanding them. She readily agreed to lend pupils to take part in travelling demonstrations, the first of which was held on 27 January 1961 at the Co-operative Hall in Peckham, with Brinson himself introducing Fewster, who conducted a 'class' for two of her pupils, Rosemary Cockayne and Keith Martin. The small group prospered and grew, and in 1963 it was presented at the King's Lynn Festival, where Belinda Wright and Jelko Yuresha gave a demonstration entitled 'The World of Giselle', tracing the growth of the Romantic ballet.

Meanwhile Brinson had approached Sir David Webster at the Royal Opera House about the possibility of setting up a formal connection with The Royal Ballet. After some discussion this was agreed, and the group was established under its new official name, 'Ballet for All' (following the style of a somewhat similar organisation 'Opera for All'). Initially its members consisted of Brinson himself – acting as administrator, author, producer, commentator and van-driver – a pianist, a stage-technician and two dancers who were changed every three months or so. When relatively important centres were visited, leading dancers were borrowed from the Touring Company whose Director, John Field, was a keen supporter and active collaborator. The first appearance of the group in its official capacity was at Portsmouth in 1964, with Brenda Last and Gary Sherwood as dancers; and over the next fourteen years it presented a long list of artists many of whom were later to become principals of The Royal Ballet Company.

Soon the number of dancers was increased to six, supported by two professional actors in place of the single commentator, with the Canadian-born Werdon Anglin as Organiser and Oliver Symons as Ballet Master. The programmes took the form of short theatrical pieces called ballet plays, scripted and directed by Peter Brinson and covering many aspects of ballet history. As well as basic demonstrations of the development of classical ballet technique and style, studies of special periods were included, and miniaturised and abbreviated reconstructions of full-scale works, such as the very popular evocations by Mary Skeaping of the eighteenth-century *The Loves of Mars and Venus*, Filippo Taglioni's *The Return of Springtime* and the original *Giselle*. They were performed on countless small stages all over the country in places which the Touring Company could never reach: from snowbound, isolated halls in the north of Scotland to mining valleys of South Wales.

Different ways of disseminating the work of the group were explored, and by 1970 it was being supported by lectures, a paperback book, and a series of television programmes. In the same year there was an interesting new development when by courtesy of the London Contemporary Dance Theatre a pair of dancers who had been trained in the modern Martha Graham style joined the group for a programme called 'On with the Dance', demonstrating the difference between the two schools of dancing. A peak in performance standards was reached when, encouraged by a generous donation from a French supporter, a reconstruction of the first Paris production of *Coppélia* was given at Richmond. In it the hero was danced by a girl, and there were handsome sets and a small orchestra. The new version was supervised by Paulette Dynalix and Lucien Duthoit who, having been trained in the Paris 'travesti' tradition, threw a new light on the ballet and on the French and Russian styles of presentation. Though important and memorable, this event revealed that the educational side of the programmes was in danger of being outweighed by its impact as pure entertainment. The popularity of 'Ballet for All' was undisputed; it was presenting over two hundred performances a year, always heavily booked and consistently showing a financial profit. But the loan of performers from the Touring Company became more and more difficult to achieve and the 'Ballet for All' engagements overlapped those of the two Companies.

Alexander Grant, who became Director when Peter Brinson resigned in 1972, concentrated his programmes more closely on illustrating the development of The Royal Ballet, but the problem of overlapping persisted and continued when, after Grant had left for Canada in 1975, David Adams, himself a Canadian, and then Adrian Grater, an ex-member of The Royal Ballet, took over. In the reorganisation following Kenneth MacMillan's resignation as Director of The Royal Ballet in 1978 the Arts Council decided that it was no longer justified in supporting the group in its current form, and it was taken over by the Royal Academy of Dancing.

10   *The School*

In de Valois' first dream of a British ballet there were three ingredients – a company, a theatre and a school, and the last came first. Her years with Diaghilev had convinced her that it was the inbred habits that we call style which provided the backbone of his most dashing experiments. Collective training, she could see, produced a harmony which was proof against individual eccentricity and the strains of change. A radical conservative by instinct, she has always believed that the future must be linked with the past. She began by nurturing roots, which in dance are put down in the student's classroom.

De Valois opened her Academy of Choreographic Art in Kensington in 1926. The fee was twenty-five shillings a week for the eight classes, six Cecchetti classes and two classes in 'composition', a kind of modern technique later christened 'plastique'. Special courses were given by two of Diaghilev's scenic artists, Vladimir Polunin and his wife, to reflect what the prospectus described as 'the growing realisation of the general knowledge a Dancer should have concerning the relation of the Dance to the Theatre as a whole'. This approach – a wide education in the arts as opposed to narrow specialisation – was de Valois' legacy from Diaghilev and was to colour her general policy. In the same way her own early training with the Italian Cecchetti, the Russian Legat and Madame Zanfretta, who had studied mime in France, shaped her plans for the teaching of dance. Her brisk empirical methods were already clearly conceived and they pervade the Royal Ballet School's teaching to this day.

The School's early years were closely bound up with the development of the Company. In the first years at Sadler's Wells de Valois and Ursula Moreton took the classes in the theatre's big rehearsal studio, now a refreshment room. Lessons were supplemented by sporadic trips for more cerebral education from a tutor in the Law Courts. When war broke out in 1939 the Company moved into the provinces but the School remained in London, superintended by Ursula Moreton, assisted by Nicholas Sergeyev. In 1940 the theatre was requisitioned as a rest centre, the administration was transferred to Lancashire and the School had to close down for three months. But after the first scare they were back at Sadler's Wells. In an attempt to rebuild the male strength of the Company scholarships were offered to likely boys. Conditions were hard. To their strenuous training routines pupils and teachers had to add slow journeys in the black-out, and when the 'flying bombs' started their practice was punctuated by much-resented interruptions while they took temporary refuge under the stage – later declared to be unsafe. But at the end of the war the school was still in full operation.

The Company's move to Covent Garden in 1946 meant finding a new home for the School and with the aid of a £5000 grant from the Arts Council a large building in Colet Gardens in the Baron's Court district of West London was purchased; to this was soon added the big house next door, where the distinguished ballet teacher Nicholas Legat once had his studios. In September 1947 the School was opened, with a modest general education added to the dance training. Arnold Haskell, a co-founder of the Camargo Society and leading supporter of British ballet in its early days, took over as Director, with

[249]

Ailne Philips (Irish-born like de Valois) in charge of the dance training. There were fifty-five pupils, all girls.

In 1948 the School, which then catered for pupils between the ages of ten and eighteen, underwent two major changes: the first batch of boys arrived and a separate home was acquired for the juniors. This permitted a large extension of numbers and a more rigorous professional approach for the older students. All the pupils at Talgarth Road (formerly Colet Gardens) are totally dedicated dance students preparing for a professional career. In spite of ever-rising fees, there is keen competition to enter the Upper School. In 1979 for example, there were two hundred and thirteen applicants out of whom forty-six were chosen, including six boys, and two more were accepted for the three-year Teacher's Course. Acceptance is the result of severe weeding out, ending in a final audition in the spring. There is no automatic limitation arising from race, colour, nationality or any other factor. By the entrance age, sixteen, almost all the applicants have had a fair standard of training; the problem is to spot the future potential. Even the entrance age is approximate, the primary requirements being average intelligence and appearance and, above all, a physique suitable for dancing: there is a rigorous physical examination.

Once accepted and established in an approved lodging (there are no boarders in the Upper School), the pupils face a routine which is as hard as in an ordinary educational institution and which is highly specialised. This is a training college, with dance, and classical ballet in particular, as the main subject. There is one class a day in academic subjects, and the pupils may – in their first year *must* – carry on their general education. The emphasis is on subjects such as music, drama and the history of ballet, with the Benesh method of dance-notation as a compulsory item. Most of the day is spent in straightforward dance training, strictly in keeping with traditional methods, with whatever modifications individual teachers may introduce from time to time. Continuity is ensured by the perpetual pupil into teacher system; occasional short visits and exchanges are made with foreign institutions, but almost all the classical ballet teachers (currently about thirteen) started their careers in the School and they return there after their time with the Company. The Company itself employs its own teachers (some of whom also still perform at Covent Garden) and they take some of the Upper School classes.

Throughout all the courses, girls are taught by women and boys by men, except in the very first lessons for new pupils, affectionately known as 'potty training'. Private lessons from outside teachers are prohibited. Special training is given in all the skills demanded today of a classical dancer, as well as the arts of mime, choreography, and stage make-up, and since 1974 there have been classes in the Martha Graham method of modern dance. Roles from the standard repertoire are studied by the senior pupils and there are courses and experimental workshops in choreography. Frequent opportunities to watch performances by The Royal Ballet are arranged, as well as occasional visits to a theatre or concert. In their last year, students in the top class are frequently called on to 'cover' roles in the corps de ballet of both Companies. The link between the School and The Royal Ballet was sealed when in the early 1950s the Company rented part of the premises for its own use as practice and rehearsal space. To begin with, strict segregation was maintained, with severe penalties for straying, or even peeping, into the 'other half', but nowadays the atmosphere is more relaxed. Students can benefit from watching professional classes and rehearsals, and they may rub shoulders in the passages with principal dancers as well as sharing the canteen.

At Talgarth Road where the senior student shades into the apprentice performer, the atmosphere is crisp and professional. In recent years new studios have been added and there is little room for the picturesque or the nostalgic. The first thing which meets the eye on entering one wing of the studios is a pile of weight-lifting equipment, and the general atmosphere is that of a gymnasium; only the incessant background noise of pounding pianos and the refreshingly slim, trim appearance of the youngsters coming and going down the corridors in a picturesque variety of practice clothes, distinguish it from a physical training establishment.

During the last few years the number of pupils in the Upper School, excluding teacher students, has fluctuated between one hundred and twenty and one hundred and thirty. Of these about one-third have 'graduated' from the Junior School, one-third have come from other schools throughout Britain and one-third are from overseas (foreign students are assessed from evidence provided by teacher's references and photographs; most of them return home at the end of the course, but about two a year are accepted into The Royal Ballet). Almost all the British pupils are assisted financially by their local Education Authorities.

Towards the end of their training, which lasts two to three years according to talent (boys are slower) the fateful moment approaches when the students' future careers are decided. There is no passing-out system. The best pupils are selected by the Directors of the two Companies for a special group known as the Graduate Class. When The Royal Ballet finds itself with vacancies they are filled from this small group. Normally the transfer takes place in the autumn, but sometimes it is at short notice. Occasionally if the School considers that the move would be premature it insists on holding on to a student for further training. Other British dance companies acquire young dancers in the same way, though The Royal Ballet always has first choice. Foreign troupes notify the School of their needs through representatives in Britain.

The employment rate of the School is high. The Royal Ballet now accepts about twelve recruits a year and ninety per cent of the remainder find places in other companies, either in Britain or abroad. The cachet of a Royal Ballet School training is a great advantage to a young dancer. For graduates from the Teacher's Course the success rate is equally high. Virtually every member of The Royal Ballet since the War has been a product of the School, and many leading dancers of foreign companies have been trained here. By agreement there is also a regular interchange of teachers with the Paris Opéra.

A feature since 1959 has been the annual School Performance, which consists of full-scale presentations of ballets, usually at Covent Garden, performed by the students exactly as they would be by the Company. The months of preparation needed for a ballet such as *Coppélia* (which with Antoinette Sibley and Graham Usher launched the series) or the full-length *Swan Lake*, *The Rake's Progress*, *The Dream* or *Concerto*, are the finest possible introduction to the routine of professional life. The experience of dancing in front of an audience is invaluable, especially since few ballets nowadays call for the troupe of child-performers which often used to be a feature of nineteenth-century productions.

It is in the annual performances that the virtues of the Royal Ballet School are most vividly demonstrated. Even an untrained eye can spot at once the uniformity of style which no amount of rigid drilling can replace – timing, the angle of the head, the emphasis in a dance-phrase, the line of arms and legs. This is the seamless material from which individual artistry can be shaped and cut. The School's training produces a way of dancing which adapts the traditional methods of Italy, France and Russia to British physique and temperament, and has become the style of The Royal Ballet, a quality which infuses every artist and gives a common identity to the two Companies. This unmistakable hallmark is slowly instilled into the students through their entire seven years' training. The final polish is applied in the Graduate Class, but the style is rooted in a process which starts with the vital primary teaching. This takes place at the Junior School, far from Talgarth Road, in surroundings which breathe a totally different atmosphere, at once sophisticated and innocent.

Looking around in 1955 for premises to accommodate the younger pupils, the Governors of The Royal Ballet lit on White Lodge, an eighteenth-century building situated in the middle of the Royal Deer Park at Richmond, a few miles outside London. This small architectural treasure – a miniature palazzo, with Palladian portico and spacious garden – belongs to the Crown. Designed by Roger Morris, it was built in 1729 as a hunting lodge for King George I and enlarged for later sovereigns. The last members of the royal family to live there were King George VI and Queen Elizabeth when they were still Duke and

Boys of the Royal Ballet Lower School at a gymnastic class, 1961, in the grounds of White Lodge.

Duchess of York. Though the handsome white-panelled rooms have now been converted for educational use, with a dance floor in the former first floor salon and two large modern dance studios added to the original building, an atmosphere of traditional elegance survives which seems entirely appropriate for a forcing-house of classical ballet.

In 1955 there were one hundred and thirty-two pupils of whom only seventy-two were boarders and only fourteen were boys. Today there are one hundred and twenty-one, of whom all except five are boarders at White Lodge. About a third of the pupils are boys, who sleep in a separate wing and take separate dance classes; the girls are accommodated in the long, low dormitories at the top of the house. For them the 'white crêpe de chine regulation dress' of de Valois' first school has been replaced by blue leotards for dance practice and dark green skirts and blazers for other classes. Pupils are accepted at the age of eleven – a few at twelve and thirteen – and, at first, dance plays only a small part in the curriculum, with only one class a day. As time goes on, dance classes gradually increase, until in their last year pupils spend about thirteen hours a week in the studios. Added to this is the study of the usual school subjects necessary to prepare them for their state-

The Royal Ballet School Annual Performance, 1967: *Swan Lake*, Act II.

approved educational examination, which is compulsory at the age of sixteen.

The atmosphere at White Lodge is much like that of a grammar school, with a shade more acceptance of discipline – a spin-off of any dance training. The boys swim, play cricket or football and listen to pop music in their spare time; the girls are more carefully nurtured, and may not participate in any activities which might disturb their physical conformation. The physique of the children is more uniform than in an ordinary school, since before being accepted for the School each child has to undergo exhaustive physical tests. Nowadays these usually include the examination of wrist-bones to ensure that no girl is likely to grow exceptionally tall, and that no boy will be exceptionally short – both serious handicaps in ballet. As few as possible are allowed to waste their youth training for a profession to which they would be ultimately unsuited. Pupils are specially encouraged to produce their own plays and concerts, and as often as possible there are excursions to watch rehearsals of The Royal Ballet. To see a row of these children sitting as quiet as mice in the darkened theatre while the stars go through the familiar sequences of *Swan Lake* or *The Sleeping Beauty* is to glimpse the thread which runs from generation to generation.

It is in the almost domestic atmosphere of White Lodge that this force of tradition becomes most palpable. The past is visible everywhere in the elegant and well-proportioned rooms, in the photographs of dancers, the prints and designs, the busts of worthies past and present which seem to proliferate in dance establishments. Beneath them the little boys and girls scamper and whisper and carry on their secret mischief like all school children, but one can feel that they are aware of the roots of history which lie under the smooth floors of the practice rooms. When each morning they troop into the studio and fall into the time-honoured formation – teacher in the centre, pupils ranged round the walls – they are taking part in a ritual performed by every dancer, boy or girl, man or woman, over three centuries: that daily homage to discipline which de Valois saw as the straight, strong trunk from which the British branch of ballet would spring. The piano strikes up, narrow shoulders straighten, slender legs bend and skimpy arms open. As they grip the barre and stretch into arabesque they seem to be holding on to the past with one hand and reaching out with the other to the future – their future, which is also that of The Royal Ballet.

Audition at the Royal Ballet School, supervised by Ursula Moreton,
Principal of the School from 1952 to 1968,
and Barbara Fewster (on left), her successor.

11 *A Structure for Dancing*

A ballet company does not consist only of dancers. Behind each performance there stands an army of administrators and technicians whose contribution can make or mar the evening as decisively as any ballerina. The scale of an organisation like the Royal Opera House is enormous. A thousand pay-slips are made out each week and of these only about one hundred and twenty are for dancers. The ballerina revolving in the Rose Adagio stands on the glittering tip of an iceberg which spreads wide and deep.

The administration and organisation of The Royal Ballet – relatively simple when it was working under the auspices of the Sadler's Wells Trust – is nowadays complex. Under the terms of the 1956 Royal Charter the two Companies became the property of the Royal Ballet Governors generally known as 'The Charter Body'. However, this Board immediately delegated its authority to the Royal Opera House Covent Garden and to the Sadler's Wells Trust respectively. In 1957 the Royal Opera House Board – acting through its General Administrator advised by a sub-Committee appointed by the Board, which meets monthly – took control of both Companies; it is this Board which appoints the Directors of the two Companies, the connecting link being the General Administrator. In theory 'The Charter Body' could, if it wished, withdraw the Companies from the Royal Opera House, though this would clearly be difficult. While the Covent Garden Company's programmes are closely interlocked with the Royal Opera House, Sadler's Wells Royal Ballet has no formal links with Sadler's Wells, Rosebery Avenue. It does however enjoy special office and rehearsal facilities rented for them by the Royal Opera House in that theatre, and it appears in Rosebery Avenue as a regular touring date.

An even greater independence is displayed in the case of the Royal Ballet School. Historically an offshoot of the Sadler's Wells Ballet, it was handed over by 'The Charter Body' to a Royal Ballet School Board and thus became completely autonomous: indeed the words 'Royal Ballet' do not even appear in the description of its purpose – 'for the education of boys and girls for the ballet'. Legally therefore it has no connection with The Royal Ballet though its primary aim is to provide both Companies with the kind of dancers they require. In fact there *is* a link, since some of its Board are appointed by the Royal Opera House. This loose arrangement in which 'The Charter Body' plays a part roughly analogous to that of a constitutional monarch is typically British, working through the simple expedient of overlapping Boards, with all real power and responsibility in the hands of one individual, the General Administrator – now called General Director – serving on both the Royal Ballet Board and the Royal Ballet School Board. Flexibility is thus coupled with stability.

The 'backroom' staff of both ballet Companies is directed by the General Administrator of the Opera House. From the public's point of view the most important are the dance staffs – the Ballet Mistress and Ballet Master, the repetiteurs, teachers and notators, not forgetting the rehearsal pianists. Vital too are those who work in the scene-painting studios, of which there are two, one in the theatre itself, where cloths are painted vertically in 'the English style', and the other at the London Opera Centre in the East End of London,

[255]

where cloths are laid on the floor and painted in 'the Continental style'. At Covent Garden are experts who make and maintain costumes, jewellery, wigs, shoes and props.

The ballet Companies have their own music staff at the head of which is The Royal Ballet's Music Director, who is also Principal Conductor for the Covent Garden Company, a post held first by Constant Lambert, then by Robert Irving, Hugo Rignold, and John Lanchbery. The present Music Director is Ashley Lawrence under whom are four other conductors. Since 1960 professional choreologists have been attached to both Companies to record new ballets in the Benesh notation system. The Companies are backed up by stage managers, wardrobe staff, press representatives, financial and other administrators, as well as the stage staff. Behind the dancers stands a support group of technicians responsible for getting on stage those productions whose impalpable magic night after night casts a spell over the audiences.

The constantly changing nature of the work of any dance company, coupled with the especially complex conditions in which The Royal Ballet operates, puts a heavy emphasis on individuals. The personality of de Valois is still easy to trace in the policies of the Company, and that of Ashton in its performances. But the administration, too, carries echoes of its founders, the first of whom was Maynard Keynes, later Lord Keynes, who as economist and art lover was an ideal figure to set the organisation on a sound course in 1946, after its epoch-making move to Covent Garden. On the dance side he was greatly helped by his ex-ballerina wife, Lydia Lopokova, who could not only charm a financier off his office stool but who had a deep knowledge of the ballet world, as well as strong views – which she was very ready to share. A champion of the Company from its Sadler's Wells days she took keen interest in its first experiences at Covent Garden. Sir Kenneth Clark, now Lord Clark, was another vigorous supporter in the early days.

Keynes was lucky from the first in working with David Webster, a music-loving businessman who had been brought down from Liverpool, where he was Chairman of the Philharmonic Society, by the Royal Opera House's licensees, Boosey & Hawkes. (Keynes was always insistent on the importance of business ability in a man running an artistic enterprise.) Webster was to remain General Administrator of Covent Garden almost until his death in 1971 (he retired in 1970). Though criticised in his day – the fate of most opera house administrators – he can be seen now to have made a striking success of a job which was both new and delicate. On the ballet side he had to work with de Valois, founder and leader of the Company, and a character of fierce determination. This suited Webster exactly. He was not obsessively industrious: he enjoyed a long lunch-hour with his cronies in the music world, and his desk was always strikingly empty. He liked to choose a director, an artist or an assistant and to give him a loose rein. Unencumbered by day-to-day routine, he was always available when some personal crisis arose, and his easy temperament was a big advantage when it came to dealing with highly strung stars and minor rebellions. He would descend on stage in times of trouble and restore order with a casual rebuke. His taste in music was wide rather than deep and he had conventional views about dance and design; but he had a flair for picking the right people and he could be surprisingly firm and energetic when faced with opposition. His handling of the crisis over the first visit by the Bolshoi was positively Churchillian, and it was he who insisted on taking Nureyev with the Company to New York when the American impresario Sol Hurok, faced with dire threats by the Russians, was hesitating: a decision in which he was backed by de Valois with unflinching nerve.

During most of David Webster's years as General Administrator he was assisted by John Tooley, who handled most of the practical problems, particularly where they concerned the ballet. When Webster retired, a very sick man, in 1970, it was Tooley who succeeded him. Predictably his way of running the ever-growing machine has been rather different. Exceptionally conscientious and hard-working, he likes to keep his eye on every detail. A more sensitive personality than Webster, he is less sweeping in his approach; his gentle strategy is better suited to modern conditions than Webster's rather lordly manner. Today Tooley, who was knighted in 1979, has to deal with several well-organised trade unions and operate in a more democratic set-up which may provide a fairer deal all round but which sometimes raises formidable obstacles in the way of making quick artistic decisions.

In recent years the task of administration has been made harder by a general and increasing financial stringency. Finance for the two Companies comes from an allotment by the Royal Opera House, which in its turn derives its income from the Arts Council (with contributions from outside sources for special projects). The School is financially independent. The Royal Opera House has always been reluctant to divide the expenses of its ballet and opera activities. on the grounds that many essential services are common to both. Successful efforts at raising outside money for productions and for its flourishing Royal Opera House Trust have been achieved, but the financial squeeze has grown tighter and tighter, posing problems which were unknown during the halcyon years of expansion. The task of The Royal Ballet administration, always hard, is likely to be harder still in the coming decade. It is in such times that the value of solid roots becomes evident.

The interlocking of ballet and opera in the same theatre has advantages as well as drawbacks – the sharing of administrative and material overheads and of the services of an orchestra, saving money, time and energy on the one hand and the inevitable competition which arises for facilities, finance, rehearsal time and space as well as for performances on the other. The struggle to achieve an equitable but economically viable balance between the two has continued amicably ever since the arrival of the Company in the Opera House; today there is a rough fifty-fifty share of performances. With the Covent Garden Company firmly housed and the Sadler's Wells Royal Ballet firmly based in its own theatre, The Royal Ballet can claim to have secured the second as well as the first item on de Valois' list of requirements for a national ballet – a home as well as a company.

12 The English Way

Ballet companies are not like individuals. There is no universal pattern of growth nor a natural limit to their age. Some may flare up and die quickly, some carry on as miniatures, some survive by change, some stiffen and wither, others fade away in an incoherent search for identity. A few take root, expand and live for years, even centuries. The Royal Ballet passes its first half-century with all the appearance of one of these long-distance runners.

The product of a character packed with fruitful contradictions – de Valois is famous for her love of drawing up rules and her zest in breaking them – it has the advantage of a soft-edged silhouette. It bears the stamp of a single founder yet it is far from a dictator's artefact. It bears a royal title but springs from a scheme to improve and entertain the working class. It has a strong individual style yet it is both eclectic in repertoire and adaptable in interpretation. It has harboured stars and engendered them but it is essentially a team. It straddles both the conservation of classics and the introduction of novelties. It has principles but no rules, a policy but no dogma; its character is easy to recognise, hard to define. In fact it is thoroughly British.

This native flavour is all-pervading; it appears in the Company's structure which is elastic, in its history which is slow and consistent, in its manner which is reserved, in its dance style which is aristocratic. It shows even in its creations. Every nation has its natural medium of expression to which it continually tends to return, as a garden plant reverts to its wild ancestor. If Russian ballet today leans towards opera, French ballet towards revue, and American ballet towards gymnastics, then our own instincts lead us back towards drama. De Valois was always insistent that ballet was part of theatre, and her judgment accords with the literary bent which runs in our national character. It is surely no accident that the Company's speciality is the narrative ballet, with flesh-and-blood characters and realism peeping out from even the most fly-away fantasy. *Symphonic Variations* may be the purest essence of English lyricism; but the ballets which carry the clearest stamp of their national origin are The Royal Ballet's dance-dramas – whether compressed like *A Month in the Country*, *The Rake's Progress* or *The Dream*, or extended into full, solidly-presented splendour in *Romeo and Juliet*, *La Fille Mal Gardée*, or *Mayerling*. The magic visions of *The Sleeping Beauty* have slowly been rounded out with a humanity which is our natural native idiom.

If a literary bias is one entrenched English quality, a love of tradition is another. What de Valois took from her experience with the Ballets Russes was its root rather than its exotic flowering, and the Company is based on a single heritage, the style of the Maryinsky classics as handed down by Nicholas Sergeyev.

Tradition is simultaneously a foundation stone and a millstone. The battle between conservation and renewal, between restoration and re-creation, has to be fought over and over again. Even a resonant victory like the 1946 production of *The Sleeping Beauty* brings its problems: should such a great achievement be embalmed, restored or replaced? The characteristic British choice would be for restoration – and for The Royal Ballet that is the natural, and probably therefore the correct, answer.

From the start, de Valois planned to include in the repertory of her Company 'works encouraging a strictly national flavour'. Only two such ballets have actually proved enduringly successful, *The Rake's Progress* and *Pineapple Poll*. The local flavour that she was determined to foster has arisen more subtly through the way in which her dancers have interpreted all ballets. The tradition handed down from Italy through France and Russia has been given a local accent. British minds working with British bodies have produced a style which is as apparent in the nineteenth-century classics as in the latest home-grown novelty.

If individuals are to be credited with the formation of this style, de Valois and Ashton are clearly the biggest influences. Mainly from de Valois flow the Company's gift for acting and the discipline that has engendered a corps de ballet which is the envy of the world. From Ashton comes its elegance and finesse and gentle lyricism. These qualities can be detected in The Royal Ballet's choreographers as much as in the dancers and they are clearly visible to foreign audiences. During the Company's very first visit to New York in 1949 one critic summed up its qualities as 'graciousness, neatness, dignity and imaginativeness'. Emotional restraint is as inherent in the dancers as is a high standard of unostentatious precision. The Royal Ballet dancer has the kind of control which results in fine shades of acting, timing, emotion and wit. Delicacy of feeling is translated into subtlety of movement and the balance which the smallest flaw or jarring accent can disturb. It is the modest simplicity of a poem by Chaucer or of a Savile Row suit in which the placing of a button is crucial.

The Company presents a seamless closely-woven texture reminiscent of fine linen, a unanimity of purpose like that which steers a flock of wheeling birds. It excels equally in the choral lyricism of the Kingdom of the Shades scene from *La Bayadère*, in the courtly ritual of *The Sleeping Beauty*, in the rapt and airy ecstasies of *Symphonic Variations* and the sharp-edged fun of *Elite Syncopations*. When it dances an abstract ballet the smallest cue will lead to a hint of character. A sense of period – natural to the history-conscious English – goes with a knowledge, born of wide experience, of the requirements and ambiance of costume, whether it be the leisurely elegance of an eighteenth-century Prince or the angular chic of a 1920s flapper.

The focal point around which the Company Style revolves is the classical technique as taught in the School and practised in the nineteenth-century classics. It is for the dancers as much as for the audience that regular performances of works such as *The Sleeping Beauty* and *Swan Lake* are important. They maintain technical standards and they also have the merit (shared by modern full-length works) of offering roles for senior artists and for dancers specialising in character parts, thus giving depth and diversity to the Company. But keeping them constantly in the repertoire raises problems. Apart from the need to nurture the star ballerinas around whom these ballets were built, there is the running difficulty of keeping old works fresh for new audiences. This lays heavy responsibilities on each Director. Like the heir to a splendid estate, each incumbent must prune and tend and plant for the future as well as for the present. More than most state companies, The Royal Ballet depends on its Director.

The imprint of de Valois is still visible and always will be; but her successors have been markedly different in personality and each has made his contribution over and above his own choreography. Ashton re-activated Nijinska and the result was the revival of *Les Biches* and *Les Noces*; MacMillan presided over the first experiments in modern dance style with Tetley's ballets *Field Figures* and *Laborintus*. Both of these Directors were promoted from inside the Company. The choice of Norman Morrice to succeed them in 1978 showed a flexibility and innovatory boldness which is the best portent for the future.

Fifty years is not a long life compared with those of some companies on the Continent. But already it is possible to trace fluctuations in The Royal Ballet's fortunes which prove that it is a living organism and not a machine. Its story divides into three periods which can be likened to the growth of a man – childhood at Sadler's Wells, adolescence during the War, and emergence as an adult at Covent Garden. In the thirty or so years that it has been centred on the Royal Opera House (with the Touring Company hovering nearby and finally finding a home at Sadler's Wells) it has seen the flowering and disappearance of a whole generation of dancers.

Disregarding small fluctuations it can now be seen that the grant of the Royal Charter in 1956 was happily timed. That year turned out to be a milestone marking the opening of a decade during which the Company was to reach its highest peak of creativity and performance. The period spanned the Directorship of de Valois and Ashton during which The Royal Ballet was enriched by three outstanding choreographers, Ashton, Cranko and MacMillan, as well as staging works by notable Russians past and present – Fokine, Nijinska and Balanchine. The list of ballets first performed by the Company between 1956 and 1966 includes (in chronological order) *Petrushka, Ondine, La Fille Mal Gardée, The Invitation, Les Deux Pigeons, The Rite of Spring, Marguerite and Armand, La Bayadère, The Dream, Les Biches, Romeo and Juliet, Les Noces, Song of the Earth* and *Apollo* – an impressive record. The dancers interpreting the ballets were equally distinguished. During these years the principals of the Company were, to name only a dozen, artists such as Fonteyn, Nerina, Beriosova, Grey, Park, Seymour and Sibley, partnered by Somes, Blair, Dowell, Grant and MacLeary. Together with the soloists surrounding them and a corps de ballet which reached the summit of perfection during those years, they made a team which will be hard to beat. The Company was also enriched by an impressive list of Guest Artists which included not only Nureyev as a regular participant but also (alphabetically) Erik Bruhn, Yvette Chauviré, Flemming Flindt, Carla Fracci, John Gilpin, Marcia Haydée, Melissa Hayden, Attilio Labis, Alicia Markova and Violette Verdy. During this decade The Royal Ballet rightly enjoyed a prestige and popularity both at home and abroad that has not been surpassed.

Such a peak proclaims the virtues of the Company but also leads to the danger of over-confidence. Students of evolution know well the perils and pitfalls of too perfect an adaptation to environment; if the environment changes, virtues may become handicaps. In terms of ballet, change can mean new tastes, new social and economic conditions, perhaps a revolution in choreography. Flexibility is vital.

No company can combine all the virtues. It would be a mistake to look to The Royal Ballet for the broad passionate flow of the Bolshoi or the speed and dynamics of New York City Ballet. To try to imitate them would be fatal; British virtues are different. But these, too, conceal an element of danger, for the risk which any ballet company runs, and to which many succumb, is the overdevelopment of intrinsically admirable characteristics. The virtues noted by the critic in New York could (and occasionally do) decline into vices. 'Graciousness' can become refinement, 'neatness' may turn into dryness, 'dignity' into gentility, 'imaginativeness' into whimsy. Most perilous of all for a British company is the gift of good taste, a deadly and well-disguised poison which has sapped our artistic vitality down the ages and is always lying in wait. Fortunately, alert management keeps a watchful eye, and regular exposure to outside influences through teachers, overseas tours and visits by Guest Artists maintain a steady sensitivity to invention and fresh tastes: the Royal Ballet remains remarkably adaptable. An inborn individualism is likely to stave off the inroads of that bureaucratic sciatica which has crippled many large companies. The curious looseness of organisation and vagueness of policy which sometimes proves baffling to outsiders provides a built-in ventilation system through which the winds of change can circulate naturally and softly.

What are the pressures that will influence those changes? The first are likely to be purely professional. The development of modern-dance techniques, as opposed to the *danse d'école* with its traditional grammar of movement, will pose questions about the possibility of grafting new growths on to old stems without damage to either. Teaching methods may have to be modified and specialisation encouraged. Conservation of twentieth-century ballets as well as nineteenth-century masterpieces, Ashton as much as Petipa, may conflict with new ways of moving. In the same way the use of electronic and other sounds not within the compass of conventional orchestras may affect the always awkward relationship between opera and ballet. Already they compete for orchestral rehearsal time; in the future, ballet may make different demands altogether.

Secondary, but sometimes even more powerful, pressures may be applied from sources altogether outside the Company. Already it suffers from inter-governmental agreements which limit the employment of dancers from the Commonwealth, formerly a prime pool of talent. These demonstrate a new social consciousness which may and indeed should be reflected in the Company's nature and activities. Another adjustment to present day society must be the reconciliation of the traditions of the Royal Opera House, a national culture centre with inbuilt undertones of royal patronage and establishment prestige, with a society moving towards greater equality and informality. Already seasons by both companies in popular regional theatres, mass auditoria and the Big Top have softened the gilded image of The Royal Ballet, while a vigorous encouragement of television coverage has widened the Company's audiences to an extent which even Lilian Baylis – who incidentally had the foresight to recognise the potential of television – could not have imagined.

The final constraint will be, as always, a financial one. Economics will affect not only the size and performance record of the Company but also its creative activity, and even the style of its ballets. Revivals of old works like *The Sleeping Beauty* cost a great deal of money – cheap material for scenery and costumes is a bad investment for a production which may last for years – and the creation of a new three-act ballet may absorb a giant share of the annual budget. A small cast in an abstract ballet is, on the other hand, the cheapest item that an opera house can offer. Clearly, planning as well as presentation could at any time be influenced by economics, though so far no choreographer has had to be frustrated by financial considerations.

The Royal Ballet today is a very different affair from the modest little group of dancers who skipped through the mixed programmes at the Old Vic and Sadler's Wells fifty years ago. Today it is, by theatrical standards, a giant. The two Companies together number over one hundred and twenty dancers, with a large back-up team in addition – artistic, directional and administrative – not to mention the two branches of the School. Nowadays it is a dynamo spreading its influence far beyond Britain. Within the last twenty years Directors of the Stuttgart Ballet, The Australian Ballet, the National Ballet of Canada, the Berlin Ballet, the Houston Ballet, the Munich Ballet, as well as London Festival Ballet and Scottish Ballet, have all been former members of the Company, and its dancers and students can be found all over the world. The Turkish Ballet was set up with the help of de Valois. Today The Royal Ballet has a large budget, complicated planning schedules, wide overseas ramifications and daunting responsibilities. From its stronghold in the country's most prestigious theatre it often goes out, not as *a* symbol of our national culture but as *the* symbol.

This is surely no accident. There are few institutions of any kind, and certainly no artistic ones, which encapsulate the British character so well. Like an expanding family it can boast of its achievements, count its celebrities, smile at its failures, welcome its new members and at the same time discipline and shape them. It is too active to be much interested in the past, too engrossed with the present to be concerned with the distant future. It does not need to cultivate a style because it is inherent in every feature, instantly recognisable and unique. It may change, but essentially it will always be the same because it is an expression of the personality of a whole nation.

With half a century behind it The Royal Ballet is an institution as well as a dance company. Seen from afar it seems massive, imposing, almost alarmingly substantial. But it is, after all, a theatrical phenomenon; it is made for magic. When at Covent Garden the lights in the auditorium are dimmed, the crimson curtains part, and the first glittering shoal of dancers floats gently on to the stage, the organisation fades away and we see the real face of the Company – eager, tender and vulnerable, renewed at each performance, and so forever young.

STATISTICS

Dancers of The Royal Ballet 265

Choreographers 271

THE ROYAL BALLET
Vic-Wells, Sadler's Wells, Royal Ballet

Repertory (I) 273

Productions in Chronological Order (I) 289

Itinerary (I) 291

SADLER'S WELLS ROYAL BALLET
Sadler's Wells Theatre Ballet, Royal Ballet Touring Company,
New Group, Sadler's Wells Royal Ballet

Repertory (II) 296

Productions in Chronological Order (II) 307

Itinerary (II) 309

The Royal Ballet School Annual Performances 315

Films and Television 316

Statistics are from 1928 to 1979 for Repertory (I) and from 1946 to 1979 for Repertory (II).
For ballets premièred Jan to Aug 1980 details include credits and first casts only.

Abbreviations

A	Abroad		orch	orchestrated
arr	arranged		OV	Old Vic Theatre
c	contract		P	Première
C	Costumes		pdd	pas de deux
CdB	corps de ballet		pds	pas de six
CG	Covent Garden branch of Royal Ballet		pdt	pas de trois
Ch	Choreography		Pr	Producer
ChC	Choreography and Costumes		Pr	production
Cr	Credits (Cr Rep I/Cr indicates see Repertory I/Repertory II)		RBchG	Royal Ballet Choreographic Group
Dir	Director		RBS	Royal Ballet School
e	evening		rec	recorded
f	female		Rep	Repertory
FP	First performance by Company		ROH	Royal Opera House
FPCG	First performance by Covent Garden Company (for date of first performance by Royal Ballet see Repertory II)		RST	Royal Shakespeare Theatre
			S	Scenery
FPTB/FPTC	First performance by Sadler's Wells Theatre Ballet/Royal Ballet Touring Company (ie for date of first performance by Royal Ballet see Repertory I)		SC	Scenery and Costumes
			sel	selected
			SMT	Shakespeare Memorial (now Royal Shakespeare) Theatre
GA	Guest Artist		Str	Stratford-upon-Avon, England
Hookham/Fonteyn	indicates name change – dancer appears on programmes under both names in the role listed		SW	Sadler's Wells Theatre
			SWB	Sadler's Wells Ballet
I, II, III	Act I, Act II, Act III		SWCG	Sadler's Wells Choreographers Group
Jenner-Last	indicates performance split between dancers		SWTB/TB	Sadler's Wells Theatre Ballet
M	Music		T	Tour (applies Rep I only – ie in UK and Abroad)
m	male		TC	Royal Ballet Touring Company (includes New Group and Sadler's Wells Royal Ballet)
m	matinée			
nc	no credit/cast (according to context)		tr	transmission
NP	New Production		Var	Variation
nr	no record		[ ]	full figures not available

Notes

The statistics cover the period from the first complete (one-act) ballet presented by the Old Vic Opera Ballet in 1928, three years before the founding of the Company in 1931.

REPERTORIES I AND II

Production credits are taken from the printed programmes and no attempt has been made to correct the attributions given.

Sources for casting are the nightly programmes, corrected, as far as possible, from Stage Management records or eyewitness accounts.

Cast statistics The number of dancers in a ballet has been included where the work has been created for the Company or where details are not readily available elsewhere (eg named roles + 4f 4m).

Performance statistics. For each ballet the annual number of performances is shown in brackets in the chronological sequence that follows production credits, eg Apollo . . .'66 (7); '67 (1) etc.

Dancer's performance dates. Where two dates follow a dancer's name in a role (eg *Prince Siegfried* Somes '53–9), these dates refer to the first and last year in which he performed that role in a particular production. A single date indicates that the work was performed in one year only.

Dancer's performance statistics. Although the Company's Seasons run from September to July, for ease of reference all details included in the statistics are based on figures for calendar years, Jan to Dec (ie performances from Jan to July and Sept to Dec).

Débuts Where a work is common to both Companies both Repertory lists should be consulted to establish the date of a dancer's début in that work.

Repertory I '52TC indicates dancer's début in role in '52 with Touring Company as well as performance in same year at Covent Garden. 52T indicates dancer's début in role in '52 with Covent Garden Company. 52(A) indicates dancer's début in '52 with CG Company abroad.

Repertory II '52CG indicates dancer's début in role in '52 with CG Company as well as performance in same year with touring company in UK. '52(3) indicates dancer's début in role in '52 with Company on tour in UK. 52A indicates dancer's début in role in '52 with Touring Company abroad. (Figures in italic type apply to performances in the provinces and Eire; figures in Roman type to London).

Dancers of The Royal Ballet

Dates given are those on which dancers' names first appear in (a) programmes (note that they may still have been students) or (b) their first contract, whichever is the earlier. Abbreviation for contract date = c.

‡indicates dancer received training at Royal Ballet Lower and Upper Schools (after 1946).
*indicates dancer received training at Royal Ballet Upper School only (after 1946)

Before 1947 many dancers received some training at the School attached to the Company, but, especially in the early years, they were student-dancers rather than full-time students.

The list does not include short-term contract artists (ie dancers whose contracts were not taken up after trial period) or students who did not become full members of the Company. NB For the 1930s it is often impossible to distinguish full Company members from student dancers, or professional dancers who appeared only once or twice, as their commitments elsewhere allowed. Unfortunately lack of space prevented us from including a complete list of dancers in this category.

GA = Guest Artist.

ABBOTT, Carolyn 1969 Oct*
ADAMS, David 1946 Oct*
ADAMS, Doreen 1931 May
ADAMS, Valerie 1952 Feb*
ADDISON, Errol 1956 Jan
AINSWORTH, Carole 1969 Oct*
AITKEN, Christine c 1966 Aug*
AITKEN, Gordon 1954 Dec*
ALDABALDETRECEE, Pirnon see TRECU, Pirmin
ALDER, Alan 1958 Apr*
ALDERTON, Christine see ANTHONY, Christine
ALDOUS, Lucette 1966 Sept*
ALEXANDER, Michael see HARPER, Michael
ALEXANDER, Susan 1953 Aug*
ALLAN, Barbara see LYNDON, Barbara*
ALLNUTT, Joanna 1972 July‡
ALPE, Elizabeth 1972 July*
AMBLER, Lynda c 1971 Nov*
ANDERTON, Elizabeth 1954 Dec* as ANDERTON, Betty
ANDREAE, Felicity 1932 Oct later GRAY, Felicity
ANDREWS, Margaret see LEE, Margaret
ANELAY, Dorothy 1958 Jan*
ANTHONY, Christine c 1956 Mar* as ALDERTON, Christine
APPLETON, John 1974 Jan‡
APPLETON, June see LEIGHTON, June

APPLEYARD, Beatrice 1939 Dec
ARGYLE, Pearl 1935 Oct
ARNEIL, Harold 1941 Dec (SWB Stage Manager)
ARNOLD, Leon 1952 Apr*
AROVA, Sonia 1962-June GA
ASHBRIDGE, Bryan 1947 Feb*
ASHBY, Sally c 1961 July‡
ASHMOLE, David 1968 Oct*
ASHMOLE, Sylvia c 1946 Feb
ASHTON, Frederick 1929 Dec
ASTILL, Marion 1951 Mar*
ATTREE, Carla c 1961 Nov*
AULD, John 1973 Aug (on staff touring section from 1970; Assistant to the Director 1972)
AUSTERBERRY, Gail 1963 Aug*
AUSTIN, Romayne 1958 Aug* also GRIGORIEVA, Romayne
AVERTY, Brenda 1948 Dec‡

BACON, Mary 1938 Mar
BADHAM, Bridget 1954 Mar*
BAKER, Allan 1944 Oct
BAKER, Dale 1977 May
BAMFORD, Freda 1928 Dec
BANKS, Joanna c 1957 Aug‡
BAPTIE, Ivan 1955 Sept*
BARBIERI, Margaret c 1965 Aug*
BARCLAY, Donald 1951 Mar*
BARKER, Keith see ROSSON, Keith
BARLOW, Kenneth 1957 May*
BARNES, Pauline 1952 Nov*
BARNES, Yvonne 1947 Sept*
BARON, Robert 1941 Oct
BARRETT, William 1950 Apr
BARRY, Bernice 1934 Jan
BART, Graham c 1969 Aug*
BARTLETT, Jane 1957 Mar‡
BARYSHNIKOV, Mikhail 1975 Oct GA
BATCHELOR, Michael 1974 Mar*
BATEMAN, Shirley 1951 Mar*
BAX, Heather 1934 Oct as LONGSTAFF, Heather
BAYLEY, Angela 1938 May
BEAGLEY, Stephen c 1975 Sept‡
BEALE, Alan 1957 Mar*
BEAR, June see BRAE, June
BEARE, Michael c 1965 Aug*
BEAUMONT, Piers 1960 Aug‡
BECK, Amanda 1974 Mar* as WILKINSON, Amanda
BECKETT, Stuart c 1975 Dec‡
BECKLEY, Christine 1956 Jan‡
BEDDOES, Ivor 1931 May
BEDELLS, Jean 1937 Jan
BEDELLS, Phyllis 1931 Nov GA
BEESON, Oona c 1978 Sept‡
BEEVERS, Lawrence 1959 Mar*
BEEVOR, Betty 1933 Oct

BELL, Marley 1931 Mar
BENESH, Joan 1951 Jan*
BENNETT, Alexander c 1956 Jan
BENNETT, Anthony 1959 Nov*
BENNETT, Austin 1959 Feb‡
BENSON, Paul 1970 Mar
BENTON, Nicholas 1958 Nov*
BERG, Bernd c 1976 Aug
BERGEN, Avril c 1961 Aug* as BERGENGREN, Avril
BERGSMA, Deanne 1958 Feb‡
BERIOSOVA, Svetlana 1950 May
BERLINER, Carol 1964 Oct*
BERTRAM, Carol 1934 Jan (From Opera Company – mime roles only)
BERTSCHER, Brian c 1964 Aug*
BEVERIDGE, Angela c 1963 Aug*
BEZANCON, Mireille 1931 May
BINTLEY, David c 1976 Aug*
BISHOP, Shirley 1948 Mar*
BIRDWOOD-TAYLOR, Joan see TAYLOR, Joan
BLAIR, David 1946 Nov as BUTTERFIELD, David
BLAKENEY, Joan 1952 Feb*
BLISS, Karen 1947 Jan‡
BLOWERS, Cynthia see MAYAN, Cynthia
BLUEMEL, Gloria 1959 Feb*
BOLAM, Margaret see DALE, Margaret
BOLTON, Brenda 1954 Sept*
BONNER, Dennis c 1976 Aug‡
BOSMAN, Petrus c 1957 July
BOSWELL, David c 1953*
BOULTON, Catherine 1950 Apr*
BOULTON, Michael 1945 June*
BOWER, Pamela 1959 Mar*
BRADSHAW, Sven 1968 Sept*
BRAE, June 1935 Sept as BEAR, June
BRASLER, Gilbert see VERNON, Gilbert
BRIGGS, Hedley 1928 Dec
BRIND, Bryony c 1978 Sept‡
BRITTON, Donald 1945 Apr
BROCKWELL, Diana 1932 Nov
BROOKE, Maurice 1933 Sept
BROOKING, Nesta 1931 Sept
BROOKS, Patricia 1946 June
BROWN, Doreen see NEIL, Sara
BROWN, Dorinda 1953 Sept‡
BROWN, Kathryn see WADE, Kathryn
BROWN, Molly 1931 May
BROWN, Paul 1960 Aug*
BROWN, William c 1949 Aug*
BRUCE, Maureen 1947 Dec
BRUHN, Erik 1962 Mar GA
BRYG, Bonita c 1969 Nov*
BULMAN, Patricia see GARNETT, Patricia
BUMPUS, Jeanetta see LAURENCE, Jeanetta
BURGESS, Janet 1958 Jan*
BURKE, Janet 1958 Jan*
BURKE, Anthony 1941 July

BURKE, Nigel see DESMOND, Nigel
BURNE, Gary 1952 May*
BURROWS, Jonathan 1979 Sept‡
BURROWS, Michael see HARPER, Michael
BURTON, Susan 1972 Nov*
BURY, Rosalind c 1967 Jan*
BUTLER, Betty 1940 Jan
BUTTERFIELD, David see BLAIR, David
BYRON, John 1934 Nov

CABOURN, Marie c 1968 Oct‡
CADZOW, Joan 1947 Nov*
CAMP, Shirley see GRAHAME, Shirley
CAREY, Dennis 1946 Feb
CARLEY, Louise 1952 Aug‡ as CARLEY,
  Marie Louise
CARLTON, Roy 1953 June* as TAYLOR, Roy
CARLTON, Susan 1960 Dec as JONES, Susan
CARNE, Anna 1949 Aug as DOWSON, Anna
CAROL, Ann 1978 Apr* as WRIGHTON,
  Carol
CARR, Christopher c 1967 Sept‡
CARRINGTON, Sally 1969 Oct‡ as HART,
  Sally
CARTER, Alan 1937 Apr
CARTER, Carlu 1951 June*
CARTIER, Yvonne 1952 July ‡
CARTWRIGHT, Hilary c 1962 Aug*
CASTLE, Katherine c 1967 Aug*
CAULEY, Geoffrey 1960 Aug‡
CAWOOD, John 1944 June
CHADWICK, Fiona c 1978 Sept‡
CHALK, Mary 1933 Mar
CHAPELL, Meryl 1964 Dec‡
CHAPMAN, Vera 1932 Oct
CHAPPELL, William 1931 Sept
CHAPIN, Harold 1930 Dec
CHARNLEY, Michael 1941 July
CHATFIELD, Philip 1942 Mar
CHATRY, Christine c 1958 Aug* as JOPE,
  Christine
CHATTING, Harry 1935 Oct
CHAUVIRE, Yvette 1958 Aug GA
CHRIMES, Pamela 1946 Feb
CHRISTIE, Elizabeth 1948 Oct
CLAIRE, Stella 1947 Feb*
CLARKE, Gilding 1931 Sept
CLARKE, Paul c 1964 Aug‡
CLARKE, Ruth 1946 Dec
CLAYDEN, Pauline 1942 Oct
CLEGG, Peter 1946 Mar
CLIFT, Clemency 1964 Jan‡
CLIPPERTON, Heather 1958 Aug‡
COLBORNE, Judith 1958 Dec*
COLEMAN, Michael 1959 Feb*
COLLIER, Lesley 1965 Nov‡
CONLEY, Sandra c 1962 Jan*
CONNETT, Kay 1962 July‡
CONNOR, Laura 1964 Oct‡
CONWAY, Anthony c 1969 Dec* as
  WRIGHT, Anthony
COOKE, Jill c 1967 Mar*
COOKE, Kerrison 1961 Dec*
COOPER, Betty c 1946 Oct
CORDER, Michael 1973 Feb‡
CORKEN, Belinda c 1971 Sept*

CORMACK, Marjorie 1932 Nov
COURTNEY, Nigel c 1975 July‡
COVENTRY, Anne 1929 May
COX, Angela c 1977 Sept‡
COX, Lambert 1958 Mar*
COX, Patricia c 1954 Mar‡
COX, Rosanne 1975 Mar‡ as COX, Ann
CRAGUN, Richard 1968 Nov*
CRANKO, John c 1946 May GA
CROFT, Robyn 1959 Feb*
CROW, Susan 1974 Mar*
CUNLIFFE, Elizabeth c 1965 July*

DADY, Margaret 1946 June
DAGLISH, Audrey 1938 Mar
DALE, Margaret 1937 Apr as BOLAM,
  Margaret
DALES, Bess 1975 Mar‡
DANIEL, Caryl c 1964 Mar*
DANILOVA, Alexandra 1949 March GA
DANTON, Henry 1944 May
DARGAVAL, Bruce 1939 Feb (From Opera
  company – mime roles only)
DARKE, Pamela 1954 Dec*
DARNBOROUGH, Hermione 1932 Oct
DARNLEY, Juliet c 1946 Oct
DARRELL, Peter 1944 Oct as SKINNER, Peter
DARWOOD, Susan 1969 Oct‡ as WOOD,
  Susan
DARYL, Jacqueline 1956 Jan* as WATCHAM,
  Jacqueline
DAVEL, Hendrik c 1964 Aug
DAVENPORT, David 1942 Oct
DAVIES, Adrian c 1973 Aug*
DAVIES, Amanda see SEATON, Amanda
DAVIES, Dudley 1952 May
DAVIES, Susan see MARLYS, Susan
DAY, Joan 1931 May
DAY, June 1946 Feb
DEACON, Olive 1939 Feb
DEANE, Derek 1972 Oct* as SHEPHERD,
  Derek
DEBDEN, Hilary 1960 Aug*
DE MARIA, Warren c 1963 Sept
DENLEY, Kathleen 1960 Aug*
DENNIS, Ann 1964 Oct*
DENYS, Maxine 1964 Feb* as GOLDSTEIN,
  Wendy
DERMAN, Vergie c 1962 Aug*
DESMOND, Nigel 1942 May as BURKE, Nigel
DE VALOIS, see VALOIS, DE
DEVINE, Jane 1974 Mar*
DE WARREN, Robert 1958 June*
DIXON, Deirdre 1950 Mar*
DIXON, Nicolas c 1975 Sept‡
DOLIN, Anton 1931 May GA
DOONE, Rupert 1932 Mar
DOUGLAS, Tom see STEUART, Douglas
DOWELL, Anthony 1959 Mar‡
DOWSON, Anna see CARNE, Anna
DOWSON, Antony 1976 Oct
DOYLE, Desmond c 1951 Feb
DRAGE, Mary 1947 Nov*
DRAISEY, Doreen 1958 Mar*
DREW, David 1955 Mar*
DU BOULAY, Christine 1939 Mar

DUBREUIL, Alain c 1973 Sept
DUKE, Valerie 1954 Mar*
DUMAS, Russell c 1971 Nov
DUNNING, Paula 1941 Oct as SPENS
  DUNNING, Topsy also Pauline
DURANT, Andrea c 1969 Aug‡
DYE, Colin c 1972 Sept*

EAGLING, Wayne 1969 Sept*
EARLY, Fergus 1962 Nov‡
EARNSHAW, Brian see SHAW, Brian
EASTLAKE, Doreen 1953 Apr*
EDE, Beryl 1928 Dec
EDGAR, Ann 1947 Jan*
EDWARDS, Leslie 1933 Jan
ELLAMS, Glynis 1958 Nov‡
ELINDEN/ELENTON, Anya see LINDEN, Anya
ELLIOTT, Jacqueline 1970 May‡
ELLIS, Richard 1933 Sept
ELLIS, Wendy c 1970 Feb‡
ELVIN, Violetta 1946 Feb as PROKHOROVA,
  Violetta
EMBLEN, Ronald 1949 Dec as student‡
  c 1962
ENGLISH, Yvonne 1951 Mar*
ENNOR, Valmai 1954 Mar*
ESCOTT, Gillian 1974 July‡
EVANS, Anya c 1969 July
EVANS, Meriel 1951 Mar*
EVANS, Rita 1957 Mar‡
EYDEN, Deirdre 1976 Nov*
EYRE, Rosalind 1958 Oct*

FAIRWEATHER, Peter 1966 Nov‡
FARJEON, Annabel 1934 Jan
FARLEY, Richard 1953 Mar*
FARNSWORTH, Claire c 1974 Nov‡
FARRANCE, Stella 1947 Dec*
FARRISS, Audrey c 1956 July*
FARRON, Julia 1935 Oct as FARRON, Joyce
FAYRE, Rowena 1938 Apr
FAWDRY, Mark 1931 Nov
FELLSTROM, Carina c 1973 Aug‡
FEUERHEER, Rosemary see VALAIRE,
  Rosemary
FEWSTER, Barbara 1946 June
FIELD, Diana 1945 Sept as FIELD, Patience
FIELD, John 1939 Dec
FIFIELD, Elaine 1946 Oct
FITZGERALD, Suzanne see STANLEY,
  Siobhan
FLEMING, Sheila see LASCELLES, Anne
FLETCHER, Graham c 1969 Dec‡
FLINDT, Flemming 1963 May GA
FONTEYN, Margot 1934, Apr as Hookham,
  Peggy also FONTES/FONTENE, Margot
FONS, Michel 1979 Aug*
FORD, Molly 1931 Mar
FORHAN, Diane 1950 Apr*
FORMAN, Doreen see WAYNE, Debra
FRACCI, Carla 1963 May GA
FRANCA, Celia 1941 Dec
FRANCIS, Elizabeth 1972 July‡
FRANCIS, Janet 1964 Oct*
FRANCIS, Mark 1976 Nov‡ as FRANCIS,
  Michael

FRANKLIN, Frederic 1949 Mar GA
FRASER, Moyra 1937 Jan
FREEMAN, Frank c 1963 Aug‡
FRENCH, Leslie 1931 May
FRENCH, Ruth 1934 Oct GA
FROST, John 1957 Mar*

GABLE, Christopher 1956 Feb‡
GAILLARD, Edward 1932 Jan
GAMBLE, Rollo 1934 Oct
GARBUTT, Sally 1973 Oct*
GARNETT, Patricia 1938 Jan as BULMAN,
    Patricia
GAY, Jennifer 1953 Mar*
GAYLE, David 1960 June* as GALE, David
GAYNOR, Pauline c 1963 Mar
GELDARD, Kathleen c 1958 July*
GERHARDT, George 1946 Apr
GIELGUD, Maina 1975 Oct GA
GIEVES, Anne 1943 Dec as SCOTT, Barbara
GILL, David 1946 June
GILL, Laurel see MARTYN, Laurel
GILLESPIE, Kenn c 1952 Nov*
GILLIES, Donald 1950 Apr*
GILPIN, John 1961 Apr GA
GILPIN, Mandy 1975 Mar
GOLD, Judy c 1946 Oct
GOLDSTEIN, Wendy see Denys, Maxine
GOODBODY, Graham c 1973 July
GOODIER, Ann 1970 May*
GOODRICKE, Bridget c 1967 Jan*
GORDON, David 1958 Mar*
GORDON, Josephine 1946 Apr
GORE, Walter 1931 Sept
GORHAM, Kathleen 1949 May*
GOULD, Diana 1933 Jan
GRAEME, Joyce 1936 Oct as PLATTS, Joyce
GRAHAM, Duncan 1941 July
GRAHAME, Shirley 1953 Oct‡ as CAMP,
    Shirley
GRANT, Alexander 1946 Apr*
GRANT, Frank see WARD, Frank
GRANT, Garry c 1963 Aug*
GRANTHAM, Joan c 1946 Oct
GRATER, Adrian 1958 Nov*
GREENWAY, Grace 1940 Aug
GREENWOOD, John 1931 Dec (From Opera
    Company – mime roles only) as
    GREENWOOD, Jack
GREGOROVA, Natalia 1932 Mar
GREGORY, Jill 1932 Nov
GREY, Beryl 1941 July
GREY, David 1937 Oct
GRIFFITH, Dennis c 1968 Aug*
GRIFFITHS, Lili 1978 Feb‡ as GRIFFITHS,
    Elizabeth
GRIFFITHS, Kenneth see MELVILLE, Kenneth
GRIGORIEVA, Romayne 1966 Mar* see also
    AUSTIN, Romayne
GROOMBRIDGE, Wendy 1972 Oct‡

HAIG, Robin 1957 Feb*
HALL, Stanley 1937 Oct
HAMBY, Greta 1946 Apr
HAMILTON, Gordon 1941 July
HAMILTON, Ian 1957 Dec‡

HAMMOND, Patricia c 1969 Aug‡
HANA, Sonya 1953 Feb
HARALD, Frank 1939 Feb also HAROLD,
    Frank
HARDING, David 1955 Sept
HARMAN, Audrey 1946 Apr
HARPER, Francis 1957 May*
HARPER, Michael c 1973 Oct* as BURROWS,
    Michael also ALEXANDER, Michael
HARRIS, Joan 1946 Apr
HARROP, Pauline 1947 Dec*
HART, John 1938 Sept
HART, Sally see CARRINGTON, Sally
HARVEY, Hermione 1951 Sept
HASKELL, Edward 1932 Jan
HASLAM, Jacqueline c 1960 July*
HATCH, Yvonne 1947 May
HAWKINS, Matthew 1976 Dec‡
HAYDEE, Marcia 1965 May* GA
HAYDEN, Melissa 1963 May GA
HAYNES, John 1967 Apr*
HAYTHORNE, Harry 1963 May GA
HEANLEY, Francis 1932 Oct
HEATON, Anne 1945 May
HELPMANN, Robert 1933 Mar as
    HELPMANN, Bobbie
HENDERSON, Audrey 1954 Sept*
HERTZELL, Eric see HYRST, Eric
HIGHWOOD, June 1968 July*
HIGGINS, David see HURD, Patrick
HILL, Anita 1928 Dec
HILL, Carole c 1962 Aug‡
HILL, Margaret 1952 Aug
HILL, Sandra 1955 Apr*
HITCH, June see VINCENT, June
HOARE, Peggy 1932 Mar
HOGAN, Michel 1946 Apr
HOLBROOKE, E(dward) G (From Opera
    Company – mime roles only)
HOLDEN, Stanley 1944 July as WALLER,
    Stanley
HOLLAMBY, Lynn c 1971 Nov‡
HOLLING, Josephine 1970 Feb‡
HOLMES, Merlyn c 1963 Aug*
HOMJI, Rashna 1968 Nov‡
HONER, Mary 1935 Sept
HOOKHAM, Peggy see FONTEYN, Margot
HOOPER, Alan c 1966 Aug‡
HORNE, Caroldene c 1966 Aug*
HORNE, Jean 1951 June*
HORRILL, Simon 1979 Sept*
HORSBRUGH, Wenda 1933 Feb
HORSHAM, Dianne 1962 July*
HOSKING, Julian 1971 May‡
HOWARD, Alison c 1968 Sept‡
HOWARD, Andrée 1948 Dec
HOWARD, Ann c 1954 July‡ as PAGE, Ann
HOWARD, David c 1957 Jan
HOWARD, Mary 1948 May
HOWARD, Norman see HYRST, Eric
HOWE, Judith c 1972 Feb‡
HOWELL, Eley c 1966 Jan* as HOWELL,
    Anthony
HOWES, Douglas 1977 Sept*
HUGUENIN, Robert c 1972 Sept*
HULBERT, Arlette 1966 Jan

HULBERT, Tony c 1965 Sept
HUNWIN, Diane 1967 Dec*
HURD, Patrick 1952 Dec‡ as HIGGINS, David
HYDE, Terence c 1968 Jan*
HUMPHREYS, Sheila 1958 Feb*
HYND, Ronald c 1952 Jan
HYRST, Eric 1943 Apr as HERTZELL, Eric
    also HOWARD, Norman

IDZIKOWSKY, Stanislas 1933 Sept GA
ILLINGWORTH, Janice c 1963 Aug*
INGLETON, Michael c 1964 Sept*
INKIN, Sally c 1967 Aug*
INNES, Joan 1932 Dec
ISOBEL, Betty 1930 Dec

JACKMAN, Angela c 1970 Dec‡
JACKSON, Jennifer c 1972 Sept*
JACKSON, Mavis 1937 Nov
JACKSON, Penelope c 1965 Aug‡
JACKSON, Rowena 1946 Nov
JAFFRAY, Daryl 1963 Oct*
JAMES, Frances 1928 Dec
JAMES, Iris 1929 Oct
JEFFERIES, Stephen c 1969 Aug*
JEFFS, Barbara 1929 Dec
JEMMETT, Suzanne c 1946 Oct
JENNER, Ann 1961 Sept‡
JOHNSON, Nicholas c 1965 Aug*
JONES, Colin 1953 Aug*
JONES, Colin 1958 Jan*
JONES, David 1959 Sept‡
JONES, Marilyn 1957 Mar*
JONES, Susan see CARLTON, Susan
JOPE, Christine see CHATRY, Christine
JUDE, Robert c 1971 Sept*
JUDSON, Stanley 1928 Dec

KARRAS, Vicki c 1964 Aug
KASSINOVA, Lana 1953 Sept
KATRAK, Nicola 1975 Jan‡
KAVANAGH, Betty 1960 July*
KEANE, Fiorella 1946 Apr
KEBBELL, Joan 1937 Oct
KEITH, Christine 1971 Jan*
KELLY, Bunty see KELLY, Margaret
KELLY, Desmond 1970 Apr
KELLY, Jonathan c 1967 Jan‡ as KELLY, John
KELLY, Margaret 1942 June as KELLY, Bunty
KEMP, Travis 1931 May
KENNEDY, Elizabeth 1936 Sept
KENNEDY, Phyllis 1948 Dec*
KENNEDY, Sherilyn 1974 July*
KENWARD, Ann 1958 June*
KERSLEY, Leo 1941 Sept
KILGOUR, Donald 1951 Mar*
KILGOUR, Murray c 1971 June
KILLAR, Ashley 1960 Aug‡
KING, Joan 1952 May*
KINGSLEY, Gillian c 1973 Dec* also King,
    Gillian
KIRKPATRICK, Donald c 1966 Aug*
KNOESEN, Margaret c 1953 Mar*
KOSHLEY, Sharon 1963 Oct*
KRAVCHENKO, Victor 1968 Jan‡
KURZ, Rosalind c 1973 Dec‡

LABIS, Attilio 1966 Nov GA
LAKE, Mollie 1929 May
LAKIER, Yvonne 1954 Sept
LAMB, Mary 1928 Dec
LAMBERT, Florence 1939 Dec
LANCHESTER, Elsa 1934 Jan GA
LANDON, Jane 1963 Oct‡ as LEACH,
   Jane
LANE, Maryon 1947 Aug*
LANSLEY, Jacqueline c 1967 Aug*
LAPERE, Gaston c 1946 Nov
LARAMAN, Judy 1948 Dec‡
LARSEN, Gerd 1944 July
LASCELLES, Anne 1942 Jan as FLEMING,
   Sheila
LAST, Brenda 1963 Jan*
LATOFF, David 1931 May
LAURENCE, James c 1971 May
LAURENCE, Jeanetta 1968 July‡ as BUMPUS,
   Jeanetta
LAVERICK, June 1948 Dec*
LAWE, Susan 1963 Nov as PRYKE, Susan
LAWRENCE, Bryan 1954 Mar‡ as
   PALETHORPE, Brian
LAWRENCE, Kit 1932 Jan
LAYLAND, Jennifer 1958 Oct*
LEACH, Jane see LANDON, Jane
LEAMAN, Joan 1934 Jan
LE COMTE, Denise 1960 Dec*
LEE, Margaret c 1954 Feb* as ANDREWS,
   Margaret
LEGERTON, Henry c 1947 Jan
LEIGEY, Veronika 1954 Mar‡
LEIGHTON, June 1943 Dec* as APPLETON,
   June
LENZ, Kurt 1931 Oct
LESLEY, June 1951 Feb* as PICKETT, June
LESTER, Keith 1932 Jan
LEWIS, Sally 1954 Sept*
LINCOLN, Julie c 1968 Jan*
LINDEN, Anya 1949 Jan‡ as ELENTON, Anya
   also ELINDEN
LINDEN, Tom 1941 July
LINDSAY, Marion 1972 Nov*
KINDSAY, Maylor 1932 Mar
LINDSAY, Rosemary c 1943 Sept as SCOTT-
   GILES, Rosemary
LINTON, Patricia 1965 Nov‡
LISNER, Charles c 1948 Aug*
LLOYD, Powell 1933 Mar (From Opera
   company – mime roles only)
LOCKWOOD, Susan c 1969 Apr*
LOFTUS, John 1932 Mar
LONGSTAFF, Heather see BAX, Heather
LOPOKOVA, Lydia 1931 May GA
LORAINE, Mary 1941 July
LORRAINE, Maggie c 1966 Aug
LORRAYNE, Vyvyan 1958 Jan*
LOWER, Barbara c 1971 Sept*
LUCAS, Susan c 1976 Aug*
LUNNON, Robert 1947 May*
LYNDALL, Vera 1932 Nov
LYNDON, Barbara 1976 Nov* as ALLAN,
   Barbara
LYNNE, Gillian 1944 May
LYONS, Margaret c 1958 July*

McALPINE, Donald 1949 Aug*
McCARTHY, Sheila 1928 Dec
McCORMACK, Graham 1947 May*
McCORMACK, Moira 1973 Jan*
MacGIBBON, Ross 1973 May‡
McGORIAN, Sharon 1977 Mar*
McGRATH, Barry c 1968 Oct
McINTYRE, Ida 1931 Mar
McLEAN, Roderick 1938 Feb
MacLEARY, Donald c 1954 July‡
MacMILLAN, Keith see MILLAND, Keith
MacMILLAN, Kenneth 1946 Apr
McNAIR, John 1931 Sept
McNAUGHT, Nancy 1946 Apr
McQUESTION, Janet see VARLEY, Janet
MADEN, Judith c 1959 July*
MADER, Arnott 1951 Sept*
MADSEN, Egon 1976 Oct GA
MADSEN, Jorn 1965 May GA
MAITLAND, Maureen c 1959 July*
MAKAROVA, Natalia 1972 June GA
MANNING, Anthony 1951 Mar* as
   MATTIUZ, Tony
MARION, Joan 1932 Mar
MARKOVA, Alicia 1932 Jan
MARLYS, Susan c 1964 May‡ as DAVIES,
   Susan
MARTIN, Alec see THOMSON, Alex
MARTIN, Enid 1939 Dec
MARTIN, Keith 1959 Sept*
MARTIN, Kenneth see SAUNDERS, Kenneth
MARTIN, Roni 1943 Oct
MARTIN, William 1946 Nov
MARTON, Andis c 1967 Aug*
MARTYN, Laurel 1935 Sept as GILL, Laurel
MASON, Kenneth 1959 Apr‡
MASON, Monica c 1958 July*
MASSEY, Guy 1931 Nov
MASSINE, Léonide 1947 Feb GA
MATHEWS, Gwyneth 1931 Sept also
   MATTHEWS, Gwyneth
MATTHEWS, Anna c 1956 Sept‡
MATTIUZ, Tony see MANNING, Anthony
MAY, Pamela 1933 Oct as MAY, Doris also
   MAYE
MAYAN, Cynthia 1952 Feb* as BLOWERS,
   Cynthia
MEAD, Robert 1957 Dec‡
MEAGHER, Alice 1929 Dec
MELLISS, Peggy 1931 Sept
MELVILLE, Kenneth 1945 May as
   GRIFFITHS, Kenneth
MENDEL, Deryk 1937 Jan
MERCIER, Margaret c 1954 July‡
MERKY, Franziska c 1978 Jan*
MERLE, Robyn c 1979 July*
MERRY, Hazel 1954 Dec‡
METLISS, Maurice 1949 May*
MICHAEL, Sylvia 1956 Jan‡
MILLAND, Keith 1949 Nov‡ as MacMILLAN,
   Keith
MILLER, Edward c 1955 July
MILLER, Elizabeth 1931 Sept
MILLER, Patricia 1947 Apr*
MILLER, Petal c 1973 May
MILLINGTON, Nicholas c 1975 Sept‡

MILLS, Jennifer 1975 Feb*
MINTY, Jeanette 1947 Nov*
MOLLOY, Clive 1956 Mar‡
MOLYNEUX, Anthony 1967 Jan‡
MONCUR, Pamela 1956 Mar‡
MONTGOMERIE, Jill 1961 Sept‡
MOORE, Andrew c 1973 Sept‡ as MOORE,
   Stephen
MOORE, Nadia see NERINA, Nadia
MORAN, Linda c 1973 Dec*
MORDAUNT, Joanna 1967 Dec‡
MORETON, Ursula 1928 Dec
MORGAN, Elaine 1952 Sept*
MORGAN, Elizabeth 1978 Nov*
MORREAU, Renée 1961 Dec*
MORRIS, Geraldine 1963 Nov*
MORSE, David 1960 Aug‡
MOSAVAL, Johaar 1951 Dec*
MOSSFORD, Lorna 1939 Mar also
   MOSSFORD, Edna
MOTTRAM, Simon 1956 Sept
MURCH, Phyllis 1938 Jan
MURDOCH, Sallie 1959 Sept‡
MURRAY, Ian 1954 Mar*
MURRAY, Lorna 1974 Mar*
MUSIL, Karl 1966 July GA
MYERS, Carl c 1968 Sept*

NAUGHTON, Henry 1951 Sept*
NAVARRE, Avril 1943 Feb
NEEDHAM, Carole 1958 Mar*
NEGUS, Anne 1944 Jan
NEIL, Sara 1950 Mar* as BROWN, Doreen
NELSON, Sheila 1945 June
NERINA, Nadia 1946 Apr also MOORE,
   Nadia
NEWHOUSE, Nadina 1929 Dec
NEWMAN, Claude 1931 Sept
NEWTON, Christopher 1952 Dec‡
NEWTON, Joy 1929 May
NIBLETT, Guy 1979 Jan‡
NICHOLSON, John 1936 May
NIELSON, Marie 1931 Sept
NISBET, Joanne 1951 July*
NORTH, Robert 1976 Oct GA
NORTH, Rosemary 1964 Oct*
NUNN, Denise 1974 Mar*
NUREYEV, Rudolf 1962 Feb GA
NURSE, Regina see WESTON, Regina
NYE, Palma 1936 Nov

O'BRIEN, Peter c 1966 Sept‡
O'CONAIRE, Deirdre c 1962 Aug
OLRICH, April 1949 Mar
O'REILLY, Sheilah 1946 Apr
ORPIN, Gillian c 1958 Aug‡
ORWELL, Cavan c 1960 Jan‡
OSBORN, Mavis 1956 Jan‡
OWEN, Ian 1970 Apr‡

PAGE, Ann see HOWARD, Ann
PAGE, Annette 1948 Apr*
PAGE, Ashley c 1975 Sept‡
PAGE, Linda 1970 Apr‡
PAISEY, Karen 1979 June‡
PALETHORPE, Brian see LAWRENCE, Bryan

PALTENGHI, David 1941 Dec
PARK, Merle 1954 Mar*
PARKER, Beverley 1972 July*
PARKER, Christina 1979 Sept‡
PARKER, Spencer 1965 Mar*
PARKINSON, Georgina 1954 Sept‡
PARRY, Guinevere 1935 Oct
PARSONS, Janice 1972 Nov*
PATRICK, Rosalind 1928 Dec
PATRICK, Sara 1934 Jan
PATTERSON, Patricia 1964 Oct‡
PEARCE, Barbara 1947 Dec
PENNEY, Jennifer 1963 Sept*
PERI, Ria 1963 Oct* as PERI, Anita
PERRIE, William c 1971 June
PHILLIPS, Ailne 1932 Jan also PHILLIPS,
   Aileen
PHILLIPS, Jeffrey 1957 Mar*
PHILLIPS, Joan see SHELDON, Joan
PIANOFF, Katherine 1975 Jan*
PICKETT, June see LESLEY, June
PICKFORD, Alexandra c 1967 Sept*
PITTS, Maud 1928 Dec
PLAISTED, Ronald 1946 Nov
PLATTS, Joyce see GRAEME, Joyce
POOLE, David 1947 Sept*
PORTER, Marguerite 1967 Jan*
PORTER, Paul c 1969 Aug‡
POWELL, Graham 1961 Mar‡
POWELL, Ray 1942 Mar
POWELL, Vicki 1972 Nov‡ as POWELL, Sally
PRICE, Roland c 1979 Jan*
PROKHOROVA, Violetta see ELVIN, Violetta
PROKOVSKY, André 1977 May GA
PRYKE, Susan see LAWE, Susan
PURNELL, Derek c 1973 Aug*

QUIXLEY, Kitty 1928 Dec

RAFIQUE, Chinko c 1967 Oct
RANDS TREVOR/RANDS, Walter see
   TREVOR, Walter
RASSINE, Alexis 1942 Mar
RATCLIFFE, Monica 1929 Dec
RAWLINSON, Margaret 1946 Feb
RAY, Mavis 1946 Jan
RAYMOND, Suzanna 1962 July* as SMITH,
   Suzanna
REECE, Valerie 1953 Aug*
REEDER, Kim 1972 Mar*
REEVES, Susan 1933 Oct
REMINGTON, Barbara c 1959 July*
RENCHER, Derek c 1953 Feb*
REPETTO, Tony 1931 Dec as REPETTO-
   BUTLER, Tony
REYMOND, Paul 1936 Aug as REYLOFF, Paul
REYN, Judith c 1962 Aug*
RICHARDS, Louanne 1958 Aug*
RICHARDS, Mary 1934 Jan
RICHARDSON, Mandy-Jane 1979 Mar*
ROADKNIGHT, Phyllis 1934 Oct
ROBERTS, Ray 1966 Mar (Actor – mime
   roles only)
ROBERTSON, Betty 1935 Apr
ROBINSON, Harold 1946 Oct (Stage Manager
   – Mime roles only)

ROBINSON, Jane 1959 Sept*
ROBSON, Joy 1931 May
RODRIGUES, Alfred c 1947 Aug as
   RODRIQUE/S, Alfred
ROOD, Sylvia 1934 Oct
ROOPE, Clover 1956 Nov‡
ROSATO, Genesia 1976 Oct*
ROSE, Julie 1978 Feb‡
ROSEBY, Margaret 1944 Oct
ROSS, Joan 1937 May
ROSSLYN, Christine 1932 May
ROSSON, Keith c 1954 July* as BARKER,
   Keith
ROWANN, Judith 1977 Aug
RUANNE, Patricia c 1962 Aug‡
RUDENKO, Anthony c 1968 Dec*
RUFFELL, Lawrence 1959 Feb*
RUSSELL, Thekla 1944 Jan
RYDER, John c 1963 Dec‡

SAIDE, Samira c 1979 July*
SALE, John 1949 Nov‡
SAMSOVA, Galina 1976 Dec GA
SAUNDERS, Kenneth c 1972 Sept* as
   MARTIN, Kenneth
SAUNDERS, Yvonne 1961 Sept*
SCOTT, Barbara see GIEVES, Anne
SCOTT-GILES/SCOTT, Rosemary see
   LINDSAY, Rosemary
SEAR, Margaret 1949 Mar‡
SEATON, Amanda 1973 Oct* as DAVIES,
   Amanda
SELLING, Caj 1959 Mar GA
SEYMOUR, Lynn c 1957 Aug* as
   SPRINGBETT, Lynn
SHAW, Brian 1944 May as EARNSHAW,
   Brian*
SHEARER, Moira 1940 Apr
SHELDON, Joan 1938 Oct as PHILLIPS, Joan
SHEPHERD, Derek see DEANE, Derek
SHERIDAN, Linda 1937 Apr
SHERIFF, Stephen c 1976 Sept‡
SHERWOOD, Gary 1959 Mar‡
SHIELDS, David 1952 Apr‡
SHORE, Anitra 1957 Mar*
SHORE, Jane 1946 Apr
SIBLEY, Antoinette 1956 Jan‡
SIBLEY, Georgina 1964 Oct*
SILVER, Mark c 1973 Sept‡
SINCLAIR, Judith 1951 Dec*
SINCLAIRE, Gary 1966 Nov*
SKEMP, Brigid c 1967 Aug‡
SKINNER, Peter see DARRELL, Peter
SLAUGHTER, Richard c 1977 Sept‡
SLEEP, Wayne 1965 Dec‡
SMITH, James c 1976 Sept‡
SMITH, Kay 1958 Nov*
SMITH, Rodney c 1969 Aug
SMITH, Suzanna see RAYMOND, Suzanna
SOKOLOVA, Lydia 1962 July GA
SOMES, Michael 1935 Feb
SOPWITH, Noreen 1948 Oct*
SOUTHAM, Caroline 1964 Oct‡
SPEED, Stephen c 1975 Jan‡
SPENCE, Mavis 1946 Feb
SPENCER, Nigel c 1970 Dec‡

SPENS-DUNNING, Topsy see DUNNING,
   Paula
SPICER, Fanny 1934 Jan also SPICER, Anne
SPIRA, Phyllis c 1960 Oct*
SPRINGBETT, Lynn see SEYMOUR, Lynn
STAFF, Frank 1934 Apr
STAFF, Helen 1958 Jan*
STANLEY, Siobhan 1975 Mar‡ as STANLEY,
   Susan also FITZGERALD, Suzanne
STEVENS, Benjamin c 1957 Mar as STEVENS,
   John (later STEVENSON, Ben)
STEUART, Douglas 1942 Mar as DOUGLAS,
   Tom
STEWART, Graham see VARDON, Douglas
STEWART, Marjorie 1931 Mar
STOKES, Jean 1947 Mar
STONE, Paddy c 1946 Oct
STRIKE, Lois c 1966 Aug*
STRINGER, Anne 1952 Nov*
STUART, Clementina 1946 Feb
STUART, Robert 1931 May
STYLES, Sheila 1974 July‡
SURTEES, Irene 1947 Oct*
SUTCLIFFE, Jacqueline c 1963 Aug‡
SWANSON, Maureen 1948 May*
SYMONS, Oliver 1954 Mar‡

TAIT, Marion c 1968 Sept*
TALBOT, Oenone 1946 Feb
TALLIS, Jacqui c 1970 Mar* as TALLIS,
   Jacqueline
TAPHOUSE, Gail 1975 May*
TARVER, Tony 1946 Mar
TAVERNER, Sonia 1954 Dec*
TAYLOR, Brenda 1949 Jan‡
TAYLOR, Bridget c 1967 Jan*
TAYLOR, Joan 1935 Oct as BIRDWOOD-
   TAYLOR, Joan
TAYLOR, Rosemary c 1967 Jan‡
TAYLOR, Roy see CARLTON, Roy
TAYLOR, Valerie 1948 Dec*
TEMPEST, Doreen 1948 Dec*
THEOBALD, Terence c 1946 Dec
THOMAS, Denise 1958 Mar‡
THOMAS, Elaine 1953 May*
THOMAS, Gail c 1964 Aug*
THOMSON, Alex 1946 June as MARTIN, Alec
THOMSON, Norman 1946 Feb
THOMPSON, Basil 1955 Jan‡
THORBURN, Patricia 1937 Oct
THOROGOOD, Alfreda c 1959 Sept‡
THOROGOOD, Patricia 1952 Sept*
TICKNER, Hilary 1967 Dec‡
TIETGEN, Daphne 1933 Feb
TIPLER, Marilyn 1968 Jan‡
TOMKINSON, Paul c 1978 Aug*
TOMLINSON, Dudley 1961 Jan*
TOYE, Wendy 1931 May
TRECU, Pirmin 1946 Sept as
   ALDABALDETRECEE, Pirnon also
   ALDABALDE, Pirnon/Pirmin
TREVOR, Elizabeth 1953 Sept‡
TREVOR, Walter 1948 Mar* as RANDS-
   TREVOR, Walter also RANDS, Trevor
TROUNSON, Marilyn c 1966 Aug*
TUCKER, Ravenna 1979 Oct‡

TUDOR, Antony 1932 Jan
TURNER, Harold 1930 Dec
TURNER, Henry 1941 July
TURNHAM, Susan 1960 Dec‡

USHER, Graham 1955 Jan listed USHER,
Colin (probably misprint for Graham)

VAIL, Veronica 1946 June
VALAIRE, Rosemary 1946 Oct as
FEUERHEER, Rosemary
VALERIE, Joan 1941 Dec
VALOIS, DE, Ninette 1928 Dec
VAN PRAAGH, Peggy 1941 Dec
VANE, Sandra 1955 Sept
VARDON, Douglas 1970 Jan* as STEWART,
Graham
VARLEY, Janet 1958 Aug‡ as McQUESTION,
Janet
VERDY, Violette 1964 Feb GA
VERE, Diana c 1962 Aug*
VERNON, Gilbert 1947 Feb* as BRASLER,
Gilbert
VINCENT, June 1936 Dec as HITCH, June
VLASIC, Paul c 1968 Dec*

WADE, Kathryn 1964 Dec‡ as BROWN,
Kathryn
WADE, Valerie 1937 Apr
WADSWORTH, Pauline 1946 Feb
WAKE, Lynne 1975 Jan‡
WAKELYN, Virginia c 1961 Apr*
WALKER, Hazel 1946 Apr

WALKER, Heather 1970 May*
WALL, David c 1963 Sept‡ (1962 Nov Brian
Wall listed probably misprint for David)
WALLER, Paul c 1971 June
WALLER, Stanley see HOLDEN, Stanley
WALLINGTON, Angela see WALTON, Angela
WALLIS, Lynn 1963 Nov*
WALTON, Angela 1950 Mar* as
WALLINGTON, Angela
WALTON, Lynne 1967 Dec*
WARD, Andrew c 1978 Sept‡
WARD, Frank 1945 Apr as GRANT, Frank
WATCHAM, Jacqueline see DARYL,
Jacqueline
WATSON, Grace 1928 Dec
WAY, Suzanne c 1971 Feb*
WAYNE, Debra 1954 Dec as FORMAN,
Doreen
WEBB, Iain 1978 Feb*
WELFORD, Mark c 1978 Aug‡
WELLS, Doreen 1954 Sept*
WESTERMAN, Diana 1952 Mar‡
WESTMORELAND, Terry 1958 Mar*
WESTON, Joan 1952 Sept*
WESTON, Regina 1960 Dec‡ as NURSE,
Regina
WHITCOMB, Phyl 1929 Oct
WHITE, Leslie 1953 Aug*
WHITE, Madeline 1952 May*
WHITE, Peter Franklin 1942 Oct also WHITE,
Franklin
WHITTEN, Rosalyn 1972 Nov*

WHITTLE, Nicholas 1974 Jan*
WICKS, Stephen 1975 Nov‡
WILES, Victoria 1963 Nov*
WILKINSON, Amanda see BECK, Amanda
WILLIAMS, Chenca c 1976 Oct‡ as
WILLIAMS, Jacqueline
WILLIAMS, Jacqueline 1959 Aug
WILLIAMS, Jacqueline see WILLIAMS, Chenca
WILSON, William 1956 Jan*
WING, Margaret 1954 Mar*
WINN, Wendy 1946 June
WITHERS, Jennifer 1972 Nov*
WOOD, Julie 1956 Jan*
WOOD, Susan see DARWOOD, Susan
WOODWARD, Christine 1967 May*
WORTHINGTON, Phyllis 1931 Mar
WRIGHT, Anthony see CONWAY, Anthony
WRIGHT, Belinda 1964 Sept
WRIGHT, Peter 1949 Jan
WRIGHTON, Carol see CAROL, Ann
WYLDE, Pippa 1972 July as BILLYEALD,
Pippa
WYNNE, Geoffrey 1968 Nov*

YOUNG, Anita 1967 Dec‡
YOUNG, Leo 1939 Dec
YURESHA, Jelko 1962 Oct

ZAYMES, Dorothea c 1946 Oct
ZINKIN, Hilda 1954 May‡
ZOLAN, Miro 1953 Sept
ZULLIG, Hans 1948 Oct

Choreographers

This list does not include divertissements nor contributions to various versions of Coppélia, Swan Lake and The Sleeping Beauty.

ANDES, Angelo
1950 El Destino
ASHTON, Frederick
1931 Regatta
1932 The Lord of Burleigh
1933 Pomona
Les Rendezvous
1935 Rio Grande
Façade
Le Baiser de la Fée
1936 Apparitions
Nocturne
1937 Les Patineurs
A Wedding Bouquet
1938 Horoscope
The Judgement of Paris
Harlequin in the Street
1939 Cupid and Psyche
1940 Dante Sonata
The Wise Virgins
1941 The Wanderer
1943 The Quest
1946 Symphonic Variations
Les Sirènes
1947 Valses Nobles et Sentimentales
1948 Scènes de Ballet
Capriol Suite
Don Juan
Cinderella
1951 Daphnis and Chloë
Tiresias
Casse-Noisette (after Ivanov)
1952 Sylvia
1953 Homage to the Queen
1955 Rinaldo and Armida
Variations on a Theme of Purcell
Madame Chrysanthème
1956 La Péri
Birthday Offering
1958 Ondine
1959 La Valse
1960 La Fille Mal Gardée
1961 The Two Pigeons
Perséphone
1963 Marguerite and Armand
1964 The Dream
1965 Monotones (later Monotones No 2)
1966 Monotones No 1
1967 Sinfonietta
1968 Jazz Calendar
Enigma Variations
1970 Lament of the Waves
The Creatures of Prometheus
1972 Siesta
The Walk to the Paradise Garden
1976 A Month in the Country
1980 Rhapsody

BALANCHINE, George
1950 Ballet Imperial
Trumpet Concerto
1964 Serenade
1966 Apollo
1973 The Four Temperaments
Prodigal Son
Agon
Allegro Brillante
1977 Concerto Barocco
Liebeslieder Walzer
BINTLEY, David
1978 The Outsider
Take Five
1979 Meadow of Proverbs
Punch and the Street Party
1980 Homage to Chopin
Adieu
BOURNONVILLE, August
1962 Flower Festival at Genzano, pas de deux
Napoli Divertissement
BRUCE, Christopher
1974 Unfamiliar Playground
BURKE, Anthony
1946 The Vagabonds
1948 Parures
BURROWS, Jonathan
1980 Catch
CARTER, Alan
1946 The Catch
1962 Toccata
1963 Night Tryst
CARTER, Jack
1975 Shukumei
1976 Lulu
CAULEY, Geoffrey
1969 In the Beginning
Lazarus
1970 La Symphonie Pastoral
1971 Ante Room
CORALLI, Jean
1934 Giselle (with Jules Perrot)
CORDER, Michael
1979 Rhyme nor Reason
1980 Day into Night
CRANKO, John
1947 Adieu
Tritsch Trash
1948 Children's Corner
1949 Sea Change
Beauty and the Beast
1950 Pastorale
1951 Harlequin in April
Pineapple Poll
1952 Bonne-Bouche
Reflection
1953 The Shadow
1954 The Lady and the Fool
1957 The Prince of the Pagodas
The Angels

1959 Antigone
Sweeny Todd
1966 Brandenburg Nos 2 and 4
Card Game
1972 Poème de L'Extase
1977 The Taming of the Shrew
1978 Brouillards
DALE, Margaret
1953 The Great Detective
DOLIN, Anton
1932 Italian Suite (with de Valois)
DOONE, Rupert
1932 The Enchanted Grove
DREW, David
1969 Intrusion
1970 From Waking Sleep
1971 St Thomas' Wake
1973 Sacred Circles
Sword of Alsace
FOKINE, Michel
1932 Le Spectre de la Rose
Les Sylphides
1933 Carnaval
1954 The Firebird
1957 Petrushka
1965 Polovtsian Dances from Prince Igor
FRANCA, Celia
1946 Khadra
1947 Bailemos
GORE, Walter
1953 Carte Blanche
HELPMANN, Robert
1942 Comus
Hamlet
The Birds
1944 Miracle in the Gorbals
1946 Adam Zero
1963 Elektra
HOWARD, Andrée
1944 Le Festin de l'Araignée
1946 Assembly Ball
Mardi Gras
1947 La Fête Etrange
1948 Selina
1952 A Mirror for Witches
1953 Veneziana
1959 La Belle Dame sans Merci
HYND, Ronald
1972 In a Summer Garden
1974 Charlotte Brontë
1980 Papillon
IVANOV, Lev
1934 Casse-Noisette
Le Lac des Cygnes, with Petipa
KILLAR, Ashley
1973 Migration
1974 The Entertainers
LAYTON, Joe
1971 Overture
The Grand Tour
1972 O.W.

MACMILLAN, Kenneth
1955 Danses Concertantes
     House of Birds
1956 Noctambules
     Somnambulism
     Solitaire
1958 The Burrow
     Agon
1960 The Invitation
1961 Diversions
1962 The Rite of Spring
1963 Symphony
1964 La Création du Monde
     Images of Love
1965 Romeo and Juliet
1966 Song of the Earth
1967 Concerto
1969 Olympiad
1970 Checkpoint
1971 Anastasia
     Las Hermanas
1972 Triad
     Ballade
     The Poltroon
1973 The Seven Deadly Sins
1974 Manon
     Elite Syncopations
1975 The Four Seasons
     Rituals
1978 Mayerling
     6.6.78
1979 La Fin du Jour
     Playground
1980 Gloria
     My Brother My Sisters
McNAUGHT, Nancy
1949 Etude
MASSINE, Léonide
1947 The Three-Cornered Hat
     La Boutique Fantasque
     Mam'zelle Angot
1948 Clock Symphony
1951 Donald of the Burthens
1962 The Good-Humoured Ladies
1963 Le Bal des Voleurs
MORRICE, Norman
1965 The Tribute
MORSE, David
1976 Pandora
1977 Birdscape
NEUMEIER, John
1977 The Fourth Symphony
NIJINSKA, Bronislava
1964 Les Biches
1966 Les Noces

NORTH, Robert
1980 Troy Game
NUREYEV, Rudolf
1963 La Bayadère, Act IV (after Petipa)
1966 Raymonda (after Petipa)
1968 The Nutcracker
PATRICK, Sara
1934 Uncle Remus
PERROT, Jules
1934 Giselle (with Jean Coralli)
PETIPA, Marius
1933 Coppélia (after Saint-Léon)
1934 Le Lac des Cygnes (with Ivanov)
1939 The Sleeping Princess
1963 La Bayadère, Act IV (arr Nureyev)
1966 Raymonda (arr Nureyev)
PETIT, Roland
1950 Ballabile
1967 Paradise Lost
1969 Pélléas et Mélisande
PROKOVSKY, André
1977 Soft Blue Shadows
ROBBINS, Jerome
1970 Dances at a Gathering
1971 Afternoon of a Faun
1972 Requiem Canticles
1973 In the Night
1975 The Concert
RODRIGUES, Alfred
1952 Ile des Sirènes
1953 Blood Wedding
1954 Café des Sports
1955 Saudades
1956 The Miraculous Mandarin
1961 Jabez and the Devil
ROSS, Herbert
1971 Caprichos
     The Maids
SAINT-LEON, Arthur
1933 Coppélia (arr Petipa)
SEYMOUR, Lynn
1976 Rashomon
1977 The Court of Love
1978 Intimate Letters
SKIBINE, George
1950 Trágedie à Vérone, pas de deux
SOMES, Michael
     Summer Interlude
TETLEY, Glen
1970 Field Figures
1972 Laborintus
1976 Voluntaries
1977 Gemini
THORPE, Jonathan
1978 Game Piano

TUDOR, Antony
1967 Shadowplay
1968 Lilac Garden
     Knight Errant
VALOIS, Ninette de
1928 Les Petits Riens
1929 The Picnic (later The Faun)
     Etude
     Homage aux Belles Viennoises
1931 Danse Sacrée et Danse Profane
     Faust, Scène de Ballet
     The Jackdaw and the Pigeons
     Cephalus and Procris
     Job
     Fête Polonaise
     The Jew in the Bush
1932 Narcissus and Echo
     Rout
     Nursery Suite
     Italian Suite
     Douanes
     The Origin of Design
     The Scorpions of Ysit
1933 The Birthday of Oberon
     The Wise and Foolish Virgins
     La Création du Monde
1934 The Haunted Ballroom
     The Jar
1935 The Rake's Progress
1936 The Gods go a'Begging
     Barabau
     Prometheus
1937 Checkmate
1938 Le Roi Nu
1940 The Prospect Before Us
1941 Orpheus and Eurydice
1943 Promenade
1950 Don Quixote
VAN DANTZIG, Rudi
1970 The Ropes of Time
VAN MANEN, Hans
1972 Grosse Fuge
1973 Twilight
     Tilt
1974 Septet Extra
1975 Four Schumann Pieces
1976 Adagio Hammerklavier
WRIGHT, Peter
1957 A Blue Rose
1964 Quintet
     Summer's Night
1975 Arpège
     El Amor Brujo
1976 Summertide

Adagio Hammerklavier FP 23 Nov 1976 ROH *Ch* Hans van Manen *M* Beethoven *SC* Jean-Paul Vroom. '76 (3). 1 Makarova (3). 2 Mason (3). 3 Penney (3). 4 Wall (3). 5 Eagling (3). 6 Silver (3).

Adam Zero P 10 Apr 1946 ROH *Ch* Helpmann *M* Arthur Bliss *SC* Roger Furse *Scenario* Michael Benthall. '46 (10); '47 (5); '48 (4). *The Principal Dancer* Helpmann '46–8 (19). *The Choreographer/The Ballerina* Brae '46–8 (15) Larsen '47–8 (4). + 4*f* 4*m* CdB.

Adieu P 29 Apr 1980 ROH *Ch* David Bintley *M* Andrzej Panufnik *SC* Mike Becket. 1 Park. 2 Mason. 3 Wall. 4 Fletcher. 5 Jefferies. + CdB.

Afternoon of a Faun FP 14 Dec 1971 ROH *Ch* Robbins *M* Debussy *S* Jean Rosenthal *C* Irene Sharaff. '71 (3); '72 (24); '73 (11); '74 (5); '76 (9). *f* Sibley '71–3 (13) Penney '72–6 (33). Bergsma '72 (4) Porter '76 (2). *m* Dowell '71–6 (19) Coleman '72–6 (12) Nureyev '72–3 (10) Wall '72–6 (11).

Agon P 20 Aug 1958 ROH *Ch* MacMillan *M* Stravinsky *SC* Nicholas Georgiadis. '58 (10). T:9. pdd *f* Linden (6) Park (4). *m* Blair (6) Doyle (4). pdt 1 Trecu (10). 2 Page (10). 3 Grahame (10). pdt 1 Lane (10). 2 Usher (10). 3 Stevens (7) Bosman (3). + 5*f* 1*m*.

Agon FP 25 Jan 1973 ROH *Ch* Balanchine *M* Stravinsky *SC* nc. '73 (14); '75 (3). *Sarabande* Dowell '73 (9) Coleman '73 (3) Nureyev '73–5 (5). *Galliard* 1 Ellis '73–5 (16) Corken '73 (1). 2 Thorogood '73 (3) Young '73–5 (13). *Bransle Simple* 1 Ashmole '73–5 (17). 2 Eagling '73–5 (16) Hosking '73 (1). *Bransle Gay* Connor '73–5 (14) Collier '73 (3). pdd *f* Derman '73–5 (9) Thorogood '73 (7) Ellis '73 (1). *m* Wall '73–5 (13) D Kelly '73 (4).

Anastasia (3 act version) P 22 July 1971 ROH *Ch* MacMillan *M* Tchaikovsky/Martinu/Studio Technical University West Berlin (Fritz Winckel/Rüdiger Rüfer) *SC* Barry Kay. '71 (13); '72 (5); '73 (3); '75 (8); '76 (6); '78 (4). T:5. *Grand Duchess Anastasia/Anna Anderson* Seymour '71–8 (28) Collier '71–8 (11). *Tsar Nicholas II* Rencher '71–8 (39) Somes '72A. *Tsarina* Beriosova '71–3 (14) Beriosova-Parkinson '71 (1) Parkinson '71–8 (19) Eyre '75–8 (5). *Mathilde Kschessinska* Sibley '71–5 (6) Park '71–5 (11) Wells '71–3 (4)/Thorogood '72–8 (6) Penney '75–8 (7) Mason '75–6 (5). Vere '72A. *Her Partner* Dowell '71–8 (20) D Kelly '71–5 (9) Wall '71–6 (12) Eagling '76–8 (3). + 6*f* 11*m* CdB.

Antigone P 19 Oct 1959 ROH *Ch* Cranko *M* Mikis Theodorakis *SC* Rufino Tamayo. '59 (7); '60 (6); '61 (9); '62 (3); '63 (7); '64 (3); '66 (4).

T:9. *Oedipus* Edwards '59–'66 (39). *Jocasta* Farron '59–'61 (15) Larsen '61–6 (24). *Polynices* Blair '59–'61 (18) Drew '61–6 (21). *Etiocles* Burne '59–'61 (10) Rosson '60–6 (26) Nureyev '63 (3). *Antigone* Beriosova '59–'66 (35) Linden '62–3 (4). *Creon* Somes '59–'63 (26) Hynd '60–6 (13). *Haemon* MacLeary '59–'66 (37) Rencher '63 (2). + 20*f* 22*m*.

Apollo FP 15 Nov 1966 ROH *Ch* Balanchine *M* Stravinsky *SC* John Craxton; from '71 nc. '66 (7); '67 (1); '68 (7); '71 (5); '72 (2); '73 (6); '74 (2); '76 (5). T:2. *Apollo* MacLeary '66–7 (3) Rosson '66–8 (5) Mead '66–8 (7) Nureyev '71–6 (15) D Kelly '73–6 (5). *Terpsichore* Beriosova '66–'71 (8) Page '66 (2) Parkinson '66–'76 (16) Bergsma '66–'73 (5) Seymour '73–6 (3) Park '74 (1). *Polyhymnia* Mason '66–'74 (14) O'Conaire '66–'71 (8) Derman '71 (2) Connor '73–6 (11). *Calliope* Parkinson '66–'73 (6) Bergsma '66 (1) Lorrayne '66–'71 (14) Vere '72–4 (6) Jenner '73–6 (5) Derman '76 (3). *Also* Rep II.

Apparitions P 11 Feb 1936 SW *Ch* Ashton *M* Liszt arr Lambert orch Gordon Jacob. *SC* Cecil Beaton (revised '49 and '52). '36 (17); '37 (10); '38 (6); '39 (2); '40 (6); '41 (4); '42 (5); '43 (9); '49 (17); '52 (6); '53 (14). T:44. *The Poet* Helpmann '36–'49 [79] Chappell '38 (2) Somes '52–3 (19) Melville '53 (1). *The Woman in Ball Dress* Fonteyn '36–'53 [82] May '37–'41 [6] Heaton '52–3 (13). + 2*m* CdB. nr '41 June 19*m*. *Also* Rep II.

Apparitions Ballroom Scene excerpt. '70 Ashton Tribute (1). *The Poet* Nureyev. *The Woman in Ball Dress* Fonteyn. + 8*f* 9*m*.

Aurora pdd *see* **Sleeping Beauty**, Act III pdd.

Baiser de la Fée, Le P 26 Nov 1935 SW *Ch* Ashton *M* Stravinsky *SC* Sophie Fedorovitch. '35 (6); '36 (12); '37 (6); '38 (5); '39 (1). T:12. *The Fairy* Argyle '35–8 (18) Appleyard '36 (3) May '36–7 (2) Brae '36–9 (7). *The Young Man* Turner '35–9 (30). *His Fiancée* Fonteyn '35–9 (30). + 29*f* 8*m*.

Baiser de la Fée, Le, excerpt Scene 3. '70 Ashton Tribute (1). *The Bride* Penney. + 8*f*.

Baiser de la Fée, Le P 12 Apr 1960 ROH *Ch* MacMillan *M* Stravinsky *SC* Kenneth Rowell. '60 (7); '61 (5); '62 (7); '65 (5). T:9. *The Fairy* Beriosova '60–5 (24). *A Young Man* MacLeary '60–5 (24). *His Fiancée* Seymour '60–5 (14) Park '61 (2) Sibley '61–5 (8). *The Gypsy* Daryl '60–1 (12) Mason '62–6 (12). + 23*f* 16*m*.

Ballabile P 5 May 1950 ROH *Ch* Petit; revised '51 *M* Chabrier arr Lambert *SC* Antoni Clavé. '50 (16); '51 (12); '52 (8); '53 (9); '54 (7); '56

(3); '60 (7). T:4. 1 Elvin '50–6 (38) Farron '51–4 (15) Navarre '53 (2) Page '60 (3) Parkinson '60 (4). 2 A Grant '50–'60 (54) Powell '52–4 (7) Chatfield '53 (1). 3 Negus '50 (13) Dale '50–3 (31) Olrich '52 (1) Benesh '54 (7) Dixon '56 (3) Park '60 (6) Lyons '60 (1) Moncur '60T. + 3*f* 4*m*, from '51 10*f* 10*m*.

Ballabile pdt. '60 (1).

Ballet Imperial (from '73 **Piano Concerto No 2**) FP 5 Apr 1950 ROH *Ch* Balanchine *M* Tchaikovsky *SC* Eugene Berman; '63 *SC* Carl Toms; '73 *SC* Terence Emery. '50 (29); '51 (30); '52 (13); '53 (21); '54 (6); '55 (6); '57 (13); '58 (11); '59 (6); '63 (10); '64 (3); '66 (7); '67 (6); '73 (3); '74 (5). T:45. 1 Fonteyn '50 (11) Shearer '50–3 (20) Elvin '50–5 (37) Farron '51 (5) Jackson '51–8 (26) Grey '52–5 (9) Nerina '57–'66 (24) Lane '58 (2) Fifield '57 (6) Sibley '59–'63 (12) Page '63 (3) Verdy '64 (2) Mason '66–'74 (11) Wells '73–4 (3). 2 Somes '50–3 (48) Field '51–5 (40) Melville '51T–3 (7) Chatfield '52–8 (17) Blair '57–'66 (25) Trecu '57–9 (5) Doyle '63 (17) MacLeary '63–'74 (9) D Kelly '73 (1). 3 Grey '50–2 (33) Lynne '50 (3) Lindsay '51–9 (56) Beriosova '52–5 (17) Linden '55–'63 (15) Park '58 (2) Grahame '57–9 (12) Bergsma '63–'73 (15) Mason '63–'73 (9) Needham '66 (2) Derman '74 (5).

Barabau P 17 Apr 1936 SW *Ch* de Valois *M/Text* Vittorio Rieti *SC* Edward Burra. '36 (9); '37 (4); '38 (6); '39 (3); '40 (2). *Barabau* Turner '36–9 (20) Newman '36 (2) Helpmann '40 (2). *Sergeant* Ashton '36–'40 (24). *A Peasant Woman* de Valois '36–7 (6) Phillips '36–7 (6) Brown '37–'40 (12). + 12*f* 6*m*.

Bayadère, La FP 27 Nov 1963 ROH *Ch* Petipa revised/*Pr* Nureyev *M* Minkus *S* nc *C* Philip Prowse. '63 (4); '64 (15); '65 (4); '67 (5); '68 (14); '69 (5); '70 (7); '71 (7); '72 (9); '73 (4); '74 (5); '75 (11); '76 (1); '77 (8); '78 (8). T:135. *Nikiya* Fonteyn '63–'73 (22) Beriosova '64–7 (5) Page '64 (7) Lorrayne '67–'72 (13) Sibley '68–'75 (18) Park '68–'78 (24) Mason '72A '73–8 (9) Connor '74 (5) Peri '75 (1) Penney '75–8 (4) Thorogood '77T '78 (1). *Solor* Nureyev '63–'75 (46) MacLeary '64–7 (5) Gable '64–5 (6) Coleman '68–'78 (22) Rosson '68–'71 (7) Wall '70–7 (11) Dowell '73–8 (5) Ashmole '75 (1) Eagling '77T–8 (4).

Bayadère, La, Entry of the Shades. '74 (1).

Belle Dame sans Merci, La FP 2 Sept 1959 ROH *Ch/SC* Andrée Howard *M* Alexander Goehr after Claude le Jeune/Clement Jannequin. '59 (3). *A Knight* MacLeary (3). *La Belle Dame sans Merci* Parkinson (3). + 8*m*. *Also* Rep II.

Biches, Les P 2 Dec 1964 ROH *Ch* Nijinska *M* Poulenc *SC* Marie Laurencin. '64 (6); '65 (3); '66 (5); '67 (4); '68 (5); '71 (10); '75 (5); '76 (2); '79 (5). T:16. *'La Garconne'* Parkinson '64–'75 (24) Page '67 (2) Derman '71–9 (7) Connor '71 (5) Makarova '75–6 (4) Penney '79 (3). *'Hostess'* Beriosova '64 (3) Bergsma '64–'75 (23) Mason '67–'76 (12) Ruanne '71 (2) Porter '79 (5). *'Athletes'* 1 Blair '64–'71 (15) MacLeary '66–8 (13) Mead '68 (1) Coleman '71–5 (9) Wall '76–9 (5) Jefferies '79 (2). 2 Rosson '64–'71 (26) K Mason '67 (3) Ashmole '71–6 (11) Dowson '79 (3) Beagley '79 (2). 3 Mead '64–'71 (30) Drew '68 (1) Eagling '71–5 (7) Myers '76 (2) Hosking '79 (3) Ashley Page '79 (2).

Birds, The P 24 Nov 1942 New *Ch* Helpmann *M* Respighi *SC* Chiang Yee. '42 (17); '43 (33). T:48. *The Hen* Fraser '42–3 [37] Nye '43T [12]. *The Cuckoo* Hamilton '42–3 [35] Powell '43 [14]. *The Dove* Rassine '42–3 [45] F White '43 [4]. *The Nightingale* Grey '42–3 [31] Shearer '43 [16]. Clayden '43 [2]. + 6f. nr '43 Oct 2m.

Birthday of Oberon, The P 7 Feb 1933 sw *Ch/Pr* de Valois *M* Purcell arr Lambert *SC* John Armstrong. '33 (6). *Spring* Appleyard (6). *Summer* Darnborough (6). *Autumn* Moreton (6) *Winter* Bamford (6). + 21f 6m.

Birthday Offering P 5 May 1956 ROH *Ch* Ashton *M* Glazounov arr/orch Robert Irving *C* André Levasseur *S* Sophie Fedorovitch (from Veneziana). '56 (7); '57 (4); '58 (2); '60 (2); '62 (5); '63 (3); '65 (1); '68 (3); '70 (3); '72 (1); '78 (7); '79 (4). T:55. pdd f Fonteyn '56–'72 (20) Beriosova '62 (3) Nerina '62–3 (3) Park '70–9 (8) Porter '78–9 (6). m Somes '56–'60 (15) Doyle '62–3 (8) Blair '65 (1) Nureyev '68 (3) MacLeary '70 (3) Wall '72–8 (4) Silver '78–9 (8). *Variations* 1 Fonteyn '56–'72 (20) Park '62–'79 (16) Porter '78–9 (6). 2 Grey '56 (7) Page '57–'63 (16) Beriosova '65 (1) Sibley '68 (4) Bergsma '70 (3) Penney '78–9 (7) Wylde '78–9 (4). 3 Elvin '56 (3) Linden '56–'63 (17) Parkinson '60–'72 (10) Lorrayne '62 (1) Thorogood '78–9 (7) Rosato '78–9 (4) 4 Nerina '56–'63 (18) Sibley '60–5 (3) Mason '62–'79 (15) Jenner '72 (1) Eyden '78–9 (5). 5 Jackson '56–8 (9) Park '57–'72 (11) Parkinson '62–3 (5) Beckley '62–3 (3) Collier '70 (3) Connor '78–9 (6) Whitten '78–9 (5). 6 Beriosova '56–'72 (17) Seymour '60–5 (3) Mason '62–3 (5) Peri '68 (3) Lorrayne '70 (3) Porter '78–9 (5) Groombridge '78–9 (6). 7 Fifield '56–7 (11) Lane '58–'65 (9) Sibley '62–3 (4) Penney '68–'72 (7) Ellis '78–9 (8) Collier '78–9 (3). + 6m ('56 Grant, Shaw, Chatfield, Blair, Doyle, Ashbridge) Solos added '65 (Blair), '68 (Nureyev).

Birthday Offering Variation 4. '70 Ashton Tribute (1). Mason.

Bonne-Bouche P 4 Apr 1952 ROH *Ch/Scenario* Cranko *M* Arthur Oldham *SC* Osbert Lancaster.

'52 (22); '53 (8). *A Mother* May '52–3 (22) Larsen '52 (8). *Her Daughter* Clayden '52–3 (22) Nerina '52–3 (6) Olrich '52 (2). *The Lover* Shaw '52–3 (30). *A Black King* A Grant '52–3 (30). + 17f 25m.

Boutique Fantasque, La FP 27 Feb 1947 ROH *Ch* Massine *M* Rossini orch Respighi *SC* André Derain. '47 (20); '48 (21); '49 (6); '50 (6); '54 (12); '55 (9). T:31. *Can-Can Dancers* f Shearer '47–9 (25) May '47–8 (16) Nerina '48–'55 (15) Dale '48–'54 (5) Danilova '49 (4) Navarre '49A '50 (4) Heaton '55 (5). m Massine '47–9 (21) Turner '47–'54 (31) Hart '48–'50 (8) Franklin '49 (4) A Grant '54–5 (7) Blair '55 (3). *Also* Rep II.

Boutique Fantasque, La Can-Can. '61 (1). f Seymour. m A Grant.

Brandenburg Nos 2 and 4 P 10 Feb 1966 ROH *Ch* Cranko *M* J S Bach *SC* Dorothee Zippel. '66 (8); '67 (3). T:6. 1 Park '66–7 (4) C Hill '66–7 (7). 2 Sibley '66 (6) Horsham '66 (2) Penney '67 (3). 3 Parkinson '66–7 (8) Vere '66 (3). 4 Jenner '66–7 (11). 5 MacLeary '66 (6) Rosson '66–7 (4) Gayle '67 (1). 6 Usher '66–7 (9) Coleman '66 (2). 7 Gable '66 (2) Bosman '66–7 (9). 8 Dowell '66–7 (6) Cauley '66–7 (5). + 4f 4m.

Card Game FP 18 Feb 1966 ROH *Ch* Cranko *M* Stravinsky *SC* Dorothee Zippel. '66 (10). *The Joker* Gable (2) Dowell (8). *Queen of Hearts* Page (5) Bergsma (5). *Two of Diamonds* Seymour (5) Jenner (5). + 2f 12m. *Also* Rep II.

Carnaval FP 24 Oct 1933 sw *Ch* Fokine *M* Schumann orch Gordon Jacob *SC* Elizabeth/Marsh Williams; '35 nc; '44 *SC* after Bakst. '33 (4); '34 (4); '35 (5); '36 (11); '37 (9); '38 (5); '39 (3); '40 (3); '44 (21); '45 (18); '46 (6). T: [78]. *Columbine* Markova '33–4 (8) de Valois '35–6 (3) Argyle '35–8 (12) Miller '36–9 (15) Fonteyn '36–'45 [30] Farron '39–'40 (4) May '40 (1) Dale '44–5 [9] Prokhorova '46 (3) Shearer '46 (3). *Harlequin* Idzikowski '33 (4) Judson '34 (3) Helpmann '34–5 (4) Gore '35 (1) Turner '35–'46 (43) Carter '40 (1) Rassine '44–6 [32]. *Pierrot* Tudor '33 (4) Kemp '34 (2) Stuart '34 (1) Gamble '34 (1) Helpmann '35–'45 [21] Ashton '35–'46 (37) Edwards '44–5 [4] Somes '45–6 (12) Paltenghi '45 (6). nr '44 Oct 14m. *Also* Rep II.

Carnaval Solo: Papillon '30. T:3.

Casse-Noisette FP 30 Jan 1934 sw *Ch* Petipa (sic) *Pr* Sergeyev *M* Tchaikovsky *SC* Hedley Briggs; '36 Act III and '37 Acts I/II *SC* Mitislav Doboujinsky. '34 (9); '35 (7); '36 (2); '37 (8); '38 (7); '39 (4); '41 (6); '42 (7). *Sugar Plum Fairy* Markova '34–5 (14) French '35–6 (3) Honer '35–'42 [21] Argyle '38 (1) Fonteyn '37–'42 [10]. *Nut-Cracker Prince* Judson '34 (7) Helpmann '34–'42 [15]. Turner '35–9 (21) Hart '41–2 [6]. nr '42 Jan 16m.

Casse-Noisette Act III. '34 (1); '35 (8); '36 (9); '37 (4); '38 (3); '42 (22); '43 (13); '44 (13). T:[152]. *Sugar Plum Fairy* French '34–6 (10) Markova '35 (1) Honer '35–'42 (14) Fonteyn '36–'44 [25] Argyle '37–8 (2) Dale '42–4 [17] May '44 (3). *Nut-Cracker Prince* Helpmann '34–'44 [37] Turner '35–8 (13) Dolin '35 (1) Hart '42 (8) Paltenghi '43–4 (13). nr '42 Oct 31m. *Also* Rep II.

Casse-Noisette Act III pdd. '36 (1); '45 (6). T:7. *Sugar Plum Fairy* French '36 (1) Fonteyn '36T '45 (4) May '45 (2). *Nut-Cracker Prince* Helpmann '36–'45 (5) Turner '36T Paltenghi '45 (2). Revived as Gala divert. C nc. '58 (1); '64 (1); '65 (1). f Fonteyn '58 (1) Nerina '64 (1) Beriosova '65 (1). m Somes '58 (1) Blair '64–5 (2). *Also* Rep II.

Cephalus and Procris FP 21 May 1931 sw *Ch* de Valois *M* André Grétry *SC* William Chappell. '31 (5); '32 (8); '33 (2). *Cephalus* Judson '31–3 (14) Doone '33 (1). *Procris* Lopokova '31 (2) McCarthy '31–3 (7) Markova '32 (3) de Valois '32–3 (3). *Aurora* de Valois '31 (2) Appleyard '31–3 (9) Newton '31–2 (2) Nielson '31–2. + 8f 4m.

Checkmate P 15 June 1937 Théâtre des Champs-Elysées, Paris *Ch* de Valois *M* Arthur Bliss *SC* E McKnight Kauffer; revised '47. '37 (11); '38 (15); '39 (8); '40 (4); '47 (14); '48 (19); '49 (3); '50 (11); '51 (13); '52 (2); '53 (4); '54 (6); '55 (1); '56 (6); '57 (8); '58 (3); '59 (2); '62 (2); '63 (6); '71 (3); '72 (3). T:[191]. *First Red Knight* Turner '37A–'48 (50) Somes '39T '40–'48 (12) Rassine '47–'51 (24) Field '50 (2) Chatfield '50A '51–7 (38) Blair '54–'63 (22) Burne '58 (1) Doyle '62 (2) MacLeary '63 (1) Nureyev '71–2 (4) Ashmole '72 (2). *The Black Queen* Brae '37A–'40 (30) May '37T–'50 (22) Grey '47–'62 (47) Elvin '47–8 (8) Lynne '50–1 (12) Farron '51–4 (9) Lindsay '54–7 (10) Beriosova '57–'63 (9) Beckley '58–'63 (4) Mason '63–'72 (6) Bergsma '72 (1). *The Red Queen* May '37A–'51 (30) Spicer '37T–'40 (4) Brae '38T–'40 (6) Farron '47–'53 (32) Larsen '47–'56 (42) B Lindsay '51–3 (4) Lynne '51 (1) Taylor '54–9 (17) Linden '57–9 (8) Henderson '62T (2) Remington '63 (6) Derman '71–2 (4) Eyre '72 (2). *The Red King* Helpmann '37A–'71 (32) Ashton '37–9 (9) Hamilton '47 (8) Edwards '47–'72 (95) Powell '48–'62 (14). + 15f 10m. *Also* Rep II.

Cinderella P 23 Dec 1948 ROH *Ch/Pr* Ashton; revised '65 *M* Prokofiev *SC* Jean-Denis Malclès; '65 *S* Henry Bardon *C* David Walker. '48 (5); '49 (44); '50 (19); '51 (17); '53 (8); '54 (6); '56 (14); '57 (4); '58 (5); '59 (12); '60 (13*); '61 (3*); '62 (7); '65 (4); '66 (16); '67 (8); '68 (1); '69 (5); '70 (6); '72 (7); '73 (3); '75 (5); '76 (2); '79 (6). T:28. *Cinderella* Shearer '48–'51 (32) Elvin '48–'56 (29) Fonteyn '49–'67 (54) Nerina '51–'66 (31) Linden '56–'62 (10) Beriosova '58–'73 (18) Seymour '60–1 (5) Page '66–7 (5) Park '69–'79 (11) Sibley '67–'73 (11) Jenner '69–'72 (4) Penney '72–9

(4) Makarova '75 (3) Porter '79 (1) Collier '79 (2). *Her Stepsisters* 1 Ashton '48–'76 (146) Powell '51 (6) Fraser '58–9 (11) Larsen '59–'62 (18) Lindsay '60–1 (8) Andrée Howard '60 (2) Anthony '62 (1) Shaw '66–'79 (15) Emblen '65–6 (8) Holden '67 (2) Coleman '79 (3). 2 Helpmann '48–'76 (92) MacMillan '50–6 (47) Clegg '54–7 (11) M Hill '58–9 (11) Lindsay '59–'60 (12) Evans '60–1 (10) Sopwith '62 (4) Andrée Howard '62 (3) Holden '65–7 (11) Bosman '67–'73 (11) Grant '75 (2) Rencher '79 (5) Drew '79 (1). *The Fairy Godmother* May '48–'50 (41) Brae '49 (9) Mossford '49–'51 (15) Lindsay '49–'57 (10) Farron '51–9 (51) B Taylor '57 (2) Page '59–66 (21) Parkinson '59–'76 (42) Remington '60–1 (10) O'Conaire '67–'70 (4) Conley '72–9 (5) Peri '72–5 (5) Mason '79 (5). *The Prince* Somes '48–'60 (77) Hart '48–'53 (26) Rassine '49–'54 (18) Blair '56–'66 (21) Doyle '56–'61 (10) MacLeary '59–'75 (22) Ashbridge '60–2 (6) Gable '65–7 (10) Mead '67–'70 (4) Dowell '67–'79 (15) Wall '72–9 (6) D Kelly '72 (1) Eagling '75–9 (2) Ashmole '75 (1) Silver '79 (1). + 41*f* 31*m*.
*9 performances '60/1 season by TC at ROH.

Cinderella Act II. '56 (1); '59 (1). *Cinderella* Fonteyn '56 (1) Beriosova '59 (1). *Her Stepsisters* 1 Ashton '56 (1) Fraser '59 (1). 2 MacMillan '56 (1) M Hill '59 (1). *The Prince* Somes '56–9 (2).

Cinderella Act II pdd. '59 (1); '70 Ashton Tribute (1). *Cinderella* Beriosova '59 (1) Park '70 (1). *The Prince* Ashbridge '59 (1) MacLeary '70 (1).

Clock Symphony P 25 June 1948 ROH *Ch* Massine *M* Haydn *SC* Christian Bérard. '48 (10). T:4. *The Princess* Shearer (8) Brae (2). *The Clockmaker* A Grant (8) Legerton (2). *The King* Edwards (10). + 18*f* 24*m*.

Comus P 14 Jan 1942 New *Ch* Helpmann *M* Purcell arr Lambert *SC* Oliver Messel. '42 (71); '43 (22); '44 (19); '45 (8). T:56. *Comus* Helpmann '42–5 [113] Paltenghi '44–5 [5]. *Attendant Spirit* Dale '42–5 [92] Jo Phillips/Sheldon '42–5 [26]. *The Lady* Fonteyn '42–5 [72] Grey '42–5 [40] Farron '43–4 (6). *Sabrina* Fraser '42–5 [118]. + 16*f* 6*m*. nr '42 Jan 16; '44 Oct 14m.

Concert, The (or The Perils of Everybody) FP 4 Mar 1975 ROH *Ch* Robbins *M* Chopin orch Clare Grundeman *C* Irene Sharaff *curtains* Ed Gorey. '75 (10); '76 (5); '77 (10); '78 (3); '79 (7). T:7. 1 Seymour '75–9 (18) Connor '75–9 (15) Harvey '78T (2) Coleman '75–9 (30) Wall '75–7 (5). 3 Parkinson '75–8 (23) Derman '75–9 (12). 4 Fletcher '75–9 (34) Carr '79 (1). + 8*f* 10*m*.

Concerto FPCG 17 Nov 1970 ROH *Cr* Rep II. '70 (8); '73 (7); '74 (3); '75 (4); '77 (5); '79 (5). T:18. *First Movement f* Penney '70–9 (18) Last '70 (4) Jenner '73A '77 (4) J Jackson '74T '75 –9 (5) Vere '74T Whitten '77 (1). *m* Coleman

'70–9 (19) Wall '70–5 (6) Sleep '74T '75–9 (4) Eagling '75–9 (3). *Second Movement f* Thorogood '70–9 (12) Seymour '70–5 (6) Collier '70–9 (5) Wells '70–3(2) Makarova '73–4 (4) Penney '74–7 (2) Corken '74T Evans '75 (1).*m* Cooke '70 (4) Blair '70 (1) Adams '70 (3) MacLeary '73A–'75 (10) Drew '73A–'77 (1) Wall '73–9 (5) Kelly '75 (1) Deane '79 (3) Hosking '79 (1). *Third Movement* Mason '70–9 (16) Connor '70–9 (10) Bergsma '73A–'74 (5) Howe '79T (1).

Concerto *Second Movement* '71 (1); '75 (1). On tour: 4. *f* Collier '71–5 (2). *m* Cooke '71 (1) MacLeary '75 (1). Ashmole '75T.

Coppélia (Acts I/II only) FP 21 Mar 1933 sw *Ch* Ivanov *Pr* Sergeyev *M* Delibes *SC* Edwin Calligan. '33 (8); '34 (3); '35 (8); '36 (3); '37 (2); '38 (2). T:5. *Swanilda* Lopokova '33 (3) de Valois '33–7 (16) French '35 (4) Miller '37–8 (2) Honer '38 (1). *Franz* Judson '33 (8) Kemp '34 (1) Gore '34–5 (6) Turner '35–8 (10) Helpmann '35 (1). *Dr Coppélius* Briggs '33–4 (9) Greenwood '34–5 (5) Newman '35–8 (12).

Coppélia (Three acts) FPNP 15 Apr 1940 sw *Ch* Petipa/Cecchetti reconstructed Sergeyev; *ch* Sergeyev (Act III dances 4, 5, 7, 9) *M* Delibes orch Act III Gordon Jacob *SC* William Chappell redesigned '46. '40 (10); '41 (10); '42 (25); '43 (25); '44 (21); '45 (20); '46 (14); '47 (6); '48 (13); '49 (16); '50 (12); '51 (8); '52 (15); '53 (4). T:[156]. *Swanilda* Honer '40–2 (37) Garnett '42 (2) van Praagh '42–5 (34) Fonteyn '42T '43–'50 (44) May '45–'52 (28) Dale '46–'52 (17) Shearer '46–'51 (17) Danilova '49 (5) Nerina '51–3 (10) Beriosova '52–3 (3) Lindsay '52T '53 (2). *Franz* Helpmann '40–1 (17) Hart '41T–'53 (50) Rassine '42–'52 (92) Turner '45–'50 (26) Franklin '49 (6) Vernon '51T–3 (6) A Grant '52–3 (2) Shaw '52T. *Dr Coppélius* Newman '40–1 (14) Greenwood '40 (1) Helpmann '41–'50 (98) Mendel '41 (2) Paltenghi '42–4 (27) Hamilton '45 (12) Edwards '46–'51 (36) Powell '50–3 (2) Ashton '51–2 (6) F White '52T '53 (1).

Coppélia Act II. '40 (1). *Swanilda* Honer. *Franz* Helpmann. *Dr Coppélius* Newman.

Coppélia Divertissement Acts I/III. '41 (4). *Swanilda* Honer. *Franz* Helpmann.

Coppélia Act III. T:[6].

Coppélia FPNP 2 Mar 1954 ROH *Ch* Ivanov/Cecchetti *M* Delibes *SC* Osbert Lancaster *Pr* Sergeyev revised de Valois. '54 (23); '55 (11); '56 (9); '57 (9); '58 (8); '59 (13); '60 (2); '61 (2); '63 (4); '64 (13); '65*(1); '68 (4); '69 (7); '70 (2). T:62. *Swanilda* Nerina '54–9 (17) Navarre '54 (4) Beriosova '54–8 (13) Lindsay '54–5 (5) Dale '54 (2) Fifield '55–7 (7) Heaton '55 (1) Linden '55–'60 (8) Lane '56–'64 (12) Jackson '57 (2) Park '58–'65 (14) Alexander '59 (1) Sibley '59–'64 (6*) Page '63–4 (3) Vere

'68–'70 (6) Jenner '68–'70 (7). *Franz* Blair '54–'60 (27) A Grant '54–9 (9) Chatfield '54–8 (12) Doyle '54–7 (7) Shaw '54–'64 (14) Burne '58–'60 (7) Britton '59 (1) Usher '59–'64 (11*) Gable '63–5 (4) Mason '63–'70 (5) Martin '68–9 (4) Sherwood '68–'70 (7). *Dr Coppélius* Ashton '54 (5) Edwards '54–'61 (23) Hart '54–9 (26) F White '54–'64 (19) Helpmann '58 (5) Legerton '59 (1) Cox '59–'65 (5*) Holden '63–9 (18) Shaw '68–'70 (5) A Grant '69 (1). *Also*: Rep II.
*+ 1 with RBS at ROH 1959.

Coppélia Act I. '60 (1). *Swanilda* Linden. *Franz* Blair. *Dr Coppélius* Edwards.

Coppélia Act I. Czardas. '59 (1).

Coppélia Act III. '54 (4); '56 (6); '57 (4); '58 (3); '59 (1). T:6. *Swanilda* Nerina '54–8 (5) Beriosova '54–7 (3) Lindsay '54 (1) Linden '56–9 (5) Fifield '57 (1) Jackson '57–8 (2) Lane '58 (1). *Franz* Blair '54–9 (8) Chatfield '54–7 (2) Doyle '54–7 (2) Shaw '56–8 (5) A Grant '56 (1).

Coppélia pdd. T:2.

Création du Monde, La FP 30 Oct 1933 ov *Ch* de Valois *M* Milhaud *SC/masks* Edward Wolfe '33 (2); '35 (4). *Man* Tudor '33 (2) Chappell '35 (4). *Woman* Moreton '33–5 (6). + 12*f* 3*m*.

Cupid and Psyche P 27 Apr 1939 sw *Ch* Ashton *M* Gerald Berners *SC* Francis Rose. '39 (4). *Pan* Somes (4). *Psyche* Farron (4). *Cupid* Staff (4). *Venus* Brae (4). + 32*f* 15*m*.

Cupid and Psyche Solo. '70 Ashton Tribute (1). *Psyche* Trounson.

Dances at a Gathering FP 19 Oct 1970 ROH *Ch* Robbins *M* Chopin *C* Joe Eula. '70 (12); '71 (13); '72 (15); '73 (9); '74 (2); '75 (4); '76 (7). T:12. 5*f* from: Connor '70–6 (51) Jenner '70–6 (45) Mason '70–6 (39) Seymour '70–6 (38) Sibley '70–4 (40) Porter '70–5 (27) Thorogood '70–3 (16) Collier '71–5 (28) Penney '71–6 (17) Park '73 (3) Parkinson '73 (3) Makarova '76 (3). 5*m* from: Coleman '70–6 (59) Dowell '70–6 (53) J Kelly '70–1 (15) Nureyev '70–6 (33) Wall '70–6 (56) Myers '70–2 (14) Ashmole '71–5 (33) MacLeary '71 (5) Eagling '72–6 (28) Hosking '72–4 (4) Sleep '73 (3) MacGibbon '76 (7).

Danse Sacrée et Danse Profane FP 5 May 1931 ov *Ch* de Valois *M* Debussy *C/masks* Hedley Briggs. '31 (5); '32 (3); '33 (2). T:3. *Danse Sacrée* Moreton '31–3 (10). *Danse Profane* Bamford '31–2 (10). + 8*f*.

Danses Concertantes FPCG 13 Mar 1959 ROH *Cr* Rep II. '59 (11); '60 (4); '62 (6). T:6. pdd *f* Lane '59–'62 (10) Wells '59–'60 (7) Park '62 (1) Seymour '62 (1). *m* Doyle '59 (11) Farley '60 (4) MacLeary '60T '62 (6). *Solo* Trecu '59 (6) Clegg '59 (3) Wilson '59 (2) Lawrence '60–2 (10).

Dante Sonata P 23 Jan 1940 sw *Ch* Ashton *M* Liszt orch Lambert *SC* Sophie Fedorovitch after Flaxman. '40 (13); '41 (19); '42 (15); '43 (21); '44 (17); '45 (15); '46 (12); '47 (11); '48 (4); '50 (4). T: [182]. *'Children of Light' f* Fonteyn '40–'50 [96] Grey '42–4 (10) Clayden '45–'50 (23) Heaton '50A. *m* Somes '40–'50 [62] Paltenghi '42–6 (59) Hart '42 (8) Field '51A. *'Children of Darkness' f* Brae '40–'50 [31] Nye '41–8 [38] Franca '42–5 (38) Grey '46–'50 (22). *m* Helpmann '40–'50 [104] Carter '40T F White '44–5 (9) Hart '47–'50 (16) A Grant '51A. + 13f 6m. nr 1941 Jan 22; 23.

Dante Sonata 'May' solo. '70 Ashton Tribute (1).

Daphnis and Chloë P 4 April 1951 ROH *Ch* Ashton *M* Ravel *SC* John Craxton. '51 (31); '52 (19); '53 (3); '54 (8); '55 (10); '56 (2); '57 (3); '58 (7); '59 (7); '61 (4); '62 (4); '64 (5); '66 (4); '69 (5); '70 (3); '73 (8); '74 (2); '75 (7). T: 31. *Chloë* Fonteyn '51–'66 (81) Clayden '51–6 (26) Park '69–'73 (6) Sibley '69–'75 (10) Penney '70–5 (9). *Daphnis* Somes '51–9 (88) Vernon '52 (1) Blair '56–'62 (9) Gable '64–6 (9) Mead '69–'70 (6) Dowell '69–'75 (13) Wall '73–5 (5) Ashmole '75 (1). *Lykanion* Elvin '51–2 (35) Farron '51–9 (51) Nerina '53 (3) Heaton '55 (1) Parkinson '61–'75 (30) Bergsma '64–'73 (8) Porter '74–5 (4). *Dorkon* Field '51–5 (58) Chatfield '51–8 (22) Hynd '58–'66 (23) Rosson '64–'70 (10) Drew '69–'75 (16) D Kelly '74–5 (2) Myers '75 (1). *Bryaxis* Grant '51–'69 (108) Drew '62 (4) Mason '70 (3) Sleep '73–5 (14) Johnson '74–5 (2) Fletcher '75 (1). + 21f 19m.

Daphnis and Chloë Scene 3. T: 1.

Daphnis and Chloë Scene 3 finale. '70 Ashton Tribute (1). *Chloë* Fonteyn. *Daphnis* Somes. *Dorkon* Hynd + 12f 12m.

Deux Pigeons, Les *see* **Two Pigeons, The**

Diversions P 15 Sept 1961 ROH *Ch* MacMillan *M* Arthur Bliss *SC* Philip Prowse. '61 (10); '62 (6); '63 (8); '64 (5); '68 (3); '79 (6). *First couple f* Beriosova '61–8 (16) Parkinson '61–8 (16) Derman '79 (3) Porter '79 (3). *m* MacLeary '61–4 (25) Nureyev '63 (3) Rosson '63–8 (4) Mead '68 (1) Deane '79 (3) Silver '79 (3). *Second couple f* Lane '61–4 (20) Mason '61–8 (12) Whitten '79 (2) Ellis '79 (4). *m* Usher '61–4 (27) Lawrence '63 (1) Dowell '64–8 (4) Coleman '79 (3) Batcheler '79 (3). + 4f 4m. Also Rep II.

Donald of the Burthens P 12 Dec 1951 ROH *Ch/Scenario* Massine *M* Ian Whyte *SC* Robert Colquhoun/Robert MacBryde. '51 (6); '52 (17). T: 2. *Donald* Grant '51–2 (15) Clegg '52 (8). *Death* Grey '51–2 (15) Lindsay '52 (8). + 38f 19m.

Don Juan P 25 Nov 1948 ROH *Ch* Ashton *M* Richard Strauss *SC* Edward Burra. '48 (9); '49 (11); '52 (7). T: 45. *Don Juan* Helpmann '48–9 (13) Hart '49–'52 (13) Melville '52T (1).

La Morte Amoureuse Fonteyn '48–9 (3) Elvin '48–'52 (23) Clayden '52 (1). *A Young Wife* Shearer '48–9 (11) Heaton '48–9 (3) Grey '49 (6) Beriosova '52 (6) Drage '52 (1). + 16f 12m.

Don Quixote P 20 Feb 1950 ROH *Ch* de Valois *M* Roberto Gerhard *SC* Edward Burra '50 (22); '51 (4); '52 (6). T: 9. *Don Quixote* Helpmann '50 (16) Field '50–2 (13) Edwards '51–2 (3). *Sancho Panza* A Grant '50–2 (32). *The Lady Dulcinea (Aldonza Lorenzo)* Fonteyn '50–2 (17) Elvin '50–2 (8) Heaton '50–2 (7). + 20f 20m.

Douanes P 11 Oct 1932 sw *Ch* de Valois revised '35. *M* Geoffrey Toye *SC* Hedley Briggs; '35 *SC* Sophie Fedorovitch. '32 (8); '33 (9); '34 (2); '35 (7); '36 (12); '37 (4). T: 14. *Cook's Man* Dolin '32 (8) Judson '33 (6) Newman '33–4 (5) Helpmann '35–7 (19) Turner '36T–7 (4). *The Tight-Rope Dancer* ('35 *Walker*) de Valois '32–7 (41) Bamford '34 (1). + 9f 2m.

Dream, The P 2 Apr 1964 ROH *Ch* Ashton *M* Mendelssohn arr John Lanchbery *S* Henry Bardon *C* David Walker; Dec '71–3 *SC* Peter Farmer (from TC); '74 *SC* as '64. '64 (17); '65 (8); '66 (4); '68 (3); '69 (3); '70 (10); '71 (5); '72 (11); '73 (6); '74 (6); '76 (12); '78 (7); '79 (9). T: 83. *Titania* Sibley '64–'74 (29) Park '64–'79 (32) Penney '66A '68–'79 (29) Wells '71–2 (3) Jenner '72–8 (2) Porter '79 (2) Collier '79 (4). *Oberon* Dowell '64–'79 (51) Au Bennett '64 (4) Mead '64A '68–'71 (9) Wall '71–9 (17) Clarke '72 (1) Coleman '72–6 (7) Nureyev '76 (2) Silver '74T '78–9 (8) Eagling '79 (2). *Puck* Martin '64–'70 (26) Morse '64–6 (9) Ruffell '66A Sleep '68–'79 (47) Mosaval '70–1 (4) Carr '72–6 (5) Molyneux '72–3 (3) Fletcher '74T '78–9 (7). *Bottom* A Grant '64–'76 (46) Holden '64–8 (15) Emblen '70–6 (14) G Grant '72–9 (26). + 7f 8m CdB. Also Rep. II.

Dream, The pdd. '70 Ashton Tribute (1). T: 1. *Titania* Sibley. *Oberon* Dowell.

Elektra P 26 Mar 1963 ROH *Ch* Helpmann *M* Malcolm Arnold *SC* Arthur Boyd. '63 (9). T: 10. *Elektra* Nerina (9). *Orestes* Blair (9). *Clytemnestra* Mason (9). *Aegisthus* Rencher (9). + 8m.

Elite Syncopations P 7 Oct 1974 ROH *Ch* MacMillan *M* Scott Joplin and others *S* nc *C* Ian Spurling. '74 (6); '75 (8); '76 (15); '77 (8); '78 (11); '79 (6). T: 37. *Calliope Rag* Mason '74–9 (39) Connor '75–9 (15). *Golden Hours f* Penney '74–8 (30) Ellis '75–9 (17) Thorogood '76–9 (7). *m* Wall '74–8 (23) Myers '75–6 (6) Molyneux '76 (2) Jefferies '77T–9 (15) Batcheler '77T–9 (8). *Stop-Time Rag* Park '74–8 (16) Collier '74–9 (19) Makarova '75–6 (3) Penney '76–9 (14) Jenner '78 (2). *Alaskan Rag f* Derman '74–9 (41) Howe '75–9 (13). *m* Sleep '74–9 (38) Fletcher '75–9 (16) Howes '79A. *Bethena Waltz f* as *Stop-Time Rag*. *m* MacLeary '74–5 (9) Hosking '74–9 (7) D Kelly '75–6 (8) Deane '76–9 (18) Wall '76–8 (8) Jefferies '77–8 (4). *Friday Night* Coleman '74–9 (38)

Ashmole '75–6 (3) Beagley '76–9 (12) Eagling '79 (1). + 1f 3m CdB. Also Rep II.

Emperor's New Clothes, The *see* **Roi Nu, Le**

Enchanted Grove, The FP 11 Mar 1932 sw *Ch* Rupert Doone *M* Ravel; Prelude Debussy orch Ravel. *SC* Duncan Grant. '32 (5); '33 (2); '34 (2). *Eros* Dolin '32 (5) Judson '33 (2) Kemp '34 (2). *Psyche* Markova '32 (5) Toye '33 (2) Gregory '34 (2). *Courier* Doone '32–4 (9). *Courtesan* de Valois '32–4 (9). + 8f 8m.

Enchanted Princess, The *see* **Sleeping Beauty, The – Blue Bird pdd.**

Enigma Variations P 25 Oct 1968 ROH *Ch* Ashton *M* Elgar *SC* Julia Trevelyan Oman. '68 (8); '69 (9); '70 (13); '71 (11); '72 (2); '73 (6); '74 (2); '75 (6); '77 (16); '79 (8). T: 25. *Elgar* Rencher '68–'79 (81). *C.A.E.* Beriosova '68–'73 (42) Mason '69–'79 (26) Eyre '74–9 (13). *H.D.S-P* Holden '68–9 (13) Sinclaire '69–'73 (17) Emblen '70–7 (34) G Grant '76T–9 (15) Benson '79 (2). *R.B.T.* Shaw '68–'79 (78) Molyneux '77 (3). *W.M.B.* A Grant '68–'77 (62) Fletcher '77–9 (18) G Grant '79 (1). *R.P.A.* Mead '68–'71 (36) Brown '70 (1) D Kelly '71–7 (20) Ashmole '75 (1) MacGibbon '77–9 (17) Hosking '77–9 (6). *Ysobel* Lorrayne '68–'74 (41) Porter '71–9 (18) Peri '73–7 (15) Conley '77–9 (7). *Troyte* Dowell '68–'77 (57) Coleman '70–9 (19) Eagling '77–9 (5). *Winifred* Parkinson '68–'77 (57) O'Conaire '69 (1) Connor '71–9 (19) Tallis '77–9 (4). *Nimrod* Doyle '68–'75 (57) Conway '77–9 (24). *Dorabella* Sibley '68–'75 (31) Jenner '68–'77 (27) Trounson '71 (2) Wells '73 (1) Collier '74–9 (16) J Jackson '76T '79 (4). *G.R.S.* Sleep '68–'79 (78) Benson '77 (2) Carr '79 (1). *B.G.N.* Edwards '68–'79 (81). ******* *(Lady Mary)* Bergsma '68–'73 (43) Beckley '69–'70 (6) Derman '74–9 (25) Groombridge '77–9 (4) Wylde '77–9 (3). + 4f 5m.

Enigma Variations 'Nimrod' '70 Ashton Tribute (1). *Elgar* Rencher. *C.A.E.* Beriosova. *Nimrod* Doyle.

Etude P 19 Dec 1929 ov *Ch* de Valois *M* Debussy *SC* nc. '29 (6); '30 (1); '31 (4). T: 3. 1 Moreton '29–31 (11) 2 Newton '29–31 (11). 3 Patrick '29–'30 (7) Bamford '31 (4).

Façade FP 8 Oct 1935 sw *Ch* Ashton *M* William Walton *SC* John Armstrong redesigned '40. '35 (9); '36 (12); '37 (12); '38 (9); '39 (8); '40 (9); '41 (35); '42 (56); '43 (41); '44 (18); '45 (17); '49 (9); '50 (17); '51 (15); '53 (4); '55 (6); '56 (2); '59 (8); '60 (6); '63 (2); '70 (5); '78 (6); '79 (6). T. [459]. *Polka* Fonteyn '35–41 [57] Miller '37–9 (8) Farron '38–'40 (9) Dale '41–5 [89] Grey '42T–4 [31] Clayden '43–'51 [20] Shearer '44–5 (11) Nerina '49 (7) Lindsay '50–6 (33) Olrich '49 (2) Evans '53 (2) Fifield '55 (6) Sibley '59–'70 (11) Park '59–'60 (10) Collier '78–9 (8) Penney '78–9 (3) Ellis '79 (1). *Popular Song 2m* from: Turner '35–'56 (54) Chappell '35–50 (53) Ellis '37–'43 [10] Hart

'40-'56 [73] Somes '40-1 [18] Field '41-3 [74] Carter '41 (2) Rassine '42-5 [50] Paltenghi '43-5 [29] Edwards '43-5 [57] F White '44-5 (26) Boulton '49-'55 (35) Britton '49 (8) Shaw '49-'63 (42) Vernon '51 (15) Clegg '50A '51-'60 (20) Grant '50A. Trecu '59 (5) Sale '59-'60 (9) Usher '63 (1) Martin '63 (1) Coleman '70-9 (12) Sherwood '70 (5) Beagley '78-9 (6) Batchelor '78-9 (5) Page '78-9 (6). *Tango: A Dago* Ashton '35-'50 [96] Newman '35-7 (4) Helpmann '41-'79 [146*] A Grant '49A '50-'70 (48) Blair '55 (2) Holden '60 (2) Deane '78-9 (6) Coleman '78-9 (5). *A Debutante* Brown '35-9 (32) Gregory '36T-9 (17) Fonteyn '39T-'79 [119*] Dale '42-'53 [75] Shearer '49-'50 (10) Brae '49-'50 (14) Nerina '50A '51 (4) Lindsay '55-'60 (20) Evans '56T Page '63 (2) Park '70-8 (8) Thorogood '78-9 (8). *includes encore 6 May '56. nr '41 Jan 15, 23; June 19m. '43 Oct 2m. *Also* Rep II.

Facade Waltz. '70 Ashton Tribute (1).
Façade Foxtrot '70 Ashton Tribute (1).

Faun, The *see* **Picnic, The**

Faust, Scène de ballet FP 5 May 1931 ov *Ch* de Valois *M* Gounod *SC* nc. '31 (5); '32 (2). T:3. *f* de Valois '31 (5) Markova '32 (2). *m* Judson '31-2 (7). NB P 9 Mar 1931 in opera *Faust* danced de Valois. Ashton.

Festin de l'Araignée, Le (The Spider's Banquet) P 20 June 1944 New *Ch* Andrée Howard *M* Albert Roussel *SC* Michael Ayrton. '44 (30); '45 (11). T:11. *The Spider* Franca '44-5 [30] Nye '44-5 [9] Grey '45 (1). *The Butterfly* Shearer '44-5 [13] Mossford '44-5 [27]. *The Mayfly* Clayden '44-5 [29]. Dale '44-5 [11]. *The Dragonfly* Danton '44-5 [38] A Burke '45 (2). + 12f 2m. nr '44 July 12m.

Fête Etrange, La FPCG 11 Dec 1958 ROH Cr Rep II. '58 (3); '59 (14); '60 (4); '63 (6); '64 (2). T:15. *A Country Boy* Trecu '58-'60 (18) Farley '59 (3) MacLeary '63 (5) Dowell '63-4 (3). *The Bride* Beriosova '58-'63 (22) Linden '60 (4) Seymour '63-4 (3). *The Bridegroom* Hynd '58-'63 (25) Rencher '59T '60-4 (4).

Fête Etrange, La pdt. '59 (1).

Fête Polonaise FP 23 Nov 1931 SW *Ch* de Valois; *Ch* Judson (Mazurka) *M* Glinka *SC* Owen P Smyth; '35 *SC* Edmund Dulac (from Camargo Soc); '41 *S* William Chappell (as *Coppélia* Act III). '31 (2); '32 (9); '33 (4); '34 (3); '35 (6); '36 (2); '41 (8). T:23. *Adagio/pdd f* Bedells '31-2 (3) Markova '32 (4) de Valois '32-3 (5) Nielson '32 (1) McCarthy '32-3 (2) French '34-5 (8) Miller '35-6 (3) May '51 (5) Honer '41 (3). *m* Judson '31-3 (12) Kemp '33 (3) Helpmann '34-6 (4) Turner '35-6 (6) Gore '35 (1) Somes '41 (5) Carter '41 (3). + 10f 4m.

Fête Polonaise excerpts. T:3.

Field Figures FPCG 16 Nov 1971 ROH Cr Rep II. '71 (4); '72 (4). T:2. **1** Bergsma '71-2 (5)

Mason '71-2 (2) Derman '72 (1). **2** D Kelly '71-2 (5) Nureyev '71-2 (3). **3** Derman '71-2 (7) Karras '72 (1). **4** Johnson '71-2 (5) Coleman '72 (3).

Fille Mal Gardée, La P 28 Jan 1960 ROH *Ch* Ashton *M* Ferdinand Hérold adapt/arr John Lanchbery from 1828 version *SC* Osbert Lancaster. '60 (17); '61 (14); '62 (14); '63 (7); '64 (11); '65 (8); '66 (5); '67 (9); '68 (6); '69 (2); '70 (8); '71 (15); '72 (9); '73 (6); '74 (5); '75 (11); '76 (9); '77 (17); '78 (10); '79 (8). T:105. *Lise* Nerina '60-7 (45) Park '60-'79 (52) Page '62-7 (8) Sibley '62TC-3 (2) Lane '64 (2) Wells '64-'71 (6) Grahame '65 (1) Last '65-'70 (3) Jenner '66A '67-'78 (21) Vere '68TC-'74 (5) Collier '71-9 (25) Connor '75A-'9 (15) Ellis '75-9 (6). *Colas* Blair '60-'73 (68) MacLeary '61-2 (5) Usher '62-8 (17) Gable '63-5 (4) Mason '67TC-'70 (5) Coleman '67-'79 (40) Wall '67-'78 (19) Sherwood '68-'72 (4) Cooke '71 (1) Dowell '73-5 (4) Johnson '74 (1) Nureyev '74A-7 (8) Ashmole '75-6 (4) Baryshnikov '77 (3) Eagling '77-9 (3) Jefferies '77-9 (7). *Widow Simone* Holden '60-'73 (89) Plaisted '61-2 (3) Shaw '66TC-'79 (39) Bosman '70-2 (6) Emblen '70-9 (48*) Gordon '71 (1) Sleep '76A-7 (2) Symons '77-9 (3). *Alain* A Grant '60-'76 (126) Ruffell '61-7 (11) G Grant '70-9 (41) Morse '71 (2) Sleep '77-8 (8) Fletcher '78-9 (3). + 24f 18m. *Also* Rep II. * + 1 with RBS at ROH 1972.

Fille mal Gardée, La Act I. '60 (1). *Lise* Park *Colas* Blair. *Widow Simone* Holden. *Alain* A Grant.

Fille mal Gardée, La Act I scene 2 pdd. '78 (2). *Lise* Ellis (2). *Colas* Coleman (2).

Fille mal Gardée, La Act II finale. '70 Ashton Tribute (1). *Lise* Park. *Colas* Coleman. *Widow Simone* Shaw. *Alain* A Grant. + 18f 15m.

Fin du Jour, La P 15 Mar 1979 ROH *Ch* MacMillan *M* Ravel *SC* Ian Spurling. '79 (6). T:4. *f* **1** Park (1) Collier (5). **2** Penney (5) Thorogood (1). *m* **1** Hosking (6). **2** Eagling (3) Jefferies (3). + CdB.

Firebird, The FP 23 Aug 1954 Empire, Edinburgh *Ch* Fokine *M* Stravinsky *SC* Natalia Gontcharova *Pr* revived Grigoriev/Tchernicheva. '54 (13); '55 (11); '56 (14); '57 (11); '58 (17); '59 (10); '60 (1); '61 (6); '62 (6); '63 (5); '64 (6); '65 (2); '72 (9); '73 (11); '78 (7); '79 (5). T:85. *The Firebird* Fonteyn '54T-62 (46) Elvin '56 (4) Nerina '56-'65 (39) Beriosova '57A '58 (2) Page '58-'64 (9) Linden '59 (2) Sibley '72-3 (5) Jenner '72-8 (8) Bergsma '72-3 (5) Park '73 (5) Mason '78-9 (6) Thorogood '79 (2) Porter '79 (1). *Ivan Tsarevitch* Somes '54T-'63 (71) Hynd '57-'65 (26) Chatfield '58 (3) Blair '61 (2) Wall '72-9 (9) D Kelly '72-3 (4) MacLeary '72-3 (5) Drew '72-9 (6) Dowell '73-8 (7) Coleman '79 (1). *The Beautiful Tsarevna* Beriosova '54T-'73 (53) Drage '55-7 (6)

Lindsay '58-'60 (15) Gay '58-9 (8) Lorrayne '59-'61 (3) Linden '61-2 (8) Bergsma '62T-'73 (18) Parkinson '72-3 (6) Conley '72-9 (10) Derman '78-9 (7). *The Immortal Köstchei* Ashton '54T-'8 (41) Hart '55-6 (5) F White '57-'65 (56) Grater '72-3 (6) Rencher '72-9 (16) Griffith '72-3 (5) Bosman '72-3 (3) Drew '78 (2).

Flower Festival at Genzano pdd FP 3 May 1962 ROH *Ch* Bournonville *M* E Helsted *SC* nc; '62 Oct *SC* Richard Beer. '62 (16); '63 (9); '64 (4); '66 (3); '75 (2). T:4. *f* Nerina '62-4 (17) Linden '62T-3 (5) Sibley '62 (2) Page '63-6 (7) Park '63 (1) Collier '75 (2). *m* Bruhn '62 (5) Blair '62-4 (15) Nureyev '62-3 (4) Shaw '62 (2) Doyle '62 (1) Usher '63 (1) MacLeary '66 (3) Sleep '75 (2). *Also* Rep II.

Foolish Virgins, The P 26 Sept 1933 SW (as **The Wise and Foolish Virgins**) *Ch* de Valois *M* Kurt Atterberg *SC* William Chappell. '33 (4); '34 (2). *The Bride* Markova '33-4 (4) Appleyard '33 (1) McCarthy '34 (1). *The Bridegroom* Judson '33-4 (5) Helpmann '33 (1). + 12f.

Four Schumann Pieces P 31 Jan 1975 ROH *Ch* Hans van Manen *M* Schumann *SC* Jean-Paul Vroom. '75 (14); '78 (5). Dowell '75-8 (19). *f* **1** Penney '75-8 (19). **2** Collier '75-8 (17) Porter '75-8 (2). *m* **1** Eagling '75-8 (19). **2** Hosking '75-8 (8) Ashmole '75 (10) Silver '75 (1). + 3f 3m.

Four Seasons, The P 5 Mar 1975 ROH *Ch* MacMillan *M* Verdi *SC* Peter Rice. '75 (11); '76 (1); '77 (4); '78 (6). T:7. *Winter f* **1** Derman '75-8 (16) Howe '75-8 (6). **2** Porter '75-8 (13) Parkinson '75-7 (7) Wylde '78 (2). *m* MacLeary '75 (4) Silver '75-8 (12) Batchelor '77T-8 (6). *Spring f* Collier '75-8 (12) J Jackson '75-6 (7) Nunn '77 (1) Thorogood '76T '78 (2). *m* **1** Ashmole '75 (10) Myers '75 (1) Fletcher '76-8 (9) Page '78 (2). **2** Eagling '75-7 (10) Corder '75-8 (4) Beagley '76-8 (8). **3** Coleman '75-8 (13) Deane '75-8 (9) Beagley '77T. *Summer f* Mason '75-8 (7) Seymour '75-8 (12) Connor '76T '77-8 (2). *m* Wall '75-8 (12) Ashmole '75-6 (2) Jefferies '77-8 (5) Moore '77T-8 (3). *Autumn f* Penney '75-8 (18) Collier '75-7 (4). *m* **1** Dowell '75-8 (10) Eagling '75-8 (10) Wall '76 (1) Beagley '77T (1). **2** Sleep '75-7 (16) Benson '78 (6). + CdB. NB 1980 SC Deborah Williams.

Four Seasons, The *Summer* '76 (1). *f* Seymour. *m* Wall.

Fourth Symphony, The P 31 Mar 1977 ROH *Ch* John Neumeier *M* Mahler *SC* Marco Arturo Marielli. '77 (4). **1** Sleep (4). **2** Seymour (4). **3** Wall (4). **4** Penney (4). **5** Eagling (4). **6** Nunn (4). **7** Coleman (4). + CdB.

Four Temperaments, The FP 25 Jan 1973 ROH *Ch* Balanchine *M* Hindemith *SC* nc. '73 (4). *Melancholic* D Kelly (4). *Sanguinic f* Jenner (4). *m* Dowell (4). *Phlegmatic* Eagling (4). *Choleric* Bergsma (2). Connor (2). *Also* Rep II.

Giselle FP 1 Jan 1934 OV *Ch* after Coralli *Pr* Sergeyev *M* Adam *SC* Barbara Allen; '35 *SC* William Chappell. '34 (9); '35 (5); '37 (8); '38 (5); '39 (3); '40 (5); '41 (9); '42 (16); '43 (15); '44 (12); '45 (13). T:[73]. *Giselle* Markova '34–5 (14) Fonteyn '37–'45 [75]. Brae '41T. Grey '44T–5 [10]. *Count Albrecht* Dolin '34–5 (5) Judson '34 (3) Helpmann '34–'45 [79] Hart '42 (1) Rassine '44T–5 [11]. *Myrtha* Darnborough '35–5 (10) Appleyard '34–5 (4) May '37–'45 [32] Brae '38–'41 (7) Franca '42–5 [25] Fraser '42–5 [21]. nr '44 July 12m.

Giselle Act II. '35 (1); '41 (7). *Giselle* Markova '35 (1) Fonteyn '41 (7). *Count Albrecht* Helpmann '35–'41 (8). *Myrtha* Appleyard '35 (1) May '41 (5) Brae '41 (2).

Giselle Act I. 'Peasant' pdd. '37 (1). T: [14].

Giselle FPNP 12 June 1946 ROH *Ch* after Coralli *Pr* Sergeyev *M* Adam *SC* James Bailey revised Sept '51. '46 (11); '47 (7); '48 (18); '49 (6); '50 (11); '51 (11); '52 (12); '53 (19); '54 (7); '55 (9); '56 (13); '57 (8); '58 (17); '59 (12); '60 (12). T:48. *Giselle* Fonteyn '46–'60 (67) Grey '46–'60 (12); Markova '48–'57 (15) Shearer '48–'53 (13) Danilova '49 (2) Elvin '51–6 (27) Clayden '54–5 (3) Heaton '54 (2) Nerina '56–'60 (11) Beriosova '56–'60 (11) Jackson '58 (1) Chauviré '58 (2) Linden '59–'60 (4) Alexander '59 (1) Page '60 (1) Seymour '60 (1). *Count Albrecht* Rassine '46–'58 (47) Helpmann '46–'50 (18) Somes '47–'60 (58) Dolin '48 (4) Franklin '49 (2) Melville '51–2 (5) Field '54–6 (5) Blair '56–'60 (14) Chatfield '56–9 (10) Ashbridge '58T–'60 (5) Selling '59 (2) Alex Bennett '59 (1) Hynd '60 (1) MacLeary '60 (1). *Myrtha* Grey '46–'53 (34) May '46–'50 (19) Lynne '47–'50 (15) Lindsay '51–'60 (50) Drage '53–7 (15) Linden '55–8 (10) Jackson '56–8 (8) M Hill '58–9 (8) Grahame '58–'60 (5) Beckley '59–'60 (9).

Giselle Act I 'Peasant' pdd. T:4.

Giselle FPNP 30 Sept 1960 Metropolitan Opera House, New York *Ch* Coralli/Perrot revised Sergeyev; *Ch* Ashton (Peasant pdd Variation *f*). *M* Adam *SC* James Bailey. *Pr* Ashton/Karsavina. '61 (16); '62 (16); '63 (7); '64 (16); '65 (4); '66 (7); '67 (6); '68 (2); '69 (5); '70 (9). T:79. *Giselle* Fonteyn '60A '61–'70 (37) Nerina '61–5 (13) Page '61–7 (5) Beriosova '61–9 (16) Linden '61–3 (6) Chauviré '62 (2) Seymour '64 (1) Park '67–'70 (5) Wells '70 (1) Anderton '70 (1) Sibley '70 (1). *Count Albrecht* Somes '60A '61 (4) Blair '61–4 (13) Hynd '61–4 (4) MacLeary '61–'70 (23) Gilpin '61 (1) Nureyev '62–'70 (33) Bruhn '62 (3) Gable '65 (1) Dowell '67 (6). *Myrtha* Linden '60A '61–3 (15) Beckley '61–3 (10) Bergsma '61–'70 (45) Needham '64–6 (6) Parkinson '64–7 (7) Mason '69–'70 (5). Also Rep II.

NB 1980 *Pr* revised Norman Morrice Redesigned James Bailey.

Giselle Act I 'Peasant' pdd Variation *f*. '70 Ashton Tribute (1).

Giselle FPCG 11 Mar 1971 ROH Cr Rep II. '71 (15); '72 (15); '73 (11); '74 (8). T:19. *Giselle* Sibley '71–3 (6) Seymour '71–3 (9) Park '71–4 (14) Beriosova-Seymour '71 (1) Wells '71–4 (6) Barbieri '71 (1) Vere '71–2 (4) Makarova '72–4 (4) Jenner '73–4 (3) Thorogood '74 (1). *Count Albrecht* Dowell '71–4 (11) Wall '71–4 (12) D Kelly '71–4 (8) MacLeary '71–4 (8) Nureyev '72–3 (9) Coleman '74T (1). *Myrtha* Bergsma '71–4 (16) Mason '71–4 (12) Derman '71–4 (10) Parkinson '72–3 (6) Mason-Conley (1) Conley '72–3 (4).

Gloria P 13 Mar 1980 ROH *Ch* MacMillan *M* Poulenc *SC* Andy Klunder. 1 Eagling. 2 Penney. 3 Hosking. 4 Ellis. + *3m 4f CdB*.

Gods go a' Begging, The P 10 Jan 1936 SW *Ch* de Valois *M* Handel arr Thomas Beecham *SC* Hugh Stevenson. '36 (21); '37 (14); '38 (8); '39 (3); '40 (4); '41 (16); '42 (26); '43 (12); '44 (18); '45 (9). T:[163]. *A Serving Maid* Argyle '36–8 (18) Miller '36–9 (15) May '36–'45 [27] Brae '39T–'41 [10] Grey '42–3 [13] Farron '42–5 [29] Shearer '42–5 [14]. *A Shepherd* Chappell '36–9 (46) Ellis '40 (3) Hart '40–2 [25] Rassine '42–5 [40] A Burke '44–5 [12]. + *13f 6m*. nr '41 Jan 20, Feb 12; '42 Nov 3; '43 Apr 23; '44 May 31.

Good-Humoured Ladies, The FP 11 July 1962 ROH *Ch* Massine *M* Scarlatti orch/arr Tommasini *SC* Léon Bakst. *Scenario* after Goldoni. '62 (17); '63 (3). *Constanza* Linden '62 (8) Bergsma '62–3 (12). *Mariuccia* Sibley '62–3 (8) Park '62–3 (9) Seymour '62 (3). *Leonardo* Hynd '62–3 (20). *Battista* Shaw '62–3 (17) Ruffell '62–3 (3). *Silvestra* Sokolova '62 (6) Larsen '62–3 (14).

Hamlet P 19 May 1942 New *Ch* Helpmann *M* Tchaikovsky *SC* Leslie Hurry. '42 (50); '43 (40); '44 (25); '45 (16); '46 (18); '47 (24); '48 (7); '49 (7); '58 (6); '64 (12). T:[204]. *King of Denmark* Paltenghi '42–6 [133] R Martin '44T Burke '45–6 (12) Davenport '47–8 (30) Edwards '48 (1) Hart '49–'58 (10) Hynd '58 (3) Rencher '64 (12). *Hamlet* Helpmann '42–'58 [159] Paltenghi '45–7 (27) Somes '47 (3) Nureyev '64 (4) Gable '64 (8). *Gravedigger* Kersley '42 (13) Powell '42–'58 [111] Vincent '43–4 [4] Hamilton '44 [7] Holden '45–'64 (23) F White '45 (1) Turner '46 (9) A Grant '46–9 (29) Milland '64 (4). *Queen of Denmark* Franca '42–5 [119] Nye '43–4 [8] Grey '46–8 (28) Farron '46–'58 (30) Brae '49 (4) Mason '64 (12). *Ophelia* Fonteyn '42–9 [124] Grey '43–4 [6] Clayden '44–9 [50] Heaton '49 (3) Linden '58 (6) Seymour '64 (10) Sibley '64 (2). + 11f 7m. nr '43 Apr 23, '44 Oct 7m, 14m, Nov 29m.

Harlequin in the Street FP 10 Nov 1938 SW *Ch* Ashton *M* Couperin orch Gordon Jacob *SC* André Derain. '38 (6); '39 (10); '40 (5); '41 (16). T:[65]. *La Superbe* Brae '38–'41 [25] May '40–1 [7]. *Monseigneur* Somes '38–'41 [32].

Harlequin Carter '38–'41 [30] Staff '39 (1) Ellis '40 (1). + *2f 5m*. nr '41 Jan 15, 22, 24, June 11e, 19m.

Harlequin in the Street ensemble. '70 Ashton Tribute (1).

Harlequin in April FPCG 5 Mar 1959 ROH Cr Rep II. '59 (6). *Pierrot* Holden (3) Powell (3). *Harlequin* Blair (5) Trecu (1). *Columbine* Sibley (3) Wells (3).

Haunted Ballroom, The P 3 Apr 1934 SW *Ch* de Valois *M* Geoffrey Toye *SC* Motley. '34 (9); '35 (16); '36 (8); '37 (2); '39 (4); '40 (4); '41 (8); '42 (14); '45 (8). T:[59]. *Master of Treginnis* Helpmann '34–'45 (68) Dolin '35 (1) Chappell '35 (3) Paltenghi '45 (1). *Young Treginnis* Bamford '34 (3) Fontes/Fonteyn '34–5 (14) Barry '35 (2) Gill/Martyn '35–6 (14) Farron '37 (2) Vincent '39–'45 (34) J Bedells '39T Leighton '45 (4). *Alicia* Markova '34–5 (17) Fonteyn '35–'45 (33) May '36–'45 (16) Farron '42 (7). + 14f 7m. Also Rep II.

Homage to the Queen P 2 June 1953 ROH *Ch* Ashton *M* Malcolm Arnold *SC* Oliver Messel. '53 (4); '54 (19); '55 (5); '56 (6); '58 (1). T:43. *Queen of the Earth* Nerina '53–8 (18) Linden '54–6 (17). *Her Consort* Rassine '53–6 (17) Blair '54–8 (18). *Queen of the Waters* Elvin '53–6 (13) Beriosova '54–5 (20) Linden '54–5 (2). *Her Consort* Hart '53–4 (17) Ashbridge '54–6 (17) Burne '58 (1). *Queen of Fire* Grey '53 (4) Jackson '54–6 (29) Lindsay '55 (1) Page '58 (1). *Her Consort* Field '53–4 (22) Chatfield '54–8 (13). *Queen of the Air* Fonteyn '53–8 (20) Clayden '54–5 (11) Fifield '56 (4). *Her Consort* Somes '53–8 (20) Doyle '54–6 (15). + 28f 12m.

Homage to the Queen Air pdd. '70 Ashton Tribute (1). *f* Parkinson. *m* Rosson.

Hommage aux Belles Viennoises P 19 Dec 1929 OV *Ch* de Valois *M* Schubert arr Norman Franklin *SC* nc; '31 *SC* Owen P Smyth; '32 *SC* Nancy Allen. '29 (6); '30 (1); '31 (8); '32 (10); '33 (1). T:1. *Tyrolese f* 1 McCarthy '29–'33 (26). 2 Bamford '29–'33 (25) Appleyard '31 (1). *m* Ashton '29–'30 (7) Beddoes '32 (1) Newman '31–3 (13) Kemp '32 (3). pdd (from Sept '31 *Mazurka*) *f* de Valois '29–'30 (7) Newton '31–3 (5) Moreton '31–2 (12) Phillips '32 (2). *m* Judson '29–'32 (23) Tudor '32–3 (3). + 12f.

Hommage aux Belles Viennoises *Tyrolese*. T:3.

Horoscope P 27 Jan 1938 SW *Ch* Ashton *M* Lambert *SC* Sophie Fedorovitch. '38 (16); '39 (8); '40 (5). T:[54]. *The Young Man* Somes '38–'40 (29). *The Young Woman* Fonteyn '38–'40 (29). *The Moon* May '38–'40 (28) Miller '39 (1). + 29f 10m.

Horoscope Solo '70 Ashton Tribute (1). *The Moon* Lorrayne.

Images of Love P 2 Apr 1964 ROH *Ch* MacMillan revised '64 Oct. *M* Peter Tranchell *SC* Barry

Kay. '64 (16); '65 (3). *Two Loves I have* 1 Nureyev '64 (4) Gable '64-5 (15). 2 Seymour '64-5 (19). 3 Gable '64 (4) MacLeary '64-5 (15). *When love begins· to sicken* ƒ Beriosova '64-5 (19). *m* MacLeary '64-5 (19). + 7ƒ 7m; from Oct '64 6ƒ 6m.

In the Night FP 10 Oct 1973 ROH *Ch* Robbins *M* Chopin *C* Anthony Dowell.'73 (3); '74 (13); '75 (3). T:2 1 ƒ Sibley '73-4 (7) Penney '73-5 (12). *m* Dowell '73-5 (12) Eagling '73-4 (7). 2 ƒ Mason '73-5 (13) Thorogood '74 (5) Vere '74 (1). *m* MacLeary '73-5 (10) Coleman '74 (9). 3 ƒ Park '73-5 (14) Connor '74 (5). *m* Wall '73-5 (11) Hosking '74 (8).

Invitation, The FPCG 13 Dec 1962 ROH Cr Rep II. '62 (2); '63 (6); '64 (3); '68 (7); '70 (4); '71 (10); '76 (4); '77 (6). T:30. *The Girl* Seymour '62-'77 (23) Trounson '68-'71 (10) Ruanne '70-1 (3) Thorogood '72A '76-7 (4) Collier '77 (2). *Her Cousin* MacLeary '62 (2) Gable '63-4 (9) Dowell '65A Sherwood '68-'71 (13) P Brown '68 (3) Fletcher '71 (3) Wall '71 (2) Eagling '76-7 (4) Deane '76-7 (4) Jefferies '77 (2). *The Wife* Linden '62-3 (8) Mason '64-'71 (6) Derman '68-'77 (15) Parkinson '68 (3) Vere '71 (4) Seymour '76-7 (4) Conley '77 (1) Connor '77 (1). *The Husband* Doyle '62-'71 (23) Hynd '68 (2) Grater '70-1 (4) Blair '71 (3) D Kelly '76 (2) Drew '76-7 (6) Wall '77 (2).

Italian Suite P 4 Mar 1932 ov *Ch* de Valois *Ch* Dolin (Serenade/pdd) *M* Lalo; pdd Cottrau; from Dec '32 Variation Cimarosa. *C* Phyllis Dolton. '32 (6); '33 (1). pdd ƒ de Valois '32-3 (7). *m* Dolin '32-3 (7). + 8ƒ 2m.

Italian Suite *Variation*/pdd. '32 (4). ƒ de Valois (3) Markova (1). *m* Dolin (4).

Jabez and the Devil P 15 Sept 1961 ROH *Ch* Alfred Rodrigues *M* Arnold Cooke *SC* Isabel Lambert. '61 (5). *Jabez* MacLeary (5). *Mary* Sibley (5). *Mr Scratch, the Devil* A Grant (5). + 14ƒ 14m.

Jackdaw and the Pigeons, The P 5 May 1931 ov *Ch* de Valois *M* Hugh Bradford *SC* William Chappell. '31 (5); '32 (10); '33 (3). T:4. *The Jackdaw* de Valois '31-3 (18). + 9ƒ.

Jar, The P 9 Oct 1934 sw *Ch* de Valois *M* Alfredo Casello *SC* William Chappell. '34 (6); '35 (12); '36 (2). T:3. *Zi'Dima Lieasi* Gore '34-5 (17) Newman '35-6 (3). *Don Lollo Zirafa* Helpmann '34-6 (13) Newman '35 (7). *Nela* Appleyard '34-6 (20). + 10ƒ 8m.

Jazz Calendar P 9 Jan 1968 ROH *Ch* Ashton *M* Richard Rodney Bennett *SC* Derek Jarman. '68 (22); '70 (10); '71 (9); '73 (3); '78 (7); '79 (4). T:12. *Monday* Derman '68-'79 (31) Peri '68-'70 (15) Penney '71 (2) Groombridge '78-9 (4) Howe '78-9 (3). *Tuesday* Park '68-'71 (22) Penney '68-'79 (15) Jenner '68-'73 (14) Collier '71 (2) Ellis '79 (2). *Wednesday* Lorrayne '68-'71 (23) Beriosova '68-'71 (16) Beckley '71 (2) Peri '73 (3) Porter '78 (3) Wylde '78-9 (4) Conley '78-9 (4).

Thursday A Grant '68-'73 (43) Fletcher '73-9 (12). *Friday* ƒ Sibley '68-'73 (22) Parkinson '68-'73 (22) Park '78 (3) Nunn '78-9 (3) Porter '78-9 (5). *m* Nureyev '68-'70 (8) MacLeary '68-'73 (28) Dowell '68-'79 (11). Wall '78 (3). Batchelor '78-9 (3). Eagling '78 (2). *Saturday* Doyle '68-'73 (44*) Drew '78-9 (10) Jude '78 (1). *Sunday* Trounson '68-'73 (37) Jenner '68-'70 (7) Ellis '78-9 (5) Whitten '78-9 (6). + 6ƒ 14m. *+ 1 with RBS at ROH 1974.

Jazz Calendar Saturday. '70 Ashton Tribute (1). Doyle + 8m.

Jew in the Bush, The P 16 Dec 1931 ov *Ch* de Valois *M* Gordon Jacob *SC* Bertrand Guest. '31 (8); '32 (5). *The Youth* Judson '31-2 (13). *The Witch* Bamford '31-2 (13). *The Jew* Ashton '31-2 (13). + 11ƒ 3m.

Job A Masque for Dancing devised Geoffrey Keynes. FP 22 Sept 1931 ov *Ch/Pr* de Valois *M* Vaughan Williams *SC* Gwendolen Raverat (after Blake); wigs/masks Hedley Briggs; '48 *SC* John Piper. '31 (3); '32 (11); '33 (5); '34 (5); '35 (13); '36 (8); '37 (4); '39 (4); '40 (3); '41 (4); '43 (3); '44 (21); '45 (4); '48 (14); '49 (7); '51 (4); '52 (3); '53 (2); '54 (2); '55 (5); '56 (4); '57 (6); '59 (4); '70 (6*); '72 (3). T:[64]. *Satan* Dolin '31-'55 (30) Helpmann '33-'49 (77) Turner '39-'48 (3) Hart '49-'55 (15) A Grant '56-7 (10) Blair '59 (3) Burne '59 (1) Cooke '70-2 (4) Davel '70 (1) Jefferies '70 (3) Drew '72 (1). *Elihu* Judson '31-4 (22) Chappell '34-'41 (26) Byron '36 (2) Ellis '37T-'48 (11) Hart '40-1 (4) Paltenghi '43-5 (28) Rassine '48-'56 (32) Trecu '55-9 (11) Farley '59 (3) Johnson '70 (6) MacLeary '72 (3). + 16ƒ 18m; '35:21ƒ; '48:28ƒ. *TC in CG production ROH.

Judgement of Paris, The P 10 May 1938 sw *Ch* Ashton *M* Lennox Berkeley *SC* William Chappell. '38 (3); '39 (2). T:2. *Paris* Helpmann '38-9 (4). Somes '39 (1). *Venus* Argyle '38-9 (3) Fonteyn '38-9 (2). *Juno* Miller '38-9 (5). *Minerva* Honer '38-9 (5). *Mercury* Chappell '38-9 (5).

Laborintus P 26 July 1972 ROH *Ch* Glen Tetley *M* Luciano Berio *SC* Rouben Ter-Arutunian *Text* Eduardo Sanguineti. '72 (7). 1 Seymour (7). 2 Nureyev (4) Wall (3). 3 Bergsma (5) Connor (2). 4 Kelly (7) Derman (7). 6 Wall (4) Ashmole (3). 7 Ashmole (4) Eagling (3). 8 Hosking (7).

Lac des Cygnes, Le *see also* **Swan Lake**

Lac des Cygnes, Le Act II FP 5 Oct 1932 sw *Ch* Petipa *M* Tchaikovsky *SC* nc. '32 (4); '33 (5). *Odette* Markova '32-3 (9). *Prince Siegfried* Dolin '32-3 (5) Judson '33 (4).

Lac des Cygnes, Le pdt FP 5 Dec 1933 sw *Ch* Petipa *M* Tchaikovsky *C* nc. '33 (2). ƒ 1 Markova (2). 2 de Valois (2). *m* Idzikowski (2). *Also* Rep II.

Lac des Cygnes, Le FP 20 Nov 1934 sw *Ch* after Petipa *Pr* Sergeyev revised '46 *M* Tchaikovsky *SC* Hugh Stevenson revised '37; 1943 *SC* Leslie Hurry revised '46, '49. '34 (3); '35 (9); '36 (4); '37 (5); '38 (4); '39 (2); '40 (5); '41 (10); '42 (22); '43 (38); '44 (35); '45 (22); '46 (7); '47 (12); '48 (18); '49 (16); '50 (17); '51 (12). T:[215]. *Prince Siegfried* Helpmann '34-'49 [104] Dolin '35 & '48 (5) Hart '42-9 (18) Paltenghi '42-7 [66] Somes '45-'51 (29). Field '49-'51 (17). *Odette/Odile* Markova '35-'47 (13) Fonteyn†/French†† '35 (1) Fonteyn†/Honer†† '36-9 (7) Honer '37-8 (4) Fonteyn '37-'51 [107] May '41-'45 [12] Grey '42-'50 [68] Clayden '44-7 (3) Clayden†/Shearer†† '45T (2) Shearer '46-'51 (11) Elvin '50-1 (11) Nerina†/ Jackson†† '51T. nr '43 Dec 4m; '44 Oct 5. †Odette ††Odile.

Lac des Cygnes, Le Act I. pdt. '35 (2); '36 (2); '37 (3); '38 (1). T:[20].

Lac des Cygnes, Le Act II. '36 (3); '37 (4); '38 (4); '39 (2); '40 (6); '41 (13); '42 (1); '44 (13); '45 (1); '47 (11); '48 (4); '49 (17); '50 (6); '51 (5). T:168. *Odette* Fonteyn '36-'49 [27] Argyle '37-8 (5) Honer '37T '39 (1) May '40-'50 [19] Grey '44-'50 [15] Shearer '47-'50 (8) Elvin '49-'51 (9) Danilova '49 (2) Nerina '51 (3). *Prince Siegfried* Helpmann '36-'49 [32] Chappell '37-9 (2) Somes '39T '41-9 (4) Paltenghi '44-7 [18] Hart '47-'50 (15) Rassine '49-'51 (10) Franklin '49 (2) Field '49-'51 (6). nr '44 Nov 29m.

Lac des Cygnes, Le Act II. pdd T:2.

Lac des Cygnes, Le Act III. '35 (1); '36 (6); '37 (2); '38 (4); '39 (2). T:[43]. *Prince Siegfried* Dolin '35 (1) Helpmann '36-9 (12) Turner '38-9 (2). *Odile* Markova '35 (1) Honer '36-9 (11) Fonteyn '36-8 (3).

Lac des Cygnes, Le Act III. pdd. T:11.

Lac des Cygnes, Le Divertissement Acts I/III. '41 (2). *Odile* Fonteyn (1) Honer (1). *Prince Siegfried* Helpmann (2).

Lac des Cygnes, Le Acts II/III. T:2.

Lac des Cygnes, Le Divertissement (unspecified) T:2.

Lac des Cygnes, Le FPNP 18 Dec 1952 ROH *Ch* Petipa/Ivanov; *Ch* Ashton (Act I: Pas de Six; Act III: Neapolitan) *M* Tchaikovsky *SC* Leslie Hurry *Pr* Sergeyev. '52 (4); '53 (28); '54 (17); '55 (27); '56 (32); '57 (18); '58 (16); '59 (31); '60 (12); '61 (7); '62 (26); '63 (7). T:188. *Odette/Odile* Grey '52-'62 (31) Nerina '52-'63 (37) Jackson '53-8 (24) Elvin '53-6 (14) Shearer '53 (2) Fonteyn '53-'63 (38) Beriosova '55-'63 (42) Fifield '56-7 (9) Linden '58-'62 (12) Seymour '59-'63 (3) Sibley '59T-'63 (3) Page '60-3 (6) Wells '62 (1) Arova '62 (3). *Prince Siegfried* Field '52-6 (31) Rassine '52-7 (18) Somes '53-9 (55) Blair '56-'63 (41) Chatfield '56-8 (19) Ashridge '58-'62 (17) Selling '59 (4)

MacLeary '59–'63 (21) Hynd '60–3 (8) Bruhn '62 (3) Doyle '62–3 (2) Gable '62 (1) Nureyev '62–3 (5). *NB* Parkinson/Lawrence danced *Odette/Siegfried* with RBS at ROH 1960.

Lac des Cygnes, Le Act I pdt. '64 (1).

Lac des Cygnes, Le Act II. '53 (16); '54 (1); '55 (2); '56 (2); '58 (4). T:25. *Odette* Beriosova '53–6 (6) Grey '53 (1) Markova '53 (6) Fonteyn '53–6 (7) Fifield '55 (1) Chauviré '58 (3) Linden '58 (1). *Prince Siegfried* Chatfield '53–6 (5) Field '53–5 (2) Somes '53–6 (12) Helpmann '53 (1) Blair '55–8 (2) Rassine '58 (3).

Lac des Cygnes, Le Act II. pdd T:2.

Lac des Cygnes, Le Act III. '54 (2). *Odile* Jackson (2). *Prince Siegfried* Field (2).

Lac des Cygnes, Le Act III pdd. '55 (1); '60 (1). T:11. *Odile* Grey '55 (1) Beriosova '60 (1). *Prince Siegfried* Field '55 (1) MacLeary '60 (1).

Lac des Cygnes, Le Act III Neapolitan. '58 (1). T:27.

Lady and the Fool, The FPCG 9 June 1955 ROH Cr Rep II. '55 (4); '56 (12); '57 (10); '58 (15); '59 (9); '61 (5); '62 (6); '63 (1); '64 (3). T:47. *Moondog* Chatfield '55–9 (37) Hynd '58–'64 (28). *Bootface* Powell '55–'61 (55) Holden '62–4 (8) Martin '62–4 (2). *La Capricciosa* Grey '55–'62 (18) Beriosova '57–'64 (34) Page '57–'62 (13). *NB* Revised version of TB '54 production.

Lady and the Fool, The Grand Adagio. '56 (1). *La Capricciosa* Grey. + 3m.

Lady and the Fool, The pdd '73 (1). *La Capricciosa* Beriosova. *Moondog* MacLeary.

Lament of the Waves P 9 Feb 1970 ROH *Ch Devised* Ashton *M* Gérard Masson *C* Derek Rencher *Light Projection Sphere* Bill Culbert. *Curtain* (from *Pélléas et Mélisande*) Jacques Dupont. '70 (10). *f* Trounson (10). *m* Myers (6) Ashmole (4).

Lament of the Waves Excerpt. '70 Ashton Tribute (1). *f* Trounson. *m* Myers.

Liebeslieder Walzer FP 19 Apr 1979 ROH *Ch* Balanchine *M* Brahms *S* David Hays *C* nc. '79 (8). *4f* from: Collier (6) Derman (6) Penney (5) Mason (4) Connor (4) Ellis (4) Porter (4) Groombridge (1). *4m* from: Hosking (7) Silver (6) Coleman (6) Deane (4) Jefferies (1) Batchelor (4) MacGibbon (2) Page (2).

Lilac Garden FP 12 Nov 1968 ROH *Ch* Tudor *M* Chausson *S* Tom Lingwood *C* Hugh Stevenson. '68 (6); '69 (2). *Caroline* Beriosova '68–9 (4) Sibley '68–9 (4). *Her Lover* MacLeary '68–9 (4) Dowell '68–9 (4). *The Man She Must Marry* Doyle '68–9 (4) Hynd '68–9 (4). *An Episode in His Past* Parkinson '68–9 (4) Lorrayne '68–9 (4). *Also* Rep II.

Lord of Burleigh, The FP 25 Sept 1932 Kongelige Theater, Copenhagen *Ch* Ashton *M*

Mendelssohn sel/arr Edwin Evans orch Gordon Jacob. *SC* George Sheringham; '37 *SC* Derek Hill. *Scenario* Edwin Evans. '32 (7); '33 (7); '35 (4); '37 (3); '38 (6); '39 (1). T:8. *Katie Willows* Markova '32A–5 (7) de Valois '32–3 (7) Phillips '33 (4) Miller '37–9 (10). *Lady Clara Vere de Vere* Moreton '32A–5 (16) Gould '33 (1) Darnborough '33 (1) Argyle '37–8 (7) Brae '38T–9 (3). *Lord of Burleigh* Dolin '32A–3 (8) Judson '33 (5) Helpmann '33–8 (8) Chappell '35–9 (7). + 8*f* 3*m*.

Lord of Burleigh, The Solo '*Lady with the Fan*' '70 Ashton Tribute (1). T:2*. Bergsma. *Bergsma with TC at Snape, pianist Benjamin Britten, 1 + encore.

Madame Chrysanthème P 1 Apr 1955 ROH *Ch* Ashton. *M* Alan Rawsthorne *SC* Isabel Lambert. '55 (15); '56 (4). T:11. *Pierre* Grant '55–6 (19). *Yves* Doyle '55–6 (19). *Mme Chrysanthème* Fifield '55–6 (19). + 17*f* 20*m*.

Mam'zelle Angot FP 26 Nov 1947 ROH *Ch* Massine *M* Lecocq orch Gordon Jacob *SC* André Derain. '47 (11); '48 (13); '49 (6); '50 (5); '51 (13); '52 (17); '53 (8); '54 (6); '55 (10); '56 (6); '58 (6); '59 (9); '64 (11); '65 (1). T:6. *Mlle Angot* Fonteyn '47 (5) Farron '47–'51 (16) Navarre '48–'54 (38) Nerina '50–9 (32) Heaton '55 (8) Lane '56–'65 (11) Park '58–'64 (8) Page '64 (4). *A Barber* Grant '47–'65 (98) Shaw '52–'64 (18) Clegg '59 (6). *The Caricaturist* Somes '47–8 (20) Field '48–'52 (33) Melville '51–3 (20) Blair '54–'64 (29) Doyle '54–6 (3) Burne '58–9 (11) Gable '64–5 (6). *The Aristocrat* Shearer '47–9 (15) Larsen '47–'53 (24) Grey '49 (3) Farron '51–6 (26) Lindsay '51–9 (19) May '52 (4) B Taylor '55–9 (14) Grahame '58–9 (5) Sibley '64 (2) Parkinson '64–5 (10). *Also* Rep II.

Mam'zelle Angot scene 1. '60 (1). *Mlle Angot* Park. *A Barber* A Grant. *The Caricaturist* Blair. *The Aristocrat* Grahame.

Manon P 7 Mar 1974 ROH *Ch* MacMillan *M* Massenet orch/arr Leighton Lucas *SC* Nicholas Georgiadis. '74 (14); '75 (4); '76 (2); '77 (7); '78 (8); '79 (7). T:26. *Manon* Sibley '74 (7) Penney '74–8 (12) Park '74A–8 (11) Makarova '74–5 (4) Seymour '76–8 (6) Collier '78–9 (2). *Des Grieux* Dowell '74–8 (14) Eagling '74–9 (16) Nureyev '74A–6 (5) Wall '76–9 (7). *Lescaut* Wall '74–9 (15) D Kelly '74–5 (8) Johnson '74A (1) Coleman '75–9 (7) Dowell '74–8 (3) Jefferies '77–9 (8). *Monsieur GM* Rencher '74–9 (39) Grater '74A–6 (3). *Lescaut's Mistress* Mason '74–9 (26) Collier '74–9 (12) Connor '78–9 (4). + 36*f* (Nov '74 35*f*) 27*m* CdB.

Marguerite and Armand P 12 Mar 1963 ROH *Ch* Ashton *M* Liszt orch Humphrey Searle *SC* Cecil Beaton. *Scenario* after Dumas Fils. '63 (7); '64 (5); '65 (5); '67 (4); '68 (3); '70 (7); '71 (6); '72 (1); '73 (3). T:27*. *Marguerite* Fonteyn '63–'73 (41). *Armand* Nureyev '63–'73 (41). *His Father* Somes '63–'73 (41). *A Duke*

Edwards '63–'73 (41). + 8*m* 1*f*. *includes 4 with TC abroad.

Marguerite and Armand excerpt '70 Ashton Tribute (1). *Marguerite* Fonteyn. *Armand* Nureyev. *His Father* Somes.

Mayerling P 14 Feb 1978 ROH *Ch* MacMillan *M* Liszt arr/orch John Lanchbery *SC* Nicholas Georgiadis. *Scenario* Gillian Freeman. '78 (17); '79 (5). T:12. *Crown Prince Rudolf* Wall '78 (9) Eagling '78–9 (7) Jefferies '78–9 (6). *Baroness Mary Vetsera* Seymour '78 (9) Collier '78–9 (8) Thorogood '78–9 (5). *Princess Stephanie* Ellis '78–9 (17) Nunn '78–9 (5). *Countess Marie Larisch* Park '78 (10) Jenner '78 (2) Conley '78 (3) Thorogood '78–9 (6) Penney '78 (1). *Bratfisch* Fletcher '78–9 (22). + 10*f* 12*m* CdB.

Miracle in the Gorbals P 26 Oct 1944 Princes *Ch* Helpmann *M* Arthur Bliss *SC* Edward Burra *Scenario* Michael Benthall. '44 (20); '45 (23); '46 (24); '47 (11); '48 (2); '49 (3); '50 (4); '58 (5). T:105. *The Suicide* Clayden '44–'50 (87) Page '58 (5). *A Beggar* Edwards '44–'58 (92). *The Official* Paltenghi '44–7 (73) Hart '47–'58 (19). *The Prostitute* Franca '44–5 (43) Farron '46–'58 (46) Larsen '49 (3). *The Stranger* Helpmann '44–'58 (74) Somes '46T–'58 (18). + 14*f* 10*m*.

Miraculous Mandarin, The P 27 Aug 1956 Empire, Edinburgh *Ch* Alfred Rodrigues *M* Bartók *SC* Wakhevitch. *Scenario* Menyhert Lengyel. '56 (10). T:3. *Mandarin* Somes T (10). *Girl* Fifield T (10). *Pimp* Grant T (10). + 8*f* 12*m*.

Mirror for Witches, A P 4 Mar 1952 ROH *Ch/C/Scenario* Andrée Howard *M* Denis ApIvor *SC* Norman Adams. '52 (14); '53 (6). *Hannah* Farron '52–3 (20). *Doll* Heaton '52–3 (14) Olrich '52–3 (6). *Titus* Chatfield '52–3 (20). *The Stranger* Hart '52–3 (20). + 26*f* 22*m*.

Monotones pdt (Trois Gymopédies) – **Monotones No 2.** P 24 Mar 1965 ROH *Ch* Ashton *M* Satie orch Debussy/Roland Manuel *C* nc (Ashton). '65 (1); '66 (3); '70 (1); '74 (1); '78 (2). T:5. *f* Lorrayne '65–'74 (6) Derman '78 (2). *m* 1 Dowell '65–'70 (5) Jefferies '74 (1) Deane '78 (2). 2 Mead '65–'70 (5) O'Brien '74 (1) Silver '78 (2). *Also* Ashmole '74T. *Also* Rep II. *See* Monotones 1 and 2.

Monotones 1 and 2 P Monotones 1 (Trois Gnossiennes) 25 Apr 1966 ROH *Ch* Ashton *M* Satie orch John Lanchbery *C* Frederick Ashton. '66 (2); '67 (6); '68 (3); '69 (3); '70 (8); '74 (2); '75 (4); .'76 (8); '77 (4); '78 (6); '79 (4). T:23. *Trois Gnossiennes f* 1 Sibley '66–8 (6) Vere '67–'70 (16) Connor '74–9 (19) Tickner '75–9 (11). **2** Parkinson '66–'75 (25) Ellis '75–9 (16) Jenner '70–8 (10). *m* Shaw '66–'70 (15) Coleman '67–'79 (23) Eagling '75–9 (12). *Trois Gymopédies f* Lorrayne '66–'75 (18) Peri '67–'76 (11) Derman '75–9 (15) Porter '77–9 (6). *m* 1 Dowell '66–'75 (25) Drew '70 (2) D Kelly '75–6 (6) Silver '76–9 (11) Batchelor '77–9 (6). **2** Mead '66–'70 (21)

Drew '70–6 (9) Ashmole '74–'75 (4) Deane '76–9 (8) Page '77–9 (6) Eagling '78 (2). *Also* Rep II.

Month in the Country, A P 12 Feb 1976 ROH *Ch* Ashton *M* Chopin arr John Lanchbery *SC* Julia Trevelyan Oman. '76 (15); '77 (5); '78 (15); '79 (4). T:26. *Natalia Petrovna* Seymour '76–8 (31) Porter '77T '78–9 (7) Park '79A Conley '79 (1). *Kolia* Sleep '76–9 (29) Fletcher '76–9 (10). *Vera* Nunn '76–9 (37) Kingsley '78–9 (2) Ellis '79A. *Belaiev* Dowell '76–8 (14) Coleman '76–9 (21) Silver '78–9 (4). + 1*f* 3*m*.

My Brother, My Sisters FP 29 Apr 1980 ROH *Ch* MacMillan *M* Schoenberg/Webern. *SC* Yolanda Sonnabend. *The Brother* Eagling. First *Sister* Penney. *Second Sister* Collier. + 3*f* 1*m*.

Napoli Divertissement FP 3 May 1962 ROH *Ch* Bournonville *M* E Helsted/H S Paulli *SC* nc; from Oct '62 *SC* Richard Beer. '62 (19); '63 (13); '64 (6); '66 (3). T:4. 4*f* from: Park '62–6 (38) Seymour '62–6 (31) Sibley '62–6 (26) Parkinson '62–6 (36) Moncur '62–3 (13) Beckley '62–3 (13) Haslam '63 (1) Jenner '64–6 (6). 3*m* from: Usher '62–6 (33) Lawrence '62–3 (14) Au Bennett '62–4 (15) Dowell '62–6 (31) Shaw '62–6 (27) Coleman '66 (3). *Also* Rep II.

Narcissus and Echo 30m Jan 1932 sw *Ch* de Valois *M* Arthur Bliss *C* William Chappell. '32 (4). *Echo* Markova (4). *Narcissus* Judson (4). + 2*f*.

Night Tryst P 12 Mar 1963 ROH *Ch* Alan Carter *M* Purcell arr John Barbirolli *C* Peter Rice. '63 (2). *The Lady of High Birth and Station* Beriosova (2). *Her Secret Admirer* MacLeary (2). + attendants.

Noces, Les FP 23 Mar 1966 ROH *Ch* Nijinska *M* Stravinsky *SC* Goncharova. '66 (9); '67 (10); '70 (4); '72 (10); '73 (4); '74 (2); '75 (6); '77 (6); '79 (5). T:3. *The Bride* Beriosova '66–'74 (31) Bergsma '70–2 (5) Derman '72–9 (13) Eyre '72–7 (6) Howe '79 (1). *The Bridegroom* Mead '66–'70 (23) Rencher '72–7 (28) Hosking '79 (5). *Friends f* Parkinson '66–'77 (23) Mason '67–'77 (18) Connor '72–9 (15). *m* Dowell '66–'77 (30) Coleman '72–9 (26).

Noctambules P 1 Mar 1956 ROH *Ch* MacMillan *M* Humphrey Searle *SC* Nicholas Georgiadis. '56 (20); '57 (5); '58 (3). T:14. *Hypnotist* Edwards '56–8 (27) Hynd '58 (1). *His Assistant* Lane '56–8 (24) Wells '56–8 (4). *The Faded Beauty* Nerina '56–8 (22) Farron '56 (1) Page '57–8 (15). *The Poor Girl* Linden '56–7 (24) Page '56 (1) Grahame '58 (3). *The Rich Man* Doyle '56–8 (27) Hynd '56 (1). *The Soldier* Shaw '56–8 (22) Trecu '56–7 (6). + 12*f* 12*m*.

Nocturne P 10 Nov 1936 sw *Ch* Ashton *M* Delius *SC* Sophie Fedorovitch. *Scenario* Edward Sackville West. '36 (7); '37 (10); '38 (8); '39 (1); '40 (10); '44 (6); '45 (12); '46 (28); '47 (6). T:59. *A Spectator* Ashton '36–'47 [78] Ellis '36–'46 (9). *A Young Man* Helpmann '36–'47 [73] Somes '45–7 (14). *A Rich Girl* (from '44 *A Young Girl*) Brae '36–'40 (36) May '44–7 [35] Grey '44T '45–6 (12) Larsen '46–7 (4). *A Poor Girl* (from '44 *A Flower Girl*) Fonteyn '36–'47 [70] Miller '37–9 (2) Clayden '46–7 (15). + 10*f* 8*m*. nr '44 Nov 29m.

Nocturne excerpt '70 Ashton Tribute (1). *A Poor Girl* Fonteyn. *A Spectator* Somes.

Nutcracker, The FP 29 Feb 1968 ROH *Ch* Nureyev; revised '73; *Ch* Vassily Vainonen (Act II: Prince's Variation) *M* Tchaikovsky *SC* Nicholas Georgiadis. '68 (25); '69 (4); '73 (5); '74 (10); '76 (4); '77 (3). T:9. *Herr Drosselmeyer/The Prince* Nureyev '68–'77 (22) Wall '68–'76 (6) Dowell '68–'74 (15) MacLeary '68 (6) Coleman '68 (2). *Clara* Park '68–'77 (26) Wells '68 (2) Sibley '68–'74 (6) Beriosova '68 (2) Penney '68–'77 (13) Collier '74–6 (2).

Nutcracker, The Act I. '68 (1). *Herr Drosselmeyer/The Prince* Dowell. *Clara* Park.

Nutcracker, The pdd. '71 (1). T:3. *Clara* Park. *The Prince* Nureyev.

Nursery Suite P 19e Mar 1932 sw *Ch* de Valois revised '35 *M* Elgar *SC* Nancy Allen; '35 *SC* William Chappell. '32 (15); '33 (6); '34 (3); '35 (5); '36 (7); '37 (1). T:3. *Little Bo-Peep* McCarthy '32–3 (14) Newhouse '32 (2) Guinness '32 (1) Brown '33–4 (6) Robson '34 (1) Farron '35–7 (11) G Gill '35–6 (2). *Georgie Porgie* Dolin '32 (8) Judson '32–3 (9) Newman '33–4 (6) Helpmann '33 (1) Birdwood-Taylor '35–6 (8) Reyloff '36–7 (5). *Prince* Dolin '32 (8) Judson '32–3 (9) Kemp '33–4 (7) Ellis '36 (3) Somes '36–7 (2). *Princess* Markova '32 (8) de Valois '32 (4) Bamford '32–3 (6) Gregory '33–4 (6) May '36 (3) Spicer '36–7 (2). + 10*f* 3*m* '35/6 performed by pupils from School – Prince/Princess omitted + 6*f*.

Olympiad FP 21 Feb 1969 ROH *Ch* MacMillan *M* Stravinsky *SC* nc. '69 (6). **1** Bergsma (3) O'Conaire (3). **2** Parkinson (3) Mason (3). **3** Derman (6). **4** Rosson (6). **5** Mead (6). + 5*m* CdB.

Ondine P 27 Oct 1958 ROH *Ch/Scenario* Ashton; revised '59 & '64 *M* Hans Werner Henze *SC* Lila di Nobili. '58 (11); '59 (18); '60 (10); '61 (14); '62 (6); '64 (5); '66 (7). T:19. *Ondine* Fonteyn '58–'66 (59) Beriosova '61–6 (8) Nerina '64–6 (4). *Palemon* Somes '58–'62 (53) MacLeary '61–6 (11) Doyle '64–6 (4) Labis '66 (3). *Berta* Farron '58–'61 (43) Linden '61–2 (11) Daryl '61 (2) Bergsma '61–6 (13) Parkinson '66 (2). *Tirrenio* A Grant '58–'66 (69) Hynd '61–2 (2). + 65*f* 73*m*.

Ondine Act III the vision of Ondine '70 Ashton Tribute (1). *Ondine* Aitken + 4*m*.

Origin of Design, The FP 1 Nov 1932 sw *Ch/Scenario* (after Blasis) de Valois *M* Handel arr Beecham *SC* William Chappell after Inigo Jones. '32 (7). *Dibutade* de Valois (7). *Eros* Judson (7). *Polydore* Dolin (7). *Apollo* Tudor (7). *Terpsichore* Markova (3) McCarthy (4). + 11*f* 3*m*.

Orpheus and Eurydice P 28 May 1941 New *Ch* de Valois *M* Gluck *SC* Sophie Fedorovitch '41 (22); '42 (8). T:[19]. *Orpheus* Helpmann '41–2 (29) Hart (1). *Love* Fonteyn '41–2 (26) Grey '42 (4). *Eurydice* May '41 (22) Farron '41T '42 (8). + 34*f* 7*m*.

Paradise Lost P 23 Feb 1967 *Ch* Petit *M* Marius Constant *SC* Martial Raysse. '67 (7). T:22. *The Man* Nureyev (7). *The Woman* Fonteyn (7). + 17*f* 21*m*.

Patineurs, Les P 16 Feb 1937 sw *Ch* Ashton *M* Meyerbeer arr Lambert *SC* William Chappell. '37 (15); '38 (13); '39 (10); '40 (9); '41 (30); '42 (30); '44 (24); '45 (21); '46 (40); '47 (12); '48 (21); '50 (25); '51 (23); '52 (15); '53 (14); '54 (11); '55 (10); '56 (20); '57 (17); '58 (9); '59 (14); '61 (12); '62 (10); '63 (6); '64 (7); '65 (2); '66 (3); '67 (5); '68 (2). T:[497]. *Variation 'Blue Boy'* Turner '37–'48 (91) Carter '40T–1 [17] Helpmann '40 (2) Mendel '41 [8] Kersley '41T–2 [12] Hamilton '41T–4 [40] Field '42 [3] Powell '44 (4) Rassine '45–8 (33) Shaw '45–'66 (123) Britton '48 (2) Vernon '50–2 (11) Boulton '50–5 (17) Clegg '52–9 (35) Usher '61–7 (17) Gilpin '61 (4) Ruffell '64 (2) Martin '67 (3) Sleep '68 (2). pdd *f* Fonteyn '37–'41 [53] Argyle '37–8 (7) Farron '39T '41–'57 [179] Dale '41–2 [12] Shearer '42–6 [25] Larsen '46 (6) Prokhorova/Elvin '46–'51 (10) Grey '47–'50 (18) May '50 (10) Lindsay '51 (4) Heaton '53–5 (8) Linden '56–'61 (29) Park '56–'63 (19) Sibley '59–'63 (17) Lorrayne '61–7 (17) Seymour '62–6 (8) O'Conaire '67–8 (3) Parkinson '68 (1). *m* Helpmann '37–'41 [48] Chappell '38–9 (7) Ellis '40T–'51 (30) Somes '40T '41 [3] Hamilton '41 [8] Hart '41–'55 [88] Paltenghi '41–7 [94] Davenport '47–8 (11) Rodrigues '47–8 (13) Chatfield '48–'54 (7) Field '50–4 (9) Ashbridge '55–8 (18) Doyle '56–'67 (39) Hynd '59 (7) MacLeary '59–'61 (9) Usher '59 (1) Rencher '61–8 (34*). *Entrée 'Blue Girls'* 2 from: Honer '37–'42 [79] Miller '37–9 (36) Martyn '37T Farron '39 (1) Garnett '39T–'42 [55] Phillips/Sheldon '41–7 [59] van Praagh '41–5 [35] Dale '44–'52 (82) Clayden '44–'54 (23) Navarre '45–'54 (97) Roseby '46 (5) Jackson '48–'58 (122) Nerina '48–'52 (27) Olrich '50–4 (33) Mayan '55 (10) Benesh '55 (2) Page '56–'63 (59) Grahame '56–9 (21) Park '57–'64 (23) Lane '58–'64 (32) Wayne '59 (8) Moncur '61–3 (16) Jenner '64–5 (5) C Hill '65–8 (9) Bergen '66 (3) Horne '67–8 (7) Vere '67 (3). + 6*f* 4*m* ('57 Mar–'66 Feb 12*f* 8*m*). *Also:* Rep II. nr '41 Jan 17, 21 Aug 2m. '42 Oct 31m. *+ 1 with RBS at ROH.

Patineurs, Les *Finale* '70 Ashton Tribute (1). *Variation* Shaw. pdd *f* O'Conaire. *m* Rencher. *Entrée* C Hill. Vere.

Pélléas et Mélisande P 26 Mar 1969 ROH *Ch* Petit *M* Schoenberg *SC* Jacques Dupont '69 (2). T:9. *Mélisande* Fonteyn (3). *Pélléas* Nureyev (3). *Golaud* Rosson (3). + *CdB*.

Péri, La P 15 Feb 1956 ROH *Ch* Ashton *M* Paul Dukas *S* Ivon Hitchens; '57 *S* André Levasseur *C* André Levasseur. '56 (11); '57 (3); '58 (5). T:21. *La Péri* Fonteyn '56–8 (19). *Iskender* Somes '56–8 (19).

Perséphone P 12 Dec 1961 ROH *Ch* Ashton *M* Stravinsky *SC* Nico Ghika *Text* Gide. '61 (5); '62 (9); '67 (5); '68 (3). *Perséphone* Beriosova '61–8 (22). *Mercury* A Grant '61–8 (20) Mason '62 (2). *Pluto* Rosson '61–8 (22). *Demeter* Larsen '61–8 (22). *Demaphoon* Rencher '61–8 (22). + 39f 28m.

Perséphone excerpt '70 Ashton Tribute (1). *Perséphone* Beriosova. *Mercury* A Grant. *Demeter* Larsen. *Demaphoon* Rencher. + 13f 8m.

Petits Riens, Les P 13 Dec 1928 ov *Ch* de Valois *M* Mozart *SC* Owen P Smyth. '28 (7); '29 (1); '31 (3); '32 (1); '33 (2). *Rosalind* de Valois '28–'32 (12) Bamford '33 (2). *Corydon* Judson '28–'33 (13) Kemp '33 (1). *Clymene* Moreton '28–'32 (9) McCarthy '31 (2) Nielson '31 (1) Newton '33 (2). *Tricis* Briggs '28–9 (8) Beddoes '31 (2) Newman '31–3 (3) Kemp '32 (1). + 8f *CdB*.

Petrushka FP 26 Mar 1957 ROH *Ch* Fokine *M* Stravinsky *SC* Alexandre Benois *Pr* revived Grigoriev/Tchernicheva. '57 (22); '58 (9); '59 (10); '60 (6); '61 (5); '62 (4); '63 (10); '66 (3); '75 (3); '76 (4). T:31. *The Ballerina* Fonteyn '57 (8) Nerina '57–'63 (36) Fifield '57 (6) Lane '57–8 (3) Park '58–'75 (16) Penney '66–'76 (7). *Petrushka* A Grant '57–'76 (48) Shaw '57–'66 (11) Helpmann '58 (3) Blair '59 (6) Nureyev '63–'75 (5) Sleep '75–6 (3). *The Blackamoor* Clegg '57–'60 (29) Burne '57–9 (14) Rosson '60–6 (26) Adams '75–6 (4) Ashmole '76 (3). *The Showman* Ashton '57 (9) F White '57–'63 (57) Holden '66 (3) Grater '75–6 (7).

Piano Concerto No 2 *see* **Ballet Imperial**

Picnic, The (from 1930 **The Faun**) P 9 May 1929 ov *Ch* de Valois; revised '30 *M* Vaughan Williams *C* Hedley Briggs. '29 (5); '31 (3). T:3. *A Satyr* ('30 *A Faun*) Turner '29 (2) Briggs '29 (3) L French '31 (1) Judson '31 (2). *A Nymph* Moreton '29–'31 (8). + 11f 1m. ('30: 10f).

Pineapple Poll FPCG 22 Sept 1959 Hippodrome Golders Green *Cr Rep II*. '59 (6); '60 (4). T:4. *Pineapple Poll* Park '59TC–'60 (6) Wells '59T–'60 (4). *Jasper* Holden '59–'60 (6) Powell '59T (2) Mosaval '60 (2). *Captain Belaye* Blair '59–'60 (7) A Grant '59TC–'60 (3).

Poème de l'Extase FP 15 Feb 1972 ROH *Ch* Cranko *M* Scriabin *SC* Jürgen Rose after Klimt. '72 (8). T:3. *The Diva* Fonteyn (8). *The Boy* Coleman (8). *Memories* 1 Drew (8). 2 D Kelly (5) Myers (3). 3 O'Brien (8). 4 Wall (8). + *CdB*.

Polovtsian Dances from **Prince Igor** FP 24 Mar 1965 ROH *Ch* Fokine *M* Borodin *SC* Nicholas Roerich *Pr* Grigoriev/Tchernicheva. '65 (4). *Polovtsian Warrior* Nureyev (4). *Persian Slave* Parkinson (4). *Polovtsian Girl* Mason (3) Vere (1).

Pomona FP 17 Jan 1933 sw *Ch* Ashton *M* Lambert *SC* Vanessa Bell; '37 *SC* John Banting *Scenario* Thomas McGreevy. '33 (7); '34 (3); '37 (6); '38 (2). T: [20]. *Pomona* Appleyard '33–4 (9) Bamford '34 (1) Argyle '37–8 (4) Fonteyn '37T (2) Brae '37–8 (2). *Vertumnus* Dolin '33 (2) Judson '33–4 (5) Helpmann '33–8 (8) Somes '37T–8 (3). + 8f 2m.

Prince of the Pagodas, The P 1 Jan 1957 ROH *Ch/Scenario* Cranko *M* Britten *S* John Piper *C* Desmond Heeley. '57 (23); '58 (5); '59 (3); '60 (3). T:10. *Princess Belle Rose* Beriosova '57–'60 (26) Linden '57–'60 (8). *Princess Belle Epine* Farron '57–'60 (23) Lindsay '57–8 (11). *Prince of the Pagodas* Blair '57–'60 (26) Hynd '57–'60 (8). *Emperor of the Middle Kingdom* Edwards '57–'60 (34). + 40f 44m.

Prince of the Pagodas Act III '59 (1) T:4. *Princess Belle Rose* Beriosova. *Prince* Blair.

Prince of the Pagodas Act III pdd '58 (1). *Princess Belle Rose* Beriosova. *Prince* Blair.

Prince of the Pagodas Act III pas de six '64 (1).

Prodigal Son FP 25 Jan 1973 ROH *Ch* Balanchine *M* Prokofiev *M* Georges Rouault. '73 (11). *Prodigal Son* Nureyev (6) Wall (3) D Kelly (2). *The Siren* Bergsma (4) Derman (4) Parkinson (3). *The Father* Grater (6) Edwards (5). *Also Rep II*.

Promenade P 25 Oct 1943 King's, Edinburgh *Ch* de Valois *M* Haydn arr Edwin Evans orch Gordon Jacob *SC* Hugh Stevenson. '43 (18); '44 (47); '45 (19). T:104. *The Lepidopterist* Hamilton '43T–4 (84). Helpmann '45A, *Rendezvous f* Grey '43T–5 (32) Fonteyn '43 (4) Shearer '43–5 (20) May '43–5 (28). *m* Paltenghi '43–5 (77) Somes '45 (7). *Promenade* Clayden '43–5 (53) Sheldon '44–5 (19) Dale '44–5 (12). + 21f 2m. *Also Rep II*.

Prometheus P 13 Oct 1936 sw *Ch* de Valois *M* Beethoven arr Lambert *SC* John Banting. '36 (7); '37 (5); '38 (3). *Prometheus* Helpmann '36–8 (11) Turner '36–7 (4). *His Wife* Honer '36–8 (11) de Valois '36 (1) Miller '36–8 (3). *The Other Woman* Brae '36–8 (10) May '36–8 (5). + 27f 9m.

Prospect Before Us, The P 4 July 1940 sw *Ch/Scenario* de Valois *M* William Boyce arr Lambert *SC* Roger Furse after Thomas Rowlandson. '40 (10); '41 (27); '42 (12); '43 (14); '44 (18); '45 (11). T: [56]. *Mr Taylor* Newman '40–1 [28] Hamilton '41–5 [59]. *Mr O'Reilly* Helpmann '40–5 [87]. *Mademoiselle Theodore* May '40–5 [34] Farron '40T '41–5 [49] Shearer '45 (4). + 22f 15m. nr '41 Jan 16, 17, 20 Feb 12. '44 Oct 7m. *Also Rep II*.

Quest, The P 6 Apr 1943 New *Ch* Ashton *M* William Walton *SC* John Piper *Scenario* Doris Langley Moore after Spenser's *The Faerie Queene*. '43 (49); '44 (30); '45 (14). T:33. *Archimago* Edwards '43–5 [92]. *St George* Helpmann '43–6 [52] Paltenghi '43–5 [37] Somes '45 (3). *Una* Fonteyn '43–5 [59] Clayden '43–5 [33]. *Duessa* Grey '43–5 [73] Fraser '43–5 [19]. + 20f 8m. nr '43 Apr 23.

Rake's Progress, The P 20 May 1935 sw *Ch* de Valois *M* Gavin Gordon *SC* Rex Whistler after Hogarth; '46 false proscenium Oliver Messel. '35 (19); '36 (10); '37 (8); '38 (4); '39 (5); '40 (6); '42 (19); '43 (22); '44 (15); '45 (10); '46 (18); '47 (13); '48 (8); '4 (5); '50 (4); '51 (13); '56 (2); '58 (6); '59 (3); '63 (5); '64 (2). T: [283]. *The Rake* Gore '35 (11) Helpmann '35–'58 [116] Ashton '36–7 (2) Carter '39–'40 (4) Edwards '44T [4] Turner '46–'50 (34) Legerton '51A (7) A Grant '51A–'64 (13) Britton '59 (1) Blair '59 (1) Shaw '63–4 (2). *The Betrayed Girl* Markova '35 (8) Miller '35–9 (26) Honer '36T–'42 [28] Fonteyn '42–6 [34] M Jackson '42–5 [15] Farron '44–'59 (49) Prokhorova/Elvin '46–'50 (13) Clayden '47–'51 (9) Heaton '51–9 (4) Alexander '59 (1) Lane '63–4 (3) Sibley '63 (2) Park '63–4 (2). + 12f 21m. nr '42 Oct 31m. '44 May 31e. '43 Oct 2m (Betrayed Girl). *Also Rep II*.

Rake's Progress, The Orgy scene. '50 (1). 21st anniversary Gala sw. *The Rake* Gore + 7f.

Raymonda Act III FPCG 27 Mar 1969 ROH *Cr Rep II*. '69 (6); '70 (4); '71 (6); '72 (7); '73 (7); '74 (3); '75 (5). T:41. *Raymonda* Beriosova '69–'73 (3) Fonteyn '70–3 (14) Seymour '71T–5 (4) Sibley '71T Parkinson '69–'75 (6) Bergsma '69–'73 (3) Mason '74–5 (5). *Jean de Brienne* MacLeary '69–'73 (8) Dowell '69–'74 (8) Rosson '69–'71 (2) Nureyev '70–5 (16) Wall '74–5 (3) Hosking '74T (1). *Hungarian f* Bergsma '69–'70 (6) O'Conaire '69–'70 (4) Eyre '71T–5 (21) Conley '72–3 (5) Howe '74T–5 (2). *m* Doyle '69–'70 (6) Mason '69–'70 (4) Mead '71T (3) Adams '71T Grater '71–5 (15) Drew '72–5 (10).

Regatta P 22 Sept 1931 ov *Ch* Ashton *M* Gavin Gordon *SC* William Chappell '31 (4); '32 (3); '33 (1). T:1. *Cabin Boy* Judson '31–2 (6) Kemp '32–3 (2). *The Foreign Visitor* de Valois '31–3 (7) Markova '32 (1). + 3f 2m.

Regatta: *Sailor's Dance*. T:3.

Rendezvous, Les P 5 Dec 1933 sw *Ch* Ashton revised 1934 *M* Auber arr Lambert. *SC* William Chappell revised '39; redesigned 1937, revised '59. '33 (3); '34 (9); '35 (12); '36 (11); '37 (6); '38 (9); '39 (1); '40 (5); '41 (4); '42 (41); '43 (36); '44 (6); '45 (13); '59 (8); '60 (14); '62 (4); '63 (19). T:[116]. *Variations/Adagio of Lovers f* Markova '33–5 (19) Fonteyn '35–'45 (43) Miller '36–9 (13) Honer '37–'42 (22) Grey '42–'63 (45) Dale '42–4 (11) May '45 (5) Nerina '59 (7) Page '59–'63 (18) Park '60–3 (6) Sibley '62–3 (2). *m* Idzikowsky '33 (3)

Judson '34 (3) Gore '34–5 (10) Helpmann '34–'42 (5) Turner '35–'45 (41) Ellis '38–'40 (4) Somes '40–1 (6) Hart '42 (19) Rassine '42–5 (65) Shaw '59–'63 (16) Trecu '59–'60 (5) Blair '60–3 (9) Burne '60 (1) Usher '62–3 (2) MacLeary '63 (2). + 10*f* 6*m*; '59: 14*f* 10*m* NB '59–'62 S used Fedorovitch set from Act I *La Traviata*. Also Rep II.

Rendezvous, Les Variation *f*. '60 (1). Page.

Rendezvous, Les *Entrée*; pdt. '70 Ashton Tribute (1). *f* Park. *m* Nureyev.

Requiem Canticles FP 15 Nov 1972 ROH *Ch* Robbins *M* Stravinsky *SC* nc. '72 (4); '73 (7). *Tuba Mirum* Eagling '72–3 (11). *Interlude* 1 Bergsma '72–3 (11). 2 Derman '72–3 (7) Connor '73 (4). 3 Ashmole '72–3 (11). 4 Eagling '72–3 (11). *Lacrimosa* Bergsma '72–3 (11). + *CdB*.

Rhapsody P 4 Aug 1980 ROH *Ch* and *S* Ashton *M* Rachmaninoff *C* William Chappell. *f* Collier *m* Baryshnikov + 6*f*.

Rinaldo and Armida P 6 Jan 1955 ROH *Ch* Ashton *M* Malcolm Arnold *SC* Peter Rice. '55 (16); '56 (2); '57 (3); '58 (6); '59 (5). T:22. *Rinaldo* Somes '55–9 (32). *Armida* Beriosova '55–9 (32). *Sibilla* Farron '55–9 (29) Larsen '58 (3) Heaton '55A. *Gandolfo* Hynd '55–9 (30) Legerton '55 (2).

Rio Grande FP 26 Mar 1935 SW *Ch* Ashton *M* Lambert *SC* Edward Burra. Text Sacheverell Sitwell. '35 (10). *Queen of the Port* Appleyard (10). *Stevedore* Gore (4) Turner (6). *Creole Girl* Fonteyn (7) May (3). *Creole Boy* Chappell (10). + 10*f* 6*m*.

Rio Grande *solo*. '70 Ashton Tribute (1). *Stevedore* A Grant.

Rite of Spring, The P 3 May 1962 ROH *Ch* MacMillan *M* Stravinsky *SC* Sidney Nolan. '62 (10); '63 (4); '64 (7); '66 (4); '68 (6); '71 (4); '72 (8); '74 (9); '79 (7). T:10. *The Chosen Maiden* Mason '62–'79 (37) Beckley '62 (1) Bergsma '64–'74 (12) Derman '72–9 (7) Collier '79 (1) Connor '79 (1). + 24*f* 21*m*.

Rituals P 11 Dec 1975 ROH *Ch* MacMillan *M* Bartók *SC* Yolanda Sonnabend. '75 (2); '76 (10); '77 (5). T:8. *Grand Master* Drew '75–7 (17). *Neophytes* 1 Eagling '75–7 (10) Coleman '76–7 (6) Beagley '76 (1). 2 Beagley '75–7 (10) Sleep '76–7 (7). *Puppets f* Derman '75–7 (11) Makarova '76 (2) Peri '76 (2) Penney '77 (2). *m* Wall '75–7 (13) Ashmole '76A (2) Rencher '77 (2). *The Mother* Seymour '75–7 (10) Thorogood '76–7 (7). *The Midwife* Mason '75–7 (10) Parkinson '76–7 (7) Eyre '76A.

Roi Nu, Le (The Emperor's New Clothes) P 7 Apr 1938 SW *Ch* de Valois *M* Jean Françaix *SC* Hedley Briggs *Scenario* Serge Lifar after Hans Andersen. '38 (9); '39 (3). T:[15]. *The Emperor* Helpmann '38–9 (11) Somes '39 (1). *The Empress* Argyle '38 (6) May '38–9 (5) Brae '38 (1). *The Empress's Lover* Turner '38–9 (12).

Tailors: 1 Ashton '38–9 (12). 2 Chappell '38–9 (12). 3 Newman '38–9 (10) Reymond '38–9 (2). + 23*f* 11*m*.

Romeo and Juliet P 9 Feb 1965 ROH *Ch* MacMillan *M* Prokofien *SC* Nicholas Georgiadis revised '78. '65 (20); '66 (7); '67 (13); '68 (10); '69 (13); '70 (11); '71 (6); '72 (13); '73 (24); '74 (9); '75 (17); '76 (7); '77 (16); '78 (5); '79 (22). T:157. *Juliet* Fonteyn '65–'76 (35) Seymour '65–'78 (28) Park '65–'79 (38) Sibley '65–'76 (24) Page '65–7 (5) Parkinson '67–'76 (18) Wells '70–4 (6) Collier '73–9 (17) Makarova '73–5 (9) Porter '76T '77–9 (6) Jenner '77 (1) Ellis '76T '77–9 (5) Barbieri '79 (1). *Romeo* Nureyev '65–'77 (46) Gable '65–6 (9) MacLeary '65–'76 (29) Dowell '65–'79 (38) Mead '67–9 (3) Wall '70–8 (24) D Kelly '72–4 (4) Eagling '73–9 (19) Baryshnikov '75–7 (6) Ashmole '76T (1) Deane '76T '77–9 (7) Silver '76T '79 (4) Jefferies '79 (1) Hosking '79 (2). *Mercutio* Blair '65–'73 (31) Drew '65–6 (17) Hamilton '67–8 (6) Mason '67–8 (13) Sherwood '68–'73 (23) Coleman '69–'79 (86) Johnson '74 (4) Wall '75–8 (6) Dowell '75T–9 (8) Myers '76T Jefferies '77–9 (6) Fletcher '79 (3). *Benvolio* Dowell '65–7 (20) Usher '65–8 (22) Mead '67–'71 (22) Coleman '68–9 (6) Rafique '69 (4) Ashmole '70–6 (47) Eagling '71–9 (34) Deane '75–8 (17) Batchelor '76T '77–9 (21). + 13*f* 12*m* + *CdB*.

Romeo and Juliet 'Balcony' pdd. '71 (1); '76 (1); '78 (2). T:9. *Juliet* Fonteyn '71 (1); Makarova '76 (1) Collier '72A '78 (2) Jenner '75A. *Romeo* Nureyev '71–6 (2) Dowell '78 (2). Also Rep II.

Ropes of Time, The P 2 Mar 1970 ROH *Ch* Rudi van Dantzig *M* Jan Boerman *SC* Toer van Schayk. '70 (7). T:4. *The Traveller* Nureyev (7). *Life* Vere (7). *Death M* Mason (7). + 10*f* 10*m*.

Rout FP 30m Jan 1932 SW *Ch* de Valois *M* Arthur Bliss *SC* nc. '32 (2) de Valois (2). + 7*f* 4*m*.

Scènes de Ballet P 11 Feb 1948 ROH *Ch* Ashton *M* Stravinsky *SC* André Beaurepaire. '48 (28); '49 (4); '50 (10); '51 (8); '52 (7); '56 (10); '58 (6); '60 (6); '62 (4); '64 (4); '65 (3); '66 (4); '68 (6); '70 (7); '71 (8); '73 (4); '74 (7); '75 (5); '79 (6). T:44. *f* Fonteyn '48–9 (11) Shearer '48–'51 (22) Grey '48 (4) Nerina '49–'62 (23) Navarre '49T '50 (4) Jackson '52–8 (12) Page '60–6 (10) Park '60 (1) Sibley '64–'75 (25) Parkinson '68 (2) Penney '70–9 (15) Collier '73–9 (8). *m* Somes '48–'52 (29) Hart '48–'52 (25) Field '52 (3) Shaw '56–'66 (23) Blair '56–'62 (10) Usher '66–8 (6) Coleman '68–'79 (27) Dowell '70–4 (10) Wall '75 (2). + 4*f* 12*m*.

Scènes de Ballet *solo* '70 Ashton Tribute (1). Sibley.

Scorpions of Ysit, The FP 15 Nov 1932 SW *Ch* de Valois *M* Gavin Gordon *SC* Sophie Fedorovitch *Scenario* Terence Gray. '32 (5); '33 (3); '34 (1).

The Goddess Ysit Appleyard '32–4 (9). *Tefen* Bamford '32–4 (9). *First Marsh Woman* Moreton '32–4 (9). + 7*f*.

Serenade FP 7 May 1964 ROH *Ch* Balanchine *M* Tchaikovsky *SC* nc. '64 (9); '65 (8); '66 (6); '67 (2); '71 (4); '72 (4); '73 (3); '76 (9); '78 (6). T:11. 1 Beriosova '64–7 (17) Lorrayne '64–7 (7) Bergsma '65–'73 (2) Parkinson '71–6 (14) Seymour '72 (2) Makarova '76 (2) Derman '76 (1) Park '78 (3) Porter '78 (3). 2 Nerina '64 (5) Mason '64–'78 (15) Lorrayne '65 (1) Page '66–7 (3) Parkinson '66–7 (5) Park '71–6 (11) Vere '71–3 (3) Jenner '72 (1) Conley '73–8 (2) Connor '76 (3) Collier '78 (1) Conley–R Taylor–Mason '78 (1). 3 Page '64–5 (11) Park '64–5 (5) Mason '65–'78 (13) Jenner '66–'76 (14) Vere '72 (1) Conley '72 (1) Connor '73 (1) Tickner '78 (1) Collier '78 (2) Penney '78 (2). 4 Blair '64–5 (9) Usher '64–5 (2) Drew '65–7 (14) Wall '71–3 (4) Rosson '71 (2) D Kelly '72–3 (5) Ashmole '76 (7) Eagling '76–8 (5) Silver '78 (3). 5 MacLeary '64–7 (10) Rosson '64–7 (15) Blair '71–2 (3) Sherwood '71–2 (5) Adams '73–6 (9) Fairweather '76 (1) Drew '76 (2) Deane '78 (3) Hosking '78 (3).

Seven Deadly Sins, The FP 19 July 1973 ROH *Ch* MacMillan *M* Kurt Weill *SC* Ian Spurling *Text* Brecht trans. Auden/Chester Kallman. '73 (6); '74 (5). T:2. *Anna I* (singer) Georgia Brown '73–4 (8) Annie Ross '73 (3). *Anna II* Penney '73–4 (8) Collier '73A–4 (3). + 13*f* 10*m* + *CdB*. + 4 singers.

Shadow, The P 3 Mar 1953 ROH *Ch/Scenario* Cranko *M* Dohnanyi *SC* John Piper. '53 (20); '54 (4); '55 (12); '56 (5); '57 (9); '58 (5); '59 (2). T:53. *A Youth* Chatfield '53–9 (49) Doyle '56–8 (8). *His Romantic Love* Beriosova '53–9 (47) Evans '54–7 (4) Boulton '57–8 (6). *The Shadow* Ashbridge '53–9 (44) Mader '54–7 (6) Rencher '58–9 (7) *A Young Girl* Lindsay '53–7 (32) Nerina '53 (9) Linden '54–6 (3) Lane '57–8 (11) Parkinson '58T Park '59 (2). + 12*f* 9*m*.

Shadow, The pdd. '56 (1). *A Youth* Chatfield. *His Romantic Love* Beriosova.

Shadowplay P 25 Jan 1967 ROH *Ch* Tudor *M* Charles Koechlin *SC* Michael Annals. '67 (11); '68 (6); '70 (3); '71 (6); '74 (4). T:8. *The Boy with Matted Hair* Dowell '67–'74 (29) Mead '70 (1). *Terrestrial* Rencher '67–'74 (30). *Celestial Park* '67–'74 (24) Jenner '68–'70 (5) Penney '71 (1). + 8*f* 9*m*.

Sinfonietta (*Elegy*) FPCG 14 Dec 1971 ROH Cr Rep II. '71 (1). *f* Wells. *m* Coleman.

Sirènes, Les P 12 Nov 1946 ROH *Ch/Scenario* Ashton *M* Gerald Berners *SC* Cecil Beaton. '46 (15); '47 (4). *La Bolero* Fonteyn '46 (9) Prokhorova '46–7 (8) Shearer '47 (2). *King Hihat of Agpar* Ashton '46–7 (13) Turner '46–7 (6). *Adelino Canberra* Helpmann '46–7 (19). + 28*f* 11*m*.

Sleeping Beauty, The FPNP 20 Feb 1946 ROH *Ch* after Petipa; *Ch* Ashton (I Garland Dance III Florestan and His Two Sisters. '52 II Var Aurora); *Ch* de Valois (III Three Ivans; Polonaise; '52 Var Prince) *M* Tchaikovsky *SC* Oliver Messel *Pr* Sergeyev; revised 1952. '46 (78); '47 (38); '48 (27); '49 (7); '50 (23); '51 (15); '52 (35); '53 (18); '54 (18); '55 (4); '56 (28); '57 (4); '58 (25); '59 (17); '60 (7); '61 (22); '62 (20); '63 (9); '64 (23); '65 (9); '66 (10); '67 (3); T:265. *Princess Aurora* Fonteyn '46–'66 (112) May '46–8 (26) Shearer '46–'53 (51) Grey '46–'59 (56) Navarre '47T Elvin '48–'56 (28) Markova '48 (3) Nerina '51T '52–'66 (60) Lindsay '51T '52 (5) Jackson '53–8 (8) Beriosova '54–'66 (40) Fifield '56 (4) Linden '57A '58–'63 (13) Chauviré '58 & '62 (3) Page '59–'67 (13) Park '61TC–7 (7) Sibley '61–5 (8) Verdy '64 (3) Wells '66 (1). *Prince Florimund* Helpmann '46–'50 (46) Paltenghi '46–7 (77) Hart '47–'55 (66) Somes '47–'61 (56) Dolin '48 (3) Field '50–5 (25) Chatfield '52–9 (17) Rassine '53–8 (15) Blair '55A '56–'66 (62) Ashbridge '58–'62 (6) Selling '59 (3) Hynd '59–'64 (8) MacLeary '60–6 (22) Doyle '60–6 (10) Rosson '61–5 (6) Gilpin '61TC–2 (2) Bruhn '62 (5) Nureyev '62–7 (5) Gable '66–7 (6). *The Fairy of the Lilac* Grey '46–'56 (93) Lynne '46–8 (34) May '47–'52 (40) Brae '47 (6) Lindsay '48–'59 (84)·Shearer '48 (1) Drage '52–7 (33) Valaire '51T '52 (1) Beriosova '52–8 (19) Linden '56–'60 (13) Boulton '58 (6) Parkinson '58–'65 (27) Lorrayne '60–7 (23) Bergsma '60–7 (51) Beckley '61–3 (5) Seymour '64TC (1) Peri '66 (3). *The Blue Birds ƒ* May '46 (1) Prokhorova/Elvin '46–'52 (91) Dale '46–8 (45) Clayden '46–'53 (20) Navarre '47–'54 (30) Shearer '49 (2) Jackson '50–8 (68) Nerina '51–2 (10) Farron '52 (1) Lindsay '53 (3) Linden '54–6 (14) Blowers '54 (2) Park '56–'65 (48) Page '56–'64 (42) Sibley '58–'65 (31) Lane '61–4 (8) Parkinson '62–7 (17) Penney '66 (4) Jenner '66–7 (2). *m* Rassine '46–'53 (118) Turner '46–8 (45) Somes '47–'50 (25) Britton '48 (1) Shaw '50–'67 (127) Vernon '51T '52 (1) MacMillan '52 (1) Clegg '52–9 (22) Boulton '53–4 (3) Blair '54–6 (17) Usher '58–'66 (63) Burne '59 (1) Lawrence '61–4 (9) Coleman '66–7 (5). *Also Rep II.*

Sleeping Beauty, The Acts I/III. '52 (2). *Princess Aurora* Lindsay (1) Grey (1). *Prince Florimund* Chatfield (1) Field (1) *The Fairy of the Lilac* Drage (2) *The Blue Birds ƒ* Navarre (1) Jackson (1). *m* Vernon (1) MacMillan (1).

Sleeping Beauty, The Act I, *Rose Adagio.* T:32.

Sleeping Beauty, The, *Rose Adagio* and Variation. '55 (1). *Princess Aurora* Elvin.

Sleeping Beauty, The Act III. '50 (1); '54 (2); '55 (1); '57 (2); '59 (1). T:71. *Princess Aurora* Fonteyn '50–4 (3) Elvin '55 (1) Markova '57 (2) Nerina '59 (1). Sibley '60A *Prince Florimund* Helpmann '50 (1) Somes '54 (2) Hart '55 (1)

Chatfield '57 (2) Blair '59 (1). MacLeary '60A *The Fairy of the Lilac* Grey '50 (1) '54/5 nc. Lindsay '57 (2) Parkinson '59 (1). *The Blue Birds ƒ* Elvin '50 (1) Navarre '54 (1) Blowers '54 (1) Jackson '55 (1) Page '57 (1) Park '57 (1) Sibley '59 (1). *m* Rassine '50 (1) Boulton '54 (1) Shaw '54–5 (2) Clegg '57 (1) Usher '57–9 (2).

Sleeping Beauty, The Act III *Florestan and his Two Sisters.* T:[15].

Sleeping Beauty, The Act III *Blue Bird* pdd '56 (1). T:[59]. *ƒ* Jackson. *m* Shaw.

Sleeping Beauty, The Act III *Blue Bird* pdd Variation *ƒ.* '60 (1). Page.

Sleeping Beauty, The Act III pdd. '56 (1); '58 (1) '59 (1); '60 (1). T:[49]. *Princess Aurora* Elvin '56 (1) Jackson '58 (1) Grey '59 (1) Fonteyn '60 (1). *Prince Florimund* Hart '56 (1) Chatfield '58 (1) Selling '59 (1) Somes '60 (1).

Sleeping Beauty, The FPNP 17 Dec 1968 ROH *Ch* after Petipa; *Ch* Ashton (Prologue: Fairy of Joy. I Garland Dance new version; II Var Prince, Awakening pdd. III Gold and Silver pdt (later Florestan and his Two Sisters *Ch* substituted as Gold and Silver pdt). *M* Tchaikovsky *S* Henry Bardon *C* Lila di Nobili/Rostislav Doboujinsky *Pr* Peter Wright. '68 (7); '69 (14); '72 (12). T:33. *Princess Aurora* Sibley '68–'72 (10) Lorrayne '68–9 (5) Park '68–'72 (6) Penney '68 (1) Fonteyn '69–'72 (7) Jenner '72 (4). *Prince Florimund* MacLeary '68–'72 (9) Dowell '68–'72 (8) Rosson '68–9 (2) Nureyev '68–'72 (11) Mead '68–9 (2) Wall '72 (1). *The Lilac Fairy* Bergsma '68–'72 (12) Peri '68–'72 (7) Derman '68–'72 (11) Lorrayne '69 (2) Porter '72A (1). *The Blue Birds* (from Mar '72 *The Blue Bird/Princess Florine*) *ƒ* Park '68–'72 (6) Penney '68–'72 (8) Collier '68–'72 (12) Jenner '69 (4) Thorogood '72 (3). *m* Coleman '68–'72 (15) Martin '68–9 (6) Sleep '68–'72 (9) Wall '72 (3) Eagling '72A.

Sleeping Beauty, The Prologue *Fairy variations.* '73 (1). *The Lilac Fairy* Derman.

Sleeping Beauty, The *Awakening* pdd. '70 Ashton Tribute (1). *Princess Aurora* Sibley. *Prince Florimund* Dowell.

Sleeping Beauty, The Act III *Blue Bird* pdd. T:2.

Sleeping Beauty, The FPNP 15 Mar 1973 ROH *Ch* Petipa; *Ch* MacMillan (I Garland Dance. II Var Aurora. III Polonaise; Jewel Fairies entrée, coda, pdt, Var 3, Var Lilac Fairy; Hop o'my Thumb. '73 Oct *Ch* Jewel Fairies revised); *Ch* Ashton (II Var Prince. III Jewel Fairy Var 2); *Ch* Fyodor Lopokov (Prologue: Var Lilac Fairy) *M* Tchaikovsky *SC* Peter Farmer *Pr* MacMillan. '73 (23); '74 (8); '75 (7). T:26. *Princess Aurora* Sibley '73–5 (5) Park '73–5 (8) Penney '73–5 (6) Thorogood '73 (4) Makarova '73 (3) Jenner–Last '73 (1) Wells '73–4 (5) Collier '74–5 (4) Mason '74–5 (2). *Prince Florimund* Dowell '73–5 (6) MacLeary '73–5 (5) Ashmole

'73–5 (4) Wall '73–5 (7) Nureyev '73–5 (9) D Kelly '73–5 (6) Hosking '74 (1). *The Lilac Fairy* Bergsma '73–4 (14) Peri '73–5 (10) Derman '73–5 (7) Porter '73–5 (6) Howe '74 (1) Wylde '75A. *The Blue Birds ƒ* Thorogood '73–4 (7) Collier '73–5 (15) Jenner '73 (1) Ellis '73–5 (5) Penney '73–5 (7) J Jackson '74–5 (2) Young '74 (1). *m* Coleman '73–5 (14) Wall '73–4 (5) Sleep '73–5 (5) Eagling '73–5 (11) Johnson '74–5 (2) Fletcher '74 (1).

Sleeping Beauty, The On tour only: Prologue *pas d'action* (1). Act III (10).

Sleeping Beauty, The Act III. pdd '74 (1). T:3. *Princess Aurora* Fonteyn. *Prince Florimund* Nureyev.

Sleeping Beauty, The FPNP 14 Oct 1977 ROH *Ch* Petipa after Sergeyev *Pr* 1939; *Ch* Ashton (as '46* + II Var Prince; Awakening pdd as '68); *Ch* MacMillan (III Hop o'my Thumb); *Ch* Fyodor Lopokov (as '73) *M* Tchaikovsky *SC* David Walker *Pr* de Valois. '77 (15); '78 (18); '79 (14). T:23. *Princess Aurora* Collier '77–79 (11) Jenner '77 (2) Park '77–9 (9) Seymour '77 (3) Penney '77–9 (11) Ellis '77–9 (5) Porter '78–9 (4) Whitten '79 (2). *Prince Florimund* Dowell '77–8 (4) Jefferies '77–9 (9) Wall '77–8 (8) Eagling '77–9 (9) Nureyev '77 (3) Deane '77–9 (5) Hosking '78 (4) Silver '79 (5). *The Lilac Fairy* Derman '77–9 (10) Wylde '77–9 (17) Porter '77–9 (14) Mason '77–9 (6) *The Blue Birds* (from '78 *The Blue Bird/Princess Florine*) *ƒ* Thorogood '77–8 (7) Ellis '77–9 (14) Collier '77–8 (4) Tickner '77–9 (5) Penney '77–8 (7) Whitten '78–9 (10). *m* Coleman '77–8 (10) Beagley '77–9 (21) Eagling '77–8 (10) D Baker '77 (1) Fletcher '78–9 (2) Jefferies '78–9 (2) Page '78 (1)'
*except *Florestan* pdt Var 1.

Sleeping Beauty, The Act III. pdd '78 (2). *Princess Aurora* Penney (2). *Prince Florimund* Eagling (2).

Sleeping Princess, The; Blue Bird pdd (The Enchanted Princess) FP 26 Sept 1933 sw *Ch* Petipa *M* Tchaikovsky *C* William Chappell. '33 (5); '34 (2); '35 (15); '36 (11); '37 (5); '38 (4). T:35. *ƒ* Markova '33–5 (15) Honer '35–8 (20) Miller '36–8 (7). *m* Idzikowsky '33–4 (5) Judson '33–4 (2) Turner '35–8 (31) Chappell '36 (1) Somes '37T–8 (3). *Also* The Sleeping Princess/Beauty below.

Sleeping Princess, The, Act III pdd (known as 'Aurora' pdd) FP 24 Oct 1933 sw *Ch* Petipa *M* Tchaikovsky *C* nc. '36 *C* William Chappell. '33 (2); '36 (6); '37 (11); '38 (3). T.16. *ƒ* Markova '33 (2) Argyle '36–8 (6) Fonteyn '36T–8 (7) Honer '36–8 (7). *m* Idzikowski '33 (2) Helpmann '36–8 (13) Turner '36–8 (7). *Also* The Sleeping Princess/Beauty below.

Sleeping Princess, The FP 2 Feb 1939 sw *Pr* Sergeyev after *Ch* Petipa *M* Tchaikovsky *SC* Nadia Benois. '39 (12); '40 (11); '41 (11); '42 (22). T:5. *Princess Aurora* Fonteyn '39–'42 (55)

May '41 (1). *Prince Charming* (from '42 Mar *Prince Florimund*) Helpmann '39–'42 (55) Hart '42 (1). *The Lilac Fairy* Brae '39–'41 [28] May '41 [3] Fraser '41–2 (23) May–Honer–Farron '41 (1). *The Blue Birds f* Honer '39–'42 [26] Miller '39 (5) May '40–1 [9] Dale '42 (11) Sheldon '42 (3). *m* Turner '39–'40 (11) Somes '39–'42 (13) Hart '41–2 [19] Rassine '42 (12). nr '41 Oct 11m (Lilac Fairy/Blue Birds).

Sleeping Princess, The Acts I/III '39 (1) Gala at ROH 22 Mar. *Princess Aurora* Fonteyn. *Prince Charming* Helpmann. *The Lilac Fairy* Brae. *The Blue Birds f* Honer. *m* Turner. NB Act III rearranged to include Prologue Fairy Variations. Jewel Fairies omitted.

Sleeping Princess, The Act III pdd. '45 (9). T [8]. *Princess Aurora* Fonteyn (8) May (1). *Prince Florimund* Helpmann (8) Paltenghi (1).

Sleeping Princess, The, *Divertissement* '41 (3). *Miss* '41 Jan 20, 22, 24.

Sleeping Princess, The. On tour only. Act III [15]. Blue Bird pdd [27].

Sleeping Princess, The pdt. '41 (1). *NB* as no pdt is listed in this production this may be a misprint for pdt from *Le Lac des Cygnes*.

Solitaire FPCG 17 Sept 1957 Metropolitan Opera House, New York Cr Rep II. '57 (9). T:18. *'The Girl'* Linden '57A (6) Hill (9). *'Polka'* Lane '57A (6) Page (3). *m solo* Blair '57A Shaw (6) Trecu (3). *m pdd* Hynd '57A (6) Usher (1) Clegg (2).

Song of the Earth FP 19 May 1966 ROH *Ch* MacMillan *M* Mahler *SC* nc. '66 (9); '67 (9); '69 (4); '70 (5); '71 (4); '72 (4); '73 (6); '74 (7); '75 (4); '77 (5); '78 (4). T:11. *The Messenger of Death* Dowell '66–'78 (33) Nureyev '66–'75 (7) Coleman '67–'78 (18) E Madsen '77 (3). *First Song* MacLeary '66–'74 (30) Doyle '67 (1) Rosson '67–'70 (7) I Hamilton '67 (2) Wall '71–8 (16) Cragun '77 (3) Jefferies '78 (2). *Second Song* Haydée '66 & '77 (8) Seymour '66–'71 (5) Mason '67–'78 (31) Parkinson '67–'74 (13) Makarova '74 (2) Collier '78 (2). *Third Song* Penney '66–'78 (51) Sibley '66–'71 (5) Collier '73A–'7 (5). *Fourth Song f* Parkinson '66–'77 (23) Jenner '67 (4) O'Conaire '69–'70 (7) Vere '71–3 (12) Derman '74–8 (13) Porter '76A '78 (2). *m* Mason '66–'70 (27) Blair '71 (2) Sherwood '71–2 (6) Ashmole '73–5 (15) Myers '75 (1) Griffith '75 (1) Eagling '77–8 (7) Moore '78 (2). + 7f 9m.

Spectre de la Rose, Le FP 4 Mar 1932 ov *Ch* Fokine *M* Weber *SC* nc. '32 Nov *C* Bakst; '44 *SC* Rex Whistler. '32 (11); '33 (7); '34 (3); '35 (5); '44 (29); '45 (13). T:42. *The Young Girl* de Valois '32 (5) Moreton '32–5 (17) Markova '33 (3) Appleyard '35 (1) Fonteyn '44–5 [26] May '44 [3] Shearer '44T–'5 [12]. *The Spirit of the Rose* Dolin '32–5 (12) Judson '33–4 (5) Idzikowsky '33 (3) Helpmann '34–5 (4) Turner '35 (2) Rassine '44–5 (40) Somes '45 (2). *Miss* '44 May 31e (Girl). Also Rep II.

Suite of Dances P 18 Dec 1930 ov *Ch* de Valois *M* J S Bach arr Eugene Goossens *SC* Owen P Smyth. '30 (5); '31 (6); '32 (2). T:3 (as *Suite de Danses*). *Gavotte* Turner '30–1 (6) Dolin '32 (2) Judson '31–2 (5). *Bourrée* de Valois '30–1 (8) Nielson '31–2 (5). + 10f 1m.

Swan Lake *see also* Lac des Cygnes, Le

Swan Lake FPNP 12 Dec 1963 ROH *Ch* Petipa/Ivanov; *Ch* Ashton (Prologue – '63–Mar '67 only). I scene 1: Waltz; Pas de Quatre. Scene 2 (formerly Act II) Dance of Four Swans. II (formerly III) Dance of Guests; Spanish; Neapolitan. III (formerly IV) entire act; *Ch* Nureyev (I scene 1: Polonaise. II Mazurka; *Ch* Maria Fay (II Czardas – '63–5 only). *M* Tchaikovsky *SC* Carl Toms *Pr* Helpmann. '63 (11); '64 (23); '65 (6); '66 (14); '67 (14); '68 (13); '69 (15); '70 (15). T:102. *Odette/Odile* Fonteyn '63–'70 (29) Nerina '63–'70 (14) Beriosova '63–9 (19) Page '63–4 (3) Sibley '63–'70 (14) Seymour '64–6 (5) Parkinson '67 (2) Bergsma '67TC–'70 (13) Mason '67TC–'70 (12). *Prince Siegfried* Blair '63–6 (16) MacLeary '63–'70 (32) Doyle '63–6 (5) Gable '63–5 (9) Nureyev '64–'70 (26) Dowell '67TC–'70 (10) Rosson '67–'70 (13).

Swan Lake Act I scene 2 (formerly Act II) T:5.

Swan Lake Act II. Neapolitan. '70 Ashton Tribute (1).

Swan Lake (revised TC *Pr* 1965) FPCG 17 Feb 1971 ROH *Ch* Petipa/Ivanov; *Ch* Ashton (as '63 except no Prologue/Dance of Swans; Dance of Guests '71–Oct '72 only); *Ch* de Valois (I: Peasant Dance); *Ch* Nureyev (I Var Prince); from Oct '72 Act IV *Ch* Ivanov; *Ch* Bruhn (I: Var Prince – Baryshnikov only) *M* Tchaikovsky *SC* Leslie Hurry *Pr* Sergeyev from Oct '72 revised de Valois. '71 (30); '72 (17); '73 (16); '74 (16); '75 (25); '76 (14); '77 (26); '78 (8); '79 (8). T:108. *Odette/Odile* Sibley '71–5 (13) Bergsma '71–4 (16) Mason '71–8 (29) Fonteyn '71–3 (12) Wells '71–3 (9) Makarova '72–7 (14) Penney '72–9 (9) Thorogood '72–4 (3) Park '73–7 (24) Collier '73–9 (18) Derman '75–9 (10) Peri '76 (1) Seymour '77 (1) Porter '79 (1). *Prince Siegfried* Dowell '71–8 (28) Rosson '71 (3) MacLeary '71–6 (21) Wall '71–8 (33) D Kelly '71–6 (14) Nureyev '71–7 (23) Ashmole '73–6 (9) Eagling '75–9 (14) Baryshnikov '75 (3) Jefferies '77–9 (2) Deane '77–9 (8) Silver '79 (2).

Swan Lake Act III. pdd '71 (1). T:6. *Odile* Bergsma. *Prince Siegfried* MacLeary.

On tour only: Act II (6). Act III: Pas de Quatre (11); Neapolitan (10); Czardas (5).

Swan Lake FPNP 5 Dec 1979 ROH *Ch* Petipa/Ivanov; *Ch* Ashton (as '71); *Ch* de Valois (as '71); *Ch* Nureyev (as '71) *M* Tchaikovsky *SC* Leslie Hurry *Pr* Norman Morrice after Sergeyev/de Valois. '79 (7). *Odette/Odile* Collier

(3) Penney (2) Porter (2). *Prince Siegfried* Wall (2) Silver (1) Dowell (3) Eagling (1).

Sylphides, Les FP 8 Mar 1932 sw *Ch* Fokine *M* Chopin orch various *SC* nc. '32 Nov *SC* Bakst; '35 *SC* Hugh Stevenson; '40 *SC* Alexandre Benois; '48 *SC* after Benois. '32 (15); '33 (10); '34 (6); '35 (17); '36 (8); '37 (5); '38 (8); '39 (8); '40 (12); '41 (36); '42 (60); '43 (44); '44 (46); '45 (26); '46 (23); '47 (30); '48 (22); '49 (12); '50 (19); '51 (20); '52 (16); '53 (10); '54 (10); '55 (23); '56 (16); '57 (14); '58 (17); '59 (2); '60 (7); '61 (8); '62 (23); '63 (9); '64 (5); '65 (2); '68 (4); '72 (1); '73 (6); '75 (8); '77 (4); '78 (7); '79 (5). T:[525]. To 1940: *Valse* Nielson '32 (10) McCarthy '32 (1) Phillips '32–7 (29) Bamford '34 (1) Miller '34–9 (14) Darnborough '34 (1) May '34–5 (6) Fonteyn '35 (1) Brae '36–7 (2) Honer '38–'40 (18) Farron '39–'40 (6). *Mazurka f* Markova '32–5 (22) Appleyard '32–5 (16) Darnborough '33 (1) Phillips '34–5 (2) Fonteyn '35–'40 (25) Argyle '35–6 (6) Honer '36–7 (3) May '38–'40 (12) Brae '40 (2). *Prelude* Moreton '32–'40 (62) Gould '33 (1) May '35–'40 (13) Argyle '38 (2) Brae '38–'40 (11). 1941–5 following dancers listed with no indication of roles danced: Fonteyn, May, Brae, Farron, Honer. '42 + Franca, van Praagh, Fraser, Grey, Nye, Shearer. '43 + Clayden. '44 + Negus, Mossford. 1946 on: *Valse* Negus '46–'50 (57) Clayden '46–'54 (28) Lynne '46–'51 (19) May '48–9 (2) Nerina '48–'53 (32) Carne '51–2 (5) Jackson '52–6 (8) Evans '52–4 (4) Heaton '53 (1) V Taylor '54 (6) Fifield '54–7 (15) Linden '55–7 (21) Lindsay '55–6 (8) Farron '56 (1) Grahame '56–'60 (22) Boulton '58 (3) Park '58–'68 (30) Sibley '59–'62 (9) Anderton '60 (2) Beckley '61–2 (10) Parkinson '63–5 (7) Penney '68 (2) Collier '72–9 (11) Connor '73–9 (8) R Taylor '75–9 (4) Ellis '74T '75–9 (7) Corken '77T (1). *Mazurka f* Fonteyn '46–'60 (18) May '46–'50 (11) Grey '46–'62 (70) Shearer '46–'50 (14) Clayden '47 (4) Nerina '47–'65 (41) Heaton '48–'55 (46) Lindsay '50–4 (12) Beriosova '52–'65 (19) Linden '55–'63 (23) Fifield '57 (4) Page '57–'63 (13) Park '58 (1) Chauviré '58 (3) Seymour '60–'75 (2) Sibley '61–2 (4) Parkinson '62–8 (6) Lorrayne '68 (2) Makarova '72–5 (3) Jenner '73 (3) Conley '73 (3) Penney '75–9 (9) Bergsma '74T Vere '74T Connor '74T Porter '75–9 (10) Mason '78 (2). *Prelude* Shearer '46–9 (10) Grey '46–7 (8) Larsen '46–'56 (74) Lindsay '47–'60 (74) Markova '48–'57 (11) Farron '51–8 (38) May '51–2 (7) Clayden '52 (1) Beriosova '52–'73 (10) Linden '56 (1) Page '58–'64 (17) Parkinson '60–'77 (21) Lorrayne '60–5 (16) Chauviré '62 (4) Fonteyn '62–'73 (10) Seymour '72 (1) Peri '75 (5) Porter '75 (1) Conley '77–9 (5) Thorogood '77T–9 (9). *Mazurka m* Dolin '32–'48 (15) Judson '32–4 (15) Idzikowski '33 (2) Helpmann '34–'45 [46] Chappell '34–9 (13) Turner '35 (2) Ashton '35–7 (13) Somes '38–'50 [44] Hart

'41–8 [39] Rassine '42–'58 [147] Paltenghi '42–5 [57] Field '42–'54 [51] Danton '46 (1) Thomson '46–7 (26) MacMillan '51–2 (4) Melville '51 (1) Chatfield '52–9 (22) Blair '55–'61 (22) Hynd '56–'62 (12) Trecu '57–8 (8) Farley '60 (1) Gilpin '61TC (1) Rosson '61–2 (6) MacLeary '61–'73 (22) Usher '62 (3) Bruhn '62 (1) Nureyev (alternative *Ch*) '62–8 (16) Dowell '72–5 (7) Wall '73–9 (10) Silver '75–9 (6) Eagling '77T–8 (5). *Valse* pdd as *Mazurka ƒ* and *m* except Fonteyn, Chauviré, Parkinson (Prelude and pdd). nr '41 Jan 16, 17, 23 June 7m. *Also* Rep II.

Sylvia (3 acts) P 3 Sept 1952 ROH *Ch* Ashton revised '65 *M* Delibes *SC* Robin/Christopher Ironside. '52 (26); '53 (7); '54 (5); '55 (12); '56 (4); '57 (8); '58 (4); '59 (8); '63 (4*); '65 (4*). T:27. *Sylvia* Fonteyn '52–'65 (23) Elvin '52–5 (8) Grey '52–6 (13) Nerina '52–'65 (17) Beriosova '54–9 (10) Linden '57–'65 (6) Wells '63–5 (3) Hayden '63 (2). *Aminta* Somes '52–9 (23) Field '52–5 (5) Chatfield '52–8 (24) Rassine '52–7 (13) Blair '57–9 (7) MacLeary '59 (2) Gable '63 (2) Flindt '63 (2) Labis '65 (4). *Orion* Hart '52–8 (50) Field '52–5 (8) Ashbridge '56–'65 (19) Hynd '59 (2) Rosson '59 (1) Rencher '59 (2). *Eros* A Grant '52–9 (63) Vernon '52 (4) Melville '52–3 (7) Sherwood '63 (4) Farley '65 (4) + 57ƒ 33m. *TC in CG production ROH only.

Sylvia Act I Variation. T:6.

Sylvia Act I *Sylvia and the Hunt.* '70 Ashton Tribute (1). *Sylvia* Bergsma + 8ƒ.

Sylvia Act III pdd. '53 (2). T:4. *Sylvia* Fonteyn (2). *Aminta* Somes (2).

Sylvia Act III solo. '59 (1). Linden.

Sylvia (1 act version) FP 18 Dec 1967 ROH Cr as above *Sylvia*. '67 (2); '68 (10). *Sylvia* Nerina '67–8 (2) Beriosova–Mason '67 (1) Bergsma '68 (3) Mason '68 (4) Beriosova '68 (2). *Aminta* Sherwood '67–8 (2) MacLeary '67–8 (4) I Hamilton '68 (1) Rosson '68 (3) Mead '68 (2). *Eros* Grant '67–8 (12). + 9ƒ 1m CdB.

Symphonic Variations P 24 Apr 1946 ROH *Ch* Ashton *M* Franck *SC* Sophie Fedorovitch. '46 (21); '47 (15); '48 (15); '49 (11); '50 (6); '51 (8); '52 (13); '53 (5); '54 (3); '55 (7); '56 (8); '57 (6); '59 (7); '61 (4); '62 (2); '63 (4); '67 (5); '68 (8); '69 (4); '70 (1); '71 (7); '72 (4); '73 (5); '74 (4); '77 (7); '79 (15). T:144. ƒ 1 Fonteyn '46–'63 (93) Navarre '46 (1) Shearer '47–'53 (19) Lindsay '51–3 (11) Clayden '52 (1) Linden '56–'62 (8) Page '53 (2) Park '67–'79 (28) Sibley '67–'73 (18) Penney '74–9 (6) Collier '77–9 (8). 2 May '46–'50 (49) Lynne '46 (3) Navarre '46 (10) Lindsay '48–'59 (41) Shearer '51 (1) Nerina '51–3 (14) Clayden '52–5 (7) Linden '61 (3) Sibley '61–7 (8) Jenner '67–'77 (34) Connor '71–3 (7) Mason '71 (1) Ellis '77–9 (14) Eyden '79 (3). 3 Shearer '46–'50 (47) Lynne '47–'51 (16) Lindsay '48–'55 (18) Clayden '51–5 (17) May

'52 (5) Nerina '52 (1) Linden '56 (2) Page '56–'61 (23) Parkinson '62–3 (6) Penney '67–'79 (33) Beckley '68 (4) Connor '72–4 (3) Mason '73 (1) Jenner '73 (1) Porter '77–9 (18). *m* 1 Somes '46–'59 (116) Hart '49A Field '51T '52 (6) Blair '56–'63 (9) MacLeary '62–'74 (19) Nureyev '63 (1) Dowell '67–'77 (22) Wall '73–9 (2) Eagling '77–9 (15). 2 Shaw '46–'63 (96) Grant '46–9 (39) Usher '67–8 (7) Mead '68–'71 (11) Coleman '68–'79 (14) Sherwood '68–'73 (11) Eagling '73–9 (8) Jefferies '77 (2) Silver '78–9 (7). 3 Danton '46 (15) Hart '46–'55 (87) Chatfield '49A Grant '55 (2) Trecu '56–9 (21) Usher '61–3 (10) Coleman '67–'79 (41) Mead '68 (3) Ashmole '74 (1) Eagling '77–9 (5) Jefferies '77–9 (4) Silver '79 (6). *Also* Rep II.

Symphony P 15 Feb 1963 ROH *Ch* Macmillan *M* Shostakovich *SC* Yolanda Sonnabend redesigned '75. '63 (7); '64 (2); '75 (6); '76 (3). T:10. 1 Sibley '63 (3) Seymour '63–'76 (12) Peri '75–6 (3). 2 Parkinson '63–4 (9) Derman '63A '75 (3) Collier '75 (3) R Taylor '76 (1) Connor '76 (2). 3 MacLeary '63–'75 (14) Ashmole '75–6 (3) Wall '76 (1). 4 Doyle '63–4 (9) Eagling '75 (6) Silver '76 (3). + 9ƒ 9m.

Taming of the Shrew, The FP 16 Feb 1977 ROH *Ch/Pr* Cranko *M* Kurt-Heinz Stolze after Scarlatti *SC* Elisabeth Dalton. '77 (18). T:4. *Katherina* Park (11) Haydée (2) Seymour (3) Collier '77T (2). *Petruchio* Wall (10) Cragun (2) Eagling (4) Jefferies (2). *Bianca* Collier (8) Porter (6) Jenner (3) Thorogood (1). + 5ƒ 13m + CdB.

Three-Cornered Hat, The FP 6 Feb 1947 ROH *Ch* Massine *M* de Falla *SC* Picasso. '47 (27); '48 (24); '49 (16); '50 (8); '52 (20); '54 (6); '55 (14); '56 (7). T:49. *The Miller* Massine '47–9 (34) Turner '48–'52 (44) Somes '48T '49–'52 (8) A Grant '52–6 (15) Vernon '52 (7) Blair '54T–5 (7) Trecu '55–6 (7). *The Miller's Wife* Fonteyn '47–9 (17) Prokhorova/Elvin '47–'56 (61) Nye '49–'50 (11) Grey '52 (5) Heaton '52–5 (15) Larsen '52T–6 (8) V Taylor '55–6 (5) Page '56T. *The Governor* Hart '47–'56 (102) Edwards '52–6 (12) F White '52–6 (8).

Tiresias P 9 July 1951 ROH *Ch* Ashton *M* Lambert *SC* Isabel Lambert. '51 (12); '52 (10); '53 (7); '54 (3); '55 (2). T:18. *Tiresias m* Somes '51–5 (33) A Grant '51 (1). *Tiresias ƒ* Fonteyn '51–4 (26) Elvin '51–5 (8). *Her Lover* Field '51–5 (26) Hart '51–3 (8). *Neophyte* Dale '51–4 (32) Nerina '51T Sinclair '55 (2). *Snakes ƒ* Clayden '51–5 (34). *m* Shaw '51–5 (30) Powell '51 (4). + 33ƒ 13m.

Triad P 19 Jan 1972 ROH *Ch* MacMillan *M* Prokofiev *SC* Peter Unsworth. '72 (12); '73 (6); '74 (4); '77 (4). T:5. *The Girl* Sibley '72–3 (7) Park '72–7 (9) Trounson '72TCA–3 (4) Jenner '73–4 (4) Penney '77 (2). *The Boy* Dowell '74 (12) Wall '72–4 (7) Clarke '72TCA (1) D Kelly '73 (2) Hosking '77 (4). *His Brother* Eagling '72–7 (20) Sherwood '72–3 (6). + 3m. *Also* Rep II.

Twilight FPCG 7e Feb 1976 ROH Cr Rep II. '76 (5). ƒ Connor (3) Seymour (2). *m* Eagling (5).

Troy Game FP 29 Apr 1980 ROH *Ch* Robert North *M* Jon Keliehor/Bob Downes *SC* Peter Farmer. 1 Wall. 2 Sleep. 3 Jefferies. 4 Coleman. + 6m.

Two Pigeons, The FPCG 16 Oct 1962 ROH Cr Rep II. '62 (5); '63 (6); '64 (11); '65 (4); '70 (8); '74 (9); '75 (4); '76 (2). T:11. *The Young Man* A Grant '62–5 (13) Gable '62–5 (9) Mason '63–4 (4) Wall '70–6 (9) Cooke '70 (1) McGrath '70 (3) Myers '74–6 (6) Ashmole '74–5 (4). *The Young Girl* Seymour '62–76 (15) Park '62TC–5 (9) Wells '62–'74 (7) Sibley '63–4 (3) Thorogood '70 (3) Collier '74–6 (9) Ellis '74 (2) Porter '75 (1). *A Gypsy Girl* Parkinson '62–'76 (25) Mason '63–'70 (6) Anderton '64 (1) Last '70–4 (5) Barbieri '70 (3) Ruanne '70 (2) Jenner '74 (3) Connor '74–6 (9) Peri '75 (1).

Two Pigeons, The Act II pdd '70 Ashton Tribute (1). *The Young Girl* Seymour. *The Young Man* Mason.

Two Pigeons, The On tour only: Acts I/II excerpts (3). Act II Gypsy Scene (1).

Uncle Remus P 19 Dec 1934 OV *Ch* Sara Patrick *M* Gordon Jacob *SC* Hugh Stevenson. '34 (4); '35 (2). *Brer Rabbit* Staff '34–5 (6). *Uncle Remus* Greenwood '34–5 (6). *Brer Fox* Newton '34–5 (6). + 10ƒ 1m.

Valse, La FP 10 Mar 1959 ROH *Ch* Ashton *M* Ravel *SC* André Levasseur. '59 (7); '60 (4); '62 (5); '67 (2); '68 (3); '77 (1). ƒ 1 Dixon '59 (7) Parkinson '60–'77 (13) Bergsma '62 (2). 2 Beckley '59–'62 (16) Lorrayne '62–8 (4) Eyre '68 (1) Derman '77 (1). 3 Daryl '59–'60 (11) Lorrayne '62 (5) Beckley '67–8 (5) Mason '77 (1). *m* 1 Burne '59 (7) Rencher '60–8 (14) MacLeary '77 (1) 2 Farley '59–'60 (11) Rosson '62 (5) Bosman '67–8 (5) Drew '77 (1). 3 Rosson '59–'60 (11) Mead '62–8 (8) Bosman '63 (2) Jefferies '77 (1). + 18ƒ 18m.

Variations on a Theme of Purcell P 6 Jan 1955 ROH *Ch* Ashton *M* Britten *SC* Peter Snow. '55 (16). 1 Fifield (14) Mayan (2). 2 Nerina (13) Linden (3). 3 Jackson (13) Park (3). 4 A Grant (15) Shaw (1). + 12ƒ 6m.

Veneziana P 9 Apr 1953 ROH *Ch* Andrée Howard *M* Donizetti arr/orch Denis ApIvor *SC* Sophie Fedorovitch. '53 (16); '54 (10). *La Favorita* Elvin '53 (13) Farron '53 (3). Beriosova '54 (10). *Punchinello* Powell '53–4 (26). + 19ƒ 16m. *Also* Rep II.

Voluntaries FP 18 Nov 1976 ROH *Ch* Glen Tetley *M* Poulenc *SC* Rouben Ter-Arutunian. '76 (7); '77 (11). 1 Seymour '76–7 (11) Makarova '76 (3) Thorogood '77 (4). 2 Wall '76–7 (15) Eagling '77 (3). 3 Derman '76–7 (15) Thorogood '77 (2) Porter '77 (1). 4 Eagling '76–7 (12) Deane '77 (4) Hosking '77 (2). 5 Silver '76–7 (11) Hosking '77 (2) Deane '77 (5). + 6ƒ 6m.

Walk to the Paradise Garden, The P 15 Nov 1972 ROH *Ch* Ashton *M* Delius *SC* William Chappell. '72 (1); '73 (4*); '74 (1); '75 (3). T:1. 1 Park '72–5 (9). 2 Wall '72–5 (9). 3 Rencher '72–5 (9). *includes 2 with TC at sw.

Wanderer, The P 27 Jan 1941 New *Ch* Ashton *M* Schubert *SC* Graham Sutherland. '41 (28); '42 (13); '45 (5). T: [27]. 1 Helpmann '41–5 [42]. 2 Fonteyn '41–5 [42]. '*Lovers*' *f* May '41–5 [26] Fraser '42 [12] Shearer '45 (4). *m* Somes '41–5 [30] Hart '42 [8] Field '42 [4]. + 9*f* 5*m*. nr '41 Feb 12, June 11e, 14e; '42 Nov 3.

Wanderer, The '*Lovers*' '70 Ashton Tribute (1). *f* Derman. *m* MacLeary.

Wedding Bouquet, A P 27 Apr 1937 sw *Ch* Ashton *M*/*SC* Gerald Berners *Words* Gertrude Stein. '37 (8); '38 (7); '39 (3); '40 (6); '41 (15); '43 (20); '44 (8); '49 (12); '50 (3); '51 (3); '64 (4); '69 (5); '79 (6). T:55. *Webster* de Valois '37–'50 (4) McCarthy '37–8 (11) Nye '38–'49 [50]. Sheldon '43–4 (13) Negus '49 (1) Olrich '51 (1) Lynne '51 (1) Mason '64–'79 (12) Inkin '79 (3). *Josephine* Brae '37–'50 [43] Fraser '41–4 [27] Nye '43–4 (8) Valaire '50–1 (4) Hamby '51A (1) Bergsma '64–9 (9) Penney '79 (4) Howe '79 (2). *Julia* Fonteyn '37–'50 [61] May '37–9 (2) M Jackson '43–4 (3) Shearer '49 (9) Heaton '49–'51 (8) Clayden '49A Page '64 (1) Jenner '64–9 (8) Porter '79 (6). *Bridegroom* Helpmann '37–'50 [77] Newman '38 (3) Hart '50A '51 (3) A Grant '64–9 (7) Holden '64 (2) Coleman '79 (4) Deane '79 (2). *Bride* Honer '37–'50 [38] Dale '43–'51 (43) Nerina '50 (2) Park '64 (4) Penney '69 (5) Collier '79 (4) Whitten '79 (2). + 11*f* 9*m*. NB Chorus replaced 1941 by Narrator – restored briefly 1949. Narrators have included Constant Lambert, Robert Irving, Robert Helpmann, Anthony Dowell. nr '41 June 11e, 14e. '40 July 30 (Webster). *Also* Rep II.

Wedding Bouquet, A Excerpt *waltz* '70 Ashton Tribute (1). *Julia* Jenner. *Webster* Eyre.

Wise and Foolish Virgins, The, *see* **Foolish Virgins, The**

Wise Virgins, The P 24 Apr 1940 sw *Ch* Ashton *M* J S Bach arr Walton *SC* Rex Whistler (no set Sept '40–May '42). '40 (11); '41 (29); '42 (17); '43 (24); '44 (2). T:[58]. *The Bridegroom* Somes '40–1 [26] Helpmann '41 (6) Hart '41T–2 [21] Rassine '43–4 (26). *The Bride* Fonteyn '40–4 [68] Brae '41 [7] Farron '42 (4). + 11*f* 6*m*. nr '41 Jan 15, 16, 24; '42 Aug 2m (second).

Wise Virgins, The *Solo* '70 Ashton Tribute (1). *The Bride* Fonteyn.

Divertissements

Amazon Forest pdd FP 23 Nov 1976 ROH *Ch* Ashton *M* Villa-Lobos *C* José Varona. '76 (1). *f* Fonteyn. *m* Wall.

Bolero P 6 Dec 1932 sw *Ch* nc (Dolin) *M* Ravel *SC* nc. '32 (3); '33 (3). T:14. Dolin '32–3 (6).

Brahms Waltzes in the Manner of Isadora Duncan FP 23 Nov 1976 ROH *Ch* Ashton *M* Brahms *SC* nc. '76 (1); '78 (2). Seymour '76–8 (3).

Cachucha FP 26 Mar 1969 ROH *Ch* after notated score by Zorn *M* Traditional arr John Lanchbery *C* nc. '69 (1). Park.

Chant du Compagnon Errant Le FP 4 Mar 1975 ROH *Ch* Bejart *M* Mahler *SC* nc. '75 (1). 1 Dowell. 2 Nureyev.

Corsaire, Le pdd FP 3e Nov 1962 ROH *Ch* after Petipa *M* Drigo/Minkus orch John Lanchbery *C* (Fonteyn) André Levasseur. '62 (3); '63 (5); '64 (3); '70 (3); '73 (1). T:11. *f* Fonteyn '62–'73 (15). *m* Nureyev '62–'73 (15). *Also* Rep II.

Corsaire, Le pdt FP 4 Mar 1975 ROH *Ch* Nureyev after Petipa *M* Minkus/Drigo *C* nc. '75 (1). 1 Derman. 2 Mason. 3 Seymour.

Daughter of Eve, A P 19 Dec 1929 ov *Ch* nc (de Valois) *M* Arensky *SC* nc. '29 (6); '30 (1). de Valois '29–'30 (7).

Divertissement P 29 Dec 1930 Pavilion, Bournemouth *Arr* de Valois *M* see individual dances *SC* nc. T:3. '31 (4). London performances indicated after relevant titles. Tour casting is shown in brackets. **Pas de deux** *M* Gluck (*f* de Valois *m* Turner). **Tambourine** *M* Manlio de Varoli '31 (4). 1 James (4). 2 Appleyard (4). **Jeunes Paysannes** *M* Thomas Dunhill. '31 (4). 1 McCarthy (4). 2 Bamford (4). 3 Newton (4). **Serenade** *M* Boccherini. '31 (4). de Valois (4). **Fantasie Espagnole** *M* Moskowski (Moreton, James, Newton). **Sunday Afternoon** *M* Arthur Somerville '31 (4). 1 McCarthy (4). 2 Bamford '31 (4). **Cossack Dance**. *M* nc (Turner). **En Bateau** *M* Debussy (Moreton, Newton, Appleyard). **Polka** *M* Johann Strauss (*f* de Valois *m* Briggs). **Valse Arabesque** *M* Theodore Cack (James). **Nautical Nonsense** *M* Bach (Bamford, McCarthy, Briggs). **Fantasie Russe** (London only) '31 (4). *M* Vladimir Rebikov. 1 de Valois (4). 2 Moreton (4). *See also*: Carnaval. Hommage aux Belles Viennoises. Etude.

Divertissements. T:2. (1959). Unspecified.

Don Juan pdd FP 4 Mar 1975 ROH *Ch* John Neumeier *M* Gluck/Thomas Luis de Victoria *C* Filippo Sanjust/Anthony Dowell. '75 (1). *f* Fonteyn. *m* Nureyev. + *CdB*.

Don Quixote pdd FP 20 May 1948 ROH *Ch* nc; 1969 *ch* after Petipa. *M* Minkus *C* nc. '48 (1); '59 (1); '60 (1); '62 (4); '72 (1); '73 (2); '75 (2). T:39. *f* Markova '48 (1) Nerina '59–'62 (3) Linden '60 (1) Arova '62 (2) Makarova '72–5 (5) Park '73A Mason '74T Collier '74T. *m* Dolin '48 (1) Blair '59–'60 (2) Bruhn '62 (2) Nureyev '62 (2) MacLeary '72 (1) Wall '73A (2) Sleep '74T Dowell '75 (2). *Also*: Rep II.

Entrée Japonaise FP 22 Mar 1956 ROH *Ch* Ashton *M* Arthur Sullivan arr Robert Irving *C* Dior. '56 (1). Fonteyn.

Gloriana P 30 May 1977 ROH *Ch* MacMillan *M* Britten *C* Yolanda Sonnabend. '77 (1). *f* Seymour. *m* 1 Eagling. 2 Coleman. 3 Beagley. + 4*m*.

Grand Pas Classique FP 12 Mar 1963 ROH *Ch* Victor Gsovsky *M* Auber *C* nc *Pr* Chauviré. '63 (2). *f* Nerina (2). *m* Blair (2).

Hamlet Prelude P 30 May 1977 ROH *Ch* Ashton *M* Liszt *C* Carl Toms. '77 (1). T (as **Hamlet with Ophelia**): 9. *Ophelia* Fonteyn. *Hamlet* Nureyev. Eagling '77A.

Hymn to the Sun FP 9m Mar 1932 sw *Ch* Dolin *M* Rimsky-Korsakov *SC* nc. '32 (5). Dolin (5).

Laurentia pas de six FP 24 Mar 1965 ROH *Ch* Vachtang Chaboukiani *repr* Nureyev *M* Alexander Krien orch John Lanchbery *C* nc. (Philip Prowse). '65 (1). T:8. 1 Nerina. 2 Park. 3 Sibley. 4 Nureyev. 5 Gable. 6 Usher. *Also*: Jenner '65A. *Also* Rep II.

Manhattan Serenade FP 14 Mar 1932 sw *Ch* Dolin *M* Louis Alter *SC* nc. '32 (3). Dolin (3).

Mirror Walkers, The pdd FP 14 Dec 1971 ROH *Ch* Peter Wright *M* Tchaikovsky *C* nc. '71 (1). T:5. *f* Park. *m* D Kelly. *Also*: MacLeary '72A. *Also* Rep II.

New Pas de deux (unnamed) P 17 July 1974 ROH *Ch* MacMillan *M* Stravinsky *C* nc. '74 (1). *f* Makarova. *m* MacLeary.

Pas de Sept (*Jewels* from The Sleeping Beauty) FP 14 Dec 1971 ROH *Ch* MacMillan *M* Tchaikovsky *C* nc. '71 (1).

Pavane P 13 Jan 1973 ROH *Ch* MacMillan *M* Fauré *C* Anthony Dowell. '73 (4); '74 (1); '77 (1). T:1. *f*. Sibley '73–4 (5) Collier '77 (1). *m* Dowell '73–4 (5) MacLeary '77 (1). *Also* Rep II.

Pride FP 3 Jan 1933 sw *Ch* de Valois *M* Scriabin *C* William Chappell. '33 (2). de Valois (2).

Raymonda, pdd, variations and coda P 3 May 1962 ROH *Ch* Ashton *M* Glazunov *C* André Levassaur. '62 (8). *f* Beriosova (8). *m* MacLeary (8). With TC Abroad: 2.

Raymonda, pdd only. '64 (1). *f* Beriosova. *m* MacLeary.

Raymonda, Scène d'Amour FP 1 Mar 1960 ROH *Ch* Ashton *M* Glazunov *C* Leslie Hurry. '60 (1). T:9. *f* Fonteyn. *m* Somes. Hynd '66A. *Also* Rep II.

Salut d'Amour à Margot Fonteyn P 23 May 1979 ROH *Ch* Ashton *M* Elgar *C* William Chappell. '79 (2 – 1 + encore). *f* Fonteyn (2). *m* Ashton (2).

Side Show P 1m Apr 1972 Royal Court, Liverpool *Ch* MacMillan *M* Stravinsky *C* Thomas O'Neil. '73 (3); '75 (3). T:4 (including première + 1 with TC in Liverpool). ƒ Seymour '73T–5 (6). *m* Nureyev '73T (3) Coleman '75 (3).

Siesta P 24 Jan 1936 sw *Ch* Ashton *m* Walton *C* (Argyle) Matilda Etches. '36 (3). T:2. ƒ Argyle (3). *m* Helpmann (3).

Spanish Dance (Danse Espagnole) FP 5 May 1931 ov *Ch* Dolin *M* Albéniz *C* nc. '31 (5); '32 (9). Dolin '31–2 (14). *incl. encore 5 May '31.

(Tchaikovsky) Pas de deux FP 16 Mar 1964 ROH *Ch* Balanchine *M* Tchaikovsky *C* nc. '64 (2). ƒ Verdy (2). *m* Blair (2).

Thaïs, Meditation from FP 14 Dec 1971 ROH *Ch* Ashton *M* Massenet *C* Anthony Dowell. '71 (1); '73 (3); '76 (4). T:5. ƒ Sibley '71–6 (8). *m* Dowell '71–6 (8).

Tritsch-Tratsch FPCG 10 Mar 1959 ROH Cr Rep II. '59 (1). T:29. *The Girl* Wells. Also Ann Howard '60A. Osborn '60A. *Two Sailors* 1 Clegg. 2 Wilson. Also Ruffell '60A. Sale '60A. Millard '60A.

Tweedledum and Tweedledee FP 22m July 1978 ROH *Ch* Ashton *M* Percy Grainger *C* lent by Bermans & Nathans Ltd. '78 (2); '79 (4). ƒ Collier '78–9 (6). *m* 1 Sleep '78–9 (6). 2 Fletcher '78–9 (6).

Valse Eccentrique FP 1 Mar 1960 ROH *Ch* MacMillan *M* Ibert *C* nc. '60 (1). T:2. ƒ Bolton. *m* 1 A Grant. 2 Holden. *Also* Rep II.

Variation P 27 Mar 1958 ROH *Ch* de Valois *M* Schumann arr Robert Irving *C* nc. '58 (1). Nerina.

Vivaldi Concerto P 13 Oct 1960 University Auditorium, East Lansing *Ch* Alfred Rodrigues *M* Vivaldi *C* Alix Stone. A:27. (Park, Sibley, Parkinson, Lawrence, Steuart, Bosman, Rosson, Rencher, Farley. Also: Beckley, Mason, Lorrayne, Burne, Linden).

Productions (I)

Ballets produced by Vic-Wells/Sadler's
Wells/Royal Ballet 1928–Aug 1980
Note Asterisks (*) indicate ballets created for the
Company

1928
Dec 13 *Petits Riens, Les
1929
May 9 *Picnic, The (revised 1930 as
       Faun, The)
Dec 19 *Hommage aux Belles Viennoises
1930
Dec 18 *Suite of Dances
1931
May 5 Danse Sacrée et Danse Profane
       *Jackdaw and the Pigeons, The
       *Faust, Scène de ballet (see
       Repertory I for première)
     21 Cephalus and Procris
Sept 22 *Regatta
       Job
Nov 23 Fête Polonaise
Dec 16 *Jew in the Bush, The
1932
Jan 30m *Narcissus and Echo
       Rout
Mar 4 Spectre de la Rose, Le
       *Italian Suite
     8 Sylphides, Les
     11 Enchanted Grove, The
     19e *Nursery Suite
Oct 5 Lac des Cygnes, Le, Act II
     11 *Douanes
     17 Lord of Burleigh, The
Nov 1 Origin of Design, The
     15 Scorpions of Ysit, The
1933
Jan 17 Pomona
Feb 7 *Birthday of Obéron, The
Mar 21 Coppélia (Acts I/II)
Sept 26 *Wise and Foolish Virgins, The
       Blue Bird, The, pdd (Enchanted
       Princess, The)
Oct 24 Sleeping Princess, The, pdd
       (Aurora pdd)
       Carnaval
     30 Création du Monde, La (*Ch* de
       Valois)
Dec 5 *Rendezvous, Les
       Lac des Cygnes, Le, pdt
1934
Jan 1 Giselle
     30 Casse-Noisette
Apri 3 *Haunted Ballroom, The
Oct 9 *Jar, The
Nov 20 Lac des Cygnes, Le
Dec 19 *Uncle Remus
1935
Mar 26 Rio Grande
May 20 *Rake's Progress, The

Oct 8 Façade
Nov 26 *Baiser de la Fée, Le (*Ch* Ashton)
1936
Jan 10 *Gods go a'Begging, The
Feb 11 *Apparitions
Apr 17 *Barabau
Oct 13 *Prometheus
Nov 10 *Nocturne
1937
Feb 16 *Patineurs, Les
Apr 27 *Wedding Bouquet, A
June 15 *Checkmate
1938
Jan 27 *Horoscope
Apr 7 *Roi Nu, Le
May 10 *Judgement of Paris, The
Nov 10 Harlequin in the Street
1939
Feb 2 Sleeping Princess, The
Apr 27 *Cupid and Psyche
1940
Jan 23 *Dante Sonata
Apr 15 Coppélia (NP Acts I/II/III)
     24 *Wise Virgins, The
July 4 *Prospect Before Us, The
1941
Jan 27 *Wanderer, The
May 28 *Orpheus and Eurydice
1942
Jan 14 *Comus
May 19 *Hamlet
Nov 24 *Birds, The
1943
Apr 6 *Quest, The
Oct 25 *Promenade
1944
June 20 *Festin de l'Araignée, Le
Oct 26 *Miracle in the Gorbals
1946
Feb 20 Sleeping Beauty, The (NP)
Apr 10 *Adam Zero
     24 *Symphonic Variations
June 12 Giselle (NP)
Nov 12 *Sirènes, Les
1947
Feb 6 Three-Cornered Hat, The
     27 Boutique Fantasque, La
Nov 26 Mam'zelle Angot
1948
Feb 11 *Scènes de Ballet
June 25 *Clock Symphony
Nov 25 *Don Juan
Dec 23 *Cinderella
1950
Feb 20 *Don Quixote
Apr 5 Ballet Imperial (from 1973,
       Piano Concerto No 2)
May 5 *Ballabile
1951
Apr 5 *Daphnis and Chloë

July 9 *Tiresias
Dec 12 *Donald of the Burthens
1952
Mar 4 *Mirror for Witches, A
Apr 4 *Bonne-Bouche
Sept 3 *Sylvia
Dec 18 Lac des Cygnes, Le (NP)
1953
Mar 3 *Shadow, The
Apr 9 *Veneziana
June 2 *Homage to the Queen
1954
Mar 2 Coppélia (NP)
Aug 23 Firebird, The
1955
Jan 6 *Rinaldo and Armida
       *Variations on a Theme of Purcell
Apr 1 *Madame Chrysanthème
June 9 Lady and the Fool, The
1956
Feb 15 *Péri, La
Mar 1 *Noctambules
May 5 *Birthday Offering
Aug 27 *Miraculous Mandarin, The
1957
Jan 1 *Prince of the Pagodas, The
Mar 26 Petrushka
Sept 17 Solitaire
1958
Aug 20 *Agon (*Ch* MacMillan)
Oct 27 *Ondine
Dec 11 Fête Etrange, La
1959
Mar 5 Harlequin in April
     10 Valse, La
     13 Danses Concertantes
Sept 2 Belle Dame sans Merci, La
     22 Pineapple Poll
Oct 19 *Antigone
1960
Jan 28 *Fille Mal Gardée, La
Apr 12 *Baiser de la Fée, Le (*Ch*
       MacMillan)
Sept 30 Giselle (NP)
1961
Sept 15 *Diversions
       *Jabez and the Devil
Dec 12 *Perséphone
1962
May 3 Napoli, Divertissement
       Flower Festival at Genzano, pdd
       *Rite of Spring, The
July 11 Good-Humoured Ladies, The
Oct 16 Two Pigeons, The
Dec 13 Invitation, The
1963
Feb 15 *Symphony
Mar 12 *Night Tryst
       *Marguerite and Armand
     26 *Elektra

Nov 27   Bayadère, La
Dec 12   Swan Lake (NP)
1964
Apr 2   *Dream, The
       *Images of Love
May 7   Serenade
Dec 2   Biches, Les
1965
Feb 9   *Romeo and Juliet
Mar 24   *Monotones pdt
       (from 1966, Monotones No 2)
       Polovtsian Dances from Prince
       Igor
1966
Feb 10   *Brandenburg Nos 2 and 4
    18   Card Game
Mar 23   Noces, Les
Apr 25   *Monotones No 1
May 19   Song of the Earth
Nov 15   Apollo
1967
Jan 25   *Shadowplay
Feb 23   *Paradise Lost
Dec 18   Sylvia (one-act version)
1968
Jan 9   *Jazz Calendar
Feb 29   Nutcracker, The (Ch Nureyev)
Oct 25   *Enigma Variations
Nov 12   Lilac Garden
Dec 17   Sleeping Beauty, The (NP)
1969
Feb 21   Olympiad
Mar 26   *Pélléas et Mélisande
    27   Raymonda Act III
1970
Feb 9   *Lament of the Waves
Mar 2   *Ropes of Time, The
Oct 19   Dances at a Gathering
Nov 17   Concerto
1971
Feb 17   Swan Lake (revised TC P 1965)
Mar 11   Giselle (TC P 1968)
July 22   *Anastasia
Nov 16   Field Figures
Dec 14   Afternoon of a Faun
1972
Jan 19   *Triad
Feb 15   Poème de l'Extase
July 26   *Laborintus
Nov 15   Requiem Canticles
       *Walk to the Paradise Garden,
       The
1973
Jan 25   Four Temperaments, The
       Prodigal Son
       Agon (Ch Balanchine)

Mar 15   Sleeping Beauty, The (NP)
July 19   Seven Deadly Sins, The
Oct 10   In the Night
1974
Mar 7   *Manon
Oct 7   *Elite Syncopations
1975
Jan 31   *Four Schumann Pieces
Mar 4   Concert, The
    5   *Four Seasons, The
Dec 11   *Rituals
1976
Feb 7e   Twilight
    12   *Month in the Country, A
Nov 18   Voluntaries
    23   Adagio Hammerklavier
1977
Feb 16   Taming of the Shrew, The
Mar 31   *Fourth Symphony, The
Oct 14   Sleeping Beauty, The (NP)
1978
Feb 14   *Mayerling
1979
Mar 15   *Fin du Jour, La
Apr 19   Liebeslieder Walzer
Dec 5   Swan Lake (NP)
1980
Mar 13   *Gloria
Apr 29   Troy Game
       My Brother, My Sisters
       *Adieu (Ch Bintley)
Aug 4   Rhapsody

Divertissements

1929
Dec 19   *Etude
       *Daughter of Eve
1930
Dec 29   *Pas de deux; Tambourine;
       Jeunes Paysannes: Serenade:
       Fantasie Espagnole; Sunday
       Afternoon;
       Cossack Dance; En Bateau;
       Polka;
       Valse Arabesque; Nautical
       Nonsense.
1931
Jan 14   *Fantasie Russe
May 5   Spanish Dance
1932
Mar 9m   Hymn to the Sun
    14   Manhattan Serenade
Dec 6   *Bolero

1933
Jan 3   Pride
1936
Jan 24   *Siesta
1948
May 20   Don Quixote pdd
1956
Mar 22   Entrée Japonaise
1958
Mar 27   *Variation
1959
Mar 10   Tritsch-Tratsch
1960
Mar 1   Valse Eccentrique
       Raymonda 'Scène d'Amour'
Oct 13   *Vivaldi Concerto
1962
May 3   *Raymonda, pdd variations and
       coda
Nov 3e   Corsaire, Le, pdd
1963
Mar 12   Grand Pas Classique
1964
Mar 16   (Tchaikovsky) Pas de Deux
1965
Mar 24   Laurentia pas de six
1969
Mar 26   Cachucha
1971
Dec 14   Pas de Sept (Jewel Fairies from
       The Sleeping Beauty) (Ch
       MacMillan)
       Thaïs Meditation
       Mirror Walkers, The, pdd
1973
Jan 13   *Pavane
       Side Show
1974
July 17   *New Pas de Deux
1975
Mar 4   Chant du Compagnon Errant
       Corsaire, Le, pas de trois
       Don Juan pdd (Ch Neumeier)
1976
Nov 23   Brahms Waltzes in the Manner
       of Isadora Duncan
       Amazon Forest
1977
May 30   *Gloriana
       *Hamlet Prelude (1978 Hamlet
       with Ophelia)
1978
July 22m   Tweedledum and Tweedledee
1979
May 23   *Salut d'Amour à Margot
       Fonteyn

Itinerary (I)

Ballet at the Old Vic, Sadler's Wells and Royal Opera House was usually in repertory with opera. London theatres are shown in italics.

1928–1930		*Old Vic*
1930		
Dec	29–31	Bournemouth, Pavilion
1931		
May	5	*Old Vic*
May	15, 21	*Sadler's Wells*
Sept	22	*Old Vic/Sadler's Wells*
1932	–6 May	
Sept	24–28	Copenhagen, Kongelige Teater
Oct	5–	
1933	–18 Apr	*Old Vic/Sadler's Wells*
Apr	20–22	Bath, Pavilion
	24– 2 May	*Old Vic/Sadler's Wells*
Sept	26–	
1934	–24 Apr	*Old Vic/Sadler's Wells*
Oct	2–	
1935	– 1 June	*Old Vic/Sadler's Wells*
June	3– 8	*Shaftesbury Theatre*
	10–15	Blackpool, Opera House
	17–22	Bournemouth, Pavilion
Aug	5–10	Glasgow, Alhambra
	12–17	Edinburgh, King's
	19–24	Manchester, Opera House
	26–31	Birmingham, Royal
Sept	2– 7	Leeds, Grand
	27–	
1936	– 1 Feb	*Sadler's Wells*
Feb	3	Cambridge, Arts
	4–25	*Sadler's Wells*
	28	Bexhill, de la Warr Pavilion
	29–17 Apr	*Sadler's Wells*
	18	Brighton, Dome
	21–15 May	*Sadler's Wells/Old Vic*
June	1– 6	Cambridge, Arts
Aug	3– 8	Birmingham, Prince of Wales
	10–15	Manchester, Opera House
	17–22	Nottingham, Royal
	24–29	Edinburgh, King's
	31– 5 Sept	Glasgow, King's
Sept	7–12	Newcastle, Royal
	22–	
1937	– 8 May	*Sadler's Wells*
May	10–15	Bournemouth, Pavilion
	17–21	*Sadler's Wells*
	31– 5 June	Cambridge, Arts
June	15–20	Paris, Théâtre des Champs-Elysées
Aug	30– 4 Sept	Newcastle, Royal
Sept	6–11	Glasgow, King's
	13–18	Leeds, Grand
	28–	
1938	–21 May	*Sadler's Wells*
May	23– 4 June	Cambridge, Arts

June	20–25	Oxford, New
	27– 2 July	Bournemouth, Pavilion
Aug	29– 3 Sept	Manchester, Princes
Sept	5–10	Dublin, Gaiety
	12–17	Cardiff, Prince of Wales
	20–29	Streatham, Streatham Hill Theatre
Oct	4–13	Golders Green, Hippodrome
	18–	
1939	–21 Mar	*Sadler's Wells*
Mar	22	*Royal Opera House*
	23–18 May	*Sadler's Wells*
	29– 3 June	Cambridge, Arts
June	5–10	Oxford, New
	19–24	Bournemouth, Pavilion
Aug	21–26	Manchester, Princes
	28– 2 Sept	Liverpool, Royal Court
Sept	25–30	Newcastle, Royal
Oct	2– 7	Leicester, Opera House
	9–14	Leeds, Grand
	16–21	Birmingham, Royal
	23–28	Southsea, King's
	30– 4 Nov	Brighton, Royal
Nov	6–11	Cambridge, Arts
	13–18	Nottingham, Royal
	20–25	Glasgow, King's
	27– 2 Dec	Bradford, Princes
Dec	26–	
1940	–27 Jan	*Sadler's Wells*
Jan	29– 3 Feb	Cambridge, Arts
Feb	5–10	Hull, New
	12–17	Leeds, Grand
	19–24	Liverpool, Royal Court
	26– 2 Mar	Leicester, Opera House
Mar	4– 9	Sheffield, Lyceum
	11–16	Manchester, Princes
	18–23	Brighton, Royal
	25–30	Bristol, Princes
Apr	1– 3 May	*Sadler's Wells*
May	6	The Hague, Koninklijke Schouwburg
	7	Hengelo,
	8	Eindhoven, Philips' Theatre
	9	Arnhem,
June	4– 6 Sept	*Sadler's Wells*
Dates unknown		ENSA tour garrison towns
Nov	18–23	Manchester, Opera House
	25–30	Stratford, Shakespeare Memorial
Dec	3– 7	Newcastle, Royal
	9–14	Blackpool, Grand
late Dec–early Jan		Dartington Hall + local engagements
1941		
Jan	14–15 Feb	*New*
Feb	17– 1 Mar	Burnley, Victoria
Mar	3– 8	Harrogate, Royal Hall
	11–15	Bournemouth, Pavilion

	17–22	Brighton, Royal
	24–29	Cardiff, Prince of Wales
Apr	7–12	ENSA tour garrison towns
	14–19	Cheltenham, Opera House
	21–26	Bath, Royal
	28– 3 May	Exeter, The Theatre
May	12–17	Cambridge, Arts
	19–21 June	*New*
July	21– 9 Aug	*New*
Aug	11–16	Liverpool, Royal Court
	18–30	Burnley, Victoria
Sept	1– 6	Leeds, Grand
	8–13	Harrogate, Royal Hall
	15–27	Manchester, Opera House
	29–25 Oct	*New*
Oct	27– 8 Nov	Edinburgh, King's
Nov	10–22	Glasgow, Royal
	24–29	Newcastle, Royal
Dec	2– 6	Sheffield, Lyceum
	24–	
1942	–31 Jan	*New*
Feb	2– 7	Cambridge, Arts
	9–14	Oxford, New
	16–21	Bournemouth, Pavilion
	23– 7 Mar	Manchester, Opera House
Mar	9–14	Liverpool, Royal Court
	16– 4 Apr	*New*
Apr	20–25	Oxford, New
May	5–18 July	*New*
Aug	3– 8	Hackney, Victoria Park Open Air Theatre
	10–22	Edinburgh, King's
	24– 5 Sept	Newcastle, Royal
Sept	7–19	Liverpool, Royal Court
	21– 3 Oct	Manchester, Opera House
Oct	5–10	Leeds, Grand
	12–17	Cambridge, Arts
	20–19 Dec	*New*
Dec	24–	
1943	– 2 Jan	York, Royal
Jan	4– 9	Bradford, Prince's
	25–13 Feb	*New*
Feb	15–27	Bournemouth, Pavilion
Mar	1– 6	Hanley, Royal
	8–13	Coventry, New Hippodrome
	15–20	Derby, Grand
	22–27	Oxford, New
	30–24 Apr	*New*
Apr	26– 8 May	Liverpool, Royal Court
May	10–22	Blackpool, Opera House
	25–26 June	*New*
	28– 3 July	Hackney, Victoria Park Open Air Theatre
July	5–24	Manchester, Opera House
	26– 8 Aug	Newcastle, Royal
Aug	26–16 Oct	*New*
Oct	19–30	Edinburgh, King's
Nov	1– 6	Glasgow, King's
	8–13	Leeds, Grand

15–20	Sheffield, Lyceum	
22–27	Bristol, Hippodrome	
30–		
1944 – 5 Feb	*New*	
Feb 7–12	Eastbourne, Garrison Theatre	
14–19	Aldershot, Garrison Theatre	
21–26	Cambridge, Arts	
28– 4 Mar	Derby, Grand	
Mar 6–11	Hanley, Royal	
13–18	Bolton, Royal	
Apr 10–22	Wimbledon, Wimbledon Theatre	
24– 6 May	Newcastle, Royal	
May 8–20	Hammersmith, King's	
22–27	Bournemouth, Pavilion	
30– 5 Aug	*New*	
Aug 28–16 Sept	Manchester, Opera House	
Sept 18–23	Birmingham, Alexandra	
27– 2 Dec	*Prince's*	
Dec 4– 9	Birmingham, Alexandra	
11–16	Hammersmith, King's	
26–		
1945 – 6 Jan	York, Royal	
Jan 29– 9 Feb	Brussels, Théâtre des Variétés	
Feb 10–11	Brussels, Théâtre Royal de la Monnaie	
12–17	Brussels, Théâtre des Variétés	
18	Brussels, Théâtre Royal de la Monnaie	
21– 2 Mar	Paris, Marigny	
Mar 6–14	Paris, Théâtre des Champs-Elysées	
16	Versailles, SHAEF	
17–20	Paris, Théâtre des Champs-Elysées	
23–28	Ghent, Koninklijke Opera	
29	Bruges, Garrison Theatre	
30	Ostend, Garrison Theatre	
Apr 17–23 June	*New*	
July 16–21	Finsbury Park, Open Air Theatre	
24–15 Sept	*Sadler's Wells*	
Sept 17– 6 Oct	Manchester, Opera House	
Oct 8–13	Glasgow, Royal	
15–27	Edinburgh, King's	
29–10 Nov	Newcastle, Royal	
Nov 19–24	Hamburg, Garrison Theatre	
26–27	Buchenburg, RAF Station	
28– 1 Dec	Hanover, Herrenhausen	
Dec 3– 8	Berlin, Theater des Westens	
11–16	Dusseldorf, Opernhaus	
1946		
Feb 20–29 June	*Royal Opera House*	
Aug 5–17	Newcastle, Royal	
19–24	Aberdeen, His Majesty's	
26–31	Edinburgh, King's	
Sept 2– 7	Glasgow, Royal	
9–14	Leeds, Grand	
16–21	Manchester, Opera House	
23–28	Coventry, Hippodrome	

Oct 5–14	Vienna, Volksoper	
25–		
1947 –21 June	*Royal Opera House*	
Aug 11–23	Manchester, Opera House	
25– 6 Sept	Edinburgh, Empire	
Sept 10–11	Brussels, Théâtre Royal de la Monnaie	
15–21	Prague, Velka Opera	
25–29	Warsaw, Teatr Polski	
Oct 1– 5	Poznán, Teatr Wielki	
12–14	Malmö, Stadsteater	
16–19	Oslo, Nationaltheatret	
Nov 12–		
1948 –10 Mar	*Royal Opera House*	
Mar 12–13	Amsterdam, Stadsschouwburg	
15	The Hague, Gebouw voor Kunsten en Wetenschappen	
16–17	Amsterdam, Stadsschouwburg	
18	Rotterdam, Schouwburg	
19	The Hague, Gebouw voor Kunsten en Wetenschappen	
24–17 July	*Royal Opera House*	
Aug 30–11 Sept	Edinburgh, Empire	
Sept 13–18	Croydon, Davis	
21– 3 Oct	Paris, Théâtre des Champs-Elysées	
Oct 6–10	Dusseldorf, Opernhaus	
12–15	Hamburg, Garrison Theatre	
18–30	Croydon, Davis	
Nov 25–		
1949 –13 May	*Royal Opera House*	
May 20–30	Florence, Teatro Comunale	
June 3–18	*Royal Opera House*	
Aug 1–27	*Royal Opera House*	
29–10 Sept	Croydon, Davis	
Sept 12–17	Woolwich, Granada	
19–24	Kilburn, Gaumont State	
Oct 9– 6 Nov	New York, Metropolitan Opera House	
Nov 7– 8	Washington, Constitution Hall	
9	Richmond, Mosque	
10–11	Philadelphia, Academy of Music	
13–20	Chicago, Civic Opera House	
21–22	East Lansing, College Auditorium	
24– 3 Dec	Toronto, Royal Alexandra	
Dec 5	Ottawa, Capitol	
6–11	Montreal, His Majesty's	
26–		
1950 – 8 July	*Royal Opera House*	
Aug 21–26	*Royal Opera House*	
Sept 10– 1 Oct	New York, Metropolitan	
Oct 2– 5	Philadelphia, Academy of Music	
6– 7	Pittsburgh, Syria Mosque	
9–10	Atlanta, Municipal Auditorium	

11	Birmingham, Municipal Auditorium	
12–13	New Orleans, Municipal Auditorium	
14–15	Houston, Municipal Auditorium	
19–28	Los Angeles, Shrine Auditorium	
30–12 Nov	San Francisco, War Memorial Opera House	
Nov 13–14	Sacramento, Memorial Auditorium	
17–19	Denver, Denver Auditorium	
20	Lincoln, University Coliseum	
21	Des Moines, KRNT	
22	Omaha, Orpheum	
24	Tulsa, Convention Hall	
25–27	Dallas, State Fair Operetta Auditorium	
28	Oklahoma City, Municipal Auditorium	
29	Memphis, Auditorium	
Dec 1– 3	St Louis, Kiel Auditorium	
4– 5	Bloomington, Indiana University Auditorium	
6– 7	Lafayette, Purdue Hall of Music	
8–10	Detroit, Masonic Auditorium	
12–13	Cleveland, Public Auditorium	
14–16	Cincinnati, Music Hall	
18–31	Chicago, Civic Opera House	
1951		
Jan 2– 5	Winnipeg, City Auditorium	
8–13	Boston, Opera House	
15	Westchester, County Center	
16–20	Toronto, Royal Alexandra	
22	Ottawa, Capitol	
23–26	Montreal, St Denis	
27–28	Quebec, Capitol	
Feb 21–12 May	*Royal Opera House*	
July 3–28	*Royal Opera House*	
30–11 Aug	Liverpool, Royal Court	
Aug 13–18	Leeds, Grand	
20– 1 Sept	Edinburgh, Empire	
Sept 4–29	*Royal Opera House*	
Oct 1–13	Croydon, Davis	
15–27	Blackpool, Opera House	
29– 3 Nov	Glasgow, Royal	
Nov 21–		
1952 –12 Apr	*Royal Opera House*	
Apr 15–23	Lisbon, Teatro Nacional de S Carlos	
25–28	Oporto, Rivoli	
May 3– 5 July	*Royal Opera House*	
Sept 3–27	*Royal Opera House*	
29– 3 Oct	Berlin, Städtische Oper	
Oct 6–18	Croydon, Davis	
20–25	Cardiff, Empire	
27– 8 Nov	Southampton, Gaumont	

Nov 15–		
1953	–27 June	*Royal Opera House*
Aug 25– 5 Sept		*Royal Opera House*
Sept 13–11 Oct		New York, Metropolitan Opera House
Oct 13–17		Philadelphia, Academy of Music
	19–24	Boston, Opera House
	27–29	Toronto, Maple Leaf Gardens
	30–31	Montreal, Forum
Nov 2– 3		East Lansing, College Auditorium
	4– 5	Detroit, Masonic Auditorium
	6– 7	Lafayette, Purdue Hall of Music
	9–11	Minneapolis, Northrop Auditorium
	12–14	Winnipeg, Winnipeg Auditorium
	17–21	Vancouver, Orpheum
	23–25	Seattle, Civic Auditorium
	26–28	Portland, Public Auditorium
Dec 1– 6		San Francisco, War Memorial Opera House
	8–16	Los Angeles, Shrine Auditorium
	18–19	Denver, Denver Auditorium
	22–	
1954	– 3 Jan	Chicago, Civic Opera House
Jan 5– 6		Atlanta, Municipal Auditorium
	7	Birmingham, Municipal Auditorium
	8– 9	New Orleans, Municipal Auditorium
	12–14	Washington, Capitol
	15–17	Cleveland, Public Auditorium
	19–21	Pittsburgh, Syria Mosque
	22–23	Baltimore, Lyric
Feb 23–16 June		*Royal Opera House*
June 18		Amsterdam, Stadsschouwburg
	19	The Hague, Gebouw voor Kunsten en Wetenschappen
	20–21	Amsterdam, Stadsschouwburg
	22	The Hague, Gebouw voor Kunsten en Wetenschappen
	24–26	*Royal Opera House*
Aug 23–28		Edinburgh, Empire
	31–25 Sept	*Royal Opera House*
Sept 27–10 Oct		Paris, Opéra
Oct 13–18		Milan, Teatro alla Scala
	20–26	Rome, Teatro dell'Opera
	28– 2 Nov	Naples, Teatro di San Carlo
Nov 5– 7		Genoa, Opera
	9–10	Venice, Teatro la Fenice
	15–20	Oxford, New
	22–27	Bristol, Hippodrome
	29–11 Dec	Manchester, Palace
Dec 16–		
1955	–25 June	*Royal Opera House*
Aug 23– 3 Sept		*Royal Opera House*
Sept 11–16 Oct		New York, Metropolitan Opera House
Oct 18–22		Boston, Opera House
	24–29	Philadelphia, Academy of Music
	31– 3 Nov	Washington, Capitol
Nov 9–16		San Francisco, War Memorial Opera House
	18–27	Los Angeles, Shrine Auditorium
Dec 1– 4		Detroit, Masonic Auditorium
	13–15	Toronto, Maple Leaf Gardens
	31–	
1956	–23 June	*Royal Opera House*
Aug 20– 1 Sept		Edinburgh, Empire
Sept 4–29		*Royal Opera House*
Oct 1–13		Croydon, Davis
	15–27	Coventry, Hippodrome
	29– 3 Nov	Oxford, New
Nov 21–		
1957	–11 May	*Royal Opera House*
May 13–18		Dublin, Royal
	21–22 June	*Royal Opera House*
Aug 20–31		*Royal Opera House*
Sept 8– 6 Oct		New York, Metropolitan Opera House
Oct 8–12		Boston, Loew's State
	14–19	Philadelphia, Academy of Music
	21–25	Washington, Capitol
	27–29	Cincinnati, Music Hall
	31– 2 Nov	St Louis, Kiel Auditorium
Nov 4– 6		Dallas, Music Hall
	8–10	Houston, Music Hall
	13–18	Los Angeles, Shrine Auditorium
	20–27	San Francisco, War Memorial Opera House
	29– 1 Dec	Seattle, Civic Auditorium
Dec 3– 7		Vancouver, Orpheum
	11–14	Minneapolis, Northrop Auditorium
	16–	
1958	– 5 Jan	Chicago, Civic Opera House
Jan 7–11		Detroit, Masonic Auditorium
	13–15	Toronto, Maple Leaf Gardens
	17–19	Cleveland, Public Auditorium
	21–24	Montreal, Forum
Feb 19–23 May		*Royal Opera House*
May 26		Brussels, Exhibition Hall
	28– 1 June	Brussels, Théâtre Royal de la Monnaie
June 3–21		*Royal Opera House*
Aug 18–13 Sept		*Royal Opera House*
Sept 15–27		Manchester, Opera House
	29– 4 Oct	Bristol. Hippodrome
Oct 6–11		Oxford, New
	27–	
1959	–20 June	*Royal Opera House*
Aug 17–12 Sept		*Royal Opera House* (joint season)
Sept 14–26		Golders Green, Hippodrome
	28–10 Oct	Streatham, Streatham Hill Theatre
Oct 19–		
1960	–25 June	*Royal Opera House*
Aug 15–17		*Royal Opera House*
	22–27	Edinburgh, Empire
Sept 11– 9 Oct		New York, Metropolitan Opera House
Oct 11–13		East Lansing, College Auditorium
	14–16	Cleveland, Public Auditorium
	18–20	St Louis, Kiel Auditorium
	22–23	Denver, Denver Auditorium
	25–26	Seattle, Orpheum
	27–29	Vancouver, Queen Elizabeth
	31– 2 Nov	Portland, Public Auditorium
Nov 4–13		San Francisco, War Memorial Opera House
	15–16	Sacramento, Memorial Auditorium
	18–20	Los Angeles, Shrine Auditorium
	22–23	San Diego, Russ High School Auditorium
	25–29	Los Angeles, Shrine Auditorium
Dec 2– 3		Houston, Music Hall
	5– 6	New Orleans, St Peter's Auditorium
	7– 8	Birmingham, Municipal Auditorium
	9–10	Atlanta, Municipal Auditorium
	12–15	Washington, Capitol
	18– 1 Jan	Chicago, Opera House
1961		
Jan 3– 4		Rochester, Eastman
	5– 8	Detroit, Masonic Temple
	10–14	Toronto, O'Keefe Center
	16–18	Montreal, Forum
	19–20	Burlington, Memorial Auditorium
	21–22	Boston, Boston Gardens
	24–26	Philadelphia, Academy of Music
	27–28	Baltimore, Lyric
	29	New York, Metropolitan Opera House
Mar 2– 3 June		*Royal Opera House*
June 15–25		Leningrad, Kirov
July 2–15		Moscow, Bolshoi
Sept 13–		
1962	– 2 June	*Royal Opera House*

June 4– 9	Coventry, Coventry Theatre
14–21 July	*Royal Opera House*
Oct 10–	
1963 – 3 Apr	*Royal Opera House*
Apr 17–19 May	New York, Metropolitan Opera House
May 21	Baltimore, Civic Auditorium
22–23	Philadelphia, Convention Hall
24–29	Boston, Music Hall
31– 2 June	Detroit, Masonic Auditorium
June 4– 9	Toronto, O'Keefe Center
11–16	Chicago, Arie Crown
19–22	Seattle, Opera House
24–26	Portland, Public Auditorium
28– 3 July	Los Angeles, Shrine Auditorium
July 5– 7	Hollywood, Hollywood Bowl
Sept 17–	
1964 –23 May	*Royal Opera House*
June 9–18 July	*Theatre Royal, Drury Lane*
Oct 8–	
1965 –13 Apr	*Royal Opera House*
Apr 21–16 May	New York, Metropolitan Opera House
May 18–19	Philadelphia, Convention Hall
20	Baltimore, Civic Auditorium
21–22	Washington, Coliseum
23	Newark, Mosque Auditorium
25–30	Boston, Music Hall
June 1– 6	Montreal, Place des Arts
8–10	Toronto, Maple Leaf Gardens
11–13	Detroit, Masonic Auditorium
15–16	Minneapolis, Northrop Auditorium
17–20	Chicago, Arie Crown
23–24	Los Angeles, Shrine Auditorium
25	San Diego, Civic
26–29	Los Angeles, Shrine Auditorium
July 1– 6	San Francisco, War Memorial Opera House
8–11	Hollywood, Hollywood Bowl
13–15	Portland, Public Auditorium
16–18	Seattle, Opera House
20–25	Vancouver, Queen Elizabeth
Oct 9–15	Milan, Teatro alla Scala
16–19	Rome, Teatro dell'Opera
21–24	Naples, Teatro di San Carlo
26–27	Bologna, Teatro Comunale

Nov 16–	
1966 – 7 June	*Royal Opera House*
June 10–11	Monte Carlo, Palace Courtyard
14–17	Athens, Herodes Atticus
21–22	Florence, Teatro Comunale
25– 1 July	*Royal Opera House*
Sept 20	Luxembourg, Nouveau Théâtre Municipal
23–25	Prague, Smetana
27–28	Brno, Janáček
30– 1 Oct	Bratislava, Slovak National
Oct 3– 5	Munich, Bayerisches Staatsoper
8–10	Belgrade, National
12–15	Sofia, Narodna Opera
17–22	Bucharest, Theatre of Opera and Ballet
25–30	Warsaw, Teatr Wielki
Nov 15–	
1967 – 8 Apr	*Royal Opera House*
Apr 18–28 May	New York, Metropolitan Opera House, Lincoln Center
May 30– 3 June	Boston, War Memorial Auditorium
June 5– 6	Philadelphia, Convention Hall
7–10	Montreal, Salle Wilfred Pelletier
12–14	Toronto, O'Keefe Center
15–16	Cleveland, Public Auditorium
17–20	Detroit, Masonic Auditorium
22–27	Chicago, Civic Opera House
30– 4 July	Los Angeles, Shrine Auditorium
July 6–12	San Francisco, War Memorial Opera House
14–18	Hollywood, Hollywood Bowl
19–20	San Diego, Civic
22–25	Seattle, Opera House
27–29	Vancouver, Queen Elizabeth
Aug 1– 6	St Louis, Municipal Opera House
Oct 12–	
1968 – 9 Apr	*Royal Opera House*
Apr 23–19 May	New York, Metropolitan Opera House
May 24–26 July	*Royal Opera House*
Oct 10–	
1969 –10 Apr	*Royal Opera House*
Apr 22– 1 June	New York, Metropolitan Opera House
June 3– 6	Philadelphia, Academy of Music
7–10	Boston, Music Hall
12–15	Chicago, Civic Opera House
17–19	Memphis, Music Hall

20–22	Atlanta, Municipal Auditorium
24–26	New Orleans, Municipal Auditorium
27–29	Houston, Jones Hall
July 2– 6	Los Angeles, Shrine Auditorium
8–13	San Francisco, War Memorial Opera House
15–16	San Diego, Civic
17–19	Hollywood, Hollywood Bowl
21–27	St Louis, Municipal Opera House
Sept 25– 6 Oct	*Royal Opera House*
Oct 10–12	Vienna, Staatsoper
23–	
1970 –11 Apr	*Royal Opera House*
Apr 21–31 May	New York, Metropolitan Opera House
June 18–23 July	*Royal Opera House*
Oct 10–	
1971 – 3 Apr	*Royal Opera House*
Apr 5–10	Southampton, Gaumont
12–24	Bristol, Hippodrome
26– 8 May	Leeds, Grand
May 10–15	Newcastle, Royal
17–22	Manchester, Opera House
28– 7 Aug	*Royal Opera House*
Oct 9–	
1972 –17 Apr	*Royal Opera House*
Apr 24– 3 June	New York, Metropolitan Opera House
June 16– 5 Aug	*Royal Opera House*
Oct 10–	
1973 –29 Mar	*Royal Opera House*
Apr 3– 5	Pôrto Alegre, Teatro Leopoldina
7– 8	Belo Horizonte, Teatro Lirico
11–15	São Paulo, Teatro Municipal
18–29	Rio de Janeiro, Teatro Municipal
29	Rio de Janeiro, Estadio Maracañazinho
May 1	Brasilia, Giñasio de Esportes
8– 3 June	*London Coliseum*
June 8– 4 Aug	*Royal Opera House*
Oct 10–15	*Royal Opera House*
17–21	Brussels, Théâtre Royal de la Monnaie
27–	
1974 –13 Apr	*Royal Opera House*
Apr 15–27	Bristol, Hippodrome
May 7–26	New York, Metropolitan Opera House
28– 9 June	Washington, Opera House, JFK Center
June 18–20 July	*Royal Opera House*
July 23– 4 Aug	Plymouth, Big Top
Oct 7–	
1975 12 Apr	*Royal Opera House*
Apr 22–24	Seoul, National
28– 2 May	Tokyo, Bunka Kaikan Hall

May 4	Yokohama, Managawa Kenmin Hall
6–7	Nagoya, Shimin Kaikan
9	Kyoto, Kyoto Kaikan
10–12	Osaka, Festival Hall
13	Kobe, Bunka Hall
15–16	Fukuoka, Shimin Kaikan
18	Hiroshima, Yubin Chokin Hall
21–23	Tokyo, Bunka Kaikan Hall
24	Chiba, Ken Bunka Kaikan
June 2–28	*Battersea, Big Top*
July 11–2 Aug	*Royal Opera House*
Sept 30–11 Oct	Newcastle, Big Top
Oct 15–	
1976 –26 Feb	*Royal Opera House*
Mar 1–13	Bristol, Hippodrome
16–7 Apr	*Royal Opera House*
Apr 19–15 May	New York, Metropolitan Opera House
May 18–6 June	Washington, Opera House, JFK Center
June 8–13	Philadelphia, Academy of Music
26–17 July	*Royal Opera House*
July 20–7 Aug	Plymouth, Big Top
Oct 15–	
1977 –21 Apr	*Royal Opera House*
May 2–14	Bristol, Hippodrome
26–1 July	*Royal Opera House*
July 4–16	*Battersea, Big Top*
21–30	*Royal Opera House*
Oct 14–	
1978 –22 Apr	*Royal Opera House*
Apr 25–29	Liverpool, Empire
May 12–19	Seoul, Sejong Cultural Centre
23–4 June	Los Angeles, Shrine Auditorium
June 6–11	Houston, Jones Hall
13–18	Chicago, Arie Crown
July 17–29	*Royal Opera House*
Aug 1–6	Athens, Herodes Atticus
Oct 19–	
1979 –31 May	*Royal Opera House*
June 5–9	Bristol, Hippodrome
26–1 July	Washington, Wolf Trap
July 3–8	Montreal, Place des Arts
10–12	Vancouver, Queen Elizabeth
14–22	San Francisco, Berkeley Community
24–29	Los Angeles, Shrine Auditorium
Aug 2–5	Mexico City, Bellas Artes
Oct 3–	
1980 – 3 May	*Royal Opera House*
May 13–24	Liverpool, Empire
26–9 Aug	*Royal Opera House*

Adieu FP 19 May 1947 Royal, Brighton *Ch* Cranko *M* Scarlatti *SC* Hugh Stevenson. '47 (53). *The Nymph* Shore (41) Heaton (12). *Her Lover* Poole (40) MacMillan (13). *A Warrior* Britton (34) Darrell (19).

Allegro Brillante FP 27 February 1973 RST, *Ch* Balanchine *M* Tchaikovsky *C* Karinska. '73 (54); '74 (6). A:3. *f* Lorrayne '73–4 (29) Ruanne '73 (11) Wade '73–4 (14) Strike '73–4 (6). *m* McGrath '73 (31) Clarke '73 (16) Waller '73 (1) Dubreuil '73–4 (11) O'Brien '74 (1). + 4*f* 4*m*.

Amor Brujo, El P 5 Sept 1975 King's Edinburgh *Ch* Peter Wright *M* de Falla *SC* Stefanos Lazaridis, asst Dimitra Maraslis. '75 (21); '76 (6). *The Ghost* Jefferies '75–6 (22) Dubreuil '75–6 (5). *Candelas* Lorrayne '75–6 (22) Barbieri '75 (5). *Carmelo* O'Brien '75–6 (21) Powell '75–6 (6). *Lucia* Highwood '75–6 (27). + 8*f* 5*m*.

Angels, The P 26 Dec 1957 ROH *Ch* Cranko *M* Richard Arnell *SC* Desmond Heeley. '57 (3); '58 (18). *The Startled* Farriss '57–8 (21). *The Morbid* MacLeary '57–8 (21). *The Strident* E Thomas '57–8 (21). *The Terrified* M Boulton '57–8 (21). *The Lyrical* Roope '57–8 (6) Anderton '58 (15). *The Vigorous* Britton '57–8 (21). *The Angel* Lakier '57–8 (21). + 6*f* 6*m*.

Ante Room P 9 June 1971 sw *Ch/SC* Geoffrey Cauley *M* Bernard Hermann. '71 (5). 1 Wells (5). 2 Ruanne (5). 3 Barbieri (5). 4 Conley (5). 5 Tait (5). 6 Aitken (5). 7 D Kelly (4). Cooke (1). 8 Johnson (5). 9 Davel (5). 10 Bart (5). 11 O'Brien (3) Jefferies (2).

Apollo FPTC 9 Nov 1970 Royal, Nottingham Cr Rep I *S* Elisabeth Dalton *C* John Craxton. '70 (16); '71 (2); '74 (3); '75 (2); '77 (3). A:4. *Apollo* Rosson '70 (7) D Kelly '70–7 (11) MacLeary '70–4 (5) Nureyev '75 (2) Ashmole '77 (1). *Terpsichore* Beriosova '70 (9) Lorrayne '70–7 (6) Bergsma '70–4 (8) Seymour '75 (2) Gielgud '77 (1). *Polyhymnia* Ruanne '70 (6) O'Conaire '70–1 (6) Derman '70–4 (5) Inkin '70 (2) Mason '74 (2) Strike '75–7 (5). *Calliope* Conley '70 (10) Lorrayne '70–5 (11) Vere '70 (2) Highwood '77 (3).

Apparitions FPTC 28 Jan 1957 SMT (Str) Cr Rep I. '57 (15). A:9. *Poet* Field (12) Alex Bennett (3). *Woman in Balldress* Heaton (14) Lee (1).

Arpège FP 14 February 1975 RST, *Ch* Peter Wright *M* François Boïeldieu *SC* Peter Farmer. '75 (35); '76 (17). *f* 1 Last '75–6 (18) Miller '75–6 (11) Strike '75–6 (19) Last – Pet Miller '75 (1) Strike – Pet Miller '76 (1). *m* 1 Dubreuil '75–6 (29) Reeder '75–6 (5) G Powell '75–6 (18). *f* 2 Lorrayne '75–6 (32) Tait '75–6 (11) Evans '75–6 (9). *m* 2 Dye '75 (12) Kilgour

'75/6 (5) O'Brien '75–6 (13) Purnell '75–6 (22). + 8*f* 8*m*. Revised version *Arpège* P 29m June 1974 RBS.

Assembly Ball P 8 Apr 1946 sw *Ch/SC* Andrée Howard *M* Bizet. '46 (59); '47 (6); '50 (8); '51 (23); '52 (29); '53 (18). A:17. *Master of Ceremonies* Kersley '46–7 (44) Britton '46–'53 (35) Blair '50–3 (47) Trecu '50–3 (17). *The Lady* Brae '46–7 (30) Harris '46–7 (35) Beriosova '50–2 (34) Claire '50–1 (7) Neil '52–3 (15) Hill '52–3 (12) O'Reilly '52–3 (10). *An Elderly Gentleman* Newman '46–7 (50) Ward '46 (1) Kersley '46 (5) Britton '46–7 (9) Holden '50–3 (74) Poole '51 (4) Davies '53A. + 8*f* 6*m*.

Aurora's Wedding. See **Sleeping Beauty, The** Act III.

Bailemos P 4 Feb 1947 sw *Ch* Celia Franca *M* Massenet *SC* Honor Frost. '47 (55). *Peasants* 3*f* from: Franca (6) Moore (39) O'Reilly (43) van Praagh (36) Field (28) Shore (1) Pat Miller (12). 3*m* from: Britton (51) Hogan (36) Boulton (54) Darrell (24). *Nobles* 3*f* from: Wadsworth (48) Chrimes (38) Shore (52) Franca (3) Hamby (24). 3*m* from: A Carter (12) A Burke (47) Cranko (43) MacMillan (40) Hogan (10) Poole (13).

Bal des Voleurs, Le FP 17 May 1963 ROH *Ch/adapted* Massine *M* Georges Auric *SC* Jean-Denis Malclès. From play by Anouilh. '63 (5). *Juliet* Fracci (5). *Eva* Grahame (5). *Peterbone* Haythorne (5). *Hector* I Hamilton (5). *Gustav* Yuresha (5). + 6*f* 8*m* + CdB.

Ballade P 19 May 1972 Teatro Nacional de S Carlos, Lisbon *Ch* MacMillan *M* Fauré *SC* nc. '72 (8). A:8. 1 Lorrayne A(8). 2 Cooke A(8) Clarke A. 3 Johnson A(8). 4 Jefferies A(8).

Beauty and the Beast P 20 Dec 1949 sw *Ch* Cranko *M* Ravel *SC* Margaret Kaye; '61 *SC* Philip Prowse; '71 *SC* Alistair Livingstone. '49 (3); '50 (42); '51 (22); '52 (5); '53 (7); '54 (18); '55 (4); '56 [24]; '57 (8); '71 (31). A:37. *Beauty* Pat Miller '49–'55 (54) Fifield '50–1 (6) Beriosova '50 (8) Page '53–5 (15) Lane '53 (2) Bolton '56–7 [2] Cox '56–7 [6] Wells '71 (7) Barbieri '71 (17) Vere '71 (7). *The Beast* Poole '49–'55 (69) Blair '50–3 (7) Wright '50–5 (23) Britton '53 (2) MacLeary '57 (2) Boulton '57 (6) Davel '71 (13) Clarke '71 (14) Sherwood '71 (4). nr 1956 Autumn tour.

Belle Dame sans Merci, La FPTC 16 Sept 1959 Grand, Leeds Cr Rep I. '59 (23). *A Knight* Gable (6) Doyle (17). *La Belle Dame sans Merci* Parkinson '59CG (12) Seymour (11) + 8*m*.

Birdscape P 11 Feb 1977 Hippodrome, Birmingham *Ch* David Morse *M* Martinu *SC*

Linda Fleckney. '77 (7). *Song Birds f* Tait (7) *m* Reeder (7). *Bird of Prey* O'Brien (7). *Birds of the Ocean f* Lorrayne (7). *m* Purnell (5) Berg (2). + 5*f* 7*m*.

Blood Wedding P 5 June 1953 sw *Ch* Alfred Rodrigues *M* Denis ApIvor *SC* Isabel Lambert *Scenario* ApIvor/Rodrigues after *Bodas de Sangre* by Lorca. '53 (34); '54 (33); '55 (44); '56 (21); '57 (33); '59 (4); '60 (15); '62 (4); '63 (42); '68 (12). A:67. *Leonardo* Poole '53–5 (81) Vernon '53–4 (4) Wright '54–5 (7) Britton '55–'63 (63) Shields '55–6 (19) MacLeary '57 (12) Doyle '60–2 (5) I Hamilton '63 (39) Davel '68 (11) Cooke '68 (1). *The Bride* Fifield '53–5 (13) Lane '53–'63 (56) Miller '53–5 (26) Neil '55–7 (34) Heaton '56–'60 (47) Lakier '57 (7) Page '59–'62 (6) Wells '62–3 (14) Anderton '63–8 (34) Aldous '68 (5). *The Bridegroom* Trecu '53–'60 (57) Britton '53–5 (35) Trevor '55–7 (29) Boulton '55–9 (50) Miller '57 (3) Alex Bennett '57–'63 (9) Doyle '60 (5) Gable '62–3 (7) Sherwood '63 (35) Wall '68 (1) Johnson '68 (1) Cooke '68A (10) + 7*f* 4*m* + CdB.

Blue Rose, A P 26 Dec 1957 ROH *Ch* Peter Wright *M* Samuel Barber *SC* Yolanda Sonnabend. '57 (3); '58 (47); '59 (7); '60 (3). A:40. *Waltz f* Alexander '57–'60 (23) Anderton '58–'60 (37). *m* Miller '57–8 (49) L White '58 (1) Mottram '59 (4) Gable '59 (2) Alex Bennett '59–'60 (4). *pdd m* MacLeary '57–9 (47) Mottram '58–'60 (13) *f* Heaton '57–9 (31) Lee '58 (16) Seymour '58–'60 (13). *Two Step f* Cox '57–8 (45) Roope '58–9 (7) Sopwith '58A–'59 (4) Geldard '59–'60 (4). *m* Boulton '57–9 (43) Mosaval '58–'60 (17). *Tango* Farriss '57–'60 (55) Lakier '58 (5). + 6*f* 6*m*.

Boutique Fantasque, La FPTC 31 Jan 1968 RST Cr Rep I. '68 (36); '69 (53); '70 (27); '78 (67). A:8. *Can-Can Dancers f* Wells '68–'70 (31) Aldous '68–'70 (32) Last '68–'78 (55) Tait '78 (25) Pet Miller '78 (13) Barbieri '78 (22) Seymour '78 (2) Kennedy '78 (3). *m* Emblen '68–'70 (47) G Grant '68–'70 (31) Mosaval '68–'70 (38) D Kelly '78 (15) Reeder '78 (11) Dubreuil '78 (36) Myers '78 (5).

Brouillards FP 3 May 1978 sw *Ch* Cranko *M* Debussy *SC* nc. '78 (21); '79 (8). *Voiles f* Tait '78–9 (16) Aitken '78–9 (13). *m* Berg '78 (9) Kilgour '78–9 (17) Waller '79 (2) Dubreuil '79 (1). *Bruyères* Ashmole '78–9 (11) Myers '78–9 (15) Kilgour '79 (3). + 5*f* 10*m* + CdB.

Burrow, The P 2 Jan 1958 ROH *Ch* MacMillan *M* Frank Martin *SC* Nicholas Georgiadis. '58 (46); '59 (13). A:20. *The Woman* Heaton '58–9 (47) Farriss '58–9 (12). *The Joker* Britton '58–9 (48) Boulton '58–9 (11). *The Outcast* Miller '58 (45) L White '58 (1) Aitken '59 (10) Howard '58 (3)

Two Adolescents ƒ Seymour '58–9 (32) E Thomas '58–9 (27) *m* MacLeary '58–9 (59). + 1oƒ6m.

Café des Sports P 24 May 1954 His Majesty's, Johannesburg *Ch* Alfred Rodrigues *M* Antony Hopkins *SC* Jack Taylor. '54 (31); '55 (66); '56 (35). '57 (6). A:19. *Urchin* Lane '54A–5 (46) Forhan '54–5 (29) White '55–7 (36) P Cox '55–7 (27). *Waiter* Vernon '54–5 (61) Zolan '55–7 (50) Boulton '55–7 (27). + 11ƒ11m.

Caprichos FP 12 Oct 1971 Wimbledon Theatre *Ch* Herbert Ross *M* Bartók *SC* nc. Based on Goya's commentaries for his Caprichos engravings. '71 (16); '72 (2). *No Te Escaparas* ƒ Ruanne '71–2 (11) Strike '71 (2) Lorrayne '72 (5). 2m from: Jefferies '71–2 (17) Morse '71–2 (17) Porter '72 (1) Bart '72 (1). *Tantalus* ƒ Tait '71–2 (13) Trounson '71–2 (5). *m* Davel '71–2 (13) Cooke '71–2 (5). *No Hubo Remedio* Karras '71–2 (14) O'Conaire '71 (2) Laurence '71–2 (2) + 2ƒ4m.

Capriol Suite FP 5 Oct 1948 sw *Ch* Ashton M Peter Warlock *SC* William Chappell. '48 (12); '49 (26); '50 (6); '51 (15). A:15. *Pavane* ƒ Shore '48–'50 (26) Claire '48–'51 (24) Barnes '51 (9). 2m from: Poole '48–'51 (30) Zullig '48–9 (32) Hogan '48–'51 (39) Gill '49–'51 (11) Wright '51 (6). + 4ƒ4m.

Card Game FPTC 3 Oct 1973 sw Cr Rep I. '73 (24); '74 (48); '75 (4); '76 (13); '77 (3); '79 (8). A:9. *The Joker* Jefferies '73–9 (54) Johnson '73 (2) Dubreuil '73–9 (29) Bertscher '73–4 (9) G Powell '76 (3) E Madsen '76 (3). *Queen of Hearts* Lorrayne '73–9 (54) Barbieri '73–7 (22) Strike '74–9 (24). *Two of Diamonds* Barbieri '73–6 (24) Wade '73–4 (39) Tait '74–9 (23) Pet Miller '74–9 (5) Last '74–6 (9).

Carnaval FPTB 21 May 1947 Royal, Brighton Cr Rep I. '47 (71); '48 (21); '49 (26); '50 (10); '51 (11); '52 (3); '53 (15); '54 (5); '55 (30). *Columbine* Heaton '47 (36) N Moore/ Nerina '47 (26) Fifield '47–'55 (52) Lane '48–'55 (23) O'Reilly '48–'53 (15) Pat Miller '50–5 (22) Bolton '55 (11) Alexander '55 (7). *Harlequin* Britton '47–'55 (55) Boulton '47–'55 (25) Kersley '47–'50 (70) Trecu '49–'54 (31) Blair '50–1 (6) Mosaval '55 (5). *Pierrot* Kersley '47 (13) Cranko '47–'51 (33) Poole '47–'55 (103) Gill '50–3 (16) Zolan '55 (9) Trevor '55 (18).

Carte Blanche P 10 Sept 1953 Empire, Edinburgh *Ch* Walter Gore *M* John Addison *SC* Kenneth Rowell. '53 (40); '54 (8); '55 (3). A:17. *Prelude* Mosaval '53–5 (49) Hurd '54A Trevor '55 (2). *Ring Master* Poole '53–4 (31) MacMillan '53–4 (8) Zolan '53–5 (12). *Trapeze Artists* ƒ O'Reilly '53 (10) Page '53–5 (40) Forhan '53 (1). *m* Britton '53–5 (46) Holden '53–4 (5). *Equestrienne* Hill '53–4 (38) O' Reilly '54A Larsen '53–4 (6) Cartier '54–5 (7) + 14ƒ4m.

Casse-Noisette Act III FPTB 8 Apr 1946 sw Cr Rep I 1937 + *Ch* Spanish Dance arr Angelo

Andes. '46 (7); '47 (7); '49 (3); '50 (46); '51 (22). *Nut-Cracker Prince* Thomson '46 (4) A Carter '46–7 (10) Blair '49–'51 (59) Poole '50–1 (12). *Sugar Plum Fairy* Dale '46 (4) N Moore/Nerina '46–'50 (14) Heaton '47 (5) Fifield '49–'51 (22) Lane '49–'51 (10) Beriosova '50–1 (30).

Casse-Noisette FPNP 11 Sept 1951 sw *Ch* Ivanov arr Ashton *M* Tchaikovsky *SC* Cecil Beaton. '51 (3); '52 (4); '53 (10). A:58. *Sugar Plum Fairy* Fifield '51–3 (13) Beriosova '52A Lane '52A (4). *Nut-Cracker Prince* Blair '51–3 (11) Trecu '52A–3 (6). NB Acts II/III only.

Casse-Noisette Act III pdd C '57 James Bailey. '53 (1); '57 (3); '58 (2). A:21. ƒ Lane '53 (1) Fonteyn '57 (3) Nerina '58 (2). *m* Trecu '53 (1) Somes '57 (3) Blair '58 (2).

Catch, The P 19 Oct 1946 sw *Ch/C* Alan Carter *M* Bartók. '46 (9); '47 (70); '48 (19). *The Elder Brother* Carter '46–7 (13) Hogan '46–8 (71) MacMillan '47–8 (14) *His Girl Friend* Harris '46–7 (13) Shore '46–8 (60) Walker '47 (17) Claire '47–8 (8). *The Younger Brother* Ward '46–7 (13) Boulton '46–8 (66) Darrell '47–8 (14) Butterfield '48 (5).

Catch P 20 June 1980 Big Top Exeter *Ch* Jonathan Burrows *m* Douglas Gould *SC* Judy Stedham. ƒ Crow, Griffiths, Lucas, Merky, Wake. *m* Bonner, Lustig, Purnell.

Charlotte Brontë P 8 Mar 1974 Alhambra, Bradford *Ch* Ronald Hynd *M* Douglas Young *SC* Peter Docherty. '74 (22). *Charlotte* Barbieri (13) Wade (9) *Emily* Lorrayne (22). *Anne* Laurence (22) *Branwell* Morse (22). + 1ƒ1m + CdB.

Checkmate FPTC 18 Apr 1961 Festival Hall, Tokyo Cr Rep I. '61 (4); '62 (43); '63 (12); '64 (3); '75 (11); '76 (19); '77 (26); '78 (5). A:13. *First Red Knight* Doyle '61A–2 (16) Gable '62–3 (12) I Hamilton '62–4 (33) MacLeary '62A (1) Dubreuil '75–8 (16) Jefferies '75–6 (13) Morse '75–7 (13) Ashmole '77–8 (13) Myers '77–8 (6). *The Black Queen* Grey 61A '62–3(4) Beriosova '61–2 (3) Layland '61–4 (32) Grahame '62–4 (23) Makarova '75 (2) Gielgud '75–7 (21) Highwood '75–7 (16) Mason '75 (2) Barbieri '76–8 (15) Lorrayne '77–8 (5). *The Red King* Legerton '61A–4 (29) Aitken '62–4 (31) F White '63 (2) Edwards '75 (3) Killar '75–7 (49) Helpmann '77 (4) Auld '78 (5). *The Red Queen* Remington '61A–2 (17) Orpin '61A '62–3 (22) O'Conaire '62A–4 (23) Lorrayne '75–8 (47) Evans '76–8 (4) Cartwright '76 (1) Aitken '77–8 (9).

Checkpoint P 27 Nov 1970 Opera House, Manchester *Ch* MacMillan *M* Roberto Gerhard *SC* Elisabeth Dalton. '70 (9); '71 (2). *The Woman* Beriosova '70–1 (9) Lorrayne '70 (2). *The Man* MacLeary '70–1 (9) Clarke '70 (2). + 7m.

Children's Corner FP 6 Apr 1948 sw *Ch* Cranko *M* Debussy *SC* Jan le Witt. '48 (49); '49 (9). *The Golliwog* Poole '48–9 (37) Butterfield/Blair

'48–9 (21). *The Wooden Doll* Shore '48–9 (43) Fifield '48 (11) O'Reilly '48–9 (4). *Mlle Piquant* Pat Miller '48–9 (26) Hamby '48 (20) Lane '48 (10) Claire '49 (2). *The Great Admirer of Mlle Piquant* MacMillan '48 (28) Trecu '48–9 (23) Holden '48–9 (7). *The Monkey of Ukubaba* Page '48 (6) Bruce '48 (42) Swanson '48–9 (10). + 3ƒ.

Cinderella TC in CG production at ROH only. *See* Rep I **Cinderella** '60: '61.

Concerto FP 26 May 1967 ROH *Ch* MacMillan *M* Shostakovich *SC* Jürgen Rose. '67 (18); '68 (29); '69 (14); '74 (39); '75 (24); '76 (9); '77 (7); '79 (10). A:48. *First Movement* ƒ Anderton '67–9 (28) Grahame '67–9 (17) Last '67–'76 (43) Strike '74–9 (23) Tait '74–9 (26) Wade '74 (1) Pet Miller '75–7 (10) Burton '76 (1) Crow '79 (1). *m* Wall '67–9 (15) Beaumont '67–9 (21) Clarke '67–9 (24) McGrath '69 (1) Johnson '69A Dubreuil '74–6 (21) Reeder '74–9 (42) O'Brien '74–6 (12) Courtney '75 (1) Sleep '75 (2) Bertscher '76–7 (4) Berg '77 (3) Ashmole '79 (3) Welford '79 (1). *Second Movement* ƒ Wells '67–9 (30) Thorogood '67–'74 (23) Ruanne '67–9 (12) Evans '74–9 (55) Homji '74–6 (16) Seymour '75–6 (3) C Aitken '76–9 (8) Tait '77 (2) Rowann '79 (1). *m* Farley '67 (8) Cooke '67–9 (35) Davel '67–9 (18) MacLeary '73A '74 (2) Jefferies '74–5 (18) Wall '74 (1) D Kelly '74–9 (21) Kilgour '74–6 (29) Ashmole '76–9 (10) Myers '77–9 (7) Purnell '79 (1). *Third Movement* Landon '67–9 (29) Aldous '67–9 (32) Grahame '69A Wade '74–5 (36) Pet Miller '74–6 (8) Strike '74–9 (22) M Lindsay '74 (1) Kennedy '74–9 (17) Gielgud '76A–7 (3) Stanley '79 (2). + 3ƒ3m + CdB. *Also* Rep I.

Concerto Second Movement '71 (4); '72 (17). A:6. ƒ Evans '71–2 (11) Wells '71–2 (4) Trounson '72 (5) Ruanne '72 (1). *m* Cooke '71–2 (11) Davel '71–2 (4) Clarke '72 (3) Blair '72 (3).

Concerto Barocco FP 26 Aug 1977 Big Top, Cambridge *Ch* Balanchine *M* J S Bach *SC* nc. '77 (25); '78 (14). A:3. 1 Lorrayne '77–8 (19) Tait '77–8 (16) Strike '77 (1) Rowann '78 (3). 2 Purnell '77–8 (18) Berg '77–8 (17) O'Brien '78 (4) 3 Highwood '77–8 (19) Strike '77–8 (20).

Coppélia FP 4 September 1951 sw *Ch* Ivanov/ Cecchetti reproduced Sergeyev *M* Delibes *SC* Loudon Sainthill. '51 (4); '52 (47); '53 (48*); '54 (52); '55 (80). A:100. *Swanilda* Fifield '51–5 (28) Beriosova '51–2 (10) Lane '51–5 (61) Pat Miller '52–5 (54) O'Reilly '52–4 (14) Page '54–5 (24) Lindsay '55 (1) Tempest '55 (20) Neil '55 (17). *Franz* Blair '51–3 (26) Trecu '51–4 (38) Britton '51–5 (75) Vernon '53–5 (33) Zolan '54–5 (43) Boulton '55 (14). *Dr Coppélius* Poole '51–5 (76) Holden '51–4 (81) Gill '52–3 (11) Zolan '54–5 (33) Mosaval '55 (15) Trevor '55 (13).
*includes 2 school mat. casts from: *Swanilda*

O'Reilly/Pat Miller *Franz* Blair/Britton *Dr Coppélius* Gill/Holden.

Coppélia FPNP 16 Jan 1956 SMT (Str) *Ch* Ivanov/Cecchetti reproduced Sergeyev *M* Delibes *SC* Robert Medley; 1958 *SC* Osbert Lancaster (as Rep I 1954) *Pr* de Valois. '56 [86]; '57 (55); '58 (46); '59 (40); '60 (58); '61 (3); '66 (55); '67 (18). A:56. *Swanilda* Tempest '56–7 [41] Neil '56–7 [26] Heaton '56–8 [38] Lee '57–8 (18) Cox '57–8 (23) Alexander '57–'60 (47) Anderton '59–'67 (52) Linden '59 (3) Farriss '59–'60 (26) Beriosova '59 (1) Nerina '51CG '61–2 (3) Park '60 (1) Wells '60–7 (19) Sibley '61 (1) Lane '66 (4) Grahame '66–7 (3) Last '66–7 (24) Aldous '66–7 (5) Wakelyn '67 (3) Thorogood '67(1). *Franz* Britton '56–'60 [73] Zolan '56–8 [54] Boulton '56–9 [70] Alex Bennett '57–'60 (38) Usher '59CG–'66 (7) Doyle '59–'60 (20) MacLeary '59 (1) Blair '60–6 (4) Burne '60 (1) Ashbridge '61 (2) Wall '66–7 (17) Mason '66 (2) Clarke '66–7 (25) Cooke '66–7 (25). *Dr Coppélius* Zolan '56–8 [43] Trevor '56–7 [54] Legerton '56–'67 [128] Holden '57–'66 (17) Miller '58 (8) Aitken '59–'67 (46) Emblen '66–7 (26) Gordon '66–7 (11) Ryder '66 (6). nr 1956 Autumn tour.

Coppélia Act III '59 (1); '61 (1). A: from '56:17. *Swanilda* Alexander '59 (1) Anderton '61 (1). *Franz* Britton '59 (1) Doyle '61 (1) *also* MacLeary '58A. *Dr Coppélius* Legerton '59 (1). '61inc.

Coppélia Act III pdd '58 (3). *Swanilda* Lee (1) Alexander (2). *Franz* Zolan (1) Alex Bennett (2).

Coppélia FPNP 15 Apr 1975 ROH *Ch* after Petipa/Cecchetti; new *Ch* Peter Wright *M* Delibes *SC* Osbert Lancaster *Pr* Peter Wright after Sergeyev/de Valois. '75 (41); '76 (57); '77 (35); '78 (8). A:4. *Swanilda* Last '75–7 (26) Park '75–6 (8) Barbieri '75–8 (31) Tait '75–8 (36) Lincoln '75–6 (7) Pet Miller '75–7 (10) Strike '75–8 (16) Wells '76 (1) Highwood '77–8 (2) Gielgud '77 (2) Jenner '78 (2). *Franz* Dubreuil '75–8 (21) D Kelly '75–8 (37) Jefferies '75–6 (18) Johnson '75 (2) Powell '75–6 (9) O'Brien '76–8 (16) Kilgour '76–8 (13) Myers '76–8 (15) Ashmole '76–8 (9) Ashmole-Kelly '77 (1). *Dr Coppélius* Jefferies '75–6 (24) Killar '75–7 (39) A Grant '75 (3) Shaw '75 (2) Auld '75–8 (49) Bintley '76–8 (16) Helpmann '77 (3) Bertscher '78 (2).

Coppélia FPNP 9 February 1979 RST *Ch* after Petipa/Cecchetti; new *Ch/Pr* Peter Wright *M* Delibes *SC* Peter Snow. '79 (72). *Swanilda* Tait (21) Strike (13) Barbieri (18) Pet Miller (5) Highwood (11) Last (1) Kennedy (3). *Franz* Dubreuil (21) Myers (13) Ashmole (18) Waller (3) Kilgour (13) O'Brien (4). *Dr Coppélius* Auld (11) Bertscher (7) Bintley (20) Wicks (20) Bonner (14).

Court of Love, The P 21 Apr 1977 Pavilion, Bournemouth *Ch* Lynn Seymour *M* Howard Blake *SC* Dimitra Maraslis. '77 (33). *Enchantress* Fitzgerald/Stanley (33). *Knight* Myers (17) Kilgour (16). *Maiden* Lucas (33). *Troubadour* Berg (33). *Queen* Lorrayne (21) Laurence (12). *King* Purnell (17) Killar (16). + 6f 3m.

Création du Monde, La P 12 Feb 1964 at RST, *Ch* MacMillan *M* Milhaud *SC* James Goddard. '64 (19). *Eve* Wells (19). *Adam* Farley (19). *The Serpent* Anderton (19). *The Great Deity* Emblen (19). *The Apple* Grater (17) Beale (2). + CdB.

Creatures of Prometheus, The P 6 June 1970 Theater der Stadt, Bonn *Ch* Ashton *M* Beethoven *SC* Ottowerner Meyer. '70 (5); '71 (4). A:7. *Prometheus* Davel '70A–1 (7) McGrath '70–1 (2). *Creatures: m* Cooke '70A '71 (3) Wall '70–1 (6). *f* Wells '70A–1 (9). *Apollo* Clarke '70A–1 (5) Rencher '70–1 (4). *Eros* Benson '70A Freeman '70–1 (9). *Thalia* Thorogood '70A–1 (7) Inkin '70A Collier '71 (2). *Mars* Grater '70A–1 (7) Drew '70–1 (2). *Melpomene* Conley '70A–1 (6) Ruanne '71 (3). *Bacchus* Morse '70A–1 (7) Sleep '70–1 (2). *Terpsichore* Last '70A–1 (8) Connor '71 (1). + 10f 14m.

Danses Concertantes P 18 Jan 1955 sw *Ch* MacMillan *M* Stravinsky *SC* Nicholas Georgiadis; redesigned 1979. '55 (38); '56 (4); '57 (4); '61 (7); '62 (10); '64 (19); '65 (9); '67 (17); '68 (9); '70 (25); '71 (22); '72 (2); '79 (12). A:59. *Solo* Britton '55–'64 (62) Vernon '55 (3) Boulton '55 (1) Shaw '61 (3) Sale '62–4 (6) Emblen '62–8 (32) G Powell '67–8 (8) Johnson '68–'71 (25) Morse '70A–1 (10) Jefferies '70–2 (6) Eagling '70 (3) Sherwood '71 (6) Cooke '71 (1) Reeder '79 (5) Price '79 (4) Corder '79 (3). pdd f Lane '55–'67 (31) Neil '55–7 (16) Bruce '55 (1) Wells '61–'71 (37) Seymour '61–4 (3) Anderton '61A '62–8 (19) Grahame '64–8 (8) Last '67–'72 (11) Aldous '67–8 (3) Hill '70–2 (14) Vere '70–1 (17) Tait '70–9 (12) Stanley '79 (3) C Kennedy '79 (3). m Poole '55 (29) MacLeary '55–7 (17) Doyle '61–2 (6) Gable '61–4 (12) Farley '64–7 (24) I Hamilton '64 (9) Grater '65–'70 (19) Clarke '68–'72 (23) Davel '68–'72 (9) D Kelly '70–1 (18) Dubreuil '79 (6) Myers '79 (3) Kilgour '79 (2) Millington '79 (1). + 8f 3m. Also Rep I.

Day into Night P 28 Mar 1980 Royal, Norwich *Ch* Michael Corder *M* Martinu *SC* Lazaro Prince. *Sun f* Kennedy. *m* Myers. *Light Moon f* Barbieri. *m* Purnell. *Dark Moon f* Highwood. *m* Wicks. *3rd Movement f* Tait. *m* Dubreuil. + 8f 8m.

Destino, El P 31 Jan 1950 sw *Ch* Angelo Andes *M* Manuel Lazareno *C* Hugh Stevenson. '50 (30); '51 (2). *Fortune Teller* Gorham '50 (25) Cadzow '50 (5) Farrance '51 (2). *Sevillian Girl* O'Reilly '50–1 (29) Shore '50 (1) Claire '50 (2). *Sevillian Boy* Trecu '50–1 (30) Blair '50 (1) Wright '50 (1). *Girl of Aragon* Lane '50–1 (19) Pat Miller '50–1 (5) Shore '50 (7) Bruce '50 (1). + 7f 6m.

Deux Pigeons, Les see **Two Pigeons, The**

Diversions FPTC 10 Feb 1971 Royal, Norwich Cr Rep I. '71 (15). 1 Beriosova (7) Lorrayne (7) Vere (1) 2 MacLeary (9) C Kelly (5) Clarke (1) 3 Last (8) Hill (7) 4 Johnson (9) Sherwood (6).

Dream, The FPTC 2 Dec 1966 New, Oxford Cr Rep I *SC* Peter Farmer. '66 (5); '67 (33); '68 (12); '69 (25); '70 (28); '75 (37); '76 (10); '78 (5). A:37. *Titania* Wells '66–'70 (43) Aldous '66–'70 (39) Grahame '69–'70 (20) Penney '66A '70–5 (3) Tait '75–8 (25) Sibley '75 (3) Barbieri '75–8 (17) Aitken '75–8 (5). *Oberon* Wall '66–9 (26) Clarke '66–'70 (45) Beaumont '67–9 (2) Nureyev '68A '75 (2) Mead '69–'70 (3) Johnson '69–'70 (20) Usher '69 (7) Jefferies '75–6 (14) Dowell '75 (3) Coleman '75 (2) Dubreuil '75–8 (26) O'Brien '75 (3) Ashmole '78 (2). *Puck* Morse '66–'78 (60) Mosaval '67–'70 (48) Johnson '67–9 (6) Bertscher '67–'78 (34) Sleep '75 (3) Reeder '78 (1) Fletcher '75 (3). *Bottom* Emblen '66–'78 (59) G Grant '66–'75 (45) Ryder '67–8 (5) A Grant '75 (5) Powell '75–6 (26) Waller '75–6 (13) Bonner '78 (2).

Elite Syncopations FPTC 10 Feb 1978 RST Cr Rep I. '78 (48); '79 (46). *Calliope Rag* Strike '78–9 (47) Pet Miller '78–9 (22) C Williams '78–9 (5) Highwood '78–9 (20). *Golden Hours f* Aitken '78–9 (38) Evans '78–9 (20) Burton '78 (2) Katrak '78–9 (17) Dales '78–9 (17) m Myers '78–9 (41) Berg '78–9 (21) Bonner '78–9 (25) Kilgour '79 (7). *Stop-Time Rag* Tait '78–9 (49) Rowann '78–9 (23) Barbieri '78–9 (8) Stanley '78–9 (14). *Alaskan Rag f* Lorrayne '78–9 (64) Rowann '78–9 (17) Powell '78–9 (13) m Bertscher '78–9 (56) Bintley '78–9 (25) Bonner '78–9 (13) *Bethena Waltz f* as Stop-Time Rag. *m* D Kelly '78–9 (26) Dubreuil '78–9 (31) Purnell '78–9 (25) Myers '78–9 (11) Bonner '79 (1). *Friday Night* Ashmole '78–9 (43) Reeder '78–9 (35) Kilgour '78–9 (16).

Entertainers, The P 2 May 1974 sw *Ch* Ashley Killar *M* Pergolesi *SC* Terence Emery. '74 (10). 1 Lorrayne (10) 2 Barbieri (8) Holling (2). 3 Reeder (10) 4 O'Brien (10). + 3f.

Etude FP 15 Mar 1949 sw *Ch* Nancy McNaught *M* Antony Hopkins *SC* Vivienne Kernot. '49 (30). *Pas seul* O'Reilly (30). *Third Movement* 1 Poole (30). 2 Zullig (28) Trecu (2). + 8f 5m. From Oct '49: 3f 3m.

Façade FPTB 29 Apr 1946 sw Cr Rep I. '46 (44); '47 (38); '48 (50); '49 (42); '50 (29); '51 (9); '52 (7); '53 (4); '54 (22); '56 (30); '57 (29); '58 (40); '59 (1); '60 (6); '61 (7); '71 (26); '72 (10); '73 (25); '74 (7); '75 (19); '76 (4). A:126. *Polka* Heaton '46–7 [37] Harman '46–7 (13) Nelson '46–7 (27) Fifield '47–'51 (80) Lane '47–'54 (78) Bruce '48–'52 (28) Beriosova '50 (6) Neil '53A–6 [16] White '57 (11) Bolton '57 (18) Farriss '58 (17) Thomas '58–'61 (17) Roope '58 (11) Alexander '59A Seymour '59A '60 (2) Lindsay '60–1 (6) Last '71–4 (16) Strike '71–5 (38) Tait '71–6 (10) C Hill '71–2 (8) Pet Miller '73–6 (19). *Popular Song* 2m from: Britton '46–'58 (180) A Grant '46 (12) Boulton

'46–'58 (*174*) Hyrst '46 (*5*) Baker '46 (*5*) Kersley '47 (*4*) Trecu '48–'54 (*110*) Gill '48–'53 (*31*) Blair '49–'51 (*55*) Holden '49 (*14*) McAlpine '50–2 (*10*) Trevor '51–7 (*25*) Vernon '54 (*9*) L White '57–8 (*59*) Hurd '58 (*3*) Gable '58 (*14*) Wilson '59 (*1*) Westmoreland '59–61 [*10*] Alder '60–1 (*9*) Johnson '71–2 (*11*) Kirkpatrick '71 (*9*) Jefferies '71–6 (*41*) Morse '71–6 (*73*) Bertscher '71 (*1*) Fletcher '71 (*3*) Porter '71–3 (*11*) Cooke '71 (*1*) Shaw '72 (*1*) Clegg '72 (*1*) Myers '72 (*1*) O'Brien '73–6 (*24*) Vardon '73 (*1*) Dubreuil '74 (*2*) Kilgour '75 (*2*). *Tango: A Dago* Ashton '46–9 (*7*) Carter '46–7 (*48*) A Burke '47–8 (*104*) Kersley '47 (*5*) Hogan '47 (*11*) Zullig '49 (*31*) Trecu '49–'50 (*2*) Holden '49–'61 (*79*) Poole '50–4 (*3*) Trevor '57 (*15*) Zolan '56–8 34 Miller '58 (*18*) Helpmann '58A Britton '59–'61 (*9*) A Grant '60–'75 (*14*) Davel '71–2 (*13*) McGrath '71–4 (*15*) Clarke '71–3 (*7*) Cooke '71–3 (*15*) Dubreuil '73–6 (*14*) Jefferies '75–6 (*8*) Killar '75 (*5*) Morse '75–6 (*3*). *A Debutante* Brae '46–7 (*34*) van Praagh '46–9 (*58*) Shore '47–'50 (*116*) Claire '49–'52 (*42*) O'Reilly '50–4 (*24*) Larsen '53–4 (*3*) M Hill '54–7 (*25*) Vane '57 (*13*) Heaton '58–'61 (*16*) Lee '58 (*19*) Farriss '58–'61 (*17*) Lindsay '60 (*2*) Ruanne '71–3 (*13*) O'Conaire '71 (*9*) Barbieri '71–6 (*39*) Merry '71 (*5*) Laurence '71–6 (*15*) Parkinson '72–3 (*8*) Highwood '75 (*1*) Homji '76 (*1*). nr: 1956 Autumn tour. '47 Nov 29e. '61 Mar 10 (Polka). '60 Jan 7, 11, 21. '61 Mar 10 (Popular Song).

Fête Etrange, La FP 25 Mar 1947 sw *Ch* Andrée Howard *M* Fauré sel Ronald Crichton orch 1 Lennox Berkeley 2 Guy Warrack *SC* Sophie Fedorovitch *Scenario* Ronald Crichton after *Le Grand Meaulnes* by Alain Fournier. '47 (*48*); '49 (*17*); '50 (*6*); '51 (*8*); '52 (*8*); '53 (*12*); '54 (*2*); '57 (*29*); '58 (*24*); '60 (*17*); '61 (*8*); '62 (*8*); '74 (*39*); '76 (*4*); '79 (*10*). A:46. *A Country Boy* Britton '47–'62 (*98*) Kersley '47–'50 (*36*) Boulton '49–'58 (*27*) Trecu '49–'61 (*20*) Poole '51 (*5*) Farley '61 (*1*) Jefferies '74 (*16*) Morse '74–9 (*33*) Bonner '79 (*4*). *The Bride* Brae '47 (*7*) Heaton '47–'61 (*94*) van Praagh '48 (*2*) Shore '49–'50 (*18*) Fifield '49–'53 (*15*) Beriosova '51–2 (*6*) Hill '52–4 (*14*) O'Reilly '54A Neil '54A E Thomas '57–8 (*16*) Seymour '60–1 (*3*) Anderton '60–2 (*5*) Sibley '61–2 (*3*) Linden '62 (*4*) Lorrayne '74–9 (*23*) Strike '74 (*10*) Barbieri '74–9 (*14*) Homji '74 (*4*) Samsova '79 (*2*). *The Bridegroom* A Burke '47 (*42*) Cranko '47 (*6*) Poole '49–'50 (*22*) Hogan '50–1 (*4*) Gill '51–4 (*23*) Wright '53–4 (*4*) MacLeary '57–8 (*25*) Miller '57–8 (*28*) Alex Bennett '60–2 (*33*) McGrath '74 (*2*) Dubreuil '74–9 (*15*) Killar '74–6 (*17*) Purnell '74–9 (*15*) D Kelly '79 (*4*). + 11*f 5m*. Also Rep I.

Field Figures P 9 Nov 1970 Royal, Nottingham *Ch* Glen Tetley *M* Stockhausen *SC* Nadine Baylis. '70 (*16*); '71 (*20*). 1 Bergsma '70–1 (*27*) O'Conaire '70–1 (*9*). 2 D Kelly '70–1 (*26*) Cooke '70–1 (*10*). 3 Derman '70–1 (*27*) Karras '70–1 (*9*). 4 Johnson '70–1 (*28*)

Kirkpatrick '70–1 (*8*). + 1*f 2m*. Also Rep I.

Fille Mal Gardée, La FPTC 9 Nov 1962 Hippodrome, Bristol. Cr Rep I. '62 (*17*); '63 (*62*); '64 (*48*); '65 (*61*); '66 (*5*); '67 (*34*); '68 (*23*); '69 (*22*); '70 (*24*); '76 (*49*); '77 (*40*); '78 (*51*); '79 (*6*). A:14. *Lise* Nerina '62–7 (*22*) Sibley '62–4 (*6*) Wells '62–'70 (*66*) Page '62CG–'64 (*7*) Park '62–'76 (*12*) Lane '63–7 (*24*) Grahame '63–'70 (*50*) Hayden '63 (*4*) Last '63–'78 (*101*) Aldous '67–'70 (*20*) Jenner '66–'77 (*8*) Vere '68 (*1*) Thorogood '69 (*2*) Wakelyn '70 (*2*) Tait '76–9 (*46*) Barbieri '76–9 (*36*) Samsova '76–8 (*17*) Kennedy '77–9 (*12*) Highwood '78–9 (*6*). *Colas* Blair '62–7 (*36*) MacLeary '62 (*3*) Gable '62–5 (*22*) Usher '62CG–'69 (*47*) Flindt '63 (*4*) Sherwood '63–8 (*29*) I Hamilton '63–4 (*19*) Usher-Sherwood '65 (*1*) Coleman '64–5 (*15*) Wall '65–'76 (*38*) J Madsen '65 (*2*) Cooke '65–'70 (*46*) Clarke '67–'70 (*28*) Mason '67–8 (*3*) Johnson '68–'70 (*4*) McGrath '70 (*3*) Jefferies '76 (*8*) Dubreuil '76–9 (*21*) D Kelly '76–9 (*39*) Myers '76–8 (*33*) Ashmole '76–9 (*27*) O'Brien '77–8 (*6*) Kilgour '77–9 (*8*). *Widow Simone* Holden '62–8 (*6*) Emblen '62–'78 (*220*) Gordon '63–'70 (*75*) Shaw '66–'77 (*30*) Mosaval '67–'70 (*16*) Morse '76–8 (*60*) Bintley '77–9 (*32*) Symons '77CG (*1*) Bonner '79 (*2*). *Alain* A Grant '62–8 (*10*) Britton '62–4 (*41*) Ruffell '62 (*5*) Alder '62–3 (*36*) Sale '63–7 (*76*) G Grant '64–'70 (*100*) Early '67–8 (*14*) Morse '69–'78 (*50*) Bertscher '76–8 (*71*) Bonner '76–9 (*37*) Bintley '79 (*2*).

Fille Mal Gardée, La pdd '72 (*1*). A:2. *Lise* Last *Colas* Johnson.

Flower Festival at Genzano pdd FPTC 27m Oct 1962 Princess, Torquay Cr Rep I. '62 (*16*); '63 (*48*); '66 (*14*); '67 (*14*); '73 (*28*); '74 (*9*); '75 (*1*). A:4. *f* Linden '62 (*6*) Page '62 (*5*) Parkinson '62 (*3*) Wells '62–3 (*15*) Grahame '63–7 (*19*) Wright '63 (*6*) Fracci '63 (*3*) Hayden '63 (*3*) Anderton '63–7 (*13*) Seymour '63 (*1*) Landon '66–7 (*11*) Cartwright '66–7 (*7*) Last '73–5 (*15*) Wade '73–4 (*20*) Tait '74 (*2*) Sibley '74 (*1*). *m* Doyle '62 (*8*) MacLeary '62 (*2*) Usher '62–3 (*6*) Gable '62–3 (*10*) Sherwood '63 (*16*) I Hamilton '63 (*16*) Gilpin '63 (*3*) Flindt '63 (*3*) Beaumont '66–7 (*16*) Clarke '66–7 (*7*) Ingleton '67 (*4*) Wall '67 (*1*) Johnson '73–4 (*10*) Bertscher '73–4 (*3*) Cooke '73 (*16*) Dubreuil '73–5 (*8*) Reeder '74 (*1*).

Four Temperaments, The FPTC 4 Oct 1976 sw Cr Rep I. '76 (*13*); '77 (*12*); '79 (*10*). *Melancholic* R Bailey '76–9 (*15*) Myers '76–9 (*20*). *Sanguinic f* Strike '76–9 (*18*) Tait '76–9 (*14*) Pet Miller '76–7 (*3*) *m* Ashmole '76–9 (*21*) Kilgour '76–7 (*7*) Reeder '77–9 (*7*). *Phlegmatic* Berg '76–7 (*16*) O'Brien '76–9 (*11*) Dubreuil '79 (*5*) D Kelly '79 (*3*). *Choleric* Gielgud '76–7 (*10*) Barbieri '76 (*4*) Lorrayne '76 (*6*) Highwood '77–9 (*5*) Strike '77 (*4*) Rowann '79 (*6*).

From Waking Sleep P 30 January 1970 RST *Ch* David Drew *M* Alan Hovhaness *SC* Ian

Mackintosh. '70 (*23*). *The Favoured* Johnson (*18*) Cooke (*5*). *His Awakening Self* Barbieri (*22*) Chapell (*1*). + 3*m* + *CdB*.

Game Piano P 12 May 1978 sw *Ch* Jonathan Thorpe *M* Prokofiev *SC* Zoltan Imre. '78 (*10*). 1 Barbieri (*10*). 2 D Kelly (*4*) Kilgour (*6*). 3 Reeder (*10*). + 4*m*.

Gemini FP 5 May 1977 sw *Ch* Glen Tetley *M* Hans Werner Henze orch Richard Blackford. *SC* Nadine Baylis. '77 (*14*). 1 Gielgud (*11*) Tait (*3*). 2 D Kelly (*14*). 3 Highwood (*12*) Strike (*2*). 4 Baker (*2*) Myers (*3*) Ashmole (*7*) Millington (*2*).

Giselle 'Peasant' pdd FP 6 Apr 1948 sw *Ch* Coralli *M* Adam/Burgmüller *C* William Chappell. '48 (*67*); '49 (*38*); '50 (*30*); '51 (*7*); '56 (*4*). A:2. *f* Lane '48–'51 (*60*) Fifield '48–'51 [*59*] Claire '48 [*3*] Pat Miller '48–'51 (*8*) Nerina '50 (*4*) Gorham '50 (*6*) Cox '56 (*4*). *m* Kersley '48–'50 [*62*] Boulton '48–'56 [*27*] MacMillan '48–9 [*22*] Trecu '48–'51 [*4*] Blair '49–'51 (*27*) Britton '51 (*2*). nr '48 June 16 m/e.

Giselle FPNP 18 Aug 1956 Plaza Porticada, Santander *Ch* after Coralli; from 1961 *Ch* Coralli/Perrot reproduced Sergeyev *Ch* Ashton ('Peasant' pdd Var *f*) *M* Adam *SC* Peter Rice*. '56 [*21*]; '57 (*48*); '58 (*43*); '63 (*11*); '64 (*34*); '65 (*37*); '66 (*30*); '67 (*14*). A:74. *Giselle* Nerina '56CG '56A '63–7 (*14*) Neil '56A–7 [*9*] Heaton '56–8 [*41*] Alexander '57–8 (*41*) Beriosova '58–'67 (*19*) Sibley '60A Grey '60A & '61A Fonteyn '61A '65 (*2*) Wells '63–7 (*38*) Page '63–5 (*7*) Linden '63 (*1*) Seymour '64–5 (*3*) Wright '64–5 (*13*) Anderton '65–6 (*18*) Aldous '66–7 (*10*). *Count Albrecht* Rassine '56A. Field '56 [*1*] Zolan '56–8 [*34*] Alex Bennett '56–'63 [*51*] MacLeary '58–'67 (*24*) Ashbridge '58–'61A (*1*) Doyle '60A '66 (*2*) Hynd '63–4 (*6*) Farley '63–7 (*42*) Blair '63–7 (*21*) Juresha '64–5 (*13*) Nureyev '65 (*2*) Wall '65–7 (*14*) Gable '65CG–6 (*4*) Musil '66 (*3*). *Myrtha* Hill '56 [*1*] Lee '56–8 [*46*] Lakier '57–8 (*23*) E Thomas '57–8 (*10*) O'Conaire '63–5 (*39*) Layland '63–5 (*17*) Landon '64–7 (*30*) Beckley '64 (*3*) Parkinson '65–6 (*2*) Saunders '65–7 (*22*) Cartwright '65–7 (*13*). nr 1956 Autumn tour. *NB* Act II produced before Act I *see* below. *NB* ROH '58 *SC* Bailey as Rep. I 1946. On tour Japan '61 Cr as Rep I *Giselle* 1960 including *SC* Bailey. Subsequent Cr on tour vary between CG Cr and Cr as above. *Seems that TC modified CG Pr on tour, with SC Rice, but used SC Bailey ROH '66. CG principals on tour used Bailey costumes.

Giselle Act II FP 28 July 1956 Jardines de Generalife, Granada Cr as above *SC* nc. A:3. *Giselle* Heaton A. *Albrecht* Field A.

Giselle Act I 'Peasant' pdd. A:7.

Giselle FPNP 15 May 1968 ROH *Ch* Coralli/Perrot; *Ch* '74 Petipa after Coralli/Perrot revised Sergeyev. *M* Adam *SC* Peter Farmer *Pr* Peter Wright. '68 (*23*); '69 (*45*); '70 (*6*); '74

(23); '75 (58); '76 (23); '77 (23); '78 (54). A:23. *Giselle* Wells '68–'70 (17) Anderton '68–9 (12) Barbieri '68–'78 (84) Aldous '68–'70 (17) Beriosova '69 (1) Ruanne '69 (4) Thorogood '69–'70 (3) Lorrayne '74–8 (43) Tait '74–8 (45) Collier '74–5 (5) Mason '75 (2) Park '75 (4) Makarova '75 (1) Seymour '75 (3) Evans '75–8 (8) Samsova '77–8 (7). *Albrecht* Wall '68–'75 (14) Johnson '68–'74 (13) Mead '68 (2) Beaumont '68–9 (16) Clarke '68–9 (10) McGrath '68–'70 (18) MacLeary '69 (3) Davel '69 (3) Usher '69 (3) D Kelly '70–8 (49) Dubreuil '74–8 (60) Coleman '74CG–5 (2) Jefferies '74–6 (25) Dye '75 (3) Dowell '75 (1) Nureyev '75 (2) O'Brien '76 (2) D Kelly/ O'Brien '77 (1) Ashmole '77–8 (24) Myers '77–8 (6). *Myrtha* Grahame '68–'70 (23) Landon '68–9 (11) Anderton '68A–'69 (15) Wade '68–'75 (32) Southam '69 (10) Strike '74–8 (56) Lorrayne '74–6 (9) Highwood '74–8 (43) Mason '74–6 (6) Parkinson '75 (7) Derman '75 (1) Gielgud '75–7 (16) Rowann '77–8 (14) Stanley '77–8 (4) Powell '78 (2). *Also* Rep I.

Gods Go a'Begging, The FPTB 10 June 1946 Cr Rep I. '46 (37); '47 (9); '48 (10); '49 (13). *A Serving Maid* Heaton '46–8 (47) Fifield '48–9 (10) Pat Miller '48–9 (12). *A Shepherd* Kersley '46–9 (36) Britton '46–7 (22) Zullig '48–9 (11).

Grand Tour, The P 10 Feb 1971 Royal, Norwich *Ch* Joe Layton *M* Noël Coward arr Hershy Kay *SC* John Conklin. '71 (51); '72 (26); '73 (4); '74 (28). A:11. *American Lady* Lorrayne '71–4 (75)· Merry '71–3 (24) Laurence '74 (10). *Steward* Jefferies '71–4 (86) Morse '71–4 (23). *Gertie Lawrence* O'Conaire '71–2 (41) Barbieri '71–4 (38) Ruanne '71–3 (11) Strike '74 (19). *Noël Coward* Sherwood '71–4 (29) Cooke '71–3 (55) Dubreuil '74 (25). *Mary Pickford* Wells '71–4 (34) Last '71–4 (52) Tait '72–4 (14) C Hill '72A (2) Pet Miller '74 (7). *Douglas Fairbanks* Clarke '71–3 (44) McGrath '71–4 (42) Kilgour '74 (23). + 3*f* 5*m*.

Great Detective, The P 21 Jan 1953 sw *Ch* Margaret Dale *M* Richard Arnell *SC* Brian Robb. '53 (23). *The Great Detective/The Infamous Professor* MacMillan (23). *His Friend, the Doctor* Holden (23). + 18*f* 13*m*.

Grosse Fuge FP 29m Apr 1972 Odeon, Golders Green *Ch/C* Hans van Manen *M* Beethoven *S* Jean-Paul Vroom. '72 (29); '73 (25) '74 (5); '75 (11); '76 (3); '78 (6); '79 (8). A:8. 4*f* from: Ruanne '72–3 (42) Barbieri '72–9 (71) C Hill '72 (9) Strike '72–9 (74) Homji '72–5 (40) Laurence '72–3 (10) Merry '72–3 (5) Porter '72–3 (9) Durant '72–3 (10) Evans '74 (5) Goodier '73 (9) Tait '74–9 (30) Highwood '75–9 (23) Katrak '79 (3) Kennedy '79 (3) Lucas '79 (3) Crow '79 (2). 4*m* from: Johnson '72–5 (30) Cooke '72–3 (42) Jefferies '72–5 (45) Clarke '72–3 (23) Porter '72–4 (39) Myers '72–9 (39) Vardon '72–9 (36) Morse

'72–9 (37) Dubreuil '74–9 (26) D Kelly '76–9 (16) Ashmole '78 (9) Kilgour '79 (5) Beckett '79 (1).

Hamlet FPTC 4 Nov 1958 Empire, Sydney Cr Rep I. '59 (3); '64 (11); '65 (12); '66 (3). A:32. *Hamlet* Helpmann '58A. MacLeary '59 (3) Farley '64–6 (20) Davel '65–6 (6). *King of Denmark* Ed Miller '58A G Aitken '59 (3) Ashbridge '64–5 (8) Grater '64–6 (14) Ryder '65–6 (4). *Gravedigger* Beale '58A Alder '59 (3) Emblen '64–6 (10) Mosaval '64A–6 (16). *Gertrude* Mossford '58A '59 (3) Humphreys '64–6 (26). *Ophelia* Linden '58A '66 (1) Heaton '58A '59 (3) Anderton '64–6 (22) Ruanne '65–6 (3).

Harlequin in April P 8 May 1951 sw *Ch* Cranko *M* Richard Arnell *SC* John Piper. '51 (13); '52 (22); '53 (11); '54 (10); '55 (1). A:51. *Pierrot* Holden '51–4 (45) McAlpine '51–2 (5) Britton '53–5 (7). *Harlequin* Blair '51–3 (25) Trecu '51–5 (32). *Columbine* Pat Miller '51–5 (51) Bruce '51–2 (3) Fifield '53 (3). + 10*f* 8*m*.

Haunted Ballroom, The FPTB 7 Jan 1947 sw Cr Rep I '47 (14); '48 (75); '49 (19); '50 (26); '51 (7); '52 (6); '53 (4); '54 (19); '56 (10); '57 (22). A:52. *The Master of Treginnis* Carter '47 (14) Poole '48–'54 (107) A Burke '48 (27) Zullig '48–9 (10) Helpmann '50 (1) Vernon '53A–4 (11) Zolan '57 (10) Alex Bennett '57 (12). *The Young Treginnis* Ward '47 (13) D Field '47 (1) Rands-Trevor '48–9 (11) Surtees '48 (62) Vail '48–'51 (26) Swanson '49–'50 (17) Page '50–2 (14) Fonteyn '50 (1) Carter '52A (2) White '53A–4 (10) King '53A Mosaval '54 (4) Reece '54 (9) P Barnes '57 (6) Cox '57 (16). *Alicia* Brae '47–8 (18) Farron '47 (1) Pat Miller '48–'54 (46) Claire '48–'53 (83) May '50 (1) Beriosova '51A '52 (3) O'Reilly '53–4 (3) Neil '54–7 [27] Heaton '57 (9) Tempest '57 (1). nr 1956 Autumn tour.

Hermanas, Las FP 2 June 1971 sw *Ch* MacMillan *M* Frank Martin *SC* Nicholas Georgiadis. '71 (24); '72 (23); '73 (5); '74 (6); '76 (3); 78 (5) '79 (3). A:5. *The Man* Sherwood '71 (10) Cooke '71–3 (22) Davel '71–2 (9) McGrath '71–4 (17) Dubreuil '74A '78–9 (3) D Kelly '76–9 (8). *The Eldest Sister* Seymour '71–8 (14) Ruanne '71–3 (22) Lorrayne '71–9 (28) O'Conaire '71 (2) Samsova '78–9 (3). *The Youngest Sister* Barbieri '71–9 (43) Chapell '71–2 (14) Trounson '71–2 (4) Homji '74 (5) Aitken '78–9 (3). + 4*f*.

Homage to Chopin P 22 Feb 1980 sw *Ch* David Bintley *M* Andrzej Panufnik *SC* Mike Becket 1 Ashmole 2 Evans 3 Katrak + 4*f*.

House of Birds P 26 May 1955 sw *Ch* MacMillan revised 1963 *M* Frederico Mompou arr/orch John Lanchbery *SC* Nicholas Georgiadis, revised 1963. '55 (56); '56 (45); '57 (40); '63 (22); '64 (11); '67 (17); '69 (11). A:20. *The Lovers* (From '67 *The Girl/The Boy*) *f* Lane '55–'67 (23) Bruce '55 (16) Neil '55–7 (53) Bolton '56–7 (41) Heaton '56 (13) Farriss '57 (3) Wells '63–7 (20) Anderton '63–9 (23)

Last '67–9 (5) Thorogood '67–9 (5). *m* Poole '55 (23) Boulton '55–7 (87) Lawrence '55–6 (16) Britton '57 (15) Gable '63 (6) I Hamilton '63–4 (21) Sherwood '63–4 (6) Clarke '67–9 (4) Wall '67 (5) Cooke '67–9 (19) *The Bird Woman* Tempest '55–7 (73) M Hill '55–7 (44) Blakeney '57 (12) Lakier '57 (12) Grahame '63–4 (13) Layland '63–4 (20) Koshley '67 (7) Saunders '67 (6) Merry '67–9 (10) Southam '69 (5). + 6*f* 6*m* (From '63: 12*f* 13*m*).

Ile des Sirènes FP 19 Sept 1952 sw *Ch* Alfred Rodrigues *M* Debussy *SC* Loudon Sainthill. '52 (7); '53 (8); '54 (1); '56 [18]; '57 (5). A:12. *The Mariner (Palinurus)* Blair '52–3 (12) Britton '53–7 [5] MacLeary '57 (4). *Siren* Fifield '52–3 (6) Lane '52–4 (10) Tempest '57 (3) Heaton '57 (2). + 6*f*. nr 1956 Autumn tour.

In a Summer Garden P 26 Oct 1972 sw *Ch* Ronald Hynd *M* Delius *SC* Peter Docherty. '72 (22); '73 (16). *f* Lorrayne '72–3 (34) Barbieri '72–3 (4). *m* McGrath '72–3 (34) Myers '72–3 (4). + 2*f* 2*m*.

In the Beginning P 17 January 1969 RST *Ch* Geoffrey Cauley *M* Poulenc *SC* Peter Unsworth. '69 (42); '70 (23). 1 Wall '69 (23) Cooke '69–'70 (37) Parker '70 (5). 2 Thorogood '69–'70 (45) Chapell '69–'70 (14) Lorraine '70 (6). 3 Aldous '69–'70 (35) Merry '69–'70 (23) Tait '70 (7). 4 Davel '69–'70 (43) Parker '69–'70 (17) Bart '70 (5). + 2*f*.

Intimate Letters P 10 Oct 1978 sw *Ch* Lynn Seymour *M* Janáček; sound collage Bob Downes *SC* Nicholas Georgiadis *Scenario* Gillian Freeman. '78 (3); '79 (3). *The Host* Wicks '78–9 (6). *The Hostess* Powell '78–9 (6). *The Woman* Samsova '78–9 (6). *Her Husband* Dubreuil '78–9 (5) Kilgour '78 (1). *The Man She Loves* Ashmole '78–9 (6). *The Man Who Loves Her* D Kelly '78–9 (6). *His Wife* Laurence '78 (3) Parsons '79 (3). *The Rival* Stanley '78–9 (6). + 4*f* 3*m*.

Intrusion FP 17 January 1969 RST *Ch* David Drew *M* Schubert *SC* Ian Mackintosh/Vincent Yorke. '69 (31). 1 Conley (31). 2 Clarke (12) Vlasic (9) Parker (10). 3 Ruanne (20) Hunwin (3) Tait (8). 4 Last (25) Wade (6). + 4*m*. P RBCh*G* 30 Mar 1968 by RBS students.

Invitation, The P 10 Nov 1960 New, Oxford *Ch* MacMillan *M* Matyas Seiber *SC* Nicholas Georgiadis. '60 (8); '61 (30); '62 (13); '64 (28); '65 (2); '66 (2); '67 (8); '74 (22); '75 (3). A:17. *The Girl* Seymour '60–4 (27) Wells '61–7 (43) Spira '62 (2) Ruanne '64–7 (19) Tait '74–5 (16) Homji '74–5 (9). *Her Cousin* Gable '60–4 (42) I Hamilton '61–4 (14) Farley '64 (12) Wall '64–6 (15) Davel '67 (6) Powell '67 (2) Jefferies '74–5 (15) Dye '74–5 (10). *The Wife* Heaton '60–1 (24) Jolaini '61–5 (32) Remington '61–2 (10) Grahame '62A '64–7 (17) Linden '65 (1) Cartwright '66–7 (4) Humphreys '66 (1) Karras '67 (2) Lorrayne '74–5 (15) Barbieri '74–5 (10). *The Husband* Doyle '60–4 (37) Alex Bennett '61–2 (18) Ashbridge '64–5 (15) Grater '64–7 (21) D

Kelly '74–5 (*14*) Dubreuil '74–5 (*10*) Killar '74 (*1*). + *17f 11m*; later *13f 9m*.

Job – TC in CG production at ROH only. *See* Rep I Job 1970.

Khadra P 27 May 1946 sw *Ch* Celia Franca *M* Sibelius *SC* Honor Frost. '46 (*51*); '47 (*58*); '48 (*18*); '49 (*17*); '51 (*5*); '52 (*4*). A:9. *Khadra* O'Reilly '46–'52 (*104*) Nerina '46–7 (*33*) Farrance '48–9 (*6*) Fifield '48 (*9*) Page '51A '52 (*1*). *The Lover* Kersley '46–9 (*114*) Hogan '46–'51 (*22*) Zullig '48–9 (*13*) Blair '52 (*4*). *His Lady* Heaton '46–7 (*80*) Harman '46 (*11*) Hamby '47–8 (*36*) Cadzow '49 (*14*) Lane '49–'52 (*7*) Beriosova '51–2 (*5*). + *6f 8m*.

Knight Errant P 25 Nov 1968 Opera House, Manchester *Ch* Tudor *M* Richard Strauss *SC* Stefanos Lazaridis. '68 (*6*); '69 (*38*). *Chevalier d'amour* Davel '68–9 (*30*) Wall '69 (*12*) McGrath '69 (*2*). *A Woman of Consequence* Landon '68–9 (*24*) Southam '69 (*20*). *Ladies of Position:* 1 Thorogood '68–9 (*29*) Inkin '69 (*15*). 2 Barbieri '68–9 (*31*) Conley '69 (*13*). 3 Anderton '68–9 (*26*) Ruanne '69 (*18*). + *5f 13m*.

Lac des Cygnes, Le Act II FPTB 16 May 1949 Arts, Cambridge *Ch* Ivanov *Pr* Sergeyev, revised 1951 *M* Tchaikovsky *SC* Hugh Stevenson. '49 (*36*); '50 (*45*); '51 (*24*); '52 (*25*); '53 (*31*); '54 (*11*); '56 (*70*); '57 (*28*); '58 (*41*). A:53. *Odette* Fifield '49–'53 (*69*) Gorham '49–'50 (*6*) Beriosova '50–8 (*47*) Nerina '50–'8 (*8*) Fonteyn '51 (*1*) Lane '52–4 (*33*) Tempest '53–7 [*53*] Heaton '56–8 [*58*] Lee '58 (*6*) Alexander '58 (*9*). *Prince Siegfried* Poole '49–'54 (*89*) Hogan '49–'52 (*33*) Somes '50–1 (*2*) Lunnon '51 (*3*) Blair '52–8 (*12*) MacMillan '52–4 (*24*) Gill '52–4 (*12*) Field '56–7 [*37*] Zolan '56–8 [*32*] Alex Bennett '56–8 [*13*]. nr '56 Autumm tour. MacLeary '57–8 (*33*) Ashbridge '58 (*1*) NB Scenery destroyed Hanley 2 June '49; from 13 June – Sept '49 used Hurry scenery from CG.

Lac des Cygnes, Le Act II pdt. '49 (*7*); '56 (*1*). *Odette* Fifield '49 (*6*) Gorham '49 (*1*) Fonteyn '56 (*1*). *Prince Siegfried* Poole '49 (*3*) Hogan '49 (*4*) Somes '56 (*1*).

Lac des Cygnes, Le (Swan Lake from Oct '61 FP 27 June 1958 ROH *Ch* Petipa/Ivanov; *Ch* Ashton (I: Pas de Six. III: Neapolitan) *M* Tchaikovsky *SC* Leslie Hurry *Pr* Sergeyev revised de Valois. '58 (*1*); '59 (*66*); '60 (*28*); '61 (*19*); '62 (*79*); '63 (*39*). A:94. *Odette/Odile* Jackson '58 (*1*) Linden '59–'63 (*39*) Seymour '58A '59–'62 (*25*) Nerina '59–'63 (*22*) Beriosova '59–'63 (*15*) Page '59–'63 (*21*) Alexander '59A–'60 (*17*) Wells '60–3 (*41*) Grey 60A & 61A '62 (*2*) Grahame '61–3 (*32*) Sibley '61–2 (*4*) Parkinson '62 (*3**) Lane '62–3 (*8*). *Prince Siegfried* Chatfield '58 (*1*) Blair '59–'63 (*24*) MacLeary '59–'63 (*20*) Ashbridge '59–'63 (*34*) Hynd '59–'63 (*21*) Doyle '59–'63 (*59*) Burne '59–'60 (*3*) Gable '60–3 (*39*) Lawrence '62 (*3**) Alex Bennett

'62–3 (*19*) Rosson '62 (*3*) I Hamilton '63 (*6*). *with RBS at CG '60.

Lac des Cygnes, Le Act II. '58 (*1*); '62 (*1*); '64 (*33*); '65 (*19*); '66 (*7*); '68 (*1*). A:21. *Odette* Heaton '58 (*1*) Fonteyn '62 (*1*) Grahame '64–6 (*28*) Page '64 (*2*) Beriosova '64–6 (*3*) Seymour '64–6 (*3*) Wright '64–5 (*13*) Wells '65 (*4*) Linden '65 (*2*) Landon '66–8 (*4*) Parkinson '66 (*1*). *Prince Siegfried* MacLeary '58–'66 (*4*) Blair '62–4 (*2*) Ashbridge '64–5 (*23*) I Hamilton '64 (*3*) Hynd '64 (*1*) Gable '64–6 (*3*) Yuresha '64–5 (*13*) Sherwood '65 (*4*) Farley '65–6 (*4*) Beaumont '66–8 (*4*) Rosson '66 (*1*).

Lac des Cygnes, Le On tour abroad only: Act I pdt (*1*). Act II pdd (*1*). Act III (*5*). Act III pdt (*1*).

Lac des Cygnes, Le from 1965 *see* Swan Lake

Lady and the Fool, The P 25 Feb 1954 New, Oxford *Ch* Cranko *M* Verdi arr Charles Mackerras *SC* Richard Beer. '54 (*46*); '55 (*29*); '65 (*22*); '66 (*19*); '67 (*15*); '72 (*56*); '73 (*34*); '74 (*3*); '76 (*14*); '77 (*14*). A:36. *Moondog* MacMillan '54 (*36*) Poole '54–5 (*25*) Wright '54–5 (*14*) Grater '65–7 (*49*) Hynd '66 (*1*) Beaumont '67 (*6*) Clarke '72–3 (*13*) Cooke '72–3 (*22*) MacLeary '72–3 (*17*) Davel '72 (*9*) Killar '72–7 (*34*) McGrath '72–4 (*11*) O'Brien '76–7 (*9*) D Kelly '77 (*5*) E Madsen '77 (*1*). *Bootface* Mosaval '54–'73 (*137*) Hurd '54 (*11*) Reece '54 (*1*) Emblen '65–7 (*24*) Morse '72–7 (*40*) Bertscher '72–7 (*37*) Fletcher '72 (*2*). *La Capricciosa* Pat Miller '54–5 (*53*) Page '54A–5 (*22*) Linden '65 (*2*) Grahame '65–7 (*22*) Anderton '65–7 (*28*) Beriosova '66–'73 (*12*) Landon '67 (*3*) Lorrayne '72–7 (*37*) Ruanne '72–3 (*24*) Barbieri '72–7 (*44*) Gielgud '77 (*3*) Strike '77 (*2*). + *7f 9m*. NB From '65 incorporates revisions made CG '55. *Also* Rep I.

Lady and the Fool, The Grand Pas. A:1.

Lazarus FP 5 Dec 1969 Grand, Leeds *Ch* Geoffrey Cauley *M* Ernest Bloch *SC* nc. '69 (*6*); '70 (*22*). A:1. *Jesus* Davel '69–'70 (*16*) Bart '69–'70 (*12*). *Mary Magdalene* Anderton '69–'70 (*18*) Ruanne '69–'70 (*9*) Karras '70 (*1*). *Lazarus* Emblen '69–'70 (*15*) Morse '69–'70 (*13*). *Mary Humphreys* '69–'70 (*18*) Castle '69 (*2*) Woodward '70 (*8*). *Martha* Karras '69–'70 (*18*) G Sibley '69 (*2*) Merry '70 (*8*). *Conscience* Gordon '69–'70 (*28*). + *6m*. P RBCG 30 Mar 1968.

Lilac Garden FPTC 12 Nov 1970 Royal, Nottingham *Cr* Rep I. *S* Elisabeth Dalton '70 (*11*); '71 (*33*). *Caroline* Barbieri '70–1 (*23*) O'Conaire '70 (*6*) Conley '71 (*3*) Ruanne '71 (*10*) Chapell '71 (*2*). *Her Lover* D Kelly '71–1 (*13*) Clarke '70–1 (*16*) McGrath '71 (*15*). *The Man She Must Marry* Grater '70 (*8*) Davel '70–1 (*20*) Drew '71 (*5*) Bart '71 (*11*). *An Episode in His Past* Derman '70–1 (*7*) Karras '70–1 (*17*) Lorrayne '71 (*17*) O'Conaire '71 (*3*).

Lord of Burleigh, The solo. *see* Rep I.

Lulu P 2 June 1976 sw *Ch* Jack Carter *M* Milhaud *SC* Norman McDowell. '76 (*17*). *Lulu* Park (*6*) Tait (*8*) Highwood (*3*). *The Ringmaster/Jack the Ripper* Jefferies (*4*) Morse (*13*). + *2f 6m* + *CdB*.

Maids, The FP 19 Oct 1971 Wimbledon Theatre *Ch* Herbert Ross *M* Milhaud *SC* William Pitkin. '71 (*2*); '72 (*26*); '73 (*6*); '77 (*3*). A:3. *Claire* Johnson '71–3 (*16*) Morse '72–3 (*18*) Reeder '77 (*3*). *Solange* Cooke '71–3 (*25*) Jefferies '72–3 (*9*) D Kelly '77 (*3*). *Madame* Lorrayne '71–7 (*18*) Ruanne '72–3 (*14*) M Porter '72–3 (*5*). *Monsieur* Bart '71–3 (*24*) P Porter '72–3 (*10*) Wicks '77 (*3*).

Mam'zelle Angot FPTC 31 Jan 1968 RST *Cr* Rep I. '68 (*26*); '69 (*9*). *Mam'zelle Angot* Aldous '68–9 (*15*) Last '68–9 (*13*) Thorogood '68–9 (*7*). *A Barber* Emblen '68–9 (*16*) G Grant '68–9 (*19*). *The Caricaturist* Wall '68–9 (*12*) Clarke '68–9 (*21*) Cooke '69 (*1*) Beaumont '69 (*1*). *The Aristocrat* Grahame '68–9 (*26*) Ruanne '68–9 (*9*).

Mardi Gras P 26 Nov 1946 sw *Ch* Andrée Howard *M* Leonard Salzedo *SC* Hugh Stevenson. '46 (*5*); '47 (*13*); '48 (*2*); '49 (*3*). *The Girl* Heaton '46–8 (*15*) O'Reilly '47–9 (*8*). *A Boy* Britton '46–8 (*20*) Trecu '49 (*3*). *A Reveller in White* Kersley '46–9 (*22*) Cranko '49 (*1*). *A Circus Dancer* Nerina '46–8 (*16*) Nelson '46–7 (*3*) Fifield '48 (*1*) Gorham '49 (*3*). + *10f 9m*.

Marguerite and Armand see Rep I.

Meadow of Proverbs P 16 March 1979 Hippodrome, Birmingham *Ch* David Bintley *M* Milhaud *SC* Mike Becket. '79 (*26*). *Pas de guitare f* Tait (*19*) Rowann (*7*). *m* Dubreuil (*19*) Purnell (*7*). *Polichinelle* Morse (*18*) Bonner (*8*). *Death Stalks the Tavern* Reeder (*19*) J Smith '79 (*5*) Webb '79 (*1*). *Souvenir de Rio f* Lorrayne (*14*) C Williams (*9*) Strike (*3*). *m* as *Pas de guitare*. + *5f 7m*.

Migration P 16 Mar 1973 Royal, York *Ch* Ashley Killar *M* Franck *SC* nc. '73 (*2*). 1 Ruanne (*2*). 2 Strike (*2*). 3 Way (*2*). 4 Durant (*2*). 5 *m* Porter (*2*). 6 Laurence (*2*). 7 Parker (*2*).

Monotones FPTC 28 May 1968 Hessisches Staatstheater, Wiesbaden *Cr* Rep I. '68 (*18*); '69 (*7*); '72 (*7*). A:23. *Trois Gnossiennes 2f* from: Wells '68A–9 (*7*) Aldous '68A–9 (*6*) Thorogood '68–9 (*18*) Last '68–'72 (*26*) Evans '72 (*7*). *m* Wall '68A–9 (*4*) Coleman '68 (*2*) Shaw '68 (*4*) Cooke '68–'72 (*21*) Johnson '69 (*1*). *Trois Gymnopédies f* Grahame '68A–9 (*14*) Landon '68–9 (*11*) Lorrayne '72 (*7*). *2m* from: Clarke '68A–'72 (*8*) Davel '68A–9 (*24*) Ingleton '68A (*17*) Beaumont '68–9 (*3*) McGrath '72 (*7*) Jefferies '72 (*2*) D Kelly '72 (*3*).

Monotones No 2 FPTC 11m Feb 1971 Royal, Norwich *Cr* Rep I. '71 (*49*); '72 (*9*); '73 (*1*). A:5. *f* Lorrayne '71–3 (*48*) Bergsma '71 (*4*) O'Conaire '72 (*7*). *2m* from: D Kelly '71 (*20*)

Drew '71 (*20*) McGrath '71–3 (*32*) O'Brien '71–3 (*11*) Clarke '71–2 (*16*) Davel '71–2 (*10*) Jefferies '71 (*9*).

Napoli Divertissement FPTC 27m Oct 1962 Princess', Torquay Cr Rep I. '62 (16); '63 (46); '66 (14); '67 (14). *4f* from: Williams '62–7 (*46*) Anderton '62–3 (*31*) Wells '62–3 (*7*) O'Conaire '62–3 (*36*) Maden '62–3 (*37*) Grahame '62–3 (*13*) Maitland '62 (*3*) Robinson '62 (*7*) Layland '63 (*24*) Spira '63 (*4*) Thorogood '63 (*3*) Saunders '63–7 (*26*) Last '63–7 (*48*) Lane '63 (*6*) Starr '63 (*5*) Holmes '66–7 (*13*) Ruanne '66 (*15*) Cunliffe '66 (*6*) Conley '66–7 (*13*) Wade '66–7 (*9*) Barbieri '66–7 (*6*) Karras '67 (*2*). *2m* (from '63 May *3m*) from: Sherwood '62–3 (*23*) Sale '62–7 (*57*) Farley '62 (*27*) Gable '62–3 (*5*) Alder '63 (*13*) Coleman '63 (*16*) Emblen '63–7 (*34*) Wall '63 (*8*) Johnson '66–7 (*28*) Bertscher '66–7 (*11*) Cooke '66–7 (*15*) Powell '66–7 (*4*).

Outsider, The P 16 Mar 1978 Hippodrome. Birmingham *Ch* David Bintley *M* Josef Boháč *SC* Mike Becket. '78 (13). *Dariol* Morse (*13*). *Renée* Strike (*13*). *Meursault* **1** Wicks (*13*) **2** Millington (*10*) M Francis (*3*). **3** Berg (*13*) **4** Vardon (*13*). *A Transvestite* Reeder (*13*). + *6f 7m*.

Overture P 8 Feb 1971 Royal, Norwich *Ch* Joe Layton *M* Leonard Bernstein *C* John Conklin. '71 (40). **1** Tait (*25*) Linton (*2*) Last (*13*). **2** Vere (*26*) Merry (*13*) Inkin (*1*). **3** Clarke (*24*) Drew (*8*) Sherwood (*8*). **4** Sleep (*33*) Johnson (*1*) Mosaval (*6*). **5** Johnson (*7*) Cooke (*26*) Kirkpatrick (*7*).

O.W. P 22 Feb 1972 sw *Ch* Joe Layton *M* William Walton *SC* John Conklin. '72 (17). *Marquis of Queensberry* Cooke (*17*). *Servant/Young Chap* Jefferies (*17*). *Sphinx* Lorrayne (*11*) Ruanne (*6*). *Oscar Wilde* Clarke (*7*) Gordon (*8*). *O.W.* Somes (*9*) Clegg (*8*). *Constance* Barbieri (*10*) C Hill (*7*). *Bosie* Johnson (*17*). + *5f 10m*.

Pandora P 30 January 1976 RST *Ch* David Morse *M* Roberto Gerhard arr David Atherton *S* nc *C* Peter Farmer. '76 (9). *Prometheus* Reeder (*6*) Bertscher (*1*) Owen (*2*). *Zeus* Jefferies (*7*) O'Brien (*2*). *Pandora* Tait (*9*). *Epemetheus* Dubreuil (*9*). + *6f 6m*.

Papillon FP 7 Feb 1980 Grand, Leeds *Ch* Ronald Hynd *M* Offenbach arr/orch John Lanchbery *SC* Peter Docherty. *Papillon* Barbieri. *The Shah* Jefferies. *Hamza* Dubreuil. *Bijahn* Myers. *Hamza transformed* Stanley. + *15f 2m* + *CdB*.

Paquita FP 17 Apr 1980 Pavilion, Bournemouth *Ch* Petipa *Pr* Samsova *M* Minkus *SC* Peter Farmer. **1** Samsova. **2** Ashmole. **3** Highwood. **4** Tait. **5** Kennedy. **6** Barbieri. + *CdB*.

Parures P 21 Jan 1948 sw *Ch* Anthony Burke *M* Tchaikovsky *SC* Vivienne Kernot. '48 (41); '49 (5). **1** Fifield '48–9 (*46*) **2** Kersley '48–9 (*46*). **3** Lane '48 (*41*) Pat Miller (*2*) Claire '48 (*3*). **4** Poole '48–9 (*33*) A Burke '48 (*13*). + *8f 4m*.

Pastorale P 19 Dec 1950 sw *Ch* Cranko *M* Mozart *SC* Hugh Stevenson. '50 (2); '51 (23); '52 (20); '53 (16). A:33. *Phillida* Pat Miller '50–3 (*42*) Lane '51–3 (*19*). *Corydon* Trecu '51–3 (*49*) Gillies '51 (*4*) MacMillan '51–3 (*8*). *Lamilia* Beriosova '50–2 (*21*) Claire '51–2 (*8*) Hill '52–3 (*17*) Neil '52–3 (*11*) Nisbet '52 (*2*) Tempest '53 (*2*). *Helanthus* Poole '50–3 (*27*) Gill '51–3 (*31*) D Davies '52 (*3*). *Damon* Blair '50–3 (*30*) Wright '51–2 (*5*) MacMillan '52–3 (*14*) Britton '52–3 (*12*). *Diaphenia* Fifield '50–3 (*28*) Harrop '51–2 (*14*) Page '52–3 (*19*). + *2f 2m*.

Patineurs, Les FPTB 23m Apr 1955 sw Cr Rep I. '55 (66); '56 [73]; '57 (50); '59 (7); '61 (7); '62 (5); '63 (32); '64 (32); '65 (18); '69 (30); '70 (20); '71 (56); '72 (26); '73 (28); '74 (12); '75 (5); '76 (1); '77 (9); '78 (15); '79 (14). A:104. *Variation 'Blue Boy'* Britton '55–'64 [*75*] Boulton '55–9 [*52*] Mosaval '55–'72 [*97*] Trevor '55–7 [*8*] Gilpin '61CG (*3*) Sale '61–5 (*20*) Coleman '63–5 (*15*) Shaw '64–5 (*5*) Usher '60A '63–9 (*17*) Bertscher '64–'79 [*102*] Hooper '69–'70 (*21*) Sleep '71–8 (*27*) Johnson '71–3 (*22*) Fletcher '72 (*1*) Reeder '73–9 (*22*). *Pas de deux f* Page '55 (*5*) Pat Miller '55 (*1*) Bruce '55 (*35*) M Hill '55–7 [*60*] Alexander '56–9 [*48*] Lee '57 (*23*) Seymour '59–61 (*5*) Anderton '61–4 (*25*) Remington '62 (*1*) Grahame '63–'70 (*72*) O'Conaire '63–'71 (*48*) Ruanne '69–'73 (*38*) Barbieri '71–3 (*16*) Lorrayne '71–9 (*46*) C Hill '72 (*5*) Evans '73–5 (*16*) Porter '73 (*3*) Wade '73–4 (*6*) Wells '73–4 (*3*) Aitken '75–9 (*13*) Highwood '77–9 (*11*) Rowann '78–9 (*7*). *m* Poole '55 (*9*) Zolan '55–7 [*73*] Wright '55 (*9*) MacLeary '55–'76 [*65*] Alex Bennett '56–'63 [*53*] Doyle '61 (*5*) Grater '63–'70 (*69*) Ashbridge '63–5 (*12*) I Hamilton '64 (*1*) Beaumont '69 (*2*) McGrath '69–'73 (*54*) Cooke '69 (*3*) Davel '71–2 (*19*) Drew '71 (*13*) Clarke '71–3 (*28*) Jefferies '72–5 (*17*) Myers '73–9 (*11*) Dubreuil '73–8 (*14*) Kilgour '74–9 (*12*) D Kelly '75 (*2*) Purnell '77–9 (*16*). *Entrée 'Blue Girls' f* 2 from: Neil '55–6 [*51*] Tempest '55–6 [*37*] Cox '55–7 [*84*] White '55–7 [*76*] Bolton '55–7 [*75*] Farriss '57–9 (*11*) Lakier '57 (*8*) Alexander '58A '59 (*4*) Anderton '59 (*3*) Moncur '59 (*3*) Wells '61 (*7*) Debden '61–'70 (*85*) Spira '62–3 (*15*) Maitland '62A (*1*) Grahame '63–'73 (*99*) Thorogood '64–'70 (*26*) J Williams '65 (*3*) Aldous '69–'70 (*16*) Wade '69–'74 (*16*) Merry '69–'72 (*32*) Tait '70–9 (*83*) Wakelyn '70 (*3*) Vere '71 (*13*) C Hill '71–2 (*34*) Evans '71–5 (*31*) Strike '71–9 (*56*) Pet Miller '73–9 (*37*) Lincoln '75 (*1*) Styles '77 (*5*) Kennedy '78–9 (*14*) Aitken '78 (*2*). nr '56 Autumn Tour. *Also:* Rep I.

Pineapple Poll P 13 Mar 1951 *Ch* Cranko *M* Arthur Sullivan arr Charles Mackerras *SC* Osbert Lancaster. '51 (28); '52 (49); '53 (38); '54 (41); '55 (78); '56 (51); '57 (54); '58 (43); '59 (3); '60 (27); '61 (6); '62 (19); '63 (13); '65 (15); '66 (29); '67 (12); '71 (56); '72 (53); '73 (35); '74 (22); '75 (18); '76 (1); '77 (19); '79 (15). A:188. *Pineapple Poll* Fifield '51–5 (*57*) Harrop '51 (*3*) Lane '51–5 (*37*) Pat Miller '52A–5 (*61*) Cartier '53–5 (*17*) Tempest '54–5 (*16*) Cox '55–8 (*108*) Bolton '55–8 (*62*) Farriss '58–'61 (*36*) Sopwith '58 (*9*) Park '59 (*1*) Wells '60–'71 (*40*) Spira '62–3 (*18*) Debden '62–3 (*13*) Anderton '65–7 (*13*) Grahame '65–7 (*9*) Last '65–'79 (*88*) Vere '71 (*10*) C Hill '71–2 (*18*) Tait '71–9 (*29*) Trounson '72 (*9*) Ruanne '72–3 (*8*) Merry '72–3 (*4*) Wade '72–5 (*29*) Strike '73–9 (*23*) Highwood '77–9 (*4*) Barbieri '79 (*3*). *Jasper* Poole '51–5 (*72*) Holden '51–9 (*55*) Britton '51A. Mosaval '52–'73 (*310*) Trevor '54–7 (*81*) Hurd '58 (*11*) Emblen '63–7 (*27*) Westmoreland '63 (*2*) Sleep '71 (*9*) Morse '71–9 (*88*) Gordon '71 (*2*) Bertscher '71–9 (*53*) Reeder '74–9 (*13*) Bonner '79 (*2*). *Captain Belaye* Blair '51–'72 (*63*) Britton '51–'62 (*175*) MacMillan '52–4 (*33*) Vernon '54–5 (*22*) Wright '55 (*11*) Boulton '55–8 (*64*) Shields '55–6 (*29*). L White '57–8 (*19*) A Grant '59A (*1*) Doyle '60–2 (*21*) Gable '62 (*4*) Alder '62–3 (*15*) Farley '62–7 (*36*) Sherwood '65–'71 (*9*) Grater '65–6 (*13*) Cooke '67–'73 (*55*) Johnson '71–5 (*34*) McGrath '71–3 (*33*) Clarke '71–3 (*18*) Dubreuil '74–9 (*19*) Jefferies '74–5 (*17*) O'Brien '74–7 (*6*) Sleep '76–7 (*2*) Myers '77–9 (*13*) Ashmole '77–9 (*8*) D Kelly '77–9 (*5*). + *8f 6m*; from '51 Sept: *10f 8m*. *Also* Rep I.

Playground P 24 Aug 1979 Big Top, Edinburgh *Ch* MacMillan *M* Gordon Crosse *SC* Yolanda Sonnabend. '79 (6). *The Youth D* Kelly (*6*). *'Girl with make-up'* Tait (*6*). *'Her Mother'* Stanley (*6*). *'Vicar'* Wicks (*6*). *'His Wife'* Rowann (*6*). + *CdB*.

Poltroon, The P 12 Oct 1972 *Ch* MacMillan *M* Rudolf Maros *SC* Thomas O'Neil. '72 (15); '73 (23). *Columbine* Last '72–3 (*19*) Strike '72–3 (*19*). *Harlequin* Jefferies '72–3 (*23*) Bertscher '72–3 (*6*) Johnson '73 (*9*). *Pierrot* MacLeary '72–3 (*11*) Cooke '72–3 (*23*) Kilgour '72 (*4*). + *4m*.

Prodigal Son FPTC 8 Aug 1973 Mann Auditorium, Tel Aviv Cr Rep I. '73 (13); '74 (42); '75 (21); '76 (5); '77 (13); '78 (21); '79 (6). A:21. *The Prodigal Son* Nureyev '73CG '73A '75 (*2*) Cooke '73A (*2*) Dubreuil '73–9 (*34*) Wall '73–5 (*4*) D Kelly '73CG–9 (*33*) MacLeary '73–4 (*3*) Jefferies '74–5 (*19*) Ashmole '76–9 (*16*) Myers '76–9 (*8*). *The Siren* Seymour '73A '75 (*1*) Lorrayne '73A–9 (*57*) Parkinson '73CG–5 (*11*) Bergsma '73CG–4 (*3*) Strike '74–9 (*23*) Gielgud '75–8 (*11*) Highwood '77–9 (*8*) Rowann '78–9 (*7*). *The Father* Auld '73A–9 (*99*) Plaisted '74–9 (*14*) Purnell '78–9 (*8*).

Promenade FPTB 8 Apr 1946 sw Cr Rep I. '46 (29); '47 (8). *Lepidopterist* Newman '46–7 (*28*) Kersley '46–7 (*9*). *Rendezvous* F Harris '46–7 (*33*) Brae '47 (*4*). *m* Gerhardt '46 (*6*) Burke

'46–7 (*31*). *Promenade* Nelson '46–7 (*27*) O'Reilly '46–7 (*10*).

Prospect Before Us, The FPTB 13 Feb 1951 SW Cr Rep I. '51 (*21*); '52 (*6*). A:24. *Mr O'Reilly* Helpmann '51 (*3*) Holden '51–2 (*24*). *Mr Taylor* Poole '51–2 (*23*) Wright '51–2 (*4*). *Mlle Théodore* Fifield '51–2 (*17*) Harrop '51–2 (*9*) Bruce '52A (*1*).

Punch and the Street Party P 20 Aug 1979 Big Top, Edinburgh *Ch* David Bintley *M* Lord Berners *SC* Mike Becket. '79 (*4*). *Punch* Morse (*4*). *Judy* Tait (*4*). *Polly* Strike (*4*). *Harlequin* Reeder (*4*). *The Thief* Myers (*4*). *Toby* Bertscher (*4*). + *4f 7m*.

Quintet FP 29 Oct 1964 New, Oxford *Ch* Peter Wright *M* Ibert *SC* Judith Wood. '64 (*18*); '65 (*13*). 1 Last '64–5 (*31*) 2 Emblen '64–5 (*31*) 3 Beaumont '64–5 (*28*) Grater '65 (*2*) Beale '65 (*1*). 4 Mosaval '64–5 (*28*) Westmoreland '65 (*3*). 5 Wall '64–5 (*22*) Davel '65–6 (*9*). *NB* UK premiere BBC tv 14 May '64 danced by RB from CG.

Rake's Progress, The FPTB 18 June 1952 Cr Rep I. '52 (*27*); '53 (*35*); '54 (*3*); '55 (*38*); '56 (*11*); '57 (*8*); '61 (*2*); '62 (*2*); '64 (*10*); '65 (*6*); '66 (*33*); '67 (*20*); '70 (*24*); '71 (*47*); '73 (*23*); '74 (*8*); '78 (*27*); '79 (*23*). A:106. *The Rake* A Grant '52–'66 (*16*) Blair '52–3 (*20*) Trecu '52–4 (*21*) Gore '52–3 (*4*) Poole '53–5 (*31*) Britton '55–'64 (*30*) Zolan '55–7 (*15*) Legerton '56 (*1*). L White '56–7 (*4*) Shaw '60A '64–6 (*2*) Wall '65–'74 (*28*) Davel '66 –'71 (*44*) Farley '66–7 (*15*) Morse '70–9 (*43*) Jefferies '70–4 (*19*) Cooke '70–3 (*22*) D Kelly '78–9 (*12*) Dubreuil '78–9 (*16*) Ashmole '79 (*4*). *The Betrayed Girl* O'Reilly '52–3 (*28*) Lane '52–'66 (*40*) Pat Miller '52–5 (*23*) Tempest '55–7 (*24*) Heaton '56–7 (*9*) Sibley '60A Anderton '61–7 (*36*) Grahame '64–7 (*20*) Thorogood '66–7 (*15*) Vere '70–1 (*18*) Barbieri '70–9 (*49*) Ruanne '70–3 (*19*) Evans '71–9 (*34*) Tait '73–9 (*23*) Homji '73–4 (*4*) Katrak '78–9 (*5*).

Rashomon P 19 Oct 1976 SW *Ch* Lynn Seymour *M* Bob Downes *SC* Pamela Marr. '76 (*7*); '78 (*3*). *Bandit* North '76 (*7*) D Kelly '78 (*3*). *Wife* Highwood '76–8 (*10*). *Husband* D Kelly '76 (*7*) Ashmole '78 (*3*).

Raymonda FP 10 July 1964 Teatro Nuovo, Spoleto *Ch* Nureyev after Petipa *M* Glazunov *SC* Beni Montresor. A:8. *Raymonda* Wells, A Fonteyn A. *Jean de Brienne* Nureyev A.

Raymonda Act III FP 7 May 1966 Suomen Kansallisoopera, Helsinki *Ch* Nureyev after Petipa *M* Glazunov *SC* Barry Kay. '66 (*24*); '67 (*21*); '75 (*22*); '76 (*24*); '77 (*8*). A:37. *Raymonda* Wells '66–7 (*14*) Landon '66–7 (*20*) Anderton '66–7 (*11*) Seymour '75 (*3*) Tait '75–6 (*8*) Lorrayne '75–7 (*15*) Barbieri '75–7 (*17*) Gielgud '76–7 (*9*) Samsova '77 (*2*). *Jean de Brienne* Rosson '66A Wall '66A–'76 (*15*) Beaumont '66–7 (*27*) Benton '67 (*1*) Blair '67 (*4*) Nureyev '75 (*2*) D Kelly '75–7 (*25*) Dubreuil '75–6 (*9*) Jefferies '75–6 (*9*) O'Brien

'76–7 (*2*) Prokovosky '77 (*2*) Ashmole '76–7 (*3*). *Hungarian Dance f* Karras '66A Landon '66–7 (*9*) Humphreys '66–7 (*30*) Saunders '67 (*6*) Highwood '75–7 (*28*) Laurence '75–6 (*23*) Tait '77 (*3*). *m* Emblen '66A Beaumont '66–7 (*12*) Clarke '66–7 (*29*) Grater '67 (*4*) Bertscher '75–7 (*38*) Morse '75–7 (*10*) Myers '76–7 (*6*). + *16f 16m*. *Also* Rep I.

Reflection P 21 Aug 1952 Empire, Edinburgh *Ch/Scenario* Cranko *M* John Gardner *SC* Keith New. '52 (*9*); '53 (*2*). *Narcissus* Poole '52–3 (*11*). *Echo* Fifield '52–3 (*8*) Lane '52–3 (*3*). *The Lovers: f* Pat Miller '52–3 (*10*) Hill '53 (*1*). *m* Trecu '52–3 (*11*). *The Tender Child* O'Reilly '52–3 (*8*) Lane '52–3 (*3*). *The Aggressive Child* Britton '52–3 (*11*). + *5f 5m*.

Rendezvous, Les FPTB 26 Dec 1947 SW Cr Rep I. *SC* William Chappell; '49 June *C* Chappell, '61 Aug *C*, Sept *S* redesigned Chappell. '47 (*2*); '48 (*97*); '49 (*44*); '50 (*21*); '51 (*15*); '52 (*18*); '53 (*21*); '54 (*47*); '55 (*4*); '56 (*14*); '57 (*3*); '61 (*16*); '62 (*43*); '63 (*10*); '71 (*20*); '72 (*50*); '73 (*13*); '74 (*11*); '75 (*11*); '76 (*11*); '79 (*18*). A:107. *Adagio des Amoureux/Variations f* Fifield '47–'52 (*148*) Lane '48–'63 (*83*) Cadzow '49 (*4*) Neil '53–7 (*40*) Page '54 (*2*) Heaton '56–7 (*11*) Wells '61A–3 (*34*) Anderton '61–3 (*24*) Sibley '61 (*2*) Park '62–'73 (*14*) Last '63–'76 (*24*) Ruanne '71–3 (*28*) Barbieri '71–9 (*19*) Lorrayne '72–6 (*22*) Tait '74–9 (*26*) Strike '79 (*7*) Highwood '79 (*1*). *m* Boulton '47–'57 (*45*) Kersley '48–'50 (*79*) MacMillan '48–'53 (*19*) Trecu '49–'54 (*72*) Blair '49–53 (*12*) Britton '51A '52–'63 (*81*) Zolan '54–6 (*12*) Gilpin '61 (*6*) Doyle '61–2 (*9*) Gable '62–3 (*14*) Sherwood '63–'73 (*7*) D Kelly '71–5 (*15*) Clarke '71–3 (*13*) Johnson '75 (*16*) McGrath '71–3 (*33*) Nureyev '72–3 (*3*) Jefferies '72–5 (*15*) Dubreuil '74–5 (*7*) O'Brien '74–6 (*7*) Kilgour '76–9 (*4*) Ashmole '76–9 (*10*) Berg '76 (*3*) Myers '79 (*6*) Reeder '79 (*1*). NB *SC* destroyed Hanley 2 June '49, replaced by new *C* designed Chappell; *S* new gates + backdrop from *Promenade*.

Rhyme nor Reason FP 30 Mar 1979 Pavilion, Bournemouth *Ch* Michael Corder *M* Stravinsky *SC* Lazaro Prince. '79 (*20*). 1 Tait (*12*) Pet Miller (*2*) Katrak (*3*) Dales (*3*). 2 Rowann (*14*) Powell (*4*) Mills (*2*). 3 Kennedy (*12*) Evans (*3*) Crow (*5*). 4 Myers (*9*) Beckett (*3*) Kilgour (*8*). 5 Reeder (*14*) Welford (*6*). P RBChG Feb '78 as *Dumbarton Oaks* by CG dancers. 7m Oct '78 SW. *SC* nc. '78 (*5*). 1 J Jackson (*5*). 2 Howe (*5*). 3 Eyden (*5*) 4 Batchelor (*5*). 6 Sheriff (*5*).

Romeo and Juliet 'Balcony' pdd FPTC 15 June 1972 Théâtre Grand, Geneva Cr Rep I. '72 (*12*); '73 (*13*); '75 (*4*). A:6. *Juliet* Fonteyn '72A Barbieri '72–3 (*11*) Ruanne '72 (*4*) Porter '72 (*1*) Parkinson '73–5 (*7*) Wells '73 (*4*) Sibley '74A Seymour '75 (*2*). *Romeo* Labis '72A D Kelly '72–5 (*5*) McGrath '72–3 (*9*) Myers '72 (*5*) MacLeary '73 (*8*) Dowell '74A Nureyev '75 (*2*).

Sacred Circles P 2 March 1973 RST *Ch* David

Drew *M* Shostakovich *SC* Terence Emery. '73 (*30*); '74 (*2*). *The Ringmaster* Johnson '73 (*15*) Drew '73 (*1*) Bertscher '73–4 (*16*). *Couple 1: f* Barbieri '73 (*24*); Strike '73–4 (*8*). *m* Cooke '73 (*24*) Clarke '73 (*6*) Dubreuil '74 (*2*). *Couple 2: f* Lorrayne '73–4 (*32*). *m* Waller '73–4 (*32*).

St Thomas' Wake FP 7 June 1971 SW *Ch* David Drew *M* Peter Maxwell-Davies *Assemblage* Peter Logan. '71 (*3*). 1 Connor (*3*). 2 Fletcher (*3*). 3 Jefferies (*3*). P RBChG 2 July '70.

Saudades (Nostalgia) P 13 Oct 1955 Royal Court, Liverpool *Ch* Alfred Rodrigues *M* Denis ApIvor *SC* Norman Adams. *Scenario* Rodrigues/ApIvor. '55 (*27*); '56 (*19*). *King* MacLeary '55–6 (*28*) Britton '55–6 (*18*). *Princess* Bruce '55 (*23*) Bolton '55–6 (*23*). *Sorceress* M Hill '55–6 (*37*) Vane '55–6 (*9*). *Merchant* ('56 *Birdseller*) L White '55–6 (*40*) Alex Bennett '56 (*6*). *Boy* Mosaval '55–6 (*46*). + *12f 9m* ('56: *12f 7m*).

Sea Change P 18 July 1949 Gaiety, Dublin *Ch* Cranko *M* Sibelius *SC* John Piper. '49 (*15*); '70 (*30*); '51 (*8*). *Skipper* Poole '49–'51 (*38*) Wright '49–'50 (*15*). *Old Woman* Shore '49–'50 (*28*) Farrance '49–'51 (*25*). *Her Son* Blair '49 (*5*) Trecu '49–'51 (*32*) McAlpine '50–1 (*16*). *A Fisherman* Hogan '49–'51 (*31*) Blair '49–'51 (*19*) Britton '49–'51 (*3*). *His Young Wife* O'Reilly '49–'51 (*42*) Lane '49–'51 (*11*). + *5f 5m*.

Selina P 16 Nov 1948 SW *Ch/C* Andrée Howard *M* Rossini arr Guy Warrack *S* Peter Williams. '48 (*6*); '49 (*36*); '50 (*26*); '51 (*2*); '54 (*2*); '55 (*10*). *Simplice* Zullig '48–9 (*26*) Poole '48–'55 (*40*) Wright '50–4 (*16*). *Selina* Fifield '48–'51 (*32*) Pat Miller '48–'55 (*40*) Nerina '50 (*5*) Harrop '51–1 (*2*) Page '55 (*3*). *Tom* Trecu '48–'55 (*49*) Boulton '48–9 (*3*) Blair '48–'50 (*19*) Mosaval '54–5 (*6*) Trevor '54–5 (*5*). *Lord Ravensgarth* Gill '48–'55 (*79*) Hogan '49 (*3*). *Agnes* Holden '48–'51 (*60*) Andrée Howard '48–'55 (*16*) Kersley '49–'50 (*4*) McAlpine '50 (*2*). *Naila* Claire '48–'51 (*49*) Drage '49–'50 (*10*) Beriosova '50 (*11*) Page '54–5 (*4*) Tempest '54–5 (*8*). + *10f*.

Septet Extra FP 12 Feb 1974 SW *Ch* Hans van Manen *M* Saint-Saëns *SC* Jean-Paul Vroom. '74 (*53*). 1 Strike (*34*) Tait (*19*). 2 Jefferies (*36*) Dubreuil (*10*) Kilgour (*3*) Reeder (*4*). + *4f 4m*.

Shukumei P 14 February 1975 RST *Ch* Jack Carter *M* Stomu Yamash'ta *SC* Norman McDowell. '75 (*29*). *The Lady* Tait (*22*) Barbieri (*6*) Seymour '75 (*1*). *The Brothers* 1 D Kelly (*20*) Kilgour (*6*) Waller (*3*). 2 Dubreuil (*26*) O'Brien (*3*). 3 Jefferies (*28*) Morse (*1*). + *2f 8m* + *CdB*.

Side Show see Rep I. Divertissements.

Siesta P 28 July 1972 The Maltings, Snape *Ch* Ashton *M* William Walton *C* nc. '72 (*7*). *f* Lorrayne (*7*) *m* McGrath (*7*). *NB Ch* not related to *Siesta* pdd '36 to same music.

6.6.78 (Tribute to de Valois on 80th birthday) P 26 Sept 1978 SW *Ch* MacMillan *M* Samuel

Barber *SC* Ian Spurling. '78 (6). *Gemini f* Tait (6). *m* D Kelly (6). + *7f 7m*.

Sinfonietta P 10 February 1967 RST *Ch* Ashton *M* Malcolm Williamson *C* Peter Rice *Optical sets* Hornsey College of Art Light/Sound Workshop. '67 (43); '68 (22). *Couple 1: f* Anderton '67–8 (20) Thorogood '67–8 (41) Karras '68 (4). *m* Farley '67 (24) Powell '67–8 (31) Hooper '67–8 (10). *Couple 2: f* Last '67–8 (39) Lorraine '67–8 (4) Debden '67–8 (22). *m* Cooke '67–8 (44) Emblen '67–8 (21). *Elegy f* Wells '67–8 (38) Aldous '67–8 (27). *m* Wall '67–8 (35) Clarke '67–8 (30). + *6f 6m*.

Sleeping Beauty, The, Blue Bird pdd FPTB 27m Dec 1949 sw *Ch* Petipa *M* Tchaikovsky *C* Hugh Stevenson. '49 (1); '50 (30); '51 (4); '56 [34]; '57 (16); '58 (41). A:8. *f* Lane '49–'51 (13) Bruce '50–1 (13) Fifield '50 (1) O'Reilly '50 (1) Gorham '50 (7) Bolton '56–7 [7] Alexander '56–8 [39] Cox '57–8 (27). *m* Kersley '49–'50 (14) Trecu '50–1 (11) Blair '50–1 (10) Boulton '56–8 [45] Britton '56 [1] Mosaval '57–8 (27). nr '56 Autumn tour.

Sleeping Beauty, The FPTC 14 Sept 1959 Grand, Leeds Cr Rep 1 1946. '59 (12); '60 (70); '61 (41); '62 (30); '63 (31); '64 (53); '65 (25); '67 (37); '68 (27); '69 (31); '70 (21). A:65. *Princess Aurora* Linden '59–'63 (26) Page '59CG–'64 (15) Alexander '59–'60 (8) Nerina '60–7 (15) Seymour '60–3 (29) Anderton '60–7 (15) Wells '60–'70 (83) Beriosova '60–9 (26) Grey 60A & 61A Sibley '60A '61–4 (9) Park '61–7 (8) Grahame '61–'70 (47) Maden '63–5 (24) Lane '63–4 (3) Fonteyn '64–'70 (10) Wright '64–5 (9) Lorrayne '67 (3) Aldous '67–'70 (25) Landon '67–9 (7) Last '67 (2) Thorogood '69–'70 (8) Barbieri '69–'70 (6). *Prince Florimund* Ashbridge '59CG–'65 (37) Doyle '59–'67 (50) Hynd '59CG–'64 (15) Burne '60A MacLeary '60A '61–'70 (31) Alex Bennett '60A–3 (39) Blair '60–7 (22) Gable '61–4 (19) Gilpin '61 (8) Rosson '61–8 (9) I Hamilton '63–4 (11) Sherwood '63–5 (29) Usher '63–9 (8) Farley '64–7 (11) Yuresha '64–5 (9) Wall '67–9 (13) Beaumont '67–9 (12) Benton '67–8 (6) Clarke '67–'70 (15) Nureyev '67 (1) McGrath '68–'70 (19) Labis '69–'70 (7) Jefferies '69–'70 (6) Cragun '70 (1). *The Fairy of the Lilac* Parkinson '59CG (6) Remington '59–'61 (63) Needham '60A–2 (68) V Taylor '60A (4) Grahame '61–4 (14) Saunders '63–9 (71) O'Conaire '63–5 (31) Starr '63–5 (22) Seymour '64 (2) Beckley '64 (8) Landon '65–9 (30) Koshley '67–8 (7) Lawe '67 (1) Ruanne '68–'70 (34) Southam '69–'70 (6) Conley '69–'70 (11). *Blue Birds f* Anderton '59–'70 (117) Farriss '59–'61 (63) Maden '60–5 (56) Spira '61–2 (11) Last '63–'70 (80) Thorogood '67–'70 (35) Lorraine '68–'70 (10) Evans '69–'70 (6). *m* Boulton '59 (12) Trecu '60 (5) Mosaval '60–5 (64) Mead '60–1 (4) Coleman '60–5 (92) Gable '61 (4) Sale '61–7 (82) Sherwood '62–3 (9) Powell '67–8 (27) Wall

'67–8 (8) Beare '67–8 (4) Cooke '68–'70 (24) Hooper '68–'70 (31) Johnson '69–'70 (12).

Sleeping Beauty, The, *Rose Adagio*. '56. A:2.

Sleeping Beauty, The, *Divertissement*. '67 (4). *Princess Aurora* Wells (1) Lorrayne (1) Aldous (1) Grahame (1). *Prince Florimund* Wall (2) Rosson (1) Beaumont (1). *Blue Birds f* Last (2) Thorogood (2). *m* Sale (2) Powell (2).

Sleeping Beauty, The, *Florestan and his Two Sisters*. '72 (7); '73 (6).

Sleeping Beauty, The pdd. '59 (9); '60 (3); '72 (3). A:35. *Princess Aurora* Linden '59 (2) Alexander '59–'60 (6) Seymour '59–'60 (3) Nerina '60 (1) Fonteyn '72A Beriosova '72 (2) Barbieri '72 (1). *Prince Florimund* Ashbridge '59 (2) Doyle '59–'60 (4) Alex Bennett '59–'60 (5) Burne '60 (1) D Kelly '70A Labis '72A MacLeary '72 (3).

Sleeping Beauty, The. On tour abroad only: Act III (2). Blue Bird pdd (1). The Three Ivans (1).

Sleeping Beauty, The Act III (**Aurora's Wedding**) FP 29 June 1976 Opernhaus, Zürich. *Ch* Petipa; *Ch* MacMillan (Hop o'my Thumb). *M* Tchaikovsky. *C* Peter Farmer. *Pr* Peter Wright. '76 (12); '77 (39). A:11. *Princess Aurora* Park '76A (1) Wells '76A Penney '76A Lorrayne '76–7 (15) Barbieri '76–7 (15) Aitken '76–7 (4) Tait '76–7 (12) Highwood '77 (4). *Prince Florimund* D Kelly '76A–7 (19) Jefferies '76A D Kelly–Dubreuil '76A O'Brien '76–7 (7) Ashmole '76–7 (13) Myers '76–7 (6) Dubreuil '77 (6). *The Lilac Fairy* Lorrayne '76A–7 (19) Barbieri '76A–7 (8) Highwood '76–7 (15) Rowann '77 (9). *The Blue Birds f* Last '76A–7 (12) Tait '76A–7 (10) Strike '76–7 (19) Pet Miller '76–7 (8) Kennedy '77 (2). *m* Dubreuil '76A–7 (2) Kilgour '76–7 (10) Berg '76–7 (20) Ashmole '76–7 (7) Myers '77 (4) O'Brien '77 (4) Reeder '77 (4).

Soft Blue Shadows FP 20 Sept 1977 sw *Ch* André Prokovsky *M* Fauré *SC* Peter Farmer. '76 (3). *f* Samsova (3) *m* Prokovsky (3). + *3f 3m*.

Solitaire P 7 June 1956 sw *Ch* MacMillan *M* Malcolm Arnold *SC* Desmond Heeley; 1978 *SC* Barry Kay. '56 [32]; '57 (52) '59 (35); '60 (6); '61 (39); '62 (18) '63 (9); '64 (36); '65 (37); '66 (12); '69 (20); '70 (18); '71 (17); '72 (43); '73 (5); '74 (17); '78 (25). A:60. *'The Girl'* M Hill '56–9 [43] Neil '57 [9] Bolton '57 (23) Alexander '57–9 (7) Anderton '59–'70 (69) Seymour '60–'78 (11) Geldard '61–2 (29) Spira '61–2 (24) O'Conaire '63–'71 (40) Thorogood '65–'70 (23) Ruanne '65–'73 (34) Chapell '69A–'72 (22) Trounson '71–2 (9) Barbieri '72–8 (20) Porter '72–3 (7) Merry '72–3 (5) Tait '74–8 (17) Homji '74 (4) Lindsay '74 (2) M Evans '78 (2). *'Polka'* Neil '56–7 [17] Bolton '57 (18) Farriss '57–'61 (53) E Thomas '57–'64 (66) Lane '60–5 (3) Wells '61 (6) Spira '61–2 (6) Debden '62–'70 (49) Last '63–'74 (108) Tait '71–8 (20) C Hill

'72 (1) Strike '71–4 (36) Wade '72–4 (9) Pet Miller '74 (4) Kennedy '78 (4). *m* solo Britton '56–'64 [78] Trevor '56–7 [16] Mosaval '57–'73 (45) Usher '59 (9) Gable '59 (1) Westmoreland '60A–5 (96) Sale '61–2 (12) Emblen '65–6 (19) Cooke '65–6 (11) Johnson '69A–'73 (39) Hooper '69–'70 (24) Kirkpatrick '71 (6) Jefferies '72–4 (3) Reeder '74–8 (7) Kilgour '74–8 (14) Berg '78 (17) O'Brien '78 (3). *m* pdd MacLeary '56–9 [65] Alex Bennett '57–'63 (75) Doyle '59–'62 (22) Gable '60A '61–4 (8) I Hamilton '63–4 (24) Farley '64–5 (7) Grater '64–'70 (67) Clarke '65–'73 (25) Davel '69A–'72 (26) McGrath '71–3 (26) Kilgour '72–8 (22) Jefferies '72–4 (6) Dubreuil '74–8 (19) Purnell '74 (3) O'Brien '74 (4) D Kelly '78 (1). + *6f 6m*. nr 1956 Autumn Tour.

Solitaire pdd '76 (1). *'The Girl'* Thorogood *m* MacLeary.

Somnambulism FP 29 May 1956 sw *Ch* MacMillan *M* Stan Kenton arr John Lanchbery *SC* nc. '56 [28]. *The Sleep: Anxiety* M Hill [7] Neil [3]. *Monotony* Britton [5] L White [5]. *Premonition* Heaton [9] Bolton [1]. + *6f 6m*. Miss 1956 Autumn tour. Revised version of *Somnambulism* P swcHG 1 Feb 1953.

Spectre de la Rose, Le FP 6 May 1946 sw Cr Rep 1. *SC* Rex Whistler; '72 *SC* Alistair Livingstone. '46 (11); '47 (23); '72 (18); '73 (23). *The Young Girl* Brae '46–7 (13) Heaton '47 (19) Moore '47 (2) Fonteyn '72 (1) Barbieri '72–3 (16) Evans '72 (5) Porter '72–3 (11) Beriosova '73 (8). *The Spirit of the Rose* Kersley '46–7 (27) Britton '47 (7) Dowell '72 (1) D Kelly '72–3 (8) McGrath '72–3 (21) Kilgour '72 (4) Johnson '73 (7).

Summer Interlude P 28 Mar 1950 sw *Ch* Michael Somes *M* Respighi *SC* Sophie Fedorovitch. '50 (45); '51 (11); '52 (7); '53 (8). *A Village Girl* Pat Miller '50–3 (54) Bruce '50–2 (16). *A Village Boy* Trecu '50–3 (55) Hogan '50–1 (8) Britton '52–3 (7); *Bathers f* Fifield '50–1 (14) Claire '50–3 (25) Beriosova '50–1 (21) Neil '52–3 (10). *m* Blair '50–3 (53) Wright '50–1 (8) MacMillan '52–3 (9). + *7f 5m*. nr '51 July 24.

Summer's Night P 29 Oct 1964 New, Oxford *Ch* Peter Wright *M* Poulenc *SC* Judith Wood. '64 (18); '65 (13). *A Young Couple f* Anderton '64–5 (25) Thorogood '64–5 (6). *m* Farley '64–5 (22) Grater '64–5 (9). *Ghosts f* Wells '64–5 (23) Ruanne '64–5 (8). *m* Sherwood '64–5 (29) Cooke '65 (2). + *9f 9m*.

Summertide P 12 Oct 1976 sw *Ch* Peter Wright *M* Mendelssohn *SC* Elisabeth Dalton. '76 (8); 77 (17); '78 (30). *f* Barbieri '76–8 (24) Lorrayne '76–8 (15) Aitken '77–8 (10) Evans '78 (6). *m* Ashmole '76–8 (29) O'Brien '77–8 (19) Berg '78 (4) Kilgour '78 (3). + *6f 7m* ('77 *4f 6m*).

Swan Lake pdt FP 20m Sept 1947 sw *Ch* Petipa *M* Tchaikovsky *C* nc. '47 (23); '48 (86); '49

(40); '50 (3); '51 (4); '52 (5); '53 (4). *f* 2 from: Heaton '47 (14) Nerina '47 (5) Fifield '47–9 (54) Wadsworth '47–8 (34) Lane '47–'53 (99) Pet Miller '47–'53 (59) Claire '48 (6) Nelson '48 (8) Bruce '48–9 (24) P Kennedy '49 (9) Gorham '49–'53 (7) Page '52–3 (6) Tempest '52 (4). *m* Kersley '47–9 (77) Boulton '47–9 (31) MacMillan '48–'52 (22) Blair '49–'51 (23) Trecu '49–'53 (5) Britton '51–3 (7).

Swan Lake FPNP 18 May 1965 ROH *Ch* Petipa/Ivanov; *Ch* Ashton (I: Pas de Six. III: Neapolitan); *Ch* de Valois (I: Peasant Dance. IV: Storm scene). *M* Tchaikovsky *SC* Leslie Hurry *Pr* Sergeyev revised Ashton. '65 (39); '66 (60); '67 (34); '68 (51); '69 (28); '70 (14). A:13. *Odette/Odile* Nerina '65–7 (9) Wells '65–'70 (39) Fonteyn '65–9 (31) Grahame '65–70 (26) Lane '65–7 (8) Sibley '65–6 (3) Beriosova '65–9 (14) Landon '65–9 (43) Parkinson '65–7 (3) Seymour '66 (7) Aldous '66–'70 (23) Mason '67 (2) Bergsma '67–8 (3) Conley†/Thorogood†† '67–8 (4) Conley '68–'70 (9) Thorogood†/Conley†† '69 (1) Thorogood '69 (1). *Prince Siegfried* Labis '65–8 (10) Wall '65–9 (63) MacLeary '65–9 (13) Beaumont '65–9 (41) Blair '65–7 (12) Nureyev '66–8 (6) Gable '66 (2) Rosson '66–8 (10) Doyle '66–7 (10) Musil '66 (2) Dowell '67 (1) Benton '67–8 (14) Clarke '67–'70 (24) Cragun '68–9 (5) McGrath '68–'70 (6) Kelly '70 (7). *Also* Rep I. †Odette ††Odile.

Swan Lake *Divertissements.* '66 (4). *Odile* Seymour (2) Landon (2). *Prince Siegfried* Gable (1) Beaumont (2) Doyle (1).

Swan Lake Act II pdd. '72 (8). A:4. *Odette* Penney (2) Thorogood (3) Seymour (3). *Prince Siegfried* D Kelly (8).

Swan Lake Act III pdd. '72 (17). A:8. *Odile* Bergsma (4) Mason (1) Parkinson (6) Lorrayne (4) Fonteyn (2). *Prince Siegfried* MacLeary (9) D Kelly (1) McGrath (5) Wall (2).

Swan Lake *Neapolitan.* A:1.

Sweeney Todd P 10m Dec 1959 SMT. (Str) *Ch/Scenario* Cranko *M* Malcolm Arnold *SC* Alix Stone. '59 (3); '60 (25); '61 (13). A:14. *Sweeney Todd* Britton '59–'61 (41). *Tobias* Mosaval '59–'61 (34) Coleman '60A–1 (7). *Johanna* Anderton '59–'61 (28) Geldard '60–1 (13). *Mark Ingestre* Doyle '59–'61 (33) I Hamilton '61 (6) Mead '61 (2). *Colonel Jeffrey* I Hamilton '59–'61 (33) Grater '61 (5) Alder '61 (3). + 3*f* 10m.

Sword of Alsace P 23 OCT 1973 sw *Ch* David Drew *m* Joachim Raff *SC* Terence Emery. '73 (16); '74 (19). *Mouchette* Barbieri '73–4 (20) Lorrayne '74 (4) Strike '74 (11). *Etienne* Jefferies '73–4 (28) Dubreuil '74 (7). *Lt André Courville* Clarke '73 (4) McGrath '73 (12) Waller '74 (13) O'Brien '74 (6). + CdB.

Sylvia TC in CG production ROH only. *See* Rep I. **Sylvia** '63; '65.

Sylphides, Les FPTB 22 Apr 1946 sw Cr Rep I.

'46 (46); '47 (62); '48 (61); '49 (36); '50 (21); '51 (6); '52 (6); '53 (16); '54 (32); '55 (53); '57 (28); '58 (5); '59 (20); '60 (11); '61 (34); '62 (49); '63 (33); '64 (8); '65 (26); '66 (32); '67 (5); '68 (27); '73 (17); '74 (69); '75 (24); '76 (7); '77 (11); '78 (31); '79 (23). A:171. '46–'51 following *f* appeared – roles not specified: '46 Clayden, Brae, Harris, Prokhorova, Heaton, Nerina Moore, June Day, Field, Chrimes, Wadsworth, Fewster + '47 O'Reilly, Fifield, Hamby, Shore + '48 Pat Miller, Claire, Lane + '49 Bruce, Cadzow, Gorham, Beriosova, Harrop. *Valse* Lane '52–'63 (11) Page '53–4 (9) Neil '53–5 (43) White '54 (5) Bruce '54–5 (15) Pat Miller '54 (2) Bolton '55–8 (16) Reece '55 (5) Lee '55 (5) Fifield '55 (1) Alexander '57–8 (16) P Barnes '59 (9) Sopwith '57 (6) Anderton '59–'64 (77) Blakeney '59 (11) V Taylor '60 (5) B Taylor '60–1 (6) Wells '61A Grahame '61–2 (10) Park '62 (1) Spira '62–3 (19) Thorogood '63–8 (22) Last '63–'75 (70) Maden '63–4 (9) J Williams '65–6 (10) Illingworth '66–7 (11) Debden '67–8 (4) Merry '68 (2) Holmes '68 (1) Tait '73–9 (19) Strike '73–9 (53) Wade '73–5 (32) Pet Miller '73–9 (19) Evans '74–8 (11) Barbieri '74 (2) Lorrayne '74 (1) Lincoln '75–6 (6) Rowann '77–9 (19) Kennedy '79 (4). *Mazurka f* Fifield '52–5 (4) Pat Miller '52–5 (18) Lane '53A–5 (11) Page '53–'65 (59) Tempest '55 (11) Neil '55 (17) Heaton '57–8 (18) Alexander '57–'60 (28) Lee '57–8 (6) Parkinson '59–'66 (9) Grey '60A & 61A Sibley '60A '61–6 (4) Seymour '60–'78 (13) Nerina '61–6 (4) Remington '61–2 (34) Anderton '61 (1) Park '62 (3) Grahame '62–8 (69) Beriosova '62 (1) O'Conaire '62–3 (14) Wright '63 (6) Fracci '63 (5) Hayden '63 (1) Ruanne '65–8 (21) Landon '66–8 (11) Aldous '66–8 (10) Barbieri '68–'79 (52) Jenner '73CG (4) Wells '73 (2) Wade '73–4 (23) Lorrayne '73–9 (55) Strike '74–9 (11) Tait '74–9 (28) Pet Miller '74 (1) Last '74 (1) Samsova '78 (4) Kennedy '79 (3) Rowann '79 (1). *Prelude* O'Reilly '52–4 (15) Neil '52 (1) M Hill '52–9 (33) Tempest '53–7 (41) Larsen '53–4 (7) Cartier '54–5 (13) English '55 (11) Reece '57 (10) Blakeney '57–'62 (48) E Thomas '57 (7) Lee '58 (2) V Taylor '59–'62 (51) Markova '60 (4) (*also Valse pas de deux*) Orpin '63–4 (23) Saunders '63–8 (38) Grahame '63–6 (8) O'Conaire '63–5 (20) Starr '64 (2) Page '65 (1) Anderton '65–8 (23) Cartwright '65–6 (11) Conley '66–8 (12) Humphreys '66 (3) Karras '68 (1) Wade '73–4 (4) Barbieri '73–9 (30) Evans '73–9 (94) Lorrayne '74–8 (11) Jenner '74 (4) Parkinson '74–5 (6) Aitken '74–9 (23) Gielgud '77 (4) Rowann '79 (6). *Mazurka m* Hyrst '46–7 (28) Carter '46–7 (26) Kersley '47–'50 (97) MacMillan '47–'54 (48) Boulton '47–9 (12) Rassine '47 (1) Zullig '49 (9) Trecu '49–'55 (42) Blair '50–1 (13) Zolan '53–5 (44) MacLeary '55–'65 (28) Lawrence '55 (7) Alex Bennett '57–'63 (105) Miller '57 (6) Hynd '59–'64 (10) Usher '59–'68 (17) Ashbridge '60–1 (7) Gilpin '61–3 (9) Mead '62

(17) Gable '63 (4) Flindt '63 (3) Farley '64–7 (25) Beaumont '65–8 (37) Rosson '65–6 (4) Wall '66–'73 (17) Johnson '68 (2) McGrath '73–4 (12) Dubreuil '73–9 (61) Kilgour '74–9 (22) O'Brien '74–9 (30) D Kelly '70A '74–9 (33) Dye '74–5 (6) Ashmole '77–9 (15).

Symphonic Variations FPTC 9 Nov 1970 Royal, Nottingham Cr Rep I. '70 (19). *f* 1 Sibley (4) Peri (11) Linton (2) Park (2) 2 Penney (4) Beckley (7) C Hill (8) 3 Connor (11) Vere (8). *m* 1 Dowell (4) Mead (4) Cooke (8) MacLeary (3) 2 Mead (4) Sherwood (7) Kirkpatrick (8) 3 Coleman (4) Ashmole (7) Johnson (8).

Symphonie Pastorale, La P 13 May 1970 ROH *Ch* Geoffrey Cauley *M* Martinu *SC* Peter Unsworth. *Scenario* after Gide. '70 (4). A:5. *The Pastor* 1 Grater (4). 2 Fairweather (4). *Gertrude* 1 Thorogood (4) 2 Chapell (4). *The Pastor's Wife* Conley (4). *Jacques* Davel (4). *Dr Martins* Gordon (4). + 3*f* + CdB.

Take Five P 26 Sept 1978 sw *Ch* David Bintley *M* Dave Brubeck *SC* Mike Becket. '78 (3). 1 Seymour (3). 2 Dubreuil (3). 3 Morse (3). 4 O'Brien (3). 5 Waller (3).

Tilt FP 2 May 1973 sw *Ch* Hans van Manen *M* Stravinsky *SC* Jean-Paul Vroom. '73 (30). 3*f* from: Ruanne (14) Barbieri (16) Strike (25) Porter (6) Homji (9) Durant (2) Tait (10) Evans (8). 3*m* from: Jefferies (20) Myers (10) Clarke (12) Porter (20) Cooke (3) Vardon (14) Dubreuil (7) Waller '73 (4).

Toccata P 14 Dec 1962 Royal, Newcastle *Ch* Alan Carter *M* J S Bach orch John Lanchbery *SC* Peter Rice. '62 (3); '63 (51); '64 (19). *Fugue* 1 Wells '62–4 (21) Anderton '63–4 (21) Starr '63–4 (30) Debden '63 (1). 2 Gable '62–3 (5) Sherwood '63 (16) Westmoreland '63–4 (29) Britton '63–4 (23). 3 Emblen '62–4 (57) Mosaval '63–4 (16). *Adagio f* O'Conaire '62–4 (60) Orpin '63 (9) Saunders '64 (4). *m* Alex Bennett '62–3 (51) Aitken '63–4 (22). *Prelude f* Spira '62–3 (25) Debden '63–4 (48). *m* Beale '62–4 (69) Grater '64 (4). + CdB.

Tragédie à Vérone (Love Duet) FP 23 Nov 1972 Grand, Leeds *Ch* George Skibine *M* Berlioz *C* Alistair Livingstone. '72 (1); '73 (21). A:4. *f* Fonteyn '72–3 (3) Ruanne '73 (1) Barbieri '73 (15) Porter '73 (3). *m* Labis '72 (1) D Kelly '73 (3) McGrath '73 (15) Clarke '73 (3).

Triad FPTC 26 May 1972 Coliseu, Lisbon Cr Rep I. '72 (12); '73 (17). A:4. *The Girl* Trounson '72A/Evans '72–4 (4) Ruanne '72–3 (24). *The Boy* Clarke '72A '73 (4) D Kelly '72–3 (12) Kilgour '72–3 (10) Cooke '73 (3). *His Brother* Johnson '72A '73 (13) Jefferies '72–3 (16).

Tribute, The P 5 Feb 1965 RST Stratford *Ch* Norman Morrice *M* Roger Sessions *SC* Ralph Koltai. '65 (34). *A Waiter* Emblen (34). *The Lady in White* O'Conaire '65 (29) Humphreys '65 (5). *The Lady in Red* Ruanne (14) Saunders (20). *Her Husband* Farley (34). *The Lady in Black* Anderton (29) Williams (5). *The Stranger* Wall (34). + 8*f* 7m.

Tritsch-Tratsch FP 20m Sept 1947 sw *Ch* Cranko *M* Johann Strauss *C* Hedley Briggs. '47 (23); '48 (101); '49 (39); '50 (31); '51 (8); '52 (6); '53 (1). A:6. *The Girl* Fifield '47–'51 [49] Pet Miller '47–'53 (85) Surtees '48 [19] Bruce '48–'52 [45] Shore '48–'50 (2) Lane '50 (1) Gorham '50 (6). *The Sailors* 2 from: Boulton '47–9 [58] Poole '47–'52 [105] Britton '47–'53 (20) Darrell '47–8 [52] Trecu '48–'51 [46] Butterfield/Blair '48–'52 [67] Holden '48–'53 (50) Cranko '50 (13) Gillies '51 (3). nr '48 June 16m/e. *Also* Rep I. Divertissements.

Trumpet Concerto P 14 Sept 1950 Opera House, Manchester *Ch* Balanchine *M* Haydn *SC* Vivienne Kernot. '50 (17); '51 (4). 1 Beriosova '50–1 (15) Pat Miller '50 (6). 2 Blair '50–1 (16) Hogan '50 (4) Poole '50 (1). 3 Fifield '50 (8) Harrop '50–1 (13). 4 Lane '50–1 (13) Bruce '50–1 (8). 5 Poole '50–1 (14) Holden '50–1 (7). 6 Trecu '50–1 (17) McAlpine '50–1 (4). + 8f.

Twilight FP 2 Mar 1973 RST (Str) *Ch* Hans van Manen *M* John Cage *SC* Jean-Paul Vroom. '73 (35*); '74 (6). f Ruanne '73 (16) Strike '73–4 (19) Lorrayne '73–4 (5) Homji '74 (1). m Clarke '73 (17) Porter '73 (14) Jefferies '73–4 (10). *Also* Rep I. *includes 1 Gala ROH.

Two Pigeons, The (Deux Pigeons, Les) P 14 Feb 1961 ROH *Ch* Ashton *M* Messager *SC* Jacques Dupont. '61 (46); '62 (18); '63 (11); '64 (15); '65 (11); '66 (11); '67 (29); '68 (14); '69 (28); '70 (20); '76 (18); '77 (55); '78 (4); '79 (49). A:11. *The Young Man* Gable '61–6 (39) Britton '61–4 (40) I Hamilton '63–4 (4) Grant '64–5 (8) Wall '64–9 (34) Powell '66–8 (10) Clarke '66–'70 (26) Cooke '67–'70 (31) Mason '69 (2) McGrath '69–'70 (9) Myers '76–9 (36) Kilgour '76–9 (25) Ashmole '76–9 (35) D Kelly '77–9 (23) Berg '77–9 (7). *The Young Girl* Seymour '61–4 (29) Wells '61–'70 (81) Sibley '61–2 (7) Park '62–7 (3) Thorogood '64–'70 (41) Aldous '66–'70 (17) Conley '67–'70 (19) Chapell '69–'70 (6) Barbieri '76–9 (44) Aitken '76–9 (21) Tait '76–9 (42) Burton '76–7 (7) Jenner '77 (3) Katrak '79 (9). *A Gypsy Girl* Anderton '61–'70 (110) Farriss '61 (4) Layland '61–5 (27) Beckley '64 (3) Barbieri '66–'79 (35) Ruanne '66–'70 (31) Wade '70 (4) Wade-Barbieri '70 (1) Last '76–7 (16) Highwood '76–9 (37) Strike '76–9 (35) Gielgud '77 (7) C Williams '77–9 (7) Stanley '77–9 (8) Rowann '79 (3). + 26f 16m. *Also* Rep I.

Two Pigeons, The. pdd. '76 (1). *Young Man* Wall. *Young Girl* Seymour.

Unfamiliar Playground P 2 Oct 1974 sw *Ch* Christopher Bruce *M* Electronic tape Anthony Hymas/Brian Hodgson *SC* Nadine Baylis. '74 (16); '75 (6). 1 Tait '74–5 (22). 2 Jefferies '74–5 (20*) Reeder '75 (1). 3 Strike '74–5 (22). 4 Dubreuil '74–5 (22). 5 Highwood '74–5 (22). + 2f 3m. *1 performance Jefferies injured – role redistributed among rest of cast.

Vagabonds, The P 29 Oct 1946 sw *Ch* Anthony Burke *M* John Ireland *SC* Vivienne Kernot. '46 (10); '47 (85); '48 (34); '49 (18); '50 (5). *The Vagabond Girl* Brae '46–8 (21) Heaton '47 (40) Moore '47 (32) Claire '47–'50 (57) O'Reilly '50 (2). *Her Lover* A Carter '46–7 (19) A Burke '47–8 (78) Hogan '47–'50 (53) Poole '50 (2). *The Other Man* Kersley '46–9 (110) Cranko '46 (13) Poole '47–'50 (27) Gill '50 (2). *His Woman* Chrimes '46–8 (68) Wadsworth '47–8 (48) Shore '48–9 (31) Cadzow '50 (3) Farrance '51 (2). + 10f 7m.

Valses Nobles et Sentimentales P 1 Oct 1947 sw *Ch* Ashton *M* Ravel *SC* Sophie Fedorovitch. '47 (29); '48 (72); '49 (25); '50 (9); '51 (13); '52 (1); '53 (9); '54 (1). A:6. 1 Heaton '47–8 (30) Fifield '48–'53 (97) Lane '48–'50 (14) Beriosova '51 (10) Pat Miller '53–4 (7). 2 Britton '47–'53 (34) Poole '48–'54 (95) Trecu '48 (7) MacMillan '48 (14) Blair '50–3 (8). 3 Boulton '47–9 (99) MacMillan '48 (6) Poole '48–'51 (3) Trecu '49–'53 (34) Blair '49–'51 (13) Britton '53A Vernon '53–4 (3). + 4f 3m. nr '51 July 24.

Veneziana FPTC 28m Dec 1957 ROH Cr Rep I. '57 (1); '58 (51); '59 (8); '61 (6). A:39. *La Favorita* Lee '57–8 (36) Heaton '58 (10) Alexander '58–9 (10) Seymour '59 (4) Needham '61 (6). *Punchinello* Mosaval '57–'61 (49) Holden '58 (3) L White '58 (3) Hurd '58 (3) Alder '59 (8).

Walk to the Paradise Garden, The *see* Rep I.

Wedding Bouquet, A FPTC 14 May 1974 sw Cr Rep I. '74 (13); '75 (5). *Webster* Last '74–5 (4) Wade '74–5 (14). *Josephine* Lorrayne '74–5 (18). *Julia* Barbieri '74–5 (12) Strike '74–5 (6). *Bridegroom* Dubreuil '74–5 (18). *Bride* Tait '74–5 (12) Last '74–5 (6).

Divertissements

Bartered Bride, The Dances from, FP 12 Aug 1946 Open Air Theatre Finsbury Park *Ch* Sasha Machov *M* Smetana *C* Reece Pemberton. '46 (4). 6f 8m. NB Ballet *Ch* for Sadler's Wells Opera production 1943.

Corsaire, Le pdd FPTC 5e Aug 1973 Binyenei Ha'oomah, Jerusalem Cr Rep I. A:4. (f Lorrayne A. m Nureyev A).

Dance of the Tumblers, The from The Snow Maiden FP 16 Dec 1946 sw *Ch* de Valois *M* Rimsky-Korsakov *S* Barbara Heseltine. '46 (2); '47 (1). 5f 5m. NB Ballet *Ch* for Sadler's Wells Opera production 1946.

Don Quixote pdd FPTC 23 Sept 1958 Empire, Sydney Cr Rep I. *C* Olivia Cranmer; from '60 *C* nc. '59 (29); '60 (1); '61 (8); '62 (5); '63 (2); 64

(15); '72 (1); '73 (17). A:62. f Linden '59 (4) Seymour '58A '59–'61 (14) Nerina '59CG–'61 (4) Alexander '59 (12) Page '59–'64 (5) Sibley '60A '61 (1) Grey '60A Wells '61–2 (5) Beriosova '62 (1) Hayden '63 (2) Grahame '64 (12) Parkinson '72 (1) Park '73 (2) Strike '73 (9) Lorrayne '73 (6). m Blair '59–'64 (6) Britton '58A '59–'61 (14) Usher '59–'64 (11) Ashbridge '59–'61 (5) Hynd '59 (2) Doyle '60A '61–2 (5) MacLeary '62 (1) Gable '62 (2) Flindt '63 (2) I Hamilton '64 (8) Sherwood '64–'73 (5) D Kelly '72–3 (3) Johnson '73 (8) McGrath '73 (6).

Dying Swan, The FP 17 Nov 1960 Hippodrome, Bristol *Ch* Fokine *M* Saint-Saëns *C* nc. '60 (2). Markova (2).

Farruca del Sacro Monte P 7 May 1948 Arts, Cambridge *Ch* Angelo Andes *M* Azagra *C* Traditional. '48 (43); '49 (9). Trecu '48–9 (52).

Forme et Ligne FP 29 Sept 1976 sw *Ch* Béjart *M* Pierre Henry *C* nc. '76 (1). Gielgud.

Four Seasons, The *Summer* pdd FP 29 Sept 1976 sw Cr Rep I. '76 (1). f Barbieri. m Kelly.

Jota Toledana P 28 Apr 1948 New, Hull *Ch* Angelo Andes revised as pdd '49. *M/C* Traditional. '48 (36); '49 (58); '50 (23); '51 (6); '52 (8); '53 (1). A:7. m Trecu '48–'53 (127) Wright '50 (5). f O'Reilly '49–'53 (89) Shore '50 (5) Bruce '52 (2).

Laurentia pas de six FPTC 26 Apr 1972 Odeon, Golders Green Cr Rep I. '72 (3). A:6. 1 C Hill (3) 2 Last (3) 3 Tait (3) 4 Jefferies (3) 5 Johnson (3) 6 Clarke (3). *also* Ruanne A. McGrath A. Cooke A.

Mirror Walkers, The pdd FPTC 16 Feb 1972 sw Cr Rep I. '72 (25); '73 (3); '74 (7); '76 (1). A:9. f Park '72–3 (7) Evans '72–4 (16) Strike '72–3 (11) Tait '74 (2). m D Kelly '72–6 (12) Jefferies '72 (8) McGrath '72–3 (8) Kilgour '72–3 (7) MacLeary '73 (1).

Nutcracker, The pdd FPTC 26 June 1968 Teatro del Generalife, Granada Cr Rep I A:3. (f Aldous A. m Nureyev A).

Pavane FPTC 15 Feb 1980 RST (Str) Cr Rep I *C* Deborah Williams. f Tait. m D Kelly.

Puerta de Tierra P 11 Dec 1953 sw *Ch* Roberto Ximenez *M* Albeniz orch Salabert *C* Anthony Boyes. '53 (2); '54 (21). Trecu '53–4 (23).

Raymonda, pdd, variations, coda *see* Rep I.

Raymonda, Scène d'Amour FPTC 5 Mar 1973 Royal, Norwich Cr Rep I. '73 (22). A:3. f Lorrayne (19) Ruanne (3). m McGrath (17) D Kelly (3) Clarke (2).

Valse Eccentrique FPTC 30 July 1972 The Maltings, Snape Cr Rep I. '72 (9); '73 (8). f Last '72–3 (11) Merry '72–3 (3) Barbieri '73 (2) Strike '73 (1). 2 m from: Cooke '72 (3) Morse '72–3 (13) Bertscher '72–3 (9) Bart '72–3 (2) Killar '72–3 (4) Porter '73 (3).

Productions (II)

Ballets produced by Sadler's Wells Theatre Ballet/Touring Company/New Group/Sadler's Wells Royal Ballet.

Note Asterisks(*) indicate ballets created for the Company

1946
Apr 8   Promenade
            *Assembly Ball
            Casse-Noisette Act III
     22   Sylphides, Les
     29   Façade
May 6   Spectre de la Rose, Le
     27   *Khadra
June 10   Gods go a'Begging, The
Oct 19   *Catch, The
     29   *Vagabonds, The
Nov 26   *Mardi Gras
1947
Jan   7   Haunted Ballroom, The
Feb   4   *Bailemos
Mar 25   Fête Etrange, La
May 19   Adieu (*Ch* Cranko)
     21   Carnaval
Sept 20m   Tritsch-Tratsch
            Lac des Cygnes, La, pdt
Oct   1   *Valses Nobles et Sentimentales
Dec 26   Rendezvous, Les
1948
Jan 21   *Parures
Apr   6   Children's Corner
            Giselle, pdd
Oct   5   Capriol Suite
Nov 16   *Selina
1949
Mar 15   Etude (*Ch* McNaught)
May 16   Lac des Cygnes, Le, Act II
July 18   *Sea Change
Dec 20   *Beauty and the Beast
     27m   Blue Bird, The, pdd
1950
Jan 31   *Destino, El
Mar 28   *Summer Interlude
Sept 14   *Trumpet Concerto
Dec 19   *Pastorale
1951
Feb 13   Prospect Before Us, The
Mar 13   *Pineapple Poll
May 8   *Harlequin in April
Sept 4   Coppélia
     11   Casse-Noisette (NP)
1952
June 18   Rake's Progress, The
Aug 21   *Reflection
Sept 19   Ile des Sirènes
1953
Jan 21   *Great Detective, The
June 5   *Blood Wedding
Sept 10   *Carte Blanche

Dec 11   *Puerta de Tierra
1954
Feb 25   *Lady and the Fool, The
May 24   *Café des Sports
1955
Jan 18   *Danses Concertantes
Apr 23m   Patineurs, Les
May 26   *House of Birds
Oct 13   *Saudades
1956
Jan 16   Coppélia (NP)
May 29   Somnambulism
June 7   *Solitaire
July 28   Giselle Act II
Aug 18   Giselle
1957
Jan 28   Apparitions
Dec 26   *Blue Rose, A
            *Angels, The
     28m   Veneziana
1958
Jan   2   *Burrow, The
June 27   Lac des Cygnes, Le
Nov   4   Hamlet
1959
Sept 14   Sleeping Beauty, The
     16   Belle Dame sans Merci, La
Dec 10m   *Sweeney Todd
1960
Nov 10   *Invitation, The
1961
Feb 14   *Deux Pigeons, Les
            (Two Pigeons, The)
Apr 18   Checkmate
1962
Oct 27m   Flower Festival at Genzano
            pas de deux
            Napoli, Divertissement
Nov   9   Fille Mal Gardée, La
Dec 14   *Toccata
1963
May 17   Bal des Voleurs, Le
1964
Feb 12   *Création du Monde, La (*Ch* MacMillan)
July 10   Raymonda
Oct 29   *Summer's Night Quintet
1965
Feb   5   *Tribute, The
May 18   Swan Lake (NP)
1966
May 7   Raymonda Act III
Dec   2   Dream, The
1967
Feb 10   *Sinfonietta
May 26   Concerto
1968
Jan 31   Boutique Fantasque, La
            Mam'zelle Angot

May 15   Giselle (NP)
     28   Monotones Nos 1 and 2
Nov 25   *Knight Errant
1969
Jan 17   Intrusion
            *In the Beginning
Dec   5   Lazarus
1970
Jan 30   *From Waking Sleep
May 13   *Symphonie Pastorale, La
June 6   *Creatures of Prometheus, The
Nov   9   Apollo
            *Field Figures
            Symphonic Variations
     12   Lilac Garden
     27   *Checkpoint
1971
Feb   8   *Overture
     10   Diversions
            *Grand Tour, The
June 2   Hermanas, Las
      7   St Thomas' Wake
      9   *Ante Room
Oct 12   Caprichos
     19   Maids, The
1972
Feb 22   *O.W.
Apr 29m   Grosse Fuge
May 19   *Ballade
     26   Triad
Oct 12   *Poltroon, The
     26   *In a Summer Garden
1973
Feb 27   Allegro Brillante
Mar   2   Twilight
            *Sacred Circles
     16   *Migration
May   2   Tilt
Aug   8   Prodigal Son
Oct   3   Card Game
     23   *Sword of Alsace
1974
Feb 12   Septet Extra
Mar   8   *Charlotte Brontë
May   2   *Entertainers, The
     14   Wedding Bouquet, A
Oct   2   *Unfamiliar Playground
1975
Feb 14   Arpège
            *Shukumei
Apr 15   Coppélia (NP)
Sept 5   *Amor Brujo, El
1976
Jan 30   *Pandora
June 2   *Lulu
     30   Sleeping Beauty, The, Act III
            (Aurora's Wedding)
Oct   4   Four Temperaments, The
     12   *Summertide
     19   *Rashomon

1977
Feb 11   *Birdscape
Apr 21   *Court of Love, The
May 5   Gemini
Aug 26   Concerto Barocco
Sept 20   Soft Blue Shadows
1978
Feb 10   Elite Syncopations
Mar 16   *Outsider, The
May 3   Brouillards
    12   *Game Piano
Sept 26   *Take Five
    *6.6.78
Oct 10   *Intimate Letters
1979
Feb 9   Coppélia (NP)
Mar 16   *Meadow of Proverbs
    30m   Rhyme nor Reason
Aug 20   *Punch and the Street Party
    24   *Playground
1980
Feb 7   Papillon
    15   *Homage to Chopin
Mar 28   *Day into Night
Apr 17   Paquita
June 20   Catch

The Company also appeared in the following Covent Garden productions during their seasons at the Royal Opera House. Casting details *see* Repertory I.
1960
Dec 14   Cinderella

1963
May 6   Sylvia
1970
Apr 23   Job
1968
May 28   Marguerite and Armand (on tour Europe only)

Divertissements

1946
Aug 12   Bartered Bride, The, Dances from (*see* Repertory II for première)
Dec 16   Snow Maiden, The, Dance of the Tumblers (*see* Repertory II for première)
1948
Apr 28   Jota Toledana
May 7   Farruca del Sacro Monte
1958
Sept 23   Don Quixote pdd
1960
Nov 17   Dying Swan, The (guest appearance Markova only)

1968
June 26   Nutcracker, The, pdd (*Ch* Nureyev)
1972
Feb 16   Mirror Walkers, The, pdd
Apr 26   Laurentia pds
June 15   Romeo and Juliet, Balcony pdd
July 28   Siesta
    30   Valse Eccentrique
Nov 23   Tragédie à Vérone, Balcony pdd
1973
Mar 5   Raymonda, Scène d'Amour
1976
Sept 29   Four Seasons, The, Summer pdd
1980
Feb 15   Pavane

Items performed by dancers from Covent Garden Company. Casting details in relevant section Repertory I.
1964
May 27   Raymonda pdd, variations and coda
1968
May 28   Corsaire, Le, pdd
1972
Apr 1m   *Side Show
July 30   Lord of Burleigh, The – Lady with a Fan
1973
Oct 23   Walk to the Paradise Garden, The

Itinerary (II)

Itinerary of performances by Sadler's Wells Theatre Ballet/Touring Company/New Group/Sadler's Wells Royal Ballet. London theatres are shown in italics.

1946
Apr 8–22 June *Sadler's Wells*
July 1– 6 Exeter, Royal
     8–13 Brighton, Royal
    15–20 Bath, Royal
    22–27 Cambridge, Arts
    29– 3 Aug Cheltenham, Opera House
Aug 5–30 Finsbury Park, Open Air Theatre
Oct 19–
1947 –10 May *Sadler's Wells*
May 19–24 Brighton, Royal
     26–31 Cambridge, Arts
June 2– 7 Cheltenham, Opera House
      9–14 Peterborough, Embassy
     16–21 Bath, Royal
     23–28 Exeter, Royal
     30– 5 July Croydon, Grand
July 7–12 Reading, Palace
     14–19 Norwich, Royal
     21–26 Harrogate, Royal Hall
     28– 9 Aug Finsbury Park, Open Air Theatre
Sept 20– 8 Nov *Sadler's Wells*
Nov 10–15 Worcester, Royal
     17–22 Stratford, Shakespeare Memorial
     24–29 Bristol, Royal
Dec   1– 6 Kidderminster, Playhouse
     13–
1948 – 7 Feb *Sadler's Wells*
Feb   9–14 Darlington, New Hippodrome
     16–21 Huddersfield, Royal
     23–28 Halifax, Grand
Mar   4–17 Apr *Sadler's Wells*
Apr 26– 1 May Hull, New
May   3– 8 Cambridge, Arts
     10–15 Reading, Palace
     17–22 Wimbledon, Wimbledon Theatre
     24– 5 June Brighton, Royal
June 7–12 Norwich, Royal
     14–19 Peterborough, Embassy
     21–26 Kilburn, Empire
     29–10 July Belfast, Grand Opera House
July 12–17 Dublin, Gaiety
     19–24 Hanley, Royal
     26– 7 Aug Finsbury Park, Open Air Theatre
Oct   2–30 *Sadler's Wells*
Nov   1– 6 Darlington, Hippodrome
     13–

1949 –19 Feb *Sadler's Wells*
Feb 21–26 Stratford, Shakespeare Memorial
Mar   3–14 May *Sadler's Wells*
May 16–21 Cambridge, Arts
     23–28 Peterborough, Embassy
     30– 2 June Hanley, Royal
June 6–11 Hull, New
     13–18 Brighton, Royal
     20–25 Mile End, People's Palace
     27– 9 July Belfast, Grand Opera House
July 11–23 Dublin, Gaiety
Sept 5–24 Manchester, Opera House
     27–
1950 –20 May *Sadler's Wells*
May 22–27 Cambridge, Arts
     29– 3 June Hull, Arts
June 5–10 Peterborough, Embassy
     12–17 Norwich, Royal
     19–24 Brighton, Royal
     29– 1 July Bournemouth, Pavilion
July 3– 8 Cheltenham, Opera House
     10–15 Finsbury Park, Open Air Theatre
Sept 4–16 Manchester, Opera House
     19–
1951 – 9 June *Sadler's Wells*
June 13–23 Bournemouth, Pavilion
     25– 5 July Oxford, New
July 9–21 Finsbury Park, Open Air Theatre
     23–28 Cambridge, Arts
Sept 1–21 *Sadler's Wells*
Oct   5– 6 Quebec, Capitol
      9–12 Montreal, St Denis
     15–20 Toronto, Royal Alexandra
     22–23 Buffalo, Buffalo Theatre
     24–25 Rochester, Eastman
     26 Cleveland, Music Hall
     27–29 Detroit, Masonic Temple
     30 East Lansing, College Auditorium
Nov   2 Grand Rapids, Auditorium
      3 Milwaukee, Pabst Theater Auditorium
      5–6 Minneapolis, Northrop Auditorium
      8 Omaha, Orpheum
      9 Sioux City, Municipal Auditorium
     10 Des Moines, KRNT Theater
     11–14 Denver, Denver Auditorium
     15–17 Salt Lake City, Capitol
     19–21 Seattle, Civic Auditorium
     22–24 Portland, Public Auditorium
     26– 1 Dec Vancouver, Strand

Dec   3– 5 San Francisco, War Memorial Opera House
      7 Sacramento, Memorial Auditorium
      8–13 San Francisco, War Memorial Opera House
     14 Berkeley, Civic Auditorium
     16 Bakersfield, Harvey Auditorium
     17 San Diego, Russ High School Auditorium
     25– 2 Jan Los Angeles, Philharmonic Auditorium
1952
Jan   3 Pasadena, Civic Auditorium
      4– 5 Los Angeles, Philharmonic Auditorium
      7 San Antonio, Municipal Auditorium
      8 Waco, Waco Hall, Gaylor School of Music
      9–10 Houston, City Auditorium
     11–12 Dallas, State Fair Auditorium
     14 Shreveport, Municipal Auditorium
     15 Little Rock, Robinson Memorial Auditorium
     16 Springfield, Shrine Mosque
     17–19 Kansas City, Music Hall
     21–27 Chicago, Civic Opera House
     29–30 St Louis, Kiel Auditorium
     31 Chattanooga, Memorial Auditorium
Feb   1 Knoxville, Alumni Memorial Auditorium
      2– 3 Atlanta, Municipal Auditorium
      5 Birmingham, Municipal Auditorium
      6 Montgomery, City Auditorium
      7– 9 New Orleans, Municipal Auditorium
     11 Daytona, City Auditorium
     12 Orlando, City Auditorium
     13–15 Miami, Dade County Auditorium
     16 Miami, Beach, Municipal Auditorium
     18 Columbia
     19 Greensboro, Aycock Auditorium
     20 Raleigh, Raleigh Memorial Auditorium
     21 Durham, Page Auditorium

Itinerary (II)

22	Norfolk, Center
23	Richmond, Mosque
25–27	Washington, Capitol
28– 1 Mar	Philadelphia, Academy of Music
Mar 3– 4	Pittsburgh, Syria Mosque
5	Columbus, City Auditorium
6	Toledo, Paramount
7– 8	Cincinnati, Music Hall
9	Indianapolis, Murat
11	Syracuse, Loew's State
12	Troy, RPI Field House
13	White Plains, RKO
14	Providence, Metropolitan
15	Hartford, Bushnell Memorial
17–22	Boston, Opera House
25– 6 Apr	New York, Warner
Apr 24– 5 July	Sadler's Wells
Aug 18–23	Edinburgh, Empire
29–18 Oct	Sadler's Wells
Oct 20–25	Oxford, New
27– 8 Nov	Leeds, Grand
Nov 10–15	Sheffield, Lyceum
17–22	Hull, New
24–29	Birmingham, Alexandra
Dec 1– 6	Norwich, New Royal
10–	
1953 – 7 Feb	Sadler's Wells
Feb 9–21	Stratford, SMT
23–28	Wolverhampton, Grand
Mar 2– 7	Blackpool, Opera House
9–14	Southport, Garrick
21– 4 Apr	Sadler's Wells
Apr 6	The Hague, Gebouw Kunsten en Wetenschappen
7– 8	Amsterdam, Stadsschouwburg
9	The Hague, Gebouw Kunsten en Wetenschappen
10	Rotterdam, Schouwburg voorstelling Zaterdag
11	Utrecht, Stadsschouwburg
12	The Hague, Stadsschouwburg
14	Antwerp, Koninklijke Nederlandse Schouwburg
15	Antwerp, Koninklijke Vlaamse Opera
16	Brussels, Théâtre Royal de la Monnaie
17	Liège, Grand Théâtre Royal
18–20	Brussels, Théâtre Royal de la Monnaie
22–23	Munich, Staatsoper
24	Nuremberg, Städtische Bühnen Opernhaus
Date unknown	Frankfurt, Althofbau
27–28	Hanover, Landestheater Opernhaus
29	Hamburg, Operettenhaus
30	Neumünster, Holstenhalle
May 1– 2	Düsseldorf, Städtische Bühnen Opernhaus
3	Cologne, Städtische Bühnen Aula der Universität
8–20 June	Sadler's Wells
July 6–18	Bulawayo, Royal
Sept 7–12	Edinburgh, Empire
14–19	Manchester, Opera House
21–26	Brighton, Essoldo
Oct 2–24	Sadler's Wells
26–31	Cardiff, New
Nov 2– 7	Liverpool, Royal Court
9–14	Coventry, Hippodrome
16–21	Birmingham, Alexandra
23–28	Nottingham, Royal
30– 5 Dec	Peterborough, Embassy
Dec 9–	
1954 – 30 Jan	Sadler's Wells
Feb 1– 6	Stratford, Shakespeare Memorial
8–13	Morecambe, Winter Gardens
15–20	Stockton-on-Tees, Globe
22–27	Oxford, New
Mar 1– 6	Wolverhampton, Grand
8–13	Bradford, Alhambra
15–20	Derby, Hippodrome
22–27	Norwich, Royal
31– 3 Apr	Sadler's Wells
Apr 27–12 June	Johannesburg, His Majesty's
June 14–26	Durban, Alhambra
28–15 July	Cape Town, Alhambra
Sept 20–25	Newcastle, Royal
27– 2 Oct	Glasgow, Royal
Oct 4– 9	Aberdeen, His Majesty's
11–16	Sheffield, Lyceum
18–23	Nottingham, Royal
25–30	Leeds, Grand
Nov 1– 6	Hanley, Royal
8–13	Birmingham, Alexandra
18–	
1955 – 5 Feb	Sadler's Wells
Feb 7–12	Stratford, Shakespeare Memorial
14–19	Preston, Gaumont
21–26	Wolverhampton, Grand
28– 5 Mar	Oxford, New
Mar 7–12	Derby, Hippodrome
14–19	Bradford, Alhambra
21–26	Stockton-on-Tees, Globe
28– 2 Apr	Norwich, Royal
Apr 4– 9	Southsea, King's
12–11 June	Sadler's Wells
June 13–18	Llandudno, Odeon
20–25	Morecambe, Winter Gardens
27– 2 July	Swansea, Empire
July 4– 9	Southampton, Gaumont
11–23	Plymouth, Palace
25–30	Brighton, Essoldo
Sept 19–24	Dublin, Olympia
26– 8 Oct	Belfast, Opera House
Oct 10–15	Liverpool, Royal Court
17–22	Leeds, Grand
24–29	Edinburgh, King's
31– 5 Nov	Glasgow, King's
Nov 7–12	Aberdeen, His Majesty's
14–19	Dundee, Gaumont
21– 3 Dec	Newcastle, Royal
Dec 5–10	Chester, Gaumont
12–17	Dublin, Olympia
1956	
Jan 6	Sadler's Wells
16–21	Stratford, Shakespeare Memorial
23–28	Preston, Gaumont
30– 4 Feb	Southend, Odeon
Feb 6–11	Ipswich, Gaumont
13–18	Norwich, Royal
20–25	Wolverhampton, Grand
27– 3 Mar	Birmingham, Alexandra
Mar 5–10	Stockton-on-Tees, Globe
12–17	Manchester, Opera House
19–24	Bradford, Alhambra
26–31	Nottingham, Royal
Apr 9–14	Southsea, King's
16–21	Bournemouth, Pavilion
23–28	Bristol, Hippodrome
30– 5 May	Sheffield, Lyceum
May 7–12	Sunderland, Empire
14–19	Hanley, Royal
21–26	Oxford, New
29–16 June	Sadler's Wells
July 18–23	Brighton, Hippodrome
26, 28	Granada, Jardines del Generalife
Aug 17–21	Santander Festival, Plaza Porticada
27– 1 Sept	Cheltenham, Opera House
Sept 3– 8	Streatham, Streatham Hill Theatre
10–15	Golders Green, Hippodrome
17–22	Cardiff, Gaumont
24–29	Newcastle, Royal
Oct 1– 6	Leeds, Grand
15–20	Leicester, De Montfort Hall
22–27	Liverpool, Royal Court
29– 3 Nov	Glasgow, Alhambra
Nov 5–10	Aberdeen, His Majesty's
12–17	Edinburgh, King's
19–24	Stockton-on-Tees, Globe
26– 1 Dec	Hull, New
Dec 3– 8	Nottingham, Royal
1957	
Jan 14–19	Brighton, Essoldo
21– 2 Feb	Stratford, Shakespeare Memorial
Feb 4– 9	Cambridge, Arts
11–16	Bournemouth, Pavilion
18–23	Wolverhampton, Grand
25– 2 Mar	Southampton, Gaumont
Mar 4– 9	Birmingham, Alexandra
11–16	Sheffield, Lyceum
18–23	Peterborough, Embassy
25–30	Norwich, Royal
Apr 8–13	Southsea, King's
15–20	Plymouth, Palace
26–23 May	Barcelona, Gran Teatro del Liceo

May	25–26	Saragossa, Iris
	28–29	Oviedo, Marquee
	31– 2 June	Bilbao, Coliseo
June	6– 7	Cologne, Opernhaus
	11–15	Zürich, Stadtheater
	18	The Hague, Gebouw voor Kunsten en Wetenschappen
	19	Amsterdam, Stadsschouwburg
	20	Rotterdam, Schouwburg
	21	Utrecht, Stadsschouwburg
	22	The Hague, Gebouw voor Kunsten en Wetenschappen
	23	Amsterdam, Stadsschouwburg
July	2–20	*Sadler's Wells*
Sept	9–14	Streatham, Streatham Hill Theatre
	16–21	Golders Green, Hippodrome
	23–28	Southsea, King's
	30– 5 Oct	Bristol, Hippodrome
Oct	7–12	Oxford, New
	14–19	Manchester, Opera House
	21–26	Edinburgh, King's
	28– 2 Nov	Glasgow, King's
Nov	4– 9	Aberdeen, His Majesty's
	11–16	Sheffield, Lyceum
	18–23	Leeds, Grand
	25–30	Hull, New
Dec	26–	
1958	–17 Jan	*Royal Opera House*
Jan	20–25	Brighton, Essoldo
	27– 1 Feb	Sutton, Granada
Feb	3– 8	Norwich, Royal
	10–22	Cambridge, Arts
	24– 1 Mar	Stratford, Shakespeare Memorial
Mar	3– 8	Wolverhampton, Grand
	10–15	Bournemouth, Pavilion
	17–22	Plymouth, Palace
	24–29	Cardiff, New
Apr	7–12	Nottingham, Royal
	14–19	Coventry, Coventry Theatre
	21–26	Liverpool, Royal Court
	28– 3 May	Dublin, Olympia
May	5–17	Belfast, Grand Opera House
	19–24	Blackpool, Grand
	26–31	Bradford, Alhambra
June	2– 7	Newcastle, Royal
	9–14	Peterborough, Embassy
	25– 3 July	*Royal Opera House*
July	7–12	Cheltenham, Opera House
Sept	11– 8 Nov	Sydney, Empire
Nov	10–	
1959	– 3 Jan	Melbourne, Her Majesty's
Jan	7–31	Adelaide, Royal
Feb	3–25	Brisbane, Her Majesty's
Mar	4– 7	Dunedin, His Majesty's
	9–21	Christchurch, Royal
	23– 4 Apr	Wellington, Grand Opera House

Apr	6–18	Auckland, His Majesty's
May	11–16	Bournemouth, Pavilion
	18–23	Cardiff, New
	25– 6 June	Birmingham, Alexandra
June	8–13	Southsea, King's
	15–20	Sutton, Granada
Aug	17–12 Sept	*Royal Opera House*
Sept	14–19	Leeds, Grand
	21–26	Newcastle, Royal
	28– 3 Oct	Sheffield, Lyceum
Oct	5–10	Liverpool, Royal Court
	12–17	Glasgow, King's
	19–24	Aberdeen, His Majesty's
	26–31	Edinburgh, King's
Nov	2– 7	Stockton-on-Tees, Globe
	9–14	Manchester, Opera House
	16–21	Nottingham, Royal
	23–28	Oxford, New
	30– 5 Dec	Bristol, Hippodrome
Dec	7–19	Stratford, Shakespeare Memorial
	28– 2 Jan	Woolwich, Granada
1960		
Jan	4– 7	Brighton, Essoldo
	11–16	Leicester, De Montfort Hall
	18–23	Southampton, Gaumont
Feb	5–29	Johannesburg, Empire
Mar	1m	Johannesburg, City Hall
	1e–19	Johannesburg, Empire
	21–22	Pietermaritzburg, Grand
	24– 9 Apr	Durban, Alhambra
Apr	12–30	Cape Town, Alhambra
May	16–28	Dublin, Gaiety
	30– 4 June	Belfast, Grand Opera House
June	6–11	Blackpool, Opera House
	13–18	Bradford, Alhambra
Aug	15–27	*Royal Opera House*
	29– 3 Sept	Nottingham, Royal
Sept	5–10	Wolverhampton, Grand
	12–17	Newcastle, Royal
	19–24	Aberdeen, His Majesty's
	26– 1 Oct	Glasgow, King's
Oct	3– 8	Sheffield, Lyceum
	10–15	Liverpool, Royal Court
	17–22	Manchester, Opera House
	24–29	Leeds, Grand
	31–12 Nov	Oxford, New
Nov	14–19	Bristol, Hippodrome
	21–26	Southsea, King's
	28– 3 Dec	Brighton, Hippodrome
Dec	14–	
1961	–12 Apr	*Royal Opera House*
Apr	17–18	Tokyo, Festival Hall
	20–24	Tokyo, Bunkyo Hall
	26–30	Tokyo, Takarazuka
May	3– 6	Osaka, Festival Hall
	9–14	Tokyo, Festival Hall
	16–17	Hong Kong, Lee
	19–21	Manila, Rizal
June	5–10	Streatham, Streatham Hill Theatre
	12–17	Golders Green, Hippodrome
	19–24	Southend, Odeon
	26–31	Norwich, Royal

Aug	29– 1 Sept	Baalbek, Temple of Bacchus
Sept	2– 3	Damascus, British Trade Fair
	6– 8	Athens, Herodes Atticus
	25–30	Bournemouth, Pavilion
Oct	2–14	Torquay, Pavilion
	16–28	Oxford, New
	30– 4 Nov	Manchester, Opera House
Nov	6–11	Glasgow, King's
	13–18	Edinburgh, King's
	20–25	Newcastle, Royal
	27– 2 Dec	Liverpool, Royal Court
Dec	4– 9	Sheffield, Lyceum
	23– 1 Jan	Monte Carlo, Théâtre du Casino
1962		
Jan	29– 3 Feb	Sutton, Granada
Feb	5–17	Stratford, Royal Shakespeare
	19–24	Brighton, Hippodrome
	26– 3 Mar	Southampton, Gaumont
Mar	5–10	Wolverhampton, Grand
	12–17	Sunderland, Civic
	19–24	Hull, New
	26–31	Leeds, Grand
Apr	2– 7	Nottingham, Royal
	9–14	Norwich, Royal
	23–28	Southsea, King's
	30– 5 May	Cardiff, New
May	7–12	Blackpool, Opera House
	14–19	Belfast, Grand Opera House
	21–26	Dublin, Gaiety
June	4– 6	Lausanne, Théâtre de Beaulieu
	11–13	Munich, Bayerisches Staatsoper
	18–23	Bath, Royal
	25–30	Shrewsbury, Granada
July	5– 7	Nervi, Teatro di Parchi
Sept	10–15	Oslo, Nationaltheatret
	18–23	Stockholm, Kungliga Teatern
	25–30	Berlin, Theater des Westens
Oct	2– 4	Hamburg, Staatsoper
	6– 7	Malmö, Stadsteater
	10–14	Copenhagen, Kongelige Teater
	22– 3 Nov	Torquay, Princess'
Nov	5–10	Bristol, Hippodrome
	12–17	Bournemouth, Pavilion
	19–24	Oxford, New
	26– 1 Dec	Manchester, Opera House
Dec	3– 8	Liverpool, Royal Court
	10–15	Newcastle, Royal
	17–22	Leicester, De Montfort Hall
1963		
Jan	7–12	Southend, Odeon
	14–19	Ipswich, Gaumont
	21–26	Brighton, Essoldo
	28– 2 Feb	Southampton, Gaumont
Feb	4– 9	Taunton, Gaumont
	11–16	Wimbledon, Wimbledon Theatre

18– 2 Mar	Stratford, Royal Shakespeare
Mar 4– 9	Sunderland, Empire
11–23	Leeds, Grand
25–30	Hull, New
Apr 1– 6	Norwich, Royal
19	Guildford, Odeon
May 6–29 June	*Royal Opera House*
Sept 9–14	Wolverhampton, Grand
16–21	Nottingham, Royal
23–28	Coventry, Coventry Theatre
30–12 Oct	Torquay, Princess'
Oct 14–19	Oxford, New
21–26	Eastbourne, Congress
28– 2 Nov	Bournemouth, Pavilion
Nov 4– 9	Paris, Théâtre des Champs-Elysées
11–16	Leeds, Grand
18–23	Sheffield, Lyceum
25–30	Stockton-on-Tees, Globe
Dec 2– 7	Newcastle, Royal
9–14	Glasgow, King's
16–21	Blackpool, Opera House
1964	
Jan 20–25	Sutton, Granada
27– 1 Feb	Taunton, Gaumont
Feb 3–15	Stratford, Royal Shakespeare
17–22	Wimbledon, Wimbledon Theatre
24–29	Southampton, Gaumont
Mar 2– 7	Brighton, Hippodrome
9–14	Bristol, Hippodrome
16–20	Birmingham, Alexandra
30– 4 Apr	Cardiff, New
Apr 6–11	Shrewsbury, Grand
13–18	Bradford, Alhambra
20–25	Sunderland, Empire
27– 2 May	Cambridge, Arts
May 7– 8	*Royal Opera House*
20–21	Wiesbaden, Hessisches Staatstheater
23–24	Düsseldörf, Deutsche Oper am Rhein
25	Duisburg, Deutsche Oper am Rhein
27–28	Lausanne, Théâtre de Beaulieu
30– 1 June	Munich, Bayerisches Staatsoper
June 3– 4	Stuttgart, Würtemburgische Staatstheater
5– 7	Zürich, Stadttheater
8–10	Brussels, Théâtre Royal de la Monnaie
11	Bremen, Théater des Freien Hansestadt
13	Cologne, Opernhaus
15	Amsterdam, Stadsschouwburg
16	The Hague, Gebouw voor Kunsten en Wetenschappen
17	Utrecht, Stadsschouwburg
18	Amsterdam, Stadsschouwburg
19	The Hague, Gebouw voor Kunsten en Wetenschappen
20	Rotterdam, Rotterdamse Schouwburg
21	Amsterdam, Stadsschouwburg
July 10–19	Spoleto, Teatro Nuovo
22–26	Baalbek, Temple of Bacchus
Sept 21–26	Coventry, Coventry Theatre
28– 3 Oct	Southsea, King's
Oct 5–10	Bournemouth, Pavilion
12–17	Eastbourne, Congress
19–31	Oxford, New
Nov 2–14	Leeds, Grand
16–21	Liverpool, Royal Court
23– 5 Dec	Manchester, Opera House
Dec 7–19	Newcastle, Royal
1965	
Jan 18–23	Southampton, Gaumont
25– 6 Feb	Stratford, Royal Shakespeare
Feb 8–13	Hull, New
15–20	Doncaster, Gaumont
22–27	Derby, Gaumont
Mar 1– 6	Cambridge, Arts
8–13	Bristol, Hippodrome
15–20	Birmingham, Alexandra
22–27	Sunderland, Empire
29– 3 Apr	Aberdeen, His Majesty's
Apr 5–10	Edinburgh, King's
12–17	Glasgow, Alhambra
May 18–17 July	*Royal Opera House*
Sept 13–18	Golders Green, Hippodrome
20–25	Coventry, Coventry Theatre
27– 2 Oct	Wimbledon, Wimbledon Theatre
Oct 4– 9	Eastbourne, Congress
11–16	Bournemouth, Pavilion
18–30	Oxford, New
Nov 1–13	Manchester, Opera House
15–20	Newcastle, Royal
22–27	Liverpool, Royal Court
29–11 Dec	Leeds, Grand
1966	
Jan 10–15	Sutton, Granada
17– 5 Feb	Stratford, Royal Shakespeare
Feb 7–12	Leicester, De Montfort Hall
14–19	Norwich, Royal
21–26	Cambridge, Arts
28– 5 Mar	Wolverhampton, Grand
Mar 7–12	Cardiff, New
14–19	Bristol, Hippodrome
21–26	Sunderland, Empire
28– 2 Apr	Glasgow, King's
Apr 4– 9	Edinburgh, King's
May 5– 8	Helsinki, Suomen Kansallisopera
10–13	Oslo, Nationaltheatret
15–16	Brussels, Théâtre Royal de la Monnaie
17	Antwerp, Zaal Koningin Elisabeth
18	Heerlen, Stadsschouwburg
19	Osnabrück, Theater am Domhof
21–22	Wiesbaden, Hessisches Staatstheater
June 9–30 July	*Royal Opera House*
Sept 26– 1 Oct	Coventry, Coventry Theatre
Oct 3– 8	Liverpool, Royal Court
10–22	Newcastle, Royal
24– 5 Nov	Leeds, Grand
Nov 7–19	Manchester, Opera House
21– 3 Dec	Oxford, New
Dec 5–10	Bristol, Hippodrome
1967	
Jan 9–14	Eastbourne, Congress
16–21	Sutton, Granada
23–28	Southampton, Gaumont
30–18 Feb	Stratford, Royal Shakespeare
Feb 20–25	Norwich, Royal
27– 4 Mar	Cambridge, Arts
Mar 6–11	Hull, New
13–18	Edinburgh, King's
20–25	Glasgow, King's
27– 1 Apr	Nottingham, Royal
May 3–29 July	*Royal Opera House*
Sept 25–21 Oct	Glasgow, King's
Oct 23–18 Nov	Manchester, Opera House
Nov 20– 2 Dec	Sunderland, Empire
Dec 4– 9	Oxford, New
1968	
Jan 8– 3 Feb	Stratford, Royal Shakespeare
Feb 5–10	Southend, Odeon
12–24	Bournemouth, Pavilion
26– 2 Mar	Norwich, Royal
Mar 4–16	Leeds, Grand
Apr 8–22 May	*Royal Opera House*
May 28–30	Wiesbaden, Hessisches Staatstheater
31– 1 June	Zürich, Opernhaus
June 7–15	Lisbon, Teatro Nacional de S Carlos
17–19	Lisbon, Coliseu
20	Coimbra, Teatro de Gil Vicente
21–22	Oporto, Coliseu
24–26	Granada, Teatro del Generalife
28–30	Nervi, Teatro dei Parchi
July 1– 3	Monte Carlo, La Place du Palais
6– 8	Lyons, Palais des Sports
9	Vichy, Théâtre du Grand Casino
11	Scheveningen, Circustheater
12–13	Amsterdam, Stadsschouwburg
15–16	Geneva, La Patinoire

18–21	Madrid, La Chopera del Parque del Retiro
23–24	Valencia, Teatro de los Viveros
25–28	Barcelona, Plaza de Toros las Arenas
30– 1 Aug	Bilbao, Teatro Coliseu Albia
Aug 2– 4	Santander, Plaza Porticada
Sept 23– 5 Oct	Coventry, Coventry Theatre
Oct 7–12	Liverpool, Royal Court
14– 2 Nov	Glasgow, King's
Nov 5–30	Manchester, Opera House
Dec 2–14	Oxford, New

1969

Jan 6–18	Stratford, Royal Shakespeare
20– 1 Feb	Eastbourne, Congress
Feb 3–15	Bournemouth, Pavilion
17– 1 Mar	Leeds, Grand
Mar 3–22	Newcastle, Royal
Apr 15– 5 July	*Royal Opera House*
Sept 4– 8	Cairo, Sphinx Theatre, Pyramids of Giza
15–20	Coventry, Coventry Theatre
23–27	Aberdeen, His Majesty's
29–18 Oct	Glasgow, King's
Oct 20– 1 Nov	Cardiff, New
Nov 3–22	Manchester, Opera House
24– 6 Dec	Leeds, Grand
Dec 8–13	Bristol, Hippodrome

1970

Jan 12–31	Stratford, Royal Shakespeare
Feb 2– 7	Hull, New
9–14	Sunderland, Empire
16–28	Liverpool, Royal Court
Mar 2–14	Oxford, New
16–28	Bournemouth, Pavilion
May 1–27	*Royal Opera House*
29–31	Wiesbaden, Hessisches Staatstheater
June 1	Antwerp, Zaal Koningin Elisabeth
6– 7	Bonn, Theater der Stadt
8	Heerlen, Stadsschouwburg
9	Aachen, Stadstheater
11–12	Toulouse, Théâtre du Capitole
16–18	Grenoble, Maison de la Culture
20–21	Vienna, Theater an der Wien
24	Munich, Bayerisches Staatsoper
26–30	Florence, Teatro Comunale
July 13–18	Oxford, New
20–25	Wimbledon, Wimbledon Theatre
Nov 9–14	Nottingham, Royal
16–21	Leeds, Grand

23–28	Manchester, Opera House
30– 5 Dec	Edinburgh, King's
Dec 7–12	Glasgow, King's

1971

Feb 8–13	Norwich, Royal
15–20	York, Royal
22–27	Stratford, Royal Shakespeare
Mar 1– 6	Bournemouth, Pavilion
8–13	Oxford, New
15–20	Cardiff, New
22–27	Liverpool, Royal Court
May 27–12 June	*Sadler's Wells*
Oct 12–23	Wimbledon, Wimbledon Theatre
25–30	Bournemouth, Pavilion
Nov 1– 6	Eastbourne, Congress
8–13	Birmingham, Alexandra
15–20	Leeds, Grand
22–27	Newcastle, Royal
29– 4 Dec	Manchester, Opera House
Dec 6–11	Nottingham, Royal

1972

Feb 16–26	*Sadler's Wells*
28– 4 Mar	Hull, New
Mar 6–11	Norwich, Royal
13–18	Oxford, New
20–25	Bristol, Hippodrome
27– 1 Apr	Liverpool, Royal Court
Apr 24–29	Golders Green, Odeon
May 14–21	Lisbon, Teatro Nacional de S Carlos
22–25	Lisbon, Coliseu
27	Coimbra, Teatro de Gil Vicente
28–29	Oporto, Coliseu
June 1– 4	Bordeaux, Théâtre de Municipal
12–14	Lausanne, Théâtre de Beaulieu
15–16	Geneva, Grand Théâtre
17–19	Monte Carlo, Théâtre du Casino
July 3– 8	Brighton, Royal
10–15	Edmonton, Regal
28–31	Snape, The Maltings
Sept 27– 5 Oct	*Royal Opera House*
Oct 9–28	*Sadler's Wells*
30– 4 Nov	Bournemouth, Pavilion
Nov 6–11	Eastbourne, Congress
13–18	Manchester, Opera House
20–25	Leeds, Grand
27– 2 Dec	Newcastle, Royal
Dec 4– 9	Nottingham, Royal

1973

Feb 19– 3 Mar	Stratford, Royal Shakespeare
Mar 5–10	Norwich, Royal
12–17	York, Royal
19–24	Sunderland, Empire
26–31	Liverpool, Royal Court
Apr 2– 7	Cardiff, New
24– 5 May	*Sadler's Wells*
May 8– 9	*London Coliseum*
14–19	Brighton, Royal
21–26	Southampton, Gaumont

28– 2 June	Birmingham, Alexandra
Aug 5m	Jerusalem, Jerusalem Theatre
5e	Jerusalem, Binyenei Ha'oomah
7– 8	Tel Aviv, Mann Auditorium
9–12	Caesarea, Roman Theatre
Sept 19–28	*Royal Opera House*
Oct 3–27	*Sadler's Wells*
30– 3 Nov	Wolverhampton, Grand
Nov 6–10	Newcastle, Royal
13–17	Leeds, Grand
20–24	Manchester, Opera House
27– 1 Dec	Oxford, New
Dec 4– 8	Eastbourne, Congress

1974

Jan 29– 2 Feb	Leicester, Haymarket
Feb 12–23	*Sadler's Wells*
25– 2 Mar	Stratford, Royal Shakespeare
Mar 5– 9	Bradford, Alhambra
12–16	Liverpool, Royal Court
19–23	Birmingham, Alexandra
26–30	Hull, New
Apr 2– 6	Peterborough, ABC
9–13	Norwich, Royal
30–15 May	*Sadler's Wells*
May 21–25	Coventry, Coventry Theatre
28– 1 June	Cardiff, New
June 4– 8	Bournemouth, Pavilion
17–18	The Hague, Nederlands Congresgebouw
19–20	Amsterdam, Stadsschouwburg
22	Rotterdam, Rotterdamse Schouwburg
July 2– 6	Oxford, New
8–13	Brighton, Royal
16–20	Southampton, Gaumont
Oct 2–26	*Sadler's Wells*
28– 2 Nov	Wolverhampton, Grand
Nov 4– 9	Leeds, Grand
11–16	Nottingham, Royal
18–23	Newcastle, Royal
25–30	Manchester, Opera House
Dec 2– 7	Eastbourne, Congress

1975

Feb 3–15	Stratford, Royal Shakespeare
17–22	York, Royal
24– 1 Mar	Norwich, Royal
Mar 3– 8	Bournemouth, Pavilion
Apr 15–16 May	*Royal Opera House*
May 19–24	Paignton, Festival
June 5–19	*Battersea, Big Top*
23–28	Athens, Herodes Atticus
Sept 1– 6	Edinburgh, King's
8–13	Nottingham, Royal
15–20	Brighton, Royal
25–18 Oct	*Sadler's Wells*
Oct 20– 1 Nov	Manchester, Opera House
Nov 3– 8	Hull, New
10–15	Leeds, Grand
17–22	Wolverhampton, Grand

	24–29	Oxford, New
Dec	1– 6	Eastbourne, Congress
	8–13	Southampton, Gaumont
1976		
Jan	26– 7 Feb	Stratford, Royal Shakespeare
Feb	9–14	York, Royal
	16–21	Liverpool, Royal Court
Mar	15–20	Norwich, Royal
	22–27	Birmingham, Hippodrome
	29– 3 Apr	Newcastle, Royal
Apr	5–10	Aberdeen, His Majesty's
	12–17	Glasgow, Royal
	19–24	Bradford, Alhambra
	26– 1 May	Cardiff, New
May	3– 8	Bournemouth, Pavilion
	25–12 June	*Sadler's Wells*
June	27–30	Zürich, Opernhaus
July	2– 3	Lausanne, Théâtre de Beaulieu
	5	Geneva, La Patinoire
	7–10	Nervi, Teatro dei Parchi
	12–15	Venice, Teatro la Fenice
	17	Cannes, Ile Ste Marguerite
Sept	28–23 Oct	*Sadler's Wells*
Oct	25– 6 Nov	Manchester, Opera House
Nov	8–13	Hull, New
	15–20	Wolverhampton, Grand
	22– 4 Dec	Oxford, New
Dec	6–11	Eastbourne, Congress
	27–	
1977	– 8 Jan	Southampton, Gaumont
Jan	31–12 Feb	Birmingham, Hippodrome
Feb	14–19	Liverpool, Empire
	21–26	Aberdeen, His Majesty's
	28– 5 Mar	Glasgow, Royal
Mar	7–12	Leeds, Grand
	16	Frankfurt, Jahrhunderthalle
	17–18	Luxembourg, Nouveau Théâtre Municipal
Apr	18–23	Bournemouth, Pavilion
	26–15 May	*Sadler's Wells*
May	16–28	Newcastle, Royal
	30– 4 June	Norwich, Royal
June	6–11	Cardiff, New
Aug	15– 3 Sept	Cambridge, Big Top
Sept	6	Antwerp, Koninklijke Vlaamse Opera
	7– 8	Ghent, Koninklijke Opera
	9–10	Brussels, Théâtre Royal de la Monnaie
	13– 1 Oct	*Sadler's Wells*
Oct	4– 7	Teheran, Rudaki Hall
	10–15	Salonika, State Theatre of N Greece
	24–29	Oxford, New
	31– 5 Nov	Manchester, Opera House
Nov	7–12	Bradford, Alhambra
	14–19	Hull, New
	21–26	Wolverhampton, Grand
	28– 3 Dec	Southampton, Gaumont
Dec	5–10	Eastbourne, Congress
1978		
Feb	6–11	Stratford, Royal Shakespeare
	13–18	Leeds, Grand
	20–25	Sunderland, Empire
	27– 4 Mar	Liverpool, Empire
Mar	6–11	Norwich, Royal
	13–18	Birmingham, Hippodrome
	20–25	Bournemouth, Pavilion
Apr	19–13 May	*Sadler's Wells*
May	15–20	Glasgow, Royal
	22–27	Inverness, Eden Court
	29– 3 June	Aberdeen, His Majesty's
June	5–10	Newcastle, Royal
	12–17	Nottingham, Royal
	26–15 July	Plymouth, Big Top
Sept	26–14 Oct	*Sadler's Wells*
Oct	23–28	Bristol, Hippodrome
	30– 4 Nov	Hull, New
Nov	6–11	Oxford, New
	13–18	Southampton, Gaumont
	27– 2 Dec	Eastbourne, Congress
Dec	4– 9	Leeds, Grand
	11–16	Coventry, Coventry Theatre
1979		
Feb	5–10	Stratford, Royal Shakespeare
	12–17	Liverpool, Empire
	19–24	Manchester, Opera House
	26– 3 Mar	Sunderland, Empire
Mar	12–17	Birmingham, Hippodrome
	19–24	Norwich, Royal
	26–31	Bournemouth, Pavilion
Apr	24–12 May	*Sadler's Wells*
May	21– 9 June	Cambridge, Big Top
Aug	20–25	Edinburgh, Big Top
Sept	5–22	*Sadler's Wells*
	26–13 Oct	Sheffield, Big Top
Oct	15–20	Hull, New
	22–27	Newcastle, Royal
	29– 3 Nov	Glasgow, Royal
Nov	19–24	Cardiff, New
	26– 1 Dec	Oxford, New
Dec	3– 8	Eastbourne, Congress
	10–15	Southampton, Gaumont
1980		
Jan	28– 9 Feb	Leeds, Grand
Feb	11–16	Stratford, Royal Shakespeare
	19– 1 Mar	*Sadler's Wells*
Mar	10–15	Liverpool, Empire
	17–22	Sunderland, Empire
	24–29	Norwich, Royal
	31– 5 Apr	Bristol, Hippodrome
Apr	7–12	Birmingham, Hippodrome
	14–19	Bournemouth, Pavilion
May	2–23	*Royal Opera House*
	26–31	Nottingham, Royal
June	3–21	Exeter, Big Top

The Royal Ballet School Annual Performances
1959–1980

Credits are as for Royal Ballet productions unless otherwise stated. Names in brackets are those under which students danced professionally. All performances took place at the Royal Opera House, unless otherwise stated.
* Indicates dancers already in the Royal Ballet.
† Indicates ballet created specially for RBS.

1959 March 21
Coppélia *Swanilda* Antoinette Sibley*. *Franz* Graham Usher*. *Dr Coppélius* Lambert Cox*. *Prayer* Deanne Bergsma.

1960 March 19
Le Lac des Cygnes *Odette* Georgina Parkinson*. *Odile* Shirley Grahame*' *Prince Siegfried* Bryan Lawrence*. *Pas de six* Jane Robinson, Rosalind Eyre, Ann Kenward, Austin Bennett, Anthony Dowell, Gary Sherwood. *Pas de trois* Susan Jones (Susan Carlton), Phyllis Spira, Karl Welander.

1961 May 13
Pineapple Poll *Pineapple Poll* Susan Jones (Susan Carlton). *Jasper* Keith Martin. *Captain Belaye* Piers Beaumont. *Gymnastic Display* David Cartwright, Kerrison Cooke, Tony Binstead, David Morse, Fergus Early, Frank Freeman, Raymond Lewis, Graham Powell, David Wall, Christopher Watson.
Les Patineurs *Variation* (*Blue Boy*) Dudley Tomlinson. *Pas de deux f* Susan Turnham, *m* Derek Rencher*. *Entrée* (*Blue Girls*) Hilary Debden, Ann Jenner.

1962 July 14
Les Sylphides *Valse* Dianne Horsham. *Mazurka* Kay Connett. *Mazurka* Geoffrey Cauley. *Prelude* Hilary Cartwright.
Dance Suite *Ch* Kenneth MacMillan. *M* Darius Milhaud. *SC* nc. *Pas de cinq* Vergie Derman, Judy Fisher (Judith Reyn), Dianne Horsham, Hilary Cartwright, Diana Fox (Diana Vere). *Pas de quatre* Elizabeth Edmiston, Carole Hill, Patricia Ruanne, Gwendoline Looker. *Pas de trois* Kerrison Cooke, Vergie Derman, Richard Cragun.
Façade *Polka* Judy Fisher (Judith Reyn). *Popular Song* Larry Beevers (Laurence Beevers), Kerrison Cooke. *A Dago* Garry Grant. *A Débutante* Sandra Conley.

1963 June 22
†Motus *Ch* Miro Zolan. *M* Benjamin Britten *SC* nc. *Variations:* 1 Jennifer Penney. 2 *f* Angela Beveridge, *m* Clinton Rothwell. 3 *f* Vivien Liver, *m* David Wall. 6&7 *f* Jane Leach (Jane Landon), *m* Nicholas Benton. 9 Sasha Davis.
Coppelia Act II *Swanilda* Merlyn Holmes. *Franz* John Ryder. *Dr Coppélius* Fergus Early.

†Etude Caractère (A demonstration of character dancing, designed to illustrate the work taught in the class-room.) *Ch* Maria Fay. *M* Mavis Barr. Hungarian, Polish, Chinese, Gypsy, Russian, Georgian. Cast included: Andrea Durant, Jeanetta Bumpus (Jeanetta Laurence), Michael Beare, Brian Bertscher, Frank Freeman, John Neumeier, Clinton Rothwell, David Wall, Geraldine Chaplin, Mary Jago, Lynn Wallis, Kathryn Brown (Kathryn Wade), Jane Leach (Jane Landon), Jennifer Penney, Gail Thomas, Victoria Wiles.

1964 June 20 (at Drury Lane)
The Sleeping Beauty *Princess Aurora* Jane Landon. *Prince Florimund* Warren de Maria*. *The Fairy of the Lilac* Ria Peri. *The Blue Birds f* Maxine Denys, *m* Fergus Early.

1965 July 17
Flower Festival at Genzano *Pas de deux f* Ann Dennis, *m* Michael Ingleton.
Napoli *Divertissement* Lynn Wallis, Elizabeth Pal, Elizabeth Cunliffe, Caroline Southam, John Travis, Wayne Sleep, Alan Hooper, Georgina Sibley, Kathryn Wade, Janet Francis, Meryl Chapell, Michael Beare, Nicholas Johnson. *The Two Pigeons The Young Girl* Lesley Collier. *The Young Man* Graham Powell. *A Gypsy Girl* Margaret Barbieri. *Her Lover* Nicholas Johnson.

1966 July 9
Coppélia Act I *Swanilda* Georgina Sibley. *Franz* Alan Hooper. *Dr Coppélius* Wayne Sleep.
Les Patineurs *Variation* (*Blue Boy*) Wayne Sleep. *Pas de deux f* Fiona Farrie, *m* Paul Vlasio. *Entrée* (*Blue Girls*) Heather Hems, Susan Watkins.
The Sleeping Beauty Act III *Princess Aurora* Caroldene Horne. *Prince Florimund* Peter Fairweather. *The Blue Birds f* Marilyn Trounson, *m* Alan Hooper.

1967 July 15
Swan Lake Act II *Odette* Hilary Tickner. *Prince Siegfried* Andis Marton.
The Rake's Progress *The Rake* Anthony Molyneux. *The Dancing Master* Michael Ho. *The Betrayed Girl* Julie Wood (Julie Lincoln). *The Gentleman with a Rope* Terence Hyde.
Les Rendezvous *Variation f* Sally Inkin. *Variation m* Christopher Carr. *Pas de trois f* Judith Beams, *m* Wayne Eagling, Michael Ho.

1968 July 6
Intrusion *Ch* David Drew. *M* Schubert. *SC* nc. (P Royal Ballet Choreographic Group 30 Mar 1968 by RBS students). Patricia Whittle (Patricia Hammond), Jiri Kylian, Anthony Rudenko, Sven Bradshaw, David Ashmole,

Paul Porter, Marion Tait, Carolyn Abbott.
Napoli *Divertissement Pas de six* Angela Jackman, Jeanetta Bumpus (Jeanetta Laurence), Judith Beams, Andrea Durant, Paul Porter, Stephen Jefferies. *Solos:* 1 Anthony Molyneux, 2 Marilyn Tipler, 3 Carl Myers, 4 Heather McCubbin, 5 Michael Ho, 6 Alison Howard, 7 Jane Buist.
Giselle Act II *Giselle* June Highwood. *Albrecht* Jiri Kylian, *Myrtha* Joanna Mordaunt.

1969 June 28
Coppélia *Swanilda Act I:* Angela Jackman. *Act II:* Carolyn Abbott. *Act III:* Andrea Durant. *Franz Act I:* Paul Porter. *Act II:* Graham Fletcher. *Act III:* Stephen Jefferies. *Dr Coppelius* David Peake.

1970 June 13
Les Sylphides *Valse* Jane Ball. *Mazurka* Helena Heatherington. *Mazurka* Julian Hosking. *Prelude* Annemarie Norton.
†Primavera *Ch* Richard Glasstone. *M* Vivaldi. *C* Heather Magoon. *Pas de quatre* Jane Ball, Ian Owen, Ian MacKenzie, Nigel Pearl (Nigel Spencer). *Pas de deux* Ann Goodier, Julian Hosking.
Façade *Polka* Christine Keith. *Popular Song* Julian Hosking, Ian MacKenzie. *A Dago* Philip Kelly. *A Débutante* Josephine Holling.

1971 No performance

1972 June 24
La Fille Mal Gardée *Lise* Jennifer Jackson. *Colas* Robert Hugenin. *Alain* Denis Bonner. *Widow Simone* Ronald Emblen*.

1973 July 7
A Living Tradition (English Folk Dancing by pupils of the Lower School.) *Pr* Bob Parker, Ronald Smedley. *M* Traditional. *C* Derek Rencher.
Solitaire *The Girl* Marion Lindsay. *Polka Girl* Rosalyn Whitten. *m* Adrian Davies, Stephen Moore (Andrew Moore), Derek Purnell.
The Dream *Titania* Lorna Murray. *Oberon* Mark Silver. *Bottom* Denis Bonner. *Puck* Jonathon Ellingham.

1974 June 29
England Dances (Traditional dances of the English countryside by pupils of the Lower School.) *Pr* Ronald Smedley, Bob Parker. *M* Traditional.
Arpège *Ch* Peter Wright. *M* François Boieldieu. *SC* nc. *Allegro Brillante: Trio 1* Lorna Murray. *Trio 2* Michael Batchelor. *Andante: Lento Attacca: f* 1 Joan French, 2 Jayne Plaisted.

Jazz Calendar *Monday* Lucinda Harper. *Tuesday* Lorna Murray. *Wednesday* Amanda Wilkinson. *Thursday* Stephen Speed. *Friday f* Denise Nunn, *m* Michael Batchelor. *Saturday* Desmond Doyle*. *Sunday* Claire Farnsworth. *Concerto First Movement f* Lorna Murray, *m* Nigel Jones (Nigel Courtney). *Second Movement f* Denise Nunn, *m* Nicholas Whittle. *Third Movement* Sherilyn Kennedy.

1975 June 28 (In the Big Top, Battersea)
Danses Concertantes Holly Lancaster, Nicholas Millington, Judith Gill, Nigel Jones (Nigel Courtney) Susan Lucas, Stuart Beckett.
The Two Pigeons *The Young Girl* Nicola Katrak. *The Young Man* Stephen Beagley. *A Gypsy Girl* Jacqueline Williams (Chenca Williams). *Her Lover* Ashley Laverty (Ashley Page).

1976 June 24
Coppélia *Swanilda* Susan Lucas. *Franz* Stephen Sherrif. *Dr Coppélius* David Bintley.

1977 May 28
The Thistle and the Rose. (Dances from England and Scotland for Jubilee Year.) *Pr* Colin Robertson (Scotland), Bob Parker, Ronald Smedley (England). *M* Traditional.
Serenade Deirdre Eyden, Deborah Kinsey, Jacqueline Barrett, Richard Slaughter, Mark Welford.
Monotones *Trois Gnossiennes* Deirdre Eyden, Fiona Chadwick, Mark Welford. *Trois Gymnopedies* Julie Mitchell, Matthew Hawkins, Andrew Ward.
Raymonda Act III *Raymonaa* Sharon McGorian. *Jean de Brienne* Matthew Hawkins. *Hungarian f* Nicola Treherne, *m* Radenko Pavlovic. *Variations:* 1 Bryony Brind, 2 Julie Rose, 3 Angela Cox, 4 Elizabeth Griffiths (Lili Griffiths).

1978 July 7
Dances from England and Scotland *Pr* Colin Robertson (Scotland), Bob Parker, Ronald Smedley (England). *M* Traditional.
Les Sylphides *Valse* Julie Rose. *Mazurka* Fiona Chadwick. *Mazurka* Andrew Ward. *Prelude* Dido Nicolson.
Diversions *1st couple: f* Clare Shepherd Wilson, *m* Ashley Wheater. *2nd couple: f* Julie Rose, *m* Roland Price.
Birthday Offering Variations: 1 Elizabeth Griffiths (Lili Griffiths), 2 Fiona Chadwick, 3 Clare Shepherd Wilson, 4 Deborah Weiss, 5 Samira Saidi, 6 Susan Pond, 7 Karen Paisey.

1979 July 11
Four Kingdoms (Traditional Dances from England, Ireland, Scotland and Wales.) *Pr* Terry Bowler (Ireland) Colin Robertson (Scotland), Bob Parker, Ronald Smedley (England). *M* Traditional. *Concerto Barocco* 1 Susan Pond, 2 Christina Parker, 3 Guy Niblett, 4 Samira Saidi.
Checkmate *First Red Knight* Robert Poole. *The Black Queen* Susan Pond. *The Red Queen* Samira Saidi. *The Red King* Simon Horrill.
Sinfonietta *1st couple f* Odette Millner, *m* Michael Crookes. *2nd couple f* Elizabeth Morgan, *m* David Peden. *Elegy f* Nicola Roberts, *m* Philip Broomhead.

1980 July 11
Concerto *First Movement f* Madonna Benjamin, *m* Philip Broomhead. *Second Movement f* Alessandra Ferri, *m* Michael Crookes. *Third Movement* Kate Strong.
The Two Pigeons *The Young Man* David Peden. *The Young Girl* Nicola Roberts. *A Gypsy Girl* Karen Donovan. *Her Lover* Mark Freeman.

The Royal Ballet Film and TV Appearances

Films

Dates are release dates.

1960 *The Royal Ballet* (Poetic Films). Paul Czinner pr for Rank Organisation. Pr/Dir Paul Czinner, Swan Lake Act II. The Firebird. Ondine. (Fonteyn, Somes). Filmed at ROH.

1964 *An Evening with The Royal Ballet* (British Home Entertainment). Pr Anthony Havelock-Allan. Dir Anthony Asquith/Anthony Havelock-Allan. La Valse. Le Corsaire pdd. Les Sylphides. Aurora's Wedding. (Fonteyn, Nureyev, Blair). Filmed at ROH.

1966 *Romeo and Juliet* (Poetic Films). Paul Czinner pr for Rank Organisation. Pr/Dir Paul Czinner. (Fonteyn, Nureyev). Shown BBC TV 10 Oct 1977.

1970 *Enigma Variations* (Argo Films) Pr James Archibald. (Original cast but Jenner for Sibley). Filmed at ROH. Shown BBC TV 15 Dec 1975 *and* 28 May 1978.

1971 *Tales of Beatrix Potter.* (John Brabourne–Richard Goodwin Production). Pr Richard Goodwin. Dir Reginald Mills. Ch Frederick Ashton. Shown BBC TV 26 Dec 1976.

1972 *I am a Dancer* (EMI). Pr Evderos Demetriou. Dir Pierre Jourdan. Marguerite and Armand and excerpts from Field Figures and The Sleeping Beauty (Fonteyn, Seymour, Bergsma, Nureyev, Somes).

1979 Stories from a Flying Trunk. Pr Richard Goodwin. Dir Christine Edzard. *Little Ida* sequence Ch Frederick Ashton.

Television

Starting with a BBC transmission of Job on 11 November 1936, over eighty television programmes have been devoted to the work of The Royal Ballet and its artists. (This excludes appearances in feature, magazine and news programmes.) The full-length ballets which have been transmitted are:

1955 12 Dec *The Sleeping Beauty* (Fonteyn, Somes) NBC/USA
1957 29 Apr *Cinderella* (Fonteyn, Somes) NBC/USA
1960 13 Apr *Cinderella* (Fonteyn, Somes) Granada
1962 27 Dec *La Fille Mal Gardée* (Nerina, Blair) BBC
1965 27 Dec *Coppélia* (Park, Gable) BBC
1968 25 Dec *The Nutcracker* (Park, Nureyev) BBC
1969 26 Jan *The Sleeping Beauty* (Sibley, Dowell) BBC
1973 24 Nov *La Fille Mal Gardée* (Park, Blair) BBC
     30 Dec *Cinderella* (Sibley, Dowell) BBC
1977 26 Dec *Romeo and Juliet* (Fonteyn, Nureyev), feature film, BBC
1978 17 June *Mayerling* (Seymour, Wall), documentary, London Weekend
     24 Dec *The Sleeping Beauty* (Park, Wall) BBC
1979 23 Dec *Cinderella* (Collier, Dowell) BBC
1980 28 July *Swan Lake* (Makarova, Dowell) Thames Television

Index